RICHARD TAYLOR

Richard
TAYLOR
Soldier Prince of Dixie
T. MICHAEL PARRISH

The University of North Carolina Press
Chapel Hill & London

96 95 94 93 92   5 4 3 2 1

Library of Congress Cataloging-in-Publication Data
Parrish, T. Michael.
Richard Taylor, soldier prince of Dixie / by T. Michael
Parrish.
    p.   cm.
Includes bibliographical references (p.   ) and index.
ISBN 0-8078-2032-6 (cloth : alk. paper)
1. Taylor, Richard, 1826–1879.   2. Generals—Confederate
States of America—Biography.   3. Confederate States of
America. Army—Biography.
4. Louisiana—History—Civil War, 1861–1865.
    I. Title.
E467.1.T24P37   1992
973.7′092—dc20
    [B]   91-46467
        CIP

FRONTISPIECE
Richard Taylor immediately after the Civil War.
Photograph by Mathew Brady (author's collection).

FOR JULIBETH

CONTENTS

MAPS

ILLUSTRATIONS

Major General Zachary Taylor in 1848, 20
President Zachary Taylor in 1849, 28
Richard Taylor, sugar planter, ca. 1860, 40
Frederick Law Olmsted, 45
Governor Alexander Mouton, 83
William L. Yancey, 88
Alexander H. Stephens, 112
Braxton Bragg, 126
Jefferson Davis, 136
Richard S. Ewell, 147
Stonewall Jackson, 159
Nathaniel P. Banks, proud political general, 172
"A Glimpse of Stonewall Jackson," 198
David French Boyd, 222
Robert E. Lee, 233
Major General Richard Taylor, 248
George W. Randolph, 249
Benjamin F. Butler, 258
Edmund Kirby Smith, 268
Henry H. Sibley, 271
Thomas Green, 280
Taylor's five-year-old son Zack, 281
Taylor's daughter Elizabeth, 282
Taylor's daughter Myrthe Bianca, 283
John G. Walker, 286
Battle of Milliken's Bend, Louisiana, 288
Richard Taylor's dressing kit, 300
Jean Jacques Alfred Alexander Mouton, 307
David D. Porter, 323
Admiral Porter's fleet at Alexandria, 326
Camille Armand Jules Marie de Polignac, 328
Nathaniel P. Banks in all his martial splendor, 343
Monument to Taylor's victory at Mansfield, 350
Thomas J. Churchill, 358

ACKNOWLEDGMENTS

In completing this study I owe a primary debt of gratitude to Norman D. Brown, my dissertation supervisor in the history department of the University of Texas, and to the members of the dissertation committee: Thomas W. Cutrer, George B. Forgie, Shearer Davis Bowman, and Don E. Carleton. Their scholarly instruction, hard work, and patient friendship proved invaluable and personally rewarding. Thanks go also to other members of the history department: Barnes F. Lathrop, George C. Wright, Richard Graham, Brian Levack, Lewis L. Gould, Howard Miller, and Mary Helen Quinn, graduate secretary.

Vital encouragement and crucial suggestions came from Gary W. Gallagher, Robert K. Krick, Charles P. Roland, James I. Robertson, Jr., Stephen Rowe, Terrence Winschel, Brandon Beck, Donald Frazier, Robert Miller, and T. E. Swenson, all of whom read the manuscript in full or in part, offering numerous criticisms and corrections.

Other friends and colleagues who provided important source materials, guidance, and moral support are Edward M. Boagni, Maury A. Bromsen, the late Jack McIlhenny, Gary Hendershott, Lawrence T. Jones, Charles V. Peery, the late Richard B. Harwell, Robert M. Willingham, Jr., Allan Purcell, Stephen L. Hardin, Jerry Thompson, Robert J. Younger, Merlin Sumner, Robert Judice, James Mundie, Jim Synnott, Bob Lurate, the late K. Jack Bauer, John Pannick, Jim Hayes, Charles Royster, Terry L. Jones, Frank Vandiver, Emily Cutrer, Eileen Gallagher, Thomas Schott, Stuart Goldman, Terry Waxham, O. Scott Petty, Evans Casso, Mary Gorman, Lucius Dabney, Harris D. Riley, Jr., Stanley Butcher, Joseph Parks, Frank Leavell, Stanley Campbell, the late Hugh Davis, Robert Reid, Robert Norris, Ken McElroy, Kenneth Kesselus, Ken Huddleston, Ron Riches, Dan Weinberg, Tom Munnerlyn, Ross Shipman, John Powers, Edith Williams, Fred White, Jr., Robert and Christine Liska, Ray and Carolyn Walton, Bill Walton, Michael Heaston, Michael and Gail Ginsberg, Elaine Brockman, Ben and Rozetta Pingenot, Bill Reese, Terry and Laura Halladay, Dorothy Sloan, and Michael Vinson.

The late John Jenkins made the Jenkins Rare Book Company a

workplace that always encouraged a productive combination of business and scholarship. His legacy was sustained ably by Maureen Jenkins, along with the Jenkins staff: Diana Japko, Leonard Lantz, and
Mark Evans. Computer consultant John Fehr also accomplished
timely transformations that streamlined publication.

The professional staffs of several research institutions responded
quickly and efficiently to my requests: George Miles (Beinecke Library, Yale University), James Gilreath, John Sellers, and James Hut-
son (Library of Congress), Michael Musick (National Archives), Katherine Adams and Ralph Elder (Barker Texas History Center,
University of Texas), Kent Keeth and Michael Toon (Baylor University), Kenneth Urquhart, Florence Jumonville, Alfred Lemmon, Susan Cole, Katherine Kahn, Jan White Brantley, and Pat McWhorter
(Historic New Orleans Collection), Wilbur Meneray and Sylvia Met-
zinger (Tulane University), Nancy Parker Booth (Rice University),
Lynda Crist (Papers of Jefferson Davis), Patricia Clark (Papers of An-
drew Johnson), the late Harold Simpson (Hill College), Arthur Ber-
geron (Louisiana State Parks Department), the late Stone Miller, Gi-
sela Lozada, and Robert Martin (Louisiana State University), Joseph
Castle, Claire Brown, and Bert Harter (Louisiana State Museum),
Collin Hamer (New Orleans Public Library), Richard Shrader and
Carolyn Wallace (Southern Historical Collection, University of North
Carolina), Robert Byrd and Samuel Hammond (Perkins Library,
Duke University), Alan Jutzi (Huntington Library), Dorothy Rush
(The Filson Club Library), Madel Morgan (Mississippi Department of
Archives and History), Frances McClure and Helen Ball (Miami Uni-
versity of Ohio), Richard Sommers (U.S. Army Military Institute), Ed-
ward Campbell (Museum of the Confederacy), Mary Willey (Knox
College), Mary Ceibert (University of Illinois, Urbana-Champaign),
Anastacio Teodoro and Richard Salvato (New York Public Library).

Matthew Hodgson and the staff of the University of North Carolina Press have served as both patient motivators and expert guides in
seeing the dissertation pushed through to completion for final publication.

From my parents, Tom and Emmy Parrish, I gained a love of learning, especially history, and the written word that makes it live.

Richard Taylor

PROLOGUE

Spanning the middle decades of the nineteenth century, Richard Taylor's life became entangled with America's struggle over slavery, secession, the Civil War, and Reconstruction. Yet in the depths of his own sentiment he dwelled continually upon another era—the eighteenth century. Throughout his adult life he seemed bent on judging all according to standards born in that distant past.

One experience in particular, during the Civil War, confirmed and illuminated within him a reverence for vanishing traditions, especially social obligations and deference between classes of people, relationships Taylor accepted as divinely inspired and ordained. In the early fall of 1862, while burdened with the command of meager, poorly equipped Confederate forces in his home state of Louisiana, Taylor journeyed for the first time through the south-central region lying along Bayou Teche. Seeking new recruits and fresh supplies and hoping to revive public morale, now so desolate after the fall of New Orleans a few months before, he discovered a sublime landscape of civilization still unharmed by the fighting. "In all my wanderings, and they have been many and wide, I cannot recall so fair, so bountiful, and so happy a land," he professed. Here he gazed upon lush sugar cane fields and houses of "opulant planters, as well as the villages of their slaves." He crossed a "broad, verdant prairie, where countless herds [of livestock] roamed." Inhabited primarily by old French and Spanish Creole families, these large plantations offered at once "the grace of the *salon* combined with the healthy cheeriness of country life." [1]

Farther up the Teche, Taylor encountered the small cabins and prosperous farms of the Acadians, descendants of French Catholics who had emigrated from Canada a century before. "What the gentle, contented Creole was to the restless, pushing American, that and more was the Acadian to the Creole," observed Taylor. Still speaking

1. Richard Taylor, *Destruction and Reconstruction*, pp. 121–24 (quotations 124). All citations of *Destruction and Reconstruction* refer to the 1955 edition, unless indicated otherwise.

only French, the Acadians worked alongside handfuls of "humble slaves," cultivating maize and sweet potatoes, as well as some cotton for making their own clothing. They owned large herds of ponies, which seemed to graze everywhere unattended. "Here, unchanged, was the French peasant," noted Taylor. "Tender and true were his traditions of la belle France, but of France before Voltaire and the encyclopedists, the Convention and the Jacobins—ere she lost faith in all things, divine and human, save the *bourgeoisie* and *avocats*."[2]

Spying an Acadian farmhouse one afternoon, Taylor stopped to rest and ask for food. A dark-eyed girl answered his knock and happily welcomed him. Noticing that her family was away, he replied politely in French, saying he would depart. But she insisted that he stay and that she would prepare him a grand luncheon. This she did, and they enjoyed a jug of claret with the festive meal. "As my hostess declined any remuneration for her trouble, I begged her to accept a pair of plain gold sleeve buttons, my only ornaments," he recounted. Delighted and exceedingly grateful for the gift, the girl reached up and kissed his cheek. "I accepted the chaste salute with all the reverence of a subject for his Queen," he recalled, "then [I] rode away with uncovered head so long as she remained in sight." Mindful of the impending Union invasion of the Teche region, Taylor lamented, "It was to this earthly paradise, and upon this simple race, that the war came, like the tree of knowledge to our earthly parents."[3]

In his view of Creole and Acadian life, Taylor conjured up a romantic yet moral ideal. Dwelling upon the contrast between these contented people and the outside world, he was captivated, almost enamored, with their social stability, a blessing that exuded ultimate faith in a hierarchy of "opulant" planters, "peasant" farmers, and "humble" servants. Unlike the great mass of Americans, the Creoles, the Acadians, and their slaves seemed to have escaped the modern evils of unbridled democracy, a malignancy Taylor saw rooted in the French Revolution. The secluded Teche region seemed to thrive like Eden, as if God had placed its inhabitants there to enjoy perfect satisfaction, free from narrow individualism, material greed, and political warfare.

2. Ibid., pp. 124–25 (quotations).
3. Ibid., pp. 125–26 (quotations 126).

Taylor had no trouble imagining his own place in such a harmonious society, in the top tier as a natural-born, eighteenth-century-style aristocrat. Yet by his own definition, he actually seemed more like one of the "restless, pushing" Americans. He had made his fortune and reputation as a sugar planter and politician immersed in the democratic tumult that gripped the nation, caught up in its competitive pursuit of wealth and jaded by its public strife. As a soldier without professional training, he had become a general officer in America's violent struggle over democracy's meaning.

Richard Taylor personified the antebellum South's most self-conscious class, the plantation aristocracy—a small group of cultured elitists who assumed that traditional prominence and leadership would be theirs, yet forced by the nation's rising tide of capitalism and democracy to compete with ambitious smaller planters and farmers for wealth and power. Taylor and his peers strove to retain an aura of dignified detachment while practical necessity relentlessly eroded the sacred ideal of benevolent paternalism toward those they viewed as social and racial inferiors. The daily rigors of controlling slaves, the disruptions of political sectionalism and secession, then the wartime uprising and exodus of bondsmen from the South's plantations, and finally the violent racial crisis of Reconstruction politics all struck at the foundation of Taylor's values. Yet paternalists like Taylor refused to relinquish their claims to a vanished aristocratic authority, reflected in the alluring image of the genteel southern planter whose sense of duty always compelled him to act selflessly in the best interests of all. Such an image had great appeal in the North as well as the South during Taylor's lifetime, and it has persisted even to the present day.

CHAPTER ONE

Young Southern Prince

I scarcely know my own children or they me.

Zachary Taylor

The earliest and most irresistible shaping of Richard Taylor's self-image came from stories told by his family's elder slaves. "In childhood I often listened with credulous ears to wondrous tales of the magnificence of my forefathers in Virginia and Maryland," he later recalled. The storytellers, "these imaginative Africans," asserted that Taylor's ancestors "dwelt in palaces, surrounded by brave, handsome sons, lovely, virtuous daughters, and countless devoted servants." The personalities of "many southern children were doubtless influenced by such tales, impressive from the good faith of the narrators," he admitted. Proudly, it seemed, the family slaves thus linked their own heritage to that of young Dick Taylor.[1]

The fact that he represented the sixth generation in a prominent Virginia-bred line always loomed starkly in his consciousness. His admiring description of fellow Confederate officer Albert Sidney Johnston's ancestry would have fit Taylor well enough: "[He was] descended from an honorable colonial race, connected by marriage with influential families." James Taylor, the first in the line, emigrated from England about 1650 and became a wealthy planter, lawyer, and

1. Richard Taylor, *Destruction and Reconstruction*, pp. 68–69 (quotations).

public official in King and Queen (later Kent) County, Virginia. His oldest son, also named James, acquired about ten thousand acres in Orange County and built the first frame house there in 1722. The second James Taylor's first child, a daughter named Frances, married Ambrose Madison, and they would become the grandparents of future president James Madison. The second James Taylor also had a son, Zachary, who served as Virginia's surveyor general, a position later held by George Washington and Thomas Jefferson. Zachary Taylor married Elizabeth Lee, of the famous family that would produce Robert E. Lee. Zachary and Elizabeth's youngest son, Richard, born in 1744, would become the father of future president Zachary Taylor.[2]

As a young man Richard Taylor became fascinated with the wilds of the frontier, despite having gained a degree from William and Mary College. In 1769, along with his older brother Hancock, he embarked on the first recorded trading voyage from Pittsburgh down the length of the Ohio and Mississippi rivers to New Orleans. After a trip back up the Mississippi to Fort Chartres and another up the Arkansas River to hunt game, the two brothers parted company. Hancock returned home via New Orleans by ship, but Richard headed overland eastward with an Indian trader, passed through Georgia and up through the Carolinas, and finally returned to Virginia after an absence of more than a year. Throughout the journey he searched for land that might prove suitable for eventual purchase and settlement.[3]

But pioneering visions fell victim to America's revolutionary conflict with Britain. Volunteering as a private in the First Virginia Regiment in 1775, Richard Taylor rose to the rank of lieutenant colonel of the Second Virginia Regiment before retiring in 1781. His distinguished service included several of the most important battles in the North under General Washington. In 1779, during the war, he married Sarah Dabney Strother, a cultured young lady whose English-

2. Ibid., p. 283 (quotation). The Taylor family's full genealogy appears in Hamilton, *Zachary Taylor: Soldier of the Republic*, pp. 21–23, 259–60. See also Padgett, "Letters of Colonel Richard Taylor," pp. 330–31.

3. K. Jack Bauer, *Zachary Taylor*, p. 1; Hamilton, *Zachary Taylor: Soldier of the Republic*, pp. 22–23.

born forebears had helped settle Virginia's central region along the Rappahannock River. The groom was thirty-five, the bride nineteen. After the war, they settled in Orange County near the rest of the Taylor family, but Colonel Taylor soon made claim to a large tract of western land (a bonus for his military service) located in Virginia's vast new frontier holding, Kentucky. In the spring of 1785 Richard and Sarah Taylor undertook a difficult journey to a small log house he had constructed the previous year, five miles east of Louisville. They brought with them their three sons. The youngest, only seven months old, was named Zachary in honor of his grandfather.[4]

Zachary Taylor grew up in rugged surroundings, a thick forest inhabited by raiding Indians who often forced his father to lead settlers in some bloody skirmishes. By about 1800, however, Louisville and the nearby area had developed into a peaceful Ohio River community that thrived on tobacco farming, whiskey distilling, and commercial trading. With a continual infusion of Virginia families, especially those of refinement like the Taylors, Kentucky soon mirrored the Old Dominion's traditions of genteel leadership. Although permanently crippled by a severe leg wound sustained during an Indian fight in 1792, Colonel Richard Taylor served as a county official, legislator, and delegate to the state constitutional convention. He also received appointment from President Washington as customs collector for the port of Louisville. Engaging mainly in land speculation and tobacco planting, by 1810 he had constructed a large brick house, Springfield, and he dressed the part of a successful gentleman planter. The owner of thirty-seven slaves, he ranked as one of the most substantial slaveholders west of the Appalachian Mountains.[5]

Little Zack and his four brothers and three sisters experienced the best kind of education the Kentucky frontier could offer. Although

4. Padgett, "Letters of Colonel Richard Taylor," p. 331; Owen, "William Strother," pp. 150–51, 165–67; K. Jack Bauer, *Zachary Taylor*, pp. 1–3; Hamilton, *Zachary Taylor: Soldier of the Republic*, pp. 23–25.

5. Padgett, "Letters of Colonel Richard Taylor," pp. 331–33; Eaton, *Growth of Southern Civilization*, pp. 17–9; U.S. House of Representatives, *Report of the Committee of Claims on the Petition of Richard Taylor*, pp. 3–8; Hamilton, *Zachary Taylor: Soldier of the Republic*, pp. 25–32; K. Jack Bauer, *Zachary Taylor*, pp. 3–4.

his letters written as a young man suffered from dreadful penman-
ship, grammar, and spelling—a problem linked to his lifelong
struggle with verbal expression—he made a determined and successful effort to improve his writing, displaying his strongly focused will
in a Spartan prose style. These painful exertions left him resolved
that his own children would receive the finest education he could afford to give them.[6]

In 1808 twenty-three-year-old Zachary Taylor put his real talents
to work by securing a commission as a lieutenant in the United States
Army's new Seventh Infantry Regiment. A military career, true to
family tradition and especially prestigious among southerners,
proved satisfying to the young officer. After seeing to local recruiting
duties and a brief assignment in New Orleans, he returned to Louisville, where in 1810 he began courting, and soon married, Margaret
Mackall Smith of Calvert County, Maryland. Peggy, as she was called,
had met Lieutenant Taylor during an earlier visit, and she had impressed him with her lack of pretension about her superior education
and cultured family background. Although a devout practicing Episcopalian, she never insisted that her husband join the church or make
religion a formal habit. It seemed to Taylor that her spiritual faith
and natural fortitude would make her an ideal army wife. As a wedding gift Colonel Richard Taylor parted with more than three hundred acres of prime land near Louisville, insuring that his son would
also have a stake in the soil.[7]

Blessings came quickly to the Taylors. By 1811 the young lieutenant had received promotion to the rank of captain, and later that
spring their first child, a daughter, Ann, was born. Living and working at Springfield with the rest of the large Taylor clan, Taylor improved his finances by purchasing bank stock and using the family
slaves to plant a few crops on his parcel of land. He soon owned two
house servants who helped Peggy at Springfield. Military duties then
called him to Indiana Territory, where Governor William Henry Har-

6. Hamilton, *Zachary Taylor: Soldier of the Republic*, pp. 27–29; K. Jack
Bauer, *Zachary Taylor*, pp. 4, 327.

7. Hamilton, *Zachary Taylor: Soldier of the Republic*, pp. 33–37; K. Jack
Bauer, *Zachary Taylor*, pp. 8–9; Wyatt-Brown, *Southern Honor*, p. 191. See also
Boller, *Presidential Wives*, pp. 95–99.

rison put him in command of Fort Knox, at Vincennes. During the War of 1812 Captain Taylor served at isolated Fort Harrison, mounting a triumphant defense against a large band of Indians allied with the British. The first American victory of the war, it garnered Taylor the rank of brevet major. Spending the rest of the war recruiting, training, and leading raw troops in fights with Indians ranging from Indiana Territory to the Mississippi River, he helped Americans in that region wrest undisputed control from the British as well as the Indians for the first time. After the war, upon learning that military authorities had restored him to the rank of captain, he made a fruitless trip to Washington to protest the dishonor and finally resigned his commission, completely disgusted with the army.[8]

By June 1815 Taylor had built his own cabin on the land he owned near Louisville. He cultivated corn and tobacco and enjoyed his family, which counted another daughter, Sarah Knox, born a year earlier at Vincennes. But a restless attraction to military life lured him back into the army a year later, this time with the well-deserved rank of major. He soon became father to another daughter, Octavia, and after two years in Wisconsin and a year's furlough that included recruiting duties in Kentucky, in mid–1819, at age thirty-four, Zachary Taylor received promotion to lieutenant colonel. About this same time his fourth daughter, Margaret, was born, and soon afterward he left for assignment in Louisiana, entrusting Peggy Taylor and the children to the care of her sister's family at Bayou Sara, on the Mississippi River about thirty miles north of Baton Rouge. An arduous routine of constructing forts and roads required Taylor's full attention. In the summer of 1820 came the crushing news of his daughter Octavia's death from a fever. Soon the illness struck Peggy and the rest of the girls. The baby, Margaret, died in October.[9]

Up to now Colonel Taylor had strongly considered buying some plantation lands and settling in Louisiana, but the deaths of his two precious daughters as a direct result of the subtropical climate pushed such thoughts from his mind. After two years of monotonous duty on the Louisiana frontier, however, in early 1823 he decided to

8. Hamilton, *Zachary Taylor: Soldier of the Republic*, pp. 37–57; K. Jack Bauer, *Zachary Taylor*, p. 10.

9. Hamilton, *Zachary Taylor: Soldier of the Republic*, pp. 58–69.

purchase a cotton plantation of almost four hundred acres in West
Feliciana Parish. He brought slaves from Kentucky to work the fields
and paid a manager to run the plantation. But the Taylors remained
in Louisiana only until February 1824, when they returned to Louisville in compliance with Colonel Taylor's new duties as superintendent general of the army's Western Department recruiting office. In
April they celebrated the birth of another daughter, Mary Elizabeth,
whom they called Betty. Early in 1826, on January 27, Peggy gave
birth to a long-awaited son. They named him Richard, in honor of
his eighty-one-year-old grandfather. He would be their only male
child.[10]

Soon after Richard's birth, Colonel Taylor served for a short time
in Washington, D.C., as a member of an advisory board of officers
working for military reforms, and in early 1827 he returned for another assignment in Louisiana. In mid–1828, however, he accepted
the challenge of commanding the country's most remote frontier
army post, Fort Snelling in Minnesota, on the upper Mississippi.
Peggy Taylor, suffering from chills and fever during the trip to the
fort, brought the children with her. Zachary Taylor found the Indians
in the vicinity to be "the most miserable set of beings I have been
among, and I presume [they] will continue to be so for the next century." After about a year the Taylors received instructions to report to
Fort Crawford at Prairie du Chien, situated on the banks of the Mississippi in the southwestern part of present-day Wisconsin. Here they
stayed for the next eight years. Except for a few months of fighting

10. Ibid., pp. 69–75. A manuscript notation in the Zachary Taylor family
Bible at the Virginia Historical Society reads: "Richard Taylor was born near
Louisville, Jefferson County, State of Kentucky, 27th of January, 1826." In
the Yale College Autograph Album Collection an unidentified student's senior class autograph album for 1845 bears a signature and notation in Richard Taylor's own hand: "Richard Taylor, Yale, April 1845. Louisville, Ky.,
January 27th, 1825." The year "1825" is incorrect. Apparently Richard wrote
it because he had just written "1845," which also ends with a "5." In his memoirs he refers to New Orleans as "my native place and home." See Richard
Taylor, *Destruction and Reconstruction*, p. 279. As an adult he made a practice
of giving New Orleans as his birthplace, although he was certainly born "near
Louisville" as stated in the Taylor family Bible. Most likely he claimed New
Orleans in order to solidify his standing as a Louisianan.

during the Black Hawk War in 1832, Colonel Taylor labored under dull conditions, describing the region as "a most miserable and uninteresting country." During a short furlough he managed to take care of some pressing financial matters, selling much of his plantation acreage in Kentucky and paying $1,500 for yet another plantation, about 140 acres in Wilkinson County, Mississippi.[11]

For young Dick Taylor, life at Fort Crawford presented little opportunity for stimulating intellectual activity. His father gave him a handsome colt and taught him to ride, and he also enjoyed playing with the other children at the fort. But he began his education in a makeshift school run by a zealous missionary whose class consisted mainly of local Indian children. Caleb Atwater, a visiting commissioner of Indian affairs, remarked after inspecting Fort Crawford that army officers should not have to serve on the frontier more than ten years because their "worthy and most interesting children" received an uncivilized form of education. Dick did not wait long to express his own displeasure. Feeling the confines of the schoolroom too much to bear, one day he and a group of Indian boys broke free and hid in the nearby woods. Two days later a search party found the small renegades fully enjoying their respite in the wilderness. Before long, however, Colonel Taylor provided his officers' children with fairly decent instruction. In 1834, when Dick had turned eight years old, his father hired a tutor, Joseph T. Wills, and shortly afterward Richard F. Cadle became a chaplain and teacher at the fort. During the fall of 1834 Colonel Taylor took leave, primarily to locate proper preparatory schools for Dick and Betty. The following year he sent Betty to a girls' boarding school in Philadelphia, and by 1836 Dick had gone to Louisville, where he entered a private school and lived with relatives. John Bliss, one of his boyhood friends at Fort Crawford, recalled, "I was awfully sorry to part with Dick, and to show the strongest evidence of my regard, [I] named one of my [pet] squirrels after him."[12]

---

11. Hamilton, *Zachary Taylor: Soldier of the Republic*, pp. 75–99 (second quotation 81); Zachary Taylor to Dr. Thomas Lawson, August 23, 1828, in Parke-Bernet Galleries, *American Historical Autographs*, item 100 (first quotation).

12. *Record of the Class of 1845 of Yale College*, p. 197; K. Jack Bauer, *Zachary Taylor*, pp. 52, 68; Hamilton, *Zachary Taylor: Soldier of the Republic*, pp. 108, 110 (first quotation), 114 (second quotation).

Before Dick left Fort Crawford, one of his sisters, Sarah Knox, began a romance with a young lieutenant from Mississippi, Jefferson Davis. A proud graduate of West Point, Davis had impressed Colonel Taylor with his fighting talents during the Black Hawk War. Although Taylor trusted Davis to act as his personal adjutant, he objected strongly to the match with his daughter. He had already given away his oldest, Ann, in marriage to Dr. Robert C. Wood, an army surgeon serving at Fort Snelling, where the couple struggled to raise two children. Burdened besides with the deaths of his two infant daughters a dozen years before, Zachary Taylor exclaimed to a friend, "I will be damned if another daughter of mine shall marry into the Army." But Knox, as she was called, having spent several years at school in Kentucky and Ohio, was a headstrong and confident young woman of eighteen. Lieutenant Davis's fiery temperament complemented Knox's sense of maturity and independence during their courtship in 1832 and 1833. Angry at Taylor's unflattering opinion, Davis briefly considered challenging him to a duel, but he gradually became accustomed to meeting his sweetheart secretly, often with the help of mutual friends. Many times Knox took Betty and Dick on walks outside the fort, where Davis waited to see her. While the children played nearby, the two carried on their clandestine romance.[13]

In mid–1833 Davis received an assignment to Fort Smith, Arkansas, where he spent two years separated from Knox. Prior to his departure, however, they became engaged, and in the summer of 1835 Davis resigned his army commission and went immediately to Louisville. There he and Knox were married in the presence of several members of the Taylor family. Keenly aware that she was tempting her father's rage, Knox had told neither of her parents about her wedding plans. In a warm but resolute letter to her mother, she wrote, "Farewell, my dearest mother; give my best love to Pa and Dick." The newlyweds then departed for Brierfield, their beautiful plantation home in Mississippi, a wedding present from Davis's father. Less than three months later all hope of happiness vanished.

13. Hamilton, *Zachary Taylor: Soldier of the Republic*, pp. 100–104 (quotation 101).

Malaria struck both Davis and his bride. In mid-September, after a slow decline, Knox died.[14]

For her parents this tragedy could only amount to the cruelest kind of irony. At first relieved that their daughter would not be wedded to an army officer after all, they now were shocked to realize that Knox had died having become a planter's wife in the very same region where they had intended one day to settle. For twenty-five years Zachary Taylor had placed his personal life far behind the demands of military duty. He had too often neglected his family. Three of his children had died, and Betty and Dick were still away at school. To a fellow officer he confided sadly, "I scarcely know my own children or they me." By 1836 the Taylors were living alone.[15]

Eleven-year-old Dick had been at school in Louisville for more than a year in March 1837 when his father gained a leave of absence so that he and his wife could visit both Dick and Betty. Before they departed, however, word came of mounting Indian hostilities in Wisconsin, forcing Colonel Taylor to postpone his leave and travel north. Again, in July, he received orders, this time to report to Florida Territory, where he ultimately spent more than two and a half years of hard service during the Second Seminole War. Taylor fought well, receiving plaudits from his superior officers and rising to the rank of brevet brigadier general. In 1840, however, three years before the war's end, a subtropical fever debilitated him so severely that he requested to be removed from his command in order to rest and finally spend time with his family. Writing to his brother Hancock, General Taylor showed the strain of his fifty-five years, stating firmly, "My days . . . of ambition . . . are passed." He had not seen his wife for almost three years, and he had not seen Betty and Dick for almost five.[16]

In May of 1840, after Peggy Taylor had joined him briefly in Florida, together they returned to Louisville, where he enjoyed only a short reunion with Dick. Concerned about Betty, General and Mrs. Taylor journeyed to Philadelphia to visit her at school and then took

14. Ibid., pp. 104–8 (quotation 106).

15. K. Jack Bauer, *Zachary Taylor*, p. 69 (quotation).

16. Hamilton, *Zachary Taylor: Soldier of the Republic*, pp. 120–41 (quotation 141).

her on a vacation trip to Niagara Falls. En route the Taylors stopped in Massachusetts for an interview with James Gordon Carter, a highly regarded educator. Founder of an excellent preparatory school at Lancaster, near Boston, Carter discussed the prospect of admitting Dick for the school's fall term, a first step toward his eventual entry to Harvard College. Having seen his father for only a few weeks during the late summer, fourteen-year-old Dick was on his way to Lancaster in September, carrying with him $400 for his tuition and living expenses along with a letter of instruction from his father to Carter.[17]

Zachary Taylor's letter revealed the unmistakable effects of continual absence from his son. "In consequence of having been seperated [*sic*] from him . . . I am not sufficiently acquainted with the progress he has made in the different branches of education," Taylor admitted, "but [I] fear he has only superficial knowledge of some of them." In particular, he wanted Dick to learn French, probably because of the language's widespread use in Louisiana. "He is a youth as far as I can know, or can learn[,] of good morals," he continued, "as well as possessing a warm and affectionate disposition." Yet he qualified this appraisal by asserting that Dick was "perhaps a little hasty as to temper, but which no doubt can be readily controlled by proper advice combined with firmness and example." Likewise, General Taylor warned Carter that because his son "may want application" toward his studies, should he not respond to "reasoning" and "encouragement," then "he must fail as a matter of course, as he is too far advanced toward manhood for any thing like coercion to be used." To keep abreast of Dick's progress, General Taylor asked Carter to write to him "fully and freely" and to remind Dick to correspond with his parents at least twice a month.[18]

17. K. Jack Bauer, *Zachary Taylor*, p. 94; Hamilton, "'A Youth of Good Morals,'" pp. 304–7.

18. Hamilton, "'A Youth of Good Morals,'" pp. 305–6 (quotations). So eager was Zachary Taylor to have Dick receive an exemplary education that he showed no worry about his son developing egotistical traits that might cause his father grief. Secure in his role as a military officer and head of his family, Taylor did not seem bent on protecting and asserting any form of perverse patriarchal power. On this subject, see Wyatt-Brown, *Southern Honor*, pp. 194–95.

Dick's erratic personality probably magnified itself in the eyes of a father who had missed seeing his only son reach the threshold of maturity. Without a personal male role model, Dick had learned to judge matters for himself, and at James Carter's preparatory school he would find fertile ground for exercising his independence. Carter had devoted his career to achieving educational innovation and reform. A Harvard graduate with credentials as the author of several textbooks and service in the Massachusetts legislature, he had helped establish the state's public common school system as well as normal schools. As a teacher he developed a scientific method of instruction based upon inductive reasoning, urging his students to work toward discovering broad, general truths by first examining specific facts. He completely discarded the traditional mode of requiring the memorization of textbooks and lectures. Thus stimulated to learn rationally and logically, Dick put his penchant for self-governing action to good use.[19]

Even under Carter's care, however, Dick's lapses of attention and stubborn behavior proved a problem. General Taylor complained to a friend in late 1841 that his son wanted to leave the school. By 1843, having reached age seventeen, Dick bluntly informed his father that he preferred to enter Yale rather than Harvard. Assenting to the decision, General Taylor wrote his son-in-law, army surgeon Dr. Robert Wood, then stationed at Buffalo, New York, and asked him to accompany Dick to New Haven and arrange for his admission to the college. At Yale Dr. Wood and Dick met with James Kingsley, eminent professor of Latin and literature. Professor Kingsley generously agreed to supervise Dick's financial affairs and to report on his general progress as a student. Having received a high level of instruction at James Carter's preparatory school, Dick qualified to join Yale's junior class in the fall of 1843.[20]

During the first half of the nineteenth century Yale College en-

19. On Carter, see Woody, "James Gordon Carter," 4:538. Cremin, *American Education*, pp. 135–37, 153–55, 174–75.

20. Zachary Taylor to E. A. Hitchcock, November 3, 1841, Zachary Taylor Papers, Manuscript Division, Library of Congress. Cited hereafter as Zachary Taylor Papers LC. Zachary Taylor to James L. Kingsley, March 6, 1844, Kingsley Memorial Collection.

joyed the reputation of offering the most complete education in
America. Harvard maintained a heavy intellectual emphasis on literature and the arts, but Yale provided more instruction in the sciences,
economics, and politics. Besides having the largest faculty and enrollment of any college, Yale attracted students from all over the country
and sent its graduates into virtually every realm of professional practice, enterprise, and public life. Yet this venerable institution also reflected a widespread stagnation in American higher education.
Rather than adjusting to the demands of increasingly individualistic
and undisciplined young men like Dick Taylor, colleges continued to
rely upon traditional regimented curricula, textbooks designed for
memorization and recitation, and pedestrian instruction by under-
paid professors who had little motivation to understand what individual students either wanted or needed. Far from adopting the reforms
then sweeping lower-level schools, colleges too often failed to challenge and inspire students to understand their own capabilities and
establish specific goals for their personal lives and employment.[21]

Comments about Dick from his classmates testify to an all-too-
common case of academic floundering. One recalled, "He was a man
of good abilities, but rather lazy, and won no special distinction in
college. But he was very popular in his class, a genial companion, full
of fun and frolic, and known as a kind-hearted, good fellow." Like
many of his uninspired contemporaries, Dick studied impulsively and
randomly. "He was a voracious, although somewhat desultory,
reader," observed another classmate. Dick especially enjoyed the heroic Greek and Roman classics as well as great works in military history. For the most gregarious students, campus literary societies, organized and promoted by the members themselves, provided
valuable intellectual enlightenment. "[The societies] filled a place in
the training of young men which the ordinary curriculum of the college does not and cannot fill," observed an appreciative alumnus.
Dick joined the Calliope Society, a group first formed in 1819 in the
wake of a dispute between northern and southern students over the
Missouri Compromise. The Calliopians always maintained a strong
southern membership. The various societies often indulged in spir-

21. Bledstein, *Culture of Professionalism*, pp. 203–47; Hofstadter, *Academic
Freedom*, pp. 209–74; Cremin, *American Education*, pp. 271–80, 400–406.

ited discussions and held formal debates over political and social issues of the day, but Dick did not distinguish himself as a public
speaker.[22]

The most lasting image Dick left with his classmates was that of a
refined southern gentleman. One described him as "handsome, always finely dressed, popular, generous, talented, and rather easy-
going." On at least one occasion he showed a streak of compassion.
One morning after compulsory prayers and a sermon in the old
Theological Chamber on campus, a collection plate for foreign mis-
sions was passed among the students. When the plate reached Dick,
he threw in a ten-dollar gold piece. "This was so extraordinary, at that
day," remembered a witness, "and for a student who was not identi-
fied with the religious activities of the college, that it made a deep
impression upon us, and was talked of for some time, to Dick's
credit."[23]

If Dick seemed to fit in comfortably at Yale, unfortunately his father and mother hardly knew anything of it. In March of 1844 Zachary Taylor wrote to Professor Kingsley asking him to report on Dick's
welfare. "From some cause unknown to me," admitted an embarrassed General Taylor, "Richard has not written either his mother or
myself since he has been at Yale." Only one message from Kingsley,
sent the previous November through Dr. Wood, had reached the Taylors. "I have no excuse to offer for troubling you in this matter, but
the anxiety of a parent," stated General Taylor. Apparently the only
kind of support Dick had needed from his family was strictly financial, because his father complained a few months later that Dick's living expenses had risen to an excessive level.[24]

In August 1845 Dick joined his class in commencement exercises.
Throughout his two years at Yale he had kept his grades at a respectable standard, averaging 2.8 on a 4.0 scale. Grading had been consis-

22. Stokes, *Memorials of Eminent Yale Men*, 2:343–45 (quotations); Cremin, *American Education*, p. 406; Meade, *Judah P. Benjamin*, p. 24.

23. C. C. Esty to Anson Phelps Stokes, Jr., November 9, 1912 (first quotation), Thomas K. Davis to Anson Phelps Stokes, Jr., May 24, 1913 (second
quotation), Stokes Autograph Collection.

24. Zachary Taylor to James L. Kingsley, March 6, 1844 (quotations),
Kingsley Memorial Collection; K. Jack Bauer, *Zachary Taylor*, p. 103.

tently severe. Only a small minority of students achieved an average
of 3.0 or slightly above. Commencement lasted most of an entire day,
with 32 of the more than 150 graduates delivering orations and reading poems. Dick neither spoke nor received any special recognition.[25]

None of Dick's family managed to attend the graduation. Once
again military duties had prevented Zachary Taylor from sharing in
his son's accomplishments. Just one week before the commencement
exercises General Taylor had received orders to proceed to Corpus
Christi, Texas, and take command of an army sent to protect the
lower Rio Grande from possible Mexican retaliation to the pending
annexation of Texas by the United States. For a decade the Mexicans
had disputed the Republic of Texas's hold on the entire area south of
the Nueces River, and they now viewed annexation as tantamount to
war. As diplomatic overtures stalled during late 1845 and early 1846,
General Taylor maintained a steady correspondence with his family.
Peggy Taylor and twenty-one-year-old Betty, now living in a secluded
cottage near Baton Rouge, had welcomed Dick back home from the
Northeast in September. Fully grown to five feet, eight and a half
inches, Dick had his father's dark hazel eyes and deep tan complexion. Slightly taller and noticeably thinner than the rather broad-
shouldered general, however, Dick showed his mother's sharp facial
features and dark brown hair. Now approaching his twentieth birthday, he seemed somewhat aimless and uncertain about his future.
His father, expressing no deep concern about the problem at the
time, wrote Betty in December 1845 advising her to study French
and other cultured subjects with her brother: "You and he should
read alternately aloud after tea in the history of England or Shake-
speare's plays, till near bedtime, [and] conclude with a chapter in the
Bible."[26]

In early 1846 Dick began considering his career more seriously.
Responding to his father's increasingly stern questions, in March he
wrote regarding the possibility of studying medicine or taking up

25. Yale College Student Record Book for the Class of 1845, Yale College
Student Record Books; *Order of Exercises at Commencement*.

26. K. Jack Bauer, *Zachary Taylor*, p. 111–17; Hamilton, *Zachary Taylor: Soldier in the White House*, p. 26; Hamilton, *Zachary Taylor: Soldier of the Republic*,
p. 114 (quotation).

plantation management. Hostilities along the Mexican border soon flared into war, and by June, after stunning military triumphs at Palo Alto and Resaca de la Palma, Zachary Taylor had vaulted from relative obscurity to national fame. In a letter to son-in-law Robert Wood, he admitted that although he felt "greatly honored" by the public's acclaim, "I would feel doubly so could I have any surety [that] it would . . . prompt my descendants to tread the path of honor by pursuing a bold, manly, and honest course in all the relations and situations of life."[27]

To resolve his course in life, Dick sought personal consultation with his father. Hoping to visit General Taylor at his headquarters in Matamoros, Dick got as far as New Orleans when he suffered an attack of rheumatoid arthritis, a painful inflammation of the muscles and joints in his limbs. Periodically afflicted so badly that he could not walk or even stand up, he seemed most vulnerable to the disease when extremely anxious or disappointed. Learning of the sudden illness, General Taylor expressed hopes that Dick would return to Baton Rouge, and he warned that Mexico "is no place for anyone in poor health."[28]

On July 5, however, Dick stepped off a vessel from New Orleans and joined his father at his Matamoros encampment. For the first time in six years they saw each other face to face. In a letter to Dr. Wood, General Taylor made only a terse mention of the reunion: "Dick got here day before yesterday; if he has learned nothing else he has learned to chew, to use tobacco." This should not have seemed entirely foolish to his father, since the general himself had a reputation for chewing and spitting with uncanny accuracy. The strained circumstances did not ease when Dr. Wood suggested that perhaps Dick might serve as an army staff aide. General Taylor dismissed the notion as improper, because so many deserving young officers had

27. Richard Taylor to Zachary Taylor, March 23, 1846, in *American Book Prices Current*, p. 2498; Samson, *Letters of Zachary Taylor*, p. 9 (quotation).

28. Samson, *Letters of Zachary Taylor*, p. 9 (quotation). Rheumatoid arthritis is still a widespread disease, and in advanced stages it can destroy internal organs and incapacitate the central nervous system. Recent research indicates that the disease stems from a mycoplasma organism akin to a bacterium or virus. See Thomas McPherson Brown, *Rheumatoid Arthritis*.

Major General Zachary Taylor in 1848, immediately after the Mexican War (Beinecke Library, Yale University).

already applied for staff positions. Dick would remain without any specific task, despite his father's concern that "idleness is here and everywhere else a growing evil." After about a week of fruitless conversations, General Taylor displayed outright exasperation. "I have not as yet made up my mind," he wrote, "as to the occupation in life it would be best for him to adopt or pursue."[29]

As August approached, the sweltering Mexican weather began taking its toll on Dick's strength, and his rheumatism flared up so sharply that his father sent him home. Characterizing his son as "talented" but "rather wild," General Taylor had gained an appreciation of Dick's youthful dilemma. "I would have been much pleased could he have remained with or near me to the end of the campaign," he wrote Dr. Wood. A month later, as he led his army toward Monterrey, he admitted that it was "better to make no very great calculations as regards the prominent positions our children are to occupy, as there are so many contingencies connected with the same, they are but rarely realized." In December the general commented on Dick in a letter to Peggy Taylor: "Let him select his own calling and I will be contented. . . . I will do all in my power to further his views and wishes. . . . Anything but idleness!"[30]

Dick spent a few weeks during August and September with his mother and sister at Pascagoula, Mississippi, a resort community on the Gulf, where he hoped to benefit from the sea breezes and warm salt water. In the spring of 1847, however, he continued to experience bouts of rheumatism and considered going to the hot springs in Arkansas to seek relief. In the meantime he had spent a few weeks in New Orleans enjoying the city's social life. "I deeply regret to hear of Dick's continued indisposition," wrote Zachary Taylor, "and [I] fear his long residence in New Orleans where there are so many temptations, was not at all favorable to his recovery." In June Dick journeyed

29. Samson, *Letters of Zachary Taylor*, pp. 25 (first quotation), 27 (second and third quotations); Hamilton, *Zachary Taylor: Soldier in the White House*, p. 23.

30. Hamilton, *Zachary Taylor: Soldier in the White House*, p. 27 (first quotation); Samson, *Letters of Zachary Taylor*, pp. 36 (second quotation), 55–56 (third quotation); Brainerd Dyer, *Zachary Taylor*, p. 259 (fourth quotation).

up the Mississippi to Arkansas, where his health gradually improved, although he failed to regain all his strength.[31]

By August, Dick had decided to try a more distant health spa, the famous hot springs in western Virginia. At White Sulphur Springs, in Greenbrier County deep in the Allegheny Mountains, he experienced effective therapy. A favorite resort and vacation spot for prominent families from across the South, White Sulphur Springs had been lavishing bodily and social benefits upon its visitors since the 1770s. In late October, however, General Taylor again began to lose patience with his prodigal son. "Dick I hope will join his mother next month nearly if not quite restored to health," he mentioned to Dr. Wood, "and will I hope be ready and anxious to commence the study of a profession or enter into business of some kind; he has already been idle too long." A month later, preparing to return home a victorious war hero and full-blown contender for the presidency, Zachary Taylor repeated his vexation regarding Dick, complaining, "he has been idle too long for his own good, or reputation."[32]

Although Dick had acted like a rakish young reprobate, he also had begun to establish himself among the upper echelon of fashionable southern society. His independent character and cultured education gave him a personable flair that assured his popularity in almost any company. Dabney Maury, a Virginian recovering at White Sulphur Springs from wounds sustained during the Mexican War, recalled the effect Dick had upon a gathering of mature, cosmopolitan men: "Even then Taylor was self-reliant and brilliant in conversation; all he said was terse, and illustrated by vivid and classical metaphor. Keen sarcasm and ready wit abounded in his talk, and in a circle of gentlemen educated in the highest social associations of this country he was pronounced by all of them the most brilliant young man they had ever met." More attuned to his personal appearance and social graces than unpretentious "Old Rough and Ready" Zachary Taylor, Dick cut a dashing figure, especially for the eligible young females of the formidable plantation families of the lower Mississippi.[33]

31. Samson, *Letters of Zachary Taylor*, pp. 56–57, 98 (quotation), 120.

32. Ibid., pp. 129, 145 (first quotation), 152 (second quotation); Moorman, *Virginia Springs*, pp. 75–193. See also Reniers, *Springs of Virginia*.

33. Maury, "Reminiscences of General Taylor," p. 568 (quotation).

One nineteen-year-old Natchez belle, Mary Conner, fell hopelessly in love with him. A daughter of wealthy cotton planter Henry L. Conner, Mary recorded in a private journal her most intimate affections for Mr. Taylor, as she properly called him. Although devoted to him to the extent of resisting the advances of several other suitors, she restrained herself in his presence, acting the traditional role of a modest and demure young southern lady. Introduced to him by her older brother Lemuel, one of Dick's classmates at Yale, Mary began spending time with him during his frequent visits to Natchez. Taking carriage rides, playing cards, conversing at dinner parties, singing and playing piano, and dancing at formal balls, they seemed the perfect couple. As early as the fall of 1846 she thought of him as "my dark eyed Don Quioxite" and delighted in the local gossips who insisted that Dick must be in love with her. "If he is not," she wrote, "he can affect the lover most admirably." During most of 1847 Mary continually pined for him while he recuperated at the hot springs in Arkansas and Virginia. The pain of separation finally abated in December when General Taylor made a triumphal visit to Natchez amid thousands of cheering citizens. "Mr. R. Taylor also came with his father," noted Mary. "He looked very well indeed, and has got a furious moustache, which I am afraid will carry my poor heart captive." At an evening party a few days later, Dick surprised Mary by suddenly taking her hand and kissing it. "I am almost inclined to think that he is very much in love with me," she exclaimed in her journal.[34]

Two months later, in February 1848 at a ball given in honor of Zachary Taylor in Woodville, Mississippi, Mary struck up a friendly conversation with the general. He confessed to her that from the time Dick began his schooling in Kentucky they had seen each other only once prior to their meeting at Matamoros during the war. He said that Dick was named for the general's father, "who was the world" to him as a boy. Now he hoped that somehow he might mean as much to Dick. "When General Taylor told me good-bye he kissed me," Mary recalled, "which took me very much by surprise."[35]

34. Conner, "Journal," typescript, pp. 6–7 (first quotation 7), 75 (second quotation), 77 (third quotation); *Catalogue of Officers and Students in Yale College*.

35. Conner, "Journal," p. 85 (quotation).

Zachary Taylor's longing for personal respect and affection from his son persisted even in the midst of the 1848 presidential campaign. Emerging as the leading prospect for the Whig party's nomination, General Taylor held interviews with party leaders and corresponded with Whig conventions and newspaper editors across the country, despite Peggy Taylor's daily prayer that he would not seek the office. After a banquet in New Orleans in January he suffered a seizure in his leg that left him confined for more than a month at the family home near Baton Rouge. While resting there he decided once and for all to put Dick to work on the Mississippi plantation. This decision was neither rash nor unfair to Dick, nor did it reflect the growing tendency among planters to force their sons into plantation agriculture rather than professional pursuits. Zachary Taylor simply could not stand to see his only son do nothing meaningful with his life. He had already informed Dr. Wood, "If we can do no better I want him [Dick] to go to the plantation and have a general supervision of the establishment, until he understands the . . . principles of planting."[36]

The plantation, known as Cypress Grove, rested on a wide bend of the Mississippi River, in Jefferson County, Mississippi, about thirty miles north of Natchez. General Taylor had purchased the property, with its 1,923 acres and 81 slaves, in 1841 at a price of $60,000 by using a combination of cash and mortgage notes. Having already sold his three smaller plantations, he transferred the slaves from those and bought more, so that eventually he maintained 127 blacks at Cypress Grove. By the end of the Mexican War, Zachary Taylor, hardly the poor career army officer, had amassed an enviable fortune as an absentee planter and investor. Besides Cypress Grove, he owned real estate in Louisville, held banking and utility stocks, and had a substantial amount of cash as well, giving him assets of about $140,000, all with minimal indebtedness against him. Slaves accounted for well more than one-third of his wealth. One of only about 1,800 planters in the entire South who owned more

36. K. Jack Bauer, *Zachary Taylor*, pp. 220–32; Hamilton, *Zachary Taylor: Soldier in the White House*, p. 25; Oakes, *Ruling Race*, pp. 69–74; Samson, *Letters of Zachary Taylor*, p. 152 (quotation).

than 100 slaves, he ranked easily in the top 1 percent among all slaveholders.[37]

For almost twenty years General Taylor had wanted to retire from the army and, as he told his New Orleans commercial factor Maunsel White, "purchase a small plantation . . . with the prospect of ease and comfort the rest of my life." A newspaper reporter from nearby Port Gibson described Cypress Grove's main living quarters as "a modest white frame house, [of] one story," and noted that "the furniture . . . is almost as plain as that of [General Taylor's] tent in Mexico. . . . No carpet covered the floor, and no mirrors hung on the walls." High cotton prices had made the plantation an attractive purchase, but in the spring of 1847 the Mississippi River flooded its banks, washing away almost all of the crop. Even worse, the general had little time to devote to his "unfortunate" plantation during the coming year of political campaigning. By early 1848 he had worried so much about Cypress Grove's "downward tendency" that he complained in a private letter that planting "has ruined me." Although he surely exaggerated the damage to his finances, his decision to cast Dick into the middle of the quagmire represented a serious risk. If a sickly social butterfly barely twenty-two years old could manage Cypress Grove for even a short time, he would at least learn the daily uncertainties and tough demands of honest work.[38]

Apparently Dick had little chance to protest, so he accepted the challenge with a characteristic air of stubbornness, finally determined

37. K. Jack Bauer, *Zachary Taylor*, pp. 107–9; Brainerd Dyer, *Zachary Taylor*, pp. 255–56.

38. K. Jack Bauer, *Zachary Taylor*, pp. 32 (third quotation), 37 (fourth quotation), 106–7 (first quotation 106, fifth quotation 107), 109. Maunsel White, an Irish immigrant, met Zachary Taylor in Louisville before setting himself up in business in New Orleans in 1801. White treated Taylor and other clients leniently during difficult financial periods, earning the general's special gratitude and praise in 1842, when Taylor and most other cotton planters found it impossible to meet their obligations on time. On White, see Eaton, *Mind of the Old South*, pp. 69–74. Undated genealogical data on the Taylor family (second quotation), Wood Papers. The exacting detail of Zachary Taylor's instructions and expectations for his plantation is evident in Currie, "Zachary Taylor," pp. 144–56.

to prove himself. Discovering that the local demand for cypress lumber had jumped recently, he convinced his father to establish a sawmill at Cypress Grove. The slaves cut, hauled, and milled a huge quantity of cypress timber, working in around-the-clock shifts to keep pace with incoming orders for lumber. In a few months the sawmill proved more profitable than the cotton crop. General Taylor visited the plantation twice during the spring, and in the meantime he corresponded with Dick, suggesting dozens of ways to improve lumber production, crop cultivation, and care of livestock. In a letter to his brother, the general expressed complete satisfaction that Dick would make "a first rate planter."[39]

Meanwhile Mary Conner began feeling the effects of neglect, noting in her journal that although Dick had visited Natchez recently, he had failed to call on her. Relatives who had seen him told her that "he looked remarkably well, and seemed perfectly absorbed in planting." Mary could hardly bear it. "I feel sometimes as if my heart will break," she wrote. In late July Dick took a short respite in Baton Rouge, where he saw one of Mary's friends, Jane Young. A few days later Jane told Mary that when she "offered to introduce him to some ladies, he said no, that he did not want to know any, and that he wished he was back on his plantation." Another friend reported to Mary that Dick "looked uncommonly well but very much sunburnt." Finally, in August, after almost eight months of separation, she saw him in Natchez at a dinner party. "Oh! the joy of those moments," she bubbled. "He appeared delighted to see me, and took a seat by me and never left it. . . . Since I saw him I have felt like a new being." Dick informed her that the Taylor family planned to visit Pascagoula in a few days and that he hoped her family would be there also. It took little time for Mary to arrange the rendezvous.[40]

During the first two weeks in September the two families gathered at Pascagoula along with scores of other favored friends and army personnel, all anticipating a climactic grand ball honoring General

39. Hamilton, *Zachary Taylor: Soldier in the White House*, p. 36; K. Jack Bauer, *Zachary Taylor*, p. 37; Brainerd Dyer, *Zachary Taylor*, p. 259 (quotation).

40. Conner, "Journal," pp. 100 (first and second quotations), 110 (fourth quotation), 112 (third quotation), 114 (fifth quotation).

Taylor. At a party given the first evening, Dick danced only once with Mary, and he spent the rest of his time with another lovely belle. "How long have I to bear this misery?" Mary asked herself. Although he acted cordially enough toward her, Dick repeated his indifferent behavior at dinners and dances over the next several evenings. "It is my constant prayer," wrote Mary, "that he may not have consciously trifled with my feelings."[41]

The ball for General Taylor was held on September 13 in the large hotel at Pass Christian, a few miles down the coast from Pascagoula. "The village of Pass Christian . . . is a place of extreme beauty," recalled a daughter of a Mississippi planter. "The houses, embosomed in the shade of live-oak, magnolia, and other beautiful trees, were dotted along the beach for four miles. The residents or sojourners were, in the main, people of culture and wealth—either citizens of New Orleans or planters of Mississippi and Louisiana, who came there to spend the summer months." At the ball held in Zachary Taylor's honor several hundred celebrants witnessed the presentation of a gold medallion bestowed upon him by Congress in commemoration of his Mexican War exploits. "I have never seen the General so much discomposed," observed Mary. "He had his address written . . . [but] could scarcely read it." As the dancing commenced he walked over to Mary and some of her friends and showed them the medallion. "I am inclined to think that I am a great pet of the General's," Mary boasted, recalling that an officer friend of his had said that "the General was courting me for Richard." Mary felt "most grateful to the dear old General, but this does not compensate for Mr. Taylor's neglect." Dick did not ask her to dance the entire evening, much to her displeasure. A few days later he accompanied the Conners onboard a steamboat returning to Natchez. "Mr. Taylor had partly promised he would stop and pass a few days with us," she recalled, "but just before we got off he concluded that he had better visit the plantation first."[42]

Instead of reappearing at Natchez, Dick decided to remain at Cypress Grove. "How strange it is that I should continue to love him," pouted Mary. "Would I have believed anyone two years ago if they

41. Ibid., pp. 118–22 (first quotation 119, second quotation 122).

42. Smedes, *Memorials of a Southern Planter*, p. 83 (first quotation); Conner, "Journal," pp. 127 (second and third quotations), 131 (fourth quotation).

President Zachary Taylor in 1849, the burdens of office already obvious
(Beinecke Library, Yale University).

had told me that my pride would so entirely forsake me?" In November the news of Zachary Taylor's election to the presidency swept the lower Mississippi Valley with excitement. Then in December the Taylor family celebrated Betty's marriage to Colonel William Bliss, the general's talented and devoted personal secretary. For some unknown reason, perhaps because of illness, Dick did not attend the wedding. In early January 1849, Mary Conner's brother William received a melancholy letter from her Mr. Taylor. William told Mary that Dick "regarded himself as an unfortunate man, that he had assumed every character in the world to please the ladies but none of them would smile upon him." Rather than resolving to give him that special smile he desired, Mary seemed consumed with helplessness. "If he would only think of me," she cried to herself. "He knows that I love him." Either Dick knew nothing of the sort, or he chose to ignore it.[43]

In mid-February Mary learned from a friend who had recently seen Dick in New Orleans that he had acted in a "most devoted" manner toward a fair young lady accompanying him to the opera. In the first week of March, however, Dick paid a surprise visit to Natchez. Mary tried to conceal her glee upon seeing him. "He took me to dinner," she exulted, "and I had more conversation with him then than I have had in years before." Dick told her that she was "a great favorite of his father's and mother's." Dick later confessed in a private conversation with Mary's uncle, Elliott Conner, that General Taylor had openly expressed his wish that Dick would find a wife. "The General referred him particularly to me," wrote Mary. "I can never cease to thank the General for this." Then, without warning, Dick sent word that he had returned to Cypress Grove.[44]

Soon afterward another flood on the Mississippi broke through the levees and inundated the plantation. Deciding to report directly to his father about the calamity, Dick took an ocean steamer to Washington in July. Not only had the flood ruined the entire cotton crop, but continual heavy rains had also forced a halt to the sawmill operation. The president tried to appear stoic. "We ought to be thankful that matters were no worse," he stated. While in Washington Dick took

43. Conner, "Journal," pp. 134 (first quotation), 153–54 (second quotation 153, third quotation 154); Hamilton, *Zachary Taylor: Soldier in the White House*, p. 26.

44. Conner, "Journal," pp. 167 (first quotation), 170–71 (second, third, and fourth quotations), 172. One of Dick's lady friends recalled, "All the fashionable young folks . . . felt the opera was absolutely necessary to their social success and happiness." See Eliza Ripley, *Social Life in Old New Orleans*, p. 67.

time to enjoy his family. His mother, whose religious devotion compelled her to attend church daily, had taken little interest in the role
of first lady, so Betty welcomed visitors to the White House and accompanied her father at formal occasions. Having been unable to attend the presidential inauguration the previous spring, Dick delighted in meeting many of the capital's political stalwarts, particularly
those of Whiggish allegiance. He also managed to accompany one of
Martin Van Buren's sons on a side trip to White Sulphur Springs,
where he gained some badly needed relaxation. Dick returned home
in October, reaching New Orleans in the middle of the month. Mary
Conner noted in her journal that some friends in Natchez told her
that he had stopped there briefly and that "he is quite well and quite
fleshy." However, he saw fit neither to call on her nor to send any
personal greeting. Their lengthy and erratic courtship had ended.
Mary never mentioned him in her journal again.[45]

In December Dick received a distinguished visitor, Lady Emmeline
Stuart-Wortley, a touring English aristocrat who had come to Amer-
ica with her daughter Victoria. She had already passed through
Washington, where President Taylor had greeted her cordially at the
White House and recommended that she stop at Cypress Grove.
Lady Stuart-Wortley and Victoria arrived there aboard the steamer
Natchez on the afternoon of December 18. Dick welcomed them "with
the kindest hospitality," recalled Lady Stuart-Wortley. He then sum-
moned all the slaves to assemble in a semicircle outside the house.
They "seemed thoroughly happy and contented," impressing the vis-
itors as "generally fine stout-looking people, and had not at all a stu-
pid air" about them.[46]

"Men, women, and children all appeared to adore Mr. Taylor, who
seemed extremely kind to them, and affable with them," observed
Lady Stuart-Wortley. As a treat, he distributed tobacco to the men,
and "they proceeded to smoke to our healths." Dick said that every
day the slaves each received a pound of meat, a ration of milk, and as

---

45. Hamilton, *Zachary Taylor: Soldier in the White House*, pp. 171, 238 (first
quotation); Jackson Beauregard Davis, "Life of Richard Taylor," p. 52; Conner, "Journal," p. 244 (second quotation).

46. Stuart-Wortley, *Travels*, pp. 86–87, 117–19 (first quotation 117, second
quotation 117, 119); Welby-Gregory, *Journal of a Tour*, pp. 83–84, 126–27.

much bread and vegetables as they wanted. On Sundays he gave them coffee, flour for pastries, butter, sugar, and salt for the week. The women wore white calico and woolen shawls, and the men were dressed comfortably in flannel. The visitors described one of the slave cabins as "a most tastefully decorated and an excellently furnished one . . . scrupulously clean and neat." When Victoria asked to meet some of the "small sable fry," at least twenty young mothers hurried forward to show off their babies. "Such a congregation of little smiling, good-natured, raven roly-polies, I never saw collected together before," wrote Lady Stuart-Wortley. Then "Mr. Taylor sent word that there were enough, thereby stopping a long line of about twenty-five more . . . each anxious to have the glory of being told that hers was the prettiest." [47]

Afterward an aged man of more than one hundred years ambled up to the porch to "see the white ladies." He greeted them with the "most Chesterfieldian bows and reverences, [and] with multitudinous respectful inquiries after our health," recalled Lady Stuart-Wortley. Dick asked him a question: "What do I owe you for those chickens you sold to me a little while ago?" The ancient gentleman answered promptly, "One dollar and five bits." Dick paid him, and Lady Stuart-Wortley added a small gratuity for his visitation, evoking from the recipient a lively demonstration of thanks punctuated by another series of deep bows. Dick later explained that he allowed this venerable slave to raise his own chickens; "and . . . I assure you," he insisted, "[the old man] invariably charges the very highest prices." [48]

Discussing living arrangements on the plantation, Dick told Lady Stuart-Wortley that he always slept "in his own shanty, surrounded by the slaves' quarters, without bolt, bar, or lock of any description on his doors, and that the negroes were not shut up in any way." She described his "shanty" as a "very nice wooden building . . . looking over the river, and [it] had a capital sitting room, very cool and pleasant." In the main house, which Victoria termed "rather primitive, though comfortable," Dick took pleasure in showing them a large li-

47. Stuart-Wortley, *Travels*, pp. 117–19 (first and second quotations 119, third and fourth quotations 117); Welby-Gregory, *Journal of a Tour*, pp. 127–28 (fifth quotation).

48. Stuart-Wortley, *Travels*, pp. 118–19 (quotations).

brary that he and his father had assembled. He seemed particularly proud of a Mexican edition of *Don Quixote* illustrated with lavish engraved plates, acquired during his sojourn to his father's camp at Matamoros during the Mexican War.[49]

Dick had a personal valet, a young slave described by Lady Stuart-Wortley as "remarkably intelligent looking." Apparently he had taught himself how to read and write. Only recently Dick had discovered the boy sitting up late at night, saving candles to provide light, and going without sleep in order to study. Although teaching a slave to read violated state law, Dick encouraged his valet's talents. As for the ultimate value of slavery, Lady Stuart-Wortley admitted that she had witnessed "the *couleur de rose*" of the institution, but she truly believed that slaves as a whole rarely received abusive treatment, except at the hands of small planters, "who have never had such power before." Her aristocratic prejudices thus guided her opinions.[50]

The Taylor "servants" unquestionably experienced the most benign sort of life slavery could offer. In 1893 the Louisville *Post* carried an interview with an elderly black woman who had been a Taylor family slave more than fifty years earlier. Aunt Mildy, as she was called, personified the easy compliance whites valued so highly, in contrast to the brashness of the younger generation of blacks. She spoke of her affection and devotion to the Taylors and said that she had accepted her proper place and the limited opportunities of a freed slave. She could not tolerate "high fluttin' niggers." The reporter neglected to ask her, however, whether she had enjoyed slavery more than freedom.[51]

Probably anticipating the difficulties facing him in the office of president of the United States, Zachary Taylor told a story in the summer of 1848 regarding another old female servant who continually grumbled about one problem or another. More than anyone he ever knew, she illustrated "the impossibility of satisfying people in this world." Hearing her say one day that she "would be perfectly happy if she had a hundred dollars," he decided to grant her wish. At first

49. Ibid., p. 118 (first, second, and fourth quotations); Welby-Gregory, *Journal of a Tour*, p. 127 (third quotation).

50. Stuart-Wortley, *Travels*, p. 119 (quotations).

51. George C. Wright, *Life behind a Veil*, p. 48 (quotations).

she seemed overjoyed and grateful, but as he walked away he heard her remark to herself, "I wish I had said two hundred."[52]

Although his affection for his slaves probably matched the feelings of the kindest southern masters, like any rational businessman Zachary Taylor had made certain that all of his property—especially his extremely valuable human property—received his abiding concern and care. Cypress Grove had proved a precarious enterprise, but his infatuation with planting persisted and even expanded while he served as president. During her visit to the White House, Lady Stuart-Wortley heard him speak of "the beauties of nature in the South" and how he "longed to return to Cypress Grove . . . his quiet home near the banks of the Mississippi." In April of 1850, however, floodwaters rose again, this time to a record level, devastating the plantation more severely than ever. President Taylor wrote gravely, "Misfortune on misfortunes have followed me in such rapid succession from floods and otherwise for the last six or eight years, I feel almost heartbroken and broken down." He even considered disposing of Cypress Grove and selling his slaves, although he had never previously sold any of them.[53]

Despite his chronic pessimism, Zachary Taylor soon authorized Dick to arrange for the purchase of yet another plantation, a large piece of property on the lower Mississippi River in St. Charles Parish, Louisiana, in the heart of the sugar cane region. Attracted to sugar's reputation for high profits, President Taylor had wanted to own such a plantation for several years, but the heavy costs of purchase and maintenance had prevented it. Dick had discussed this goal with his father, and now, having discovered a prime opportunity, he pushed it to fruition. The plantation, known as Fashion, comprised more than 1,200 acres, a large and elegant main house, and all necessary machinery and tools, along with 64 slaves. Situated about 30 miles upriver from New Orleans and owned by G. W. Fullerton, Fashion carried a purchase price of $115,000, a sum requiring a cash payment of $19,500 and a series of notes payable over the next four years.

52. Smedes, *Memorials of a Southern Planter*, pp. 117–18 (quotations 118).

53. Stuart-Wortley, *Travels*, p. 87 (first quotation); Brainerd Dyer, *Zachary Taylor*, pp. 261–62; Zachary Taylor to Richard Taylor, May 9, 1850 (second quotation), Zachary Taylor Papers LC.

Dick's father urged him to make absolutely sure that the plantation would present no major difficulties and, most of all, to see that its levees were secure from flooding. "The loss of one [year's] crop might have the effect to embarrass me," he warned, "and the loss of two might result in utter ruin." In the sugar region the prospect of handsome returns brought with it serious risks.[54]

Had Fashion fallen on hard times, Zachary Taylor would have seen his finances somewhat strained, but not broken. He could have made a much larger cash payment at the time of purchase; but he always preferred to maintain liquid funds, and during the same period he invested rather heavily in bank stocks as well. His income, coupled with his annual chief executive's salary of $25,000, had risen considerably, despite the calamities at Cypress Grove. He decided to retain Cypress Grove rather than sell it, and in mid-June he instructed Dick "to carry on the saw mill without interruption, and indeed . . . run it day and night, as soon as the Mississippi falls sufficiently." He also encouraged his son to take with him to Fashion "as many hands from Cypress Grove as can be employed to advantage." The president's only worry about Fashion's work force stemmed from an apparent lack of "young negroes, which is always a very bad sign. . . . [But] I hope you will be able to have it corrected." Asking Dick to report regularly on "our money concerns and prospects," he predicted that with "proper industry and economy, we can hardly fail to meet all our engagements as they fall due." Cypress Grove would likely remain only marginally profitable, if at all, but as for Fashion, Taylor and son expected to net $20,000 or more annually, an extremely good profit on their original investment.[55]

Zachary Taylor's vicarious devotion to "the great art of planting," as he called it, had taken an ambitious leap forward, largely because of Dick's aggressive designs to purchase Fashion. Only a few weeks later,

54. Zachary Taylor to Richard Taylor, May 9, 1850 (quotation), Zachary Taylor Papers LC; Jackson Beauregard Davis, "Life of Richard Taylor," pp. 52–53.

55. K. Jack Bauer, *Zachary Taylor*, pp. 109–10; Hamilton, *Zachary Taylor: Soldier in the White House*, p. 386; Zachary Taylor to Richard Taylor, June 11 (quotations), 12, 1850, Zachary Taylor Papers LC.

however, the president fell ill after attending a long Fourth of July ceremony at the Washington Monument. After suffering for several days with a painful intestinal inflammation and fever, on July 9 he died. After a state funeral at the White House and temporary inter- ment in Washington, Peggy Taylor arranged for burial at the Taylor family cemetery near Louisville. The president's brother Joseph and son-in-law William Bliss accompanied his remains to Kentucky. Peggy Taylor, with Ann and Betty, left for New Orleans and arrived there in early November. Dick had found it impossible to join his family in the sad tributes to his father. "I have been very ill indeed with congestion of the brain brought on by anxiety and exposure to the sun on [the] plantation . . . and am now barely able to sit up," he explained to Col- onel Bliss. After spending several weeks at Pass Christian to regain his strength, he met with the entire family in New Orleans, where an excellent attorney, Judah P. Benjamin, handled the Taylor estate's settlement.[56]

The dispersal of Zachary Taylor's properties went smoothly. The total value of the estate, including the mortgage value of Fashion, amounted to more than $225,000. Peggy Taylor and her two daugh- ters received and divided among themselves the bank stocks, the Louisville real estate, some cash, 48 slaves, and the Cypress Grove plantation, which they eventually sold. The family agreed to allow Dick to retain ownership of Fashion, with its 64 slaves. He also re- ceived $21,000 in cash and 83 more slaves, valued at $43,825, who had lived at Cypress Grove. Altogether, Dick garnered well over half of the estate's tangible assets. His holdings in slaves alone, a total of 147, now carried a value of at least $75,000.[57]

Twenty-four-year-old Dick Taylor could call himself a substantial planter. But Fashion also represented an immense financial obliga- tion involving a debt of almost $100,000 and only a few years to can-

56. Zachary Taylor to Richard Taylor, June 12, 1850 (first quotation), Zachary Taylor Papers LC; K. Jack Bauer, *Zachary Taylor*, pp. 316–19; Rich- ard Taylor to William W. S. Bliss, August 31, 1850 (second quotation), Mis- cellaneous Manuscripts Collection, Filson Club.

57. K. Jack Bauer, *Zachary Taylor*, pp. 313–20; Hamilton, *Zachary Taylor: Soldier in the White House*, pp. 398–99.

cel it in full. His mother and sisters became so worried about the risk that for a while they wanted "to get rid of Fashion . . . even at a sacrifice." But Dick persuaded them to let him keep it. Without any experience in the intricate problems of running a sugar plantation, and saddled with acutely delicate health, he lurched headlong toward a challenge his father had never meant for him to face alone.[58]

58. Hamilton, *Zachary Taylor: Soldier in the White House*, p. 399; K. Jack Bauer, *Zachary Taylor*, p. 320; Richard Taylor to William W. S. Bliss, August 31, 1850 (quotation), Miscellaneous Manuscripts Collection, Filson Club.

CHAPTER TWO

Paternalistic Planter

Oh! no, sir, I'd rather be free!

William, one of Richard Taylor's slaves

Owing fundamentally to his father's personal guidance and financial legacy, Richard Taylor had gained enough confidence to manage Fashion by himself. By channeling his independent temperament and energetic mind into serious work, he would soon accustom himself to the rigors of complete ownership. His periodic bouts with severe illness, rather than discouraging him, only seemed to harden his will to succeed on his own.

Thanks also to his father, Dick had experienced a first-class education, an advantage that spurred within him a lofty self-image to match his determination. Hardly satisfied to settle down to business alone, he had achieved considerable social standing among the South's plantation aristocracy. His father's frontier-style crustiness and outward humility had left no impression upon Dick. Now a gentleman planter in the region of Dixie that boasted the largest per capita wealth in the nation, he would not be mistaken for a common farmer as his father often had been. One of his socially sophisticated friends later observed, "Dick Taylor had a magnetic personality, which overshadowed the fact [that] he was the only son of . . . the President." His intellect and polished manners and his heritage—the aristocratic colonial Virginia heritage the old family slaves had

dramatized for him when he was a child—would reassure him profoundly of his fitness for a role of prominence and leadership. Richard Taylor did not aspire to compete for honor and power; he assumed it would be his duty to accept them, just as he had accepted
the responsibility of building upon his father's fortune.[1]

To a privileged young man like Taylor, the southern plantation system provided the legitimate source of all productive vitality and social
stability. Like so many of the South's elite families situated for generations on the tidewater lands and along the fertile lower Mississippi
River Valley, he embraced the plantation's enduring strength as a unifying force in the face of potentially divisive economic interests and
social differences among white southerners. Proud of their colonial
forebears (particularly if they had rendered service during the Revolution), sedate and dignified in their religion (usually Episcopalian),
and imbued with English-style notions of aristocratic noblesse oblige,
the planter gentry firmly upheld the tradition of benevolent leadership along with their assumption of continuing wealth, despite the
nineteenth-century South's increasingly democratic and commercially competitive environment.[2]

According to this conservative ideal, the plantation system gave the
South a harmonious blend of aristocracy and democracy, springing
from a pastoral agrarian culture that flourished with widespread productivity and growing economic opportunity. The heart of the syn-
thesis lay in planters' paternalistic attitudes, manifested in the social
behavior they displayed on a daily basis. Most significantly, they believed that by acting with kindness and care toward their slaves they
would engender loyalty and affection from these servants, who would
therefore adhere gladly to the discipline necessary to make the plantations prosper. Likewise, an understanding of proper roles played
by yeoman farmers and other common whites reinforced the notion
of a hierarchical but interdependent free white society. Planters supposedly deserved aristocratic prestige and political prominence along
with undisputed economic strength, while lesser folk enjoyed social

1. Eliza Ripley, *Social Life in Old New Orleans*, p. 144 (quotation).
2. Oakes, *Ruling Race*, pp. 190–216; Eaton, *Growth of Southern Civilization*,
pp. 19–22; Kolchin, *Unfree Labor*, pp. 157–67.

respect, a democratic voice in politics, and opportunities to improve their positions, even to become planters themselves.[3]

Publicly softening class distinctions among whites by emphasizing racial superiority to all blacks, planters assumed that their longstanding claims to leadership had unquestioned democratic support. But if privilege meant power, it also demanded the responsibility to serve the best interests of all, both black and white; to lead by example and mutual trust rather than to dominate and exploit; to place the general welfare above personal profits; and to temper southerners' own brand of American political individualism, materialism, and racial antagonism with a sense of organic unity. As a permanent ideal, the plantation system thus evoked an incentive for all members of a diverse society to act in concert for the stability and well-being of the whole. With the greatest duty resting upon the shoulders of the planters, stability depended entirely upon the South's acceptance of paternalism's benevolent intent and civilizing effect.[4]

Owning an excellent property like Fashion enabled Taylor to project an image of grand wealth and stability as completely as any planter could have dreamed. Travelers to Louisiana's sugar district often wrote of the serene view offered from the decks of the steamboats passing up and down the Mississippi. "The villas of the planters are thickly planted in the midst of green fields," remarked one observer during a summer sojourn. "These fields, level as a billiard table, are of the brightest green crops of maize and sugar." The plantations seemed to embody an incomparable prosperity, with thousands of acres of tall cane spreading back toward cypress forests sev-

3. The pervasive influence of planter paternalism is argued most strongly in Genovese, *Roll, Jordan, Roll,* pp. 3–158; and Genovese, *World the Slaveholders Made,* pp. 95–102, 165–244. See also Kolchin, *Unfree Labor,* pp. 103–91. For a critical view of paternalism, see Gutman, *Black Family in Slavery and Freedom,* pp. 309–18.

4. Edgar T. Thompson, *Plantation Societies,* pp. 3–40, 69–111; Potter, *Impending Crisis,* pp. 456–57; Greenberg, *Masters and Statesmen,* pp. 3–22; Hesseltine, "Four American Traditions," pp. 3–32. See also the excellent description of antebellum southern society in Escott, "Failure of Confederate Nationalism," pp. 18–24.

Richard Taylor, sugar planter, ca. 1860. A friend commented on Taylor's prosperous countenance, "Dick is fat as a Dutchman." Portrait by Julius Hoening (Louisiana State Museum).

eral miles in the distance. Because each estate had a narrow front on the river, usually no more than a half-mile to a mile in width, the road running along the levee seemed like the main avenue of a spacious village. The large houses, with their stately pillars and wide verandas, stood surrounded by several outbuildings and long, neat rows of whitewashed slave cabins. Perfect classical symmetry and harmony of design met the eye at every bend of the great river.[5]

The mansions stood as the most salient evidence of a planter's success, but these graceful structures also manifested several practical features. Usually constructed of thick cypress timbers and bricks made of river clay, they possessed great strength and durability. Their high pitched roofs extended outward, normally on all four sides, thereby forcing off the frequent rains as well as providing shade from the intense, semitropical sunlight. Taylor's domain received its most telling description from Frederick Law Olmsted, the famed travel journalist who later became America's foremost landscape architect. He noted that Taylor's house echoed the traditional Creole style, having a lower story constructed of brick and an upper story of wood, with a broad veranda all around. Round brick columns with connecting arches supported the entire structure beneath the veranda, and a wide stairway at the front of the house led to the upper floor's main living quarters: two parlors, a library, and bedrooms. Several small dormer windows were spaced evenly across the roof.[6]

Exercising a sharp eye for horticultural elegance, Olmsted noted that Fashion's grounds flaunted rows of orange and fig trees, sculpted evergreens, and colorful beds of violets and other flowering plants. In the rear of the house was a vegetable garden an acre or more in size. Several other buildings stood behind the house: the kitchen, the domestic servants' quarters, a stable and carriage house, and barns for the blacksmiths, coopers, and carpenters. A road led farther back to the sugar works, a huge brick smokestacked building housing machinery for processing the cane crop into sugar. Nearby Olmsted

5. Russell, *My Diary North and South*, p. 254 (quotation); Thorpe, "Sugar and the Sugar Region," pp. 749–50; Prichard, "Tourist's Description of Louisiana," pp. 1112–13.

6. Sitterson, *Sugar Country*, pp. 73–74; Roland, *Louisiana Sugar Plantations*, pp. 1–9; Olmsted, *Seaboard Slave States*, p. 659. On Olmsted, see Roper, *FLO*.

found "the negro settlement," thirty-six comfortable-looking cabins. From there the cane fields spread outward, the whole expanse of almost a thousand acres surrounded by a sturdy fence of cypress posts and rails. A well-traveled man not easily impressed, Olmsted called Fashion "a capital plantation."[7]

As Fashion flourished, so too did Taylor's personal life. During the difficult months of mid–1850, when he battled illness and adjusted to the impact of his father's death, he had the good fortune of receiving moral support from a beautiful sixteen-year-old girl, Myrthe Bringier. Mimi, as she was called, daughter of the well-known French Creole family with extensive sugar plantation holdings in Ascension Parish, had first met Taylor in 1848 at a dinner party honoring his father. The party's host, Duncan F. Kenner, was a prosperous sugar planter and state legislator who had married into the Bringier family. He was the husband of Mimi's sister Nanine. Taylor soon began courting Mimi. Her younger siblings teased her about Taylor's dandified appearance, especially his stylish long hair and wide-skirted coats. In the summer of 1850, during Taylor's convalescence at Pass Christian, the Bringier family happened to stay at the same hotel, allowing the couple to devote themselves to romance. "There was Dick Taylor," recalled a friend, "propelled in a wheel chair over that hotel veranda . . . his valet so constant in attendance that we wondered how the young man ever got an opportunity to whisper sweet nothings into the ear of lovely Myrthe Bringier—but he did!" At Pass Christian he asked for her hand in marriage, and in early February 1851, shortly after Mimi's seventeenth birthday, the wedding ceremony took place at Melpomene, the Bringier family house in New Orleans.[8]

Mimi's vivacious personality provided a perfect complement to her husband's polished demeanor. Frederick Law Olmsted described her

7. Olmsted, *Seaboard Slave States*, pp. 658–59 (first quotation 659); Menn, *Large Slaveholders of Louisiana*, p. 346; Beveridge and McLaughlin, *Papers of Frederick Law Olmsted*, p. 213 (second quotation).

8. Undated genealogical data on the Taylor family, Wood Papers; Melvin J. White, "Duncan Farrar Kenner." On Kenner, see also Craig A. Bauer, "A Leader among Peers." Eliza Ripley, *Social Life in Old New Orleans*, p. 144 (quotation).

as "a devil of a Creole wife—young, childish, whimsical, comical." Dabney Maury, a longtime friend of the family, observed, "In his domestic relations he was singularly happy." The marriage also reflected a certain practicality, especially on Taylor's part. Although well-to-do Creole families had traditionally maintained a distinct, rigidly Catholic and conservative culture, during the 1840s and 1850s they began intermarrying frequently with Anglo-Americans, particularly with young men eager to solidify or enhance their social and economic standing. In New Orleans and most of southern Louisiana the passive ways of the Creoles gradually gave way to modern manners and values. Taylor had purchased Fashion from an elderly Creole, an indication that land and wealth were flowing to the more aggressive Anglo-American planters. By moving into the Bringier and Kenner circle, Taylor had made the most advantageous decision of his life.[9]

Within a year after their wedding Dick and Mimi Taylor had a baby girl, Louise Margaret, named for Mimi's own given first name and for Taylor's mother. In July 1854 another girl was born, Elizabeth, called Betty, the same as Taylor's sister. Then in June 1857 they had their first son, Zachary, named in honor of Taylor's father and nicknamed Zack. In June 1860 another son was born, named Richard after his father and nicknamed Dixie. Taylor's mother lived at Fashion for only a short time, keeping with her there General Taylor's personal papers and military relics. Varina Howell Davis, Jefferson Davis's second wife, recalled, "When General Taylor died [I] was with the family [in Washington, D.C.]. . . . Mrs. Taylor was worn to a shadow and lay without uttering a sound. . . . [It was] the last crushing sorrow of a lifetime, which she survived but a very short time." She died in August 1852, shortly before her sixty-fourth birthday, while staying at her cottage on the Gulf near Pascagoula. She had lived long enough to enjoy her granddaughter Louise's first eight months. Dabney Maury, having an opportunity to observe Taylor's private life during this period, later

9. Beveridge and McLaughlin, *Papers of Frederick Law Olmsted*, p. 213 (first quotation); Maury, "Reminiscences of General Taylor," p. 569 (second quotation); Sitterson, *Sugar Country*, p. 76; Ralph A. Wooster, "Wealthy Southerners," pp. 146–47; Wyatt-Brown, *Southern Honor*, pp. 212–13; Oakes, *Ruling Race*, p. 45.

commented, "He was true and devoted to his family, and free and affectionate in his intercourse with them."[10]

Along with the joys and responsibilities of marriage, Taylor undertook the continual care of Fashion's other families, his numerous slaves. The remarkable eyewitness account by Frederick Law Olmsted affords a glimpse of a southern master and his bondsmen in a genuine manner that few outsiders were privileged to see. Although Olmsted opposed slavery, he shunned abolitionist doctrine, instead viewing the institution as an economic and social hindrance to modern progress in the South. He refused to blame southerners alone for slavery, which he preferred to call "an unfortunate circumstance." Believing that gradual voluntary emancipation would eventually solve the problem, Olmsted hoped to engender mutual understanding and conciliation between the North and the South. Intent on presenting an accurate picture of southern society for readers of the fledgling New York *Times*, and with help from some of his brother's former Yale classmates, he contacted Taylor and received an invitation to visit Fashion. Stopping in New Orleans on the way, he heard the distressing rumor that "Dick Taylor was nearly dead," the victim of a fever brought on by his rheumatoid arthritis. After proving the rumor false, Olmsted took a steamer upriver and spent three full days, February 23–25, 1853, interviewing Taylor and Fashion's slaves.[11]

"He is a man of more than usual precision of mind, energetic and humane," Olmsted wrote of Taylor, "and while his negroes seem to be

10. Tucker, *Descendants of the Presidents*, p. 104; Elizabeth Taylor Stauffer to Gaillard Hunt, June 30, 1922, Zachary Taylor Papers LC; Hamilton, *Zachary Taylor: Soldier in the White House*, p. 399; Varina Howell Davis, "Gen. Zachary Taylor. Mrs. Jefferson Davis' Recollections of Him," undated clipping in biographical files, United Daughters of the Confederacy Library, Waco, Tex. (first quotation); Maury, "Reminiscences of General Taylor," p. 569 (second quotation).

11. Beveridge and McLaughlin, *Papers of Frederick Law Olmsted*, pp. 4–11, 210 (first quotation), 470; White and Kramer, *Olmsted South*, pp. xviii–xix (second quotation xviii), 52–53. Taylor became so ill during the first half of 1853 that the rumor of his imminent death was complicated by yet another rumor that he had gone insane. See Braxton Bragg to his wife, June 9, 1853, Bragg Papers.

Frederick Law Olmsted, ca. 1860
(Fabos, Milde, and Weinmayr, Frederick Law Olmsted*).*

better disciplined than any others I had seen, they evidently regarded him with affection, respect, and pride." When Olmsted and Taylor began their tour of Fashion late in the morning, the slaves had not seen their master for several weeks during his illness. About a dozen young women, returning from the fields to take a two-hour break for nursing their infants, encountered Taylor and his visitor first and offered an excited greeting. "Oh, master! how is 'ou?" they inquired.

"Well, I'm getting up," replied Taylor. "How are you, girls?" He then inquired about their children and showed particular concern about one baby who had been sick. A boy driving a cart stopped nearby, removed his hat respectfully, and inquired after his master's health. "I'm getting well, you see," said Taylor, and then he remarked, "If I don't get about and look after you, I'm afraid we shan't have much of a crop." The boy took the claim in jest and chuckled, "Ha!—look heah, massa!—you jus' go right straight on de ways you's goin'; see suthin' make you laugh," thereby indicating that the slaves had all been hard at work to insure the sugar cane's healthy growth.[12]

Olmsted found the slave cabins at Fashion "neat and well-made," comparing them to cottages he had seen in New England company towns. As a rule, slave cabins in the South were crudely constructed, had dirt floors, and cramped the families living in them. Taylor had destroyed the existing cabins when he purchased Fashion and had replaced them with much better ones. Olmsted noted that they looked like structures he had seen on a particularly prosperous Georgia rice plantation, except that Fashion's also had broad verandas. Each cabin measured twenty-one by twenty-one feet, dimensions almost double the largest size typically recorded by contemporary observers. "The clothing furnished the negroes, and the rations of bacon and meal, were the same as on other good plantations," wrote Olmsted. Taylor always purchased clothing for his slaves, rather than expecting them to make their own. During the course of one year he spent almost $1,800 on winter and summer clothing, including coats, pants, shirts, frocks, and chemises. The large garden usually produced plenty of corn and other vegetables, or Taylor purchased enough to make up the difference. He also provided weekly rations of pork, flour, coffee, and tobacco. During the cool months the slaves continually enjoyed hot molasses made from the sugar cane. Unlike many planters, Taylor made certain that the slaves received regular medical attention. He retained a physician's services for frequent visits at an annual fee of $250, thereby reducing the occurrence and

12. Olmsted, *Seaboard Slave States*, pp. 657–58 (quotations). In his book Olmsted referred to Taylor as "Mr. R," a method used to protect southerners from any stigma that might result from public knowledge of their identities. See Beveridge and McLaughlin, *Papers of Frederick Law Olmsted*, pp. 463–64.

severity of sickness. Olmsted concluded, "The Negroes [were] well taken care of and comfortable as possible." [13]

By all accounts the slaves who worked on Louisiana's sugar plantations experienced the most arduous physical tasks required of any bondsmen in the South. Although respite from labor came on Sundays and a few holidays, as well as on special occasions such as marriages and funerals, a relentless series of demands faced the slaves from the time they were small children able to carry the lightest loads. In late January all field hands, including men, women, and children, divided into gangs, usually by families, to begin plowing the soil and carefully planting small cuttings of cane saved from the previous year's harvest. "From the time the cane is put in the ground it is the source of constant anxiety," wrote one observer. "At least every two weeks, for nearly half the year, every part of the cane field is wrought over until it possesses a garden-like neatness that commands the admiration of the person most indifferent to agricultural pursuits." Continual hoeing of weeds and replowing of furrows to insure the proper balance between moisture and drainage as well as soil depth, depending on the temperature and rainfall, gradually brought the tender green cane shoots to a height of four or five feet by July. The slaves then took to the swamps at the rear of the plantation, where they cut and hauled back great loads of wood for the fuel necessary to make sugar. They also cleaned the deep ditches that drained the

13. Olmsted, *Seaboard Slave States*, pp. 659–61 (first quotation 659, second quotation 660), 422; Blassingame, *Slave Community*, pp. 254–55; David et al., *Reckoning with Slavery*, pp. 292–98; statements of accounts current for Richard Taylor with Martin Gordon, Jr., February 15, 1854–June 15, 1858, Richard Taylor Papers in the possession of Edward M. Boagni, Baton Rouge. Cited hereafter as Taylor Papers, Boagni Collection. Invoice from Hebrard & Co. to Richard Taylor, September 7, 1860, invoice from Hebrard & Co. to Richard Taylor, March 1, 1861, receipt from Thomas E. Broaddus, M.D., to Richard Taylor, April 1, 1858, Zachary Taylor Papers LC; receipt from Sam W. Logan, M.D., to Richard Taylor, January 14, 1852, and receipt from M. R. Brickinnough, M.D., to Richard Taylor, January 1, 1856, Taylor Papers, Boagni Collection; Whitten, "Medical Care of Slaves," pp. 153–80; William K. Scarborough, "Slavery—The White Man's Burden," pp. 115–16; Joe Gray Taylor, "A New Look at Slavery in Louisiana," pp. 190–208; Beveridge and McLaughlin, *Papers of Frederick Law Olmsted*, p. 213 (third quotation).

fields, reconditioned the roads running through the cane, gathered wild hay for the winter, and prepared the machinery in the sugar works for the period of harvesting cane and making sugar—the all-important grinding season.[14]

For three or four months a year, from October through December and often into January, sugar production went on around the clock, even on Sundays and usually through Christmas. Taylor told Olmsted that during the grinding season "nearly every man, woman, and child on his plantation, including his overseer and himself, were at work fully eighteen hours a day." (Taylor's recent physical breakdown had probably resulted from the grinding season finished a few weeks earlier.) Out in the fields the strongest workers wielded hooked machetes that cut the thick, ten-foot cane stalks and stripped them of their leaves in four rapid, sweeping strokes. Others loaded and carted the cane away to the sugar works. With the approach of cold weather and the possibility of a freeze, any delays might prove disastrous. In the sugar works the slaves fed the cane stalks into steam-powered presses with heavy cylinders that ground the cane and squeezed out the sweet juice. Filtered through charcoal and then boiled in airtight metal drums, the juice gradually reduced to a thick syrup that cooled into dark brown sugar crystals, while molasses separated itself and drained off from the sugar. "The amount of fuel consumed in the production of sugar is enormous," commented an observer. "Three cords [of wood] are on an average necessary for the manufacture of one hogshead of sugar." The hogsheads, large wooden barrels made by the slaves, each held a thousand pounds of sugar or seventy gallons of molasses. Once filled and sealed, they stood ready for shipment to market in New Orleans.[15]

14. Rice, *Rise and Fall of Black Slavery*, p. 287; William K. Scarborough, "Slavery—The White Man's Burden," pp. 111–15; Thorpe, "Sugar and the Sugar Region," pp. 756–57 (quotation 757); Olmsted, *Seaboard Slave States*, pp. 665–67; Prichard, "Routine on a Sugar Plantation," pp. 171–73; Moody, "Slavery on Louisiana Sugar Plantations," pp. 232–38. For a particularly informative account of operations on a sugar plantation, see Whitten, *Andrew Durnford*.

15. Olmsted, *Seaboard Slave States*, pp. 667–73 (first quotation 668); Sitterson, *Sugar Country*, pp. 112–56; Prichard, "Routine on a Sugar Plantation,"

Despite the grinding season's constant pressures, Taylor told Olmsted that "his negroes were as glad as he was himself to have the time for grinding to arrive, and they worked with greater cheerfulness than at any other season." Olmsted surmised that this cheerfulness resulted from the extra food and limitless helpings of fresh coffee and molasses available to the slaves, as well as the cooperative atmosphere—the feeling of a "degree of freedom . . . and a variety of occupation which brings a recreation of the mind . . . and pleasure in their labor." At the same time, they looked forward to a Christmas celebration that would last several days, although it might come a week or two into January. As an added incentive and a kind of reward, at Christmas Taylor divided among the heads of each family money representing one dollar for each hogshead produced on the plantation. If any slave had shown "careless or lazy" behavior during the year, "it was remembered at this Christmas dole." Although the gifts averaged only two or three dollars for each slave, the money seemed to boost morale, noted Olmsted, because it gave them "a direct interest in the economical direction of their labor." Prosperity for all thus depended upon a unified effort, true to the plantation system's timeless ideals.[16]

For those who refused to submit to paternalism's beneficent guidelines, however, punishment came as surely as did rewards. Rather than attempting to reason with an erring slave, most masters and their overseers resorted to impersonal methods such as imposing extra work, confinement, or decreased rations. The most extreme method, of course, remained the whip. Even considering the cash value represented in a prime field hand or skilled workman, one outspoken Louisiana planter professed, "If the law was to forbid whipping altogether, the authority of the master would be at an end." Yet Olmsted made no direct mention of whippings or of even seeing a whip at Fashion, thus leaving the impression that Taylor rarely, if ever, engaged in the practice. Olmsted merely stated in passing, "Men

---

p. 175; Moody, "Slavery on Louisiana Sugar Plantations," pp. 238–42; Thorpe, "Sugar and the Sugar Region," p. 758 (second quotation).

16. Olmsted, *Seaboard Slave States*, pp. 668 (first quotation), 660 (second and third quotations); Boles, *Black Southerners*, p. 81; Moody, "Slavery on Louisiana Sugar Plantations," pp. 248, 253–56.

of sense have discovered that when they desire to get extraordinary exertions from their slaves, it is better to offer them rewards than to whip them; to encourage them, rather than to drive them." It seemed quite clear that Taylor preferred to foster mutual responsibility between master and slave rather than mutual abuse.[17]

The most serious discipline problems at Fashion arose from the unavoidable contact Taylor's slaves had with the outside world. On a few small farms bordering Fashion lived some Acadians (commonly called Cajuns), whose presence disturbed Taylor intensely. By 1853 he had managed to buy much of their property and incorporate it into his own acreage, but most of them had refused to sell, even at prices two or three times actual worth. He told Olmsted that they acted like "lazy vagabonds, doing but little work, and spending much time in shooting, fishing, and play." The Acadians lured his slaves into doing "little services" for them by promising "luxuries" Taylor did not wish the slaves to have. Most of all, however, he worried that the Acadians' example of laziness "was not favorable to good discipline" and that it "demoralized" his slaves. "Seeing them living in apparent comfort, without much property and without steady labor, the slaves could not help thinking that it was not necessary for men to work as hard as they themselves were obliged to; that if they were free they would not need to work." Although Olmsted neglected to ask Taylor whether any of his slaves had ever attempted to make a run for freedom, Taylor's attitude exhibited less concern about their ultimate loyalty than about their immediate behavior. Any slave, he realized, might decide to resist a master's demands, even if that slave did not harbor freedom as an ultimate goal.[18]

The worst kind of aggravation from outside whites occurred when petty traders stopped at Fashion. Floating silently downriver on small boats during the night, these crafty peddlers tempted slaves, usually young males, into stealing small but expensive pieces of equipment

17. Blassingame, *Slave Community*, pp. 264–65; William K. Scarborough, "Slavery—The White Man's Burden," pp. 120–22; Oakes, *Ruling Race*, pp. 154–63, 167 (first quotation); Olmsted, *Seaboard Slave States*, pp. 668–69 (second quotation).

18. Olmsted, *Seaboard Slave States*, pp. 673–74 (quotations 674); Boles, *Black Southerners*, p. 83.

from a planter's sugar works. The slaves sold the equipment to the traders at a small fraction of real value and then normally used the money to purchase liquor from the traders themselves. Although selling liquor to slaves clearly violated the law in every southern state, thefts by slaves and their subsequent dealings with such black-market merchants posed a chronic problem on virtually all large plantations. Holding little or no tangible property of their own, slaves generally believed that their masters could easily afford such losses. Olmsted noticed that thievery seemed especially frequent along the lower Mississippi. Planters tried to keep each other informed when a trader came into their vicinity, but most of the boats escaped detection. Local police had virtually no effect in either deterring or catching the traders. If cornered, they easily disposed of all evidence by tossing it overboard into the river. "The law is entirely inadequate to protect us against the rascals," Taylor complained. "We can never get them punished, except [when] we go beyond or against the law ourselves." Successful vigilante action usually led to the seizure of a boat and its cargo and sometimes to a trader's death by hanging, particularly if he turned out to be a midwesterner who could be accused of espousing free labor principles among the slaves.[19]

Taylor told Olmsted quite pointedly that he preferred "that negroes never saw anybody off their own plantation; that they had no intercourse with other white men than their owner or overseer," and "especially it was best that they should not see white men who did not command their respect, and whom they did not always feel to be superior to themselves, and able to command them." This statement underscored Taylor's outright disdain for common whites who upset the conservative ideal of a rigid social hierarchy. Believing in permanent class inferiority for both common whites and blacks, paternalistic masters like Taylor conceived that blacks, as slaves, simply stood at the lowest level on the social scale. His genteel class consciousness thus muted his racism. Blacks who accepted their subordination to all whites played their proper role in the hierarchy, not so much because

19. Olmsted, *Seaboard Slave States*, pp. 674–75 (quotation); Stampp, *Peculiar Institution*, pp. 125–27; Joe Gray Taylor, *Negro Slavery in Louisiana*, pp. 204–7; Moody, "Slavery on Louisiana Sugar Plantations," pp. 256–60; Russell, *My Diary North and South*, p. 289.

they were black as because they were slaves. Free blacks stood on a slightly higher level, still posing no threat to a planter's social stature. But planters also recognized that freedom for large numbers of blacks would prove intolerable to common whites. If slaves even imagined themselves as equal or superior to common whites, they shook the foundations of social stability and harmony. If they ever saw themselves as deserving of freedom, they robbed a paternalistic master like Taylor of all justification for their care and protection.[20]

Olmsted discovered the limits of paternalism at Fashion in a long conversation with a house servant named William. Riding together in a buggy on the road back to New Orleans, a distance of some twenty miles, Olmsted and William had ample time to get acquainted. William said he was about thirty-three years old and that he had been raised in Virginia, where he was taken from his mother at the age of thirteen and sold in Louisiana. He had lived and worked at Fashion for two decades and had been sold twice with the plantation. Taylor was his third master. A trusted servant with a quick mind, he handled French fluently and seemed at ease with Olmsted, calling him "massa." "He spoke rapidly, garrulously," recalled Olmsted, "and it was only necessary for me to give a direction to his thoughts, by my inquiries."[21]

William at first displayed curiosity about Olmsted's home state of New York and other parts of the North, particularly about black people who lived there. Talk soon turned to Africa, and William spoke with a serious and concerned expression. "I've heered, massa, dat dey sell one another dah, in de fus place. Does you know, sar, was dat so?" Olmsted described the "savage custom of making slaves of prisoners of war, and . . . the constant wars of the native Africans. I told him that they were better off here than they would be to be the slaves of cruel savages, in Africa." William looked Olmsted in the face "anxiously . . . like a child," and asked, "*Is* de brack folks better off to be herc, massa?" Olmsted tried to explain this common belief, but William paused and asked shrewdly why whites wanted to send free blacks to the African colony in Liberia. Rather than admit that most

20. Olmsted, *Seaboard Slave States*, p. 674 (quotation); Oakes, *Ruling Race*, pp. 209–11.

21. Olmsted, *Seaboard Slave States*, pp. 676–78 (quotation 676).

whites viewed all blacks, slave and free, as racially inferior and unacceptable in white society, Olmsted skirted the question.[22]

As they slowly passed other plantations in the vicinity, William pointed out the hard conditions endured by the slaves, especially those owned by free blacks and Creoles. "If I was sold to a brack man, I'd drown myself," he asserted; as for the Creoles, "dey whip dar niggers most to deff—dey whip de flesh off of 'em." The Anglo-American plantations surpassed these in every respect, he assured Olmsted. "Didn't you see de niggers on our plantation, sar? . . . Why, dey all looks fat, and dey's all got good clothes, and dey look as if dey all . . . hadn't got no work to do." Then he let out a laugh. "But dey does work, dough. Dey does a heap of work." Without any inducement from Olmsted, he substantiated Taylor's claim that the slaves enjoyed the grinding season most of all, "because—oh, it's merry and lively." William proudly called Fashion "the best plantation in the state, and he believed there was not a better lot of negroes." He said that Taylor allowed them to raise their own corn, potatoes, pumpkins, and other vegetables on patches of ground at the edge of the swamps. They worked these private gardens on Sundays and at night, and once the grinding season ended, they had Saturday afternoons off as well.[23]

Then Olmsted sprang the question he had wanted to ask the most: "Well, now, wouldn't you rather live on such a plantation than to be free, William?" "Oh! no, sir, I'd rather be free!" the slave answered excitedly. "Why would you?" asked Olmsted. "If I was free—if I was *free*, I'd have *all* my time to myself. I'd rather work for myself. I'd like dat better," William explained. "But then, you know, you'd have to take care of yourself, and you'd get poor," insisted Olmsted. "No, sir, I would not get poor, I would get rich," William affirmed, "for you see . . . then I'd work *all de time* for myself." Asked what he would do with his freedom, he said he would visit his mother in Virginia and then go to work on a plantation and earn enough money to buy his own house and farm, get married, and raise a family. Other slaves, if

22. Ibid., pp. 676–79 (first quotation 678, second quotation 678–79, third quotation 679).

23. Ibid., pp. 680–83 (first quotation 680, second and third quotations 681, fourth quotation 682).

emancipated, would do the same, working "*harder* dan dey do now to get more wages—a heap harder." [24]

Sensing William's deep feelings on the subject, Olmsted asked whether the other slaves at Fashion spoke of freedom with the same passion. William responded instantly, "Oh! yes, sir; dey talk so; dat's what dey tink." But when Olmsted asked whether they discussed freedom to a great extent, William became more guarded. "Yes, sir," he answered in a halting voice. "Dey—dat is, dey say dey wish it was so; dat's all dey talk . . . dat's all, sir." Unlike almost any other examples of contemporary conversations with slaves, Olmsted's encounter with William revealed the widespread notion of freedom as an ultimate ideal among bondsmen. William had displayed remarkable candor, and the sudden prudence and reticence in his final statement reflected a concern that he might have betrayed himself and his fellow slaves by appearing dissatisfied or disloyal. "His caution was evidently excited," Olmsted noticed, "and I inquired no further." William's remarks confirmed that Taylor recognized the immense value of humane treatment for his slaves. More consistently than most other masters, he managed to assert his authority without losing his slaves' outward loyalty and respect, at least the great majority of the time. Yet neither a paternalistic master nor the fellowship and security found in Fashion's slave community could divert or distract them from their deepest and most cherished longing. William's ultimate dreams centered upon the opportunities he could possess only by gaining freedom: to reestablish his family ties from the distant past, to work productively and one day own a farm and other property—in essence, to join American society and become his own master. [25]

24. Ibid., pp. 679–80, 683–84 (first, second, third, and fourth quotations 683, fifth quotation 684).

25. Ibid., p. 684 (quotations); Van Deburg, *Slave Drivers*, pp. 62–66; Blassingame, *Slave Community*, pp. 148–51, 160–66, 191–92, 213–17; Gutman, *Black Family in Slavery and Freedom*, pp. 257–326. On the limits of communal bonds and attachments among slaves, see Kolchin, "Reevaluating the Antebellum Slave Community," pp. 579–601. See also Kolchin, "American Historians and Antebellum Southern Slavery," pp. 87–111.

As for Taylor, when Olmsted asked him to express his own opinion about slavery, he offered none of the racist rhetoric so popular among southern planters. On the contrary, like many conservative paternalists, he admitted that slavery represented "a very great evil, morally and economically." He even called it "a curse upon the South" and said that "nothing would be more desirable than its removal, if it were possible." The effect upon the character of whites seemed "most deplorable" of all to Taylor, causing him to regret "that his children would have to be subject to it." Yet he could not tolerate the moralistic rantings of northern abolitionists, who seemed to harbor particular contempt for slavery in Louisiana, where the most barbarous conditions allegedly existed. In his memoirs Taylor referred to Harriet Beecher Stowe's *Uncle Tom's Cabin* as "dramatic talent prostituted to the dissemination of falsehood."[26]

Taylor told Olmsted that "eventually" he would like to liberate his bondsmen and send them to the free black colony in Liberia, "if he were able to afford it." Taylor's visions of shipping his slaves to Africa seemed consistent with paternalistic desires to protect freedmen from abusive common whites in the South, but his dominant worry about his own financial welfare unmasked his most essential goal. Slavery had made both his father and himself rich men, and he meant for it to make him richer still. Even a planter with the strongest paternalistic values realized that slaves not only guaranteed social prestige among southerners, but more crucially, slaves also offered the most immediate potential for producing enough wealth to reap uncommon luxuries, physical security, and personal freedom for himself and his heirs. Virtually all planters and would-be planters aspired to possess such wealth. Supposedly an incidental, even crass pursuit among conservative paternalists, this fundamental commitment to material prosperity forced men like Taylor into a painful dependence upon slavery. Even the kindest treatment of their slaves and the most sincere recognition of slavery's immorality by such planters still left

26. Olmsted, *Seaboard Slave States*, pp. 675–76 (first, second, third, and fifth quotations); Oakes, *Ruling Race*, pp. 118–19; Harwood, "Abolitionist Image of Louisiana and Mississippi," pp. 281–308; Richard Taylor, *Destruction and Reconstruction*, p. 275 (fourth quotation).

black persons defined as valuable, productive property first and human beings second.[27]

Rather than confessing any moral guilt or personal responsibility for perpetuating slavery, Taylor considered the institution an unavoidable and unfortunate circumstance. He continued to cling to the self-image of a benevolent social paternalist, despite having demonstrated to Olmsted that the respect and authority he had among both slaves and common whites depended not so much upon paternalistic relationships as upon direct control, a method dictated by his devotion to personal wealth. Unlike the multitude of planters who defended their right to profits on the basis of race, Taylor defended his right to genteel racism on the basis of profits. He had simply reversed the equation. Either way, the results were the same: slavery and wealth defined each other, and in turn, they defined a planter's identity. Even the great necessity of maintaining racial control—so valuable in preserving common whites' support for planters' power—could not have justified slavery's existence unless the institution had made profits for a huge majority of planters year after year.[28]

The plantation system's primary capacity as a money-making boon brought the South unparalleled wealth during the 1850s. The largest planters like Taylor benefited by far the most from the upsurge in

27. Olmsted, *Seaboard Slave States*, p. 676 (quotation); Oakes, *Ruling Race*, pp. 119–20; Potter, *Impending Crisis*, pp. 454–55. A Louisiana law passed in 1852 typified increasing southern stringency against the manumission of slaves, prohibiting masters from freeing slaves without sending them out of the United States, preferably to Liberia. But planters who were determined to free their slaves within the state usually found a way to do so. Besides, Louisiana had a large population of free blacks with a longstanding status that gave them most of the legal rights enjoyed by whites. Like Taylor, most planters continued to insist that they would only endanger their slaves by setting them free, whether subjecting them to abusive whites within the South or sending them on the harsh passage to Liberia. Berlin, *Slaves without Masters*, pp. 129–42; Sterkx, *Free Negro in Ante-Bellum Louisiana*, p. 171.

28. On the pervasive absence of guilt about slavery among planters, see Foster, "Guilt over Slavery," pp. 665–94. On the compatibility of capitalism and conservative paternalism among planters, see Bowman, "Antebellum Planters and *Vormarz* Junkers," pp. 779–96, and Greenberg, *Masters and Statesmen*, pp. 89–102, 137–38. See also Fogel, *Without Consent or Contract*.

demand by the industrial world, most notably the Northeast and England, for cotton, sugar, tobacco, and other staple crops. Straining to
meet their share of this demand, many Louisiana sugar planters invested heavily in expensive modern processing equipment and machinery, experimented with scientific methods of cultivation, and
managed their plantations with utmost efficiency. Because a high federal tariff helped to offset competition from cheaper sugar grown in
the rich soil of the West Indies, planters pushed their own production
up rapidly, and they normally enjoyed annual net profits of 10 percent or more. Taylor informed Olmsted, "Three or four years ago
there was hardly a planter in Louisiana or Mississippi that was not in
very embarrassed circumstances. . . . [But] the good crops of the last
few years have set them all on their legs again; and this year all the
jewelers' shops, and stores of rich furniture and dry goods, in New
Orleans, were cleared out by the middle of the season, and everybody
feels strong and cheerful." An Englishman traveling through the city
in 1853 alluded to its commercial frenzy, commenting dryly, "New
Orleans [offers] surprising evidence of what men will endure, when
cheered on by the hopes of an ever-flowing tide of all-mighty dollars
and cents." By now the Crescent City was the largest port in the South
and one of the largest in the world, thanks almost entirely to the
power of the plantation system.[29]

By the time Olmsted visited Fashion in early 1853, Taylor had produced "three good crops in succession." Although an early frost had
limited his first crop to 175 hogsheads, the latest had yielded 530,
plus 1,200 barrels of molasses. The molasses alone had covered his
overhead expenses, and the sugar had given him a 25 percent profit
against his debts, a figure far above the profit margins achieved by
most sugar planters. Taylor "modestly credited his extraordinary success to 'luck,'" noted Olmsted, "but I was satisfied . . . that intelligence,

29. Heitmann, *Modernization of the Louisiana Sugar Industry*, pp. 8–9, 25;
Schmitz, *Economic Analysis of Antebellum Sugar Plantations in Louisiana*, pp.
239–44; David et al., *Reckoning with Slavery*, pp. 349–51; Whitten, "Sugar
Slavery," pp. 423–42; Sitterson, *Sugar Country*, pp. 70, 162, 170, 178, 180–
82; Whitten, "Tariff and Profit in the Antebellum Sugar Industry," pp. 226–
33; Olmsted, *Seaboard Slave States*, pp. 661–62 (first quotation); Murray,
Lands of the Slave and the Free, p. 139 (second quotation).

study, and enterprise had seldom better claims to reward." Discovering that a much more substantial plantation adjoining Fashion had produced only about half as much sugar and molasses, Olmsted asked Taylor if the other planter simply owned inferior soil. "I think not," he answered. Citing Fashion's extensive drainage system as his chief advantage, Taylor said that his best cane had actually come from a previously undeveloped section of land that "had been considered too low, wet, tenacious, and unfertile" to cultivate. Good drainage and replowing of the furrows during the fall had made the fallow land extremely productive. Among the thirty-six sugar planters in St. Charles Parish, only three had produced larger crops than Taylor's. He assured Olmsted that with one more good crop he would be able to discount his outstanding notes and own Fashion outright, two years ahead of his original schedule of six years.[30]

By owning such an expanse of prime acreage with a labor force to match, Taylor enjoyed a huge advantage over the many less affluent planters. By 1860 Louisiana's largest planters (those with fifty or more slaves) comprised only 7 percent of all slaveholders in the state, yet they owned about half of all slaves and produced about half of all the cotton and about three-quarters of all the sugar grown. All classes of whites benefited from the unprecedented prosperity of the 1850s, but modest planters and nonslaveholding farmers faced rising costs that enabled only large planters to afford substantial purchases of more land and more slaves. A widening gap between the wealth of a few and the assets of the great majority, part of a national trend during the previous decades, now typified a formula that would dominate the American economy into the twentieth century. Large-scale operations like Taylor's plantation reflected heavy capitalization in property and sure access to credit, technology, and labor on a mass scale, bringing the greatest possible productivity and profits. By 1860, with his personal wealth in property and slaves valued at upward of $400,000, he ranked in the top 10 percent of Louisiana's elite large

30. Olmsted, *Seaboard Slave States*, pp. 662–63 (quotations); Champomier, *Statement of the Sugar Crop Made in Louisiana in 1850–51*, pp. 19–20, 46. Issued annually and cited hereafter as Champomier, *Sugar Crop in Louisiana* with appropriate dates. Champomier, *Sugar Crop in Louisiana, 1851–52*, pp. 19–20; Champomier, *Sugar Crop in Louisiana, 1852–53*, pp. 19–20.

slaveholders and in the top 15 percent of those Louisianans whose wealth was valued at more than $100,000. At thirty-four years of age, with four of five of his peers older and more experienced, and with Louisiana already boasting the greatest proportion of wealthy individuals for any state population in the South, Taylor ranked as one of the richest of the rich.[31]

Taylor readily admitted, however, that even owning a plantation as magnificent as Fashion was still "essentially a gambling operation . . . as much trusting to luck as betting on a throw of dice." Like any other large-scale business enterprise, high profits carried high costs. Immediately after financing Fashion's purchase, Taylor added to his indebtedness by making several major improvements: the completely new sugar works, the new slave cabins, a sawmill, stables, and a doubling of the plantation's existing stock of mules and oxen. These improvements, he casually informed Olmsted, had cost him more than twice the amount of capital he had invested in purchasing Fashion. The sugar works alone required an outlay of more than $40,000, a typical figure on large plantations. He also added continually to his property by buying bordering parcels of farmland and undeveloped swampland, so that by 1858 Fashion reached its fullest extent, about 2,000 acres. By 1860 his force of slaves had grown from 147 to 197, mainly the result of a positive ratio of births to deaths rather than purchases of new slaves. When Taylor did buy slaves, like any rational planter he acted according to a strategy of labor and land use efficiency rather than from a desire to own more slaves simply for the sake of social prestige. During the 1850s prices for the best bondsmen rose at a stiff rate. Taylor paid $1,100 for a male slave in 1857 and $1,600 for another two years later. In his largest single purchase he

31. Oakes, *Ruling Race*, pp. 64–67; Menn, *Large Slaveholders of Louisiana*, pp. 1–12, 23–24, 346–47; Coles, "Some Notes on Slaveownership and Land-ownership in Louisiana," pp. 393–94; Shugg, *Class Struggle in Louisiana*, pp. 33, 78; Main, "Inequality in Early America," pp. 559–82; Soltow, *Men and Wealth in the United States*, pp. 133–36; Pessen, "How Different from Each Other Were the Antebellum North and South?," pp. 1119–49; Olsen, "Historians and the Extent of Slave Ownership," p. 111; U.S. Bureau of the Census, *Agriculture in the United States in 1860*, p. 247; Ralph A. Wooster, "Wealthy Southerners," pp. 135–46.

paid $16,200 for 11 adults, including several field hands, some saw-yers, and a washerwoman. One-third of this price he paid in cash, and the rest he financed with two equal notes, one due after six months and the other after a year.[32]

Taylor considered his plantation a gamble because he realized that success in agriculture depended ultimately upon the uncertain forces of nature. After Olmsted's visit to Fashion in 1853, Taylor enjoyed three more years of good crops. But in the fall of 1856 a heavy and sustained freeze inflicted the worst devastation ever seen in the sugar region. Taylor lost his entire crop. Like other sugar planters, his sur-vival demanded immediate financial credit. Continual indebtedness, either as way of capitalizing on rising profits or weathering a year of poor crops or low prices, had long insured that planters would stay prosperous, despite their loud complaints about being burdened by financial obligations. Taylor had intended to free himself altogether from his debts, a wise goal considering the inflated costs of improving and operating a sugar plantation during the 1850s. But now he ap-pealed to his close friend and business associate Martin Gordon, Jr., for help. For several years Gordon had served as Taylor's factor, act-ing as his commission merchant in New Orleans and overseeing the sales of Fashion's annual shipments of sugar and molasses. Factors often provided small advance payments on open accounts to planters, but when necessary they also negotiated with banks for large loans on a planter's behalf and sometimes even endorsed these notes in order to secure them. New Orleans bankers eagerly sought such arrange-ments. The great bulk of all loans went to large planters, thus making

32. Olmsted, *Seaboard Slave States*, pp. 660–61 (quotation 661), 670; Ro-land, *Louisiana Sugar Plantations*, pp. 3–4; plan of the estate of Richard Tay-lor, Parish of St. Charles, Louisiana, November, 1856, Taylor Papers, Boagni Collection; Jackson Beauregard Davis, "Life of Richard Taylor," p. 53; Menn, *Large Slaveholders of Louisiana*, p. 346; Joe Gray Taylor, *Negro Slavery in Loui-siana*, p. 105; Sitterson, *Sugar Country*, p. 61; authorization by the St. Charles Parish Recorder for Richard Taylor to purchase a male slave for $1,100, Jan-uary 20, 1857, Taylor Papers, Boagni Collection; bill of sale conveying male slave from J. M. Wilson to Richard Taylor, May 11, 1859, Zachary Taylor Collection, Louisiana State Museum.

Louisiana one of the nation's foremost suppliers of banking capital. As expected, Martin Gordon quickly went to work to ease Taylor's financial crisis.[33]

Fortunately for Taylor, Gordon was also his brother-in-law. Taylor's wife, Mimi, was a sister to Gordon's wife, Louisa, and the Bringier family connection proved crucial to handling Taylor's dilemma. Gordon spoke to their mother-in-law, Aglae Bringier, the widowed matriarch of the family, and convinced her to rescue Taylor from ruin. The Bringier family's wealth, undergirded by a substantial sugar plantation in Ascension Parish, had actually benefited Gordon's business dealings for several years. In 1853 Gordon told one planter that Madame Bringier's signature "will enable me to get all the money I want at eight percent interest." He even bragged that "the capitalists [bankers] now *apply to me* for the Bringier paper." A family member later recalled that Aglae Bringier "leaned for advice on her son-in-law Martin Gordon, and he induced her to endorse the multitudinous notes of Dick Taylor." Gordon himself was so confident about the arrangement that he agreed to sign many of the notes himself. On October 1, 1856, Madame Bringier and Gordon allowed Taylor to remortgage Fashion against an ongoing series of notes for $204,000 in the Bringier name and an additional $125,000 in Gordon's name, thus giving Taylor a guaranteed credit of $329,000 at only 8 percent interest. He was soon making regular payments. The rest of the family seemed unaware of or unconcerned about the situation. "Money was flowing from the plantations in golden streams," one of the Bringiers later remarked, "and Fashion was assuredly good for a few hundred thousands. . . . In fact, matters seemed to jog

33. Champomier, *Sugar Crop in Louisiana, 1853–54*, p. 19; Champomier, *Sugar Crop in Louisiana, 1854–55*, p. 18; Champomier, *Sugar Crop in Louisiana, 1855–56*, p. 18; Champomier, *Sugar Crop in Louisiana, 1856–57*, p. 18; Sitterson, *Sugar Country*, pp. 18–19, 72, 162–65, 191–92, 196–98; Martin Gordon, Jr., to Richard Taylor, October 17, 29, December 27, 1855, January 9, 1856, statements of accounts current for Richard Taylor with Martin Gordon, Jr., February 15, 1854–June 15, 1858, Taylor Papers, Boagni Collection; Green, *Finance and Economic Development in the Old South*, pp. 5, 20, 29, 174, 177–82.

along for all in the most haphazard and happy way. The skies looked very blue."[34]

Although Taylor possessed the assets to stand behind his notes, his original goal of freeing himself from debt had evaporated completely. The effects of the 1856 freeze shook Louisiana commerce to its foundations. A year later, in October 1857, Martin Gordon nervously awaited reports on the new agricultural season, hoping to find relief from his own financial pressures. "I am as near run mad as a man can be," he wrote a planter. "Mental excitement alone keeps me up." Taylor's 1857 crop came in at 520 hogsheads, reflecting a generally good year throughout the sugar region. Over the next three years, however, his production averaged about 470 hogsheads, and market prices remained flat. For the entire decade of 1850–60, not including the debacle of 1856, he produced nearly 4,500 hogsheads. Including the molasses that accompanied each crop, Taylor grossed an average of $30,000 to $40,000 each year. Overhead and marketing expenses generally cost a sugar planter 40 to 50 percent of his gross. Taylor therefore earned an average annual net profit of at least $15,000 to $20,000, a handsome income. But after remortgaging Fashion, he dropped ever deeper into debt. Upon paying a series of notes, he simply reborrowed, only to pay and reborrow again and again. During one nine-month period alone, from September 1858 through May 1859, he made successive payments on 63 notes amounting to $299,000.[35]

34. Sitterson, *Sugar Country*, p. 198 (first and second quotations); undated interview notes by Trist Wood, vol. 4 (third and fourth quotations), Bringier Family Genealogy Collection; mortgage agreement between Richard Taylor, Aglae Bringier, and Martin Gordon, Jr., October 1, 1856, Taylor Papers, Boagni Collection. The Bringier family had been generous to Duncan Kenner and his wife early in their marriage, loaning them at least $150,000; Kenner later returned the favor by giving Bringier family members similar financial help. Craig A. Bauer, "A Leader among Peers," pp. 132–33.

35. Sitterson, *Sugar Country*, pp. 162, 191–92, 202 (quotation); Champomier, *Sugar Crop in Louisiana, 1857–58*, p. 18; Champomier, *Sugar Crop in Louisiana, 1858–59*, p. 18; Champomier, *Sugar Crop in Louisiana, 1859–60*, p. 18; Champomier, *Sugar Crop in Louisiana, 1860–61*, p. 18; statement of notes discounted and matured, September 2, 1858–May 18, 1859, Taylor Papers, Boagni Collection.

Taylor could have liquidated some of his assets to help meet his obligations, but in order to make any significant headway against the huge amounts owed, he would have had to sell many of his slaves, an act that ran against his paternalistic grain. Taylor of course knew that indebtedness had become a way of life for many prominent planters, and besides, he had accustomed himself to partaking in the sumptuous and elegant luxuries enjoyed by the wealthiest of his peers. He cultivated expensive tastes in food, wine, cigars, and clothes. Commenting on Taylor's aura of boundless prosperity, a friend wrote in 1858, "Dick is as fat as a Dutchman." In nearby New Orleans, where commerce and pleasure held the planter class in such firm sway that the city became known as the southern Babylon, he and his family enjoyed some of the finest dining, entertainment, and shopping available anywhere. In January 1860, during the worst period of his debt payments, he spent $726.58 for wines and liquors purchased on an open account during the previous year. By the beginning of 1861 he had spent another $692.51 on such liquid luxuries. The Taylors also continued to frequent the gentry's favorite resorts along the Gulf Coast and made several extended trips to White Sulphur Springs, Virginia, still the pinnacle of southern social circles. Dabney Maury recalled a more modest summer outing taken with the Taylors via steamboat up the Mississippi during the late 1850s. "We were about a week upon the journey, and a more pleasant one I cannot recall," noted Maury. "[Taylor] was the life of the company." If he ever worried about his debts, he masterfully avoided showing it.[36]

Conspicuous consumption among the antebellum South's elite probably differed little in degree from indulgences relished by rich

36. Sitterson, *Sugar Country*, pp. 75–81, 164–65, 183; Joe Gray Taylor, *Negro Slavery in Louisiana*, pp. 92–93; Robert C. Wood to his wife, September 24, 1858 (first quotation), Wood Papers; Shugg, *Class Struggle in Louisiana*, pp. 35–38; Eaton, *Growth of Southern Civilization*, pp. 125–49; Eliza Ripley, *Social Life in Old New Orleans*, pp. 58–59; invoice from Samuel Stuart to Richard Taylor, April 11, 1859–April 6, 1860, Taylor Papers, Boagni Collection; invoice from D. H. Holmes to Mrs. Richard Taylor, August 1, 1860, invoice from L. Malus & Co. to Richard Taylor, January–December, 1859, invoice from L. Malus & Co. to Richard Taylor, February–December, 1860, Zachary Taylor Papers LC; Maury, *Recollections*, pp. 224–25 (second quotation 225).

families north of the Mason-Dixon line. Yet Taylor practiced the art of living beyond one's means so perfectly that he had almost no trouble maintaining his status as an aristocratic son of the plantation system. Above all, his penetrating intellect and magnetic wit worked to his advantage. Because southerners placed a premium on gentility and social grace, his self-assured presence and refreshing personality convinced virtually every prominent individual he encountered, from his in-laws to his many wealthy friends, that he fully deserved high esteem as well as money and power. Erudite and more cosmopolitan than other planters, most of whom confined their reading and conversation to agricultural prices, current politics, and an occasional popular novel, Taylor enhanced his superior education by immersing himself in classical and modern philosophy, science, literature, poetry, and history—especially military history. Fluent in both French and Spanish, he bought books and periodicals regularly and in quantity, building an outstanding library. "He seemed to have read and studied everything affecting the progress and history of mankind, and to remember all he had read," wrote one of his admiring friends. This wellspring of knowledge he deftly used to entertain and fascinate his favorites among the southern gentry. "The charm of his conversation dominated every social circle in which he moved," another friend recalled. "It was said of him that to dine with Taylor, when he was in form and mood, was better than going to a play." [37]

Nothing sanctified a planter's sociability more than the sport of horse racing. By the 1850s, together with the bizarre parades and lavish balls surrounding the hedonistic Mardi Gras season in New Orleans, local racing tracks had made the city a mecca for festive celebration on a grand scale. Established by affluent planters, merchants,

37. Pease, "A Note on Patterns of Consumption," pp. 381–93; Wyatt-Brown, *Southern Honor*, pp. 89–101; Sitterson, *Sugar Country*, pp. 83–84; Jackson Beauregard Davis, "Life of Richard Taylor," p. 54; invoice from Brookes & Pursglove to Richard Taylor, April–December, 1858, invoice from J. B. Steel to Richard Taylor, November 4, 1850–February 9, 1852, Taylor Papers, Boagni Collection; Maury, "Reminiscences of General Taylor," p. 567 (first quotation); Fenner, "Richard Taylor," pp. 5199–5203 (second quotation 5199–5200).

and professionals, the New Orleans tracks attracted so many outstanding horse owners that Louisiana became the nation's most prestigious center for thoroughbred racing. A correspondent for a well-
known sporting journal affirmed, "The horses are fast, and the
people are fast." The city's most extravagant track, the Metairie
Course, had an avid patron in Dick Taylor. Owned by several flam-
boyant Louisiana and Mississippi turfmen, including Taylor's
brother-in-law Duncan Kenner, the Metairie Course was sponsored
by the exclusive Metairie Jockey Club, which counted Taylor among
its sustaining members. Races took place virtually every week, but the
climactic events came twice a year, usually in the spring and fall, with
several races held each day for six consecutive days. Turfmen from
across the South, and even an occasional Yankee, brought their
horses and jockeys to compete, producing some of racing lore's most
legendary contests. The rotunda of New Orleans's fashionable St.
Charles Hotel brimmed nightly with throngs of owners, breeders,
and lovers of horseflesh tossing about hearty boasts and making liberal bets on the upcoming races. In the afternoons as many as twenty
thousand people, all dressed in their most formal attire, crowded into
the canopied grandstand, stood on the infield, and circled the outer
railing, cheering on the young slave jockeys mounted on their masters' swiftest horses.[38]

Duncan Kenner served as an enviable model for serious racehorse
owners in the lower Mississippi Valley. With a reputation as the region's unrivaled king of the turf, he maintained a private track and
stables for training dozens of Kentucky and English-bred thoroughbreds for which he routinely paid several thousand dollars each. Although Taylor could not hope to match his brother-in-law's prowess,
he did purchase a few fine horses for his own competitive pleasure.
Yet he experienced only minor success. His best horse, Bonnie Lassie,
won three races in 1858 with purses of a few hundred dollars each,
and she then placed second in race in 1859, sharing in a purse
amounting to $2,000. Winners' purses, most of which came out of the

38. Wyatt-Brown, *Southern Honor*, pp. 339–50; Somers, *Sports in New Orleans*, pp. 3–4, 9–11, 21, 23–34; Arvilla Taylor, "Horse Racing," pp. 2–5, 19,
37–38, 62–64, 132 (quotation); *Historical Sketch Book and Guide to New Orleans*,
p. 241.

pockets of the Metairie Jockey Club's members, actually paled in comparison to the costs of buying and maintaining a racing thoroughbred. Gentlemanly rivalry and the spirit of competition reigned over monetary considerations, but personal wagering often raised the stakes to serious sums. Taylor's high standing as a racing enthusiast led him in 1860 to serve as chairman of a committee comprising Kenner, William J. Minor, and Thomas J. Wells, the club's most respected members, cooperating with jockey clubs across the country in formulating a national system of uniform rules. This marked Taylor's most significant contribution to the sport.[39]

Taylor achieved an equally impressive place in New Orleans high society by gaining membership in the Boston Club, one of the most exclusive private men's clubs in the country. Named for the popular game of Boston, the forerunner of bridge, the club included only the cream of the city's merchants and lawyers, along with the surrounding area's most respected planters and the state's leading politicians. With a strictly limited roll of 150, the club maintained a long waiting list, and each candidate had to receive unanimous approval from the membership. A few years prior to his acceptance in the Boston Club, Taylor joined the Orleans Club, a less restrictive group of about 400, mainly young men with appetites for horse racing, drinking, and gambling. A notorious lack of discipline among its members, compounded by emotional arguments over politics, sent the Orleans Club into a swift decline in the late 1850s, but Taylor continued to maintain his membership even after joining the Boston Club. Founded in 1841, making it the third oldest private club in the country, the Boston Club epitomized the South's most refined male tastes and attitudes. As one member observed, "Propriety of demeanor and proper courtesy are alone exacted within its portals." Meeting in a large, comfortable building in the heart of the city, members enjoyed superb dining, elegant balls, and quiet hours of reading, conversation, billiards, and card playing. Taylor's intelligence and personality made

39. Arvilla Taylor, "Horse Racing," pp. 24–25, 37–38; Russell, *My Diary North and South*, p. 286; Jackson Beauregard Davis, "Life of Richard Taylor," p. 54; Somers, *Sports in New Orleans*, p. 30; *Historical Sketch Book and Guide to New Orleans*, p. 205; Charles Stone to Richard Taylor, May 10, 1860, Taylor Papers, Boagni Collection.

him a natural favorite. "He was a high type of man . . . the ideal club man," wrote the club's historian.[40]

Gaiety and gambling also had their places in Boston Club activities. Like the Orleans Club and others, the Boston Club frequently patronized the Metairie Course by putting up high-stakes purses to help offset the Jockey Club's expenses. On the eve of the the Metairie Course's spring races in 1858, the New Orleans *Picayune* commented, "The Boston Club . . . being composed of gentlemen who know 'what's what' . . . insured not only a numerous but a distinguished attendance upon the occasion." As if to pay homage to the large purse put up by the club, the *Picayune* remarked, "In the betting circles last evening . . . the wagering was spirited and lively, and a good deal of money will change hands upon the result." Although gambling at cards behind the club's doors met with increasing disfavor among most members, this sober sentiment frequently went ignored. Duncan Kenner, a longtime member, allegedly lost $20,000 at one sitting of Boston. Kenner could actually afford such a setback, and no one would have accused him of irresponsible behavior. Meanwhile Taylor became infatuated with playing whist, a variation on Boston more closely resembling bridge.[41]

More serious pursuits, particularly the art of politics, intertwined easily with entertainments at the Boston Club. The membership included the most powerful men in state government as well as several national figures, most notably Senators Judah P. Benjamin and John Slidell, who together with Pierre Soulé and Randell Hunt comprised the so-called big four of Louisiana politics. In no other setting did the pervasive conservatism of the state's foremost planters, merchants, and lawyers receive a more sublime consecration. Here they found a perfect forum for arguing their views and promoting the measures that decided Louisiana's future. During the 1850s Richard Taylor joined them in facing the greatest challenge to their wealth, prestige, and power: the national controversy over slavery.[42]

40. Landry, *History of the Boston Club*, pp. 3, 9–10, 47, 50, 60–61, 206, 329–30 (second quotation), 332–34; *Historical Sketch Book and Guide to New Orleans*, pp. 94–96; Reinders, *End of an Era*, pp. 158–59 (first quotation).

41. Landry, *History of the Boston Club*, pp. 57–58 (quotation), 203.

42. Meade, *Judah P. Benjamin*, pp. 82–83.

CHAPTER THREE
_____

Aristocrat in Political Bedlam

[Taylor] was never an aspirant for political office,

but was a power in his personal character.

Dabney Maury

Almost from the time Richard Taylor acquired Fashion in the early
1850s, public issues fascinated him deeply, luring him into politics.
The increasingly common American notion that a politician should
have to curry public approval, however, never motivated him in the
least. His self-image as an aristocratic paternalist, the personification
of the plantation system's social and economic virtues, precluded any
overt ambition for political popularity and honor. The personal
charms he displayed privately to the affluent and powerful quickly
disappeared in public. "Dick Taylor was a man of haughty bearing
and rather saturnine temper, repelling familiarity, except from his
friends," observed one of his contemporaries. "He had not the oratorical temperament, and seldom indulged in public speaking on the
hustings and elsewhere." To his friend Dabney Maury, Taylor himself
stated the matter more bluntly: "I am utterly unfitted for the business
of oratory." In the same manner that he played the role of prominent
planter, intellectual socialite, and suave gamester, he approached politics with a sense of high calling and destiny rather than partisan cal-
culation. Like a Virginia-bred colonial patrician, he intended to rep-

resent the people as he saw fit, and if he meant to impress anyone, he worried only about those he considered to be his true peers, those who could fully appreciate his sophisticated and subtle powers of enlightenment and persuasion. "He was never an aspirant for political office," wrote Maury, "but was a power in his personal character."[1]

Taylor's political initiation came in August 1851 when he served as a delegate from St. Charles Parish to the Whig party convention in Donaldsonville to nominate a congressional candidate for Congress. Called upon to put his skills of personal persuasion to work, he received appointment to a committee formed to resolve a dispute over apportionment between some questionable delegates from New Orleans and some from outlying parishes. Taylor convinced the rest of the committee that the New Orleans delegates' claims to voting privileges in the convention were valid, and the convention decided to abide by this view. Party leaders also wanted to place Taylor's name in nomination for election to the Louisiana senate, but they discovered that he did not yet meet requirements for length of residency in his home parish. Only twenty-five years old at the time, Taylor had already achieved a reputation for integrity and forthright opinions. The traditional demand by influential southerners that a young office seeker should possess political connections and social standing had seldom seen a more satisfactory prospect.[2]

It made perfect sense for Taylor to have joined the Whig cause. His father had been elected president on the party's ticket. Although Zachary Taylor had made a firm stand against a coalition of southern Democrats and Whigs who threatened secession over his proposal to restrict slavery's extension into the western territories, Whiggery continued to serve, North and South, as a bastion against the Democratic party's shameless appeal to the common man. Formed in outrage toward Andrew Jackson's administration, the Whig party sought to abate the tide of democracy that had widened suffrage, blocked fed-

1. Fenner, "Richard Taylor," p. 5199 (first quotation); Richard Taylor to Dabney H. Maury, May 8, 1876 (second quotation), Brock Papers; Greenberg, *Masters and Statesmen*, pp. 45–64, 72–84; Maury, *Recollections*, p. 225 (third quotation).

2. Jackson Beauregard Davis, "Life of Richard Taylor," pp. 54–55; Wyatt-Brown, *Southern Honor*, pp. 85–86.

erally financed internal improvements, and killed the national banking system. Heirs to the Federalist party's nationalistic vision of a
great American economic empire, Whigs tended to favor benevolent
leadership by educated, talented, and commercially motivated men
who held property and productive capital. They criticized Democratic leaders as unprincipled demagogues who catered to the growing mass of foreign immigrants and irresponsible small entrepre-
neurs thriving on blind individualism, narrow localism, and a
perverse distrust of taxation and positive government. Whigs wanted
to foster an underlying social unity based upon a nationally integrated economy of diverse yet interdependent producers and con-
sumers. But they also clung firmly to traditional Anglo-American
standards of social uniformity, as dictated by their own position at the
top of a hierarchy comprising a small number of enlightened, dispas-
sionate leaders and subclasses of rational followers. Democrats, in
turn, labeled their opponents as the party of the rich and as elitist
enemies of the Jeffersonian agrarian tradition of independence and
equality. Democrats also tended to believe that a moral devotion to
individual rights and personal interests would guarantee the common good. Whigs tended to believe that a moral devotion to the common good would guarantee individual rights and personal interests.
Both parties advocated opportunity for individuals to acquire property and prosper, yet each accused the other of endangering traditions of community and public order. Both parties wanted economic
progress, yet each accused the other of restricting such progress
through the abuse of governmental power.[3]

In the South large planters like Taylor generally supported the
Whig party not only because of its conservatism but also because the
plantation system's paternalistic ideals fitted neatly into the party's vision of a nationally integrated, commercially diverse economy that
would produce prosperity for all. Yet much like the conflict between
profits and paternalism on the plantation itself, political warfare with
the Democrats, especially in the Lower South, undercut Whiggish no-

3. K. Jack Bauer, *Zachary Taylor*, pp. 271, 303, 321–24; Thomas Brown,
Politics and Statesmanship, pp. 183–85, 215–17, 229–30; Howe, *American
Whigs*, pp. 20–31, 47–52; Oakes, *Ruling Race*, pp. 146–47. See also Ash-
worth, "*Agrarians*" *and* "*Aristocrats*."

tions of social and economic harmony. In Louisiana this partisan political struggle reached a climax in 1852, when Whig planters and their merchant and lawyer allies supplanted the Democratic-inspired revisionist state constitution of 1845 with a new constitution fostering the creation of corporations, banks, and railroads through state aid and monopolistic legal advantages. More importantly, the new constitution also apportioned representation in the legislature on the basis of total population, slave as well as white, thus giving parishes with large numbers of slaves a disproportionately high number of legislators. This afforded the wealthiest planters and their New Orleans merchant allies tight control over the state's most powerful branch of government against upstate farmers and other common whites, most of whom were Democrats. Less than one-third of the state's white population now elected more than half of the legislators. Large slaveholders in the rest of the South likewise managed to take the reins of power during the 1850s, but only in Louisiana did they resort to counting their own slaves as part of the population. A bold conservatism, characterized by fear of Democratic demagoguery and radicalism, had gained an advantage, not by virtue of Whiggish ideals of commercial unity and benevolent paternalistic leadership, but through the sheer assertion of economic and social dominance.[4]

In mid–1855 Taylor received nomination to represent St. Charles and Jefferson parishes in the Louisiana senate, and in November he won an easy election. His victory, however, came not at the behest of the Whigs but as a result of his new allegiance to the American party. The Whigs had disintegrated as a national party during the recent revival of sectional hostilities regarding slavery's extension into the western territories. With southern Democrats acting as the self-proclaimed protectors of proslavery expansionist rights, southern Whigs seemed almost disloyal by comparison. Largely owing to southern support, Democrat Franklin Pierce won the presidency in 1852. The party had begun attracting large planters, thus giving most

4. Sellers, "Who Were the Southern Whigs?," pp. 335–46; Howe, *American Whigs*, pp. 130–31; Robert A. Wooster, *People in Power*, pp. 9, 15, 17–19; Perry H. Howard, *Political Tendencies in Louisiana*, pp. 71–74; Ralph A. Wooster, "Structure of Government in Late Antebellum Louisiana," pp. 362–63; Meade, *Judah P. Benjamin*, pp. 81–82.

southern legislatures Democratic majorities. Most Whigs in the
South, however, still adhering to a conservative distaste for Democratic rabble-rousing, refused to join their rivals. Instead, during
1854 and 1855 southern and northern Whigs alike transferred almost en masse to the new American party, commonly called the
Know-Nothings, a loosely knit group united primarily by a nativist
disdain for immigrants, especially Irish Catholics flocking to the seaboard cities and enlisting as Democrats. In Louisiana, with New Orleans's mushrooming immigrant population posing an acute menace,
Know-Nothing strength concentrated there as well as in the large
slaveholding parishes, attracting even Catholic Creoles hoping to resist the Democratic onslaught. In this atmosphere of flux and tension,
Taylor gained election to the state senate as a Know-Nothing.[5]

Early in 1856 Taylor took his seat in the legislature. Although continually present during the 1856 and 1857 sessions, in typical fashion
he did not deliver any speeches or engage in any debates. He served
on various minor committees and on the important Committee on
Internal Improvements. By now, however, the Know-Nothing party,
like the Whig party before it, had fallen prey to sectionalism. Southern Know-Nothings had blithely expected their northern comrades
to back proslavery measures like the Fugitive Slave Act and the
Kansas-Nebraska Act along with the doctrine of popular sovereignty
in the territories, all in an effort to prevent southern Democrats from
using these heated issues as political proof of loyalty to the South. But
northern Know-Nothings balked at the strategy, refusing to antago-
nize their own constituents, and many in the northern wing of the
party shifted their loyalties to the new majority party in the North,
the Republicans. In the 1856 presidential election Know-Nothings in
the South reacted by turning in droves against the party's chosen candidate, Millard Fillmore, and casting enough votes for Democrat
James Buchanan to defeat Republican John C. Frémont. Even in Tay-

5. Jackson Beauregard Davis, "Life of Richard Taylor," p. 55; Cooper,
South and the Politics of Slavery, pp. 341–65; William H. Adams, *Whig Party of
Louisiana*, pp. 244–69; Cooper, *Liberty and Slavery*, pp. 244–46; Perry H.
Howard, *Political Tendencies in Louisiana*, pp. 74–84; Carriere, "Louisiana
Know-Nothing Party," pp. 183–86. See also Jeanfreau, "Louisiana Know-
Nothings," pp. 222–64.

lor's own St. Charles Parish, once considered a stronghold of Know-Nothing support, voters gave Buchanan a majority of more than 60 percent.

Taylor, along with Senator Judah P. Benjamin and most other prominent Louisiana Know-Nothings, willingly joined the Democratic ranks. As a national party the Know-Nothing cause was dead. The Republican party, increasing its popularity in the North, advocated a doctrine of free soil and free labor in the territories, exactly what most southerners could not abide. With Democrats in the North now in a minority, southerners had achieved a powerful position in the party. Buchanan, a Pennsylvanian, had depended upon Senator John Slidell of Louisiana for securing his nomination as the party's presidential candidate. Without the South's overwhelming support Buchanan would not have been elected. The Lower South in particular now devoted itself to one party, the Democrats, in an alarmed reaction to the threat of Republican dominance. National politics thus degenerated into a bitter, sectionally aligned contest as a direct result of the popular furor over slavery, and most former Whigs in the South such as Taylor, always loathful toward any popular outcry, became newly christened Democrats caught in the midst of the struggle.[6]

True to his Whiggish and nativist beliefs, but more especially because of his unwavering conservatism, Taylor viewed the rise of the Republican party, as well as the ensuing Democratic outrage, as products of the greater problem of democracy—a mass society intoxicated by the ballot box. He therefore cast heavy blame for the political strife over slavery essentially upon a "vast immigration that [had] poured into the country" since 1840, foreign hordes consisting of Germans, Scandinavians, and Irish whose "numbers were too great to be absorbed and assimilated by the native population" (meaning the more virtuous citizens of English origin). Pointing to an impassioned demagoguery practiced by far too many political leaders, Taylor asserted that "the modes of political thought were seriously disturbed, and a

6. Jackson Beauregard Davis, "Life of Richard Taylor," p. 55; Cooper, *South and the Politics of Slavery*, pp. 365–72; Perry H. Howard, *Political Tendencies in Louisiana*, pp. 75–84; Greer, *Louisiana Politics*, pp. 131–39, 147, 154–55; Meade, *Judah P. Benjamin*, pp. 103–4.

tendency was manifested to transfer exciting topics from the domain of argument to that of violence." His condemnation of political sensationalism in both the North and the South typified conservatives' fears throughout the country. The issue of slavery represented an illegitimate form of extremism, a phantom issue that only rampant democracy could have produced.[7]

Despite his rather general disgust, Taylor clearly saved his most indignant ridicule for the abolitionists. Comparing the condition of national politics to an increasingly "exhausted" human body susceptible to a ravaging disease, he described abolitionism as a "malignant fever" that had "failed to attract public attention for many years" but that gradually, "by unwearied industry, [and] by ingeniously attaching itself to exciting questions of the day, with which it had no natural connection, it succeeded in making a lodgement in the public mind." In the South, although large slaveholders and merchants were gaining control over state and national offices through the Democratic party, sectionalism had infected many ambitious party leaders with a tendency to resort to emotional oratory and moralistic drama as the most effective tactics to win voter approval. Ironically, the Whigs had already accustomed themselves to using a liberal dose of exaggerated campaign rhetoric, particularly during presidential elections. Taylor's father had achieved the Whig nomination and then won the presidency almost entirely because of his popularity as a war hero. The strident cry from southern politicians for the defense of proslavery rights in the territories incensed Richard Taylor and other conservatives almost as deeply as did the opposite cry from antislavery northerners. As a wealthy slaveholder and genteel politician, Taylor seemed irritated and perplexed rather than challenged by slavery's central role in the political and constitutional failure to reach a consensus about the nation's westward expansion and development.[8]

7. Richard Taylor, *Destruction and Reconstruction*, p. 4 (quotations). For an illuminating discussion of the political agitation caused by democracy's ascendancy during the antebellum era, see Somkin, *Unquiet Eagle*, pp. 175–84.

8. Richard Taylor, *Destruction and Reconstruction*, p. 4 (quotations); Oakes, *Ruling Race*, pp. 206–9; Robert A. Wooster, *People in Power*, pp. 42–46, 111, 134–38; Greenberg, *Masters and Statesmen*, pp. 3–22; Eaton, *Growth of Southern Civilization*, pp. 322–24.

The Democrats' crucial goal of defending proslavery rights within the Union ultimately depended upon maintaining party unity, North and South, against surging Republican popularity. Democratic unity required leaders to control passions generated by internal disputes, especially the passions of southerners. But the most ardent southern Democrats, the fire-eaters, concentrated in the Lower South, thrived like no others on stirring up extreme proslavery demands that not only struck at party unity but also glorified disunion and the establishment of a separate southern nation. With no strong rival Unionist party in the Lower South to challenge them openly and defeat them for state office, the fire-eaters saw no reason to restrain themselves, least of all to consider the unity of the national party. Every Republican victory, in fact, made the fire-eaters' vision of disunion a greater possibility, assuming enough southern Democrats would push their states into secession upon the election of a Republican president.

Emboldened in 1857 by the Supreme Court's Dred Scott decision, which implicitly approved taking slaves into a territory, the fire-eaters spearheaded the South's outcry against Congress's rejection of a Kansas territorial constitution written by a minority proslavery convention, the so-called Lecompton Constitution. With Kansas now assured a rightful territorial government under the antislavery majority, southerners lambasted northern Democrats, and in particular Senator Stephen Douglas of Illinois, for having joined Republicans in Congress in defeating Kansas's proslavery constitution. Although President Buchanan had supported the constitution, his deeper desire to maintain party unity backfired against Douglas's unshakable commitment to popular sovereignty, pure majority rule by the populations living in the territories. The fire-eaters deftly accused Douglas of driving a wedge between the northern and southern wings of the Democratic party. With renewed vehemence, they now pushed their program for destroying the Union.[9]

In a widely publicized effort to rally support for disunionist sentiment, some of the best-known fire-eaters, led by William L. Yancey of Alabama, Edmund Ruffin of Virginia, and Robert Barnwell Rhett of South Carolina, used the annual meetings of the Southern Commer-

9. Potter, *Impending Crisis*, pp. 297–327; Holt, *Political Crisis of the 1850s*, pp. 221–36; Cooper, *South and the Politics of Slavery*, pp. 373–74.

cial Convention as a platform for their demands. Since 1837 the convention had espoused various means of economic development for the South, usually to the benefit of large planters, but during the 1850s fire-eaters gradually converted the meetings into political extravaganzas full of outrageous oratory and caustic debate. Their most alarming exertions centered upon a proposal to abolish the fifty-two-year-old constitutional prohibition against the African slave trade. For several years the convention had rejected all resolutions on the subject, but in 1859, at the meeting held in Vicksburg, a large majority of the delegates voted for such a resolution. Taylor attended the Vicksburg meeting, having already witnessed the 1858 meeting in Montgomery, Alabama, but he did not participate in any of the proceedings. As expected, the slave-trade resolution had no effect in Congress, except for a series of defensive explanations by southern representatives who came under criticism. Only in the state legislatures of the South would the issue have any chance for creating real trouble.[10]

During the late 1850s several southern states flirted with proposals to reopen a supervised slave trade with Africa. But in Louisiana a strong, concerted movement reached the point of threatening outright defiance of the Constitution and precipitating a federal crisis. In January 1858 Henry St. Paul, a leading fire-eater popularly known as the Hotspur of the Senate, proclaimed to his colleagues, including Taylor, that he intended to submit for approval an African apprentice bill. Most of the members reportedly appeared dazed upon hearing St. Paul's message. All understood that so-called apprentices would eventually become slaves, thus effectively reviving the slave trade. Shock turned to astonishment when the House passed the bill and sent it to the senate for a vote. The fire-eaters' strategy of inciting common whites into joining their program for disunion cropped up clearly in Senator Edward DeLoney's argument in favor of the bill. DeLoney, another prominent fire-eater, insisted that the accelerating

10. Potter, *Impending Crisis*, pp. 395–401, 467–69; Jackson Beauregard Davis, "Life of Richard Taylor," p. 57. On the Southern Commercial Convention's annual meetings, see Van Deusen, *Ante-Bellum Southern Commercial Conventions*, and Wender, *Southern Commercial Conventions*.

prices of slaves had made it impossible for the average farmer to afford to become a slaveholder and that an influx of fresh Negroes would therefore reduce prices, widen the extent of slave ownership, and thus strengthen the South's capacity for sending more slaveholders into the western territories. Anyone opposed to such benefits, DeLoney concluded, would deserve to be called an abolitionist, the worst accusation imaginable in the South at the time.[11]

On March 11 the bill came up for a vote in the senate. Already aware that the proposal commanded the favor of a slight majority (twelve of twenty-three senators), Taylor and eight others who opposed the bill suddenly rose and walked out of the chamber, thereby leaving the body without a quorum. Two days later the bill received the same clever yet drastic treatment, and on March 15, upon the third and final reading, a motion for indefinite postponement passed by a vote of fifteen to thirteen, finally putting the matter to rest. The bill's opponents had successfully maneuvered the senate into resignation. Although Taylor never made any arguments explaining his position, any one of several motives might have accounted for his opposition. Had the bill become law, he would have seen a decided decline in the value of his two hundred slaves, and as a sugar planter he would have risked losing the protection of a federal tariff on foreign sugar. All of the senators from the sugar growing areas of the state opposed the bill with Taylor. Practical politics influenced him as well. So profoundly did the bill jeopardize Senator John Slidell's standing with President Buchanan's administration that Slidell put direct pressure on several senators to kill it, warning that its passage would "seriously embarrass" the president in Washington. A pro-Slidell newspaper editor asserted that a revival of the slave trade would "precipitate a collision between state and Federal authorities," a crisis Republicans could have exploited to discredit all Democrats. As the avowed strongman of the Democratic party in Louisiana, Slidell knew the fire-eaters would stoop to any political trick for the sake of disrup-

11. Takaki, *A Pro-Slavery Crusade*, pp. 170–72 (quotation 170); Hendrix, "Efforts to Reopen the Slave Trade," pp. 97–106; Joe Gray Taylor, "Foreign Slave Trade in Louisiana," p. 40.

tion. "As to the Rhetts, Yanceys, and others," he told a southern colleague in Congress, "the sooner and more effectively we get rid of them the better." Accomplishing such a purge would remain impossible, however, as long as the fire-eaters continued to exploit slavery as an issue. In effect, slavery and disunion had become inseparably linked, and the Slidell-Buchanan majority in the party could offer no remedy.[12]

By now Taylor had joined the Slidell-Buchanan wing of the party in promoting southern unity as the only way to convince the northern wing of the party that Stephen Douglas's doctrine of popular sovereignty was unconstitutional and dangerous. Southerners strained under the reality of territorial governments like Kansas's holding ultimate power, if not the legal authority, to exclude slavery by popular will. Buchanan, who supported the southern view, experienced much the same difficulty in his protracted efforts to purchase Cuba and annex it as a territory, thus creating another slave state. Congressional Democrats, including Douglas, generally viewed such Caribbean expansion as inevitable and even desirable. But Republicans, unalterably opposed to the extension of slavery on any terms, blocked Buchanan's scheme. Years later Taylor alluded to "the lust of rule and territory always felt by democracies, and nowhere to a greater degree than in the South." But in 1859, any Whiggish distrust he might have harbored toward southern expansionists for their lust to push slavery westward and southward hardly prevented him from acclaiming Buchanan's policies, at least in public. Serving as a delegate to his congressional district's nominating convention in June, Taylor presented a series of resolutions wholeheartedly endorsing the president. In an ongoing effort to play the role of loyal Democrat as well as loyal southerner, Taylor, like so many other former Whigs, deferred to the urgent proslavery rhetoric that seized increasing numbers of southern Democrats in its grip. If he had any hope of influencing events, he would have to go with the prevailing current. In doing so, he would also have to compromise his conservative, Whiggish scruples just to stay afloat. He had fallen into a rapid, swirling,

12. Hendrix, "Efforts to Reopen the Slave Trade," pp. 106–23; Takaki, *A Pro-Slavery Crusade*, pp. 172–74 (quotations).

democratic whirlpool, and the only rudder of any strength seemed locked in a fire-eating position.[13]

In October of 1859 the fire-eaters received a perfect gift in the form of John Brown. The South reeled in unprecedented trauma over his apocalyptic raid upon the United States arsenal at Harpers Ferry, Virginia. Despite Brown's absurd failure, southerners now had little reason to doubt fire-eaters' claims that Republicans, by allegedly condoning and even sanctioning the raid, not only intended to prohibit slavery in the territories but also to eradicate it from the South. Brown had sparked the national embroilment of emotions he and other abolitionists had craved for so long. To southerners, the most horrific fact was that Brown had planned to raise an army of slaves for inciting a wild tidal wave of black insurrection. Louisiana fire-eater Edward DeLoney, the senator who had recently championed reopening the slave trade, declared in an article written for *De Bow's Review* that "actual aggressive hostilities have been commenced by the North upon the slave states, and a revolutionary or guerrilla warfare upon our Southern borders has been planned and sanctioned by a large number of Abolition members of Congress." Although Republicans generally decried Brown as a treasonous fanatic, his trial and execution by hanging produced so many northern supporters and eulogists exalting him as a righteous martyr that southerners became all the more convinced that the Republican party differed little in essence from John Brown's envisioned army of slaves.[14]

"I have heard men of good sense say that the union of the states any longer was impossible," observed William Tecumseh Sherman, the newly appointed superintendent of the Louisiana state seminary at Alexandria. Taylor had acted as one of his strongest supporters in securing him the position, having first met the Ohio native in 1852 during Sherman's command of the the army's commissary depot at

13. Potter, *Impending Crisis*, pp. 399–402; Roy F. Nichols, *Disruption of American Democracy*, pp. 227–30; Richard Taylor, *Destruction and Reconstruction*, p. 8 (quotation); Jackson Beauregard Davis, "Life of Richard Taylor," pp. 57–58; Howe, *American Whigs*, pp. 238–41.

14. Potter, *Impending Crisis*, pp. 356–84; DeLoney, "The Union Broken," p. 604 (quotation); Bragg, *Louisiana in the Confederacy*, pp. 4–5.

New Orleans. A stern West Point graduate, Sherman now held the responsibility of reviving the seminary by transforming it into a military school financed by the state. "Taylor . . . is a very plain, straightforward man, of great independence, candid, honest and clearheaded," wrote Sherman. "Whatever he promises we may rely on, as he has great influence." Working under increasingly delicate political circumstances, Sherman's task inevitably grated on his own patriotic feelings as a former army officer. "I have heard a great deal lately . . . that the Southern States by military colleges and organizations were looking to a dissolution of the Union," he informed his wife in late 1859. "If they design to protect themselves against negroes and abolitionists I will help; if they propose to leave the Union on account of a supposed fact that the northern people are all abolitionists like . . . [John] Brown then I will stand by Ohio and the Northwest." Taylor and other friends assured him that the school's martial atmosphere would merely impose discipline upon increasingly unruly and lazy planters' sons so that they could learn standard academic subjects. For the time being Sherman appeared satisfied with this explanation, and he enjoyed the challenge at hand.[15]

Tensions in Louisiana heightened, however, when the new Democratic governor, Thomas O. Moore, delivered an address to the legislature in January 1860. A wealthy planter generally considered a puppet of Senator John Slidell, Moore vowed that "Louisiana, as dearly as she loves the Union, will never separate herself from her sister slave states." Sherman tried to remain optimistic about the situation, hoping that the state would not jump blindly into a southern secession movement. "Louisiana is not ultra," he observed, "but her people and representatives are nervous on the nigger question." Taylor and other close associates kept Sherman from becoming alarmed. "I am coaxed and begged not to leave them," Sherman noted with gratitude, and he later recalled that Louisianans always treated him with "the greatest kindness and courtesy."[16]

15. Lloyd Lewis, *Sherman*, pp. 26, 87, 110–25; Fleming, *Sherman*, pp. 43–45 (first and third quotations 44–45), 81 (second quotation).

16. Greer, *Louisiana Politics*, pp. 221–22 (first quotation); Fleming, *Sherman*, pp. 174–75 (second quotation 174–75, third quotation 175); Sherman, *Memoirs*, 1:147–48 (fourth quotation 147).

These warm but fragile relations received a severe test one evening in February when Sherman attended a New Orleans dinner party hosted by Governor Moore. Several political leaders, including Taylor, as well as Colonel Braxton Bragg, now a prominent sugar planter, gathered for the occasion at the governor's residence with other respected and genteel citizens. After dinner, the ladies having left the room, the men fell into a serious exchange. Governor Moore characterized Sherman's brother John, a Republican congressman and leading candidate for Speaker of the House, as an outright abolitionist. "Some of our people wonder that you should be here at the head of an important state institution," said Moore, who then asked Sherman to explain his own views on slavery. Without a hint of agitation, Sherman corrected Moore politely, pointing out that his brother's antislavery principles did not approach abolitionist extremes. "He would not of himself take from you by law or force any property whatever, even slaves," Sherman stated firmly but calmly. As for slavery as an institution, Sherman said that if he personally held a position of influence and power in Louisiana he would try to "bring the legal condition of slaves nearer the status of human beings" by forbidding the separation of family members and by allowing all slaves to learn to read and write. Suddenly Lieutenant Governor Henry M. Hyams, a cousin to Senator Judah P. Benjamin, pounded the table and exclaimed, "By God, he is right!" The conversation continued in a lively and positive manner, with Sherman's opinions receiving fair consideration. This relieved him greatly, he later admitted, "because at the time all men in Louisiana were dreadfully excited on questions affecting their slaves, who constituted the bulk of their wealth." [17]

Taylor's fears about the Republican party stemmed from his deeply conservative abhorrence of antislavery's source of power—of mass democratic politics. Popular agitation only encouraged and even glorified John Brown's violence and similar forms of moralistic terrorism. Democracy at its divisive worst, devoid of rational leadership, seemed to fuel the Republican lust for power. Taylor knew that only a united national Democratic party could prevent what most southerners feared more than anything: the election of a Republican president. Yet now the Democrats lurched into a deep sectional rift, dem-

17. Sherman, *Memoirs*, 2:148–50 (quotations).

onstrating their own proclivity for untamed democratic politics. In the fevered wake of John Brown's raid, the fire-eaters made gigantic strides, inciting widespread support in the Lower South for their most extreme demand: a federal slave code with full congressional approval, in order to protect slavery's extension into all western territories, despite any local antislavery sanctions. Such a law had absolutely no chance for passage in Congress because virtually all northern Democrats opposed this most blatant manifestation of proslavery aggression. But with Douglas poised as the leading contender for the Democratic nomination for president, the Lower South meant to block his candidacy unless he came out in favor of a slave code. James Buchanan, now disinclined to run for a second term, failed to provide the leadership necessary to persuade the fire-eaters and the Douglasites to reach a compromise prior to a hostile confrontation at the upcoming Democratic convention. Taylor later observed, "The aged and feeble President, Buchanan, unfitted for troublous times, was driven to and fro by ambitious leaders of his own party." The Democrats had drawn internal battle lines according to their own sectional animosities, playing further into the hands of their Republican enemies.[18]

Having risen to the influential chairmanship of the Louisiana senate's Committee on Federal Relations, Taylor was selected at the March 5 Democratic state convention in Baton Rouge as one of twelve delegates to attend the national Democratic convention in Charleston, South Carolina, in late April. As expected, the proceedings at Baton Rouge fell under the orchestration of Senator John Slidell, who wielded a huge majority against Pierre Soulé's pro-Douglas wing of the state party. All twelve of the delegates chosen to go to Charleston enjoyed Slidell's blessings, most of them wealthy planters who owned at least sixty slaves each. Only one was a lawyer, and only two, former governor and former United States senator Alexander Mou-

18. Potter, *Impending Crisis*, pp. 403–4; Richard Taylor, *Destruction and Reconstruction*, p. 4 (quotation). On the growing volatility of national party politics during the antebellum era, see Foner, "Politics, Ideology, and Civil War," pp. 15–34. On the social and economic changes that contributed to political turmoil, see Wiebe, *Opening of American Society*, pp. 129–68, 229–43, 348–75.

Governor Alexander Mouton, leader of the Louisiana delegation at the
Charleston Democratic convention, 1860
(Jenkins Rare Book Company).

ton and Taylor, had any experience in political office. In a resounding
series of votes, the convention passed several resolutions designed to
guide its delegates in Charleston. Declining to give instructions regarding a preferred presidential nominee, the convention pledged to
support the party's choice. But Louisiana's antipathy for Douglas sur-

faced full blown in a resolution denouncing popular sovereignty in the territories and asserting, "It is the duty of the General Government to interpose by active exertion of its constitutional powers to secure the rights of slaveholders." This unequivocal call for a federal slave code received further impetus from another resolution stating that if a Republican were elected president in November, Louisiana should then join the rest of the southern states in considering the best means of defending their collective interests.[19]

Taylor arrived in Charleston with the Louisiana delegation on Friday, April 20, prior to the Democratic convention's opening session on Monday. Hardly a neutral site, Charleston proved extremely irritating and often unnerving to northern delegates. Overcrowded accommodations and the nearly one-hundred-degree afternoon heat, combined with the Carolina low country's constant humidity, taxed the patience and reasoning powers of even the coolest minds. Charleston's famous elegance and colonial charm vanished in an atmosphere charged with sectional distrust, and William Lowndes Yancey, the Alabama fire-eater, intended to use that sectionalism to his complete advantage. Realizing that southerners had failed to agree upon a candidate who could challenge Douglas, Yancey approached the Louisiana delegation with an invitation to join several other delegations from the Lower South in a meeting planned for Friday evening in order to determine a concerted course of action. Yancey had come to Charleston with his state party's authorization to withdraw his delegation from the convention if the nominee did not demand a federal slave code as a plank in the Democratic election platform. The Louisianans, however, declined to attend Yancey's Friday night caucus. "This invitation and the terms in which it was conveyed argued badly for the harmony of the convention," Taylor observed.[20]

The convention assembled about noon on Monday in Institute Hall, boasting more than three thousand persons, with delegates mill-

19. Jackson Beauregard Davis, "Life of Richard Taylor," pp. 56, 58; Greer, *Louisiana Politics*, pp. 223–25; Bragg, *Louisiana in the Confederacy*, pp. 6–8 (quotation 8).

20. Roy F. Nichols, *Disruption of American Democracy*, pp. 288–96; Nevins, *Emergence of Lincoln*, pp. 204–13, 225; Richard Taylor, *Destruction and Reconstruction*, pp. 4–5 (quotation 5).

ing about on the floor and spectators jamming the galleries. In a sweltering, noisy commotion, the selection of officers proceeded, with
New Yorker Caleb Cushing, an anti-Douglas man, securing the presidency of the convention. The Louisiana delegation selected the venerable Governor Mouton as its president and Taylor as its vice-
president. Taylor recalled that his colleagues "held moderate views,
and were ready to adopt any honorable means to preserve the unity
of the party and country." He had confidence in Mouton, whom he
considered "a man of high character." A New Orleans newspaper correspondent, however, described the Louisianans as "not generally regarded as being of the ultra stripe, though two or three of them are
as much so as Yancey himself." At a caucus of southern delegates late
Monday evening, Governor Mouton had the honor of presiding
while Yancey argued forcefully for the delegates to demand a slave
code plank. Taylor remembered Yancey simply as "an able rhetori-
cian" who advocated "the extreme Southern view as to the rights of
citizens in the territories." Many at this meeting voiced their agreement, especially those from Mississippi, Texas, Florida, and Arkansas, delegations Taylor called "the fiery spirits" in step with Yancey's
Alabamians. When Yancey called for a vote to determine which delegations would support him in bolting the convention if the slave code
plank failed, the Louisianans, with Governor Mouton showing a
deepening streak of radicalism, joined the "fiery spirits" in promising
to follow Yancey's lead. Taylor acquiesced in this brazen strategy. At
one point during the caucus a North Carolina delegate stood up to
question the constitutional right of Congress to pass a slave code for
the territories, but he was instantly stifled by jeering and laughter.
The South Carolina delegation, a surprisingly conservative group
wary of Yancey's recklessness, agreed to cooperate with him only as a
last resort. Taylor later wrote admiringly of the South Carolinians:
"Representing the most advanced constituency in the Convention,
they were singularly reticent, and abstained from adding fuel to the
flames."[21]

21. *Proceedings of the Democratic Convention*, pp. 3–10; Bragg, *Louisiana in
the Confederacy*, pp. 8–9 (first quotation 9); Richard Taylor, *Destruction and
Reconstruction*, pp. 6–7 (second quotation 7, third, fourth, fifth, and sixth
quotations 6).

By Thursday, sectionalism in the convention reached a discomforting level as various delegations tried to influence the writing of the
platform by offering resolutions from the floor. Governor Mouton,
one of the first to speak out in favor of a slave code, proclaimed, "It is
the duty of the General Government to interpose, by active exertion
of its constitutional powers, to secure the rights of slaveholders." His
statement received a heartfelt round of applause from southerners
on the floor and in the galleries. On Friday, with Douglas supporters
boasting that they held a majority of delegates favoring a platform
that would exclude a slave code plank, southerners embarked on a
series of long-winded speeches, goading their opponents into fruitless debate far into the evening. Yancey rose to the occasion and delivered the crowning oration of his career, asserting that the South had
submitted far too long to the delusion that slavery should be viewed
as an evil institution to be restricted by national policy. Southern
rights and political equality depended on slavery as a recognized virtue, he concluded, a virtue that must never be publicly degraded or
threatened. Shocked at Yancey's arrogance, northern delegates then
demanded a vote on the platform, but southerners protested the
move as an attempt to gag further debate. Chaos broke out on the
floor as delegates shouted insulting accusations at each other. Spectators urged on the uproar. Finally both sides succumbed to frustration
and weariness, and about ten o'clock the convention adjourned. On
Saturday the stalemate continued, with more resolutions, filibustering, and parliamentary jousting preventing a vote on the platform.
Southerners knew that during the brief Sunday recess they would
have to collect their wits and courage before an inevitable confrontation on the slave code.[22]

"Charleston presents today a novel scene," wrote a reporter on
Sunday, April 29. "The excitement is very great, greater than it has
been yet, and the breach in the party wider than it was before, with
hardly a hope of reconciliation." Until now, Taylor had merely
watched the deliberations, conforming silently to his colleagues' sup-

22. *Proceedings of the Democratic Convention*, pp. 14–28 (quotation 16); Roy
F. Nichols, *Disruption of American Democracy*, pp. 300–302; Potter *Impending
Crisis*, pp. 408–9.

port of Yancey's dangerous strategy. But that evening, as a heavy spring rain drenched the city, Taylor became "filled with anxious forebodings" about the ramifications of disrupting the convention. On his own initiative he called upon Senator Slidell, who had come to Charleston from Washington in hopes of engineering Douglas's defeat. Senators James Bayard of Delaware and Jesse Bright of Indiana, two other members of the lame duck Buchanan political machine, also listened to Taylor's opinion regarding "the certain consequences of Alabama's impending action." Conflict over slavery aside, Taylor viewed party unity as the fundamental catalyst for halting the Republican menace. To bolt the convention would only discredit the Democratic cause nationally and throw the nomination to Douglas. Douglasites had even stated openly that if enough southern delegates walked out, victory for the "Little Giant" would come even more easily. Nomination required a two-thirds vote, however, and at this point Douglas had a slim majority. Taylor soon convinced Slidell, Bayard, and Bright that if the southern delegates could offer a widely acceptable candidate, such as James Guthrie of Kentucky, and then simply reaffirm the vague and equivocal proslavery plank in the 1856 party platform, they might still defeat Douglas outright. "I made an earnest appeal for peace and harmony, and with success," Taylor recalled. Yet it still hinged on convincing Yancey to stay in the convention.[23]

Shortly before midnight Taylor contacted Yancey and persuaded him to join the discussion. The stern Alabamian listened to Taylor's argument and gradually discerned the logic. He promised to call his delegation together immediately and speak to its members. Yancey's eagerness to compromise did not mean that he had altered his goals. He still intended to force the party into accepting a presidential candidate who, either by choice or through the party platform, would denounce Douglas's loathsome policy of popular sovereignty in the territories. Yancey's plotting for ultimate disunion thus continued un-

23. Bragg, *Louisiana in the Confederacy*, p. 9 (first quotation); Richard Taylor, *Destruction and Reconstruction*, p. 6 (second, third, and fourth quotations); Venable, "Douglas and Yancey Forces," pp. 238–41; Nevins, *Emergence of Lincoln*, pp. 219, 226.

William L. Yancey, king of southern fire-eaters
(*Johnson and Buell*, Battles and Leaders of the Civil War).

diminished. If the party ran a presidential candidate who happened to alienate enough northern voters to insure Republican victory and thereby push the South toward secession, Yancey would be ecstatic. But because of Douglas's power in the convention, Yancey had only intended that a walkout by southern delegates would represent a first step toward whipping the party into accepting either a proslavery platform or a proslavery candidate. At this point he actually underestimated his own power to ruin the party and precipitate a sectional crisis. He never expected that a walkout by one or more delegations might cause a permanent sectional division in the party. Taylor, however, fully perceived Yancey's destructive potential. In persuading the Alabamian to agree to forestall a walkout, he hoped to champion a dark horse from one of the border states who might wrest the nomination from Douglas and also project an image as a moderate candidate worthy of intersectional support, an absolute necessity for any Democrat to win the presidency.[24]

In Monday's early morning darkness Taylor and the three senators waited for Yancey to return. By dawn they knew he had failed to convert the Alabama delegation. Taylor later learned that Yancey's old rival, former governor John A. Winston, refused to bend to the argument. Having fought the walkout strategy before coming to Charleston, Winston and his followers in the delegation now sought to discredit Yancey and the fire-eaters in the eyes of Alabama Democrats by forcing him to carry through on his radical threats. Winston intended to follow Yancey out of the convention in order to appear a loyal Alabamian victimized by Yancey's reckless leadership. Like Yancey, Winston wanted the national party unified by a complete commitment to slavery, and also like Yancey, he did not expect a walkout to ruin the party but only to give the South enough leverage to coerce the party into compliance. Yet Winston also wanted to take control of Alabama politics from Yancey and the fire-eaters. By walking out of the convention, Winston would, as he put it, "force those who had brought the trouble from Alabama to stand by their work." He also knew that Yancey would have to fulfill his threat or face a damaging loss of prestige among fire-eaters throughout the South. To Taylor, this petty, convoluted struggle among Alabama Democrats only underscored the senseless volatility of slavery as a divisive issue in the grip of uncompromising politicians driven by lust for popularity and power. Commenting on Winston's cynical strategy, Taylor later wrote in a tragic vein, "Thus the last hope of preserving the unity of the National Democracy was destroyed, and by one who was its earnest advocate."[25]

On Monday morning, April 30, the convention assembled amid uncertainty and speculation about the action southerners might take

24. Richard Taylor, *Destruction and Reconstruction*, pp. 6–7; Thornton, *Politics and Power*, pp. 382–91; Venable, "Douglas and Yancey Forces," pp. 240–41.

25. Thornton, *Politics and Power*, pp. 392–94 (first quotation 392); Richard Taylor, *Destruction and Reconstruction*, p. 7 (second quotation).

concerning the impending vote on the platform. "It was not long," wrote a journalist, "before every observer saw that the long looked for explosion was at hand." With the gallery depleted of northern spectators who had spent their money and left for home, the proceedings reeled along in an atmosphere of boisterous southern radicalism. The crowd erupted in applause and shouting when Yancey appeared on the floor wearing a cocksure grin. "He had evidently made up his mind," noted the journalist. "He was not perplexed by saucy doubts and fears." The crucial slave code plank quickly came up for a vote. The southern delegations, voting almost entirely as a unit, lost 165 to 138, as expected. The Douglasites had triumphed hands down. Leroy Pope Walker, speaking for the Alabamians, then rose slowly, gained the chair's permission to speak, and proclaimed his delegation's determination to withdraw from the convention. After making a short speech about the gigantic injustice perpetrated upon the South by the traitorous Douglasites, he turned and led his colleagues out of the room amid a dead silence, as if the other delegates and the spectators could not believe what they were witnessing. The Mississippi delegation made the next move, walking out in the same defiant manner, with one of their delegates, D. C. Glenn, predicting the advent of a united South within sixty days. Suddenly a raucous torrent of cheering broke forth from the gallery. Delegates from South Carolina and Louisiana contended with each other for recognition by the chair.[26]

Governor Mouton gained the right to speak on Louisiana's behalf. Proclaiming that the Democratic party had reached an irreconcilable impasse, he offered little hope for a solution. He chose to face the Ohio delegates as he argued his point, prompting one of them to attempt to laugh off the remarks, a tactic that made him appear even more "hopeless and forlorn." In order to fight the "Black Republicans" the Democratic party must present "a bold front," Mouton declared. "We say that the Douglas principles . . . can never be the principles of the South." After a few more remarks defending the radical

26. Hesseltine, *Three against Lincoln*, pp. 79–84 (first quotation 79, second quotation 80); Potter, *Impending Crisis*, p. 410. For a cogent summary of events leading up to the walkout, see Johannsen, *Frontier, the Union, and Douglas*, pp. 146–64.

demand for a federal slave code to protect "the property of Southern citizens in all the territories," he led the Louisiana delegation out of the convention. "He made a very decided impression," wrote a witness, "and called down rapturous applause from the swarming galleries." Taylor, loyal to the delegation's wishes, joined the walkout. Two Louisianans, Charles Jones and James McHatton, stubbornly refused, prompting Mouton to point a disdainful finger at them and shout his condemnation as he strode down the aisle. In quick succession the delegations from South Carolina, Florida, Texas, and parts of those from Delaware and Arkansas repeated the tactic and bolted the convention. All the while spectators in the galleries shouted and applauded in wild delight. Most of the remainder of Arkansas's and all of Georgia's delegation walked out the next day, making a total of fifty renegade southerners.[27]

The fire-eaters had won an ominous victory. By exploiting the southern desire for a slave code plank as a necessary pretext to preventing Douglas's nomination, they had inflicted a far more serious blow to Democratic party unity than most southerners realized. Even the fire-eaters themselves failed to perceive the damage they had done. When the bolters assembled a few blocks away at St. Andrew's Hall on Monday evening, they made no effort to nominate their own presidential candidate but instead waited for the convention to cave in to their demands and send some kind of compromise proposal that would justify their returning to the Democratic fold. Full southern rights within the party, and within the Union, remained their only realistic hope and expectation. Yancey and his followers, however, made the most of the moment, parading with a brass band through the streets of Charleston late into the night and delivering passionate disunionist speeches to throngs of worshipful citizens. "Every ultra sentiment was applauded with mad enthusiasm," wrote a journalist. In one breath Yancey spoke of vindicating the South's constitutional rights, and in the next he predicted a "new revolution." When someone bellowed, "Three cheers for the In-

27. Hesseltine, *Three against Lincoln*, pp. 84, 74 (quotations); Roland, *Louisiana Sugar Plantations*, p. 19; Diket, *Senator John Slidell*, p. 206; McHatton-Ripley, *From Flag to Flag*, pp. 46–47; Potter, *Impending Crisis*, p. 410.

dependent Southern Republic," the crowd thrilled at yelling each brazen "hurrah!"[28]

Calling themselves the Constitutional Democratic Convention, the bolters reassembled on Tuesday, May 1, at the Charleston Theater. For reasons unknown, Taylor had not attended the previous evening's boisterous proceedings, waiting until Tuesday to register his name as a delegate alongside that of James McHatton, one of the two Louisianans who had first refused to take part in the walkout. The other, Charles Jones, still declined to join the bolters, but he too would soon relent. Senator Bayard, receiving election as president of the rump convention, reflected the cautious approach supported by most of the delegates when he effectively quelled the fire-eaters' attempts to recommend a presidential nominee to challenge Douglas. Still holding out hope for an invitation to rejoin the regular convention, they sat dumbfounded when on May 3 the regular convention decided to adjourn and meet again in Baltimore on June 18. Douglas had actually rejoiced at seeing the fifty southerners bolt, because he had expected their absence to give him the nomination. But Caleb Cushing, much to Douglas's displeasure, had ruled that the vote would require two-thirds of the original number of delegates present, thus barring Douglas from victory. Failing to nominate a candidate, the regular convention headed for Baltimore, where Douglas anticipated seeing a new slate of southern delegates much more sympathetic to his candidacy.[29]

The bolters could do little more under the circumstances than to schedule a meeting of their own for June 11, in Richmond, in order to be near Baltimore. Senator Bayard made some closing remarks at Charleston extolling the necessity of preserving the Union, but fire-eater A. B. Meek of Alabama, smelling blood, stood up and cried that their purpose should be not to preserve the Union but to preserve the Constitution. On this shrill note the convention of bolters closed. Taylor, a silent witness to it all, returned to Louisiana completely embar-

28. Roy F. Nichols, *Disruption of American Democracy*, pp. 306–8; Channing, *Crisis of Fear*, p. 210; Hesseltine, *Three against Lincoln*, pp. 86–87 (quotations 86).

29. *Statement of Proceedings of the National Democratic Convention*, pp. 26–36; Channing, *Crisis of Fear*, p. 210; Roy F. Nichols, *Disruption of American Democracy*, pp. 308–9; Potter, *Impending Crisis*, p. 411; Hesseltine, *Three against Lincoln*, pp. 88–117.

rassed and incensed at having participated in the self-torture and near destruction of the Democratic party. He resolved to have nothing more to do with politics. A fellow delegate wrote to him soon afterward, commenting, "You left Charleston in such immeasured disgust with politics and politicians." In an attempt to reinstill in Taylor a "confidence in the eventual triumph of principle over expediency," his colleague insisted that the party could be reunited, and he pleaded with Taylor to help initiate the healing. "The future welfare of the country, if not the preservation of the Union, will depend in great measure on the solution of present difficulties, and your share of the responsibility should not be delegated to others," he asserted. Taylor had only a few days to make a decision; Louisiana Democrats would reconvene June 4 in Baton Rouge to confirm delegates to the convention of bolters in Richmond.[30]

Only reluctantly did Taylor attend the Baton Rouge meeting, but once there, he agreed to serve as a delegate to the convention in Richmond. Although Pierre Soulé's pro-Douglas Louisiana Democrats held their own meeting and selected a delegation to the regular convention in Baltimore, Taylor and his colleagues received sanction to go to Baltimore as well, making for rival delegations. A similar situation prevailed in several other states in the Lower South. Thus did the Democratic party set about haphazardly to restore unity, now in the full knowledge that the Republicans had already nominated their own candidate, Abraham Lincoln of Illinois.[31]

The bolters assembled in Richmond at Metropolitan Hall, again calling themselves the Constitutional Democratic Convention. The meeting lasted only two days, June 11 and 12, with delegates anticipating attendance and full acceptance at the regular convention in Baltimore the following week. The great hope of forcing Douglas or some other candidate to accept a slave code plank still captivated the bolters, although Taylor realized its futility. In Richmond he listened to John Erwin of Alabama call for "making one more attempt at reconciliation" with the Douglasites. "But we must yield nothing," he warned. "The serpent of 'squatter sovereignty' must be strangled."

30. Hesseltine, *Three against Lincoln*, pp. 114–15; [?] to Richard Taylor, May 10, 1860 (quotations), Taylor Papers, Boagni Collection.

31. Greer, *Louisiana Politics*, pp. 229–30; Roy F. Nichols, *Disruption of American Democracy*, pp. 313–14.

The delegates responded with earnest applause. When a member from a group of sympathetic New Yorkers in attendance stood up and started delivering an appeal for "party peace" and "national love," W. F. Barry of Mississippi interrupted, saying that he "had abused the courtesy of the Convention." Delegates took this insulting remonstrance as a convenient cue to adjourn for Baltimore on June 18.[32]

By selecting Baltimore as the site for reconvening, party leaders hoped to recapture the same sense of sectional neutrality that had helped make the city the choice for every Democratic convention from 1832 through 1852. But all attempts at compromise misfired from the very beginning. Douglas's captains had the upper hand, and they refused to relinquish it. "They had long been stung by the taunts of their Republican neighbors that they were serfs of southern masters," observed a reporter, "and in the new demands and arrogant intolerance of the South, they felt that they were regarded as inferiors." The question of which delegations from the Lower South to admit into the convention quickly degenerated into a nasty contest of wills. After several days of negotiations Douglas grudgingly agreed to accept the bolter delegations, excluding those from Alabama and Louisiana. The forces of Yancey and Slidell, vowed Douglas, would not taint the convention. One Douglas supporter was heard to say, "The southerners have been ruling over niggers so long they thought they could rule white men just the same." The pro-Douglas delegations from Alabama and Louisiana thus took their seats. The upheaval resulting from this action surpassed even the chaos at Charleston. Even anti-Douglas northerners, incensed at Douglas's power to decide the issue, joined all the southerners, except for the few Douglas supporters, in staging a mass walkout. Douglas, having altered the voting rules to require only a two-thirds majority of those delegates present, thereby won an easy victory as the Democratic presidential candidate.[33]

32. Hesseltine, *Three against Lincoln*, pp. 178–84 (quotations 182–84).
33. Cooper, *Liberty and Slavery*, p. 263; Hesseltine, *Three against Lincoln*, pp. 259–64 (first quotation 260–61, second quotation 263); Roy F. Nichols, *Disruption of American Democracy*, pp. 314–18; Potter, *Impending Crisis*, pp. 412–13.

The delegates who had walked out assembled on June 23 at Market Hall in Baltimore and dubbed themselves the true Democratic convention. Taylor joined them in affirming a platform calling for a federal slave code. Rapidly offering nominations from the floor, they selected Vice-President John C. Breckinridge as their candidate for president and Senator Joseph Lane of Oregon as his running mate. Both were avowed partisans of southern rights, yet they conceivably might appeal to some northerners as well. As the convention spiraled to a finale, calls rang out for Yancey to deliver a closing speech. "The storm clouds of faction have drifted away," he proclaimed triumphantly. "I am, however, no worshiper at the shrine of the Union." Spouting that he was "neither for the Union nor against the Union—neither for disunion nor against disunion," he proudly claimed that Douglas's "friends . . . have buried him today beneath the grave of squatter sovereignty." Most of the audience apparently had heard enough, however, and they soon began to tire of Yancey's self-serving tones. Several hundred sauntered out during the speech. Just as Yancey started building toward crescendo, someone on the floor interrupted, and a quick motion to adjourn put an end to the evening. The great Democratic party, which still might have commanded a national majority of voters if only it could have united behind a single candidate, now lay in shambles, bitterly divided and thus completely vulnerable to a Republican victory. Yancey himself publicly denied any part in promoting such a disaster. Calling the accusation "an infamous calumny," he claimed to be a loyal Democrat who would campaign vigorously for Breckinridge. The fact that neither Breckinridge nor Douglas had much hope against Lincoln seemed beside the point.[34]

As if to dramatize the nation's political splintering even more completely, a third group calling itself the Constitutional Union party had already formed and had nominated John Bell of Tennessee, one of only a handful of southern senators in Congress who had resisted proslavery measures. Appealing to former Whigs and Know-

34. Roy F. Nichols, *Disruption of American Democracy*, pp. 319–22; Hesseltine, *Three against Lincoln*, pp. 265–77 (first and second quotations 275–76); Potter, *Impending Crisis*, pp. 413–14; Thornton, *Politics and Power*, pp. 396–98 (third quotation 398).

Nothings, the new party sought to restore harmony across sectional lines. In the South, where Douglas had no real chance, Bell, as a southerner, posed a real threat to Breckinridge. Proclaiming the Union as the paramount hope of all, Bell supporters pushed Breckinridge men into arguing that Bell's only chance of winning would depend on crossover votes from Republicans.[35]

In Louisiana this attempt to paint Bell as a Republican in disguise emerged most conspicuously in the form of a broadside circular titled *To the People of the State of Louisiana*, which received full endorsement from the Democratic State Central Committee. The circular's authors included Richard Taylor, along with three other members of the Louisiana delegation recently returned from Baltimore. Branding Bell's ex-Whig supporters as "a portion of the life-long and ancient enemies of the Democratic party," the circular asked pointedly, "Can any true Southern man conscientiously give his support to such a ticket?" Louisiana's sovereignty and equality were at stake, and with these the institution of slavery, "shown to be fraught with incalculable benefits," economic as well as social. "Distinction of color . . . has obliterated all other social distinctions, placing all white men, whether rich or poor, on a common equality. . . . Upon the preservation of this institution, intact under the Constitution, depends our political existence as a State and Nation." The circular expressed "the most cheering hopes" of Breckinridge's election; but in case of a Republican victory, the appeal concluded, "Be true to yourselves, to your principles, to your Constitutional rights, and to your sister states of the South."[36]

35. Potter, *Impending Crisis*, pp. 416–17; Greer, *Louisiana Politics*, p. 233.

36. Hatch et al., *To the People of the State of Louisiana* (n.p., [1860]), undated broadside circular (quotations), in Taylor Papers, Boagni Collection. This circular was actually written entirely by Hatch, one of the four delegates, including Taylor, whose names appeared as authors. Hatch assumed Taylor's compliance in the matter because he informed Taylor in a letter dated August 29, 1860, that "the delicacy and responsibility of speaking for others" had prompted him to submit the text to the Democratic State Central Committee, which endorsed it prior to publication. Apparently Hatch did not have time to secure Taylor's personal approval before attaching his name to it. Regardless, he probably would not have stated a position conflicting with

As Louisianans anticipated the upcoming election, public campaigning reached a high-pitched level. Torchlight parades, mass meetings, and barbecues throughout the state provided political speakers with forums to stir the people. An especially exciting event unfolded with the arrival of William L. Yancey in New Orleans on October 29. Militiamen marched, bands played, cannon fired, and tens of thousands of spectators crowded into Canal Street, with flags and banners waving from every building. In the cool of twilight, standing on a platform erected in front of the famous statue of the Great Compromiser, Henry Clay, Yancey spewed forth an utterly uncompromising defense of state sovereignty as a right of the people under the Constitution. "He held his audience spell-bound for two hours," a witness recalled, "and such was the enthusiasm aroused that it really seemed as though he could have led the crowd into the Mississippi River had there been an enemy there to charge." Yancey could not have timed his appearance in the South's largest city any more perfectly. Rumors of slave revolts, poisonings of slaveowners and their families, and burnings of plantations and entire towns by abolitionist-inspired slave armies had swept the white population of the South into a frenzy unequaled since John Brown's raid. In effect, the campaign for the presidency had been thoroughly distorted by an escalating fear among southerners that Lincoln's election would spark a mass uprising of bondsmen. "People here now talk as though disunion was a fixed thing," wrote William T. Sherman to his wife. "Men of property say that as long as this constant . . . danger of abolitionism exists, they would rather try a Southern Confederacy."[37]

On election day, November 6, to virtually no one's surprise, Lincoln triumphed with an overwhelming electoral vote, the result of the North's growing wave of popular support for the Republican party. Only in the Upper South did Lincoln's name even appear as a candidate on the ballot. Yet he actually needed no southern support to win.

Taylor's views. No evidence of Taylor's reply to Hatch survives. See F. H. Hatch to Richard Taylor, August 29, 1860, Taylor Papers, Boagni Collection.

37. Greer, *Louisiana Politics*, pp. 236–39; DuBose, *Life and Times of Yancey*, 2:529–33; Rainwater, *A Civilian's Recollections*, pp. 77–78 (first quotation 78); Fehrenbacher, *South and Three Sectional Crises*, pp. 62–65; Reynolds, *Editors Make War*, pp. 97–117; Fleming, *Sherman*, pp. 301–2 (second quotation).

Breckinridge took the southern states, except for Kentucky, Tennessee, and Virginia, which went to Bell. Douglas made a miserable electoral showing, winning only Missouri and sharing New Jersey with Lincoln. Even as a purely sectional candidate, Lincoln exploited the huge electoral advantage of the North over the South, a reflection of total population, and his success depended even less than expected on the disarray of his opponents. In Taylor's view, all hope of defeating Lincoln had evaporated in the chain reaction he had foreseen in April at the Democratic convention in Charleston. In his memoirs he wrote painfully, "The withdrawal of Alabama, followed by other Southern States, the adjournment of part of the Convention to Baltimore and another part to Richmond and the election of Lincoln by votes of Northern States, require no further mention." It all became virtually inevitable when Yancey first bolted the Charleston convention and carried the rest of the Lower South with him. Now Lincoln's election seemed to make secession and disunion equally inevitable.[38]

Many southerners, however, still believed that Unionist sentiment in the South would keep the fire-eaters from fomenting a hysterical secession movement. In Louisiana the two Unionist candidates, Bell and Douglas, had won a combined majority of votes but had lost to Breckinridge's plurality. Across the rest of the Lower South, Bell and Douglas fared only slightly worse, polling all together a total of 49 percent of the popular vote. But Lincoln's victory severely damaged the legitimacy of Unionist loyalty. Most Unionists in the Lower South could not abide a Republican president, but they were unable to formulate attractive alternatives to the fire-eaters' clamor for states to secede immediately. "Even the conservatism which seemed a month ago to view the coming storm with calmness now gives way to consternation," admitted a Baton Rouge Unionist newspaper editor. "The excitement spreads like an evil contagion." Senator John Slidell, like Taylor, considered secession a foregone conclusion in the Lower South. Writing to President Buchanan, Slidell lamented, "I see no probability of preserving the Union, nor indeed do I consider it desirable to do so if we could." At Slidell's prompting Governor Moore

38. Potter, *Impending Crisis*, pp. 442–47; Richard Taylor, *Destruction and Reconstruction*, p. 7 (quotation).

issued a call for the legislature to meet in a special session on December 10 to consider secession and, with it, military preparedness.[39]

As the political storm intensified, Taylor played an increasingly visible role. At the Southern Rights Mass Meeting in New Orleans on November 23 he had the honor of acting as a vice-president. That same day William T. Sherman wrote to his wife, "Many gentlemen who were heretofore moderate in their opinions now begin to fall into the popular current and go with the mad foolish crowd that seems bent on dissolution [of the Union]." On November 29 Dr. Benjamin Palmer of the First Presbyterian Church in New Orleans delivered a Thanksgiving Day sermon that gave the crisis an extra emotional dimension. Relying on apocalyptic passages from the Old Testament, Dr. Palmer spoke for more than two hours on the sinister purposes of Republican party power, which he equated with atheism. The heart of his message came from Psalms 94:20: "Shall the throne of iniquity have fellowship with thee, which frameth mischief by law?" Newspapers across the state printed the sermon in its entirety, and tens of thousands of pamphlet copies were issued to meet public demand. At the same time, another series of fantastic rumors of slave unrest swept across the South. Planters began predicting that Lincoln's inauguration in March would spark a mass rebellion of slaves. In Taylor's home parish of St. Charles the police jury ordered two pro-Union individuals expelled because they had "tampered" with slaves, had "hurrahed" for Lincoln, and had expressed "sentiments at the present hostile to the interests of the parish." The imagined horrors of Republican power, described so well by Dr. Palmer in his Thanksgiving Day sermon, had struck a chord of fear that reverberated all the louder as legislators assembled in Baton Rouge on December 10.[40]

39. Greer, *Louisiana Politics*, pp. 240, 244 (first quotation), 247, 250 (second quotation); Perry H. Howard, *Political Tendencies in Louisiana*, pp. 90–93; Potter, *Impending Crisis*, p. 472; Roland, "Louisiana and Secession," pp. 391–92.

40. Jackson Beauregard Davis, "Life of Richard Taylor," p. 59; Fleming, *Sherman*, p. 305 (first quotation); Lane C. Kendall, "Interregnum in Louisiana," pp. 185–87 (second quotation 185); Potter, *Impending Crisis*, pp. 452–55, 519; Bragg, *Louisiana in the Confederacy*, p. 27 (third quotation).

Governor Moore opened the special session of the legislature with a call for swift action. "I do not think it comports with the honor and respect of Louisiana, as a slaveholding state, to live under the government of a Black Republican President," he announced decisively. Although he conceded Lincoln's election as completely legal, the governor also warned in a self-righteous tone reminiscent of Dr. Palmer's sermon that "the greatest outrages, both upon public and private rights, have been perpetrated under forms of law." Arguing that a state's clear constitutional right to secede from the Union helped distinguish the United States' system of government from the revolutionary extremism that plagued the despotic nations of Europe, he urged, without realizing the contradiction, that the South take action against the threat of Republican coercion just as the American colonies had done against England during the American Revolution. Although Moore said he favored a conference of southern states to form a concerted front against the North, he wanted to suffer no hesitation on Louisiana's part to move on her own initiative prior to Lincoln's inauguration. The governor also asked the legislature to fund the expansion of the state militia and to call for the popular election of a convention of delegates to consider Louisiana's place in the Union.[41]

As chairman of the Louisiana senate Committee on Federal Relations, Taylor took the responsibility of presenting a bill designating January 7, 1861, as the date for a statewide election of delegates to a convention that would assemble in Baton Rouge on January 23. The legislature, firmly attuned to Slidell's and Moore's wishes, quickly passed the bill. The immediate question of Louisiana's position on secession hinged on voters' selection between two choices: cooperationist delegates, who supported a meeting of southern states to discuss the issue; or immediate secessionists, who demanded Louisiana's sovereign right to act alone and secede from the Union. Across the rest of the Lower South a similar situation prevailed. Meanwhile Republicans in Congress rejected all proposals to compromise on the issue of slavery's westward extension. Many believed that southerners were bluffing, and Lincoln seemed to expect that loyal Unionists in

41. Greer, *Louisiana Politics*, pp. 247–48 (quotations 248); Lane C. Kendall, "Interregnum in Louisiana," p. 182.

the South would arrest or at least blunt the secession fever. By now Taylor and most other moderate leaders had resisted secession by reaching into the depths of their own loyalty to the Union. Yet they also had grown to distrust the Republican alternative so completely that little hope for a solution surfaced anywhere. "I observe such men as Dick Taylor, the general's son, are in favor of immediate secession," Sherman wrote despairingly to his wife on December 15. "I have scarce room now to doubt that Louisiana will quit the Union in January." A few days later he added, "The opinion is universal that disunion is resolved on, and the only questions are what states will compose the Southern Confederacy." South Carolina, as expected, made the first brash step; on December 20 a state convention passed an ordinance of secession proclaiming her ties with the rest of the Union legally dissolved.[42]

South Carolina's secession provided the rest of the Lower South a bold example. If any one state might have resisted secession at the time, however, Louisiana seemed most likely. Because Bell and Douglas had received a combined majority of Louisiana's vote for president, the Unionist sentiment supporting a cooperationist position lifted expectations of winning a majority of delegates to the convention. But the advocates of immediate secession ran a ruthless campaign, openly branding all cooperationists as "submissionists" ready to make any compromise necessary to placate the Republicans. In the election on January 7, cooperationists won fifty seats in the convention, while immediate secessionists tallied eighty seats, one of which went to Richard Taylor. Although the popular vote reflected only a slim majority for the immediate secessionists, the legislative-style apportionment of delegates gave a sharp advantage to parishes with heavy slave populations, where support among large planters and their neighbors for immediate secession ran highest. Most of the sugar parishes, however, showed a slight cooperationist majority, presumably because sugar planters depended on a federal tariff for high prices and on northern markets for sales. St. Charles Parish elected a

42. Lane C. Kendall, "Interregnum in Louisiana," pp. 192–93; Potter, *Impending Crisis*, pp. 522–34; Richard Taylor, *Destruction and Reconstruction*, p. 7; Jackson Beauregard Davis, "Life of Richard Taylor," p. 59; Fleming, *Sherman*, pp. 315–16 (first quotation 315, second quotation 316).

divided delegation of three: two cooperationists and Taylor as the lone immediate secessionist.[43]

Delegates to the Louisiana state convention met in Baton Rouge on January 23, now fully aware that every other state in the Lower South except Texas had already seceded. Most immediate secessionists, regardless of state, represented areas with the largest slaveholders and the most slaves, demonstrating slavery's grip on slaveholders and nonslaveholders alike. Governor Moore had already ordered state militia units under Braxton Bragg, now a member of the state militia board, to seize Forts Jackson and Saint Philip on the Mississippi River below New Orleans as well as several other federal installations, including the United States arsenal at Baton Rouge. Anxious to remove the same specter of federal coercion evident at Fort Sumter in Charleston Harbor and at Fort Pickens near Pensacola, Governor Moore justified this unusual action by citing the immediate secessionists' victory in the recent election as virtual proof that Louisiana would break its ties with the Union in only a few days. For W. T. Sherman, this blatant defiance of federal authority proved intolerable. Resigning his position as superintendent of the state seminary, he informed his wife, "All these are acts of war. The revolution has begun."[44]

The convention elected as its president Alexander Mouton, the former head of the Louisiana delegation at the ill-fated Charleston Democratic convention. Taylor received appointment to a committee of three to welcome commissioners from South Carolina and Alabama, thus bringing him face to face with his antagonist at Charleston, John A. Winston of Alabama. Along with John L. Manning of South Carolina, Winston addressed the convention, calling for Louisiana to waste no time in joining the tide of secession. Now firmly

43. Perry H. Howard, *Political Tendencies in Louisiana*, pp. 95–103; Dew, "Who Won the Secession Election?," pp. 18–32; Roland, "Louisiana and Secession," pp. 393–95; Dew, "Long-Lost Returns," pp. 355–58, 367. See also McCrary, Miller, and Baum, "Class and Party in the Secession Crisis," pp. 429–57.

44. Robert A. Wooster, *Secession Conventions*, pp. 115–20; Bearss, "Seizure of the Forts," pp. 401–9; Lloyd Lewis, *Sherman*, pp. 141–42; Fleming, *Sherman*, p. 333 (quotation).

committed to a separate nation of slave states, Winston boasted that within two years an independent southern republic would stand as the greatest country in history. True to all expectations, on January 26 the convention approved an ordinance of secession by a vote of 113 to 17. Most of the cooperationists had conceded, voting with the majority for secession. One of the few staunchly Unionist delegates stood up and accused the convention of perpetrating a revolutionary act that would result in social anarchy and a destructive war, but a chorus of immediate secessionists shouted him down and then voted to strike his comments from the record of proceedings. Taylor voted in favor of the secession ordinance, later explaining, "Indeed, similar action having already been taken by her neighbors [in the Lower South], Louisiana of necessity followed." Mouton announced solemnly that Louisiana was now fully confirmed as "a free, sovereign, and independent power." Amid cheers of unrestrained joy and patriotic pride, Governor Moore and several other state officials unfurled a large Louisiana flag with its distinctive pelican design and draped it dramatically across the podium upon which Mouton presided.[45]

The convention soon had to relocate to New Orleans, however, because of Baton Rouge's inadequate living quarters. Reconvening on January 29 in the public assembly room of the New Orleans City Hall, delegates heard an opening prayer by Dr. Benjamin Palmer. Spectators filled the galleries and crowded behind railings on the floor. The matter of electing representatives to a convention to form a southern Confederacy became the main priority. A provisional Confederate government with Jefferson Davis appointed president would soon reach consummation in Montgomery, Alabama. Rather than submitting candidates to a popular election, the Louisiana convention voted to avoid delay and select representatives of its own accord. One of the six seats went to Duncan Kenner. Although Taylor's name did not receive attention during nominations, his friend Alexander Mouton

45. Richard Taylor, *Destruction and Reconstruction*, pp. 7–8 (first quotation 8); *Official Journal*, pp. 5, 8, 15, 18 (second quotation); Jackson Beauregard Davis, "Life of Richard Taylor," pp. 59–60; Bragg, *Louisiana in the Confederacy*, pp. 30–32; Robert A. Wooster, *Secession Conventions*, pp. 110–11; Roland, "Louisiana and Secession," p. 398.

honored him in the final balloting with a single vote, an exceedingly gracious gesture.[46]

Taylor played his most important role in the state convention as chairman of the Committee on Military and Naval Affairs. On February 2 he reported that Louisiana lay defenseless, completely open to an invasion by naval vessels via the Mississippi River. Fort Jackson below New Orleans needed extensive repairs, and the state militia, barely five hundred strong, appeared wholly inadequate and poorly armed besides. He recommended a minimum militia force of two regiments (about 1,800 men) and more generous funding (over the $500,000 recently approved by the legislature) to be drawn from the Swamp Land Fund, thus providing a budget of $1.2 million. These proposals passed without opposition, but Taylor's arguments for additional measures went largely ignored. Horace S. Fulkerson, a Mississippi businessman, had already approached Louisiana officials with a proposal to act as purchasing agent for a large quantity of English Enfield rifles. But the officials scorned his offer, declaring that the "United States government would not, and could not, deny the right of the State to withdraw" from the Union. Appealing to state militia board member Braxton Bragg, Fulkerson sustained another rude jolt. "Col. Bragg . . . received me and heard me, and then in his sententious, brusque manner informed me, with the wave of his hand, that Louisiana had all the arms she needed . . . meaning the old United States flint-lock muskets which had been seized at the arsenal," Fulkerson recalled. Taylor considered his own efforts in the state convention similarly futile. "More would have been desirable in the way of raising troops, but the temper of men's minds did not then justify the effort," he recounted disgustedly. "The Governor declined to use his authority to purchase arms, assured as he was on all sides that there was no danger of war, and that the . . . arsenal at Baton Rouge . . . would furnish more than we could need."[47]

46. Lane C. Kendall, "Interregnum in Louisiana," pp. 639–45.

47. *Official Journal*, pp. 33–36; Jackson Beauregard Davis, "Life of Richard Taylor," p. 60; Lane C. Kendall, "Interregnum in Louisiana," p. 653; Rainwater, *A Civilian's Recollections*, pp. 44–50 (first quotation 44–45, second quotation 45); Richard Taylor, *Destruction and Reconstruction*, pp. 7–8 (third quotation).

One of only a small minority of secessionists willing to acknowledge the South's overt, aggressive hostility toward the North, Taylor warned his colleagues in vain about the extreme probability of a terribly violent struggle. By now Lincoln was stiffening in his public statements regarding secession, but southerners sought a multitude of reasons to believe the North would not fight. A New Orleans newspaper editor contended that the Republicans would never resort to war because they wanted to avoid incurring political chaos and untold financial burdens on the northern public. Taylor's friend Braxton Bragg agreed completely with this blindly optimistic assessment. "We hope this course will lead to a peaceable solution," he informed Sherman. "Why should there be any strife over it?" Sherman, his political conservatism and sympathy for the South shaken, viewed Bragg's notion as an "an absurd impossibility." The South was surely doomed, Sherman told David French Boyd, a faculty member at the seminary. "Only in your spirit and determination are you prepared for war," he warned. "This country will be drenched in blood."[48]

As Taylor listened to his fellow delegates at New Orleans, he gradually received a stunning revelation. Only now did he realize that the dynamics of disunion, starting with the deliberate breakup of the Democratic party at Charleston and leading to the very act of secession, had depended upon a widespread conviction among southerners that the Republicans would not use force to protect federal military property in the South, that they would back down as before and let the South leave the Union in peace. "At the time and since, I marveled at the joyous and careless temper in which men, much my superiors in sagacity and experience, consummated these acts," Taylor recounted. "The attachment of the northern and western people to the Union; their superiority in numbers, in wealth, and especially in mechanical resources; the command of the sea . . . all these facts were laughed to scorn, or their mention was ascribed to timidity and treachery." Louisiana's secessionists seemed supremely nonchalant about what the Yankees might do. "They're all a set of cringing cowards!" asserted one delegate. "If there was money in it, maybe they'd

48. Dumond, *Southern Editorials on Secession*, pp. 464–65; Fleming, *Sherman*, pp. 351 (first quotation), 348 (second quotation); Boyd, "Gen. W. T. Sherman," pp. 412–13 (third quotation).

fight." Some did concede that war appeared likely, but they insisted it would be short and a victory for the South. One secessionist bragged confidently, "We are ready; we have been getting ready for years. A hundred thousand men are ready to take Washington and overrun the northern states in less than a month."[49]

Such contagious confidence stirred up a climate of unremitting public revelry and celebration, even by New Orleans standards. On February 12, acting in his capacity as chairman of the Committee on Military and Naval Affairs, Taylor made arrangements for official recognition of Louisiana's new self-proclaimed independence with a ceremony inaugurating the state flag. Escorted by a company of state militiamen, delegates assembled on the green in Lafayette Square to witness the raising of the flag on a staff atop the New Orleans City Hall. The Washington Artillery, the most elite of Louisiana military units, unleashed a twenty-one-gun salute as a huge crowd of citizens cheered. A journalist reported, "As the breeze unfurled the heaven-born hues of Louisiana's flag against the sky, displaying the beauteous harmony of its combined colors, a thrill of joy and admiration filled the spectators." The delegates then walked proudly past the militiamen, inspecting their ranks, and the soldiers honored them with a presentation of arms and stiff salutes.[50]

As the convention proceeded with its business, Taylor made a final, desperate effort to convince the other delegates that the state's military defenses required immediate attention. He had a single ally in P. G. T. Beauregard, the colorful Creole whose Mexican War service and expertise as a captain of army engineers had recently gained him a short-lived appointment to the superintendency of West Point. Now a private citizen, Beauregard responded promptly to the Louisiana Military Board's request for advice on strengthening the Mississippi River against a naval attack on New Orleans. He recommended an elaborate series of floating booms connected with large chains or heavy wire that would span the river just below Forts Saint Philip and

49. Richard Taylor, *Destruction and Reconstruction*, p. 8 (first quotation); Jane Martin Johns, *Personal Recollections*, pp. 88–90 (second and third quotations 89).

50. *Official Journal*, p. 51; Lane C. Kendall, "Interregnum in Louisiana," pp. 667–68 (quotation 668).

Jackson. The concept impressed the board, but state officials, especially Governor Moore, decided to approve only a partial execution of Beauregard's plan. New Orleans and the rest of southern Louisiana would therefore remain needlessly vulnerable to invasion.[51]

Taylor's intense frustration over military preparedness did not keep him from taking part in the convention's final deliberations. Although he avoided debate, he listened to delegates argue over necessary changes to the state constitution and over pressing financial matters. By now a large lithographed copy of the manuscript secession ordinance sat on display for all to examine, and on the front wall hung portraits of Jefferson Davis and George Washington. On the streets of New Orleans celebrating heightened as citizens anticipated Louisiana joining the Confederacy. A New York newspaper reporter working undercover commented on the public spirit, "I could fully understand how many strong Union men had at last been drawn into the almost irresistible tide." On March 21 the convention approved and ratified the Confederate constitution by a vote of 101 to 7. Taylor of course voted with the majority. A Unionist delegate's resolution asserting that state law had been violated because the constitution had not been submitted to a popular vote for ratification met an equally huge rejection from the convention. Taylor also supported the majority on this issue. Although Louisiana had become a Confederate state, he felt overcome by profound disillusionment and foreboding. "As soon as the Convention adjourned, finding myself out of harmony with prevailing opinion as to the certainty of war and necessity for preparation, I retired to my estate," he recalled. He vowed to give no service to the new southern nation unless called.[52]

Years later, looking back on the secession movement, Taylor expressed unvarnished alienation and contempt. He viewed the event as the direct result of a divisive popular battle inherent to the nation's democratic form of politics. With the federal government ultimately in a position to exert the power of majority will over minority interests, conflict seemed almost unavoidable. In his memoirs he men-

51. Winters, *Civil War in Louisiana*, pp. 18–19.

52. *Official Journal*, pp. 51–101; Richardson, *Secret Service*, pp. 42–44 (first quotation 44), 72–76; Richard Taylor, *Destruction and Reconstruction*, p. 8 (second quotation).

tioned Patrick Henry, Luther Martin, and other honest patriots who had opposed ratification of the Constitution because they feared the federal government's unmitigated authority to coerce states and individuals. Crises such as the Whiskey Rebellion, the Hartford Convention of New England states, and South Carolina's nullification movement Taylor cited as forerunners to the secessionist South's minority stand against the threat of tyranny from the northern majority. Likewise, he believed that a significant minority of southerners had opposed secession but that the majority had dominated all decisions on the issue. "Yet, so far from modifying in the smallest degree the will and conduct of the majority, this multitude of men [the minority] dared not give utterence to their real sentiments," Taylor argued. "A government of numbers, then, is not one of virtue and intelligence, but of force, intangible, irresistible, irresponsible." Such disdain for popular politics reflected an attitude common among archconservatives throughout the country at the time. A traveling English journalist observed, "As at New York, so at New Orleans. Universal suffrage is denounced as a curse, as corruption legalized, [as] confiscation organized." The apparent chaos of sheer majoritarian democracy, a gigantic brute springing from America's mass society, repulsed Taylor so deeply that he clearly wished he had never allowed himself to be pulled into the political maelstrom.[53]

Immediately after the war a friend spoke with Taylor about the secession movement, asserting, "You always used to say that you would go with the southern leaders very far, but that when it came to secession, you would oppose them as you did not wish to break up the Union." Taylor replied that the South's leadership should take no blame. "It was, on the contrary, a movement of the southern people," he explained, "and they were so unanimous in their determination that it became a question of whether we should let them go in by themselves or whether men of capacity and experience should take the reins. This decided me." But in his memoirs he admitted that the politicians, himself included, had played upon public fears in order to win support for secession. "Aggrieved by the tendencies of the Fed-

53. Richard Taylor, *Destruction and Reconstruction*, pp. 3–4, 255–56 (first quotation); Russell, *Civil War in America*, p. 140 (second quotation); Persons, *Decline of American Gentility*, pp. 16–17.

eral Gov't, and apprehending worse in the future, a majority of the people of the South approved secession as the only remedy suggested by their leaders," he confessed. Southern politicians had followed the fire-eaters' example by exploiting extremist tendencies in the sectional struggle. After his fruitless efforts at compromise during the Charleston convention, Taylor had taken up the cause of the secessionists, believing they comprehended the movement's drastic essence as a rebellious act. By their refusal to acknowledge the probability of war as a consequence of their actions, they demonstrated to Taylor democracy's worst kind of mass delusion.[54]

Taylor fully appreciated that secession, driven by revolutionary fury, was an unconstitutional action that would justify the North's use of military force. Like many wealthy planters whose Whiggish conservatism had bred in them nationalistic pride, he considered the Union a permanent legal entity under the Constitution, even with the government now in the hands of the hated Republicans. Taylor agreed with southern politicians that Republicans represented an intolerable form of tyranny over the southern minority, but he scoffed at the "Calhoun school" of secessionists, who espoused the doctrine of state sovereignty and the constitutional right of peaceable secession. Uncompromising popular will had infested politics so thoroughly, North and South, that Taylor held no illusions about the legal legitimacy of so-called states' rights. Secession meant revolution, a patently illegal action that simply enjoyed the Lower South's popular approval. Yet southern leaders refused to speak of secession as revolutionary. "There was to be no revolution," Taylor observed wryly, "for this, though justified by oppression, involved the recognition of some obligation to the Union." In other words, by claiming constitutional sanctions, southerners merely masked their raw determination to reject Republican rule. In Taylor's view, the South's revolutionary popular will had challenged the North's constitutional popular will. Only a few other southern leaders, most notably Robert E. Lee,

54. Marks and Schatz, *Between North and South*, p. 241 (first and second quotations); Richard Taylor, *Destruction and Reconstruction*, p. 286 (third quotation). Support for secession from the great majority of southerners is demonstrated persuasively in Ralph A. Wooster, "Secession of the South," pp. 117–27.

acknowledged the mammoth responsibility of joining such a movement. Although many secessionists did compare themselves to courageous colonists of the Revolutionary era, they denounced Republicans as the real radical insurgents and praised each other as
conservative patriots who understood and protected the paramount
rights of sovereign states. Nevertheless, the Union—something precious and sacred—now stood forsaken for an uncertain future.[55]

In a doubly disheartening realization, Taylor recognized that Confederate leaders, after taking the huge risk of revolution against the
Union, did not go nearly far enough in correcting the problems of
democratic politics. Like so many conservatives, especially among
those large slaveholders who wanted to rid the South once and for all
of the corrupting influence of demagogues and popular whim, Taylor asserted that the Confederacy's "paper constitution" failed to fulfill the reactionary ends he had envisioned as secession's only possible
virtue. Although the Confederate constitution's framers represented
the elite of southern leadership, Taylor bemoaned the lost opportunity to establish a southern nation administered by a small number of
wise and benevolent aristocrats, much like himself, who would refuse
to cater to popular demands. "The powers of different [government]
departments were as carefully weighed as are dangerous drugs by a
dispensing chemist," he grumbled. The Congress, with its bicameral
organization, he ridiculed as a "refuge for mischievous twaddlers to
worry the executive and embarrass the armies." Likewise, the Confederacy's governors readily exploited the doctrine of states' rights, "reasoning that one State had as much right to disagree with eleven as
eleven with twenty, [and] declared each of their hamlets of more importance than the cities of others." A few of the state secession conventions did grapple with proposals to restrict suffrage in order to
consolidate planters' and merchants' power over farmers and other
common whites. But such measures saw no chance of approval, since
they would have required thousands to vote in favor of relinquishing
their own right of suffrage. Much to Taylor's distaste, the Confeder-

55. Beringer et al., *Why the South Lost*, p. 73; Oakes, *Ruling Race*, pp. 220–
42; Richard Taylor, *Destruction and Reconstruction*, pp. 285–86 (quotation
286).

acy would function with the same kinds of democratic factionalism and localism he blamed for destroying the Union in the first place.[56]

Ultimately, however, Taylor adopted the popular dogma that secession erupted from a sincere desire for political liberty and not for the sake of slavery. He denied that at the heart of the problem lay southern demands for a slave code in the territories and concomitant fears of slave revolts fueled by Republican agitation. "The common belief that slavery was the cause of the civil war is incorrect," he stated flatly. Comparing the South's fundamental rights to the principles first set forth in the Magna Charta, he claimed that southerners strove only "for that which brought our forefathers to Runnymede, the privilege of exercising some influence in their own government." On this particular issue Taylor harbored relentless enmity toward Alexander Stephens of Georgia, the Confederate vice-president. In March 1861 Stephens delivered a widely publicized speech proclaiming slavery's function as the "cornerstone" of the new Confederacy. To Taylor this statement only benefited their enemies, especially the abolitionists, "the humanitarians," as he called them, "whose sympathies were not much quickened toward us thereby." Although the demand for securing the future of slavery not only dictated the course of secession but also prompted the Montgomery convention to write it into the Confederate constitution, Taylor would never accept slavery's true primacy in the sectional struggle. The democratic political process remained the overwhelming evil—a needless provocation for slavery becoming such a sensational public issue from the beginning. Instead of slavery leading to a crisis in democratic politics, he always believed that democratic politics, exploited by ambitious, mediocre, even incompetent leaders, had spawned the political manipulation of slavery for partisan advantage and personal prestige. "Yet we fought for nothing but slavery, says the world, and . . . Mr. Alexander Stephens reechoes the cry," Taylor declared angrily.[57]

56. Roark, *Masters without Slaves*, pp. 18–24; Richard Taylor, *Destruction and Reconstruction*, p. 286 (quotations); Faust, *Confederate Nationalism*, pp. 22–40.

57. Richard Taylor, *Destruction and Reconstruction*, pp. 4 (first quotation), 291 (second and fourth quotations), 27 (third quotation); Jesse T. Carpenter,

Alexander H. Stephens, Confederate vice-president
(*Johnson and Buell,* Battles and Leaders of the Civil War).

In almost every important phase of his life, Taylor's ideals had col-
lided with reality. His self-image as an aristocratic gentleman of education and talent—a man apparently destined by the plantation system's paternalistic traditions to enjoy wealth, prominence, and
leadership—had suffered under economic, social, and political forces
that continually thwarted his expectations. In order to maintain at

South As a Conscious Minority, pp. 245–49. On the prominence of proslavery
ideology in the Confederacy, see Faust, *Confederate Nationalism,* pp. 58–81.
For a different perspective emphasizing ideological principles of classical re-
publicanism as more important than slavery to southerners, see Holt, *Political
Crisis of the 1850s,* pp. 240–60. Holt fails to accept that, without the need to
protect slavery, there would have been no need for proslavery arguments
avowing republican principles. Had slavery not existed, no conflict would
have erupted.

least a semblance of authority and purpose, he found himself compelled to compromise his high principles, to adopt the very sort of materialistic, democratic, and racist methods that genteel aristocrats supposedly abominated. To a large extent, his dilemma typified the lives of many large planters in the Lower South on the eve of the Civil War.

As a sugar planter Taylor had used personal effort and innovative skill to achieve financial success in his first few years at Fashion. But the loss of his crop to the freeze of 1856 set him on a course of staggering indebtedness that he deliberately abused in order to maintain his stature as one of the South's most affluent planters. Meanwhile, his habit for gambling on horse races and card games confirmed that stature but surely complicated his strained finances. In December 1860 Martin Gordon, Jr., alerted him to the increasingly tenuous circumstances at hand, reminding him of an impending payment due for $72,000 on several notes his mother-in-law, Aglae Bringier, and Gordon had willingly endorsed. "We will have to be in a very good vein of luck—almost extraordinary," wrote Gordon. "I fear the result, my friend." As before, however, Taylor managed to pay his obligations by simply reborrowing, each time a larger amount. The crop he planted in the spring of 1861 produced a record yield, 930 hogsheads, reflecting a prosperous year in the sugar region. He had almost doubled the production of his best years, but even this impressive harvest proved far too small to pull him out of debt. "At the time the Civil War broke out, [Mrs. Bringier's] signature was on his notes for quite a fortune," recalled a Bringier family member. In April 1861 Taylor began defaulting on his note payments. Because of the economic chaos that soon came with the war, Gordon fell into an equally ruinous state, forcing Aglae Bringier to bear the entire burden of debt. Rather than allow her son-in-law to suffer the disgrace of losing Fashion, she agreed with the banks to pay off the notes, now amounting to more than $300,000, over an extended period of several years. Combined with the shock of Union invasion and widespread agricultural collapse, this huge financial obligation against Taylor's unpaid notes brought the Bringiers hardship from which they never fully recovered. Following the war Duncan Kenner generously propped up the family's finances in order to save various properties from foreclosure. Still, none of the Bringiers ever complained of Taylor having done anything dishonorable.[58]

Had Zachary Taylor lived, he never would have tolerated his son's lapse into profligacy. A hardened soldier whose Spartan and frugal conduct had always enabled him to keep his debts under control, Zachary Taylor had made a fortune through wise investments and conservative use of his capital, patiently accumulating a considerable sum of cash in order to protect his finances. Now that fortune lay in ruins, a victim of Dick Taylor's shortsighted desire to project an image of aristocratic wealth, the basis of his presumed right to social favor and political power. Yet even the grand image itself had failed to deliver the effortless influence he believed he deserved.

The most disturbing affront to Taylor's aristocratic visions came from his slaves. Even more than his financial problems, his relations with his slaves proved inherently vexing, undermining his paternalism, the fundamental sense of responsibility and benevolence that should have defined and gently shaped the whole of southern society, black and white alike. On the eve of the Civil War an English journalist in Louisiana observed, "There is one stereotyped sentence [from planters] which I am tired of: 'Our negroes, Sir, are the happiest, the most contented, and the best off of any people in the world.'" Against Taylor's expressed wishes, the slaves at Fashion resisted his authority in several ways: they habitually fraternized with poor white Acadians, whom he considered a bad influence on slave discipline and morale; they also pilfered expensive equipment from Fashion's sugar works to sell to common white traders. The ideal of paternalistic trust gave way to the necessity of continual surveillance and periodic punishments, never cruel in degree, yet indicative of slavery's unavoidably coercive purpose as forced labor for a master's profit. Although they

58. Martin Gordon, Jr., to Richard Taylor, December 19, 1860 (first quotation), Richard Taylor Papers, Boagni Collection; Champomier, *Sugar Crop in Louisiana, 1861–62*, p. 18; undated interview notes by Trist Wood, vol. 4 (second quotation), Bringier Family Genealogy Collection; promissory notes by Richard Taylor to Aglae Bringier and Martin Gordon, Jr., with protests of nonpayment dated April 27 and May 28, 1861, February 21, March 3, and March 31, 1862, and February 10, 1863, Richard Taylor Papers, Boagni Collection; Craig A. Bauer, "A Leader among Peers," pp. 398–402.

obviously revered Taylor with deep loyalty and affection, appreciating his generosity and fair treatment, his slaves hoped fervently for freedom, and their frequent forays into undisciplined behavior only confirmed their ultimate desires.[59]

The traditional conservative notion of paternalism's kind persuasion and mutual respect faltered in the face of Taylor's necessary assertion of control, just as the notion of secure aristocratic wealth, free from overt materialism, faltered in the face of his necessary pursuit of profits. Finally, the primal fear among virtually all southern whites—that they actually might lose control of the slaves—emerged most conspicuously after Lincoln's election, when local authorities in plantation districts organized armed patrols to crush any hint of slave sabotage and insurrection. In Taylor's St. Charles Parish, patrols searched slave quarters, prevented all contact with unauthorized parties, and punished slaves who left plantations without written passes. "A number of dogs are also loosed," recorded a visitor near Fashion, "but I am assured that the creatures do not tear the negroes; they are taught 'merely' to catch and mumble them, to treat them as a well-broken retriever uses a wounded wild duck." Any slave who tried to avoid arrest could be shot by the patrols.[60]

In a moment of candor Taylor admitted to Frederick Law Olmsted that slavery was a moral and economic evil for the South and that he wished he could free his bondsmen. But slavery produced his wealth, and therefore his stature, as a large planter. The institution defined his identity, and although he deplored this in the abstract, he continued to depend on its tangible benefits, especially after falling so deeply into debt. Out of sheer necessity, he asserted a discomforting control over his slaves because their lapses in discipline and their aspirations for freedom so often undermined his paternalistic efforts to provide for their welfare and happiness under his protection. Convinced not so much of blacks' racial inferiority as he was of their permanent social inferiority—much like the permanent inferiority of common whites—Taylor refused to recognize paternalism's manifold

59. Russell, *Civil War in America*, p. 121 (quotation); Olmsted, *Seaboard Slave States*, pp. 656–86; Oakes, *Ruling Race*, pp. 179–220.

60. Roland, *Louisiana Sugar Plantations*, p. 33; Russell, *My Diary North and South*, p. 265 (quotation). See also Oakes, *Slavery and Freedom*, chaps. 2–4.

weaknesses. Instead, he redoubled his sense of aristocratic purpose. The war would soon witness massive numbers of slave refugee families fleeing into the Union lines, eventually giving rise to almost two hundred thousand black volunteer soldiers. Yet Taylor asserted in his memoirs that the slaves "worked quietly in the fields until removed by the Federals. This is the highest testimony to the kindness of the master and the gentleness of the servant." His own experience as master, even as one of the kindest, failed to prove such a claim.[61]

While he struggled to bolster his finances and to control his slaves, Taylor experienced the same manner of frustration in politics. Rather than seeking the kind of public honor other southern politicians craved, Taylor served with a sense of duty, confirming his self-image of benevolent leadership, which was supposed to have tempered southern democracy. But these visions of social harmony, of combining planter rule with democratic power, broke apart under the weight of political warfare, pushing Taylor to compromise his ideals and to join the dirty game of bitter competition between large planters and common whites as well as embroiling him in the even more antagonistic sectional conflict.[62]

Taylor's Whiggish conservatism, part of the plantation ideal of elite leadership for the common good of a hierarchical society, floundered on the shifting sands of democratic politics. Rather than an organic and interdependent society of cooperation and deference to social distinctions, democracy meant harsher economic competition and far less public respect for the refined tastes and opinions of men like Taylor. "Years upon years have been found necessary to induce the masses to consider, much less adopt, schemes for their own advantage," he later observed haughtily. Control of the unruly masses, rather than skillful inducement and leadership by example, became the necessary tactic in the hands of Whig planters. But unlike slaves, white voters refused to bend so often and so easily. Even after gaining the constitutional sanction for disproportionate legislative representation, Louisiana's Whigs saw Democrats use the sectional issue of

61. Olmsted, *Seaboard Slaves States*, pp. 675–76; Howe, *American Whigs*, pp. 38–39; Richard Taylor, *Destruction and Reconstruction*, p. 257 (quotation).

62. Frederickson, "Aristocracy and Democracy," pp. 97–104; Howe, *American Whigs*, p. 262.

slavery in the territories to stir the public's emotions and destroy the Whig party. Rather than give up all hope of political influence, southern Whigs like Taylor, their loyalty to the South under public scrutiny, joined the Democrats in droves. The old Whig goal of preserving the Union through compromise over slavery soon collapsed under the extremism of the most ambitious southern Democrats, the fire-eaters, whose final demand for a federal slave code for the territories alienated northern Democrats. Taylor's desperate attempt to preserve the party and the Union at the Charleston convention confirmed his attachment to the old ways of sectional compromise, but in doing so, he embodied a faint echo of Whiggish principles rendered irrelevant by the fire-eaters' relentless efforts to destroy the Union.[63]

In the same way that the plantation system's commercial purpose demanded cash profits and control over slaves, the stake of large planters in the contest against Republican power compelled Taylor to support the demand for a federal slave code. Any prospect of maintaining traditional claims to political influence required genteel conservatives like Taylor to conform to the pervasive forces of commercial capitalism, racial control, and finally, the volatile politics of democracy. Yet even after jumping headlong into the radical politics of secession, Taylor indulged in the delusion that secession would somehow forge a new southern nation unified by the same elitist visions of aristocratic paternalism and Whiggish conservatism that had always failed him. Despite his forthright view of secession as an unconstitutional revolution—disturbingly glaring proof of democracy's vulnerability to popular upheaval—he expected the Confederate government suddenly to repress democracy and make full-scale preparations for a war to defend the plantation system's myth of unchallenged leadership by a beneficent ruling class. Clearly, Confederate leaders refused to adopt such reactionary and militant measures.

63. Richard Taylor, *Destruction and Reconstruction*, pp. 255–56 (quotation). The instability of southern legislatures, plagued by high rates of turnover and thus controlled by inexperienced and excitable members, is demonstrated in DeBats, "An Uncertain Arena," pp. 423–56. The gradual abandonment of paternalism as a political tactic among large slaveholders, including Whigs, is demonstrated persuasively in Siegel, "Paternalist Thesis," pp. 246–61. See also Greenberg, *Masters and Statesmen*, pp. 129–41.

Likewise, instead of pushing for a buildup of troops and new weaponry, they spoke confidently of peaceable secession or, at worst, a
short and glorious war. Instead of framing a government free of fac-
tional politics and claims of state sovereignty, they entangled themselves in the same kinds of popular conflict that had destroyed the
Union. Taylor's hope for a southern version of the Union as it should
be, perhaps something akin to the counterrevolutionary conservative
regimes taking control in Europe, remained an alluring, distant mirage on a swirling ocean of democratic politics.

Watching the crisis escalate following Lincoln's inauguration in
March, Taylor brooded over his own powerlessness. Like a scripted
drama, the failures at sectional compromise and the military confrontation at Fort Sumter took on the appearance of an inevitable cata-
clysm. It happened with "such bewildering rapidity," he lamented,
"and the human agencies concerned seemed as unconscious as scene-
shifters in some awful tragedy." Only a few days before the firing on
Fort Sumter, Taylor received a letter from his old friend ex-governor
Alexander Mouton, the politician who had done so much to insure
disunion in Louisiana. Mouton expressed bewilderment over the
"considerable excitement" caused by Lincoln's dispatching of Federal
troops to reinforce Sumter's small garrison, "indicating a determination [by Lincoln] . . . to bring on a war with us." Mouton concluded
dreamily, "For myself I have doubts yet of the correctness of the report." Of the Confederacy's subsequent triumph at Charleston, Taylor wrote morosely, "The capture of Fort Sumter, with its garrison of
less than a hundred men, was hardly Gibralter; yet it would have put
the grandiloquent hidalgoes of Spain on their mettle to make more
clatter over the downfall of the cross of St. George from that historic
rock." The South's rapturous celebration failed to ease Taylor's agony
over the magnificent American Union, finally shattered and at war
with itself.[64]

Other southerners, including many ardently patriotic Confederates, likewise mourned the necessity of dissolving the Union. To an
extreme degree, however, Taylor carried lasting feelings of tragedy

64. Richard Taylor, *Destruction and Reconstruction*, pp. 9 (first quotation),
29–30 (third quotation); Alexander Mouton to Richard Taylor, April 11,
1861 (second quotation), Richard Taylor Papers, Boagni Collection.

stemming from personal anger and regret—anger over the excesses of democracy having produced political fear and hostility between the sections, and regret over having consented to participate in the resulting conflict between two visions of the American democratic ideal of popular rights and power. By retreating to Fashion and swearing to abandon the Confederacy, he seemed like an outcast, part of a group of conservative planters and other old Whigs who believed in the old Union as the best protector. Yet Taylor attached an important proviso to his vow. He would serve only if called, just as he had done so often in the past. Although he despaired over what the South had done to itself and to the Union, he completely despised the power of the Republican party.[65]

Once hostilities began, like many in the South who had tried to remain neutral, Taylor quickly made his allegiance known. On April 20, one week after the firing on Sumter, he responded to an invitation to speak to a mass meeting of citizens at Napoleonville, in nearby Assumption Parish, in order to raise money and encourage volunteers for the Confederate Army. Together with Louis Bush, a prominent local lawyer and politician who had supported Douglas for president, Taylor issued a stirring appeal. In this, his only known occasion to deliver a public speech, Taylor displayed an uncharacteristic degree of passion, assailing the enemy as "the aggressor North." Citizens responded generously, especially wealthy planters, promptly contributing large sums to equip the growing ranks of volunteer soldiers. Similar outpourings of money and men came from across the rest of the South during April and May. Local companies organized and began to drill, all eager for the chance to fight.[66]

Hundreds of thousands of southerners would soon go to war with little thought of protecting slavery. The immediate struggle required defending their families and property—usually small farms and businesses—and their communities and states rather than their ideas and interests involving slavery. Similarly, few northerners intended for the war to destroy slavery, but rather to suppress rebellion and preserve the Union, with slavery most likely left intact. Most conservative

---

65. Stampp, *Southern Road to Appomattox*, pp. 13–14; Beringer et al., *Why the South Lost*, p. 67; Richard Taylor, *Destruction and Reconstruction*, p. 8.

66. Lathrop, "Pugh Plantations," p. 23 (quotation).

northerners, like Taylor's friend William T. Sherman, condemned the South for abusing and perverting democracy in rejecting the North's legal right to majority rule. "This is the real trouble," asserted Sherman, "it is not slavery, it is the democratic spirit which substitutes mere opinion for law." For southern conservatives like Taylor, it would have seemed particularly absurd to admit that slavery had caused secession and that the South had taken up arms to keep Republicans from inciting slave uprisings. Not only would he have had to accept slavery as the fundamental source rather than simply the illegitimate catalyst of the popular discord between the sections, but he also would have had to concede to Republicans their assertion that slavery's coercive purpose as a means of commercial profit and racial control had belied the plantation system's tradition of paternalistic benevolence. Republicans' concerns about the immorality of slavery paled in comparison to their concerns about slavery's power as a dominant institution spreading into the western territories and even into the free states. Northerners in general, and Republicans in particular, viewed free white labor and industrial expansion as the key to America's social and economic future. Southerners in general, and slaveholders in particular, viewed plantation slavery in the same terms. The highly touted battle over democratic power—the South's minority rights clashing with the North's majority rule—thus cloaked the deeper confrontation over slavery.[67]

As a self-styled aristocrat of talent and virtue, Taylor believed that he could have prospered without the advantage of slavery. He told Olmsted that the South would have been better off had the institution never existed but that emancipation, although desirable, appeared impossible because of common whites' virulent racism. Taylor would never admit that slavery, more than his highly bred character and acumen, had produced his wealth and defined the cultural prestige and political influence he had known. Most of all, he would never admit that because slavery constituted the most extreme form of pri-

67. Reid Mitchell, "Creation of Confederate Loyalties," pp. 94–95; Lloyd Lewis, *Sherman*, p. 134 (quotation); Bowman, "Antebellum Planters and *Vormarz* Junkers," pp. 796–808. On the Republican majority's condemnation of the South, see McPherson, "Antebellum Southern Exceptionalism," pp. 230–44.

vate property and productive capital within the realm of American economic enterprise, large planters like himself stood out as mere moneyed aristocrats, continually wrestling for profits, social esteem, and political power in a climate of increasing economic competition, blurred class lines, and democratic rivalry. The traditional European aristocrat of hereditary nobility, by contrast, still felt secure and stable enough in his wealth, title, and political influence to practice paternalistic noblesse oblige, taking for granted respect and deference from the rest of society. Taylor's southern plantation world, its own version of hierarchy continually challenged and undermined by dissension from common whites and resistance from slaves, clearly lacked true aristocratic security and stability. His disdain for common whites and his distrust for slaves exposed his failure to live up to the ideals of a harmonious organic society nourished by paternalism. Yet he steadfastly refused to abandon those ideals, despite the impossibility of achieving them. To have surrendered them he would have had to acknowledge his own grasping, competitive materialism, his own subtle racism, and his own political stake in slavery's survival. The grand role of aristocratic paternalist—justified by the plantation system's supposedly stable blend of democracy and aristocracy, of private capitalism and a sense of welfare for all, of social mobility and hierarchical structure—had affected him so deeply with a self-image of natural authority and duty to serve, that he and many other prominent planters continued to cultivate the self-image as intently as they cultivated their crops.[68]

Thus did Taylor detach himself intellectually and emotionally from any personal responsibility for slavery and from any desire to see it

68. Boney, "Southern Aristocrat," pp. 140–56. The failure of slaveholders to maintain their authority by means of aristocratic paternalism is argued most persuasively in Diggins, "Comrades and Citizens," pp. 614–23. See also Shalhope, "Race, Class, Slavery, and the Southern Mind," pp. 557–74. On the growing prevalence of America's competitive materialism during the nineteenth century, see Burns, *Success in America*, pp. 43–47. For a superb discussion of slavery as an inescapable dilemma that made aristocratic conservatives disdainful of northern antislavery agitation and thus finally vulnerable to the proslavery argument, see McCoy, *Last of the Fathers*, pp. 323–69.

protected, while at the same time acquiescing in proslavery demands for a federal slave code and even helping to bring secession. He had prepared himself as well to join the Confederacy in its military struggle, not wanting so much to defend the South's democratic minority rights as to resist the moralistic North's far more dangerous democratic majority. The future of slavery, he had convinced himself, seemed irrelevant compared with the manifold political evils of Republican power. As much as anything, he possessed a visceral sense of duty to defend the South for what still might remain of its old virtues as he saw them, to recapture its mythic roots in the plantation's harmonious, unifying image of benevolent paternalism.[69]

In fact, Taylor believed the democracy-plagued Confederacy had little chance of victory. If he would serve such a foolish and risky cause, he would act not out of his fundamental dependence on slavery but according to his self-image as a direct descendant of colonial Virginia's plantation aristocracy. He would act not as a mere moneyed aristocrat mired deeply in debt, not as a politician enmeshed in the democratic confrontation over the Union's future, but surely as a man of cultivated talent and ingrained virtue, motivated by duty to the southern people rather than by any hope of public honor. He later observed solemnly, "It was not for me, then, to whimper when the cards were bad; that was the right of those who were convinced there would be no war, or at most a holiday affair, in which everybody could display heroism."[70]

In August of 1847 Zachary Taylor had asserted to Jefferson Davis that the struggle over slavery had been "brought about by the intemperate zeal of the fanatics of the North, and the intemperate zeal of a few politicians of the South." Yet despite his strong sense of national-

69. Weaver, *Southern Tradition at Bay*, pp. 178–92.

70. Richard Taylor, *Destruction and Reconstruction*, p. 252 (quotation). The similarity between Taylor's and Robert E. Lee's decision to support the Confederacy despite its democratic weaknesses is evident in Edmund Wilson, *Patriotic Gore*, pp. 301, 334–35. On the persistence of devotion to moral duty among southern conservatives, a trait at odds with the South's democratic cult of public honor, see Wyatt-Brown, *Southern Honor*, pp. 68–69, 95–111. See also William R. Taylor, *Cavalier and Yankee*, pp. 34–35, 72–73, 124–30, and the excellent background summary in Singal, *War Within*, pp. 11–21.

ism and devotion to the Union, General Taylor declared that if the North ever exceeded its "right and proper" constitutional power, "let the South act promptly, boldly and decisively with arms in their hands if necessary, as the Union in that case will be blown to atoms, or will be no longer worth preserving. But I pray to God this state of things will not occur in my day or in your[s], or that of our children or children['s] children, if ever." As president in 1849 and 1850 Zachary Taylor stood rigidly against southern secessionist threats regarding slavery's status in the new western territories. But he also believed the Constitution would, and must, protect slavery where it existed in the South, not because it constituted a positive good, but because it undergirded and bespoke the South's every hope of economic, social, and political stability. Thus like their Revolutionary fathers, even the most conservative southern Unionists—Zachary Taylor among them —almost always behaved as southerners first, acting from their deepest conviction: the inviolability of slavery. It was the thorniest of legacies. Now at the end of the path his forebears had forged with a mixture of relish and dread, Richard Taylor grasped tightly that legacy: a white southern rose in full bloom, its sharp thorns as black as any slave.[71]

71. McIntosh, *Papers of Jefferson Davis*, pp. 210–11 (quotations). On the ambivalence and mixed feelings of southerners with strong Unionist principles, see also Fehrenbacher, *Constitutions and Constitutionalism*, pp. 33–56.

CHAPTER FOUR

Tamer of Louisiana Tigers

Thoughtless fellows for such serious work.

Stonewall Jackson

During late April of 1861 Richard Taylor watched and waited while prominent Louisianans displayed an ever increasing degree of enthusiasm for the southern cause, giving their money and pledging their own services to the swelling ranks of Confederate troops. St. Charles Parish's planters did their part, contributing $10,000 to support the outfitting of a local volunteer unit. Over the next six months about 30,000 Louisianans, most of them young and blindly ecstatic about the chance to kill Yankees, would leave their state in response to President Jefferson Davis's call to defend the South. Taylor, however, remained at Fashion, refusing to take any action on his own, his political pride still wounded by those state leaders who had rejected his proposal to provide soldiers and weaponry not only for the war in the East but also for the war that would surely come to Louisiana.[1]

In early May, Taylor received a letter from his friend Brigadier General Braxton Bragg, Confederate commander at Pensacola on the Florida coast, in charge of training thousands of raw volunteers pouring in from the surrounding states. "Give us the benefit of your

1. Roland, *Louisiana Sugar Plantations*, p. 25; Cassidy, "Louisiana," p. 95.

counsel," Bragg wrote, expressing confidence that Taylor's sense of patriotic duty would compel him to come at once. Taylor responded positively to the request, but he also took time to handle some personal affairs before arriving in Pensacola a few weeks later.[2]

For a West Pointer and Mexican War veteran like Bragg to seek Taylor's expertise hardly seemed logical. But Bragg knew Taylor well enough to recognize his potential value as an advisor. "Dick Taylor was a born soldier," observed Charles Fenner, a close friend. "Probably no civilian of his time was more deeply versed in the annals of war, including the achievements and personal characteristics of all the great captains, the details and philosophies of their campaigns, and their strategic theories and practice." Perusing the writings of outstanding soldiers, especially Napoleon, Julius Caesar, Frederick the Great, Henri Jomini, French marshals Villars, Turenne, Bugeaud, and many others, had inspired Taylor as no other intellectual pursuit. Undaunted by his lack of formal military training, Taylor actually viewed the West Point curriculum and the subsequent assignments given to young officers as often detrimental. In a conversation with Dabney Maury, himself a West Pointer and seasoned officer, Taylor declared, "Take a boy of sixteen from his mother's apron-strings, shut him up under constant surveillance for four years at West Point, send him out to a two-company post upon the frontier where he does little but play seven-up and drink whiskey at the sutler's, and by the time he is forty-five years old he will furnish the most complete illustration of suppressed mental development of which human nature is capable, and many such specimens were made generals on both sides when the war began."[3]

Serving on Bragg's staff as a civilian extra aide-de-camp without rank, Taylor confronted a slew of disturbing problems at Pensacola. Bragg seemed extremely irritated over having to play a secondary role in the Confederate high command's military strategy. After the

2. Richard Taylor, *Destruction and Reconstruction*, p. 10; Urquhart, "General Richard Taylor," p. 13 (quotation).

3. Fenner, "Richard Taylor," p. 5200 (first quotation); Bergeron, "General Richard Taylor," p. 38; Maury, *Recollections*, p. 229 (second quotation). See also Richard Taylor, *Destruction and Reconstruction*, pp. 113–14.

Braxton Bragg
(*Johnson and Buell,* Battles and Leaders of the Civil War).

fall of Fort Sumter, Jefferson Davis turned his back on Bragg's proposal to attack the Union garrison occupying Fort Pickens in Pensacola Harbor. Now Davis fixed his attention on Virginia, hoping to
mass enough troops to win an overwhelming victory, perhaps even to
capture Washington, and thus force the North to concede the South
its independence. Davis meant for Pensacola to serve only as a training ground for thousands of men destined for the war in Virginia.[4]

The conglomeration of green volunteer soldiers under Bragg's
care would have exasperated even the most tolerant commander.
"Full of enthusiasm for their cause, officers and men were, with few

4. McWhiney, *Braxton Bragg,* pp. 155–77.

exceptions, without instruction," noted Taylor. This problem appeared all the more unassailable because, in accordance with long-standing tradition among volunteer armies, enlisted men insisted on electing their own officers, a practice Taylor considered a "vicious system . . . [that] struck at the very root of that stern discipline without which men cannot be converted into soldiers." Bragg agreed completely with Taylor on this sore point, having informed him in early April, "Most of my trouble here has been from election of officers. It took a week's big drunk to get the Alabama Regiment I found here organized."[5]

Taylor soon determined to take such embarrassments in stride. "He is cool, sagacious and devoted to the cause and to me," observed Bragg. With the debilitating heat of summer in the Lower South setting in, an English journalist on the scene wilted under a sun "blazing so fiercely as to force one to admit the assertion that the average temperature is as high as that of Calcutta." Bragg also began to show signs of strain. "He was the most laborious of commanders, devoting every moment to the discharge of his duties," Taylor recalled, and "as a disciplinarian . . . his method and manner were harsh." Bragg's volunteers rapidly grew weary of such inglorious conditions. They "had become tired of living like flounders and crabs in the deep sands of Pensacola," complained a Louisianan. Throughout the camps a common cry rang out: "On to Richmond!"[6]

Apparently satisfied in his role as a civilian advisor, Taylor continued to balk at the idea of offering himself for military service. In early July, however, he received a telegram from Governor Thomas Moore abruptly granting him rank as a full colonel with command of the newly formed Ninth Louisiana Infantry Regiment, with orders to prepare at once to leave for the seat of war in Virginia. Apparently convinced that his political reputation had received some measure of

5. Richard Taylor, *Destruction and Reconstruction*, p. 10 (first and second quotations); Braxton Bragg to Richard Taylor, April 6, 1861 (third quotation), Taylor Papers, Boagni Collection.

6. McWhiney, *Braxton Bragg*, p. 182 (first quotation); Russell, *Civil War in America*, p. 110 (second quotation); Richard Taylor, *Destruction and Reconstruction*, p. 117 (third quotation); Terry L. Jones, *Lee's Tigers*, p. 1 (fourth quotation).

vindication, Taylor returned to New Orleans to meet with Governor Moore. Bragg viewed Taylor's departure as a grievous loss. "I sincerely regret it," wrote Bragg. "He had become about a necessity to me." Bragg had even recommended him to the War Department for a commission as brigadier general. Taylor had indeed performed well. Military experts were soon describing the troops trained at Pensacola as among the finest in the Confederacy.[7]

Although he referred to his new officer's commission as an appointment, Taylor had actually gained his colonelcy through the despised means of election by subordinates. The captains of the Ninth Louisiana had chosen him primarily because he was Jefferson Davis's brother-in-law, a family association they assumed would assure the regiment quick passage to Richmond. At the time, the pervasive concern among all volunteers in the Lower South was that they might not get into the fighting before the war ended. Yet despite their ulterior motive, the Ninth's soldiers placed surpassing confidence in Taylor as a competent commander. "The officers were elected yesterday," wrote a private, "and I think we have as good ones as the world could afford us." Another boasted, "With such officers this regiment will certainly make a name in history."[8]

While in New Orleans, Taylor witnessed war fever at the boiling point. "The tailors are busy day and night on uniforms, the walls are covered with placards for recruits, the seamstresses are sewing flags, . . . newspapers are crowded with advertisements relating to the formation of new companies of volunteers," declared a traveling journalist. Taylor found his regiment at Camp Moore, about eighty miles north of the city, deep in the piney woods, where thousands of Louisiana troops were receiving rudimentary training. One witty observer remarked that "it would require months of discipline to enable them to pass for soldiers, even at the North." But Taylor's men had the good fortune of a preliminary dose of drilling under Lieutenant Colonel

7. Richard Taylor, *Destruction and Reconstruction*, p. 11; McWhiney, *Braxton Bragg*, p. 182 (quotation); Urquhart, "General Richard Taylor," p. 27.

8. Richard Taylor, *Destruction and Reconstruction*, p. 11; Gunby, *David French Boyd*, p. 7; R. A. Pierson to James F. Pierson, July 3, 1861 (first quotation), Pierson Family Papers; Casey, *Story of Camp Moore*, p. 46 (second quotation).

Edward G. Randolph, a Mexican War veteran whom Taylor described as "a well-instructed officer for the time." A private in the Ninth considered Randolph "an excellent disciplinarian and drill-master, and to him the regiment owed all its knowledge of tactics and the greater part of its efficiency."[9]

Taylor had time only to make a cursory inspection of his regiment, which comprised ten companies, a total of about one thousand men. Although he wistfully remembered them as gentleman planters and sons of planters like himself, most in fact came from small farms in upstate Louisiana, and the remainder included a mixture of rural merchants, clerks, German laborers, Irish ditch diggers, and a few small-town lawyers, doctors, and preachers. "They are all whole souled country boys," affirmed one of their own. After ordering Randolph to secure the regiment transportation by rail to Virginia, Taylor made a brief stop in New Orleans, where he coaxed state authorities into giving him one hundred thousand rounds of ammunition along with other field equipment. There he also spent a few final hours with his family, said his farewells, and boarded an express train bound for the Confederate capital. One man chose to accompany him: Tom Strother, the slave Taylor had known as "foster brother and early playmate." As a youth Tom had assisted his uncle, Charles Strother, as body servant to Zachary Taylor in camp and battle in both Florida and Mexico. Tom had a large family, and "on this account I hesitated to bring him to Virginia," Taylor recalled, "but he would come, and was a model servant."[10]

Convinced that the South faced a lengthy and bitter war, Taylor reflected, "I had cut into this game with eyes wide open, and felt that in staking life, fortune and the future of my children, the chances were against success." A gambler in the most serious game of all, he

9. Russell, *Civil War in America*, p. 138 (first and second quotations); Richard Taylor, *Destruction and Reconstruction*, p. 11 (third quotation); Cummer, *Yankee in Gray*, p. 30 (fourth quotation).

10. Richard Taylor, *Destruction and Reconstruction*, pp. 11–12, 49 (first quotation), 69 (third quotation); Urquhart, "General Richard Taylor," p. 18; R. A. Pierson to James F. Pierson, July 3, 1861 (second quotation), Pierson Family Papers.

chose familiar cards, a suit long on duty and short on any hope of public honor.[11]

For Louisiana's ten regiments and five battalions of more than twelve thousand men journeying to Richmond during the spring and summer of 1861, the first, superficial flush of glory came in massive doses as they passed through Dixie. Drunk on liquor and anticipation, Taylor's regiment preceded him on July 11, encountering along its route the cheers of ardent young females waving handkerchiefs and patriotic banners. "In many places they ran out to the train with fruit and bouquets and threw them into the cars," recounted a soldier. Crowded onto flatcars and into boxcars, the southern boys rarely slept while rolling across Tennessee and upward through Virginia via Lynchburg, finally reaching Richmond on July 17. They camped with throngs of other volunteers outside the city on the fairgrounds, and the next day they thrilled to the sight of President Davis himself and several aides riding through their midst on an informal inspection visit. As Davis raised his hat the Louisianans greeted him with shouts so loud that one private recalled, "the whole earth seemed to tremble at the sound."[12]

Taylor arrived in Richmond on July 20. The Confederate capital was in a frenzy, riddled with rumors of fighting at Manassas about ninety miles to the north. "A multitude of wild reports, all equally inflamed, reached my ears," he remembered. Quickly finding his regiment, he assembled the men and told them he intended to take them into battle as soon as possible, a prospect that overjoyed every one of them. Late that afternoon he sought out Leroy Pope Walker, the new Confederate secretary of war, to obtain specific orders. On the way to Walker's office, accompanied by a young orderly sergeant, Taylor halted suddenly, noticing that the sergeant's pistol showed signs of rust. "Looking me straight in the eye," the startled soldier recalled, "he sternly said, 'If your gun is not in condition for inspection by nine o'clock, sir, I will have you punished.'" Humiliated at this upbraid, the

11. Richard Taylor, *Destruction and Reconstruction*, p. 252 (quotation).

12. Terry L. Jones, *Lee's Tigers*, p. 1; R. A. Pierson to [W. H. Pierson], July 12 (first quotation), 19 (second quotation), 1861, Pierson Family Papers; Cummer, *Yankee in Gray*, p. 32.

orderly soon decided to decline further service to his exacting colonel, and within a few days he had willingly returned to the ranks as
an ordinary private.[13]

Secretary Walker's office presented Taylor with a ridiculous scene
of chaos and frustration. A cultured Alabama gentleman without a
hint of managerial aptitude, Walker had gained his position at the
insistence of his political friend William L. Yancey, the old fire-eater.
Walker moaned to Taylor about the thousands of men languishing
outside Richmond waiting for the government to give them ammunition and equipment. A glaring example of the Confederacy's early
incapacity to mount a concerted war effort, Walker's quagmire forced
him to refuse service to dozens of regiments. During the first year of
the war as many as two hundred thousand impatient volunteers eventually returned home, their regiments disbanded for lack of basic military necessities. Upon discovering that Taylor had already procured
ammunition and equipment for his regiment, Walker gleefully issued
orders for the Ninth Louisiana to board a Manassas-bound train at
9:00 that evening. With darkness falling, Taylor trotted his men
through Richmond's streets toward the railway station. Anxious citizens cheered them on, one group of ladies shouting in unison, "Farewell brave soldiers!"[14]

At the station the regiment waded through crowds of people
spreading more unfounded rumors about a terrible battle at Manassas. Some claimed a southern victory, but others said the army had
been severely beaten and that several general officers had been killed.
Taylor expected his train at any moment, but an hour passed and
then two more before it finally appeared, well after midnight. The
troops jumped aboard, anticipating arrival at the battle front by early
morning. But this proved a painful delusion. The locomotive engine,
"a machine of the most wheezy and helpless character," lumbered
along at a pathetic pace, requiring the soldiers to leap off the cars in

13. Richard Taylor, *Destruction and Reconstruction*, p. 12 (first quotation);
Roby, "Reminiscences," pp. 548–49 (second quotation 549).

14. Richard Taylor, *Destruction and Reconstruction*, pp. 12–13; Donald, *Liberty and Union*, p. 98; Cummer, *Yankee in Gray*, p. 32; Urquhart, "General
Richard Taylor," p. 20 (quotation).

order to climb steep hills. Throughout the morning of July 21 they heard gunfire, constant and clear, echoing off the Blue Ridge mountain range far to the west. "At every halt of the wretched engine," Taylor recounted, "the noise of battle grew more and more intense, as did our impatience." Choice cursing flew from Taylor's lips in a steady stream. "I hope the attention of the recording angel was engrossed that day in other directions," he later mused.[15]

At last, near dusk the Ninth Louisiana disembarked at Manassas Junction, where they learned of the Confederate victory gained that very day. Just then another train loaded with dead and wounded soldiers came into full view. "Filled with wonder," wrote a private, "we wandered about gazing upon the wounded and the prisoners collected at the R. R. station . . . gradually acquiring a slight perception of the horrors of war." Ordering his men to bivouac nearby and remain ready for combat at short notice, Taylor searched through the darkness and confusion on the battlefield for General Beauregard's headquarters. There he found a staff officer who said that the commanding general's orders would come to Taylor the following morning. Excited speculation about an immediate advance on Washington made sleep difficult for the Louisianans, but Taylor's morning orders simply instructed him to select a suitable campsite and await further word from headquarters.[16]

Already crestfallen over having missed the fighting, Taylor's men listened with jealous discomfort to the bragging of the "veterans" who camped nearby. Taylor tolerated such bravado as the "natural" result of a great victory. "They had achieved all, and more than all, that could have been expected of raw troops," he wrote. Later asserting, as did many other southerners, that "a strong brigade" of Confederates could have stormed into Washington and Baltimore on the heels of the routed Yankees, Taylor cited Napoleon's axiom that a victorious army, despite its exhaustion and confusion, should always pursue a defeated foe. Yet, "if there be justification in disregarding an

15. Urquhart, "General Richard Taylor," p. 21; Richard Taylor, *Destruction and Reconstruction*, p. 13 (quotations).

16. Roby, "Reminiscences," p. 549; Cummer, *Yankee in Gray*, p. 33 (quotation); Richard Taylor, *Destruction and Reconstruction*, p. 13.

axiom of Napoleon," he admitted, "the wild confusion of the Confederates after Manassas afforded it."[17]

For several days chaos continued in the camps. "Regiments seemed to have lost their colonels, colonels their regiments," Taylor recalled. Many soldiers actually believed they had already won the war. Outbursts of celebrating brought flurries of small arms fire, disrupting the camps with stray bullets that accidentally killed several Confederates. By July 25, however, General Beauregard reasserted control by organizing his corps into eight brigades. Colonel Taylor's Ninth Louisiana was brigaded with the Sixth, Seventh, and Eighth Louisiana regiments, along with Major Roberdeau Wheat's Special Battalion, the fearsome Louisiana Tigers. Beauregard gave command of the Louisiana Brigade to Brigadier General William H. T. Walker of Georgia, a fifty-four-year-old West Pointer who had served in the Seminole War and the Mexican War. During both conflicts Walker had recovered from serious multiple wounds. One Louisiana soldier wrote of the new brigadier, "The permanent evidences of his sufferings remained in a painfully spare frame and a pale cadaverous complexion, which always suggested a ghost on horseback."[18]

Walker's physique only faintly disguised his military prowess. Initiating a heavy and constant dose of drill and tactical training, he disciplined his officers and men so well that they soon possessed a reputation as a model brigade. "We are all proud of our General Walker—he has the entire confidence of his men," wrote one of the privates. Under such a severe regimen Taylor's own passion for soldierly duty flourished. "Col. Taylor is a regular martinet in the line of discipline, and aspires to have the most orderly regiment in the service," remarked one of his men. Yet much like Walker, Taylor tempered his demands with fair treatment. "Our colonel seems to have a great deal of sympathy for his men," wrote another. "True, he is quite

17. Urquhart, "General Richard Taylor," p. 23; Richard Taylor, *Destruction and Reconstruction*, pp. 14–16 (quotations).

18. Richard Taylor, *Destruction and Reconstruction*, p. 13 (first quotation); Alison Moore, *Louisiana Tigers*, pp. 47–49; Cummer, *Yankee in Gray*, p. 33 (second quotation).

rigid in his discipline as all military commanders should be, but he is a gentleman in every sense." [19]

Preparations for another anticipated Union offensive suffered an alarming setback, however, as huge numbers of Confederates gradually succumbed to camp diseases, the scourge of both armies throughout the war. Living in close quarters with poor sanitation, the rural-bred southerners fell victim to rampant outbreaks of measles, mumps, typhoid, pneumonia, dysentery, and whooping cough. Driven from camp at Manassas by the stench of decaying horses and trash left on the battlefield, the army moved several miles north to Centreville, about twenty miles from Washington. Healthier surroundings here helped only slightly to check the epidemic. Taylor's regiment fared as badly as any, losing almost one hundred men to medical discharge and death. By September he could muster barely three hundred soldiers free of sickness. By the end of the month a total of some fifteen thousand Confederates, about one-third of the entire army, lay sick, many without any hope of recovery. "The death of one of our poor soldiers is hardly noticed," wrote one of Taylor's privates. "One of the Bossier boys died day before yesterday and one of ours today and it seemed to me that it was not noticed no more than if a dog had died." [20]

Taylor became personally involved in the ordeal of illness, recalling, "I passed days in hospital, nursing the sick and trying to comfort the last moments of many poor lads, dying so far from home and friends." Working under such a physical and emotional strain, Taylor felt his own strength deteriorating. By the end of September he lay bedridden, paralyzed with the chronic rheumatoid arthritis that had stalked him since his youth. Gaining a leave of absence to recover, he spent the first week of October in Richmond in the home of his friend Judah P. Benjamin, the new secretary of war. Taylor then traveled

19. W. Ezra Denson to John F. Stephens, October 10, 1861 (first quotation), Miscellaneous Manuscript Collections, Louisiana State University; Cummer, *Yankee in Gray*, p. 91 (second quotation); Meade, *Judah P. Benjamin*, p. 194; R. A. Pierson to [W. H. Pierson], August 17, 1861 (third quotation), Pierson Family Papers.

20. Richard Taylor, *Destruction and Reconstruction*, p. 19; Cummer, *Yankee in Gray*, pp. 33, 90; Terry L. Jones, *Lee's Tigers*, pp. 24–26 (quotation 25–26).

twenty miles to Fauquier Springs, a short distance south of Manassas, where his sister Elizabeth Dandridge had come from her home in Winchester in order to nurse him back to health. Widowed upon the death of Colonel William Bliss in 1853, Betty had married Dr. Philip Dandridge of Winchester in 1858. "Col. Taylor is still absent, sick," noted one of his men at Centreville. "Doubts are expressed as to whether he will be able for duty this winter."[21]

Taylor lifted all concern for his health when he returned to Centreville on October 30, there to face a new problem: his promotion by President Davis to the rank of brigadier general with command of the Louisiana Brigade. As part of a plan to give the army greater cohesiveness, Davis had decided to brigade all regiments by states. He therefore assigned General Walker to a Georgia brigade and gave Taylor the Louisiana Brigade. "This promotion seriously embarrassed me," Taylor recalled. The brigade's three other colonels far surpassed him in training and experience, having already led their men in battle at Manassas. Taylor had never even experienced combat. As a sad result, Walker abruptly resigned from the service, outraged at having lost the brigade he had trained and finally deciding that Davis had deliberately ignored his merit by promoting inexperienced officers to responsible positions of command. "I will not condescend to submit any longer to the insults and indignities of the Executive," he informed Secretary of War Benjamin.[22]

Taylor's discomfort stemmed from the fact that he was Davis's brother-in-law, a relationship he feared "would justify the opinion

21. Richard Taylor, *Destruction and Reconstruction*, pp. 19–20 (first quotation); Meade, *Judah P. Benjamin*, pp. 186, 194; Urquhart, "General Richard Taylor," p. 26; Tucker, *Descendants of the Presidents*, p. 103; W. Ezra Denson to John F. Stephens, October 10, 1861 (second quotation), Miscellaneous Manuscript Collections, Louisiana State University. A modern physician who has studied Taylor's illness concludes that it might have been a psychologically induced reaction to stress, fatigue, and depression. See Riley, "General Richard Taylor," pp. 67–86.

22. Richard Taylor, *Destruction and Reconstruction*, pp. 20–21 (first quotation 20); Urquhart, "General Richard Taylor," pp. 27–29; Alison Moore, *He Died Furious*, pp. 89–90 (second quotation). On Walker's career, see Stephen Davis, "A Georgia Firebrand," pp. 447–60.

Jefferson Davis
(Jenkins Rare Book Company).

that my promotion was due to favoritism." Members of the Louisiana Brigade only confirmed this worry. "One thing is true of Mr. Davis," remarked one officer. "He has his favorites whom he promotes at all hazards, whether competent or not." The president's wife, the sagacious Varina Howell Davis, asserted openly that "Mr. Davis" had only two faults: he was "too fond of West Point officers and his first wife's relations." The New Orleans *Daily Delta* published a letter from a soldier in the brigade who commented angrily on Taylor's extraordinary promotion, "A more shameful piece of business has not transpired during the war."[23]

Amid this furor Taylor hurried to Richmond to ask Davis to cancel his commission as brigadier. "After an affectionate reception, the

23. Richard Taylor, *Destruction and Reconstruction*, p. 20 (first quotation); Goree, *Thomas Jewett Goree Letters*, p. 98 (second quotation). A new edition of Goree's Civil War letters is being prepared by Thomas W. Cutrer. Marks and Schatz, *Between North and South*, p. 153 (third quotation); New Orleans *Daily Delta*, November 6, 1861 (fourth quotation).

president listened to the story of my feelings," he remembered. Davis responded by saying he would reflect upon the matter for one day and notify Taylor of his decision by mail. But when Taylor returned to Centreville on November 3, he learned that Davis had written not to him but instead to the Louisiana Brigade's three senior colonels, Harry T. Hays, Isaac G. Seymour, and Henry B. Kelly. Davis's letter, Taylor discovered, "went on to soothe the feelings of these officers . . . so effectually as to secure me their hearty support." Davis had won this round in the ongoing public controversy regarding his appointments of general officers. He knew he could trust Taylor to remain loyal, especially considering the growing number of "political generals" pushed upon him by state leaders. Davis wanted the most respected and cultured men available for these positions, and he meant to hold them to the same standards as the West Pointers he preferred so much. One military observer commented in a waggish vein, "Dick Taylor is superior to any [West Pointer] and [has] more brains than all of them put together. If Davis was too fond of his first wife's relations, tis a pity there were not more like Taylor."[24]

Despite all the tension over Taylor's promotion, mutual esteem between Walker and Taylor survived unshaken. As a friendly gesture Walker left his successor a tent and some field equipment. Walker would eventually return to the army, serving under Joseph E. Johnston in the western theater and becoming a major general. His superb training of the Louisiana Brigade rendered Taylor's new assignment all the more manageable. As autumn wore on, turning to Indian summer and then to cold and rainy weather, the Federal army made no aggressive movements, and both sides settled into a long stalemate interspersed with tiresome rumors of imminent attack. A Louisiana officer soon remarked, "We have about given up the idea of a fight at this point." Yet Taylor determined to keep his men in shape, occasionally leading them on marches up to the front lines and back again the same day. "Owing to the good traditions left by my predecessor,

24. Richard Taylor, *Destruction and Reconstruction*, pp. 20–21 (first quotation 20, second quotation 20–21); Urquhart, "General Richard Taylor," pp. 30–31; McWhiney, *Southerners and Other Americans*, pp. 89–95, 100–101; Donald, "Confederate As a Fighting Man," pp. 186–93; Marks and Schatz, *Between North and South*, p. 246 (third quotation).

Walker, and the zeal of officers and men, the brigade made great progress," he recalled. Yet zeal often gave way to exhaustion. One of Taylor's planter-soldiers vowed, "If I ever get home I will give the negroes a heap more Saturday evenings than I ever did before. Bless the name of Saturday."[25]

Even under Taylor's demanding routine the brigade managed to enjoy an uncommonly comfortable camp life. Regimental bands kept the men entertained with concerts. The Louisianans also received shipments of extra clothing and blankets from state authorities as well as personal bundles from home that included some of the best food and drink outside Paris. Officers began to compete in producing the most exotic dishes, and Taylor often joined them in the feasting. Their new general thus gradually charmed them into a warm comradeship of affection mixed with soldierly respect. David French Boyd, the Ninth Louisiana's commissary officer, described Taylor as "genial, full of humor and very witty, his dark brown eyes a-sparkling, and with his rich, melodious voice, he was the most brilliant and fascinating talker that I remember in the Southern army." Another officer reflected warmly, "When that pleasant smile glowed upon his face, and he began to smoke his corn-husk cigarette and talk, what a treat it was to sit around and listen to Dick Taylor." Sergeant Fred Gruber, a loquacious German wit from the Seventh Louisiana, cultivated a special affinity for Taylor's camaraderie, often visiting his headquarters and exchanging verbal barbs that attracted listeners from all over the camp. But Gruber always approached Taylor's tent with caution, first asking a staff officer whether the general's rheumatism had flared up recently. On one occasion, discovering Taylor to be indisposed, the sly sergeant retorted, "Isn't it bad enough for the General to have 'rheumatiz' without my 'catching fits.'" Boyd recalled how harsh weather often aggravated Taylor's illness, giving him a violent nervous headache and leaving his right side, and sometimes all of his limbs, partially paralyzed. "Often in Virginia in the wet,

25. Urquhart, "General Richard Taylor," p. 30; Warner, *Generals in Gray*, pp. 323–24; Richard Taylor, *Destruction and Reconstruction*, pp. 19, 21 (second quotation); Stafford, *General Leroy Augustus Stafford*, p. 37 (first quotation); R. A. Pierson to Miss M. C. Pierson, November 5, 1861, Pierson Family Papers; Terry L. Jones, *Lee's Tigers*, pp. 21–24 (third quotation 23–24), 55–56.

cold weather he had to be helped on and off his horse; and then his disabled leg would hang limp, like a rope, from his saddle. . . . When he was sick he was 'ugly,' and we had to keep away from him," wrote Boyd, "yet it was seldom that he would allow himself to go 'off duty.'"[26]

Taylor's explosive temper soon became as palpable as his witty banter, and nothing inflamed him more than poor discipline. During the late fall of 1861, the pain Taylor detested worse than his physical illness came from a thorn in his side known as the Louisiana Tigers. Commanded by Major Rob Wheat, a six-foot four-inch, 240-pound giant, the Tigers combined a legendary reputation for combat ferocity with a nasty proclivity for drinking and brawling. Taylor had no personal quarrel with Wheat, whom he remembered as a favorite of Zachary Taylor's in Mexico. Although he allegedly had more actual experience under fire than any man in North America at the time, Wheat seemed genuinely humble and earnest, a trait that endeared him to his Tigers. Besides serving in the Mexican War, he had engaged in Latin American filibustering expeditions and had fought for Garibaldi in Italy. As late as November he had not fully recovered from a life-threatening wound received while leading the Tigers in a magnificent charge at Manassas. But Taylor wanted so badly to rid himself of Wheat's battalion that he appealed directly to General Joseph Johnston, who now commanded the Confederate Army in Virginia. Realizing that no other brigadier would willingly accept such a riotous unit, Johnston flatly refused to transfer the Tigers. Taylor later recalled, "He promised, however, to sustain me in any measures to enforce discipline."[27]

26. Stafford, *General Leroy Augustus Stafford*, p. 37; Terry L. Jones, *Lee's Tigers*, pp. 28–29; Urquhart, "General Richard Taylor," pp. 36–37; anonymous undated manuscript leaf (second quotation), Miscellaneous Manuscript Collections, Louisiana State University; Boyd, *Reminiscences of the War*, pp. 13 (first and fourth quotations), 32 (third quotation). On Boyd's service as a commissary officer under Taylor, see Germaine M. Reed, *David French Boyd*, pp. 34–39.

27. Dufour, *Gentle Tiger*, pp. 130–46; Terry L. Jones, *Lee's Tigers*, p. 54; Alison Moore, *He Died Furious*, pp. 10–13; Richard Taylor, *Destruction and Reconstruction*, pp. 21–23 (quotation 21).

Late on the cold night of November 28, long after tattoo, Taylor ordered several Tigers confined to the guardhouse for creating a disturbance in camp. After a short time, a small band of their comrades, outraged and extremely drunk, attacked the posted guard in a bungled attempt to liberate the prisoners. Two Tigers, Dennis Corkeran and Michael O'Brien, admitted to being the ringleaders. The next morning they faced a court-martial that sentenced them to death by firing squad. Drinking liquor, a pastime that clearly violated army regulations (except among officers), had become virtually impossible to suppress, especially during long stretches of inactivity. One Louisianan recalled that several army doctors had argued that "it would be very advantageous to the health" of the many victims of disease, but Taylor still refused to allow enlisted men even "a single drop of whiskey." With irresistible guidance from the always resourceful Tigers, however, the rest of the Louisianans learned happy disobedience. "Taylor's Louisiana Brigade . . . being mostly city or river men, 'knew the ropes,' and could get liquor from Richmond," recollected a Georgian in the same division. "Our men could not." By now, much to Taylor's embarrassment, the name Louisiana Tigers had attached itself in popular parlance to his entire brigade.[28]

Fed up with the problem of drunkenness in camp, Taylor decided to make an example of the two guilty Tigers by having them executed by members of their own company. Discovering this, Wheat rushed to Taylor and earnestly requested pardons. One of the two soldiers had braved enemy gunfire in helping carry Wheat's wounded body from the field at Manassas. Although both men had spotty records of personal behavior, Wheat explained that their stern company commander, Captain Alex White, had been away on leave during the melee at the guardhouse. But Taylor stood his ground, refusing to pardon the prisoners. Wheat then informed him that the Tigers might mutiny at the idea of executing two of their own. At this Taylor stiffened and glared at Wheat, calmly warning him that

28. Richard Taylor, *Destruction and Reconstruction*, pp. 21–22; R. A. Pierson to Miss M. C. Pierson, August 5, 1861 (first quotation), Pierson Family Papers; James Cooper Nisbet, *Four Years on the Firing Line*, pp. 24–25 (second quotation); Terry L. Jones, *Lee's Tigers*, pp. 34–35.

such blatant disobedience to orders would surely bring "serious consequences." [29]

On December 9 the entire division, under the command of Major General Edmund Kirby Smith, turned out to witness the Army of Northern Virginia's first military execution. Corkeran and O'Brien, dressed in their full Zouave uniforms, stood before two white stakes ten feet apart. Two coffins lay nearby. A priest prayed with them as they knelt down to receive blindfolds and have their hands tied behind them to the stakes. The previous night they had issued a joint statement to their fellow soldiers. "We acknowledge the justice of our sentence," they wrote. "May the rendering up of our lives prove a benefit . . . and a lesson to all to guard against the vice of drunkenness." Claiming, "we die a soldier's death," they yielded to the "altar of military order and discipline." To their executioners they made one request: "Do not mangle us; aim at our hearts!" Their message concluded with, "Tigers, a last farewell." [30]

A firing squad of twenty-four Tigers, half of them given blanks for their muskets, stood fifteen paces away from the condemned pair. The regiments of the division lined up on three sides around, watching in silence. By Taylor's secret orders a company from Colonel Henry Kelly's Eighth Louisiana, their guns loaded, stood on the front row directly behind the firing squad, ready to prevent any hint of mutiny from the Tigers. Major Wheat, unable to bear the spectacle, remained in camp, refusing to leave his tent. Corkeran and O'Brien, their shirts pulled open to their waists, kneeled and waited, motionless, as their captain, Alex White, slowly shouted the orders: raise muskets, aim, fire. Death came instantly. The two bodies pitched forward. Suddenly a Tiger, Daniel Corkeran, ran from the ranks toward the bodies. Weeping uncontrollably, he fell to his knees and held his brother Dennis in his arms. Tears filled the eyes of many of the stunned and silent witnesses. [31]

29. Dufour, *Gentle Tiger*, p. 161; Alison Moore, *He Died Furious*, p. 101; Richard Taylor, *Destruction and Reconstruction*, p. 22 (quotation).

30. Dufour, *Gentle Tiger*, p. 161; unidentified newspaper clipping (quotations), Confederate States of America Archives.

31. Richard Taylor, *Destruction and Reconstruction*, p. 22; Dufour, *Gentle Tiger*, p. 161; Boyd, "Major Bob Wheat"; Richard Lewis, *Camp Life of a Confederate Boy*, p. 25.

The execution stood out as the most memorable event in the army that winter. Southern newspaper editors, holding General Johnston ultimately responsible, debated the legitimacy of executing soldiers for a noncombat incident. A Yankee editor called it an example of Confederate officers' prejudice against Irish-born soldiers. David Boyd later commented, "It was whiskey that was to blame—not these hard fighters." Observing pointedly that similar crimes resulted in less severe punishments during the rest of the war, Boyd concluded, "We had another and better use for our men than shooting them ourselves." But Taylor never regretted the act. The deaths of Corkeran and O'Brien, he noted, "produced a marked effect" upon his brigade.[32]

General Taylor had finally achieved absolute authority over the Louisiana Brigade. He had convinced every man, especially the Tigers, that neither liquor nor any other distraction could subvert his control, whether in camp or in battle. If the Confederate Army had any hope of avoiding a debacle of disorder like the one following the Manassas battle, every commander would have to heed Taylor's lesson. If the South's shameless wealth of proud soldiers, officers and enlisted men alike, had any hope of winning their independence, they would have to submit to unconditional discipline.

Soon afterward, ironically enough, Taylor had to confront southern pride at its highest level. General Joseph Johnston, deeply resentful at President Davis for appointing him fourth in rank among the army's recent promotions to full general, prevailed upon Taylor's apparent influence with Davis to argue his case for the supreme rank. Because Johnston had served most recently as quartermaster general in the United States Army prior to the war, he insisted that Davis should have placed him ahead of Samuel Cooper, Albert Sidney Johnston, and Robert E. Lee, each of whom had ranked no higher than colonel. "[Joseph] Johnston was the beau ideal of a soldier," observed Taylor, "and no officer . . . had seen so much actual service with troops." But Davis viewed Johnston's quartermaster general's rank as merely a staff position. The other three had been serving at

---

32. Alison Moore, *Louisiana Tigers*, pp. 45, 54–55; Boyd, "Major Bob Wheat" (first quotation); Richard Taylor, *Destruction and Reconstruction*, p. 22 (second quotation).

the time as field commanders, and all had held seniority to Johnston during his previous stint as a line officer. Rejecting this reasoning, Johnston dispatched a reluctant Taylor to Richmond to confront Davis.[33]

The president listened patiently to Taylor's eloquent plea, but during their conversation Taylor gradually perceived "the estrangement growing up between these two eminent persons." Davis remained obstinate in his decision, a trait he would perfect as the war continued. Taylor returned to Johnston and explained the president's position. Johnston and Davis then exchanged bitterly defensive letters on the matter, and "time but served to widen the breach," Taylor remembered. Davis's critics in the Confederate Congress used the feud as political ammunition, thus "weakening the influence of the head of the cause for which all were struggling." Davis had gladly rewarded his old friends Samuel Cooper and Albert Sidney Johnston in making the appointments, and Robert E. Lee had used his genteel charm and humility to win the president's personal trust. Unfortunately for Joseph Johnston, a charming demeanor toward his superiors had never graced his personality. "Destiny willed that Davis and Johnston should be brought into collision," Taylor concluded. "Each misjudged the other to the end."[34]

In mid-December Taylor moved his brigade from Centreville to a camp situated a few miles from Manassas. The weather, cool and clear, brought improved health to the ranks. On Christmas Day he hosted a sumptuous dinner for his staff and other officers. A New Orleans correspondent in camp described the affair as a huge success and noted a grand spirit of unity throughout the brigade. "Gen. Taylor," he reported, "is daily gaining the confidence and affection of the officers and men by his unwavering and straightforward course, and . . . will, no doubt, when opportunity presents, prove himself a 'chip off the old block.'" All was not unity and comradeship yet, however,

33. Richard Taylor, *Destruction and Reconstruction*, pp. 23–25, 42–43 (quotation).

34. Ibid., pp. 24 (first quotation), 45 (second quotation); Thomas, *Confederate Nation*, p. 141. Johnston's side of the debate is thoroughly defended, with sharp criticism of Taylor's conclusions, in Robert M. Hughes, *General Johnston*, pp. 78–90.

because Major Wheat remained conspicuously absent from Taylor's Christmas celebration. Taylor had sent the Tigers several miles away to spend the holiday season performing outpost duty. As it turned out, Wheat and his officers enjoyed a Christmas of revelry with a group of Virginia cavalrymen in a deserted tavern, a setting more to their liking than Taylor's dinner table.[35]

By early 1862 snow covered the ground, and the Louisiana Brigade worked quickly to finish the small log cabins that would serve as winter quarters. "We are constantly prepared for an advance of the enemy but scarcely expect it," wrote one of the men. Throughout February they huddled close to their fireplaces as heavy blizzards raged across Virginia. The army's strength declined severely at the same time, however, because thousands opted for furloughs, which General Johnston had granted in great numbers on the condition that these soldiers would reenlist for the duration of the war once their twelve-month enlistments ended in the spring. As throngs of men left for home, leaving the whole of Virginia open to invasion, Taylor thought only of the Confederate Congress's initial "folly of accepting regiments for the short period of twelve months," a legacy of the misguided belief that the war would last only a few weeks or months. Likewise, he blamed a rising contingent of anti-Davis congressmen, and in particular Vice-President Alexander Stephens, for publicly pressuring Johnston into approving the mass of furloughs. According to Taylor, Stephens had asserted that Confederate soldiers "were as capable of judging of the necessity of their presence with the colors as the commanders of the armies," and that "when no fighting was to be done, they had best be at home attending to their families and their interests." Taylor's unmitigated antipathy for the vice-president dated from the speech in which Stephens pronounced slavery the "cornerstone" of the Confederacy. Taylor also doubtless recalled Stephens's political maneuverings as a congressman against President Zachary Taylor during the sectional battle over the status of western territories won from Mexico. Now the diminutive Georgian seemed bent on undermining Davis and the army at any cost. He took

35. Urquhart, "General Richard Taylor," p. 41; New Orleans *Daily Crescent*, January 10, 1862 (quotation); Alison Moore, *Louisiana Tigers*, p. 56.

great pains years later to deny Taylor's accusations, calling them "fig-
ments of a disordered imagination." [36]

Fortunately for Johnston's diminished regiments, continually
muddy roads in the region precluded any danger of an enemy attack.
"An army could no more have marched across Virginia than across
Chesapeake Bay," wrote Taylor. In late February, however, Johnston
predicted Union general George B. McClellan's plan to make a grand
flanking movement with one hundred thousand men within a few
weeks. Johnston prepared to withdraw his forty-thousand-man army
about forty miles south toward Orange Court House, safely below the
Rappahannock and Rapidan rivers, where he could operate along interior lines of communication and supply in order to defend either
Fredericksburg or Richmond. Taylor's brigade was now under the divisional command of recently promoted Major General Richard Ewell, a Virginia cavalry officer who had replaced Edmund Kirby Smith.
Ewell's division departed Manassas on March 9, the Louisianans serving as a rear guard against McClellan's advance forces. Leaving behind blackened logs as artillery decoys, so-called Quaker guns that
successfully slowed and embarrassed McClellan, Taylor's men
trudged southward through a cold wind often laced with rain and
sleet. Three days of marching through deep mud and across swollen
streams left many of the Louisianans sick and straggling. A private
commented, "We had a wet, miserable time of it." [37]

Taylor had special plans for Wheat's Tigers during the retreat. Assigned the crucial role of skirmish unit for the brigade's rear guard,
the Tigers burned bridges and clashed with the enemy on a daily basis. Because Taylor routinely had to halt his column to wait for stragglers, he and the other mounted officers rode close to the rear, encouraging and sometimes carrying those who suffered most. He gave

36. Urquhart, "General Richard Taylor," pp. 41–42; Cummer, *Yankee in
Gray*, p. 92 (first quotation); Richard Taylor, *Destruction and Reconstruction*,
pp. 10, 25–27 (second quotation 25, third quotation 27); Stephens, *Comprehensive and Popular History*, pp. 991–93 (fourth quotation 992).

37. Richard Taylor, *Destruction and Reconstruction*, pp. 26 (first quotation),
34–35; Urquhart, "General Richard Taylor," pp. 43–44; Hamlin, *"Old Bald
Head,"* p. 71; Terry L. Jones, *Lee's Tigers*, pp. 64–65 (second quotation 65).

the men advice on bathing and binding their swollen and bleeding feet, and he soon noticed with some satisfaction that they "held it a disgrace to fall out of ranks." Before reaching the Rappahannock, however, some of the slowest fell captive to the rapidly pursuing Federals. Once across the river, Taylor's brigade joined the rest of Ewell's division. At this point Ewell's orders were simple: keep the enemy from taking the one bridge in the vicinity and thereby provide front-line protection to the remainder of Johnston's army, now situated farther to the south, across the Rapidan.[38]

Ewell's division would remain at the Rappahannock bridge for more than a month. As usual Taylor refused to allow his men to lapse into idleness. Having experienced the grave reality of rapid marching in brutal weather conditions, the Louisianans trained more vigorously than ever. "Before a month had passed the brigade learned how to march," Taylor recalled with satisfaction. The persistence of cold, wet weather and poor foraging made the task extremely onerous, but fortunately the brigade's commissary officer, Major Aaron Davis, had such a "fine nose for bullocks and bacon" that the entire division depended upon his skills. At one point, however, General Ewell became so alarmed at the impending shortage of food that he set out one day on a foraging expedition of his own. Having learned the art of survival while commanding a small body of United States dragoons on the frontier, he paraded back into camp that afternoon with a single bull. "With a triumphant air Ewell showed me his plunder," Taylor recounted. Admitting that the bull was certainly "a most respectable animal," Taylor pointed out, however, that it would hardly begin to feed the division's eight thousand men. "Ah!" exclaimed Ewell. "I was thinking of my fifty dragoons."[39]

The joke about the general and his bull only enlivened Ewell's genuine popularity with his troops. Taylor had known this curious little officer since the war in Mexico, where Ewell gained a superior repu-

38. Alison Moore, *He Died Furious*, pp. 119–21; William Calvin Oates, *War between the Union and the Confederacy*, p. 89; Richard Taylor, *Destruction and Reconstruction*, p. 35 (quotation); Terry L. Jones, *Lee's Tigers*, pp. 65–66; Urquhart, "General Richard Taylor," p. 44.

39. Richard Taylor, *Destruction and Reconstruction*, pp. 35 (first quotation), 38 (second and third quotations).

Richard S. Ewell, divisional commander of Taylor's brigade
(Jenkins Rare Book Company).

tation as a cavalry commander. Now they cultivated a close friendship based upon mutual honesty and an appreciation of each other's talents. The forty-five-year-old Ewell projected large, luminous eyes, a long hooked nose, and a bulbous bald head, features Taylor described as giving him "a striking resemblance to a woodcock." Displaying a nervous streak whereby he surpassed even Taylor for eccentric effect, Ewell "fancied that he had some mysterious internal malady" and often droned on about it with clinical relish. He passed many a fitful night "curled around a camp-stool in positions to dislocate an ordinary person's joints," Taylor remembered. Although possessed of "a fine tactical eye on the battlefield," Ewell always sought confirmation from other officers for the plans he formulated, and he often seemed uncomfortable giving orders, preferring instead to pitch into a fight like a brigadier or colonel. Only recently promoted to divisional command, on several calm nights in camp he broke the silence by asking aloud in his excited lisp, "General Taylor! What do you suppose President Davis made me a major-general for?" Attributing Ew-

ell's question to "singular modesty," Taylor never doubted his ability
to lead a division.[40]

One afternoon in mid-April, enemy artillery fire from across the
Rappahannock disrupted Taylor's camp near the southern end of
the bridge. Ordering his men to prepare for battle, Taylor rushed to
the bridge and found Ewell with a small body of Confederates already returning the enemy's fire. The Federal battery, only two guns,
quickly withdrew, but Taylor was suddenly shocked to see that Ewell
had ordered his soldiers to torch the bridge, which now burned rapidly. Noticing Taylor's pained expression, Ewell remarked, "You don't
like it." Taylor realized that Ewell would have had to destroy the
bridge at any rate, since Johnston had sent orders to move the division south within a few days. Taylor explained to Ewell, however, that
he had once read an account of one of Napoleon's colonels who used
a similar situation to supreme advantage by leaving the bridge intact
and ordering only part of his command to retreat. Remaining hidden
nearby with the majority of his men, he easily ambushed and overwhelmed the enemy force as it crossed the bridge. Hearing this, Ewell
yelped in exasperation, "Why did you keep the story until the bridge
was burnt?" Taylor admitted his negligence, but the incident did
serve to enhance a priceless candor between them. "He drew from
me whatever some reading and a good memory could supply," Taylor
asserted, "but his shrewd remarks changed many erroneous opinions
I had formed, and our 'talks' were of more value to me than to him."[41]

On April 18 Ewell's division broke camp and marched south, crossing the Rapidan the following day and camping near Gordonsville to
await further orders. Now prepared for the certainty of swift marching, each man carried only his gun and ammunition, an extra outfit
of clothing and shoes, and one blanket. Tents gave way to the necessity of using whatever shelter the countryside afforded. All Taylor
required for himself, including a small fly tent and a single change of
underwear, he carried on his horse. A Confederate lieutenant described Taylor as wearing a black hat and black overcoat, and like

40. Warner, *Generals in Gray*, pp. 84–85; Richard Taylor, *Destruction and
Reconstruction*, pp. 36–37 (quotations).

41. Richard Taylor, *Destruction and Reconstruction*, pp. 38–40 (first quotation 39, second and third quotations 40).

other officers, he tended to keep the overcoat on, even during warm weather, to protect against a sudden chill or rain. Tom Strother, his servant, rode alongside, equally Spartan in his accoutrements. "My people grumbled no little at being 'stripped,'" Taylor recalled, "but soon admitted that they were better for it," despite the shock of several more violent storms. "Winter returned with renewed energy, and we had for several days snow, sleet, rain, and all possible abominations in the way of weather."[42]

By now McClellan had launched his 100,000 men down the Atlantic coast to the Virginia Peninsula for an attack on Richmond from the east. Yet the imperious Federal commander's abiding fear of massive numbers of Confederate defenders allowed Joseph Johnston time to reinforce the skeleton units protecting the capital. In mid-April Johnston possessed about 60,000 men to resist the invaders. But Robert E. Lee, President Davis's new principal military advisor, worried even more about the danger posed by an additional 40,000 Federals under Major General Irvin McDowell moving down from Fredericksburg to help McClellan crush Johnston. McClellan, however, hesitated at every opportunity. With his doubts confirmed by inaccurate reports from scouts and spies estimating Confederate strength at upward of 150,000 soldiers, McClellan told President Abraham Lincoln that unless McDowell's force marched south toward Richmond, McClellan's Army of the Potomac would continue to sit idly, and expensively, on the Peninsula, incapable of matching the Army of Northern Virginia's sheer manpower.[43]

Nothing would have pleased Lincoln more than to send McDowell to McClellan's aid. This remained his firm intention throughout the Peninsula Campaign. But one overwhelming concern gnawed at the president: the defense of Washington, D.C. If he allowed McDowell to leave Fredericksburg to join McClellan, the capital would lay open to a Confederate flanking movement from the west. In mid-March Lincoln had tried to reinforce McDowell by ordering Major General Nathaniel P. Banks to send 25,000 men from the Shenandoah Valley

42. Urquhart, "General Richard Taylor," p. 45; McHenry Howard, *Recollections*, p. 119; Richard Taylor, *Destruction and Reconstruction*, pp. 40 (first quotation), 42 (second quotation).

43. McPherson, *Ordeal by Fire*, pp. 235–39.

to Manassas. But this maneuver fell victim to a snakebite from Major General Thomas Jonathan Jackson, who had standing orders to prevent any Federals in the Valley from reinforcing armies to the east. On March 23, south of Winchester, near Kernstown, Jackson's small command of 4,200 Virginians attacked Banks's detachment under Brigadier General James Shields. Although he suffered a complete rout, Jackson shocked Lincoln into believing the Confederates had a large force operating in the Valley, a force that might sweep eastward toward Washington at any time. In order to guarantee the capital's safety, Lincoln detained McDowell's 40,000 men at Fredericksburg throughout April, refusing to send them to McClellan's support yet still expecting McClellan to move against Richmond. Jackson had achieved a strategic victory by immobilizing McDowell. If Jackson could hold the Federals in check, the Confederates could build up Richmond's defenses, bring in more volunteers, and possibly even catch McClellan off guard and drive him from the Peninsula.[44]

Lee believed he had found in the Shenandoah Valley an Achilles' heel to the Union giant. Jackson agreed, having warned repeatedly that losing the Valley would be tantamount to losing the war in Virginia. Indeed, the Valley corridor might afford complete control over the Union army in the East. To make the next snakebite even more venomous, however, Jackson's fatigued and demoralized soldiers would need help.[45]

In late April, at Lee's behest, Jackson ordered Dick Ewell to march his division from Gordonsville westward toward Swift Run Gap, the nearest pass over the Blue Ridge. With the addition of Ewell's men, Jackson's Army of the Valley would number barely seventeen thousand. For General Taylor the ten days spent at Gordonsville had proved extremely unpleasant. Besides enduring freezing weather, the Louisiana Brigade had faced "reorganization" under the new Confederate Conscription Act, which gave the men in the ranks the opportunity to elect new company and regimental officers. Taylor assumed this procedure would involve the mere reelection of all current officers, and he made his expectation firmly known to the entire

44. Tanner, *Stonewall in the Valley*, pp. 110–61.
45. Ibid., pp. 40–42.

brigade. All units complied except for an artillery battery of Virginians Ewell had assigned to him. When Taylor learned they had elected a new captain, he flew into a fit of cursing, calling the whole battery "worthless," and promptly relieved them from further duty. He quickly replaced them with infantry soldiers from the brigade's ranks and installed the original captain as the battery's commander. Incensed at Taylor's extraordinary behavior, the ousted artillerymen filed a formal protest with the War Department in Richmond, and although they won their appeal, more than a month would pass before they returned to serve under their chosen captain.[46]

A Virginia cavalryman serving as a courier about this time confronted Taylor's temper at its petulant worst. Arriving at Ewell's headquarters one day to make a report, the courier mentioned to the officers gathered there, including Taylor, that he had "passed Taylor's Brigade." "How dare you speak in that manner!" snarled Taylor, insulted at the courier's failure to use his rank in describing his brigade. "I am *General* Taylor, sir!" Suddenly Ewell shot an acrid look at Taylor. "This is *my* courier, sir," he snapped. The rebuke left Taylor speechless. The astonished cavalryman later observed, "Taylor was undoubtedly a splendid officer, but he was proud as Lucifer, and therefore unpopular . . . and not one of the men would have acted as courier for Gen. Dick Taylor, if they could have avoided it."[47]

Taylor's demeanor could not have improved as Ewell's division made its way over the Blue Ridge through Swift Run Gap in a frightening mountain thunderstorm on April 30. "We have nothing but march, march, and halt and sleep in wet blankets and mud," wrote a private. Yet when the men began to descend into the Shenandoah Valley, bright sunlight brought a hint of spring at last, encouraging Taylor to believe they had finally "left the winter and its rigors behind." The Louisiana Brigade led the way as the division's several brass bands played in unison the popular melody "Listen to the Mockingbird." Long icicles still hanging thickly in the trees rapidly melted, water rushing down the mountains in refreshing jets, and

---

46. Urquhart, "General Richard Taylor," pp. 45–56; McPherson, *Ordeal by Fire*, p. 239; Terry L. Jones, *Lee's Tigers*, pp. 64–65 (quotation 64).

47. Myers, *Comanches*, p. 39 (quotations).

Taylor gazed out on an unforgettable scene. "The great Valley of Virginia was before us in all its beauty," he recorded. "Fields of wheat spread far and wide, interspersed with woodlands, bright in their robes of tender green." Prosperous farmhouses and grain mills dotted the rolling landscape, displaying the region's immense importance as an agricultural boon to the Confederacy. "But the glory of the Valley," Taylor reflected, "is Massanutten[,] . . . this lovely mountain . . . rising abruptly from the plain near Harrisonburg" and extending fifty miles northward to Strasburg, running parallel to and west of the Blue Ridge. Blessed with steep slopes and high, intermittent peaks, Massanutten provided dozens of superb positions for signal stations to scan the entire length of the Valley.[48]

When Ewell reached the Blue Ridge's base late that afternoon, he expected to find General Jackson waiting, but instead he stumbled into a deserted campsite. Having held only a smattering of correspondence with Jackson, for at least two weeks Ewell had operated in complete ignorance of Jackson's whereabouts and strategic intentions. Even worse, Jackson had given him no certain idea of the locations of enemy troops in the region. Finally Ewell had exploded into a foul rage, shaking all over and swearing that Jackson was surely insane. Ewell had in fact dreaded moving into the Valley from the first instant he learned Jackson would be his new commander. David Boyd, one of Taylor's officers, remembered clearly, "Ewell didn't like it, and Dick Taylor didn't like it," because "they were afraid Jackson would lead them into some awful scrape." Indeed, since gaining accolades as the Stonewall of Manassas, Jackson had borne the dishonor of criticism from Confederate authorities for his ill-fated winter fighting in the Virginia mountains, a controversy that brought his temporary resignation. His defeat at Kernstown, although having served to stall McClellan's designs on Richmond, still haunted Jackson's reputation. Most of all, however, he had done absolutely nothing to dispel his image as the humorless, perversely secretive, puritanical religious

48. Terry L. Jones, *Lee's Tigers*, pp. 66–67 (first quotation 67); Richard Taylor, *Destruction and Reconstruction*, pp. 45–47 (second and third quotations 45, fourth quotation 46); William Calvin Oates, *War between the Union and the Confederacy*, p. 93.

fanatic his cadet students at Virginia Military Institute had ridiculed as "Fool Tom."[49]

Together, Ewell and Taylor judged Jackson's disappearance from the area of Swift Run Gap so disturbing that they decided to take matters into their own hands. For several days they had discussed the best means of freeing themselves from Fool Tom, finally agreeing upon two possibilities: either gain a transfer of Ewell's division to Johnston's army near Richmond or convince Jefferson Davis to order another general officer to the Valley to outrank Jackson. Taylor now insisted that Ewell allow him to go immediately to Richmond to argue these methods. Ewell agreed, and that evening, April 30, Taylor departed, although his painful illness forced him to ride in an ambulance rather than on horseback. Still he made good time, reaching Richmond a few days later. There he spoke with President Davis and Secretary of War Benjamin, both of whom agreed that Jackson should have a ranking commander in the Valley. Much to Taylor's satisfaction, they suggested Major General James Longstreet for the role. His mission completed, Taylor rambled triumphantly back across the Blue Ridge. David Boyd met him at Ewell's campsite, now abandoned, and explained that Ewell had moved the division further into the Valley in obedience to Jackson's orders. "Well . . . there is one consolation," Taylor remarked jovially. "We won't be under this damned old crazy fool long. General Longstreet is coming up here to take command."[50]

Taylor found Ewell camped only a short distance away, at Conrad's Store, near the banks of the Shenandoah River's south fork. To Taylor's horror, however, Ewell informed him that dispatches from General Lee received during the past several days had mentioned nothing about the prospect of General Longstreet coming to the Valley. Placing the highest trust in Jackson's ability, Lee apparently had persuaded Davis and Benjamin to drop the plan to supersede Jackson with Longstreet. Jackson had positioned Ewell at Conrad's Store in

49. Tanner, *Stonewall in the Valley*, pp. 143–45, 180; Boyd, *Reminiscences of the War*, pp. 7–8 (quotation); Richard Taylor, *Destruction and Reconstruction*, p. 51.

50. Boyd, *Reminiscences of the War*, pp. 8–10 (quotation 9–10).

order to prevent Banks's twenty-two thousand men at Harrisonburg from making a possible advance south to Staunton, where the Virginia Central Railroad provided a vital east-west supply line from the Valley to Richmond. More importantly, Jackson instructed Ewell to stop any movement by Banks eastward that might reinforce the Federal drive against Richmond.[51]

Ewell and his division then sat in place as Jackson launched west in early May into the Allegheny Mountains, more than fifty miles distant. Jackson's intention was to keep Major General John C. Frémont from combining forces with Banks. Frémont seemed to be pushing south through the Alleghenies from western Virginia to join Banks at Staunton in the Valley. Lee emphatically urged Jackson to strike immediately, no matter the enemy. On May 8 Jackson's six thousand troops attacked Frémont's three-thousand-man advance guard at McDowell, high in the Alleghenies, successfully discouraging the timid Frémont from any further advance. With his troops worn down, hungry, and apparently verging on mass mutiny after suffering heavy casualties at McDowell, Jackson returned to the Valley to rejoin Ewell. Throughout this brief campaign Ewell alone had received messages from Jackson regarding his movements, an honor Ewell had great trouble appreciating. In risking his precious secrecy, however, Jackson repeated to Ewell the necessity of remaining in the Valley and monitoring the enemy's movements there. Now Ewell's added strength would become vital to Jackson as he finally prepared to confront Banks.[52]

During Jackson's absence Ewell writhed and ranted, choking on the leash of a commander he considered hopelessly mad. In speaking with an officer about Jackson, Ewell bellowed, "I tell you, he is as crazy as a March hare." After several such outbursts Ewell's men began to doubt their own leader's sanity as well. Colonel Isaac Seymour, commander of the Sixth Louisiana, admitted in a private letter, "We are all exceedingly dissatisfied with Gen. Ewell, who is very eccentric and seems half the time not to know what he is doing." But Ewell's ire only

51. Hattaway and Jones, *How the North Won*, pp. 176–78; Tanner, *Stonewall in the Valley*, p. 185.

52. Lang, Hennessee, and Bush, "Jackson's Valley Campaign," pp. 38–45; Tanner, *Stonewall in the Valley*, pp. 158–86.

intensified when he received alarming messages from Lee regarding enemy movements. On May 6 Banks had evacuated Harrisonburg and gone north to Strasburg, sending Shields's division in advance, apparently in preparation for another movement eastward to reinforce McDowell at Fredericksburg. For the time being Lincoln believed Jackson and Ewell posed no immediate threat to Washington, and Lee knew that as soon as Shields joined McDowell, the long-delayed Union campaign against Richmond would begin. Lee therefore urged Ewell to take any action necessary to prevent Shields from moving toward Fredericksburg.[53]

As late as May 12, however, Jackson continued to hold a tight rein on Ewell. Champing at the bit to pursue Shields, Ewell swore to a fellow officer, "This man Jackson is certainly a crazy fool, an idiot." To his niece he wrote a letter confessing that he had spent the unhappiest two weeks of his life waiting for "that enthusiastic fanatic" Jackson. Finally, with an inflamed stomach disorder keeping him from getting any rest, he warned Jackson with a cold, blunt message, "On your course may determine the fate of Richmond." By May 17 Shields had already left the Valley, crossing the Blue Ridge with seven thousand men and marching through Front Royal on his way to Fredericksburg. Banks, with the bulk of his force still in the Valley at Strasburg, had sent about one thousand men to garrison Front Royal, thus giving Shields an extra rear guard. That same day, May 17, Ewell received a confusing message from Jackson saying that if Shields had indeed left the Valley, Ewell should only follow him rather than pursue him. Jackson still had Banks in his sights as the most important target, but Ewell could make no sense at all of Jackson's vague and contradictory orders. He therefore determined to speak with the mysterious Stonewall himself about the whole mess.[54]

Early on May 18 Ewell rode into Jackson's camp about twelve miles southwest of Harrisonburg. Together the two generals scanned a map of the Valley, pinpointing enemy positions. Gradually their wearied minds surged with the electrifying realization that Frémont and

53. Tanner, *Stonewall in the Valley*, pp. 160–61, 186–88 (first quotation 188); Terry L. Jones, *Lee's Tigers*, pp. 63–64 (second quotation 63).

54. Tanner, *Stonewall in the Valley*, pp. 187–91 (first quotation 187, second quotation 189, third quotation 190).

Shields had separated themselves from Banks to such an extent that Banks now sat with only ten to fifteen thousand men at Strasburg, effectively vulnerable to a deep Confederate thrust northward down the Valley. Shortly, Jackson received a letter from Lee arguing the essential need for this very action. Lee implored Jackson to drive Banks back toward the Potomac and thus appear to be planning to use the Maryland corridor to Washington. If Jackson and Ewell had any opportunity whatsoever of compelling Lincoln to send Shields back to the Valley, they would have to attack Banks immediately. By now, however, Shields was only thirty miles from Fredericksburg, and Richmond seemed doomed to an overwhelming Federal siege.[55]

Ewell's appetite for fighting had finally received some satisfaction. Returning to Conrad's Store, he prepared his division for hard marching and waited eagerly for instructions from Jackson, who remained near Harrisonburg. The next day, May 19, Jackson ordered Ewell to march north to Luray, but first to detach Taylor's brigade and send it in the opposite direction, around the southern base of Massanutten and then north to New Market, where Taylor would join Jackson. Taylor could hardly fathom such orders. When he asked Ewell what good the circuitous movement could accomplish, Ewell confessed that he had not the faintest notion, declaring, "If Gen. Jackson were shot down I wouldn't know a thing of his plans!" "What!" Taylor retorted. "You, second in command, and don't know!" Swelling up in frustration, Taylor insisted, "If I were second in command I would know!" Ewell only smiled and cocked his head, responding, "You would, would you?" Taylor stood silent. "No," Ewell continued, "you wouldn't know any more than I do now." Still smiling a painful smile, Ewell summed up the fundamental problem vexing both of them: "You don't yet know the man."[56]

By calling for Taylor's brigade to join him, Jackson had already set in motion his grand strategy for the Valley Campaign. Without realizing it, Taylor would perform a crucial diversion, prompting any Federal scouts in the vicinity to believe that Jackson meant to concen-

55. Lang, Hennessee, and Bush, "Jackson's Valley Campaign," pp. 45–46; Tanner, *Stonewall in the Valley*, pp. 192–98.

56. Tanner, *Stonewall in the Valley*, p. 198; Boyd, *Reminiscences of the War*, p. 12 (quotations).

trate his forces west of Massanutten at New Market and then strike
northward down the smooth Shenandoah Valley Pike toward Banks
at Strasburg. Despite his intense displeasure at leaving Ewell, Taylor
meant to follow Jackson's orders in the grandest fashion possible. His
Louisianans were on the road at dawn on the twentieth, a delightful
spring day, and by late afternoon they had marched more than
twenty miles, maintaining perfect formation the entire distance. Approaching New Market, Taylor received orders from one of Jackson's
couriers to encamp beyond the Stonewall Brigade's camp, just south
of town. As Taylor's men marched along in tight, rigid rows, Jackson's
tired, ragged veterans assembled and made a half decent attempt at
"present arms" on both sides of the road, standing agog at the Louisianans' European-style spit and polish élan. "It was the most pictur-
esque and inspiring martial sight that came under my eyes during
four years of service," wrote one of Jackson's men. Never had the Virginians seen such uniforms—fresh gray with spotless white gaiters
and leggings, the officers "brilliant with gold lace, their rakish slouch
hats adorned with tassels and plumes." The Louisiana pelican
adorned the colorful unit flags, which seemed peculiarly exotic compared to other Confederate banners. As the regimental bands paced
the proud brigade in faultless marching measure, a sea of three thousand polished bayonets gleamed in the rich horizontal light of the
setting sun. Taylor remembered this performance with deep pride,
affirming that "no man with a spark of sacred fire in his heart but
would have striven hard to prove worthy of such a command."[57]

Along with Major Rob Wheat's Tigers, who hailed from the New
Orleans riverdocks and other port towns upriver, the brigade presented a spicy mixture of volunteers from all over Louisiana. Taylor's
old regiment, the Ninth, commanded by Colonel Leroy Stafford, consisted of upstate farm boys, small-town professionals, and a smattering of planters and their sons. Isaac Seymour's Sixth Regiment, laborers and mechanics recruited mainly in New Orleans, showed a
preponderance of Irish natives, "stout, hardy fellows," said Taylor,

57. Chambers, *Stonewall Jackson*, 1:517; Worsham, *One of Jackson's Foot Cavalry*, p. 81; James Cooper Nisbet, *Four Years on the Firing Line*, p. 41 (first and
second quotations); Richard Taylor, *Destruction and Reconstruction*, pp. 50–51
(third quotation 51).

"turbulent in camp and requiring a strong hand, but responding to kindness and justice, and ready to follow their officers to the death." Rounding out the Sixth were 140 Louisiana natives, 130 from other southern states, and more than 100 German-born immigrants. Harry Hays's Seventh Taylor described forcefully as "a crack regiment." Hailing from New Orleans and surrounding parishes on the lower Mississippi, these men had worked as farmers, merchandising clerks, and common laborers, about one-third of them claiming Irish roots, another third being Louisiana-born, and the rest coming from other southern states. Mixed in were a few Germans and Englishmen. Except for the bloodthirsty Tigers, the soldiers of the Seventh offered the brigade's best fighting unit, thanks largely to the fiery Hays. Henry B. Kelly's Eighth comprised the most colorful group of all, including several companies of French-speaking Acadians, or Cajuns, from the forests and lush farmlands of southern Louisiana's beautiful Teche region. Possessing "all the light gayety of the Gaul," Taylor recalled, "few spoke English, fewer still had ever before moved ten miles from their natal *cabanas*; and the war to them was 'a liberal education.'" Although the majority of the regiment consisted of Louisiana- and southern-born Anglo-Americans, as well as 142 Germans, the Acadians gave the Eighth its conspicuously romantic and colorful flavor.[58]

While his men settled into their new surroundings, Taylor walked along the pike a short distance to Jackson's camp, seeking to introduce himself to the strange man in whose hands Robert E. Lee had placed so much promise. Finding a staff officer, Taylor asked Jackson's whereabouts. The officer pointed to a rigid figure sitting atop a fence near the road. He was alone, looking out over a broad, empty field in the twilight. Taylor walked up, saluted, and stated his name and rank. Jackson registered no response except to focus slowly upward, raising his chin in order to peer from under the black visor of his old kepi. Immediately Taylor noticed a wrinkled pair of cavalry

58. Richard Taylor, *Destruction and Reconstruction*, pp. 48–49 (first and third quotations 49, second quotation 48); Terry L. Jones, *Lee's Tigers*, pp. 238–44, 249–50. The Eighth Louisiana even included a free black, Charles F. Lutz, who doubtless presented himself as white. Bergeron, "Free Men of Color in Gray," pp. 248–49.

Stonewall Jackson
(*Johnson and Buell,* Battles and Leaders of the Civil War).

boots "covering feet of gigantic size," and then "a heavy, dark beard, and weary eyes." Jackson wore an old gray army coat that had started fading to brown. His kepi was already a dark mustard yellow from continual exposure to the sun.[59]

Taylor's new commander spoke in "a low, gentle voice," asking the brigade's route and distance marched that day. "Keazletown road, six and twenty miles," Taylor replied proudly. "You seem to have no stragglers," said Jackson. "Never allow stragglers," Taylor asserted, even more proudly. "You must teach my people; they straggle badly," said Jackson sullenly. Completely pleased at this, Taylor responded with an aristocratic bow. Suddenly a band began to play a lively tune.

59. Richard Taylor, *Destruction and Reconstruction,* pp. 51–52 (quotations 52); Cooke, *Stonewall Jackson,* pp. 196–97.

Jackson and Taylor looked toward the Louisiana camp, where the Acadians had begun a boisterous bit of waltzing with each other in pairs, a pastime Taylor had become accustomed to seeing them practice "with as much zest as if their arms encircled the supple waists of the Celestines and Melazies of their native Teche." Stonewall stared intently at them, lifted a half-eaten lemon to his mouth, and sucked on it, a habit that supposedly eased a chronic case of intestinal dyspepsia. Then he grumbled, "Thoughtless fellows for such serious work." Taylor made no apology for his Acadians but merely said he hoped "the work would not be less well done because of the gayety." Jackson continued squeezing the lemon, apparently unimpressed. After a long, uneasy silence Taylor dismissed himself and departed.[60]

Jackson's cryptic mixture of compliment and criticism left Taylor coolly amused. He did not have to like Tom Fool Jackson in order to serve under his command. In background, personality, and values, the two men had nothing in common. But late that evening Jackson surprised Taylor by visiting his campfire. He said the army would move at sunrise; the direction he did not mention. He asked Taylor a few specific questions about the methods he used in compelling his men to march long distances, and then he sat for several hours without speaking. Taylor made no attempt to converse with him. "If silence be golden, he was a 'bonanza,'" reflected Taylor, hardly expecting Jackson to compromise his sacred thoughts of strategy. One of Jackson's staff officers, Lieutenant Henry Kyd Douglas, later admitted that he doubted whether Jackson "could have discussed his plans satisfactorily if he had desired. . . . 'Mystery, mystery is the secret of success,'" Jackson had declared tersely. Regardless, neither Taylor's penchant for witty campfire stories nor even casual military discussion could have distracted the puritan Stonewall from his ritual of prolonged inner concentration, the wellspring of his indomitable determination as a professional soldier. "Praying and fighting appeared to be his idea of the 'whole duty of man,'" Taylor observed almost scornfully. If, as Ewell had declared, Taylor "did not yet know the man," now he wondered whether anyone ever could.[61]

60. Richard Taylor, *Destruction and Reconstruction*, p. 52 (quotations).
61. Ibid., p. 52 (first and third quotations); Henry Kyd Douglas, "Stonewall Jackson and His Men," pp. 647–48 (second quotation).

A few hours later, as Taylor assembled his brigade on the pike just before dawn, Jackson rode up and told him to march north. This put Taylor's men in the forefront, setting the pace, but it also put Jackson riding alongside him. The two exchanged few words. Now, in the full light of day, Taylor took careful note of Jackson's martial bearing on horseback. He rode a "sorry chesnut," his stirrups holding "huge feet with outturned toes." His kepi, with its "low visor," contributed to a certain "wooden look." More amused than astonished, Taylor concluded dryly, "our new commander was not prepossessing." Shortly they reached New Market, and Jackson suddenly turned the swiftly moving column east, up toward Massanutten and the mountain pass leading to Luray, where Ewell waited. This, Taylor realized, would simply bring his brigade full circle, close to the location whence he had started two days earlier. "I began to think Jackson was an unconscious poet, . . . an ardent lover of nature" who wanted to display to the Louisianans "the beauties of his Valley," Taylor mused in bewilderment.[62]

In the evening, near Luray, Jackson and Taylor united with Ewell, giving the Army of the Valley its full strength of seventeen thousand men and fifty artillery pieces. What Jackson intended to do puzzled everyone, especially in light of Lee's pleas for action to divert the ominous threat to Richmond. Ewell, who knew only that Banks was the target, had recently confessed to Taylor that he "never saw one of Jackson's couriers approach without expecting an order to assault the north pole." But Jackson continued to keep his own counsel, and the next morning, May 22, he gave Taylor a single instruction: march north. With the Louisiana Brigade again in the vanguard and Jackson again at Taylor's side, the army trudged northward down the Luray Valley over a road terribly inferior to the smoothly paved Shenandoah Valley Pike to the west. Unlike the gently rolling terrain covered by the pike, here the ground undulated sharply in an endless series of inclines and dips. Yet Taylor had made certain that his men were in "superb condition" for the ordeal. Jackson had obviously become so impressed by the Louisianans that he had taken them from Ewell's immediate authority to use them as an advance

62. Richard Taylor, *Destruction and Reconstruction*, pp. 52–53 (quotations 53).

guard. He meant for them to set a crippling pace, and that they did.[63]

The Stonewall Brigade and the rest of Jackson's Virginians struggled in agony to keep up, and by late afternoon the lengthening column had progressed only fifteen miles. Having had only four days of rest after 230 miles of marching with poor food through wretched weather, the Virginians verged on complete exhaustion. Major Robert L. Dabney, a prominent Presbyterian preacher serving as Jackson's chief of staff, began to wonder if his commander cared any more about his men than he did about the enemy. "The latter he kills, the former he works nearly to death," Dabney wrote to his wife. Taylor had heard Jackson assert that "it was better to lose one man in marching than five in fighting," hence his determination to surprise the enemy with rapid movement. By using the methods Taylor had taught him regarding marching discipline, however, Jackson obtained the utmost from his army. Once an hour he halted the column for ten minutes, allowing the men a brief enough rest to keep their muscles from stiffening. Officers prodded and assisted stragglers, making certain that blistered feet received proper attention. Beyond this, invaluable support came from local citizens, who seemed to adore Jackson and his men as their protectors. "The devotion of all to the Southern cause was wonderful," Taylor recalled. "To the last, women would go [great] distances to carry the modicum of food between themselves and starvation to a suffering Confederate."[64]

Now more than ever Jackson realized that he might have to sacrifice some men, even his own Virginians, for the sake of speed. McClellan had inched to within five miles of Richmond, where President Davis, Robert E. Lee, and Joseph Johnston waited impatiently for Jackson to strike a blow in the Valley. Johnston had just informed Ewell, "The whole question is whether or not General Jackson and yourself are too late to attack Banks." Shields had already reached Fredericksburg. There McDowell planned to honor Lincoln and sev-

63. Tanner, *Stonewall in the Valley*, pp. 204–5; Richard Taylor, *Destruction and Reconstruction*, pp. 37 (first quotation), 48 (second quotation), 53.

64. Tanner, *Stonewall in the Valley*, pp. 203–5; Dabney, *Life of Jackson*, p. 266 (first quotation); Richard Taylor, *Destruction and Reconstruction*, pp. 91 (second quotation), 47 (third quotation).

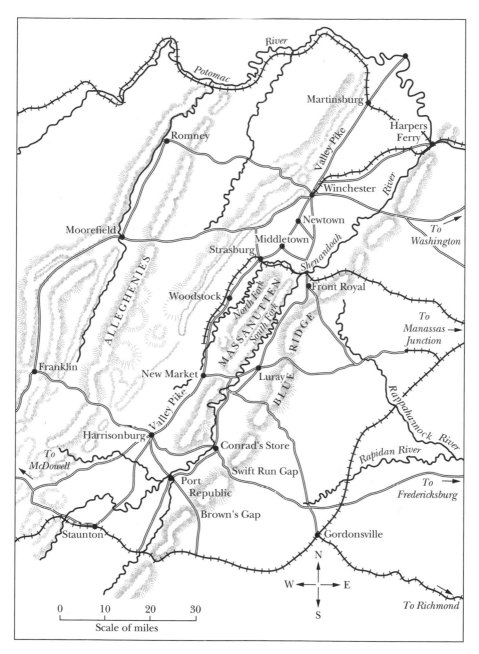

Map 1. Shenandoah Valley Region, 1862

eral of his cabinet members with a grand review of his army before marching in concert with McClellan and achieving a climactic siege and capture of Richmond. The spring of 1862 had already dealt the Confederacy a series of demoralizing blows. Most of Tennessee had fallen to a Union invasion, and at Shiloh a large southern army had suffered ten thousand casualties, among them General Albert Sidney Johnston, whom Taylor considered "the foremost man of all the South." For the Louisiana troops in Virginia, however, the fall of New Orleans ranked as the most devastating catastrophe of all. Many believed that the city's commander, Major General Mansfield Lovell, had engaged in cowardly, even traitorous conduct. One Louisianan wrote, "Curses, not loud but deep, are freely bestowed on General Lovell."[65]

With the weight of the South's plummeting fortunes squarely upon his shoulders, Jackson halted his little army the night of May 22 about ten miles south of Front Royal, a town garrisoned by only a thousand Federals. Twelve miles to the west, at Strasburg, Banks had about eight thousand men. A former Speaker of the United States House and Massachusetts governor without any military training or experience, the jaunty Major General Banks ranked highest among the "political generals" Lincoln had reluctantly appointed early in the war. Still laboring under the impression that Jackson meant to move north down the Valley pike from Harrisonburg to Strasburg, Banks had no inkling that his enemy had cut east across Massanutten with Taylor in order to rejoin Ewell for a swift flanking movement via Front Royal. Several of Banks's own officers had pointed to Front Royal as a vulnerable key position, but Banks only mentioned to Washington that the Front Royal-Strasburg line was "hopelessly indefensible" with so few troops at his disposal. Although he had received vague scouting reports of Confederate activity between Luray and Front Royal on May 21, Banks did not bother to inform Colonel John R. Kenly, the commander at Front Royal, of this danger. Instead, Banks had become completely distracted by a cavalry detachment Jackson had deftly sent from Harrisonburg toward Strasburg several days earlier

65. Tanner, *Stonewall in the Valley*, pp. 193, 201 (first quotation), 206–8; Richard Taylor, *Destruction and Reconstruction*, p. 285 (second quotation); Terry L. Jones, *Lee's Tigers*, p. 28 (third quotation).

to serve as a decoy to his movement against Front Royal. Thus far Jackson's use of deception and speed had worked splendidly. He could not have asked for a foe more ignorant and exposed than Kenly at Front Royal.[66]

Early in the afternoon of May 23, as the head of Jackson's column came within a short distance of Front Royal, a mounted officer rode up from the rear and asked Jackson to come back with him. While Jackson was absent, Taylor and several other officers noticed a young woman running out of the woods toward them. It was Belle Boyd, the renowned spy. In a breathless voice she told them that the enemy camp lay on the west side of the Shenandoah River, just beyond the town, and that the small Federal garrison lay completely open to attack. Although one prominent resident of the Valley later contended that Miss Boyd "loved notoriety and attention, and was as far below . . . the pure and noble womanhood of the South as was a circus rider," Taylor noted that she spoke "with the precision of a staff officer making a report, and it was true to the letter." Her information was "news to me," Taylor recalled, and now he realized that Jackson had known everything all along and that he had formed his plans accordingly. "There also dawned on me quite another view of our leader than the one from which I had been regarding him for two days past," he admitted. Taylor had begun to appreciate Jackson's all-consuming silence and, with it, his firm grasp of military strategy.[67]

With Jackson still at the rear of the column, Taylor decided to act upon Belle Boyd's enticing report. Intending to sweep down and surprise the Federal garrison singlehandedly, Taylor ordered his men forward at a double-quick pace. "I felt immensely 'cocky' about my brigade and believed that it would prove equal to any demand," he recalled. Before the overeager Louisianans had proceeded very far, however, Jackson galloped up from the rear and put a stop to Taylor's

66. Lang, Hennessee, and Bush, "Jackson's Valley Campaign," p. 46; Tanner, *Stonewall in the Valley*, pp. 205–6; Harrington, *Fighting Politician*, pp. 69–70 (quotation 70).

67. Richard Taylor, *Destruction and Reconstruction*, pp. 53–54 (second, third, and fourth quotations 54); Ashby, *Valley Campaigns*, p. 141 (first quotation); Henry Kyd Douglas, *I Rode with Stonewall*, pp. 51–52. See also Ruth Scarborough, *Belle Boyd*, pp. 49–52.

rashness. He calmly ordered Taylor to spread his lead regiment out on either side of the road as skirmishers and to follow slowly with the rest of his brigade. Jackson then called up Colonel Bradley T. Johnson's First Maryland Regiment to the head of the column and attached it to Taylor's brigade. Because Front Royal's garrison consisted entirely of Unionist Marylanders, Jackson wanted to take complete advantage of the hatred Johnson's men had for Yankees from their home state. Therefore he ordered Johnson to take the lead. As the Marylanders passed to the front Taylor halted his brigade and brought it to attention. "Present arms!" he shouted, and the Louisianans added spontaneous cries of "Give 'em hell, Maryland!"[68]

Emerging from the woods, Taylor's command topped a rise and gazed down about a mile toward Front Royal. He remembered this as a "surpassingly beautiful" sight, the Allegheny Mountains in the far distant background and Massanutten's northernmost peak sloping downward about ten miles to the west. The confluence of the Shenandoah River's north and south forks appeared about a mile northwest of the town. Between the town and the south fork lay the Federal camp. Running parallel to each other, a wagon bridge and a railroad bridge crossed the north fork and led up to a ridge, Richardson's Hill, where an enemy battery overlooked the river and town. Jackson quickly ordered Johnson's Marylanders and Wheat's Tigers, with the Sixth Louisiana following in support, to move around to the right and prepare to rush the town from the east. He then sent Taylor with his remaining three regiments to the left with orders to charge from the southwest. Jackson's weary Virginians would trail behind these movements as soon as they arrived from the rear.[69]

The men under Taylor's immediate command, the Seventh, Eighth, and Ninth regiments, formed several long parallel lines facing toward the town and extending down toward the river to the left. From here Taylor could see enemy soldiers farther downriver on the opposite bank, and he decided to ride to the water's edge to get a better look through his field glasses. While he scanned the Federal

68. Richard Taylor, *Destruction and Reconstruction*, p. 54 (first quotation); Hale, *Four Valiant Years*, p. 147 (second quotation).

69. Richard Taylor, *Destruction and Reconstruction*, p. 55 (quotation); Dufour, *Gentle Tiger*, p. 175.

positions, his horse gradually walked down to the water and then stepped into it to take a drink. Suddenly a series of long-range rifle volleys from unseen Yankee soldiers on the opposite bank sent up showers of water around and over him. This was Taylor's first exposure to enemy fire, and although his attitude was rather foolhardy in itself, with his own men looking on from a distance he steeled himself into false passivity. Determined that he "must 'strut' one's little part to the best advantage," he sat motionless while his thirsty horse continued to drink, oblivious to the gunfire. "A provident camel, on the eve of a desert journey, would not have laid in a greater supply of water than did my thoughtless beast," he recounted. At last his horse looked up, apparently satisfied, then turned and lumbered back up the bank. "This little incident was not without value," he concluded, "for my men welcomed me with a cheer."[70]

These dramatics apparently failed to impress the inscrutable Jackson. Glancing back, Taylor noticed only that his commander "seemed lost in thought." By now the Federal battery on Richardson's Hill had started firing toward Taylor's men. The battle had begun. Taylor led his regiments down through a series of fields and thickets toward the town, where Wheat and Johnson already had the few enemy troops there flying in a panic, forcing them across the river. Jackson watched in disgust, however, as the Tigers stopped to loot the enemy camps, thus allowing scores of Federals to escape. Yet Jackson's attention quickly turned to the immediate need for artillery to punish the foe and silence the enemy battery that continued to fire on the advancing Confederates. Discovering that none of his long-range guns had come up from the rear, Jackson exploded in indignation. "Oh, what an opportunity for artillery! Oh, that my guns were here!" he shouted. "Order up every rifled gun, and every brigade in the army," he commanded one of his staff officers.[71]

Halting his men in town, Taylor rode back to Jackson and sug-

70. U.S. War Department, *The War of the Rebellion: A Compilation of the Official Records of the Union and Confederate Armies*, series 1, 12(1):800. Cited hereafter as *O.R.* (All citations refer to series 1, unless otherwise stated.) Richard Taylor, *Destruction and Reconstruction*, pp. 55–56 (quotations).

71. Richard Taylor, *Destruction and Reconstruction*, p. 56 (first quotation); Tanner, *Stonewall in the Valley*, pp. 212–13; James Cooper Nisbet, *Four Years*

gested that, rather than attempting to cross the river on the wagon bridge, where the Federal battery bore down directly, he could take his brigade downriver and cross the railroad bridge. To this Jackson simply "nodded approval." Taylor sent orders to Henry Kelly's Eighth Louisiana to lead the charge. Kelly sent his regiment forward, and when he reached the railroad bridge he dismounted to lead the way. Stepping carefully on the freely suspended railroad cross ties while enduring volley after volley of rifle fire, Kelly's men could offer no resistance. Several lost their balance and fell through the open cross ties into the river and disappeared beneath the dark, swirling current, now swollen high by several weeks of heavy rainfall.[72]

The Eighth Louisiana's bravery served as a signal to the rest of the southerners to charge across the wagon bridge. This breakthrough forced the Federals back across a third bridge spanning the river's north fork. But as they retreated, they set fire to the structure. Seeing this, Jackson shuddered in disbelief. Up to now he had dearly wanted to capture the entire enemy garrison. Without the bridge he would have to find another crossing farther upstream, a delay he could ill afford. He had already ordered a cavalry detachment from the west to cut the telegraph lines between Front Royal and Strasburg. But if even one Federal escaped from Front Royal, word of the Confederate strike would surely reach Strasburg, thus giving Banks time to evacuate the Valley. A single flaming bridge might destroy all of Jackson's plans with it.[73]

At this point Taylor grasped only one possible action: storm across the bridge before the fire completely enveloped it. Again he looked to Jackson for approval, and again Stonewall gave a silent nod. Taylor ordered his men across, sending Wheat's Tigers in the lead. They seized the challenge with gleeful fury. "I shall never forget the style in which Wheat's battalion passed us," recalled one of Ewell's men. The massive Wheat "was riding full gallop, yelling at the top of his voice . . . the men following after—all running—all yelling—all looking like fight." Kelly's gallant regiment came next, its lead company

on the Firing Line, p. 41; Dabney, Life of Jackson, pp. 365–66 (second quotation).

72. Richard Taylor, Destruction and Reconstruction, p. 56 (quotation).

73. O.R., 12(1):702; Tanner, Stonewall in the Valley, pp. 213–14.

assigned to swim into the swift current and climb up the bridge's support beams in order to form a kind of vertical bucket brigade by filling their hats and canteens with water to fight the fire. Two of Kelly's men drowned in the river, but the rest of the company continued throwing water on the flames, giving their comrades precious time in crossing the bridge. "Come on boys," yelled Kelly, "we will have them!"[74]

Pressing through the thick, black billows of smoke, which served somewhat to obscure them from enemy fire, Taylor's men lurched backward when a long section of bridge flooring collapsed beneath them. Now forced to move single file to the right, they slowed their pace only slightly. Fire scorched their uniforms and many suffered severe burns on their hands as they ripped flaming brands from the bridge and threw them into the water. Taylor himself, once safely across, noticed Jackson riding at his side. "How he got there was a mystery, as the bridge was thronged with my men going at full speed," he marveled, "but smoke and fire had decidedly freshened up his costume." Even more miraculously, Kelly's men soon had the flames under control, saving the bridge from complete destruction.[75]

With the Federals now retreating at full speed, Jackson realized he must take action before the rest of his army crossed the bridge. Immediately he called upon Colonel Thomas Flournoy's Sixth Virginia Cavalry to take up pursuit. Personally leading the 250 horsemen, Jackson caught up with the enemy after riding only a few miles. Near the town of Cedarville Flournoy's men executed a series of charges into the teeth of hundreds of muskets, finally breaking through, slashing, shooting, and surrounding virtually all of the exhausted and confused Yankees. Even Jackson admitted that he had never seen such a fearless display by mounted troops. As the Virginians rounded up their prisoners and headed back toward Front Royal in the late afternoon, Jackson reflected on his victory. He had taken his first step

74. Richard Taylor, *Destruction and Reconstruction*, p. 56; Terry L. Jones, *Lee's Tigers*, pp. 73–74 (first quotation 74); William Calvin Oates, *War between the Union and the Confederacy*, p. 97; Opelousas *Courier*, September 6, 1862 (second quotation).

75. Tanner, *Stonewall in the Valley*, pp. 213–14; Richard Taylor, *Destruction and Reconstruction*, pp. 56–57 (quotation 57); O.R., 12(1):702.

in crushing Banks, who apparently still had a faulty notion of Jackson's location. He had captured Front Royal's garrison, its battery of rifled artillery, and large quantities of guns, ammunition, and supplies. A civilian witness of the Confederate sweep through Front Royal recalled that it all happened so quickly that "no one was hurt, and the disorder was more like a police riot than a fight between soldiers." A private in the Ninth Louisiana confessed, "Our regiment did not get a shot, as the Yankees ran immediately after they were attacked." Confederate casualties for the day, even after Flournoy's daring attack near Cedarville, amounted to no more than one hundred men.[76]

Among the dead, however, Taylor discovered the body of Major Aaron Davis, his brigade's commissary officer. Separated from Taylor after crossing the burning bridge, Davis had joined the cavalry attack. "Led on by fatal impetuosity, Major Davis rode with a group of cavalrymen . . . and met his death charging at its head," Taylor reported. Taylor had depended heavily upon Davis's talents to forage for rations, a responsibility vital to the brigade's well-being. Davis's loss stunned soldiers throughout the army. "I never heard of any other quartermaster [or] commissary . . . being killed," wrote one officer. Taylor later recalled, "He was much beloved by the command, and many gathered quietly around the grave. As there was no chaplain at hand, I repeated such portions of the service for the dead as a long neglect of pious things enabled me to recall." Soon afterward Taylor submitted a request for a brigade chaplain, and the rigid Protestant Jackson showed remarkable sensitivity by appointing a priest, since most of the Louisianans were Catholic.[77]

76. Tanner, *Stonewall in the Valley*, pp. 214–15; *O.R.*, 12(1):702; Ashby, *Valley Campaigns*, p. 115 (first quotation); R. A. Pierson to W. H. Pierson, June 11, 1862 (second quotation), Pierson Family Papers.

77. *O.R.*, 12(1):800 (first quotation); James Cooper Nisbet, *Four Years on the Firing Line*, p. 42 (second quotation); Richard Taylor, *Destruction and Reconstruction*, pp. 57–58 (third quotation); Henry Kyd Douglas, "Stonewall Jackson and His Men," p. 650. Following Davis's death, David French Boyd, commissary officer of the Ninth Louisiana, assumed duties as the Louisiana Brigade's commissary officer with the rank of major. Germaine M. Reed, *David French Boyd*, pp. 37–38.

Late that night Jackson appeared at Taylor's campfire, made himself comfortable, and mentioned that the Louisiana Brigade would move again with him the next morning. He then fell into his usual silence, making no reference to the day's fighting. Taylor could not help but believe, however, that Jackson was pleased. "I fancied that he looked at me kindly, and interpreted it into an approval of the conduct of the brigade." Lingering excitement, growing anticipation, and deep sorrow over Major Davis's death kept Taylor from sleeping, so he could only watch Jackson, who sat utterly still, gazing at the fire. "I took up the idea that he was inwardly praying, and he remained throughout the night," Taylor remembered. But Jackson did much more than pray. His ultimate goal, to trap and destroy Banks, hinged upon his enemy's next move. In his official report, written months afterward, Jackson revealed succinctly the burden of his thoughts: although "the enemy's flank was turned and the road to Winchester opened . . . if we moved directly to Winchester [Banks] might move [east] via Front Royal toward Washington." Jackson meant to prevent this at all costs, since Banks would then give added support to McDowell's impending march from Fredericksburg upon Richmond. On the other hand, if Jackson tried to block such a move by heading due west toward Banks at Strasburg, Banks "might escape [north] toward the Potomac," where he could choose superior defensive positions to thwart Jackson indefinitely.[78]

This pressing strategical problem—how to catch Banks before he escaped the Valley—weighed all the more heavily upon Jackson because of several even more tangible concerns. Jackson always sought to attack with superior numbers against an enemy's most vulnerable position. This he had done successfully at Front Royal. But now erroneous Confederate reports estimated Banks's force at a figure comparable to Jackson's own, as high as fifteen thousand men (about double Banks's real strength). Likewise, Jackson always meant to use speed, maneuverability, lightning-quick attacks, and sustained pursuit against an enemy. According to this formula, the fighting at Front Royal had proved the army's power in only a piecemeal and

78. Richard Taylor, *Destruction and Reconstruction*, p. 58 (first and second quotations); *O.R.*, 12(1):703 (third and fourth quotations); Tanner, *Stonewall in the Valley*, pp. 215–17.

Nathaniel P. Banks, proud political general
(*Johnson and Buell,* Battles and Leaders of the Civil War).

erratic manner. Taylor's Louisianans, along with Johnson's Maryland-ers, had performed admirably enough. But the frenzy of looting by Wheat's Tigers and the unexplained absence of artillery had given the Federals extra time to escape. Although Ewell's men, including Tay-lor's brigade, appeared strong and capable of rapid marching, Banks's command would be fresh after several weeks of only light marching and extended rest. Jackson would have to depend almost entirely upon Ewell and Taylor to move swiftly cross-country to block Banks if he retreated north toward Winchester. The key would be to know precisely when Banks moved one way or the other, either east or south.[79]

Jackson explained in his official report, "In order to watch both directions, I determined, with the main body of the army, to strike the [Valley] turnpike near Middletown, a village 5 miles north of Strasburg and 13 [miles] south of Winchester." By 6:00 A.M. on May 24 Jackson had started from Front Royal. The column received sup-port from the cavalry of Colonel Turner Ashby, a brash, talented Vir-ginian whose official role of independence from direct army control had always chafed Jackson's stern sensibilities. The previous night Banks had received conflicting telegraph messages from some offi-cers who had made their way to Winchester after avoiding capture at Front Royal. Refusing to interpret the fight at Front Royal as any-thing more than a diversionary raid, and continuing to believe that Jackson's main force lay south of Strasburg, Banks took time to enjoy a night's rest. Early on the twenty-fourth he received word from scouts that Confederates had shown up in large numbers near Front Royal. Banks finally decided to abandon Strasburg and head for Win-chester, but the last of his infantry units did not march until 9:00 A.M. "Jackson and Ashby are clever men," wrote one Federal. "We are slow-w-w!"[80]

By mid-morning, however, no Confederate displayed even a hint of either cleverness or speed. Still uncertain of Banks's intentions, Jackson halted his army and waited for scouting reports. Ewell's divi-

79. Tanner, *Stonewall in the Valley*, pp. 217, 254–55.
80. *O.R.*, 12(1):703 (first quotation); Tanner, *Stonewall in the Valley*, pp. 218–19; Eby, *A Virginia Yankee*, p. 39; Harrington, *Fighting Politician*, pp. 67–93 (second quotation 67).

sion, minus Taylor's brigade, had not joined Jackson but instead had proceeded several miles north of Cedarville on the road to Winchester. Jackson apparently intended to hedge his bets by sending Ewell in a race for Winchester if necessary. Banks's cumbersome supply wagons intermingled with soldiers in full gear and hundreds of black refugees, causing the Federal column to string out for almost ten miles along the Valley pike. One of Banks's staff officers recorded in his diary, "It seemed impossible that Jackson, with the force attributed to him, having opened the campaign with so vigorous and successful a blow, should permit our weak column, encumbered with so much coveted and needful spoil, to walk away intact at its leisure."[81]

Toward noon Jackson finally learned from his wayward scouts that Banks had in fact started for Winchester and that the Federal column had made itself highly vulnerable to a broadside attack. At once Jackson determined to make a thrust northwest toward Middletown and attempt to demolish Banks's caravan. Allowing Ewell with most of his division to continue marching north toward Winchester, Jackson again detached Taylor's brigade to accompany him, along with Ashby's cavalry and a battery of artillery. Jackson's weary Virginians followed as best they could. "Major Wheat, with his battalion of 'Tigers,' was directed to keep close to the guns," wrote Taylor. "Sturdy marchers, they trotted along with the horse and artillery at Jackson's heels." But a poor road and many steep hills, muddied by a light rain that began to fall, and some unexpected harassment from Union cavalry, slowed Jackson's advance, turning the short seven miles to Middletown into a three-hour ordeal. Except for the Tigers, who managed to keep up with the artillery and Ashby's cavalry, Taylor's brigade soon lagged about a mile behind Jackson.[82]

About 3:30 in the afternoon Jackson reached a crest overlooking the Valley pike just north of Middletown. The Tigers formed a single battle line while the artillery unlimbered at a range of less than a thousand yards to level their aim at the circuslike parade of unsus-

81. Strother, "Personal Recollections of the War," pp. 423–49 (quotation 443).

82. Tanner, *Stonewall in the Valley*, pp. 220–21; William Calvin Oates, *War between the Union and the Confederacy*, p. 97; Richard Taylor, *Destruction and Reconstruction*, p. 58 (quotation).

pecting Federals clogging the length of the pike in either direction as far as the eye could see. Then, like one massive firing squad, the southerners opened up on their victims with bullet and shell. "In a few moments," wrote Jackson, "the turnpike, which had just before teemed with life, presented a most appalling spectacle of carnage and destruction." Squeezed tightly between waist-high stone walls along both sides of the narrow pike, lurching horses and wagons trampled scores of wounded as the column heaved forward in complete panic. "The road was literally obstructed with the mingled and confused mass of struggling and dying horses and riders," Jackson reported. Ashby's cavalry swept down on the far right, attempting to cut off escape. Then the Tigers rushed forward, shooting delirious Federals and seizing wagons to search for plunder.[83]

The remainder of Taylor's brigade, still marching on the road to Middletown, heard the gunfire and quickened their pace. "A volley in front, followed by wild cheers, stirred us to a 'double,'" he recalled. Major Robert Dabney remembered seeing the Louisianans as they approached: "General Taylor, throwing his advance regiment into line, advanced at a double quick to the center of the village, his men cheering and pouring a terrific volley into the confused mass which filled the street." Henry E. Handerson, a private in the Ninth Louisiana, recounted, "As we jumped over the stone wall onto the pike, however, a vicious volley of bullets whistled through our disordered ranks, splintering the rails of a neighboring fence and wounding several of my comrades, and, looking down the road toward Strasburg, I saw a company of Zouaves behind a stone wall firing vigorously upon our advance." This retaliation fazed the Ninth for only a moment. "Hastily leaving the open pike," continued Handerson, "we rushed forward under the protection of houses and fences until, emerging from the southern end of the village, we found our enemies in rapid retreat."[84]

Looking for Wheat's Tigers in hopes of adding their deadly force to the rout, Taylor found them, true to form, still distracted by the

83. *O.R.*, 12(1):703 (quotations); Tanner, *Stonewall in the Valley*, p. 221.

84. Richard Taylor, *Destruction and Reconstruction*, p. 58 (first quotation); Dabney, *Life of Jackson*, p. 371 (second quotation); Cummer, *Yankee in Gray*, p. 42 (third and fourth quotations).

enemy booty. "The gentle Tigers were looting right merrily, diving in and out of wagons with the activity of rabbits in a warren," he recalled, "but this occupation was abandoned on my appearance, and in a moment they were in line, looking as solemn and virtuous as deacons at a funeral." The firing began to wane as Taylor's men chased down about two hundred prisoners, many of whom were found crouching behind the pike's stone walls in a feeble effort to avoid detection. When a group of Union cavalrymen surrendered at gunpoint, Taylor ordered them to dismount. Hailing from New England, where, as Taylor observed, "horsemanship was an unknown art, . . . some of the riders were strapped to their steeds . . . and were given time to unbuckle." Oddities of Yankee warfare did not cease here. Some cavalrymen even wore breastplates and other pieces of armor, as if they "were recurring to the customs of Gustavus Adolphus." Noticing one of them lying dead in the road, a single bullet hole through his breastplate, Taylor concluded, "Iron-clad men are of small account before modern weapons." [85]

About 4:00 P.M. Jackson questioned several civilians in Middletown regarding the actual number of Banks's force that had passed along the pike, but the answers he received seemed all too vague. Then Federal artillery to the south began shelling the town, leading Jackson to surmise that he had succeeded in blocking the majority of enemy troops in their flight northward. Anticipating a conclusive fight, Jackson took the Tigers, part of the Seventh Louisiana, and Ashby's horsemen north to clean up what he believed would be the advance elements of Banks's column. He entrusted Taylor to drive the main body of Federals southward, back toward Strasburg. Taylor sent his men into the fray by ordering several volleys of musket fire, but the Yankees retreated about a mile, drawing up on a ridge west of the pike, near Cedar Creek. "Their numbers were unknown, and for a moment they looked threatening," he noted. As the Louisianans formed in skirmish lines and moved forward, an artillery shot downed several of the men. As Taylor rode up to get a better view, a shell exploded directly beneath his horse, tearing away the saddle

85. Richard Taylor, *Destruction and Reconstruction*, pp. 58–59 (quotations); *O.R.*, 12(1):703; Dabney, *Life of Jackson*, pp. 371–72.

cloth on both sides and covering him with dirt. To his amazement, "neither man nor horse received a scratch." Quickly the Confederate artillery unlimbered and returned the fire, and the Federals scurried westward on the heels of several well-placed shells that sent some of their supply wagons flying into the air. Taylor's men found knapsacks on the ground in perfect rows where whole companies had left them in order to speed their flight into the hills west of the pike. With no other enemy troops in sight, Taylor marched his men back through Middletown to catch up with Jackson.[86]

Several miles to the north Jackson met stiff resistance from a large body of Federals. Suddenly it became obvious he was fighting a rear guard that protected the bulk of Banks's column. By spending two hours fighting at Middletown, Jackson had allowed most of the enemy force to slip through his fingers. When Taylor's men overtook Jackson they could hardly believe they would have to continue pursuing Banks. "The excitement of battle had begun to wear off, and we soon felt the fatigue and hunger of men who had been marching all day with little or no food," wrote a Louisianan. "Yet our orders were to press forward to Winchester, distant some thirteen miles." By now, late in the afternoon, Banks and his staff had already reached Winchester, and the rest of his troops would continue to appear gradually, well into the evening. There they learned that the townspeople had been busy all day cooking dinners and cakes, expecting Jackson's army to arrive at any moment to liberate them. "We laughed heartily at their fatuity," recalled one Federal officer, who believed, as did Banks, that Jackson had still not left Front Royal. "Their cavalry was annoying our flank and rear, hoping to ease us of some superfluous baggage, and to clean out a few of our sutlers and perambulating whiskey merchants, which I thought would be advantageous to both parties."[87]

86. Tanner, *Stonewall in the Valley*, pp. 221–22; Richard Taylor, *Destruction and Reconstruction*, pp. 59–60 (quotations); Dabney, *Life of Jackson*, pp. 372–73; Cummer, *Yankee in Gray*, p. 42; *O.R.*, 12(1):704.

87. Tanner, *Stonewall in the Valley*, p. 222; Cummer, *Yankee in Gray*, p. 42 (first quotation); Strother, "Personal Recollections of the War," p. 443 (second quotation).

For several miles between Middletown and Newtown, wrecked and abandoned wagons littered the pike in the wake of the Federal retreat, tempting Ashby's cavalrymen to load themselves down with plunder rather than to chase the enemy. Without cavalry support, Jackson's artillery and small contingent of infantry made slow headway against the Federal column's rear guard. "Up to the present moment," Jackson professed in his official report, "there was reason to believe, if Banks reached Winchester, it would be without a train, if not without an army." He blamed Ashby for the debacle, but he realized this swashbuckling Virginian had little control even over his own men, except in battle. Reflecting Jackson's own jaundiced view, Taylor later gave vent to the army's growing resentment toward Confederate cavalry units. "Living on horseback, fearless and dashing, the men of the South afforded the best possible means for cavalry," he observed, admitting also that they "rendered much excellent service." But Taylor accused them of one shortcoming: "They had every quality but discipline." Unbridled democracy had always distressed Taylor's aristocratic instincts of class structure and duty. The South's war for democratic rights, however, often resulted in concessions to individual and local demands. Like no other part of the military effort, the whims of Confederate cavalrymen typified this problem.[88]

About dusk Taylor's men caught up with Jackson just north of Newtown. The pace slowed as plunging temperatures brought stiffness to the soldiers' sore and expended muscles. Yankee ambushers added to their pain, forcing them into blind skirmishes at uncertain intervals. Taylor rode at the head of the column with Jackson, who seemed alert yet unconcerned by the danger. "Charge them! Charge them!" shouted Jackson with a ring of defiant impatience. Taylor later wrote, "I quite remember thinking at the time that Jackson was invulnerable, and that persons near him shared that quality." Throughout the night the jaded southerners, now including Jackson's Virginians in the lead, stumbled along, barely able to stand up, shivering in the

88. Tanner, *Stonewall in the Valley*, pp. 223–24; *O.R.*, 12(1):704 (first quotation); Richard Taylor, *Destruction and Reconstruction*, pp. 65–66 (first quotation 66, second quotation 65). For a strong defense of Ashby and his horsemen, see Bushong, *General Turner Ashby*, pp. 133–51.

near-freezing cold and longing for sleep. "The army had been marching for weeks," recalled Kyd Douglas, and "was exhausted, broken down, and apparently unfit for battle." But Jackson had no intention of stopping. He wanted to reach the hills south of Winchester in order to give his artillery a commanding position the next morning. "So important did I deem it to occupy before dawn the heights overlooking Winchester, that the advance continued to move forward," he reported.[89]

At one point during the night Jackson's chief quartermaster rode up and reported that many wagons had bogged down on an impassable road far to the rear. "The ammunition wagons?" Jackson asked tersely. "All right, sir," the quartermaster reassured him, explaining that he had given them double teams of horses. "Ah!" sighed a relieved Jackson. Overhearing the conversation, Taylor remarked to the quartermaster, "Never mind the wagons. There are quantities of stores in Winchester, and the General has invited me to breakfast there to-morrow." Missing the joke completely, Jackson turned a solemn expression on Taylor, then reached out his hand and touched him on the arm, as if to thank him for his confidence that Winchester would be theirs. "Without physical wants himself," Taylor also reflected, "[Jackson] forgot that others were differently constituted, and [he] paid little heed to commissariat; but woe to the man who failed to bring up the ammunition!"[90]

By 3:00 A.M. the entire Army of the Valley was faltering pathetically. One by one soldiers lost consciousness and collapsed along the pike. Since sunset they had managed to advance only about five miles against a tormenting combination of enemy sharpshooters and surprise attacks from skirmishers. Winchester lay just two miles distant, but Jackson realized that if he did not order a halt, morning would find his ranks depleted and virtually useless for battle. Relenting to allow them a brief but welcome two hours of rest, Jackson remained

89. Dabney, *Life of Jackson*, p. 375 (first quotation); Richard Taylor, *Destruction and Reconstruction*, p. 60 (second quotation); Edward A. Moore, *Cannoneer under Jackson*, pp. 55–56; Henry Kyd Douglas, *I Rode with Stonewall*, p. 55 (third quotation); *O.R.*, 12(1):704 (fourth quotation).

90. Richard Taylor, *Destruction and Reconstruction*, pp. 60–61 (quotations).

vigilant as they stopped in their tracks and fell to the ground. Several miles to the east General Dick Ewell, having continued marching northward on the road directly from Front Royal to Winchester, halted his division at a point comparable to Jackson's, about two miles south of town. That night Ewell received a single-sentence message from Jackson devoid of all subtlety: "Attack at daylight."[91]

91. Tanner, *Stonewall in the Valley*, pp. 225–26 (quotation 226); Edward A. Moore, *Cannoneer under Jackson*, p. 56; Henry Kyd Douglas, *I Rode with Stonewall*, pp. 56–57; *O.R.*, 12(1):779.

CHAPTER FIVE

Jackson's Swift Sword in the Valley

To General Taylor and his brigade belongs the honor of

deciding two battles.

Richard Ewell

Sunday, May 25, dawned with a cool mist and gray fog hanging over the rolling wheat fields and orchards surrounding Winchester. At the first hint of light Jackson gave the order to march. "We . . . arose from the ground . . . stiff and sore," recalled one of Taylor's men, and "pushed on toward Winchester." Expecting to find the enemy's artillery and infantry positioned on a high ridge a few hundred yards south of town, Jackson sent forward Brigadier General Charles S. Winder, commander of the Stonewall Brigade, to dislodge the Union guns. But Winder met only faint resistance from skirmishers, allowing Jackson to take easy advantage of the position, his primary goal. This stroke of good fortune Major Dabney attributed to "the will of God." In fact it had more to do with the will of Nathaniel P. Banks. Believing Jackson had given up the chase, Banks had left the task of selecting defensive positions to his subordinate officers, who simply formed their lines along the town's outskirts. Now the early morning greeted them with the sight of the Stonewall Brigade and its artillery occupying the ridge opposite them.[1]

Quickly recovering their composure, the Federals opened a pin-point barrage of shelling that sent Winder's men scrambling for cover. By now Banks had no more than four thousand soldiers to defend Winchester, but the blanket of early morning fog mingled thickly with gunpowder smoke to help the Yankees conceal their true numbers. Far to Jackson's right Dick Ewell fell victim to the same problems. The sound of battle to the west had spurred him forward, but his men broke ranks, confused by the fog and soon pinned down by the enemy's concentrated firing. Ewell decided to pull back, circle slowly to the right, and try to find the Federal left flank. In the mean-time he hoped his partner Jackson would play a trump card.[2]

The Army of the Valley had reached an all-too-uncomfortable im-passe, but Jackson studied his opponent before revealing his hand. Finally, with Winder yelling to him that somehow they must assault the enemy's right flank, Jackson agreed, responding firmly, "I will send you up Taylor." Immediately he turned and ordered Kyd Doug-las to find Taylor and bring him to the front. Douglas raced about a mile to the rear and urged Taylor to bring his brigade forward at a double-quick. In a few minutes Taylor saw Jackson trotting up the pike to meet him. The Louisianans halted and removed their hats in respect. Returning the salute, Jackson rode up to Taylor and asked pointedly, "General, can your brigade charge a battery?" "It can try," Taylor answered. "Very good; it must do it then," said Jackson. "Move it forward."[3]

Taylor then galloped ahead with Jackson to survey the Confederate

1. Tanner, *Stonewall in the Valley*, pp. 226–28; Cummer, *Yankee in Gray*, p. 42 (first quotation); Dabney, *Life of Jackson*, pp. 376–77 (second quotation 376); Harrington, *Fighting Politician*, pp. 74–75. For a concise description of this battle at Winchester, see Beck and Grunder, *Three Battles of Winchester*, pp. 9–15.

2. Dabney, *Life of Jackson*, pp. 377–79; Tanner, *Stonewall in the Valley*, pp. 226–29.

3. Tanner, *Stonewall in the Valley*, pp. 229–30 (first quotation 229); Henry Kyd Douglas, *I Rode with Stonewall*, pp. 57–58 (second quotation 58); Richard Taylor, *Destruction and Reconstruction*, p. 61.

position overlooking Winchester. The prolonged, brutal effect of the enemy artillery on Jackson's Virginians at once alarmed Taylor. "Several regiments were lying down for shelter, as the fire from the ridge was heavy and searching," he recalled. "A Virginia battery, [the] Rockbridge artillery, was fighting at a great disadvantage, and already much cut up. . . . With scarce a leg or wheel for man and horse, gun or caisson, to stand on, it continued to hammer away at the crushing fire above." Jackson, however, "impassive as ever," pointed to the position occupied by the enemy toward the left and said, "You must carry it." After a hurried inspection of the terrain, Taylor joined his brigade just as it arrived, ordered it to file to the left, and conducted it westward along Abraham's Creek at the ridge's southern base, thus affording his men a measure of temporary protection.[4]

After a few moments Taylor noticed Jackson riding at his side. Such direct exposure to enemy fire was "not the place for the commander of the army," Taylor remarked, but Jackson ignored him. As the brigade filed past an open depression along the banks of the creek, the Federal artillery focused directly on the area, causing several casualties. Vulnerable and defenseless, the Louisianans cringed and ducked with each explosion. "What the hell are you dodging for?" shouted Taylor. "If there is any more of it, you will be halted under this fire for an hour." His soldiers stiffened at the wrathful warning, and so did Jackson. "I shall never forget the reproachful surprise in Jackson's face," Taylor recalled. Placing his hand on Taylor's shoulder, Jackson said gravely, "I am afraid you are a wicked fellow." He then turned around and rode back toward the pike.[5]

If Taylor seemed like a poor lost sinner, at least Jackson had seen no need for any preaching about field tactics. Shortly before 7:00 A.M. Taylor faced his column toward the enemy line just as the sun began to illuminate the Blue Ridge. With the fog and mist now clearing away, Robert Dabney witnessed the Louisianans at work: "Under a shower of shells and rifle-balls, this magnificent body of troops wheeled from column into line, with the accurateness and readiness

4. Richard Taylor, *Destruction and Reconstruction*, pp. 61–62 (quotations 61); *O.R.*, 12(1):759.

5. Richard Taylor, *Destruction and Reconstruction*, pp. 62–63 (first and second quotations 62, third quotation 63).

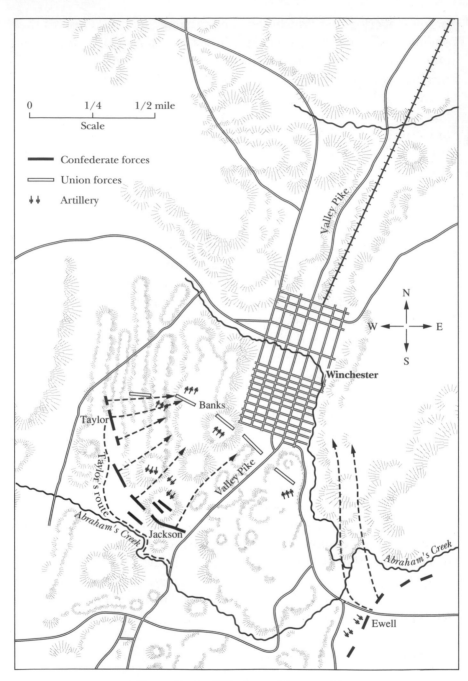

Map 2. *Battle of Winchester, May 25, 1862*

of a parade." Taylor ordered the men forward at a steady marching gait. "This full brigade," wrote Kyd Douglas, "with a line of glistening bayonets bright in the morning sun, its formation straight and compact, its tread quick and easy as it pushed on through the clover and up the hill, was a sight to delight a veteran."[6]

Taylor rode at the front of the brigade, his sword drawn, turning his horse at times or twisting in the saddle and glancing backward to make certain the advance continued without any hesitation. Alert and calm under the enemy's fire, for an instant he even caught sight of a bluebird flying past with a worm in its beak. "Birdie had been on the war path, and was carrying home spoil," he reflected. Although he later confessed to feeling "anxiety amounting to pain for the brigade to acquit itself handsomely," the peacock in him refused to have its plumage ruffled. "The excitement of battle seemed to soothe him," recalled David Boyd, "and he would become pleasant and playful as a kitten." Now Taylor enjoyed complete freedom from the physical pain of his debilitating disease. The adrenalin of the moment incited the instinct of a pure fighter. Colonel Joseph L. Brent later noted, "I only recollect, among the many I heard, two voices of high officers in battle which preserved their ordinary and usual tones. One was Gen. Gustavus Smith, and the other was Gen. Dick Taylor."[7]

Responding quickly, Federal officers shifted several regiments to their right to bolster their strength against the Louisiana Brigade's approach. "They were received with a destructive fire of musketry," reported a Union colonel, yet they "moved on, but little shaken." Taylor noticed in particular old Colonel Isaac Seymour, "on foot, with sword and cap in hand, his thin gray locks streaming," expertly pacing the Sixth Louisiana and shouting, "Steady men!" Then suddenly a detachment of enemy cavalry charged down on Taylor's far left. He immediately sent orders instructing Lieutenant Colonel Francis T. Nicholls of the Eighth, on the left near Wheat's Tigers, to delay slightly and turn toward the horsemen. A single volley from Nicholls's

6. Ibid., p. 63; Dabney, *Life of Jackson*, p. 379 (first quotation); Henry Kyd Douglas, *I Rode with Stonewall*, p. 58 (second quotation).

7. Worsham, *One of Jackson's Foot Cavalry*, p. 87; Richard Taylor, *Destruction and Reconstruction*, p. 63 (first quotation); Boyd, *Reminiscences of the War*, p. 13 (second quotation); Brent, *Memoirs*, p. 148 (third quotation).

men sent dozens of Federal horses and riders reeling to the ground, and Wheat used the opportunity to sweep even farther to the left, thereby posing a more serious threat to the enemy flank. A minute or two later Nicholls's left arm was shattered by a single minié ball, imperiling his life from loss of blood. The brigade surged onward, its casualties mounting. "Closing the many gaps made by a fierce fire, steadied rather by it," wrote Taylor, "the brigade, with cadenced step and eyes on the foe, swept grandly over copse and ledge and fence."[8]

About halfway up the hill Taylor grasped the utter ripeness of the situation. Private John H. Worsham of the Stonewall Brigade remembered watching, mesmerized, as Taylor rose in his saddle and delivered "in a loud commanding voice, that I am sure the Yankees heard, the order to charge!" In an instant the entire brigade lunged forward. Another storm of bullets and shrapnel, even more deadly than before, cut into the Louisianans. A Union officer recalled, "Here at Winchester, the range was so good, and the enemy so massed, that with any aim at all, it was simply impossible to miss." "For a moment," wrote another Federal, "the enemy seemed to stagger, but only for a moment; for feeling confidence in their great strength, they charged . . . with deafening cheers." Far over on the right, Dick Ewell's men knew instantly what had happened. "Ah, me boys," howled one of Ewell's Irishmen, "that's Taylor; that's the jenewine Irish yell." An envious Private Worsham later admitted, "This charge of Taylor's was the grandest I saw during the war."[9]

Positioned on the ridge near the pike, Jackson and his staff scrutinized Taylor's advance. Robert Dabney noticed his commander at first showing "an air of eager caution, peering like a deer-stalker." But as the Louisiana Brigade gained momentum, Jackson perceived the disruption developing along the enemy front. Kyd Douglas recalled

8. *O.R.*, 12(1):617 (first quotation); Richard Taylor, *Destruction and Reconstruction*, pp. 97 (second quotation), 63–64 (third quotation 64); Casso, *Francis T. Nicholls*, p. 78.

9. Worsham, *One of Jackson's Foot Cavalry*, p. 87 (first and fourth quotations); Tanner, *Stonewall in the Valley*, p. 231; E. R. Brown, *Twenty-Seventh Indiana Volunteer Infantry*, pp. 144–48 (second quotation 146); *O.R.*, 12(1):624 (third quotation); William Calvin Oates, *War between the Union and the Confederacy*, p. 98 (fourth quotation).

that Jackson appeared "evidently surprised," then he turned to Douglas and exclaimed, "Order forward the whole line, the battle's won." Spurring his horse, he shouted to the rest of the officers near him, "Forward, after the enemy!" The Stonewall Brigade and the other Virginia regiments nearby leaped up and threw themselves into the fight. In the same urgent manner, Ewell already had seized the initiative on the right. For Jackson, all the demeaning frustrations of the past year, the immense pressure to relieve Richmond by defeating Banks, and the very sight of Winchester, the town he had known and loved all his life, ignited within him a display of emotion never before seen by his soldiers. Waving his kepi in the air, he roared, "Very good! Now let's holler!" Dabney could scarcely believe the sight, Jackson galloping at full speed, "his face inflamed with towering passion and triumph, with the leading pursuers, urging them upon the enemy." [10]

"On every side above the surrounding crest surged rebel forces," wrote a Union officer who saw his men sustain "a sharp and withering fire of musketry" accompanied by the "yells of a victorious and merciless foe." One of Taylor's men recalled, "We rushed forward, whooping and yelling, [even] as they poured volley after volley into us. We routed them from their position after having to climb over three stone walls and a fence." Jackson later reported that he saw the Louisianans "mounting the hill, and there fronting the enemy, where he stood in greatest strength, the whole line swept magnificently down the declivity and across the field, driving back the Federal troops and bearing down all opposition before it." Near the top of the hill, as Taylor organized his men into a column to pursue the enemy, Jackson rode up and extended his hand, a gesture Taylor considered "worth a thousand words from another." [11]

As the Yankees bolted through the streets of Winchester, citizens did all they could to impede the despised fugitives. A Federal officer recoiled at the sight of men and women "firing from the houses,

10. Dabney, *Life of Jackson*, pp. 379–80 (first and third quotations 379, fifth quotation 380); Henry Kyd Douglas, *I Rode with Stonewall*, pp. 58–59 (second and fourth quotations 59); Chambers, *Stonewall Jackson*, 1:541.

11. *O.R.*, 12(1):617 (first quotation), 705 (third quotation); Opelousas *Courier*, September 6, 1862 (second quotation); Richard Taylor, *Destruction and Reconstruction*, p. 64 (fourth quotation).

throwing hand grenades, hot water, and missiles of every description." Then, as another described the scene, "The Confederates . . .
poured in at every street like a flood of dirty water . . . gray ragged,
and unwashed, clad in all fashions." Banks finally came to his senses
and joined his men in the streets, trying to rally them by bravely exposing himself to gunfire. Confederate pursuit did falter for several
minutes, but not because of Banks's leadership. Hundreds of civilians, even women with small children and babies in their arms,
clogged the streets, rushing to meet their liberators. "They were fran-
tic with delight, only regretting that so many Yankees had escaped,"
wrote Taylor. When a pretty young woman ran up and cried, "Oh!
You are too late—too late!" an Acadian from the Eighth Louisiana
took his cue, embracing her passionately, planting a lusty kiss on her
lips, and declaring in French, "I never arrive too late." Scurrying away
with a twinkle in her eye, she seemed scarcely insulted by either the
kiss or the fits of laughter from Taylor's soldiers.[12]

Jackson took little time to enjoy the celebration. Because of a lack
of empty wagons to carry supplies and ammunition, Banks had set
fire to several storage buildings, sending clouds of smoke through the
the streets. "I actually saw a lady waving her handkerchief from the
front of her house when the rear was in flames," remembered one
citizen. "They said they didn't care if the whole town burnt so long as
the Yanks were driven off." Jackson ordered soldiers and civilians
alike to fight the flames and save the priceless enemy supplies. Then
his attention turned again to Banks's retreating regiments. "Push on
to the Potomac!" he shouted. On the northern outskirts of town the
Confederates formed irregular lines to chase the Federals, capturing
scores of stragglers. Jackson searched for his cavalry officers to make
easy work of Banks's pitifully vulnerable masses, but no horsemen
arrived. "Never have I seen an opportunity when it was in the power
of cavalry to reap a richer harvest of the fruits of victory," he later
asserted. A staff officer suggested sending the horse-drawn artillery
as a substitute, and Jackson responded, "Yes; go back and order up
the nearest batteries you find!" To another officer he added enthusi-

12. *O.R.*, 12(1):617 (first quotation); Eby, *A Virginia Yankee*, pp. 49–50 (second quotation); Richard Taylor, *Destruction and Reconstruction*, p. 64 (third
and fourth quotations).

astically, "Order every battery and every brigade forward to the Potomac!" By 9:00 A.M. Jackson had joined Taylor north of town, where
the Louisianans were straining to keep up with the rear of Banks's
column. "Where is the cavalry?" asked Taylor; but Jackson only
"glowered and was silent." [13]

Soon the artillerymen came forward to take up the pursuit. Jackson
prodded them ruthlessly, ordering them to unlimber at regular intervals to rake the enemy. One Federal soldier recalled, "At every shell
that burst . . . I could see our columns shake with a convulsive start,
as a single body." Before long, however, the artillery teams were plod-
ding along much too slowly for Jackson's liking, so he ordered the
gunners to unhitch their horses and mount them as makeshift cavalrymen. Riding with unusual eagerness, these artillerymen shot down
dozens of stragglers, gaining vengeance for the hour or more of pun-
ishing fire from enemy batteries they had endured earlier that morning on the ridge south of Winchester. According to a Federal officer,
the artillerymen "slew the weary and jaded," ignoring their "cries for
mercy," only screaming, "Give no quarter to the damned Yankees!"
The horses, however, lasted but a few miles more, and as the pursuit
gradually died out, Jackson's thoroughly drained army fell along the
roadside and then made camp near Martinsburg. By day's end only
3,500 Union soldiers, about half of Banks's command, had crossed
the Potomac to safety. He had left behind nearly 500 killed and
wounded and about 3,000 prisoners in Jackson's possession. [14]

Every witness agreed that Taylor's brigade had carried the day. "In
truth," Taylor admitted none too modestly, "it was a gallant feat of
arms." Jackson had used the Louisianans like an elite unit of shock
troops, keeping them in the forefront on the march and throwing
them into the thickest of the fighting. Jackson had fully expected Taylor's charge against the elevated enemy position to win the battle. Yet

13. Hale, *Four Valiant Years*, p. 157 (first quotation); Henry Kyd Douglas, *I
Rode with Stonewall*, pp. 59–60 (second quotation 60); *O.R.*, 12(1):706 (third
quotation); Dabney, *Life of Jackson*, p. 381 (fourth quotation); Richard Taylor,
Destruction and Reconstruction, p. 65 (fifth quotation).

14. Tanner, *Stonewall in the Valley*, pp. 232–33; Strother, "Personal Recollections of the War," p. 445 (first quotation); *O.R.*, 12(1):617 (second quotation).

considering the enemy's heavy concentration of firing against the Virginians in the center and against Ewell's division on the right, Jackson could have done little else than summon Taylor to make the charge on the left. Once Taylor began moving forward, he gradually extended his left flank far beyond and around the Union right, taking advantage of Jackson's superior overall manpower. Despite the extraordinary courage shown by the Louisiana Brigade, it had achieved victory against unseasoned and outnumbered soldiers virtually devoid of competent leadership. Up to now, after the fights at Middletown and Winchester, Jackson's army counted only about 400 casualties to add to the 100 suffered at Front Royal. Taylor reported his brigade's casualties for the same three-day period, including Winchester, as amounting to only 21 killed and 109 wounded, an astonishingly low figure considering the action his men had seen. Ewell's entire division, including Taylor's brigade, had a scant 39 killed and 172 wounded. The Louisianans had served as Jackson's thoroughbreds, but the true hell of a sustained battle against a powerful foe had not yet tested them.[15]

Jackson set aside the next day, Monday, May 26, as a time of religious devotion in order to atone for Sunday's combat. Regimental chaplains held several services of thanksgiving, merely momentary distractions for soldiers intent on feasting upon the captured Yankee rations—potted meats, fruits, liquor of all kinds, and real coffee, all commodities by now difficult to obtain in the South. One appreciative Confederate reflected that "later on in the war, when rations became scarce . . . [we] would have been glad to have got another whack at Banks's commissary train." The army also garnered large droves of cattle and sheep, thousands of additional small arms, two more cannon, and badly needed medical supplies—so much booty that Jackson's chief quartermaster John A. Harmon could not find enough wagons to haul all of it. While in Winchester, Taylor took time to visit his sister Elizabeth Dandridge. He also read Jackson's official proclamation thanking the army for its suffering and bravery. "Every man was satisfied with his apology," wrote Private John Worsham. "To accomplish so much with so little loss, we would march

15. Richard Taylor, *Destruction and Reconstruction*, p. 64 (quotation); Tanner, *Stonewall in the Valley*, p. 233; *O.R.*, 12(1):780–81, 801.

six months! The reception at Winchester was worth a whole lifetime of service." [16]

Without realizing it, Jackson himself had performed a lifetime's worth of service to the Confederacy. Although he had wanted to obliterate Banks's force, the victory at Front Royal three days before had already prompted Lincoln to suspend the massive Union movement toward Richmond scheduled for May 25. On the afternoon of May 24, immediately after learning of Jackson's strike against Front Royal, Lincoln had ordered McDowell to leave Fredericksburg with twenty thousand men, about half of his command, and move into the Shenandoah Valley to help Banks and Frémont deal with the ubiquitous Stonewall Jackson. At this point Lincoln seemed more intent on swatting Jackson away rather than acting to protect Washington. But when he learned of Banks's rout at Winchester on the twenty-fifth, coupled with unconfirmed reports of thousands of Confederate cavalrymen galloping through central Virginia toward Manassas, Lincoln began to worry about Washington's safety. "Jackson's movement is a general and concerted one," he informed McClellan, "such as could not be if he was acting upon the purpose of a very desperate defense of Richmond." Lincoln had blundered badly; Jackson's entire campaign in the Valley was desperate by any measure. Had he attacked Front Royal even one day later, he would have failed in his mission. A Federal siege of Richmond would have been under way. Now McDowell's shift to the Valley became irrevocable, and McClellan was left to stew on the Peninsula and grudgingly confront Richmond's defenses by himself. Neither Lee nor Jackson had ever expected to accomplish so much. The best they had hoped for was a delay, perhaps to confuse Lincoln and force him to doubt his ability to move against the Confederate capital and protect Washington at the same time. Instead, they had gained the indefinite suspension of the most vital part of the Federal campaign. [17]

16. Hale, *Four Valiant Years*, p. 156; Tanner, *Stonewall in the Valley*, pp. 233, 258–59; McClendon, *Recollections of War Times*, p. 59 (first quotation); Richard Taylor, *Destruction and Reconstruction*, p. 66; Worsham, *One of Jackson's Foot Cavalry*, p. 88 (second quotation).

17. Lang, Hennessee, and Bush, "Jackson's Valley Campaign," pp. 46–47; Tanner, *Stonewall in the Valley*, pp. 238–46 (quotation 244).

On May 28 Jackson moved north to appear to threaten an invasion of Maryland and an eastward thrust toward Washington. "We then were sure of going into Maryland," wrote a Louisianan, "and were highly elated at the thought." The next day, however, Jackson sent Taylor's brigade on an assignment several miles to the east, placing him in a position to decoy or, if necessary, thwart the division under Brigadier General James Shields now moving west toward Strasburg from McDowell's army at Fredericksburg. Ashby's cavalry, operating in the same vicinity, served the same purpose and succeeded in confusing Shields, forcing him to slacken his pace. Jackson had willingly put himself in the middle of a triangular pincers movement, with Shields to the southeast, Frémont's fifteen thousand men to the southwest, and Banks apparently ready to turn on him from the north. Both Shields and Frémont made slow progress, however, and by May 30 Jackson knew their exact locations. As the pincers began to tighten, Jackson ordered the various units of his command to move south in a race for Strasburg. Confident to the point of even taking a nap for several critical hours, Jackson intended to save his entire army, plus some 2,300 prisoners and several hundred overloaded wagons of captured supplies, by pushing through Strasburg before the Yankees closed in for the kill. Disdainful of the soldierly abilities of each of his adversaries, Jackson seemed more worried about the supply wagons than anything else. "The importance of preserving the immense trains filled with captured stores, was great," Taylor recalled, "and would engage much of [Jackson's] personal attention. . . . The men said that his anxiety about the wagons was because of the lemons among the stores." [18]

Taylor received his orders to depart for Strasburg on May 31. Stopping briefly in Winchester to evacuate the Confederate wounded still there, he visited Colonel Francis Nicholls, whose arm had been amputated after his wounding at Winchester. Taylor wanted to bring Nicholls along, but his physical condition was still far too serious. "The surgeons forbade his removal, so that, much to my regret

18. Tanner, *Stonewall in the Valley*, pp. 263–70; Opelousas *Courier*, September 6, 1862 (first quotation); Hattaway and Jones, *How the North Won*, pp. 180–81; Richard Taylor, *Destruction and Reconstruction*, pp. 66–67 (second quotation 67).

and more to his own, he was left," Taylor recalled. The townspeople, aghast at being abandoned again to certain occupation by Yankee troops, hated to see Taylor depart. A Louisiana private remembered with bitterness the "cries and wailings of the ladies, imploring us to remain and give them protection." [19]

On the night of the thirty-first, after pushing his brigade more than thirty miles, Taylor reached Strasburg. There Jackson met him with undisguised anticipation and concern. "Jackson sat some time at my camp fire that night, and was more communicative than I remember him before or after," Taylor recalled. Jackson said his scouts had located Frémont only a few miles to the west. But Shields, rather than closing in from the east, had started moving south, up the Luray Valley, with the apparent intention of crossing over Massanutten to New Market or continuing south and then cutting east, around Massanutten's southern base, in order to block Jackson's army from reaching Harrisonburg. As an essential first step in his plan to outrun Shields, Jackson wanted Taylor to rejoin Ewell's division and help fend off Frémont the next morning. The entire Army of the Valley, exhausted and miserable, would have to fight on the run. Yet Jackson still seemed more worried about his hundreds of supply wagons than about his soldiers. A captive Union officer observed caustically, "Stonewall Jackson's men will follow him to the devil, and he knows it." [20]

Jackson's confidence only increased as he became more convinced of his adversaries' weaknesses. Frémont showed a mystifying lack of initiative the following morning, Sunday, June 1, when Taylor joined Ewell to confront Frémont just west of Strasburg. A thick forest hid the enemy from view. Offering only some intermittent artillery shelling, Frémont seemed satisfied to wait for Ewell to make the first move. But Jackson had given Ewell explicit orders to refrain from committing himself to a fight. Growing exceedingly impatient, Ewell

19. Terry L. Jones, *Lee's Tigers*, p. 82; Richard Taylor, *Destruction and Reconstruction*, p. 67 (first quotation); Casso, *Francis T. Nicholls*, p. 81; Opelousas *Courier*, September 6, 1862 (second quotation).

20. Richard Taylor, *Destruction and Reconstruction*, p. 67 (first quotation); Tanner, *Stonewall in the Valley*, pp. 271–73; Henry Kyd Douglas, *I Rode with Stonewall*, p. 70 (second quotation).

remarked to Taylor, "At this rate my attentions are not likely to become serious enough to engage anyone." Taylor volunteered to take
his brigade far to the right to search out the enemy's position there.
"Do so," said Ewell. "That may stir them up. I am sick of this fiddling
about." When Taylor reached Frémont's left flank, he wheeled his brigade around, opened fire, and then moved forward, crushing the
Federal line in a perfect "walk-over" maneuver. "Sheep would have
made as much resistance as we met," he recorded. "Men decamped
without firing, or threw down their arms and surrendered, and it was
so easy that I began to think of traps." The only casualties among the
Louisianans came from the misdirected shots of their own skirmishers.[21]

While taking prisoners Taylor discovered that this part of Frémont's army consisted of German immigrants who spoke no English.
Commenting years later on the martial reputation of the German nation, Taylor insisted in his typically condescending manner that "they
require a cause and leaders. . . . We have millions of German citizens,
and excellent citizens they are. Let us hope that the foregoing facts
may be commended to them, so their ways may be ways of peace in
their adopted land." Although he failed to understand that timidity
on the part of these German Yankees typified the widespread lack of
confidence in the hapless General Frémont, Taylor was honest
enough to admit that his attack had been "rash and foolish," the result
of his own nervousness. Earlier during the morning, while under fire
from the enemy artillery, he confessed to Ewell that he felt a distressing lack of confidence. "Whether from fatigue, loss of sleep, or what,
there I was, ducking like a mandarin," he admitted. "It was disgust-
ing, and, hoping that no one saw me, I resolved to take it out of
myself [at] the first opportunity." Thus he had determined to attack
Frémont's flank, an act he later regretted. "Alarm and disgust at
my own nervousness occasioned it, proving weak nerves to be the
source of rash acts." Jackson had wisely instructed Ewell to refrain
from engaging the enemy, realizing that "he could not waste time
chasing Fremont," Taylor affirmed, "but we, who looked from a lower

21. Richard Taylor, *Destruction and Reconstruction*, pp. 71–72 (first quotation 71, second quotation 72).

standpoint, grumbled and shared the men's opinion about the *lemon wagons*." [22]

Tom Strother, Taylor's body servant, showed far more poise than his master during the fight near Strasburg. Left alone on a nearby hill to wait for Taylor, Tom soon found himself within range of roving artillery shells exploding all around him. Jackson happened to ride past and suggested that Tom move to a safer area, but the loyal slave told the general that his master had instructed him to stay put at that spot. Besides, he assured Jackson, "he did not believe [the] shells would trouble him." A few days later, while seated at Taylor's camp fire one evening, Jackson related the story to Taylor and then, with great reverence, stood up and shook Tom's hand. "I used to fancy there was a mute sympathy between General Jackson and Tom, as they sat silent by the camp fire, the latter respectfully withdrawn," observed Taylor, "and [the] incident here at Strasburg cemented this friendship." [23]

Taylor's brigade rejoined the rest of Ewell's division about dusk on June 1 and moved along the Valley pike south of Strasburg, watching to see whether Frémont would follow. Shortly, Jackson rode up and ordered Taylor to move his brigade several hundred yards west of the pike in order to protect the withdrawing Confederate column, although Jackson did not expect any enemy pursuit that night. Camping on a hillside overlooking the pike, the Louisianans maintained silence, went without fires, and ate cold rations. Taylor tried to sleep, but the incessant clatter of wagons and animals on the pike's stone surface made him restless. After a few hours he heard distant gunfire. Through pitch blackness he rode down to the pike and learned from some Confederate stragglers that enemy cavalry units from both Frémont and Banks had just forced Colonel Thomas T. Munford's Virginia cavalrymen into a running fight from Strasburg. With the gunfire growing more pronounced, Taylor roused his disgruntled men from their slumber, and with many complaints and much swearing they stumbled through the darkness toward the pike. Be-

22. Ibid., pp. 70–73 (first and third quotations 73, second quotation 70, fourth quotation 72).

23. Ibid., pp. 69–70 (first quotation 70, second quotation 69–70).

cause the rest of Jackson's infantry had already marched several miles up the pike, Taylor realized that his brigade and Munford's cavalry alone would have to resist the unknown numbers of Union cavalry.[24]

Taking two companies of Irishmen from the Sixth Louisiana to serve as a rear guard, Taylor marched his brigade at a rapid pace in an effort to catch up with Jackson. In a few minutes, however, a group of horsemen charged through the Louisianans' ranks, proving to be a swirling mixture of Confederate and Federal cavalrymen involved in a running skirmish. Confused by the darkness and gunfire, part of the Seventh Regiment fired on some of Munford's horsemen by mistake. The Federals, realizing their vulnerability, quickly retreated, but they soon attacked several times more, displaying a degree of fortitude none of Taylor's men had expected. "They were bold and enterprising, and well led, often charging close up to the bayonets," wrote Taylor. As usual with mounted troops, however, the Federals fired rather wildly, leaving Taylor's Irishmen with only a few minor casualties. On through the night the brigade marched. "The white of the pike alone guided us," he recalled. "Owls could not have found their way across the fields." After a few hours the enemy sent forward some artillery to harass Taylor's men. Since the Federals were firing from the hills above the pike, however, their aim was too high to inflict much damage, and the Louisianans kept up their march without halting to return the fire.[25]

"It was a fine night intirely for diversion," according to the one of the Irishmen. Although Taylor had some trouble sharing their enjoyment, he was proud of their performance. "They were as steady as clocks and chirpy as crickets, indulging in many a jest." When he suggested at one point that they might need some relief, they quickly protested, "We are the boys to see it out." Indeed, they seemed eager for more combat. When they learned from Taylor that they might confront Shields very soon, one of them remarked that Frémont's "Germans is poor creatures, but Shields's boys will be after fighting." Taylor told them he believed they could beat Shields, to which the Irishmen responded loudly, "You may bet your life on that, sar." Tay-

24. Ibid., pp. 73–74; Terry L. Jones, *Lee's Tigers*, pp. 83–84.
25. Richard Taylor, *Destruction and Reconstruction*, pp. 74–75 (quotations 75); *O.R.*, 12(1):730–31.

lor later noted, "As Argyle's to the tartan, my heart has warmed to an Irishman since that night."[26]

Just after dawn on June 2 Charles Winder brought his Stonewall Brigade back to relieve Taylor. Although exhausted, Taylor's Louisianans remained close at hand as they continued marching. But Winder's Virginians held their ground without trouble, expertly resisting several charges by Federal cavalrymen throughout the day. A Confederate private recalled, "The enterprise displayed by the cavalry of Frémont and Banks was very creditable. In the absence of these two generals their forces were more effective." In the late afternoon a heavy rain drenched the Valley, but Jackson refused to halt his jaded army. One southerner remembered that they slogged along "shoe-mouth deep in mud," that his feet were "blistered all over," and that several times he fell asleep while marching. Again, Taylor ascribed Jackson's merciless pace to his desire to protect his precious supply wagons. "In advance, his trains were left far behind," Taylor noted. "In retreat, he would fight for a wheelbarrow."[27]

Many of Jackson's men could not endure such demands. Thousands of stragglers fell prisoner or simply deserted, including scores from Taylor's own brigade. By now Jackson counted no more than twelve thousand men in his army, a force reduced by almost one-fourth from its original size. Those remaining, however, gloried in the Confederacy's outpouring of praise for their commander as a new southern hero as well as in their own popular reputation as "Jackson's Foot Cavalry," a name reflecting their unsurpassed ability to march rapidly over long distances. During one of their brief halts Jackson happened to ride from the rear of the column all along its length to the front, prompting the army to make a memorable display of affection and devotion. "As he came on the men pressed in shoals to the road and waved their hats and cheered enthusiastically," wrote a soldier. "I never saw a more thrilling scene. . . . Gen. Jackson himself seemed much affected, and as he rode on, uncovered and

26. Richard Taylor, *Destruction and Reconstruction*, pp. 75–76 (first and second quotations 75, third, fourth, and fifth quotations 76).

27. Ibid., pp. 76–78, 61 (third quotation); James Cooper Nisbet, *Four Years on the Firing Line*, p. 49 (first quotation); William Calvin Oates, *War between the Union and the Confederacy*, p. 101 (second quotation).

"A Glimpse of Stonewall Jackson." Sketch by A. C. Redwood
(*Johnson and Buell,* Battles and Leaders of the Civil War).

bowing constantly, I doubt not he esteemed it the proudest and happiest hour of his life."[28]

Fortunately for Generals Winder and Taylor, relief from rear
guard action came in the form of Turner Ashby's cavalrymen, who
easily kept the Federals under control. Marching in a pouring rain,

28. Tanner, *Stonewall in the Valley,* p. 277; Power, "'There Stands Jackson,'"
p. 73 (quotation).

Taylor's brigade crossed the bridge over the Shenandoah River's North Fork on June 3 and camped near Mount Jackson with the rest of the army. After burning the bridge, Jackson gave his men thirty-six hours of desperately needed rest, although rain continued to fall almost constantly. Realizing that Frémont would soon build a pontoon bridge and that Shields would continue marching southward up the Luray Valley to his east, Jackson had to keep his two antagonists from combining forces. Therefore he decided to continue up the Valley, march through Harrisonburg, leave the Valley pike, and head southeastward to Port Republic. There he could cross the South and North Rivers, just above the point where they combined to form the Shenandoah River's South Fork. Expecting Frémont and Shields to converge on Port Republic as well, Jackson hoped to use the swollen rivers to keep the two enemy forces apart, choosing the time and place to confront them separately. He also intended to maintain an escape route eastward across the Blue Ridge. On June 5 Jackson's army passed through Harrisonburg, stretching out so far that the supply wagons in the lead had already reached Port Republic as soldiers in the rear marched into Harrisonburg. Taylor's brigade, having rejoined Ewell's division, camped that night a few miles beyond Harrisonburg.[29]

By now torrential rains had transformed the road from Harrisonburg to Port Republic into a sea of churning mud, sinking Jackson's column into a fitful crawl. Continuing to protect the rear, General Ashby's cavalry proved its mettle throughout the day of June 6, skirmishing with enemy horsemen and infantry near Harrisonburg. Late in the afternoon several units of Federals attempted to make a serious move forward, and Ashby responded too rashly, leading a counterattack into an enemy position concealed by dense woods. Ashby's men gained the upper hand, but their brave leader fell wounded. Rising to rally his men on foot, Ashby was killed by a volley of gunfire at close range. Although Jackson had vehemently protested Ashby's promotion to brigadier general a few weeks earlier, he now admitted he had lost the best cavalry officer he had ever known. The army

29. Richard Taylor, *Destruction and Reconstruction*, pp. 77–79; Tanner, *Stonewall in the Valley*, pp. 278–79, 286–87; Chambers, *Stonewall Jackson*, 1:568–69; Hamlin, *"Old Bald Head,"* p. 100.

likewise viewed Ashby's death as a demoralizing blow, but Taylor minced no words in his appraisal of this colorful horseman. Commenting later on the lack of organization and discipline that so often negated the southern cavalryman's courage in battle, Taylor argued, "Graceful young cavaliers, with flowing locks, leaping cannon to sabre countless foes, make a captivating picture. . . . 'Tis beautiful, but 'tis not war; and grave mishaps have been occasioned by this misconception. . . . Valor is necessary . . . but disciplined, subordinated valor, admitting the courage and energies of all to be welded and directed toward a common end."[30]

During the day of June 7 Jackson moved forward to a position seven miles from Port Republic, near the hamlet of Cross Keys. After attempting unsuccessfully to lure Frémont into a fight, he then decided to divide his army, leaving Ewell's division at Cross Keys to resist Frémont. Jackson took the rest of his force, along with the supply wagons, to Port Republic in order to be in a position to confront Shields. At first Jackson viewed neither Frémont nor Shields as an immediate threat, but late that night he learned from scouts that Shields had advanced to a point only a few miles north of Port Republic. As the news circulated in the Confederate camps, Major Dabney heard men whispering, "Jackson is surrounded." Still confident that he could deal handily with both Shields and Frémont, however, Jackson informed Dabney that he expected a sermon to be delivered to the Stonewall Brigade the following morning, a Sunday. "I shall attend myself," he promised, "that is, if we are not disturbed by the enemy."[31]

Sunday, June 8, proved more disturbing than Jackson had anticipated. Early in the morning one of Shields's cavalry regiments and some artillery descended on Port Republic. If they could only destroy the bridge, they would not only be able to capture Jackson's supply wagons, which had already crossed, but they would also trap Jackson's army, still camped on the same side of the river as Frémont. Jackson immediately called up an artillery battery and ordered an infantry

30. Tanner, *Stonewall in the Valley*, pp. 279–85; Richard Taylor, *Destruction and Reconstruction*, pp. 79–81.

31. Tanner, *Stonewall in the Valley*, pp. 286–88; Dabney, "Stonewall Jackson," p. 146 (quotations).

brigade forward to meet the threat. He also dispatched a courier to Taylor at Cross Keys with instructions to bring his Louisianans at a double-quick. "Such a message from Jackson meant business," Taylor affirmed. Once again Stonewall wanted Taylor where the challenge seemed most formidable. But the Louisianans had covered more than two miles when another courier from Jackson told Taylor to halt. In about thirty minutes Jackson himself appeared and said that his artillery had effectively expelled the enemy from Port Republic. Jackson had narrowly avoided capture while riding alone with his staff through the town. The Federals, at first believing they could hold the bridge, had hastily retreated without destroying it, thus insuring Jackson free rein to fight on his own terms. He then ordered Taylor to rejoin Ewell, who had already begun skirmishing with Frémont near Cross Keys.[32]

Taylor's brigade arrived on the field at Cross Keys in the early afternoon, just after Ewell had successfully resisted several bungled attacks by Frémont. Although outnumbered by his opponent by more than two to one, Ewell told Major Dabney that "he felt all day as though he were again fighting the feeble, semi-civilized armies of Mexico." With Frémont apparently muzzled, Taylor halted and ordered his men to stack arms near Brigadier General Isaac R. Trimble's brigade. The Irishmen from the Sixth Louisiana wasted little time in pilfering personal belongings from the bodies of dead Federals. Trimble's men, not yet callous enough to participate in such scavenging, watched as one Irishmen turned over a body and quipped, "This fellow will not need his watch where he has gone, as time is nothing there, and the burial corps will soon get everything that's left."[33]

Trimble, occupying a position on Ewell's right, wanted Taylor to help him convince Ewell to pursue the enemy and deal a death blow, but Taylor declined, saying that his men needed food and rest after a morning of hard marching. Leaving Trimble to stew, Taylor took his

32. Tanner, *Stonewall in the Valley*, pp. 288–93; Richard Taylor, *Destruction and Reconstruction*, pp. 81–83 (quotation 82); Dabney, *Life of Jackson*, pp. 414–18; Stephen Davis, "A Federal Writes of Port Republic," p. 32.

33. Dabney, *Life of Jackson*, p. 418 (first quotation); James Cooper Nisbet, *Four Years on the Firing Line*, pp. 53–54 (second quotation 54).

brigade to the rear, behind the center of the Confederate position. Late in the afternoon Ewell contemplated making a move against Frémont but then changed his mind. By nightfall Trimble was still anxious, convinced that the southerners could rout if not capture Frémont's entire force. But Ewell informed him that Jackson himself would have to authorize such an offensive, so Trimble rode to Port Republic to see Jackson. There Jackson gave Trimble only tacit approval and deferred the matter to Ewell's judgment. Returning to Cross Keys, Trimble confronted Ewell and Taylor, both of whom argued against attacking in the dark. Trimble even asked for permission to use only his brigade, but Ewell replied succinctly, "You have done well enough for one day, and even a partial reverse would interfere with Jackson's plans for [tomorrow]." In his official report Trimble criticized Taylor for extreme laggardness and for infecting Ewell with the idea that attacking Frémont was not worth the effort. Taylor made only a passing reference to the controversy, writing, "We did not persist far, as Shields was near upon us."[34]

Although the great majority of Shields's twenty thousand men had not yet arrived in the immediate vicinity, Jackson clearly intended to exert his best efforts against this foe. Jackson's staff, however, assumed he would take advantage of the darkness and escape from Port Republic, thereby saving his army and his supply wagons. "But the General seemed to like traps," wrote Kyd Douglas, "and, at any rate, was not yet satisfied with the risks he had run and the blows he had inflicted." Displaying supreme confidence in his ability to manhandle both of his enemies, Jackson planned to take his army over the river, defeat Shields by 10:00 A.M. the following morning, and then recross the river and whip Frémont the same day.[35]

Jackson's audacity had never soared so high. Without even knowing Shields's true strength, he had devised a plan that would surely jeopardize his army if he failed to move his men rapidly into position to deliver Shields a decisive blow. Perhaps Jackson wanted to avenge

34. *O.R.*, 12(1):713–14, 797–98 (first quotation 798); Tanner, *Stonewall in the Valley*, pp. 293–95; Richard Taylor, *Destruction and Reconstruction*, p. 82 (second quotation).

35. Tanner, *Stonewall in the Valley*, pp. 295–98; Henry Kyd Douglas, *I Rode with Stonewall*, pp. 88–89 (quotation 89).

the humiliating defeat he had suffered at Shields's hands the previous winter at Kernstown. Perhaps he yearned for the fame that would be his by winning a brilliant double victory over both Shields and Frémont, a victory comparable in its virtuosity to that of Napoleon. Taylor in fact had begun to detect in Jackson a brooding Cromwellian temperament, a passionate inner conflict between towering pride and Christian humility. "His ambition was vast, all-absorbing," Taylor later reflected. "He loathed it, perhaps feared it; but he could not escape it—it was himself—nor rend it—it was his own flesh. He fought it with prayer, constant and earnest—Appollyon and Christian in ceaseless combat."[36]

If Jackson seemed tortured by personal vainglory—a Puritan's most deadly sin—he also managed to face fundamental demands of strategy. If he decided to desert Port Republic, first destroying the bridge, Frémont and Shields could still throw a temporary bridge across the river, combine their forces, and then be able to chase Jackson indefinitely, causing him to lose even more stragglers and deserters or even forcing him into a battle against forces several times larger than his own. Even worse, Shields might give up the chase and then march his twenty thousand men back to Fredericksburg to rejoin McDowell for the campaign against Richmond. For Jackson to fail to confront his enemies now might mean surrendering his supremacy as master of the Valley and savior of Richmond.[37]

Jackson also took some precautionary measures before fighting Shields. He wisely sent his supply wagons out of danger, east across the Blue Ridge, through Brown's Gap, a road he also viewed as an eventual escape route. In order to keep Frémont from occupying the bluffs overlooking Port Republic, a position affording an excellent artillery platform, Jackson instructed Colonel John M. Patton's and Trimble's brigades to hold Frémont in check several miles from town. Brigadier General William B. Taliaferro's brigade occupied the bluffs as an added safeguard. Jackson therefore intended to use only Winder's Stonewall Brigade and Ewell's three brigades, including Taylor's, to deal directly with Shields on the southern side of the river. Before daybreak he ordered these units to march through the town, cross

36. Richard Taylor, *Destruction and Reconstruction*, p. 91 (quotation).
37. Lang, Hennessee, and Bush, "Jackson's Valley Campaign," p. 49–51.

the bridge, and prepare to fight by early morning. From the very beginning, however, Jackson's plans soured. First the narrow bridge over the North River delayed the predawn movement, and then a makeshift footbridge Jackson had ordered hastily constructed over the smaller South River also proved extremely troublesome. The Stonewall Brigade had crossed by 5:00 A.M., but as more men tested the footbridge, the wagons and planks used in its construction gradually broke apart, leaving a single plank that allowed crossing only by single file, slowly and precariously. Major Dabney, the staff officer in charge of the footbridge, could neither figure a means to repair it nor persuade the fearful soldiers to wade into the swollen current, which normally allowed easy crossing via a shallow ford at the same location.[38]

The sun had already risen when only a fraction of the southerners had successfully crossed both rivers. Agitated and impatient at the delay, Jackson refused to wait for all of the brigades to arrive. Winder's Stonewall Brigade, arriving first with two batteries of artillery, moved directly toward the position manned by Shields's advance force of about three thousand men, mostly rugged midwesterners, commanded by Brigadier General Erastus B. Tyler. "The enemy had judiciously selected his position for defense," Jackson admitted in his official report. Looking northeast for a mile across a narrow plain of lush green wheat fields, he observed a line of Federal soldiers massed between the river on his left and a forested spur of the Blue Ridge to his right. At the edge of the spur, on a plateau that had once served as a coaling (a shallow pit used for making charcoal), sat a battery of six, long-range enemy guns already sweeping the wheat fields with blasts of deadly grapeshot. Another battery near the center of the line was also firing at a rapid clip. Throwing Winder forward directly into the maelstrom, Jackson also sent two Virginia regiments to the right through heavy thickets on a mission to execute a surprise flank attack on the battery atop the coaling. The Union infantry, despite its limited strength, started a slow advance while its artillery effectively bullied Winder into a virtual halt. The Confederate gunners tried to retaliate but soon began to run out of ammunition and had to wait for

38. Tanner, *Stonewall in the Valley*, pp. 297–99; Dabney, *Life of Jackson*, p. 421.

more to arrive from ordnance wagons far in the rear. "The air was full of screaming fragments of exploding shell," wrote an artilleryman, "and I thought I was a goner."[39]

Meanwhile, Taylor's brigade, the leading element in Ewell's division, had not yet appeared on the field. Still without any specific orders from any of Jackson's staff, Taylor had allowed his men to camp and begin making breakfast after struggling across the footbridge at Port Republic. Hearing an increasingly steady eruption of cannon fire in the distance, he ordered the brigade to form ranks and march at once. Taylor then galloped ahead about a mile in search of Jackson. When he reached the battlefield, Taylor witnessed the stunning spectacle of the enemy's artillery working in tandem with the oncoming blue-clad infantry. "Federal lines, their right touching the river, were advancing steadily, with banners flying and arms gleaming in the sun." Winder's brigade bravely attempted to stand its ground. "This small force was suffering cruelly, and its skirmishers were driven in on their supporting line," Taylor observed.[40]

A Union officer later reported, "The enemy contested nearly every inch of ground, but we drove his superior force for nearly half a mile, and continued to drive him. . . . The loss of the enemy was greater than ours, for grape and canister were poured into them with terrible effect, and the ground was strewn with their dead." Kyd Douglas knew this encounter would prove to be Jackson's most severe trial. "For the first time in my life," he wrote, "I saw a regiment, from Ohio I believe, change front to rear on first company, under fire, and with admirable precision. I knew then that it would be no easy matter to defeat such troops. . . . Jackson found that he had met men of like mettle to his own." A Confederate artilleryman felt the sting of both fear and envy, recalling succinctly, "More accurate shooting I was never subjected to."[41]

39. *O.R.*, 12(1):714 (first quotation), 728, 802; Dabney, *Life of Jackson*, p. 422; Tanner, *Stonewall in the Valley*, pp. 298–302; Neese, *Three Years in the Confederate Horse Artillery*, p. 74 (second quotation).

40. Richard Taylor, *Destruction and Reconstruction*, p. 83 (quotations).

41. *O.R.*, 12(1):700 (first quotation); Henry Kyd Douglas, *I Rode with Stonewall*, pp. 89–90 (second quotation); Edward A. Moore, *Cannoneer under Jackson*, p. 75 (third quotation).

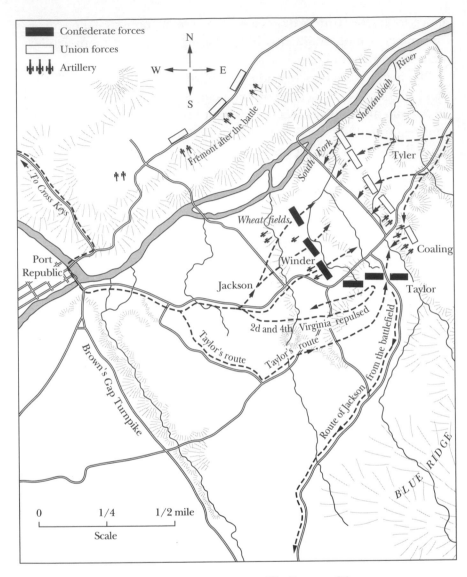

Map 3. *Battle of Port Republic, June 9, 1862*

Taylor located Jackson near the front, watching the action in a prayerlike trance. Seeing Taylor ride up, Jackson remarked in his usual staid manner, "Delightful excitement." If this seemed like an uncharacteristic attempt at ironic humor on Jackson's part, Taylor took the bait, answering that "it was pleasant to learn that he was enjoying himself, but thought he might have an indigestion of such fun if the six-gun battery [on the coaling] was not silenced." Jackson said nothing except to turn to an officer nearby, Lieutenant Robert M. English, instructing him to serve as Taylor's guide for a crucial flanking movement up the wooded hillside to the right in order to emerge undetected and assault the battery. Jackson had planned for Taylor to accomplish this movement much earlier in the morning, but because the Louisiana Brigade took so long to cross the footbridge, Jackson had sent two Virginia regiments on the mission; but they had failed badly, turning back in the face of the battery's heavy shelling. With Winder's men now suffering terribly, Taylor's responsibility loomed as absolutely vital. As a final requirement, however, Jackson ordered Taylor to leave Harry Hays's Seventh Louisiana at Winder's disposal. Unfortunately, Taylor expected to have Hays's men returned to him once he reached a position with the rest of the brigade to attack the enemy battery on the coaling.[42]

Jackson's apparent humor and composure had only masked his anger at having been forced to wait for Taylor's arrival. He had already sent at least three messengers back to the Louisiana Brigade in a frenetic effort to hurry it forward to the front. Because Taylor had remained at the rear of his brigade as it crossed the footbridge, Jackson's pleadings had fallen upon Colonel Henry Kelly, commander of the Eighth Louisiana, the first regiment to cross the river. Kelly therefore brought the brigade forward and pushed it up into the woods without Taylor present. Once Taylor received his orders he hurried back to the rear to make sure all of his brigade was moving. Only a few minutes later Jedediah Hotchkiss, Jackson's mapmaker, who supposedly had accurate knowledge of the area, appeared on the scene. Jackson immediately pointed toward the enemy battery and repeated

42. Richard Taylor, *Destruction and Reconstruction*, p. 84 (quotations); *O.R.*, 12(1):719, 728, 801–2; Imboden, "Stonewall Jackson in the Shenandoah," pp. 293–98.

the orders he had given to Taylor's guide, Lieutenant English, instructing Hotchkiss, "Take General Taylor around and take those batteries." Hotchkiss found the Louisianans and tried to lead them as best he could, although he apparently never saw either Taylor or Kelly. Without help from any guide, Kelly moved the Louisianans forward through the thick woods, ordering them into line of battle, with skirmishers in front, expecting to encounter Federal infantry at any moment. The woods hid the brigade from the enemy's view, but the undergrowth of thickets made for slow going, and Kelly had to rely on the sound of the battery on the coaling to guide his movement forward. Meanwhile Taylor brought up the rear, prodding the Sixth Regiment, whose tardiness had resulted from the bottleneck at the footbridge. With help from his guide, Lieutenant English, Taylor led the Sixth farther to the right along a road that provided a fairly easy route toward the battery. In this confused and time-consuming manner Taylor's brigade executed its crucial flanking movement.[43]

43. The surviving evidence regarding Taylor's flanking movement is complex and often contradictory. In his published memoirs Taylor stated that, after receiving Jackson's orders, he met his brigade as it approached and that he led it, guided by Lieutenant English, up into the woods along a narrow path, moving rapidly toward the battery. Richard Taylor, *Destruction and Reconstruction*, p. 84. But in his official report, written a few days after the battle, Taylor stated that the movement was slow because of the thickly wooded terrain on the hillside. He was not clear about exactly how he received Jackson's orders, whether directly from Jackson or someone else, and he did not mention having the advantage of a guide. *O.R.*, 12(1):802. Jedediah Hotchkiss, writing more than thirty years later in a letter to Major Robert Dabney, criticized Taylor's memoirs by asserting that Taylor never saw Jackson, that Taylor received Jackson's orders through Hotchkiss, and that Hotchkiss met Taylor as he approached with his brigade, leading Taylor up into the woods himself. Jedediah Hotchkiss to Robert L. Dabney, August 4, 1897, Hotchkiss Papers. But in his private journal, written on the day of the battle, Hotchkiss mentioned only that he received Jackson's orders just as Taylor's brigade was arriving, that he met the brigade (not Taylor), and that he led it up into the woods, where it formed in line of battle with skirmishers in front, expecting to meet enemy resistance as it moved forward through the woods. Neither in his letter nor in his diary did Hotchkiss mention following a path or road. McDonald, *Make Me a Map of the Valley*, p. 55 (quotation). Hotchkiss did not

For more than an hour the Louisianans under Kelly hacked and tripped their way through the thickets, fortunately meeting no enemy resistance. "The advance was continued along the crest of the hills for about three-quarters of a mile, while the battle was raging in the open fields between the hills and the river," Kelly recalled. At the very moment that Kelly finally sighted the Federal battery on the coaling, Taylor came galloping up with the Sixth and immediately gave orders for the brigade to deploy under cover of the woods for an attack. "The sounds of the battle to our rear appeared to recede," Taylor recounted, "and a loud Federal cheer was heard, proving Jackson to be hard pressed." Down in the wheat fields Jackson had become worse than "hard pressed," having thrown Hays's Seventh Louisiana in with Winder's Stonewall Brigade to make a valiant charge that had merely stalled the enemy advance for a short time. For Jackson's Virginians the situation began to evoke memories of the awful rout they had suffered at Kernstown. Although Taylor had not fully completed his deployment, he realized he could wait no longer. "It was rather an anxious moment, demanding instant action," he recalled.[44]

---

issue an official report, but a topographical engineer under his supervision reported that Hotchkiss guided Taylor's brigade through the woods. *O.R.*, 12(1):719. Colonel Kelly, in a book written almost twenty-five years after the battle, criticized Taylor severely by asserting that he (Kelly) received orders from Dabney as well as from Major Rob Wheat, who apparently had gone forward to find Jackson, and that he (Kelly) personally guided the brigade, except for the tardy Sixth Regiment, through the woods without the help of a guide. Kelly also said that Taylor brought up the rear with the Sixth, having come guided by Hotchkiss along a road, and that he (Kelly) saw Taylor come up just as the brigade had gained a position to make the charge against the battery. Taylor then took command of the brigade and led the charge himself. Kelly apparently bore a grudge against Taylor for his failure to praise, either in his official report or in his memoirs, Kelly's arduous service in leading the vanguard of the brigade through the woods. Kelly, *Port Republic*, pp. 15–18. See also Lyman, "Cross Keys and Port Republic," typescript, which is generally supportive of Kelly and critical of Taylor.

44. Kelly, *Port Republic*, pp. 17–18 (first quotation); Richard Taylor, *Destruction and Reconstruction*, p. 84 (second and third quotations); Terry L. Jones, *Lee's Tigers*, pp. 87–88; Tanner, *Stonewall in the Valley*, pp. 302–4.

A deep, wooded ravine separated the Louisianans from the battery on the coaling a few hundred yards in the distance. Enemy infantry stood in support nearby, and a contingent of skirmishers lay hidden up on the wooded slope to Taylor's right. With the element of surprise in his favor, Taylor ordered his brigade to charge the battery. A Union artillery officer on the coaling recalled, "The thick undergrowth prevented our seeing [the Confederates] until they were quite near us." Federal infantry hurried into position and opened fire, and the battery's gunners wheeled their pieces around, frantically trying to measure an accurate range. Down in the wheat fields, soldiers on both sides fixed upon this sudden interruption in shelling from the coaling. "I saw General Dick Taylor's Louisianans debouching from the undergrowth," recalled a southerner, "and like a wave crested with shining steel rush toward the fatal coaling and deadly battery with fixed bayonets, giving the Rebel yell like mad demons." Down into the ravine and up toward the coaling they charged. Kelly's Eighth Louisiana reached the battery first, and the others rushed in behind, driving off the Federal gunners. "By the impetus of the charge over the rough ground all formation was lost," wrote Kelly, "and officers and men were all thrown into one unorganized mass around the captured guns."[45]

In the swirling smoke atop the coaling the Louisianans cheered and celebrated, climbing all over the guns and dancing in delight at their triumph. But the glory of apparent victory exploded with a barrage of artillery shells that suddenly came screaming in from the other enemy battery now repositioned only a few hundred yards away, near the center of the original Federal line. Several enemy regiments that had been advancing against Jackson in the wheat fields also shifted rapidly to their left and rear and provided reinforcements to the troops driven from the coaling. This clearly took the pressure off Jackson but only heaped all the more upon Taylor. Within a few minutes Yankees "swarmed like so many hornets . . . about the lost battery," recalled Kelly. Lieutenant Colonel William R.

45. Terry L. Jones, *Lee's Tigers*, p. 88; Richard Taylor, *Destruction and Reconstruction*, p. 85; *O.R.*, 12(1):693 (first quotation); Neese, *Three Years in the Confederate Horse Artillery*, pp. 74–75 (second quotation 74); Kelly, *Port Republic*, p. 19 (third quotation).

Peck of the Ninth Louisiana remained cool, however, shouting orders to kill the battery's horses so the Yankees would not be able to carry away the guns. Soldiers turned their rifles upon the helpless beasts, shooting dozens of them. Rob Wheat unsheathed his long Bowie knife and slashed several horses' throats. "It was a sickening sight," wrote a Confederate. "Major Wheat was as bloody as a butcher."[46]

Around the batteries the combatants clashed in hundreds of hand-to-hand death struggles. "Many fell from bayonet wounds," wrote Taylor. "'Twas claw for claw." One southerner observed in near disbelief, "Panting like dogs—nine tenths of them bareheaded . . . men beat each other's brains out with muskets which they have no time to reload." Another remembered seeing dead and wounded "men in gray and those in blue piled up in front and around the guns and with the horses dying and the blood of men and beasts flowing almost in a stream." For a few minutes the Louisianans lost possession of the battery and reeled backward down into the ravine. But they quickly rallied and reformed to mount another charge. Soon they held the battery again, but under a terrific storm of bullets they retreated, only to surge forward yet another time. Finally, Taylor's men began to buckle under the sheer strength of Federal numbers concentrated on the coaling. Attempting to stand defiantly, his officers yelled out orders to the men, but in the noise of battle few soldiers heard or even hoped to obey. "It was impossible to reform or organize them or to hold the ground they occupied," wrote Kelly, "and they fell away to the wooded hillsides of the vicinity."[47]

Kelly noticed Taylor and a few other officers in the woods with small groups of soldiers searching for a safe haven, completely disorganized and jumbled except for a partial line of men from the Sixth Louisiana that had somehow managed to stay together. "None of the other regimental colors were there," Kelly recalled, "men and officers of the brigade being dispersed, in irregular bodies, on the hillsides

46. Terry L. Jones, *Lee's Tigers*, pp. 88–89; Kelly, *Port Republic*, pp. 19–20 (first quotation 20); Buck, *With the Old Confeds*, p. 38 (second quotation).

47. Richard Taylor, *Destruction and Reconstruction*, p. 85 (first quotation); Alison Moore, *He Died Furious*, p. 161 (second quotation); Buck, *With the Old Confeds*, p. 38 (third quotation); *O.R.*, 12(1):802–3; Kelly, *Port Republic*, p. 20 (fourth quotation).

along the road, and on both sides of the ravine." Then the battery on
the coaling unleashed a torrent of canister into the woods, but Taylor's men remained defiant, responding stubbornly, if fitfully, with
musket fire. After about fifteen minutes they saw several Federal regiments forming their lines for a concerted attack. "There seemed
nothing left but to set our backs to the mountain and die hard," wrote
Taylor.[48]

What Taylor described as "a solid wall" of bluecoats then marched
briskly toward the Louisianans. At this very moment a solitary, familiar figure, Dick Ewell, enthusiastic beyond all reason, came galloping
up from the wheat fields, slashing his way through the underbrush
into open view with a wildly quixotic look to him. Taylor's men
cheered heartily at seeing this lone reinforcement, and in another
moment a pair of Ewell's Virginia regiments, the Forty-fourth and
Fifty-eighth, appeared on his heels, inspiring the Louisianans to
throw themselves into an assault against the advancing Federal infantry. A shell exploded beneath Ewell's horse, killing the animal but
leaving the rider unshaken, his eyes still fixed upon the battery. Now
running on foot, Ewell urged the Louisianans and Virginians forward by waving his kepi in the air.[49]

The Federal infantry, bracing itself for a fight, halted and sent skirmishers forward to test this unwarranted display of southern inso-
lence. Suddenly a shell from a distant Confederate artillery piece
screamed across the Yankee line and exploded. From the wheat fields
came more reinforcements—the survivors from the Stonewall Brigade and Hays's Seventh Louisiana, surging up the hill. Several other
Virginia regiments, stymied for so long by the footbridge at Port Republic, also lent support. All at once Jackson was finally able to assert
his numerical superiority against the three thousand Federals. "Loud
Confederate cheers reached our delighted ears, and Jackson, freed
from his toils, rushed up like a whirlwind," wrote Taylor. The Yankees
blanched and stiffened at the sight, fired a hurried, poorly aimed vol-

48. Kelly, *Port Republic*, pp. 20–21 (first quotation 20); Richard Taylor, *Destruction and Reconstruction*, p. 85 (second quotation).

49. Richard Taylor, *Destruction and Reconstruction*, pp. 85–86 (quotation
85); *O.R.*, 12(1):786; Hamlin, *"Old Bald Head,"* p. 104; Kelly, *Port Republic*,
p. 22.

ley, and began a wholesale retreat. Because Taylor's men had already killed the battery's horses, Federal soldiers managed to save only one gun by dragging it off the field by hand. "We turned the captured guns on them as they passed, Ewell serving as a gunner." Searching for a horse, Ewell spied a stout-looking steed bridled to a supply wagon, mounted it bareback, and led the pursuit of the beaten foe for several miles before encountering organized rear guard resistance.[50]

Atop the coaling Taylor and his men gloried in their victory. "Jackson came up, with intense light in his eyes, grasped my hand, and said the brigade should have the captured battery," wrote Taylor. "I thought the men would go mad with cheering, especially the Irishmen." One of them, sitting proudly astride a cannon barrel, his whiskers burned with gunpowder and one eye swollen shut, bellowed to Taylor, "We told you to bet on your boys." More than any other soldiers in his brigade, these New Orleans Irishmen of Isaac Seymour's Sixth Louisiana had indeed become Taylor's "boys." They had joined him for a wild and jovial night of action during the retreat up the Valley pike; here at Port Republic they had received his personal guidance during the flanking movement so that he would be certain to have them when he attacked the battery; and they suffered the most casualties in his brigade, eleven dead and fifty-five wounded. In his memoirs Taylor described them with admiration and affection. Yet his deeply aristocratic streak of Anglo-American chauvinism also tinged his memory of them, prompting him to wonder about their ethnic character: "Strange people, these Irish! Fighting every one's battles, and cheerfully taking the hot end of the poker, they are only found wanting when engaged in what they believe to be their national cause." The fact that they had become southerners fighting against northern Irishmen and other immigrant citizens never impressed him as much as their seemingly peculiar traits.[51]

Combatants on both sides at Port Republic gave Taylor complete

50. Richard Taylor, *Destruction and Reconstruction*, pp. 85–86 (first quotation 85, second quotation 86); *O.R.*, 12(1):786; Tanner, *Stonewall in the Valley*, pp. 305–6; Hamlin, *"Old Bald Head,"* p. 104.

51. Richard Taylor, *Destruction and Reconstruction*, p. 86 (quotations); *O.R.*, 12(1):787.

credit for the final triumph. "The hero par excellence of this bloody little battle was Dick Taylor," wrote a Confederate from Georgia. In his official report Jackson lauded the tactical effect of Taylor's charge on the enemy battery: "While Winder was in . . . critical condition [in the wheat fields] the gallant and successful charge of General Taylor on the Federal left and rear diverted [the enemy's] attention from the front, and led to a concentration of their force upon him." Likewise, a Federal officer reported that when his commander, Brigadier General Tyler, "saw the disaster that had befallen his left [where Taylor charged the battery], he at once hurried his infantry in that direction to regain the road that was our only line of retreat." Colonel Henry Kelly of Taylor's brigade underscored this fact, asserting proudly, "From the first instant the batteries were first taken by the Louisiana infantry . . . what, up to that moment, was a disastrous defeat to Confederate arms, was changed to certain victory." Thus did Taylor's initial charge allow the rest of Jackson's army to take the offensive with superior numbers and finally overpower Tyler's forces. By killing the artillery horses, Taylor's men also insured that the battery would be theirs. General Tyler himself admitted regretfully, "The loss of our artillery we feel almost as keenly as we should to have lost our colors, yet it was impossible to save them without horses."[52]

Dick Ewell's report on Port Republic added immeasurable luster to Taylor's laurels. "To General Taylor and his brigade belongs the honor of deciding two battles, that of Winchester and this one," wrote Ewell. Jackson's complete reliance upon the Louisianans to set the army's rapid marching pace and then to spearhead the most critical fighting had culminated spectacularly at Port Republic. Taylor not only saved Jackson's reputation, but he also saved the Army of the Valley from horrendous casualties, perhaps even a total rout, a blow the South could not afford either psychologically or materially. Jackson's gratitude far exceeded his act of awarding the Louisianans the captured battery. Although he routinely rendered to God the credit for his victories, he compared Taylor's feat to an outright miracle.

52. James Cooper Nisbet, *Four Years on the Firing Line*, p. 58 (first quotation); *O.R.*, 12(1):715 (second quotation), 697 (fifth quotation); Huntington, "Operations in the Shenandoah Valley," p. 28 (third quotation); Kelly, *Port Republic*, p. 21 (fourth quotation).

Locating Ewell after the battle, Stonewall proclaimed passionately, "General, he who does not see the hand of God in this is blind, sir, blind!"[53]

Considering how carelessly he had handled his army at Port Republic, Jackson had every reason to thank the Almighty for sending Taylor to his rescue. "The fact is, Jackson went into the fight impetuously and was disappointed," wrote his discerning aide Kyd Douglas. "Had he waited to get his troops up and into formation, his victory would have been easier and his loss less." Having no clear knowledge of Shields's full strength, Jackson had expected to crush him and then turn back on Frémont by mid-morning, an imposing schedule soon aborted when he started throwing his regiments piecemeal against an imposing enemy position. By squandering his two-to-one advantage against Shields's advance force of three thousand under Tyler, Jackson displayed a rigid puritan will that showed no mercy for his dying soldiers. Taylor understated the situation when he later observed, "Had Shields himself with his whole command been on the field, we should have had tough work indeed."[54]

Fortunately also for Jackson, the hand of God received help from the hand of Yankee incompetence. According to General Tyler's subordinate officers, their leader committed a series of mistakes that led directly to defeat. Early in the battle, infantry commander Colonel Samuel S. Carroll and artillery commander Colonel Philip Daum urged Tyler to provide strong infantry support for the artillery on the coaling. "I impressed upon him the need of sustaining the batteries upon our left," wrote Carroll. When Jackson first sent the two Virginia regiments on their unsuccessful flanking movement through the woods toward the coaling, Colonel Daum became extremely concerned. "I now demanded of Gen. Tyler to push forward some more infantry into the woods to the left of the guns, whereupon he rebuked me for asking or suggesting to him," wrote Daum. Instead of strengthening support of the battery, however, Tyler ordered two

53. *O.R.*, 12(1):786 (first quotation); Tanner, *Stonewall in the Valley*, p. 308; Henry Kyd Douglas, *I Rode with Stonewall*, p. 91 (second quotation).

54. Tanner, *Stonewall in the Valley*, p. 308; Henry Kyd Douglas, *I Rode with Stonewall*, p. 90 (first quotation); Richard Taylor, *Destruction and Reconstruction*, p. 86 (second quotation).

nearby regiments, the 84th and the 110th Pennsylvania, to join the
main advance against Jackson's force in the wheat fields. This left only
one regiment and two companies to protect the guns. When Tyler saw
the Confederates begin to collapse in the wheat fields, he did send the
84th and 110th back toward the coaling, but, as Colonel Daum reported, "they were placed [by Tyler] in the wrong direction," thereby
preventing them from reacting in time to Taylor's attack on the battery. Tyler, however, considered Taylor's success unavoidable. "So
rapid was this movement [by Taylor's men]," asserted Tyler, "that they
passed the line on which the 84th and 110th Penn. were ordered
unobserved, making a dash upon the battery so sudden and unexpected as to compel the cannoneers to abandon their pieces." This
forced Tyler to order two more regiments away from the wheat fields
to resist Taylor, thus insuring Jackson's ability to rally his superior
forces and claim the victory.[55]

When General Shields learned the details of the battle, he erupted
in anger over Tyler's mishandling of the troops entrusted to him. Tyler's men "were compelled to abandon the field . . . by a fatal mistake
of General Tyler's in stripping the left flank of all infantry support,"
reported Shields. Furthermore, he insisted, Tyler should never have
fought Jackson at all. "The advance [under Tyler], instead of falling
back upon the main body [of Shields's division] as it should have
done, gave battle and was repulsed." Colonel Carroll had even argued
for a withdrawal prior to the battle, but Tyler refused. Another Federal officer later reflected, "Our position was by no means indefensible, had we been strong enough to occupy it properly, or as we might
have done had the whole division been present. . . . There was, probably, not a man who stood in our thin battle-line at Port Republic who
did not know that our defeat was only a question of time. There was
a grim determination [however] to make that time as long as possible." Given the distress of Jackson's men in the wheat fields, the Federals still could have pushed hard enough and held on long enough
to win. Had Taylor's brigade remained entangled in the woods much
longer or had he emerged at a point too far from the battery to make
an effective assault, Jackson would have had little hope of stemming

55. *O.R.*, 12(1):699 (first quotation), 692 (second and third quotations),
697 (fourth quotation).

the enemy tide. Regardless, had Tyler protected the battery properly, Taylor would have encountered a force that even men like Wheat's Tigers and Seymour's Irishmen could not have overpowered. As it turned out, Tyler's blunders exceeded Jackson's blunders by only the slimmest margin, barely enough to give the Confederates a victory.[56]

Years later many of Jackson's men continued to believe they had defeated Shields's entire force, Taylor being one of the few exceptions. A Federal officer wrote, "I have talked with a number of Confederate officers who were at this battle, and all insisted that Shields's whole division was present." This impression doubtless persisted because of the inordinate number of casualties. "This was one of the severest battles of the war," recalled a southerner. "I never saw more stubborn fighting or more killed in the same length of time where only small forces on either side could be brought into action." Confederate killed and wounded amounted to more than 800, compared to about 500 Federals, although Jackson did take 450 prisoners. General Tyler reported, "The loss of the enemy must have been very heavy. . . . [We] mowed them down like grass before a well-served scythe." Harry Hays's Seventh Louisiana, detached by Jackson to help Winder's Virginians in the wheat fields, suffered more casualties than any other regiment, a total of 8 killed and 110 wounded. Hays himself received a serious wound that incapacitated him for several months. Colonel Carroll, the Federal officer, made special reference to the Seventh's sacrifice, reporting, "A Louisiana regiment on our right was almost annihilated."[57]

After Port Republic Taylor's men took singular pride in the fact that Jackson now called them his Iron Brigade. With a total of 288 casualties, the most of any brigade, the Louisianans had endured a tremendous shock. "Though it had suffered heavy loss in officers and men, [the brigade] was yet strong, hard as nails and full of confidence," Taylor recalled. This did not make the awful aftermath of

56. Ibid., pp. 685 (first and second quotations), 699; Huntington, "Operations in the Shenandoah Valley," pp. 24–29 (third quotation 24, 29).

57. Huntington, "Operations in the Shenandoah Valley," p. 29 (first quotation); Buck, *With the Old Confeds*, p. 39 (second quotation); Tanner, *Stonewall in the Valley*, pp. 306–7; *O.R.*, 12(1):698 (third quotation), 700 (fourth quotation).

battle any easier to bear. Describing the area around the coaling where so much savage fighting had occurred, Taylor wrote, "I have never seen so many dead and wounded in the same limited space." Among those killed lay Lieutenant Robert M. English, the young Virginian who had served as Taylor's guide. Rather than turning back, he had joined the Louisianans in charging the coaling. With the rest of the survivors, Taylor spent the afternoon and early evening tending to the wounded. "[I] performed the last offices to the dead, our own and the Federal," he recounted. For a short time the punchless, almost forgotten General Frémont made his presence known by lobbing shells onto the battlefield from the far side of the river. David Boyd noted that the Federal guns "seemed to play generally on the Port Republic field, hurting his Union friends about as much as he did us." Soon realizing the absurdity of firing on wounded soldiers and burial parties, Frémont retired in frustration. The Confederates continued their somber task in silence. Taylor later recalled that he "lunched comfortably" from the haversack of a dead Yankee soldier. "It is not pleasant to think of now," he confessed, "but war *is* a little hardening."[58]

Conquered without bringing even one-quarter of his forces into the fight against Jackson, Shields could not restrain his indignation. "This man [Jackson], who dared to insult our capital . . . who fell back in haste before my whole division, not deeming himself safe until he put five miles between us, is left to escape," Shields howled in his official report. "The plan for Jackson's destruction was perfect," he insisted. "This division has not been defeated." For several days preceding the battle, however, Shields's entire command had been operating under torturous conditions. Forced to slog their way through the muddy Luray Valley while Jackson's army raced along the macadamized Valley pike, the Federals had almost broken down under the strain. "About half my command are barefoot and foot-sore," admitted Shields. When his demoralized soldiers retreated northward through Front Royal a few days after the battle, citizens witnessed a

58. Terry L. Jones, *Lee's Tigers*, p. 92 (first quotation); *O.R.*, 12(1):787, 745; Richard Taylor, *Destruction and Reconstruction*, pp. 86–88 (second quotation 88, third and fourth quotations 86, sixth quotation 87); Boyd, *Reminiscences of the War*, p. 14 (fifth quotation).

stream of Yankees "worn out, ragged, and half starved." Colonel Carroll told one of the townspeople, "Old Jackson gave us hell." Fortunately for the Confederates, the Luray Valley's wretched marching terrain had given Shields's men more hell than even Stonewall Jackson could have mustered. Through a combination of cunning and luck, Jackson had made the Shenandoah and Luray valleys his own. Not only had he used their physical features—their mountains, rivers, and mud—to thwart his enemies, but he had also used his brilliant skills of deception, speed, and relentless, often reckless determination to intimidate each Union commander he faced.[59]

Having made a habit of circulating exaggerated accounts of his army's strength for the benefit of enemy intelligence, for the next few weeks Jackson enjoyed the luxury of outrageous rumors about an influx of southern reinforcements giving him as many as eighty thousand men. Without even moving, Jackson's forces seemed to be everywhere at once in overwhelming numbers, marching rapidly and descending on Federal positions up and down the Valley. For several days he remained poised to return to the Valley if necessary, but with such rumors working to his advantage, he finally found time to rest his battered army. The Confederate strategy of using Jackson to distract the Federal hordes and thereby relieve Richmond had succeeded beyond all expectations. By dispersing his limited forces along interior lines, Robert E. Lee had compelled the Federals to disperse their own forces, a classic Napoleonic maneuver. By doing so, he had freed Jackson to strike with superior numbers against scattered and inferior enemy troops under poor leadership. Now Lee turned his full attention to McClellan, betting that the same tactics would work on the Peninsula and that McClellan's leadership would prove just as deficient, perhaps even worse.[60]

59. *O.R.*, 12(1):685 (first and second quotations), 683 (third quotation); Ashby, *Valley Campaigns*, p. 137 (fourth quotation).

60. Tanner, *Stonewall in the Valley*, pp. 326–28; Connelly and Jones, *Politics of Command*, pp. 174–75; Hattaway and Jones, *How the North Won*, pp. 176–77.

CHAPTER SIX

Spectator on the Peninsula

The success with which he has managed his Brigade . . .

makes it my duty as well as my pleasure to

recommend him for promotion.

Stonewall Jackson

During the evening of June 9, after burying the dead at Port Republic, Jackson moved his army several miles to the southeast, up into the
Blue Ridge toward Brown's Gap, where the men would find a safe
encampment. Riding at the head of his brigade as it trudged up the
foothills, Taylor noticed immediately ahead a Virginia artilleryman
riding on a caisson to avoid marching, an act in direct violation to an
order Jackson had recently issued. Taylor rode up and reprimanded
the offender, a private named Walter Packard, and ordered him to
get down at once. Highly pugnacious, with an irritating habit of engaging all comers in verbal jousting, Packard turned around and retorted, "Who are you and what the devil do you have to do with my
riding on a caisson?" Another soldier nearby recalled that "Taylor
seemed astounded for a moment and then opened on poor Walter
with a volley of oaths that our champion swearer, Irish Emmett,
would have envied." Impressed neither by Taylor's rank nor by his
cursing, Packard replied blithely, "Excuse me, General. I have my

Captain's permission to ride." Either too tired or too amazed to deal with such perverse impudence, Taylor turned and rode back to his brigade.[1]

Taylor's aggravations only continued when the army stopped for the night. A cold, steady rain began to fall as he rode forward in search of his brigade's supply wagons so that his hungry men could at least have some food before retiring. Near the top of the mountain, at the head of the long single file of wagons parked along the entire length of the winding road, Taylor finally located his supplies. "I rather took it out of the train-master for pushing so far up," he recounted. Later, after a wet and miserable meal, his troubles took an even more exasperating turn. Forced to find comfort on the steep mountainside, soldiers climbed under wagons, huddled in rock crevices, straddled tree trunks, and propped themselves up against outcroppings while the rain poured and water flowed in streams down the slopes. But the Louisiana Brigade's feisty commander refused to accept such conditions gracefully. "When Taylor saw his 'camp' he made things 'blue' around him," recalled David Boyd. "The rest of us were more resigned[,] . . . but our General only got the madder and 'cussed' the louder." Tom Strother dutifully prepared his master a bed by piling up some leaves and spreading blankets on top, and Taylor surrendered to exhaustion, quickly falling asleep despite the rain and the thirty-degree angle of repose.[2]

Before long, Boyd awoke to the sound of "Taylor's deep voice calling loudly above the storm for Major T. R. Heard, the quartermaster. Taylor in his sleep had turned in his steep bed, and he, bed and all were sliding down the mountain!" Upon Heard's approach, Taylor unleashed his full wrath, demanding to know "why he had chosen such a damned camp for him!" Heard explained that no other site was available, but this "only made Taylor swear the more and the louder." In a few minutes the whole camp was stirring, the men laughing and joking at "the wordy duel 'twixt General and quartermaster." Too weary to join in the fun, Boyd fell back into a deep slum-

1. Edward A. Moore, *Cannoneer under Jackson*, p. 80 (quotations).
2. Richard Taylor, *Destruction and Reconstruction*, p. 87 (first quotation); Buck, *With the Old Confeds*, p. 39; Boyd, *Reminiscences of the War*, pp. 14–15 (second quotation 15).

David French Boyd, perceptive commissary officer of the Louisiana Brigade
(Louisiana State University).

ber. About daybreak he heard Taylor calling his name. "What now?" Boyd wondered. "Had he tired of Heard and wanted a fresh victim? No, he was as gentle as a lamb. . . . Taylor was happy again, and all the more pleasant and agreeable to everyone, as was his custom after explosions of temper, for his ugly mood and fretfulness the night before." He politely asked Boyd to go to Jackson's headquarters, farther down the mountainside, and simply ask permission to find a more suitable campsite. This Boyd did, and Jackson granted the request.³

Two days later, on June 12, Jackson led his army back down into the Valley, several miles southwest of Port Republic. "We were encamped near Weyer's Cave," remembered a Louisianan, "where we enjoyed the luxuries of a good bath, an abundance of food, clean clothes, and the rest which we all so much needed." During the respite Taylor gained deeper insight into Jackson's character in a series of encounters involving Brigadier General Charles Winder of the Stonewall Brigade. Winder surprised Taylor one day by telling him that he had resigned from the army because Jackson had declined to grant him a brief furlough to resolve some pressing personal affairs in Richmond. Furthermore, for several weeks Jackson had been undermining Winder's authority in the management of his old brigade. This represented only the latest in a series of personal clashes between Jackson and several of his subordinate officers. Taylor recalled, "Holding Winder in high esteem, I hoped to save him to the army, and went to Jackson, to whose magnanimity I appealed." Instead of emphasizing Winder's merits, however, Taylor "dwelt on the rich harvest of glory [Jackson] had reaped in his brilliant campaign." Jackson listened intently. "Observing him closely, I caught a glimpse of the man's inner nature," wrote Taylor. "It was but a glimpse. The curtain closed, and he was absorbed in prayer. Yet in that moment I saw an ambition boundless as Cromwell's, and as merciless."⁴

Jackson sat without speaking, and Taylor, believing he had failed in

3. Boyd, *Reminiscences of the War*, pp. 15–16 (first quotation 15, second, third, fourth, and fifth quotations 16).

4. Cummer, *Yankee in Gray*, p. 43 (first quotation); Tanner, *Stonewall in the Valley*, p. 309; Richard Taylor, *Destruction and Reconstruction*, p. 89 (second, third, and fourth quotations).

his mission, rose to leave. Then Jackson stood up and said he would ride with Taylor back to his camp. As they rode, Jackson remained utterly silent, and reaching Taylor's camp, he merely turned and departed. That evening Taylor received a note from Winder saying that Jackson had persuaded him to withdraw his resignation. Taylor had succeeded with Jackson, he believed, only by having gently exposed the solitary Stonewall's explosive ambition and prideful intolerance, thereby prodding him to succumb to his equally formidable Christian scruples. Taylor had finally come to know and understand the inner man, perhaps as well as anyone could.[5]

Jackson's ambition and pride had indeed risen to stratospheric heights. Fortified by popular praise comparing his Valley Campaign to legendary triumphs of military geniuses such as Napoleon and Julius Caesar, he sent a request to Jefferson Davis and Robert E. Lee for reinforcements amounting to forty thousand men to march into Pennsylvania. Davis and Lee flirted with the idea for several days but finally decided that such massive numbers of troops could not be stripped from Richmond's defenses. "I think the sooner Jackson can move this way the better," Lee informed Davis. "The object now is to defeat McClellan. The enemy in the Valley seems at a pause." In order to save Richmond and ultimately win the war, Lee meant to crush the Army of the Potomac rather than simply transfer the major theater of action to Pennsylvania. With so many Federals still distracted by Jackson's phantom movements in the Valley, McClellan seemed temporarily vulnerable. He had also taken up positions outside Richmond precarious enough that Lee perceived an opportunity to deliver the timid Yankee commander a fatal stroke. Davis agreed, and on June 16 Lee ordered Jackson to prepare to join the fight against McClellan.[6]

The next day Jackson's men started for Richmond, but Taylor was not among them. He had already gone to the city after requesting a brief leave in order to gain information about his wife and children, whom he had not heard from for more than a month. Enervated from the strain of the recent campaign and acutely concerned about

5. Richard Taylor, *Destruction and Reconstruction*, p. 90.

6. Power, "'There Stands Jackson,'" pp. 74–77; Tanner, *Stonewall in the Valley*, pp. 310–17 (quotation 316).

his family's safety since the fall of New Orleans, he came dangerously close to experiencing a recurrence of the severe rheumatoid arthritis that had incapacitated him the previous autumn. But at the War Department office in Richmond he discovered several letters from his family telling him they had fled New Orleans with Governor Thomas O. Moore just prior to Rear Admiral David G. Farragut's seizure of the city. Moore had taken them to live with friends near his plantation on the Atchafalaya River. Relieved and refreshed at this news, Taylor also encountered an official at the War Department who hinted that "if I knew what was afoot, my stay in Richmond would be short." With this piece of advice Taylor returned immediately by train to Charlottesville, where he rejoined Jackson's army.[7]

Jackson camped the night of June 20 on the road between Charlottesville and Gordonsville, in Orange County, near the old Taylor family homestead, the birthplace of Taylor's father. That evening a distant cousin appeared and invited Taylor to breakfast the following morning, and Taylor agreed, provided the meal could be served "at the barbarous hour of sunrise" so that he could return to his command in time to march. Before dawn a slave came on horseback to escort Taylor and his body servant, Tom Strother, along with a young aide, Lieutenant James Hamilton, the few miles to the cousin's plantation house, "a fine old mansion, surrounded by well-kept grounds." Welcomed by their host and "his fresh, charming wife," Taylor and Hamilton sat with them on the veranda exchanging pleasantries while a "white-headed butler . . . with ebon face beaming hospitality" served "from a huge silver goblet filled with Virginia's nectar, mint julep." Cooled with cracked ice, sweetened with "a mass of white sugar," and laced with "luscious strawberries" and "sprigs of fragrant mint," this lavish bourbon drink provided an early morning intoxication long enjoyed by genteel Virginians. "Ah! that julep," Taylor marveled years later. "Mars ne'er received such tipple from the hands of Ganymede."[8]

The breakfast, served in the dining room with formal place set-

7. Richard Taylor, *Destruction and Reconstruction*, pp. 90, 92 (quotation), 120.

8. Ibid., pp. 92–93 (first quotation 92, second, third, fourth, and fifth quotations 93).

tings, consisted of hot pancakes "of wondrous forms, inventions of the tropical imagination of Africa." Taylor took care to exercise moderation in his eating, "but the performance of Hamilton was gargantuan, alarming." Soon departing, Taylor expressed his gratitude by giving his hostess a kiss, "the privilege of a cousin." The overstuffed Hamilton "wore a sodden, apoplectic look, quite out of his usual brisk form." But he recovered during the ride back to camp, and "for many days he dilated on the breakfast with the gusto of one of Hannibal's veterans on the delights of Capua." This part of Virginia, where war had not yet come, proved no less bountiful for hundreds of others of Jackson's men who availed themselves of crops and livestock from nearby farms, causing citizens to complain loudly. One soldier recalled that these "professional stragglers who stayed behind to live off the fat of the land" had to be rounded up and brought into camp.[9]

Jackson's command then continued moving toward Richmond, passing through Louisa Court House. A Louisianan recounted, "This movement . . . was for several days shrouded in mystery even to our own officers, while the country was filled with all sorts of contradictory rumors relative to our destination and objects." "The advance frequently halted or changed direction," wrote Taylor. "We were pushing between McDowell [at Fredericksburg] and McClellan's right, over ground recently occupied by the enemy." A few weeks earlier, on May 31 and June 1, General Joseph Johnston had tried to take advantage of McClellan's divided army on the Peninsula by attacking two corps of Federals at Seven Pines, south of the Chickahominy River. McClellan, having advanced slowly toward the outskirts of Richmond, had sent his other three corps north of the river in hopes of linking up with McDowell for an encirclement of the city. Although indecisive in its outcome, the battle of Seven Pines left both sides with heavy casualties, among them Johnston himself, whose wounding proved so serious that Lee took over field command of the Army of Northern Virginia. Convinced that Lee's troops outnumbered his own huge force of more than one hundred thousand men by as much as two to one, McClellan continued to maintain a divided front on

9. Ibid., pp. 93–94 (first, second, and third quotations 93, fourth quotation 93–94, fifth quotation 94); James Cooper Nisbet, *Four Years on the Firing Line*, p. 63 (sixth quotation).

SPECTATOR ON THE PENINSULA

either side of the Chickahominy, protesting the prospect of more needless casualties and demanding reinforcements from Lincoln, who instead wanted action. Lee, like Johnston before him, now determined to beat McClellan to the punch by attacking first.[10]

A Georgia private who happened to see Jackson's men on their march to Richmond noticed Taylor's brigade in particular. Stopping to inspect the battery the Louisianans had captured at Port Republic, he recalled, "The bullet marks and the blood-spattered guns showed the nature of the fighting at the hands of the Louisiana Tigers." Their horses, wagons, and other equipment looked used up and almost worthless. "But the soldiers!" he remarked. "How lean and ragged, yet how game and enthusiastic! And when they stood up in line on dress parade under their tattered colors, their regiments were not larger than companies." These veterans appeared ready to fight McClellan, but their commander clearly was not. The attack of rheumatoid arthritis Taylor had fended off several days earlier returned with a fury on June 25 shortly after Jackson's command camped at Ashland, twelve miles north of Richmond. Stricken with pain in his head and loins so intense that he could not mount his horse the next morning, Taylor gave up control of the Louisiana Brigade to Isaac Seymour, the senior colonel. Barely conscious yet unable to sleep in his agony, he spent the twenty-sixth lying on the floor of a vacant house in Ashland, his arms and legs almost fully paralyzed.[11]

Unfortunately for Lee, stress and fatigue had exacted an equally cruel toll on Stonewall Jackson. Still running more on nervous adrenalin and prayer than on decent rest since the Valley Campaign, Jackson failed in the critical assignment Lee gave him on the twenty-sixth. Lethargic to the point of apathy, he marched slowly all day, although his eighteen thousand-man division, now reinforced by eight thousand men under Brigadier General William H. C. Whiting, encountered only sporadic resistance from Federal cavalry. Moving south from Ashland, Jackson was ordered to execute a flanking assault on

10. Cummer, *Yankee in Gray*, p. 43 (first quotation); Richard Taylor, *Destruction and Reconstruction*, p. 95 (second quotation); Terry L. Jones, *Lee's Tigers*, pp. 93–95.

11. Bradwell, "Soldier Life in the Confederate Army," p. 21 (quotations); Richard Taylor, *Destruction and Reconstruction*, pp. 95–96.

Brigadier General Fitz John Porter's corps of thirty thousand Yankees firmly positioned along Beaver Dam Creek on the northern side of the Chickahominy near the hamlet of Mechanicsville. Having amassed three other divisions besides Jackson's to make the attack on Porter, Lee expected Jackson to link up with Major General D. H. Hill's division on the left. Unable to find Hill, however, and convinced that nothing more could be gained by sunset, Jackson ordered his men into camp near Totopotamoy Creek. Yet he sent no message to Lee requesting instructions or reporting his position. Just as the men settled down for the evening, they heard heavy gunfire only a few miles away in the direction of Beaver Dam Creek, where Lee had started the battle without Jackson. Porter easily resisted Lee's attack, and during the night he withdrew farther down the Chickahominy's northern edge to an even stronger position near Gaines's Mill. Jackson's soldiers sat helpless, wondering how he could have denied his "foot cavalry," so famous for speed and surprise, from reaching the battlefield at Mechanicsville. E. Porter Alexander, one of Lee's staff officers, later observed, "A further advance [by Jackson] that afternoon of 3½ miles would have completely cut off the retreat of Fitz John Porter's whole corps."[12]

Taylor actually received more information than Lee did about Jackson's whereabouts that day. But to Taylor, in a state of near delirium at Ashland, the several reports delivered by his staff made little sense. Still suffering incessantly, he spent another sleepless night but finally drifted into exhausted unconsciousness near dawn on the twenty-seventh and managed to rest for several hours. Early in the afternoon an easterly wind carried the rumbling of artillery fire, heavy and unremitting, causing Taylor to stir. "Tom raised me to a sitting posture, and administered a cup of strong coffee," he remembered. "The sound of battle continued until it became unendurable." With help from Tom and the driver of an ambulance nearby, Taylor struggled into the vehicle, made himself as comfortable as possible, and rolled slowly toward the sound of the fighting. "After weary hours of rough road, every jolt on which threatened to destroy my remaining vitality, we approached Cold Harbor and met numbers of wounded," he re-

12. Dowdey, *Seven Days*, pp. 168–210; Terry L. Jones, *Lee's Tigers*, p. 101; Gallagher, *Fighting for the Confederacy*, pp. 99–100 (quotation 100).

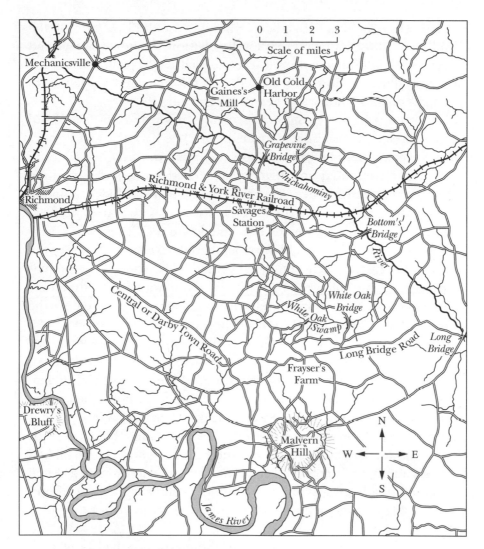

Map 4. Area of the Seven Days, near Richmond, June–July 1862

called. Here he saw Brigadier General Arnold Elzey, one of the
wounded, whose aide said that Ewell's division, including Elzey's and
Taylor's brigades, had endured severe casualties. "This was too much
for any illness," Taylor recounted, "and I managed somehow to
struggle on to my horse and get into the action." [13]

"It was a wild scene. Battle was raging furiously. Shot, shell, and
ball exploded and whistled," wrote Taylor. Lee had attacked Porter's
corps near Gaines's Mill along Botswain's Swamp, where the Federals
occupied an elevated and firmly entrenched semicircular position
about a mile and a half in length. Enemy artillery, hidden among
trees in the rear, pounded the Confederate lines with fearsome effect,
while Lee's own artillery made little impact on the Federals' superior
position. A Confederate soldier remembered, "Not a single one of the
enemy was visible, being concealed behind a breastwork of logs, hidden by the dense foliage of the Chickahominy swamps. We fired only
at the smoke of their guns." Ewell's division, having arrived before the
rest of Jackson's command, received orders from Lee to support Major General A. P. Hill's division near the center of the Federal line.
Meanwhile Jackson, who remained completely ignorant of the area,
had taken a wrong turn in his effort to find the enemy's right flank.
There D. H. Hill waited with his division as he had done the day before, with orders to attack only after Jackson's arrival. With daylight
fading and Jackson nowhere in sight, Lee determined that Ewell, with
the Louisiana Brigade, must break the Federal center. A. P. Hill had
already attempted the feat several times without success, and as Ewell
prepared to advance, Porter bolstered the center with extra troops,
anticipating this very attack. McClellan had ordered Porter to hold at
all costs. [14]

A Louisiana private, one of Taylor's brigade, described Ewell's advance: "The necessity for prompt action was so great that we were
hurriedly formed in line of battle . . . and were rapidly marched
under a terrific fire from the artillery as well as the infantry." Ewell
ordered a charge through the thick forest and down into the swamp,
where the men opened fire and tried to climb up the long slope to-

13. Richard Taylor, *Destruction and Reconstruction*, p. 96 (quotations).
14. Ibid., pp. 96–97 (first quotation 96); Dowdey, *Seven Days*, pp. 211–28;
Cummer, *Yankee in Gray*, p. 96 (second quotation).

ward the Federals, three deep in their elevated breastworks. "Many of us were wounded, and all within a space of thirty yards, and that was as far as our brigade went," recalled a soldier in the Sixth Louisiana. Colonel Seymour, leading the brigade in Taylor's absence, was one of the first to fall, killed instantly by a hail of bullets. Confused and overcome by the slaughter, hundreds bolted toward the rear, where they encountered some southerners from General Isaac R. Trimble's brigade coming up on their left. "Boys, you are mighty good," shouted a Louisianan, "but that's hell in there." Major Rob Wheat, totally irate at the sight of his Tigers getting whipped for the first time, rode slowly through the underbrush up the hill toward the front, searching for a weak point in the Federal line. Suddenly a bullet passed through his skull and he toppled over dead. "Now was the critical time when a voice of authority to guide our uncertain steps and a bold officer to lead us forward would have been worth to us a victory," asserted a member of the Ninth Louisiana. "But none such appeared. Gen. Taylor was sick and absent." [15]

Taylor located his brigade shortly before dusk. "Mangled and bleeding, as were all of Ewell's, it was holding the ground it had won close to the enemy's line, but unable to advance," he recorded. A Louisiana soldier wrote of their plight, "To halt before such a volcano was madness. The only hope was to storm it rapidly." With darkness approaching, Lee had one chance to win the battle. Calling up the brigades of Brigadier General John Bell Hood and Colonel Evander M. Law, a total of about four thousand fresh troops, Lee ordered them to charge the Federal center. With Jackson and D. H. Hill finally pressing down on Porter's right, Lee would have his entire force engaged for the first time. Hood and Law eagerly led their men down into the swamp and up the slope toward the center. Running at full speed without firing a shot, they let forth a continuous, high-pitched rebel yell. Hood's Texans and Georgians took the brunt of the punishment, losing one-fourth of their numbers before piercing the enemy breastworks and causing a rout at the center that led to a grad-

15. Walshe, "Recollections of Gaines's Mill," pp. 54–55 (first quotation 54, second quotation 55); James Cooper Nisbet, *Four Years on the Firing Line*, p. 64 (third quotation); Cummer, *Yankee in Gray*, pp. 45–46 (fourth quotation 45); Terry L. Jones, *Lee's Tigers*, pp. 102–5.

ual collapse along the entire length of the Federal line. Porter managed to withdraw in an orderly fashion because Confederate pursuit soon faltered in the face of timely Federal reinforcements. Although defeated, Porter had preserved his corps and had bought McClellan time to change his army's base of supply from the York River to a safer position farther to the south, on the James. Lee had successfully turned the enemy away from the gates of Richmond, but in failing to annihilate Porter, he had suffered almost nine thousand casualties, compared with Porter's seven thousand.[16]

"The loss in my command [a total of 32 killed and 142 wounded] was distressing," wrote Taylor. "I had a wretched feeling of guilt, particularly about Seymour, who led the brigade and died in my place." Taylor also genuinely regretted the death of Major Wheat, whose talents he had grown to admire fully during the Valley Campaign. A week prior to Gaines's Mill he had written to President Davis suggesting that Wheat's Tigers, now reduced to fewer than one hundred men, should be combined with several other Louisiana battalions to form a regiment with Wheat promoted to command as colonel. "Nothing could be more just," Taylor argued to Davis. "I am happy in the belief that [Wheat's] habits have materially changed for the better, and this belief is founded on the experience of several past months." But after Wheat's death the Tigers lost their collective identity and pride as a combat unit. "With all Dick Taylor's will and power he could do nothing with them," observed David Boyd. "They would fight in any other command to which they might be assigned, but as Wheat's Battalion never again would they fire a gun."[17]

By Saturday, June 28, the day after Gaines's Mill, Porter had reunited his corps with the rest of the Army of the Potomac on the southern side of the Chickahominy. Lee could only guess at McClellan's next move. Still unaware of McClellan's intentions regarding

16. Richard Taylor, *Destruction and Reconstruction*, p. 97 (first quotation); Cummer, *Yankee in Gray*, p. 47 (second quotation); Dowdey, *Seven Days*, pp. 234–45.

17. Richard Taylor, *Destruction and Reconstruction*, p. 97 (first quotation); *O.R.*, 11(2):609; Richard Taylor to Jefferson Davis, June [19,] 1862 (second quotation), Davis Papers, Louisiana Historical Association Collection, Tulane University; Boyd, "Major Bob Wheat" (third quotation).

Robert E. Lee
(Jenkins Rare Book Company).

Richmond, Lee wanted only to catch him off guard in the open and destroy him, a task made all the more difficult by McClellan's decision to consolidate his army and remain on the defensive. Believing correctly that the Federal supply line running from the York River base held the key to McClellan's true aims, Lee placed Ewell's division, with support from Brigadier General J. E. B. Stuart's cavalry, along the northern side of the Chickahominy to watch the several bridges McClellan would have to use if he intended to maintain his supply line from the York. Meanwhile McClellan placed troops on the southern side of the bridges to protect himself from a Confederate attack against his rear. Ewell ordered Taylor, now healthy enough to retake command of the Louisiana Brigade, to watch Bottom's Bridge.[18]

That evening Robert E. Lee paid Taylor a personal visit. "General Lee informed me that I would remain the following day to guard Bottom's [Bridge] and the railway bridges," Taylor recalled. Realizing by now that McClellan probably intended to abandon his supply base on the York River and withdraw southward during the night, how-

18. Dowdey, *Seven Days*, pp. 246–58; Richard Taylor, *Destruction and Reconstruction*, p. 102.

ever, Lee told Taylor that he planned to concentrate most of his divisions south of the Chickahominy the next morning in an effort to keep McClellan from reaching the James. Lee "expressed some confidence that his dispositions would inflict serious loss on McClellan's army, if he could receive prompt and accurate information on that General's movements," wrote Taylor. "Meantime, I would remain until the following (Sunday) evening, unless sooner convinced of the enemy's designs, when I would cross Grapevine Bridge and follow Jackson." Once again Lee expected Jackson to make a crucial attack on the Federal right flank. Colonel E. Porter Alexander of Lee's staff asserted, "It was plain that we had the enemy on the jump, and that a great opportunity was before us." [19]

Taylor awoke Sunday, June 29, to discover that the Federals had destroyed the center portion of the railroad bridge leading to Savage's Station south of the Chickahominy. During the afternoon the sound of battle came from Savage's Station, less than two miles away, but a dense forest hid the action from Taylor's view. Major General John Bankhead Magruder, under orders from Lee, had advanced his division against two enemy divisions there while the rest of Lee's army probed farther south. The overly nervous Magruder, expecting help from Jackson at any moment, made a fitful series of attacks that failed completely. Jackson, who spent the morning repairing the Grapevine Bridge, simply informed Magruder that he was engaged in another important assignment. Near sunset Taylor's brigade crossed the Grapevine Bridge with the rest of Jackson's command and camped on the river's southern bank. "A heavy rain came down, converting the ground into a lake, in the midst of which a half-drowned courier, with a dispatch, was brought to me," he recounted. Having taken several hours just to find Taylor, the courier brought a pathetic plea from Magruder for reinforcements. With the lethargic Jackson having spent a leisurely Sabbath refusing to move, Magruder had been left to fend for himself, even to send a wayward message to Taylor begging for aid. Sadly, the battle at Savage's Station had dramatized Lee's lack of an effective staff system for gathering intelligence and

19. Richard Taylor, *Destruction and Reconstruction*, p. 102 (first and second quotations); Dowdey, *Seven Days*, pp. 259–69; Gallagher, *Fighting for the Confederacy*, p. 105 (third quotation).

conveying orders to coordinate his field commanders' movements and bring them into action.[20]

June 30 dawned clear and warm, but the rain the night before left Taylor weak and in pain, forcing him to ride in an ambulance to conserve his strength. Joining the rear of Jackson's column, he proceeded south along the road leading to White Oak Bridge, whence came artillery fire around noon. Stopping on the road while a staff officer went forward to determine the situation, Taylor noticed Brigadier General Wade Hampton and Confederate senator Louis T. Wigfall riding up to see him. A vain Texan who consistently opposed Jefferson Davis's policies, Wigfall said that he hoped a brigade commander would be killed so that his friend Hampton, recently promoted but still without a brigade, would become a replacement. "Finding me extended in an ambulance, he doubtless thought he had met his opportunity, and felt aggrieved that I was not *in extremis*," mused Taylor. A wealthy, aristocratic South Carolinian, Hampton enjoyed Taylor's respect as a fine cavalry officer, but his blustery sidekick Wigfall was impossible to tolerate. A vociferous fire-eater and secessionist, Wigfall personified the persistence of radical states' rights doctrine, a position Taylor viewed as treacherous to the Davis administration in particular and to the South's unity as a fledgling nation. Serving as Hampton's temporary volunteer aide, Wigfall informed Taylor that "he proposed to attach himself and see the fun." Such flippancy only sharpened Taylor's disdain for politicians of Wigfall's stripe.[21]

An artillery duel continued most of the afternoon near White Oak Bridge, where the road traversed a swamp drained by a slough. Finally deciding that his gunners could not hold their own against the

20. Richard Taylor, *Destruction and Reconstruction*, pp. 102–3 (quotation 103); Dowdey, *Seven Days*, pp. 270–81; Gallagher, *Fighting for the Confederacy*, pp. 105–6.

21. Richard Taylor, *Destruction and Reconstruction*, pp. 104 (quotations), 66; Warner, *Generals in Gray*, pp. 122–23, 336–37. Taylor's memory of his encounter with Hampton and Wigfall was faulty; Hampton had already received temporary command of one of Jackson's Virginia brigades following the death of Colonel Samuel Fulkerson at Gaines's Mill. Taylor probably saw Hampton and Wigfall immediately before or after Gaines's Mill. See Dowdey, *Seven Days*, p. 312.

Federals' rifled cannon, Jackson ordered his batteries to withdraw. "Our loss, *one* artilleryman mortally wounded, proved that no serious effort to pass the slough was made," wrote Taylor, "yet a prize was in reach worth the loss of thousands." True to his form of the last several days, Jackson refused to see the urgency in moving forward against McClellan's right flank near Frayser's Farm. Instead, he dallied with repairing White Oak Bridge and made no serious attempt to discover a passable ford through the swamp, only a mile upstream. Echoing Taylor's opinion of Jackson's inactivity, E. P. Alexander later observed, "Never, before or after, did the fates put such a prize within our reach." About 4:00 P.M. Lee threw A. P. Hill's and James Longstreet's divisions into the strongest part of the Federal lines drawn up near Frayser's Farm. "Again, fractions against masses," Taylor noted despairingly. Lee's poor staff work had prevented his other divisions nearby from arriving on the field in time to help Hill and Longstreet, and Jackson's absence loomed even more conspicuous as a result. Several hours of bloody Confederate assaults left Lee with more than 3,600 casualties and McClellan with only about 2,900. McClellan withdrew his army farther south during the night to a much stronger position on Malvern Hill. That evening Jackson overheard his staff officers speculating aloud on the reasons for his disturbing lack of usual audacity, prompting him to blurt out, "If General Lee had wanted me at Frayser's Farm, he would have sent for me!"[22]

"Malvern Hill was a desperate position to attack in front," wrote Taylor. "By its height, [it] dominated the ground to the north, the James River, and the Newmarket road on which we approached." Federal artillery, comprising a total of 250 available guns, raked the Confederates throughout the afternoon of July 1 while Lee struggled to align his divisions in a semicircle around the hill's northern edge. Lee had determined that a mass frontal assault offered the only chance of preventing McClellan's final escape to his new supply base on the James River, where Union gunboats could provide him full

22. Richard Taylor, *Destruction and Reconstruction*, pp. 104–5 (first and third quotations 105); Dowdey, *Seven Days*, pp. 282–315; Gallagher, *Fighting for the Confederacy*, pp. 106–11 (second quotation 109); Robertson, *Stonewall Brigade*, p. 120 (third quotation).

protection. E. P. Alexander later surmised, "Gen. Lee . . . seemed to have such supreme confidence that his infantry could go anywhere, that he took comparatively little pains to study out the easier roads [leading to the right and rear of Malvern Hill]." And, much as before, Lee's loosely worded initial orders and glaring lack of staff work caused his divisional commanders to flounder in confusion before a ruthless enemy bombardment. The climactic encounter of the Seven Days battles thus degenerated into another haphazard and fruitless wasting of southern lives.[23]

Although held in reserve to support the rest of Jackson's division near the center, Taylor's brigade fell into the prevailing bedlam by mistake. Colonel Leroy A. Stafford, having taken field command because Taylor was still unable to walk or ride, wrote in his official report that shortly after sunset an unidentified officer with apparent authority, most likely one of Lee's staff, suddenly appeared and ordered the Louisianans to move forward. "This charge resulted in the loss of some valuable lives," a total of 24 killed and 91 wounded, reported Stafford. A member of the Ninth Louisiana, one of many soldiers in that regiment who mercifully failed to hear the order to advance, witnessed the aftermath: "We found the whole brigade so scattered and disorganized that a halt for the remainder of the day was necessary to collect the stragglers. Indeed the whole battle of Malvern Hill seems to have been conducted . . . without system or mutual cooperation, and with the natural result of a complete defeat." By midnight Lee had suffered 5,355 casualties and McClellan barely 3,200, leaving casualties for the entire Seven Days battles standing at more than 20,000 Confederates and about 16,000 Federals. Lee had lost about a quarter of his entire army; McClellan had lost 20 percent of his.[24]

23. Richard Taylor, *Destruction and Reconstruction*, pp. 105–7 (first quotation 105–6); Gallagher, *Fighting for the Confederacy*, pp. 111–14 (second quotation 111); Dowdey, *Seven Days*, pp. 316–46.

24. *O.R.*, 11(2):619–20 (first quotation 620), 609; Cummer, *Yankee in Gray*, p. 50 (second quotation); Hattaway and Jones, *How the North Won*, pp. 199–200. Strangely, Taylor stated in his memoirs that his brigade did not participate in the action at Malvern Hill. See Richard Taylor, *Destruction and Reconstruction*, p. 107.

In his memoirs Taylor described Lee's strategy during the Seven Days as "magnificent" and filled with potential for "resplendent success." Yet "this opportunity was lost by tactical mistakes, occasioned by want of knowledge of the theatre of action, and it is to be feared that Time, when he renders his verdict, will declare the gallant dead . . . to have been sacrificed on the altar of the bloodiest of all Molochs—Ignorance." Taylor viewed the fighting as a "series of blunders, one after another, and all huge. The Confederate commanders knew no more about the topography of the country [surrounding Richmond] than they did about Central Africa." Lee's army was operating in one of the oldest, most civilized areas in North America, "and yet we were profoundly ignorant of the country, were without maps, sketches, or proper guides." The Federals actually possessed better knowledge of the ground, McClellan having sent scouts into the tangled maze of woods, streams, and swamps to chart the network of roads and connecting paths. This seemed all the more appalling to Taylor, considering that Johnston, Lee, and Davis all had West Point training and practical experience before the war as topographical engineers. "Every one must agree that it was amazing," he observed. "Even now, I can scarcely realize it."[25]

Unfortunately, no detailed maps of the South even existed at the time, and the Confederate Engineer Bureau lacked personnel to do much more than locate and survey the best sites for constructing defensive positions around Richmond. Although Lee had requested a comprehensive reconnaissance and mapping of the area, McClellan's ominous presence hampered the effort severely, forcing Lee to rely on an incomplete and often inaccurate general map to conduct the Seven Days battles. "That some of our generals had maps of the principal county roads there can be no question," recalled a Confederate officer, "but the by-roads were not laid down." The problem proved particularly detrimental to commanders who attempted to follow Lee's vague instructions with scant help from staff communications and qualified guides. Only after suffering this hard lesson did the

25. Richard Taylor, *Destruction and Reconstruction*, pp. 107 (first and second quotations), 99–100 (third and fourth quotations 99, fifth quotation 100); Hattaway and Jones, *How the North Won*, p. 194.

Confederate Engineer Bureau begin to supply the army with detailed and accurate maps of Virginia.[26]

General Lee, however, sternly discounted poor maps as a primary reason for tactical failures during the Seven Days. "Blunders came not from the lack of intelligence of the countryside, but [from] inattention to orders and lack of energy by a few subordinate commanders," Lee told a topographical officer. Yet his tendency to rely upon his generals to carry out discretionary orders, with faulty coordination by staff officers during combat, would continue to plague the army, especially during complex offensive operations similar to the Seven Days. "In truth, the genius of Lee for offensive war had suffered by a too long service as an engineer," Taylor later contended. "[The offensive] was not his forte." Referring to Lee's faulty intelligence about enemy movements during the Antietam and Gettysburg campaigns, Taylor observed, "In both, too, his army was widely scattered, and had to be brought into action piecemeal." Taylor neglected to mention, however, Lee's offensive brilliance at Second Manassas and at Chancellorsville. Although he admired Lee's spotless character and selfless sense of duty, Taylor blamed West Point's inadequate training in practical battlefield command as the fundamental cause of Lee's errors. The want of good maps only underscored this handicap.[27]

Taylor's memoirs did discuss Jackson's failure to execute Lee's orders regarding critical flanking movements at Gaines's Mill and Frayser's Farm. But these lapses Taylor attributed specifically to inferior maps and Lee's lack of staff communications rather than to Jackson's fatigue and stubbornness. Jackson's talented mapmaker Jedediah Hotchkiss, who had proved the absolute necessity of accurate maps during the Valley Campaign, had been detached to another assignment during the Seven Days, thereby exacerbating Jackson's confu-

26. James L. Nichols, *Confederate Engineers*, pp. 80–86; Lamb, "Malvern Hill," p. 218 (quotation).

27. Campbell, "Lost War Maps of the Confederates," p. 479 (first quotation); Richard Taylor, *Destruction and Reconstruction*, pp. 111–14 (second and third quotations 112). On military maps and mapmaking during the Civil War, see Stephenson, *Civil War Maps*, pp. 1–26.

sion and lack of initiative. Hotchkiss's presence might not have shaken Jackson out of his lethargy, but in Taylor's opinion Jackson's talents went wasted during the Seven Days. "What limits to set on his ability, I know not," wrote Taylor in unabashed reverence, "for he was ever superior to occasion." Jackson's single fault, his towering ambition, he seemed to have controlled and channeled well enough to insure his greatness as a commander. "In Valhalla, beyond the grave, where spirits of warriors assemble, when on the roll of heroes the name of Jackson is reached, it will be for the majestic shade of Lee to pronounce the highest eulogy known to our race—'Died on the field of duty,'" Taylor concluded fervently. Ascendancy to Valhalla instead of a Protestant's heaven surely would have rankled both Jackson's and Lee's souls, but at least Jackson had overcome the limitations of a West Point education in Taylor's estimation.[28]

Such worshipful appreciation for his commander perhaps stemmed in part from the knowledge that Jackson recommended Taylor for promotion to the rank of major general. Although Taylor did not realize it at the time, on June 10, one day after the victory at Port Republic, Jackson sent a message to Confederate Adjutant General Samuel Cooper, stating, "The success with which [Taylor] has managed his Brigade in camp, on the march, and when engaged with the enemy at Front Royal, Middletown, Winchester, and yesterday at Port Republic, makes it my duty as well as my pleasure to recommend him for promotion." Among the worthy brigadiers who had served Jackson during the Valley Campaign only Taylor received this honor. Except for the dashing J. E. B. Stuart, who received promotion only shortly before him, Taylor, at thirty-six years of age, became the youngest of the thirty major generals then serving in the Confederate Army. Only three others, John C. Breckinridge, T. C. Hindman, and William W. Loring, were non–West Pointers like Taylor. Shortly after the Seven Days he received the news of his increased rank, which became official on July 25.[29]

Immediately before learning of his promotion, however, Taylor

28. Richard Taylor, *Destruction and Reconstruction*, pp. 101–2, 104–5, 91–92 (first quotation 91, second quotation 92).

29. Terry L. Jones, *Lee's Tigers*, p. 92 (quotation); Charles C. Jones, *Roster of General Officers*, pp. 14–16.

suffered yet another attack of rheumatoid arthritis that left his legs paralyzed. Taken to Richmond to receive proper medical care, he rested there for about a month before regaining his strength. On the evening of July 24 President Davis met with him to discuss the future. They agreed that he would serve best in a completely new role, as commander of Confederate forces in Louisiana. Davis wrote Lee about this decision the next day, explaining that Taylor would recruit fresh troops for the Army of Northern Virginia. Lee replied at once, "In regard to detaching Genl. Taylor, his presence in La. will no doubt hasten the enrollment and expedite the recruiting of regts. If it should establish his own health, it would be an additional benefit to the service. I would therefore on the latter ground alone recommend it." With the news of Taylor's impending departure Lee also attempted to assuage Jackson's concerns about his division's severely depleted manpower, especially among Louisiana regiments recently brigaded together under his command. "The regiments assigned to you are those that will be first filled up with recruits from Louisiana," Lee assured Jackson. "Genl. Taylor, still an invalid, will go to Louisiana to hurry on the men." [30]

Davis failed to emphasize to Lee, however, that recruiting men for the war in Virginia would not comprise Taylor's major responsibility. As early as May 21, a few weeks after the fall of New Orleans, Governor Thomas O. Moore of Louisiana complained in an emotional letter to Davis, "I am stripped of everything I have—guns, munitions, forces and commissary stores. . . . A part of my State is now in possession of our ruthless enemy—the remainder is prey to internal dissension and the perils of demoralization." Thirty thousand soldiers had left Louisiana to defend Virginia, Tennessee, and other parts of the Confederacy, but Governor Moore still had not a single officer "to advise with or a man to execute an order." Clarifying this need, Moore stated in a desperate tone, "I beg that a general may be assigned to whatever department Louisiana may be placed in, very soon." By late July, Moore became so exasperated that he joined with the governors of the other states west of the Mississippi in demanding

30. Richard Taylor, *Destruction and Reconstruction*, pp. 107–8, 116; *O.R.*, 51(2):597; Freeman, *Lee's Dispatches*, pp. 34–36 (first quotation 36); Dowdey and Manarin, *Wartime Papers of R. E. Lee*, pp. 238–39 (second quotation 239).

immediate action from Davis. More than a month later Davis responded, confirming Taylor's assignment to Louisiana and explaining that "while Virginia was pressed by the whole force of the United States Government, with our capital threatened, and even closely invested . . . it was impracticable to detach such commanding officers to the Trans-Mississippi Department."[31]

Taylor regretted leaving his comrades in Virginia, especially Ewell. "Dear Dick Ewell," he wrote affectionately in his memoirs. "Virginia never bred a truer gentleman, a braver soldier, nor an odder, more lovable fellow." Not to be outdone for warm familiarity, Ewell confided to another officer upon Taylor's departure that he admired "Taylor's genius and military ability, but that he feared, so eccentric was he, his mind would lose its balance." Ewell thus affirmed the honest intimacy of their friendship, each seeing the other's hopeless eccentricities. Taylor also recalled with sadness, "In leaving Virginia I was separated from my brigade, endeared by so many memories. . . . A braver command never formed a line of battle." His old regiment, the Ninth Louisiana, demonstrated its loyalty by presenting him with a formal request to accompany him to Louisiana. "You have made soldiers of us," wrote Colonel Leroy Stafford and the other officers on behalf of the regiment. "Wherever you go, we desire to go, and let your destiny be our destiny." The Ninth would stay in Virginia, however, and the Louisiana Brigade would often still find distinction informally as "Taylor's brigade" long after he had gone. It would eventually participate in every major battle fought by Lee's army, and the Ninth would suffer higher casualties than any other Louisiana regiment in the entire war. Had he remained in the East, Taylor would have proved a fine divisional commander. Douglas Southall Freeman, eminent historian of Lee's campaigns in Virginia, observed trenchantly, "The Army was poorer for Taylor's departure."[32]

In mid-August Taylor journeyed westward by rail, stopping in

31. *Correspondence between the War Department and General Lovell*, pp. 116–17 (first, second, and third quotations 116); *O.R.*, 13:879–80 (fourth quotation 879).

32. Richard Taylor, *Destruction and Reconstruction*, pp. 89 (first quotation), 116 (third quotation); "Jackson and Ewell," pp. 32–33 (second quotation); Urquhart, "General Richard Taylor," pp. 73–74 (fourth quotation 74); James

Chattanooga to confer with his old friend Braxton Bragg, now a full general in command of the Army of Tennessee. Mindful of the excellent service Taylor had performed as his advisor at Pensacola the year before, Bragg had recently asked Davis to appoint Taylor as his chief of staff. Taylor's impending duties in Louisiana had nullified Bragg's request, but he decided to stop and visit with Bragg personally at Davis's suggestion. During his two days at Chattanooga, Taylor discovered that Bragg's appeal reflected more serious problems. Dissatisfied with the appointments to command Davis had made in the Army of Tennessee, Bragg had already transferred or court-martialed several officers, desiring instead to choose all of his own subordinates. But Davis refused to cooperate with Bragg. Abusive toward the officers he could not eliminate, Bragg groused to Taylor, "The Government is to blame for placing such men in high position." Taylor respected Bragg's love of absolute loyalty and discipline, "but his method and manner were harsh, and he could have won the affections of his troops only by leading them to victory." Feverishly preparing to launch a campaign into Kentucky within a few weeks, he also appeared victimized by poor health, a condition Taylor blamed for the campaign's eventual failure. Without Taylor to help him, Bragg would determine to act as his own chief of staff, burdening himself with distractions that further sapped his energy and produced disorganization throughout the army. "From that hour I had misgivings about General Bragg's success," Taylor recalled, "and felt no regret at the refusal of authorities to assign me to duty with him."[33]

Although he had lost Taylor's services, Bragg wished his fellow Louisianan well in his new responsibilities. Later that year he praised Taylor openly, stating that he was "the right man in the right place, for if anybody *could* do anything in Louisiana *he would*, as he had great energy and intelligence." Although eager to return home, Taylor also recognized the gigantic task weighing on him, that indeed he might be facing a quagmire. His experience in Virginia with soldiers

---

Cooper Nisbet, *Four Years on the Firing Line*, p. 85; Terry L. Jones, *Lee's Tigers*, pp. 227–54; Freeman, *Lee's Lieutenants*, 1:668 (fifth quotation).

33. Richard Taylor, *Destruction and Reconstruction*, pp. 116–19 (first and third quotations 118, second quotation 117); McWhiney, *Braxton Bragg*, pp. 278–81.

like Jackson, Ewell, and Lee, as well as the negative example set by
Bragg, had strengthened his capacity for higher command. But the
Trans-Mississippi posed a far more complex set of problems: unwilling soldiers; unpatriotic, even treacherous civilians; rebellious slaves;
and an invading enemy bent on crushing Louisiana completely. Taylor would soon confront the savagery of total war.[34]

34. R. L. Pugh to Mary Williams Pugh, December 16, 1862 (quotation),
Pugh Papers.

CHAPTER SEVEN

Defender of Louisiana

General Taylor has done everything that was

possible with the resources at his command.

Edmund Kirby Smith

On August 19, 1862, Major General Richard Taylor crossed the Mississippi near the mouth of the Red River and returned to his home state. Having traveled all night, shortly before dawn he found his family near Washington, a small town in St. Landry Parish, where they were living with friends. "I had the happiness to embrace wife and children after a separation of fourteen months," he recalled. But within a few hours he departed for Opelousas, a short distance south, where he met with Governor Moore. A crossroads in the Teche region of southern Louisiana, Opelousas now served as the temporary state capital following the enemy's occupation of Baton Rouge a few weeks earlier. There Tayor spent two days recovering from his journey and conferring with Governor Moore.[1]

"Melancholy indeed was the condition of the . . . command of which I was assigned," he remembered. "The Confederate Government had no soldiers, no arms or munitions, and no money, within

1. Richard Taylor, *Destruction and Reconstruction*, pp. 119–20 (quotation 120), 127.

the limits of the district." Moore could provide him with nothing more than a handful of poorly trained and ill-equipped militia units. Taylor appealed to his immediate superior, Lieutenant General Theophilus H. Holmes, the fifty-eight-year-old commander of the Trans-Mississippi Department, headquartered at Little Rock. But Holmes replied that all of his resources would have to be used for defending Arkansas. Taylor also sent a message to Governor John J. Pettus of Mississippi, asserting, "We are so destitute of material on this side of the river." Like Holmes, Pettus professed an inability to provide relief of any kind. Increasingly isolated from the rest of the Confederacy, pressed back by invading Union forces, and fraught with internal weaknesses, the Trans-Mississippi Department would remain a neglected stepchild while also facing mounting political and military pressure from Confederate authorities to aid the costly war effort in the East.[2]

General Holmes, nicknamed "Granny" because of his wrinkled appearance and lack of energy, did little to meet the challenge. Rather than molding the department into a coordinated command system, he decided to relinquish virtually all authority to his district commanders, thus leaving Taylor to his own devices. Establishing the District of West Louisiana's headquarters at Alexandria in the central part of the state, Taylor began to come to grips with the responsibility of unifying Louisiana (excluding the parishes east of the Mississippi). Working without telegraph lines or railway connections for communications, he spent most of his time traversing the state in an ambulance, relying on fresh teams of mules at various relay points. Soon it seemed that he "almost succeeded in being two places at once." He deemed his personal presence in the field especially vital because of the population's distressingly low morale. "I addressed myself to the heavy task of arousing public sentiment, apathetic if not hostile from disaster and neglect," he recalled. But these initial forays proved acutely discouraging. "I can assure you that at times I am almost disheartened by the want of patriotic feeling here," he wrote a friend in Virginia. "The people think or affect to think that our State has been

2. Ibid., pp. 120–21 (first quotation 120), 127; Geise, "Hindman and Hebert Divide Command," p. 115; Dufour, *Nine Men in Gray*, p. 25 (second quotation); Woodworth, "'Dismembering the Confederacy,'" pp. 1–13.

neglected by the government in Richmond, and because soldiers are not sent to defend them they are unwilling to do anything to defend themselves. In the lower part of the State this feeling is almost universal, and of course I as the representative of the government am abused on all sides for not accomplishing impossibilities."[3]

Almost immediately Taylor discovered that he would have to raise public morale while also conscripting men into the army. Wasting no time in the expectation of large numbers of volunteers, he issued orders requiring a military draft in accordance with recent Confederate conscription laws. Northern Louisiana had already seen heavy volunteering for service outside the state, but many men in the southern part continued to shun enlistment, especially in the parishes with large Acadian populations. Here Taylor registered thousands of conscripts by sending out detachments of militiamen to sequester them for instruction and training in camps near Opelousas. By October he reported a total force of 5,840, including volunteers, state militia, partisan rangers, and new conscripts. At least another 8,000, however, he classified as deserters, runaway conscripts, and draft evaders. Most of Taylor's fledgling army had inadequate weapons, ammunition, and equipment, but Major Joseph L. Brent, the district's ordnance officer, set out to remedy the dilemma. Establishing machine shops at New Iberia, Alexandria, Monroe, and Franklin, he also contracted with a private foundry at Shreveport and opened supply lines linked to Confederate arsenals and ordnance depots east of the Mississippi. Within a few months, thanks to Brent's production as well as to the timely capturing of enemy arms and munitions during various engagements, Taylor no longer had to rely on shipments from the East but was in fact sending excess lead to arsenals across the river.[4]

3. Geise, "General Holmes Fails," pp. 171–72; Richard Taylor, *Destruction and Reconstruction*, pp. 127–28 (first quotation 128), 121 (second quotation); Bragg, *Louisiana in the Confederacy*, pp. 255–56 (third quotation).

4. Ethel Taylor, "Discontent in Confederate Louisiana," pp. 412–14, 416, 421; Winters, *Civil War in Louisiana*, pp. 153–54, 157; Geise, "General Holmes Fails," p. 172. See also Joseph L. Brent's masterwork on technical, strategic, and tactical aspects of artillery warfare, *Mobilizable Fortifications, and Their Controlling Influence in War*.

Portrait of Major General Richard Taylor by an unknown artist, the original of which is lost. Wartime photograph by Andrew D. Lytle, Baton Rouge (Louisiana Office of State Parks).

George W. Randolph, Confederate secretary of war
(*Johnson and Buell,* Battles and Leaders of the Civil War).

The Confederacy's leaders, however, had given Taylor a far more grandiose mission than merely to act as a supplier of munitions. Prior to his leaving Richmond, he had met with President Davis and Secretary of War George Wythe Randolph to formulate an ambitious secret scheme to recapture New Orleans from Union major general Benjamin F. Butler's fifteen-thousand-man army of occupation. Taylor's transfer to Louisiana therefore carried broad strategic ramifications. Until now the notion of Confederate troops reconquering territory lost to Federal invasion and occupation had seemed almost unthinkable. But New Orleans's relatively small and inexperienced enemy garrison appeared vulnerable, and the prospect of reestablishing Confederate control of the lower Mississippi River proved irresistible to Randolph, especially considering the influence it might have in strengthening diplomatic support from the European powers. More importantly, Randolph was the first member of the Confederate high command to recognize and act upon a growing realization that the outcome of the war would likely hinge upon the fate of the Mississippi Valley and the Lower South rather than Virginia. Randolph gave Taylor authority to detach troops from Texas, Mississippi, and Alabama in order to launch a concerted, multipronged attack on New Orleans. He also hoped that Taylor's public image as a native son would inspire Confederate loyalists in New Orleans to rise up, along with certain unscrupulous Unionist businessmen eager for economic benefits, in a conspiracy to help overthrow the Federals.[5]

On the very day he arrived in Louisiana, August 20, Taylor sent a forceful letter to Brigadier General Daniel Ruggles, commander of the Confederate bastion at Port Hudson on the Mississippi above Baton Rouge. He confidently informed Ruggles, "I am about to undertake an expedition which I anticipate will place me in possession of the Opelousas Railroad up to the vicinity of Algiers" on the outskirts of New Orleans. He also asked Ruggles to establish a line of couriers to improve communications with Richmond and with Major General Earl Van Dorn at Jackson, Mississippi. Apparently Taylor intended to take whatever forces he could muster and march toward New Orleans almost immediately.[6]

Secretary Randolph's desire to maintain secrecy about the plan appeared threatened in mid-September, however, when Ruggles telegraphed Richmond with his own proposal to lead an assault on New Orleans. Completely ignorant of Taylor's purposes, Ruggles provoked an angry Randolph to reply tersely, "Major General Taylor has already been assigned by the president to the very responsible duties referred to." Warning Ruggles not to "interfere with the authority vested in Major General Taylor," Randolph also upbraided him for risking "publicity through the medium of the telegraph to suggestions which should have been regarded . . . as private and are so regarded in the instructions to General Taylor." By now, however, the

---

5. Shackelford, *George Wythe Randolph*, pp. 123–37; Vandiver, *Rebel Brass*, pp. 49–54.
6. *O.R.*, 15:802 (quotations).

secretary's grand design was already losing ground to more daunting pressures upon the Confederacy. Troops in Mississippi that would have been necessary to attack New Orleans were instead contending with Federal forces pushing to control vital railroad lines in the Tennessee-Mississippi border region. On September 29 Davis sent Governor Moore a reassuring but evasive message: "I beg you . . . to believe that you cannot more earnestly desire than I do the speedy expulsion of the invaders from the soil of Louisiana. I am taking further measures which I hope soon to have the pleasure of communicating to you with a view to expedite this result."[7]

Although Randolph had become disillusioned with the president's waning enthusiasm regarding New Orleans, he refused to give up on the venture. This was patently evident in his letter of September 30 to Lieutenant General John C. Pemberton, the new commander at Vicksburg, whose authority extended over Mississippi and East Louisiana (the portion east of the Mississippi). "If a favorable opportunity offer[s] for an attack on New Orleans, you will avail yourself of it, and act in concert with Major General Richard Taylor," Randolph instructed Pemberton. "You will communicate with him as speedily as possible and concert with him a joint plan of operations for the defense of the [Mississippi] river and the capture of New Orleans." Pemberton received a shock a few days later, however, when Major General Earl Van Dorn's forces suffered a total defeat in an attempt to dislodge enemy forces holding the railhead at Corinth, Mississippi. Pemberton would be unable to spare Taylor any troops, especially considering his primary responsibility: preparing Vicksburg for a Federal campaign down the Mississippi. Then, on October 8, Bragg's invasion of Kentucky met a reversal at Perryville, forcing him to abandon the state. "The retreat of Bragg from Kentucky and the defeat of Van Dorn at Corinth change the condition of affairs," wrote Davis in a letter to General Holmes on October 21. By December,

7. Archer Jones, "George W. Randolph's Service," pp. 307–11; *O.R.*, 15:810 (first and second quotations); Shackelford, *George Wythe Randolph*, pp. 137–42; Jefferson Davis to Thomas O. Moore, September 29, 1862 (third quotation), Moore Papers.

Davis was speaking no longer in terms of driving the Federals from Louisiana but was instead simply holding out hope to Governor Moore that somehow Taylor would be able to "baffle the enemy in his designs upon the Mississippi valley."[8]

Remarkably, despite the myriad of obstacles to recapturing New Orleans, Randolph and Davis had placed great faith in Taylor, a non–West Pointer and a sickly brigadier only a few months earlier. Entrusted with discretionary authority over two senior officers, first Holmes and then Pemberton, he had possessed a fleeting opportunity to achieve a magnificent stroke for the Confederacy. A concurrent series of disappointments for Randolph, culminating in his unauthorized attempt to order troops from the Trans-Mississippi across the river, soon left him so embittered toward Jefferson Davis that he resigned as secretary of war in mid-November. His successors never considered reviving the plan to retake New Orleans. Taylor mentioned nothing about the abortive scheme in his memoirs, although he might have enhanced his historical stature by doing so. Faced with the immediate problem of raising troops from Louisiana's demoralized citizenry, he recognized the mammoth difficulties inherent in carrying out Randolph's plan. Yet Taylor personally refused to abandon the dream of recapturing New Orleans. Even with little or no help from other quarters of the Confederacy, he would work constantly toward the day when he could gather enough strength to deliver the city into the hands of his fellow Louisianans. Realizing the heavy odds against him, however, he harbored no illusions of heroic grandeur.[9]

With an attack on New Orleans now impossible, Taylor's desire to press southeastward toward the city still made sense as an effort to relieve nearby parishes of the oppressive Federal presence. For several months Butler had been sending troops on forays into the Lafourche region on the western side of the Mississippi above New Orleans. "We are prisoners in every sense of the term," wrote a local militia commander, "as we have [enemy] gunboats passing up and

8. *O.R.*, 17(2):716–17 (first quotation 717); Archer Jones, "George W. Randolph's Service," p. 310; Rowland, *Jefferson Davis*, 5:356 (second quotation), 381 (third quotation).

9. Shackelford, *George Wythe Randolph*, pp. 140–50, 171.

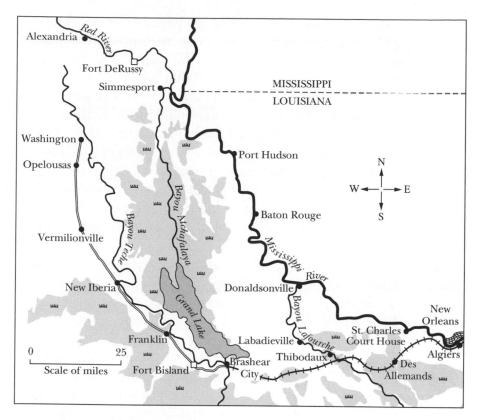

Map 5. *New Orleans, Lafourche, and Teche Regions*

down the River, and the proximity of the city renders expeditions from that place an easy matter. Were we to attempt exercising any military authority, we would be arrested and our families harassed. Where is our protection to come from?" Taylor answered the plea by sending Major Edward Waller's unit of mounted Texas riflemen, described by a grateful militia officer as "a splendid battalion of cavalry." The only trained and experienced troops then under Taylor's command, Waller's men arrived in Louisiana in late October primed for a fight. On September 4 a detachment of the Texans, along with a militia unit, struck the Federal outpost at Des Allemands and forced its garrison back toward New Orleans. "This trifling success," wrote Taylor, "the first in the State since the loss of New Orleans, attracted attention, and the people rejoiced." [10]

Capturing enough Yankee rifles to replace many of their outmoded flintlocks and shotguns, Waller's men also recovered piles of booty the Federals had stolen during a recent raid upon nearby plantations. "Books, pictures, household furniture, finger rings, breast pins and other articles of feminine adornment and wear, attested [to] the catholic taste and temper of these patriots," observed Taylor. The enemy had in fact swept through Taylor's home parish, St. Charles. His plantation, Fashion, left in the care of an overseer during his family's absence, had suffered some of the worst desecration and looting. "It is one of the most splendid plantations that I ever saw," wrote a Vermont private in a letter describing Fashion. "I wish you could have seen the soldiers plunder this plantation." Not only did they confiscate all of the stock animals, but they also forced Taylor's slaves to help them ransack the house and barns. The spoils included "hundreds of bottles of wine, eggs, preserved figs and peaches, turkeys, chickens, and honey in any quantity. . . . The camp is loaded down with plunder—all kinds of clothing, rings, watches, guns, pistols, swords, and some of General [Zachary] Taylor's old hats and coats, belt-swords—

10. Lathrop, "Lafourche District in 1862: Militia and Partisan Rangers," pp. 230–44 (first quotation 234); Morris, "Battle of Bayou des Allemands," p. 16 (second quotation); Richard Taylor, *Destruction and Reconstruction*, pp. 131–32 (third quotation 131). See also Spurlin, *West of the Mississippi with Waller's Cavalry*.

and, in fact, every old relic he had is worn about the camp. . . . Nothing is respected."[11]

Robert Butler, one of the militiamen with Waller in the attack on Des Allemands, described their midnight march along the Mississippi in the aftermath of destruction: "It was one continual scene of desolation and sadness—nearly every place on the route had been despoiled and plundered—even to the huts of the poorest creoles." When they reached Fashion, the soldiers stopped for a closer look, the militiaman recalling, "The officers entered the house—it was a complete wreck, the furniture smashed, the walls torn down, pictures cut out of their frames, while . . . scattered over the floor, lay the correspondence and official documents of the old General while President of the U.S.—the barbarians had respected nothing but the portrait of General [Winfield] Scott upstairs." At the recapture of Brashear City in the summer of 1863, Louisiana captain Raney Greene recovered from a Vermont officer a letter written by Taylor to his father in 1850. Upon receiving the letter from Greene, a grateful Taylor remarked that it was the "sole object left in his possession which had belonged to his father."[12]

One of Fashion's slaves, William Henry Hawkins, a butler and valet to Taylor, later testified to the quantity of plunder the Federals had reaped: 130 horses, 200 head of sheep, and several hundred hogsheads of sugar, along with virtually all of the family's personal possessions. He said that about 175 slaves had been working on the plantation when the soldiers arrived. Hawkins expressed a continued sense of loyalty to his master and regretted seeing Fashion sacked. But another slave interviewed at the same time, Washington Kelly, said he left Fashion rejoicing that he was forever "free from slavery."[13]

11. Richard Taylor, *Destruction and Reconstruction*, pp. 131–32 (first quotation 132); Lathrop, "Federals 'Sweep the Coast,'" pp. 62–68; "Plunderers in Louisiana," p. 538 (second and third quotations).

12. Robert Butler to his sister, September 22, 1862 (first and second quotations), Butler Papers; Lathrop, "Federals, 'Sweep the Coast,'" pp. 63–64 (third quotation 64).

13. Statements by William Henry Hawkins and Washington Kelly, June 1, 1914 (quotation), Stauffer Papers.

Once they had gained their freedom, however, Taylor's slaves could not simply go wherever they wished. Unlike the slaves of local planters who had declared loyalty to the Union and who therefore continued to hold their slaves as legal property, Taylor's blacks received treatment as the confiscated property of a traitor. Much like the livestock herded away from Fashion by the soldiers, the slaves officially became contraband of war. Taken by the Federals to a camp at Algiers, near New Orleans, they congregated with tens of thousands of other blacks, now ostensibly free yet wholly dependent upon the Yankees for support. While General Butler and his advisors grappled to determine how to put them to productive tasks, many of the freedmen agreed to work for the army as laborers, and some volunteered to enlist as soldiers in the Louisiana Native Guard, a regiment of black soldiers—the first black unit in the United States Army—recently formed by Butler on an experimental basis. But the others, at least thirty thousand of them, remained in the contraband camps, barely surviving in repulsive conditions, without enough food and medical care. About this time Taylor's brother-in-law Martin Gordon, Jr., still living in New Orleans, received a desperate message from Taylor's former slaves asking him to "get word to Mars Dick that they were dying of disease and starvation. Thirty had died that day." Gordon immediately appealed to a Federal officer for some kind of action; but the officer only responded dispassionately, "It is working out as I expected. . . . Their strong men we put in the army. The rest will disappear like cotton after a frost."[14]

During October of 1862 General Butler initiated a plan requiring Federal officials to take over abandoned and confiscated plantations like Fashion and put freedmen to work on them as wage laborers. A considerable number of Taylor's former slaves returned to Fashion, and by the spring of 1863 a Federal inspector reported a total of 351 freedmen, about 150 more than Taylor ever owned, were living and working on the plantation. About 900 acres of sugar cane and 400

14. Messner, *Freedmen and the Ideology of Free Labor*, pp. 1–20; Joe Gray Taylor, "Slavery in Louisiana during the Civil War," pp. 27–29; Oakes, *Slavery and Freedom*, pp. 182–88; Chesnut, *Mary Chesnut's Civil War*, p. 467 (quotations). See also C. Peter Ripley, *Slaves and Freedmen in Civil War Louisiana*, pp. 25–68, 102–25.

acres of corn were in full cultivation. In August an inspector reported that "the crops of corn and cane equal anything I have seen." He described discipline among the freedmen as "very good—the negroes have great confidence in the U.S. Gov't and the overseer, and cheerfully comply." Much like other portions of the occupied South, the region near New Orleans saw masses of freedmen back on the plantations, many of them working for their former masters. The Union military command had established an economic and racial policy for controlling black labor that would endure throughout the war and afterward. With little opportunity to buy their own land, most blacks submitted to an agricultural economy based on sharecropping, enmeshing themselves in an almost hopeless cycle of debt and poverty that seemed almost the mirror image of slavery.[15]

When Taylor learned of the extent of wanton looting and ravaging the Federals had perpetrated prior to the fight at Des Allemands, he could hardly contain his rage. On September 8 he persuaded R. C. Wickliffe, a former Louisiana governor, to deliver a letter to General Butler under a flag of truce. Taylor's letter berated Butler for allowing "a ruthless soldiery" to engage in "lawless and inhuman acts . . . the horror of which no language can exaggerate." He also informed Butler that in reprisal for each subsequent act of this kind he would execute ten of the Union soldiers captured at Des Allemands. Although both the United States and Confederate governments had recently authorized executions of prisoners as retribution for the enemy's killing of civilians, as well as for civilians who killed soldiers, Taylor had taken the law into his own hands by vowing such punishment for the destruction of private property alone. Butler responded

15. Roland, *Louisiana Sugar Plantations*, pp. 56, 72–73; Howard A. White, *Freedmen's Bureau in Louisiana*, pp. 45–47; Messner, *Freedmen and the Ideology of Free Labor*, pp. 32–43, 184–87; Moses Greenwood to Richard Taylor, November 19, 1864, Richard Taylor Papers, Louisiana State Museum, Louisiana Historical Center; plantation report by Captain S. W. Cozzens, May 15, 1863, United States Army, Records of Continental Commands, Letters Received (file C–77–1863); report by George Hanks on Taylor and Payne Plantations, August 6, 1863 (quotations), United States Treasury Department, Records of the Third Special Agency, Civil War Special Agencies of the Treasury Department, (vol. 71).

Benjamin F. Butler, infamous "Beast" of New Orleans
(Jenkins Rare Book Company).

with a stern but placid letter. Assuring Taylor that no Federal soldier had the right to damage anything, Butler also reminded Taylor that "unlicensed acts . . . committed by troops in marching is the well-known fact of all civilized warfare." He also mentioned that he possessed thirty prisoners of his own whom he judged to have engaged in equally detestable guerrilla-style tactics at Des Allemands and that he had hundreds of others as well, many of whom had committed indiscriminate acts of terrorism over the past several months. "I shall make no threats of reprisal," Butler stated passively. "No hair on the head of any one of my captured soldiers ought to be touched. . . . I trust you will reconsider your determination to do so in any event." Promising to deal harshly thereafter with any Federal soldier caught destroying private property, Butler concluded, "That I punish the guilty marauders with promptness, the women and children of New Orleans who sleep in calm undisturbed quiet under our flag will tell you." [16]

Taylor made no reply to Butler, thus allowing his threat to stand. A few days later Butler communicated with southern partisan Brigadier

16. Benjamin F. Butler, *Private and Official Correspondence*, 3:265–69 (first quotation 265–66, second quotation 266, third quotation 268–69, fourth quotation 269); Richard Taylor, *Destruction and Reconstruction*, p. 132.

General M. Jeff Thompson, who had been attempting to arrange an exchange of prisoners with Butler from eastern Louisiana, outside Taylor's district. Enclosing a copy of Taylor's "extraordinary communication," Butler informed Thompson that any further prisoner exchanges would be completely unwarranted until he could be certain Taylor would not act upon the "ill-judged determination" to execute captured Union soldiers. "That Genl. Taylor may have some personal feeling because of the deprivation of some property upon his plantation, taken by my men, and for the loss of his father's sword . . . I can readily understand," wrote Butler. "But that his 'private griefs' should incite him to forget his duty as a soldier . . . I shall not believe unless constrained by the fact." Presumed private griefs aside, Taylor soon became satisfied that Federal soldiers would no long commit depredations. He later observed that "the conduct complained of was speedily stopped . . . by orders from General Butler." Taylor was so pleased by the result that he actually maintained lasting respect for "Beast" Butler. But this confrontation with Federal military power would prove only temporarily beneficial. The enemy's destructive proclivities portended worse calamities for Louisiana. Taylor had received a foretaste of total war.[17]

In order to protect the Lafourche region from any further intrusions, and to reap its potential for supplies and new recruits, Taylor instructed Major Waller to patrol the area along the Mississippi River. He also warned Waller specifically to avoid entrapment by enemy troops who might land both above and below him, since his only escape would be through the treacherous swamps several hundred yards from the river. But Waller acted negligently. On September 8, four Federal regiments, using the very tactics Taylor had feared, descended on Waller near St. Charles Court House and chased his cavalrymen into the swamps. In their confusion and panic Waller's men abandoned more than two hundred horses and many of their weapons, including four artillery pieces. "The battalion was shattered and went to pieces . . . wading through the swamps . . . [and] made their way to Bayou des Allemands in squads of 15 or 20," wrote a Confed-

17. Butler, *Private and Official Correspondence*, 3:302–3 (first and second quotations 303); Richard Taylor, *Destruction and Reconstruction*, p. 132 (third quotation).

erate. Taylor later observed of Waller's laxity, "The constant watchfulness . . . that is necessary in war, can only be secured by discipline which makes duty a habit."[18]

Despite Waller's humiliating defeat, Taylor still had reason to expect success in defending the Lafourche region. In mid-October Brigadier General Jean Jacques Alfred Alexander Mouton, son of former governor Alexander Mouton, arrived with the Eighteenth Louisiana Regiment. A thirty-three-year-old West Pointer and hero of Shiloh, where he had been gravely wounded, Mouton took command of about 2,500 men, including nearly 1,000 inexperienced militiamen and conscripts formed into regiments. From his headquarters at Thibodaux, Mouton spread his forces out at various points throughout the Lafourche region to detect Federal movements. On October 27 Brigadier General Godfrey Weitzel led about 5,000 Yankees from New Orleans up both sides of Bayou Lafourche to Thibodaux, routing Mouton's skeleton forces, many of whom deserted without firing a shot. "The terror, destruction, and confusion that reigned here at that time can only be described by those who remained to witness it," wrote a swift-footed Confederate. A few miles up the bayou, near Labadieville, Weitzel attacked a larger portion of Mouton's command. "This entire force," recalled one of Mouton's men, "was badly armed with guns of inferior quality." Once again the rich Lafourche region had fallen under Federal domination.[19]

Taylor later asserted that, had Mouton concentrated all of his regiments rather than leaving them spread out, he "would have defeated Weitzel and retained possession of the Lafourche country." Considering Weitzel's superior manpower and Mouton's poorly armed and

18. Lathrop, "Lafourche District in 1862: Confederate Revival," p. 315; Carpenter, *History of the Eighth Regiment*, p. 70; Spurlin, *West of the Mississippi with Waller's Cavalry*, pp. 48–49; Morris, "Battle of Bayou des Allemands," p. 16 (first quotation); Richard Taylor, *Destruction and Reconstruction*, p. 133 (second quotation).

19. Arceneaux, *Acadian General*, p. 53; Lathrop, "Lafourche District in 1862: Invasion," pp. 175–86; Raphael, *Battle in the Bayou Country*, pp. 41–46; Winters, *Civil War in Louisiana*, pp. 159–62; Bergeron, *Uncle Silas*, pp. 107–10 (first quotation 107, second quotation 106).

undisciplined troops, however, Taylor had demanded far too much. In his report to the War Department he admitted that conscripts were deserting at a high rate, thereby proving "the impolicy of employing troops in the immediate vicinity of their own homes." Furthermore, legal exemptions from conscription for planters and their sons had virtually ruined "the expectation of any serviceable addition being made to the number of conscripts now in service." Fortunately for Taylor, the Federals advanced no farther than Berwick's Bay and established headquarters at Thibodaux, where General Weitzel supervised Butler's program for operating plantations for cultivation by free black labor. Had he known of Mouton's inability to resist further attacks, Weitzel could have continued raiding at will across the whole of southern Louisiana.[20]

As yet unaware of Mouton's debacle at Labadieville, Taylor had engaged himself in strategic concerns of far-reaching significance. Responding to Lieutenant General John Pemberton's request for a conference, he spent several days at Vicksburg during late October discussing possible means of cooperation. "It was of vital importance to control the section of the Mississippi receiving the Red and Washita [Ouachita] Rivers," he recalled, not only to protect central Louisiana from invasion but also to allow troops and supplies to continue crossing the Mississippi. Vicksburg's defenses would have to receive support in tandem from Port Hudson, downriver. "I undertook to supply Vicksburg and Port Hudson with corn, forage, sugar, molasses, cattle, and salt," wrote Taylor. Providing salt, an especially scarce commodity throughout the Confederacy, became one of Taylor's most crucial responsibilities following the discovery of huge beds of pure rock salt at Judge D. D. Avery's island in Vermilion Bay, south of New Iberia. There Taylor established a mining operation with slave labor and constructed meat packing facilities for curing beef. After his conference with Pemberton, however, he began to doubt President Davis's wisdom in appointing such an apparently ordinary artillery offi-

20. Richard Taylor, *Destruction and Reconstruction*, p. 134 (first quotation); *O.R.*, 15:175–76 (second quotation 175, third quotation 176); Ethel Taylor, "Discontent in Confederate Louisiana," p. 415; Winters, *Civil War in Louisiana*, pp. 163–64.

cer to a pivotal command like Vicksburg. "Davis could have known nothing of Pemberton except that his military record was good," Taylor later observed. Pemberton's lack of ability seemed too obvious to ignore. "President Davis should have known all about it," Taylor asserted, "and yet he made a pet of Pemberton." For the time being at least, much the same could have been said about Taylor.[21]

In order to prevent enemy gunboats from invading Louisiana's interior, Taylor initiated the construction of several small forts, terming them "mere water batteries." Fort DeRussy stood near the mouth of the Red River, and Fort Beauregard at the mouth of the Ouachita. Another, Fort Burton on the Atchafalaya at Butte a la Rose, would help secure the transportation route of supplies eastward and would also prevent enemy gunboats from ascending the Atchafalaya to its junction with the Red River. Garrisoned by no more than one hundred men each and armed with only a few moderately heavy guns, these three forts would always remain vulnerable to enemy assaults unless rapidly supported by Taylor's army. "It was not supposed that they could be held against serious land attacks," he noted pessimistically.[22]

After learning of Mouton's defeat at Labadieville, Taylor groped for a plan to defend the Teche region of south-central Louisiana against an invasion that he knew must come. He ordered Mouton to construct earthworks on either side of Bayou Teche and the road running parallel to it a few miles upstream from Brashear City. Called Fort Bisland, this position stood vulnerable to a flanking attack if enemy troops used transports to land above on Grand Lake. "This danger was obvious," he recalled, "but the people [in the Teche region] were so depressed by our retreat from [the] Lafourche that it was necessary to fight even with this risk." Fears of invasion had grown so pronounced that many planters and other citizens had left

21. *O.R.*, 15:174–75; Geise, "General Holmes Fails," pp. 172–73; Richard Taylor, *Destruction and Reconstruction*, pp. 135–39 (first and second quotations 137, third quotation 138, fourth quotation 139); Lonn, *Salt As a Factor*, pp. 70–71; Raphael, *Battle in the Bayou Country*, pp. 54–55.

22. *O.R.*, 15:175; Richard Taylor, *Destruction and Reconstruction*, pp. 140–42 (quotations 141); Geise, "General Holmes Fails," p. 173; James L. Nichols, *Confederate Engineers*, pp. 58–59.

the Teche region, taking their slaves with them in a westward exo-dus.[23]

In an attempt to rally morale and patriotism, Taylor issued a public appeal on November 8 to the citizens of St. Mary, St. Martin, and Lafayette parishes. "I regret the causeless panic which has led so many of the inhabitants of the parishes bordering on the Teche to abandon their homes," he stated. "I assure the residents . . . that the means already under my control are ample to repel any attempt which the enemy might be disposed to make to occupy this portion of the State; and reinforcements are on the way and will shortly arrive." He also asked planters to furnish slaves as laborers on the earthworks at Fort Bisland and to provide supplies "for the comfort of the men who are engaged in defending their homes and their property." Yet scores of Mouton's newest soldiers proved unworthy of such support. A Union officer reported on December 8, "The conscripts are desert-ing the rebels . . . from the other side of Berwick's Bay; we have a number come in every day."[24]

Desperate to compensate for the increasing rate of desertions, Tay-lor implored General Pemberton at Vicksburg for help. "One good regiment of infantry not subject to such influences would be of incal-culable service to me," he wrote. Hardly impressed, Pemberton re-plied sharply, "I am utterly unable to afford you any assistance . . . as I regard the defense of this valley of much greater importance than that of West Louisiana." Curbing his pride, Taylor addressed Pember-ton in a conciliatory tone, expressing an understanding of the specter of twin Federal campaigns, one against Vicksburg from Tennessee and the other against Port Hudson from New Orleans. "In asking for a regiment from your side of the river it was for the purpose of giving some confidence and backbone to the raw levies, composing the prin-cipal part of my little force," he explained. "Were it not for the salt

23. Richard Taylor, *Destruction and Reconstruction*, pp. 142–43 (quotation 143); *O.R.*, 15:859–60.

24. *The Confederate States*, November 15, 1862 (first and second quotations). Taylor's proclamation, titled *To the People of the Parishes of St. Mary, St. Martin, and Lafayette* (New Iberia, November 5, 1862), was also issued in broadside circular form, a copy of which is in the Museum of the Confederacy, Rich-mond, Va. Allen, *Pickering Dodge Allen*, p. 80 (third quotation).

mine I would feel like taking the responsibility of going over to you with every man and gun." Yet Taylor also repeated to Pemberton the handicaps under which he was operating. "To defend the lower part of this district against an enemy supreme on the water is simply an impossibility," he lamented. "The country is penetrated in every direction by large, deep bayous and lakes, the defense of which would require a large army."[25]

By early 1863 New Orleans had a new Federal commander, Major General Nathaniel P. Banks, Taylor's old adversary during the Shenandoah Valley Campaign. Taylor later explained Banks's appointment with the supposition that his "blunders served to endear him to President Lincoln." No Confederate, however, could afford to scoff at the thirty thousand troops Banks now had at his disposal. Lincoln meant for Banks to act aggressively to subdue the whole of Louisiana and to use his political background to cultivate Unionist sentiment in forming a reconstructed state government. As his first goal, however, Banks set his sights on capturing the southern stronghold at Port Hudson in order to clear the Mississippi River northward for Union vessels to aid Major General Ulysses S. Grant in his impending siege of Vicksburg. To succeed, Banks would have to rid the western side of the Mississippi of interference from Taylor. Not only did Banks determine to prevent Taylor from sending more supplies and any reinforcements to Port Hudson, but he also wanted to shield New Orleans from a possible attack by Taylor since the large majority of Federal troops would be away from the city.[26]

In mid-January Banks sent General Weitzel with forty-five hundred men up along Bayou Teche with orders to capture Fort Burton on the Atchafalaya and thereby enable Federal gunboats to reach the mouth of the Red River. Outnumbered by more than three to one, Mouton gave Weitzel little resistance. The lone armed vessel at Mouton's disposal, a converted steamboat called the *Cotton*, could not even maneuver well within the Teche's narrow channel, so Mouton ordered it scuttled to prevent its capture. Fortunately, the *Cotton*'s

25. *O.R.*, 15:859–60 (first quotation 860), 868 (second quotation), 873 (third and fourth quotations).

26. Richard Taylor, *Destruction and Reconstruction*, p. 132 (first quotation); Winters, *Civil War in Louisiana*, pp. 166–67, 212.

sunken hull helped to impede the advance of the Federals' four small gunboats, so Weitzel decided to withdraw, satisfied that he had intimidated Mouton. In mid-February, Taylor learned that a gunboat, the *Queen of the West*, one of many Union vessels on the Mississippi, had successfully run past the Confederate batteries at Vicksburg. Informed on the fourteenth that the gunboat had entered the Red River, Taylor rode rapidly the thirty miles from the Atchafalaya through sleet and hail to Fort DeRussy on the Red. There at dusk he discovered that Confederate artillery had disabled the *Queen*, forcing its crew to abandon the boat near the riverbank. Taylor ordered the vessel towed up to Alexandria for repairs. "She was an ordinary river steamer, with her bow strengthened for ramming," he recalled. "A heavy bulwark for protection against sharp-shooters, and with embrasures for field guns, surrounded her upper deck."[27]

Almost immediately Taylor learned that another enemy vessel, the powerful ironclad *Indianola*, had also cruised past Vicksburg's batteries and was terrorizing Confederate traffic on the Mississippi. "We had barely time to congratulate ourselves on the capture of the *Queen* before the appearance of the *Indianola* deprived us again of the navigation of the great river, so vital to our cause," he wrote. "To attempt the destruction of such a vessel as the *Indianola* with our limited means seemed madness; yet volunteers for the work promptly offered themselves." Soldiers from the garrison at Fort DeRussy eagerly boarded the *Queen* when it arrived from Alexandria on February 19. A converted steamer, the *Webb*, clad with cotton bales and fortified for ramming, also received more than enough volunteers. Yet Major Joseph Brent, Taylor's choice to command the expedition, had trouble convincing local planters, whose slaves had been building the fort's earthworks, to agree to lend their valuable bondsmen to serve as stokers for the two gunboats. "It was a curious feature of the war that the Southern people would cheerfully send their sons to battle, but kept their slaves out of danger," Taylor later complained. Such reluctance reflected a growing tendency among planters living in war zones to doubt the Confederate government's ability to protect what

27. Kerby, *Kirby Smith's Confederacy*, pp. 24–28; Winters, *Civil War in Louisiana*, pp. 212–14; Raphael, *Battle in the Bayou Country*, pp. 67–76; Richard Taylor, *Destruction and Reconstruction*, pp. 142–46 (quotation 146).

they perceived as their most vital interest, slave labor for commercial profit. Unable to gain the planters' compliance, Major Brent boldly laid hold of a gang of slaves by force, put them aboard the *Queen* and *Webb*, and departed. "A famous din was made by the planters, and continued until their negroes were safely returned," Taylor noted.[28]

On February 24 Brent found the *Indianola* about twenty-five miles below Vicksburg, near the western bank of the Mississippi. "I doubt whether any commander ever had an expedition of poorer promise against as formidable and well equipped an enemy," Brent later professed. But his own audacity and the advantage of surprise gave him a brief chance for success. Under cover of darkness he ordered the *Queen* and *Webb* to ram directly into the Union vessel. The *Queen* attacked first, plowing through a coal barge at the *Indianola*'s side. The *Webb* struck another coal barge on the other side, ripping it apart and fortunately avoiding shots from the *Indianola*'s forward guns. The *Queen* then crashed into the ironclad's paddle box and into the armor, and the *Webb* closed in for the kill, striking the same spot with such speed that the armor collapsed. After about an hour the *Indianola* was sinking, her crew clamoring for mercy. "Thus we regained control of our section of the Mississippi," wrote Taylor, "and by an action that for daring will bear comparison with any recorded of Nelson or Dundonald." Brent's heroics achieved no lasting effect, however, because in mid-March Rear Admiral David G. Farragut ran two large ships past the Confederate batteries at Port Hudson in order to prevent Taylor from sending more supplies downriver to the fort. Even before Banks's and Grant's sieges of Port Hudson and Vicksburg had reached full scale, Taylor realized that "the navigation of the great river was permanently lost to us."[29]

28. Richard Taylor, *Destruction and Reconstruction*, pp. 146–47 (first quotation 146, second and third quotations 147); Escott, "Failure of Confederate Nationalism," p. 26; Powell and Wayne, "Self-Interest and the Decline of Confederate Nationalism," pp. 30–31.

29. Kerby, *Kirby Smith's Confederacy*, pp. 28–29; Brent, *Lugo Case*, pp. 33–84 (first quotation 33); Richard Taylor, *Destruction and Reconstruction*, pp. 147–49 (second quotation 149); Edmonds, *Guns of Port Hudson*, 1:103; Irwin, "Capture of Port Hudson," pp. 589–90.

One week earlier Taylor had welcomed to the Trans-Mississippi Department a new supreme commander, Lieutenant General Edmund Kirby Smith. A Florida native with a West Point education and experience in the Mexican War and Indian fighting on the Texas frontier, Smith had risen rapidly in the Confederate military hierarchy. Winning Jefferson Davis's favor for his success as a brigade and divisional commander in Virginia, he took over the District of East Tennessee and led a corps during Braxton Bragg's invasion of Kentucky in the summer of 1862. Yet Bragg's growing animosity toward Smith prompted Davis to seek to use him elsewhere, and the Trans-Mississippi's mismanagement under Holmes spurred Davis to replace him with Smith. Scholarly and religious by nature, Smith wore spectacles and had a receding hairline, making him appear older than his thirty-eight years. Taylor seemed pleased with Smith's appointment, calling him "an excellent selection." [30]

Moving the department's headquarters from Little Rock to Alexandria, Smith considered his primary responsibility, according to orders from the War Department, to be the disruption of enemy movements against Vicksburg and Port Hudson. This would require the defense of Taylor's district from invasion by Federals under Banks's command. Recognizing Taylor's need for reinforcements, President Davis assigned Brigadier General Henry Hopkins Sibley's Texas cavalry brigade to service in Louisiana. Although his troopers had seen hard service in New Mexico and had also driven enemy troops from Galveston, the forty-six-year-old Sibley was a notorious alcoholic who had recently gone to Richmond in order to clear himself of charges of drunkenness and cowardice. Davis ignored Sibley's failings and expressed assurance in his capacity as an officer. Taylor likewise placed high expectations in Sibley and his Texans. "I have the utmost confidence in your ability to whip all the raw Yankees that Weitzel can bring against your position," wrote Taylor shortly after Sibley's arrival in early March. "Your fine artillery and superior cavalry will give you great advantage." Taylor intended this extra

30. Parks, *Edmund Kirby Smith*, pp. 251–53; Kerby, *Kirby Smith's Confederacy*, p. 29; Richard Taylor, *Destruction and Reconstruction*, pp. 150–51 (quotation 151).

Edmund Kirby Smith, assertive commander of the Trans-Mississippi Department
(Stephen M. Rowe).

firepower and mobility to do no less than "clear out our side of the river."[31]

Upon inspecting Sibley's thirteen hundred men assembled at Fort Bisland, however, Taylor began to worry. Like so many of the cavalrymen who came from the Lone Star State, Sibley's presented a thoroughly unmilitary appearance. "The men were hardy and many of the officers brave and zealous," recalled Taylor, "but the value of these qualities was lessened by lack of discipline." On one occasion Taylor made a frustrating search in camp for a Texas cavalry colonel, finally locating him sitting in the shade of a grove of trees with several of his men gathered around him in a strangely devoted manner. Approaching nearer, Taylor discovered the colonel was dealing a hand of monte, a Mexican card game popular among Texas frontier gamblers. One of the Texans later described his fellow troopers as "the gamblingist, most profane group of men I had ever met. They would bet on the way a bird would fly." None of the soldiers in the circle bothered to give Taylor much notice, but the colonel did offer to deal his new commanding general into the hand. Taylor ordered the game stopped at once and berated the colonel. "Learning that I would not join the sport, this worthy officer abandoned his amusement with some displeasure," wrote Taylor. "It was a scene for that illustrious inspector Colonel Martinet to have witnessed."[32]

General Banks's plan to secure his western flank in the Teche region before moving up the Mississippi to seize Port Hudson mirrored his previous efforts in the Shenandoah Valley. Unless Banks swept the Teche clear of Confederate forces, New Orleans, like Washington, would lay open to a Stonewall Jackson-style threat from Taylor, thus jeopardizing the operation against Port Hudson, much like McClellan's operation against Richmond. "The Teche country was to the war in Louisiana what the Shenandoah Valley was to the war in Vir-

31. Parks, *Edmund Kirby Smith*, pp. 255–59; Jerry Thompson, *Henry Hopkins Sibley*, pp. 311–14; Richard Taylor to Henry Hopkins Sibley, March 2, 1863 (quotations), Sibley Letters.

32. Richard Taylor, *Destruction and Reconstruction*, pp. 149–50 (first quotation 149, third quotation 150); Duaine, *Dead Men Wore Boots*, pp. 28–29 (second quotation 28); Jerry Thompson, *Henry Hopkins Sibley*, pp. 322–23.

ginia," observed a perceptive Federal soldier. "It was a sort of back alley, parallel to the main street [the Mississippi River] . . . and one side or the other was always running up or down the Teche with the other side in full chase after it." The Shenandoah Valley's agricultural wealth also found a counterpart in the Teche region, whose abundance of supplies gave Banks another enticement for making a foray. Taylor had no more than four thousand men in the area to resist the offensive, but like his mentor Jackson, he would continually have the advantage of operating against troops who had little stomach for marching long distances into a country with a hostile climate and against a highly mobile, often unseen enemy.[33]

By April 10 Banks had moved sixteen thousand men, three divisions of his Nineteenth Army Corps, to Brashear City, about fifteen miles below Fort Bisland. Just as Taylor expected, Banks sent four thousand men under Brigadier General Cuvier Grover on floating transports up the western edge of Grand Lake to attempt to land above Fort Bisland and threaten Taylor's rear while the rest of Banks's troops attacked his front. As a Union officer described the movement, "Our force was so much stronger than Taylor's as to suggest the idea of capturing him . . . as otherwise he might retire indefinitely into the vast open country behind him and return at his leisure at some inopportune moment." Determined to oppose both movements at the same time, Taylor later insisted that "to retreat without fighting was, in the existing condition of public sentiment, to abandon Louisiana." Positioning a detachment of cavalry and some artillery on Grand Lake to stall Grover's arrival, Taylor braced himself with most of his manpower at Fort Bisland. In the late afternoon of the twelfth, Banks appeared and drove in Taylor's skirmishers. "The enemy were in force," wrote a Confederate soldier. "They were advancing with cavalry, artillery, and heavy columns of infantry on both sides of the Bayou. . . . Thirty-nine pieces of artillery on our side opened the ball at half past 4 o'clock, p.m.; four thousand muskets supported the music from behind our breastworks." Banks responded with his own symphony of long-range shot and shell; but within three hours dark-

33. De Forest, *A Volunteer's Adventures*, pp. 85–86 (quotation 85); Edmonds, *Guns of Port Hudson*, 1:202; Kerby, *Kirby Smith's Confederacy*, pp. 97–98.

Henry H. Sibley, Taylor's weak right arm
(*Johnson and Buell,* Battles and Leaders of the Civil War).

ness had put a halt to the barrage, and both sides settled into camp for the night.[34]

Surmising that Banks would likely wait for Grover's movement toward the rear to develop, that night Taylor rode thirteen miles up to Franklin, near Grand Lake, to assess Grover's progress. Before leaving, however, he ordered Sibley to prepare his seasoned brigade for a counterattack against Banks's left at sunrise. Confident that Sibley would hit Banks hard enough to force him to withdraw Grover and suspend the entire operation, Taylor learned at Franklin that, fortunately, Grover had not yet landed. At dawn Taylor returned to Fort

34. Raphael, *Battle in the Bayou Country*, pp. 86–95; Irwin, "Capture of Port Hudson," pp. 590–91 (first quotation 590); Richard Taylor, *Destruction and Reconstruction*, pp. 153–55 (second quotation 155); Noel, *Old Sibley Brigade*, p. 46 (third quotation).

Bisland to discover that Sibley had failed to make any preparations to strike Banks. "The supineness of that officer [Sibley] . . . and his positive declaration of the impracticability of carrying the plan into execution for want of time frustrated the scheme," Taylor complained in his official report. Now he would have to wait for Banks to make the next move.[35]

A thick fog lifted over Bayou Teche on the morning of the thirteenth to reveal Banks's infantry advancing slowly, his artillery delivering a tremendous outpouring of screening support. "At times the firing was so brisk that one could scarcely discern any pause whatever," wrote a Texan. Taylor estimated that the enemy had about sixty artillery pieces, many of them heavy rifled guns. Noticing that the Louisianans behind the breastworks on the right showed "much consternation" because they had not seen serious combat before now, Taylor worried that even a halfhearted Federal assault might result in a breakthrough. "It was absolutely necessary to give the men some morale," he recalled. Mounting the breastwork, he casually rolled a cigarette and proceeded to walk up and down the line, smoking with utter nonchalance while peering at the advancing foe and ignoring the artillery fire that continued to rake the position. Inspired by Taylor's example, Captain Robert Bradford of the Twenty-eighth Louisiana volunteered to climb a nearby tree and gain a better view of the enemy's movements. Taylor handed Bradford his field glass, "and this plucky youngster sat in his tree as quietly as in a chimney corner, though the branches around were cut away." The Louisianans responded with a new confidence, a few even exposing themselves too rashly, "and some casualties were suffered in consequence." Having first seen the necessity of demonstrating to his brigade in Virginia his willingness to risk his own life, Taylor now did the same on the breastwork at Bisland, much to the satisfaction of his raw troops.[36]

35. Richard Taylor, *Destruction and Reconstruction*, pp. 154–55; Jerry Thompson, *Henry Hopkins Sibley*, p. 325; Winters, *Civil War in Louisiana*, pp. 222–23; *O.R.*, 15:388–89 (quotation 389).

36. Noel, *Old Sibley Brigade*, p. 47 (first quotation); *O.R.*, 15:389–90; Richard Taylor, *Destruction and Reconstruction*, p. 155 (second, third, fourth, and fifth quotations); Bergeron, *Guide to Louisiana Confederate Military Units*, p. 138.

Throughout the day the bombardment continued, but Taylor knew "there was nothing to be done but submit to the pounding." The Federals poured their heaviest fire on the gunboat *Diana*, which some of Sibley's artillerymen and Waller's troopers had captured from the enemy a few weeks earlier. Positioned in the bayou between the breastworks and armed with a thirty-pound gun, the largest in Taylor's arsenal, the *Diana* received a series of direct hits from Federal Parrotts, leaving it temporarily disabled. Taylor went immediately to assess the damage. "An officer came to the side of the boat to speak to me, but before he could open his mouth a shell struck him, and he disappeared," Taylor recalled. Even after losing the *Diana*, however, the southerners remained calm as they watched Banks arrange his regiments for an apparent movement forward against the breast-works. "I hoped an attack would be made," wrote Taylor, "feeling con-fident of repulsing it." But the attack never came. Although Banks did attempt to apply pressure on both flanks, he met stiff resistance, and with daylight fading, he finally backed down, obviously waiting for Grover to disembark at Grand Lake and fall on Taylor's rear.[37]

Grover's tardiness worried Banks, but it gave Taylor an added dose of encouragement. Still believing that his cavalry at Grand Lake would detect Grover's appearance in time to allow a detachment of Confederates from Bisland to prevent a landing, Taylor waited for a report from the rear. "No news seemed good news," he recalled. But about 9:00 P.M. word came that Grover had landed in force and had already pushed back Taylor's cavalry to within two miles of Franklin, thus threatening to block their only escape route from Bisland north-ward through the cane fields and swamps. "Here was pleasant intelli-gence!" Taylor recounted. "There was no time to ask questions. I hoped to cut my way through, but feared the loss of wagons and ma-terial." Ordering his officers to begin an immediate evacuation of Bis-land, Taylor rode north to Franklin to determine Grover's exact loca-tion. Just beyond the town he discovered that the bridge across Bayou

37. Richard Taylor, *Destruction and Reconstruction*, pp. 156–57 (first and second quotations 156, third quotation 157); *O.R.*, 15:390–91; Raphael, *Battle in the Bayou Country*, pp. 77–85, 95–98; Allen, *Pickering Dodge Allen*, pp. 100–101; Arceneaux, *Acadian General*, pp. 78–80; Jerry Thompson, *Henry Hopkins Sibley*, pp. 325–26.

Yokely stood unoccupied, a stroke of good fortune he could hardly believe. A short distance to the east, on the far side of a wooded area, he saw the camp fires of Grover's troops. "Grover had stopped just short of the prize," wrote Taylor. "Thirty minutes would have given him the wood and the bridge, closing the trap on my force."[38]

Realizing that he must intimidate Grover in order to give the retreating Confederates from Bisland enough time to escape across the Bayou Yokely bridge, Taylor led his available forces, no more than twelve hundred men, directly toward Grover's camp. With the first faint signs of dawn on April 14 Taylor ordered a charge as the Federals started to move cautiously forward in line of battle, their vision still clouded and their footing unsteady in the cane fields muddied by recent rains. All at once they reeled backward under the screaming southerners' gunfire, leaving a battery on their left so helplessly exposed that Taylor and his staff, riding forward at a full gallop, compelled the groggy-eyed gunners to abandon their artillery pieces. "All this was easy enough," Taylor recorded. "Surprise and the uncertain light had favored us; but broad day exposed our weakness, and the enemy threw forward a heavy line of skirmishers." With casualties mounting and Grover's superior manpower gradually threatening to overwhelm Taylor's thin line of soldiers, suddenly the *Diana* appeared churning its way up Bayou Teche, its big gun's shells ripping apart the Federal lines. Then the most advance units from Bisland started to arrive, and by noon Taylor's column of troops and supply wagons had safely crossed the Bayou Yokely bridge, taking the road to New Iberia. Taylor ordered the bridge burned and the *Diana* destroyed to keep the enemy from capturing the vessel.[39]

In his official report General Banks described the actions at Fort Bisland and Franklin (also known as Irish Bend) as great successes,

38. Richard Taylor, *Destruction and Reconstruction*, pp. 157–58 (first and second quotations 157, third quotation 158); Raphael, *Battle in the Bayou Country*, pp. 99–100; *O.R.*, 15:391; Winters, *Civil War in Louisiana*, pp. 224–26.

39. *O.R.*, 15:391–92; Richard Taylor, *Destruction and Reconstruction*, pp. 158–59 (quotation 159); Winters, *Civil War in Louisiana*, pp. 226–29; Raphael, *Battle in the Bayou Country*, pp. 109–20; Tiemann, *159th New York Volunteers*, pp. 28–30; Noel, *Old Sibley Brigade*, pp. 47–48.

but one of his officers overheard him moan, "We had the rebels in a bag, and Gen. Grover held the strings . . . but the damn string was rotten, and they slipped through." Another officer later admitted, "Taylor had made a gallant fight and had extricated himself cleverly." Indeed, Taylor himself recalled the results with great pride. "The object sought in holding Bisland was attained," he asserted. "From this time forward I had the sympathy and support of the people, and my troops were full of confidence."[40]

Taylor had a right to boast about saving his little army, but his sanguine view of the homefront in southern Louisiana masked his inability to protect private property and engender consistent public loyalty. As his men marched north, burning bridges in an attempt to slow the pursuing foe, state officials in Opelousas decided to move the state capital all the way to Shreveport, where General Smith now maintained the Trans-Mississippi Department's headquarters. Citizens in the Teche region fled before the invaders. "The entire force of the Yankees moved on up the Bayou Teche, plundering and stealing everything they could put their hands on," wrote a Confederate prisoner who marched with them. A Federal soldier confessed, "We have left an awful scene of desolation behind us. In spite of orders not to pillage, burned and sacked houses mark our course." Brigadier General William H. Emory complained to Banks of "grave disorders" among "stragglers" who made thievery a full-time occupation. "The inducements for plunder in this country are so great that unless high-handed measures are taken, many men will be lost to the ranks," Emory warned. But Banks was distracted with a more official and profitable kind of plundering. Along the route he supervised the systematic confiscation of immense stores of cotton, sugar, and other valuable commodities and began shipping them to New Orleans. Soon after reaching Opelousas on April 20, Banks estimated that he had already seized as much as $10 million in private property. His soldiers also destroyed the Confederate salt works at Avery Island. In the meantime thousands of slaves escaped their masters and poured into

40. Flinn, *Campaigning with Banks*, p. 56 (first quotation); Irwin, "Capture of Port Hudson," p. 592 (second quotation); Richard Taylor, *Destruction and Reconstruction*, pp. 160–61 (third quotation).

the Federal lines. The New Orleans *Era*, a Unionist newspaper, reported gleefully, "Our army is rolling like a ball of fire through the
finest portion of Louisiana."[41]

Taylor clearly had no cause to rejoice about such devastation, yet
the condition of his own troops should have seemed just as discouraging. During the retreat to Opelousas hundreds deserted. Louisianans returned to their homes to protect their families while many
Texans headed west for the border of their own state. "Our regiment
lost heavily by desertion and fatigue," wrote a soldier in the Eighteenth Louisiana. "Many of the men had but little to eat, had been up
for two nights, and were unable to travel." Thus hundreds more fell
captive to the enemy. "Stragglers in gray and butternut dropped back
among us," noted a Federal soldier, "for although we could not catch
the Texan horsemen, we were marching the Louisiana infantry to tat-
ters. . . . They told us that their officers were driving the men on with
drawn sabers, or the whole force would have gone to pieces under the
exhaustion of the retreat." Over the next several days Taylor would
lose more than twelve hundred men, about one-third of his command, to straggling and desertion.[42]

Although he expressed in his official report his "regret" that a
"very considerable number" had deserted, Taylor did not seem
deeply concerned. By now he had begun to accustom himself to
seeing his soldiers—especially conscripts—leave to attend to private
affairs only to return and fight again. The previous December he had
granted thirty-day deferments to many conscripts who begged to go
home to care for their starving and ill families. The rigid discipline
he had once demanded of his brigade in Virginia now seemed unde-
sirable, if not impossible. Realizing that the paucity of forces available

41. Arceneaux, *Acadian General*, pp. 87–90; Haas, "Diary of Julius Giesecke," p. 28 (first quotation); Moors, *Fifty-Second Massachusetts Volunteers*, pp.
132–39 (second quotation 133); William H. Emory to Richard B. Irwin, May
2, 1863 (third and fourth quotations), Emory Papers; Raphael, *Battle in the
Bayou Country*, pp. 125–44; Lonn, *Salt As a Factor*, pp. 192–93; Allen, *Pickering Dodge Allen*, p. 109 (fifth quotation).

42. Bergeron, *Uncle Silas*, p. 122 (first quotation); De Forest, *A Volunteer's
Adventures*, p. 92 (second quotation); *O.R.*, 15:387.

to him might dwindle even further if he exerted tight control, Taylor reported candidly, "It is to be hoped [the lack of discipline] will be corrected" so that these "excellent" soldiers might give "more efficient service to our cause." Taylor distinguished harshly, however, between deserters and jayhawkers, the latter being lawless bands of mounted marauders who preyed on civilians. By late spring he had routinely begun ordering parties of soldiers to track down jayhawkers in an effort to quell their robberies and depredations. If evidence proved their guilt, or even if they resisted arrest, they suffered immediate execution, especially when they happened to be renegade Yankees. Confederate deserters often turned up during such operations, but unless they had become jayhawkers themselves, these wayward soldiers were simply returned to the army. A few months later a Louisiana officer recorded in his diary that Taylor "is celebrated for having never punished a deserter."[43]

If Taylor had a right to be angry about poor discipline during the retreat to Opelousas, he blamed the problem on one man: Brigadier General Henry Hopkins Sibley. Already disgusted with Sibley's failure to prepare and initiate an attack at Fort Bisland on the morning of April 13, Taylor had also ordered him to coordinate the evacuation of the army's supply wagons from Bisland late in the evening. Sibley apparently had been feeling sick, because throughout the day's fighting he rested comfortably at his headquarters far from the fighting. After receiving Taylor's orders for evacuation, he delegated the responsibility to a subordinate and promptly went to bed. The next day, during the hectic race through Franklin, Sibley dutifully ordered his men to set fire to the Bayou Yokely bridge without realizing that Mouton's command had not yet crossed. Mouton's Louisianans luckily escaped across the burning bridge just before it collapsed. Sibley topped this blunder by ignoring Taylor's orders to transport the sick and wounded in wagons, ambulances, and other available vehicles. Instead he put them on a steamboat headed

43. *O.R.*, 15:394 (first and second quotations); Ethel Taylor, "Discontent in Confederate Louisiana," p. 415; Bragg, *Louisiana in the Confederacy*, pp. 198–99; Arceneaux, *Acadian General*, pp. 139–41; Pellet, *114th New York Volunteers*, pp. 184–86; Hyatt diary, p. 68 (third quotation).

up Bayou Teche, only to see the vessel easily captured by the enemy.[44]

Sibley's incompetence proved even more detrimental, however, during the final stages of the retreat. Trusting Sibley to carry out one last order, Taylor personally instructed him to prevent all straggling and to maintain firm control over the column during the march to Opelousas. Later that afternoon Taylor discovered that "the men were straggling without order over the whole line of march and adjacent country." Sibley himself was not even in the vicinity. Instead, he had taken a road completely different from that of the troops. Late in the evening he finally appeared, informing Taylor that once again he had become ill. Shortly afterward Taylor entered charges against Sibley for his multiple transgressions and ordered him court-martialed. Although no evidence arose indicating that Sibley had been drinking, his erratic conduct fit this well-known pattern of behavior. Departmental inefficiency delayed the trial until August, and the passage of time apparently favored Sibley's case. Ruling that he had not deliberately disobeyed Taylor's orders, the court-martial panel acquitted him on all counts. Having gone without a command in the meantime, however, he failed to convince his superiors of his worthiness for a new assignment. Blaming Taylor for this humiliation, Sibley wrote him in mid-October requesting "reparation for the injury you have inflicted upon me." Taylor responded in an amiable but stubborn tone, "I am not conscious of having voluntarily inflicted any injury upon you, and consequently have to decline acceding to [your] request."[45]

Sibley's fall from grace left his brigade under the command of Colonel Thomas Green, who had taken charge unofficially after Sibley's incapacitation at Bisland. The forty-eight-year-old Green was a genuine Texas hero. A veteran of San Jacinto, an Indian-fighting Texas

44. Jerry Thompson, *Henry Hopkins Sibley*, pp. 326–28; Bergeron, *Uncle Silas*, p. 121.

45. *O.R.*, 15:393 (first quotation); Jerry Thompson, *Henry Hopkins Sibley*, pp. 328–31; Henry Hopkins Sibley to Richard Taylor, October 16, 1863 (second quotation), Richard Taylor to Henry Hopkins Sibley, October 21, 1863 (third quotation), Richard Taylor Papers, Louisiana Adjutant General's Office. Cited hereafter as Taylor Papers, Jackson Barracks.

Ranger, and an officer under Zachary Taylor in the Mexican War, Green also had a reputation as a heavy drinker, but apparently he held his liquor well. "Upright, modest, and with the simplicity of a child, danger seemed to be his element, and he rejoiced in combat," wrote Taylor. "To me he was a tried and devoted friend, and our friendship was cemented by the fact that, through his Virginia mother, we were related by blood." Soon after Green's crucial service in directing rear guard action during the retreat from Bisland, Taylor secured his promotion to brigadier general and appointed him commander of all cavalry units.[46]

After abandoning Opelousas, Taylor sent Green and Mouton west, hoping they would find good foraging and would revive their men for a strike against Banks's rear, thereby threatening his lines of communication and supply. Taylor took about one thousand remaining Louisiana infantry, a cavalry regiment, his artillery, and the supply wagons north to Alexandria, arriving on April 24. But Green and Mouton had to go all the way to the Sabine, more than one hundred miles distant, to find sufficient forage. Banks's army therefore continued unfettered along Bayou Teche toward Alexandria, throwing the Red River Valley's population into mass panic. Taylor fled farther upriver with his small force to Natchitoches, and on May 8 Banks marched arrogantly into Alexandria. Underscoring the Federals' gargantuan presence, nine gunboats commanded by Admiral David D. Porter steamed up the Red River past Fort DeRussy, which Taylor had ordered abandoned. Almost immediately Banks resumed his wholesale confiscation of cotton and other property for shipment to New Orleans. When a committee of terrified Alexandria citizens approached him seeking some kind of compensation, Banks only sneered, "Believe it gentlemen, as if you heard God himself speak it, I will lay waste to your country . . . so that you will never organize and maintain another army in this department."[47]

Although Edmund Kirby Smith now feared that the Federals

46. Barr, "Tom Green," pp. 39–41; Faulk, General Tom Green, p. 53; Richard Taylor, Destruction and Reconstruction, pp. 215–16 (quotation 216).

47. Kerby, Kirby Smith's Confederacy, pp. 100–109; Arceneaux, Acadian General, pp. 90–91; Official Report Relative to Federal Troops, pp. 144–45 (quotation 145); Winters, Civil War in Louisiana, pp. 230–38.

Thomas Green, trusted and aggressive cavalry commander
(Jenkins Rare Book Company).

would continue sweeping unopposed up the Red River to capture
Shreveport with its abundance of supplies and even to invade Texas,
he refused to blame Taylor. "General Taylor has done everything that
was possible with the resources at his command," Smith reported to
the War Department. Taylor still believed, however, that Banks would
soon veer back to the Mississippi to besiege Port Hudson. Yet this did
not make the forced retreat of more than 150 miles any easier for
him to bear. "Taylor is a very quiet, unassuming little fellow, except on
a retreat, when he is really noisy," observed Lieutenant Colonel Arthur W. Hyatt. "On these occasions he has been known to curse and
swear at mules and wagons, but this is overlooked as it is . . . only done
for effect." By now his use of profanity seemed more palpable, because his chronic rheumatoid arthritis had flared up again. "I came
across Gen. Dick Taylor cussing [and] crippled but full of fight and
blasphemy," recalled a cadet at the Louisiana state seminary who
joined the evacuation from Alexandria. "The boys told of him that he
could cuss a blue streak. . . . But in passing him I saw a keen-looking,
intelligent man, and one who looked the brave man that soldiers said
he was."[48]

48. Kerby, *Kirby Smith's Confederacy,* pp. 105–9; *O.R.,* 15:387 (first quotation); Richard Taylor, *Destruction and Reconstruction,* p. 160; Hyatt diary, p. 68
(second quotation); Henderson, "Boys of '63," p. 86 (third quotation).

Taylor's five-year-old son Zack, dressed in Confederate gray,
less than a year before his death in April 1863
(Edward M. Boagni).

Pain and anger turned to deep personal sorrow when Taylor learned that the older of his two sons, Zack, died of scarlet fever on April 27. Only two days earlier, at Alexandria, Taylor had put his family on a steamboat headed up the Red River for Shreveport with other refugees. "A moment to say farewell," he recalled, and his wife, Mimi, with their two girls and two boys departed, "all pictures of vigorous health." Five-year-old Zack died before they reached Shreveport. Mimi described her feelings to her niece Wilhelmine Trist. "My little man Zack was manly to the last," wrote Mimi. "I thought my heart would break when I saw that dearest little face covered with Death's icy hand, [and] when those beautiful, bright eyes closed forever. . . . I felt as if I had lost all in this world." Some Confederate officers onboard constructed a small coffin, and a recently married young woman gave part of her bridal dress to line and cover it. When the family reached Shreveport, the child's body was taken to a church, where the same officers stood watch during the night. Although the other Taylor children also showed

Taylor's daughter Elizabeth, ca. 1865. Photograph rather crudely retouched (Edward M. Boagni).

symptoms of scarlet fever, a local citizen, Ulger Lauve, offered to care for them and comfort Mimi in his home, risking his own family's exposure.[49]

"I was stunned by this intelligence, so unexpected," Taylor recalled, "and it was well perhaps that the absorbing character of my duties left no time for the indulgence of private grief." Still unable to join his family, Taylor received word a few weeks later that his younger son,

49. Richard Taylor, *Destruction and Reconstruction*, pp. 162–63 (first quotation 162); Myrthe Bringier Taylor to Wilhelmine Trist, June 5, 1863 (second quotation), Trist Family Papers; Tucker, *Descendants of the Presidents*, pp. 103–4; undated genealogical data on the Taylor family, Wood Papers.

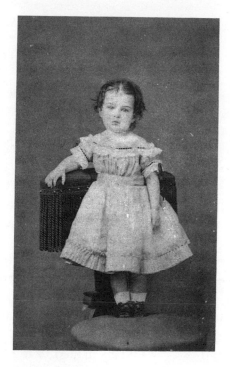

Taylor's daughter Myrthe Bianca, born in November 1864,
pictured at the age of twenty months
(Edward M. Boagni).

Richard, Jr., affectionately called Dixie, had died on May 20, almost a month short of his third birthday. "My sweet little Dixie lingered for three weeks," wrote Mimi. "Nothing, scarcely nothing, was left of him. It was enough to soften the hardest heart to witness the sufferings my sweet little man went through the last 24 hours of his short happy life." With her at the time was Clarice Hewitt, wife of James Hewitt, a sugar planter whose family had escaped to Shreveport from his plantation on Bayou Lafourche. "I have been all day with Mrs. Taylor," she wrote in her diary. "It is marvelous, her courage and sweet resignation to the will of God, as both her darling boys are dead. . . . In the midst of her overwhelming sorrow she is unselfishly thinking of what a terrible grief it would be to her husband who is with the army, fighting gallantly in defense of our country." General Smith, acting in Taylor's absence, made arrangements for the burials of both boys.

Fortunately, the two daughters, Louise and Betty, older and stronger, gradually recovered from the illness.[50]

Taylor finally saw his family several days later, yet only for an hour. He did his best to provide a source of strength. "Poor husband!" wrote Mimi. "It nearly breaks my heart when he speaks of those dear departed Angels. He tries so to console and comfort me, when the blow has fallen as heavily on him." Although the Taylors later had another daughter, Myrthe Bianca, born November 29, 1864, Mimi never recovered fully from the crushing loss of her sons and the continual hardship she endured during the war. Only twenty-nine years old in 1863, she began to suffer a slow, steady decline in health. For Taylor, the personal tragedy of the deaths of Zack and Dixie, a result of the larger tragedy of violence inflicted upon the South, received graphic emphasis when he returned to Fashion shortly after the war. Hoping to recover remnants of his family's personal belongings, he found the house in ruins. Walking to a small barn, one of the few remaining structures on the plantation, he gazed upon a horrifying spectacle: the dried hides of a Welsh and a Shetland pony, animals his sons had once loved as favorite pets, nailed to the barn door by the Union soldiers who had plundered Fashion almost three years earlier.[51]

By mid-May 1863, Banks had withdrawn from Alexandria, moving his men overland directly toward Port Hudson, ambitious to overwhelm its defenders, invoke his superior rank to supplant Grant, and then lead a huge combined army that would finally capture Vicksburg. Although he began a siege of Port Hudson in early June, Banks made no headway against the massive breastworks. Even worse, his failure to destroy Taylor's small but potent force had left southern Louisiana open to a Confederate counterthrust that might endanger

50. Richard Taylor, *Destruction and Reconstruction*, p. 163 (first quotation); Tucker, *Descendants of the Presidents*, p. 104; Myrthe Bringier Taylor to Wilhelmine Trist, June 5, 1863 (second quotation), Trist Family Papers; *O.R.*, 26(2):30; Fearn, *Diary of a Refugee*, pp. 33–34 (third quotation 34).

51. Richard Taylor, *Destruction and Reconstruction*, pp. 163, 303; Myrthe Bringier Taylor to Wilhelmine Trist, June 5, 1863 (quotation), Trist Family Papers; Tucker, *Descendants of the Presidents*, p. 104; McIlhenny interview.

Banks's communications and supply lines on the Mississippi. New Orleans itself would also lay vulnerable to Taylor's designs for revenge.[52]

Asserting this very strategy to General Smith, Taylor believed that by moving against New Orleans he would compel Banks to abandon Port Hudson, thereby allowing its garrison to reinforce Joseph Johnston's small army in its operations against Grant east of Vicksburg. In attempting such a campaign, Taylor would now have an added advantage in the form of Major General John G. Walker's Texas Division, recently arrived from Arkansas. A forty-year-old Missourian who had fought in the Mexican War, Walker came to the Trans-Mississippi with a solid record as a divisional commander in the Army of Northern Virginia. Over the past several months he had prepared his Texans to fight. "Seconded by good brigade and regimental officers, he had thoroughly disciplined his men, and made them in every sense soldiers," wrote Taylor. Smith, however, had no faith in Taylor's plans for Walker. "I know your desire is naturally great to recover what you have lost in lower Louisiana, and to push on toward New Orleans," he informed Taylor on May 20, "but the stake contended for near Vicksburg is the Valley of the Mississippi and the Trans-Mississippi Department; the defeat of General Grant is the *terminus ad quem* of all operations in the west this summer; to its attainment all minor advantages should be sacrificed." Smith firmly believed that by cutting off Grant's supply lines opposite Vicksburg on the Mississippi, Taylor would "reduce him to starvation or a change of base."[53]

In belittling a campaign toward New Orleans as a "minor advantage," Smith completely ignored the strategic soundness of Taylor's reasoning. Always pushing for an opportunity and a sufficient force to liberate the city, Taylor also recognized it as Banks's Achilles' heel. In much the same way that Jackson had used the Shenandoah Valley

---

52. Edmonds, *Guns of Port Hudson*, 1:237–39; Irwin, "Capture of Port Hudson," pp. 592–95; Winters, *Civil War in Louisiana*, pp. 238–41.

53. Richard Taylor, *Destruction and Reconstruction*, pp. 164–65, 179 (first quotation); Kerby, *Kirby Smith's Confederacy*, pp. 112–13; Bearss, "Trans-Mississippi Attempt to Relieve Vicksburg," pt. 1, pp. 59–60; *O.R.*, 26(2):12–13 (second and third quotations 13).

John G. Walker, energetic commander of the Texas Division under Taylor
(*Johnson and Buell,* Battles and Leaders of the Civil War).

as a corridor to threaten Washington, Taylor could threaten New Orleans and thereby force Banks to retire from Port Hudson. Perhaps
Taylor was too optimistic in expecting Port Hudson's garrison then to
move north and aid Johnston in his fight against Grant east of Vicksburg. Regardless, Taylor viewed Smith's plan of severing Grant's supply lines on the Mississippi's western bank as utterly senseless. The
many Federal gunboats monitoring the river held a distinct advantage, and the concept of trying to aid Pemberton seemed illogical.
Most absurd of all, Pemberton had resolved to keep his thirty thousand men within Vicksburg's fortifications, bringing them closer
to starvation every day, rather than to force his way out and defeat Grant. "The problem was to withdraw the garrison, not to reinforce it," Taylor later insisted. Although Pemberton claimed that
without reinforcements he would have to remain on the defensive,
Grant himself later commented, "I didn't think the rebels would

be such fools as to shut up thirty thousand troops there for me to capture."[54]

Taylor continued to plead his case for a strike against New Orleans, but Smith resisted adamantly. According to Taylor, Smith informed him that Pemberton and Johnston, as well as the Confederate high command, were demanding "some effort on our part in behalf of Vicksburg, and that public opinion would condemn us if we did not *try to do something*. To go two hundred miles and more away from the proper theatre of action [New Orleans] in search of an indefinite *something* was hard; but orders are orders." Ironically, when Grant's sixty-three-mile supply lines opposite Vicksburg had been most vulnerable several weeks earlier, Smith had retained Walker's Texans in northern Louisiana because of Banks's temporary threat to Shreveport. By now Grant had shortened his supply lines considerably, allowing much stronger protection from armored gunboats on the Mississippi, a menace Taylor recognized as extremely hazardous. Thus Pemberton was the loser to Smith's and Taylor's fundamental fixation on events in their own department. As for grand strategy, Smith and Taylor had diverged completely in their opinions about the Trans-Mississippi. Smith clearly viewed the northern front as most important, with an eventual sweep into Missouri and the recapture of St. Louis as strategically paramount. "The movement into Missouri is the *terminus ad quem* of all my hopes," he informed the War Department. "Complete success on the Mississippi will, I trust, enable its realization." Failing to convince Taylor of either the likelihood or the desirability of achieving such a goal, Smith displayed a stubbornness that merely outranked Taylor's. Smith gave "much of his mind to the recovery of his lost empire, to the detriment of the portion yet in his possession," Taylor later observed; thus "the substance of Louisiana and Texas was staked against the shadow of Missouri and northern Arkansas."[55]

54. Richard Taylor, *Destruction and Reconstruction*, p. 164 (first quotation); Parks, *Edmund Kirby Smith*, pp. 268–69; Simon, *Papers of Ulysses S. Grant*, 16:139 (second quotation).

55. Richard Taylor, *Destruction and Reconstruction*, pp. 165 (first quotation), 150 (third quotation); *O.R.*, 26(2):41–42 (second quotation 42). The strategic

Battle of Milliken's Bend, Louisiana
(Jenkins Rare Book Company).

The heated disagreement between Smith and Taylor regarding Vicksburg showed signs of evolving into a bitter feud. On June 3, with Taylor already near Vicksburg, Smith complained to Taylor's adjutant at Alexandria, Major Eustace Surget, about rumors "misrepresenting my relations with General Taylor, and otherwise calculated to injure me. These reports are said to come from your headquarters." Smith instructed Surget to "counteract any misstatement," assuring him, "I have General Taylor's interests at heart." Apparently the rumors involved the possibility of Smith replacing Taylor with a "senior officer" who might come to Louisiana with reinforcements, whereupon Smith would "take to the field in person" as overall commander. No such senior officer seemed likely to appear, however, and Smith expressed confidence that Taylor would arrive opposite Vicksburg "in time to complete Grant's destruction."[56]

Insistent on action, Smith informed Taylor that a trustworthy civilian had reported that Federal positions near Vicksburg were "guarded by convalescents and some negro troops"; therefore "no

and tactical execution of Confederate operations opposite Vicksburg is described in Bearss, *Campaign for Vicksburg*, 3:1153–1206.

56. *O.R.*, 26(2):29–30 (quotations).

danger was anticipated." His scouts having confirmed this view, Taylor decided to divide Walker's Division and to launch simultaneous assaults against Milliken's Bend and Young's Point, enemy positions lying several miles apart along the Mississippi's western bank. Leaving personal supervision to Walker and his brigade commanders, Taylor remained at Richmond, a town several miles to the west. At Milliken's Bend, the more heavily fortified position, Brigadier General Henry E. McCulloch's brigade moved against a part of the Twenty-third Iowa and a small black brigade composed of former slaves from Louisiana and Mississippi commanded by white officers. Altogether the Federals had no more than a thousand men. With barely two weeks' experience in uniform and armed with inferior muskets, the black troops apparently offered easy prey. "Strict orders had been given to drive the enemy into the river, so as to permit no time for escape or re-enforcements," noted Taylor. Several days earlier Banks had used other black units in a charge upon Port Hudson, the first time any such troops had seen combat, and they had performed with unusual bravery.[57]

Shortly before dawn on Sunday, June 7, McCulloch's fifteen hundred Texans attacked, pushing the outnumbered Federals back toward the river, where two parallel levees allowed defensive positions replete with breastworks bolstered by heavy cotton bales. "The enemy opened a terrible fire of musketry," wrote one of McCulloch's men. "After firing a volley . . . we were ordered to charge them with the bayonet." Another recalled, "The Texas yell was the only response the enemy got from us until we reached them with our bayonets. . . . We mounted the embankment and turned loose our war dogs, and let me tell you . . . they howled!" Many of the blacks failed to reload their muskets properly or did not even try to fire them. "But to their credit . . . they never flinched but made a desperate resistance," wrote a white Federal soldier. "So it came to thrusting at each other with their bayonets, clubbing muskets, and dashing each other's brains out." The Texans seemed determined to give no quarter, bayoneting

57. O.R., 26(2):15 (first quotation) and 24(2):457–59 (second quotation 459); Bearss, "Trans-Mississippi Attempt to Relieve Vicksburg," pt. 1, pp. 61–70; Quarles, Negro in the Civil War, pp. 220–21; Winters, Civil War in Louisiana, pp. 198–200; Palfrey, "Port Hudson," pp. 35–36.

wounded blacks to death and simply shooting others who had thrown down their arms in trying to escape. "I saw one poor darky who had six bayonets thrust [into him] after having fallen by a shot," a Yankee observed. Another remembered, "It was a horrible fight, the worst I was ever engaged in—not even excepting Shiloh. The enemy cried 'No quarter!' but some of them were very glad to take it when made prisoners."[58]

By mid-morning two Union gunboats appeared on the river, shelling the Confederates and gradually forcing them to retire. Mc-Culloch sent word to Walker asking him to come with Colonel Horace Randal's brigade, which had been held in reserve several miles in the rear. When Walker and Randal arrived, they found their men too exhausted from the high temperature to attempt a second assault. "It is true the heat was intense, the thermometer marking 95 degrees in the shade," Taylor reported, "but, had common vigor and judgment been displayed, the work would all have been completed by 8 A.M." Taylor was thoroughly rankled. "In this affair General McCulloch appears to have shown great personal bravery, but no capacity for handling masses," he informed General Smith. His anger only intensified when he learned that Brigadier General James M. Hawes, assigned to attack Young's Point the same morning, had refused to risk his brigade to the heat and the three Federal gunboats on the river. Taylor reported to Smith, "I beg [you] to believe that I used every personal exertion to insure success. . . . Nothing was wanted but vigorous action in the execution of the plans. . . . Unfortunately, I discovered too late that [Walker's] division was possessed of a dread of gunboats."[59]

In his memoirs Taylor professed in an irritated tone, "As foreseen,

58. Norman D. Brown, *Journey to Pleasant Hill*, pp. 234–36; Blessington, *Walker's Texas Division*, pp. 95–97 (first quotation 96); Gravis, *Twenty-Five Years on the Outside Row*, pp. 27–28 (second quotation 28); Hatch, *Dearest Susie*, pp. 53–54 (third and fourth quotations 54); Glatthaar, *Forged in Battle*, pp. 131–35; McPherson, *Negro's Civil War*, pp. 186–87 (fifth quotation 186); Quarles, *Negro in the Civil War*, pp. 222–23; Berlin, *Freedom*, pp. 531–33. See also Hargrove, *Black Union Soldiers*, pp. 139–50.

59. *O.R.*, 24(2):459–60 (first and second quotations 459, third quotation 460), 462–65, 471–72.

our movement resulted, and could result, in nothing." His own lack of enthusiasm for the operation, however, was reflected in faulty planning, poor communications, and the surrender of field command to Walker and his subordinates. By allowing Walker to divide his forces and keep Randal's brigade in reserve several miles distant from both Milliken's Bend and Young's Point, in effect Taylor counted on Randal not having to reinforce either location. He also had expected both McCulloch and Hawes to win their objectives before daylight, fearing that their attacks, if delayed until the heat of the day, would surely flounder, even with support from Randal. Had Taylor kept Walker's Division together, moving against one objective and then the other, not only would he have wielded greater firepower at both points, but he also would have relieved Walker and his officers of the necessity of making difficult field command decisions. Completely frustrated, Taylor admitted to Smith that the operation had convinced him to "rely upon myself not only to devise . . . plans, but also to execute them, in order to insure their being carried out vigorously." [60]

At any rate, the enemy gunboats had proved decisive. In his official report, Walker defended the actions of McCulloch and Hawes, declaring, "The enemy, behind a Mississippi levee, protected on the flanks by gunboats, is as securely posted as it is possible to be, outside a regular fortification." Taylor himself had argued to Smith the prowess of these gunboats as reason enough not to attempt the operation from the beginning. When Walker later protested to the War Department that Taylor's official report had reflected badly on his conduct, Taylor called it a misconception and admitted, "The plan was mine, and the position held by General Walker was strictly in accordance with my orders." Although he had gone into the operation expecting poor results, Taylor was still disappointed with Walker's Division, and only reluctantly did he accept responsibility for defeat. Coming on the heels of Smith's outright rejection of New Orleans as the primary strategic focus, along with the terrible deaths of Taylor's only

60. Richard Taylor, *Destruction and Reconstruction*, p. 166 (first quotation); Bearss, "Trans-Mississippi Attempt to Relieve Vicksburg," pt. 2, p. 55; *O.R.*, 24(2):461 (second quotation).

sons, the abortive effort to aid Vicksburg left Taylor deeply discouraged.[61]

The aftermath of combat also produced disturbing complications. Following the battle at Milliken's Bend, Taylor learned that McCulloch's brigade had captured about fifty black soldiers and two of their white officers. No evidence exists indicating that Taylor personally instructed McCulloch to give no quarter during the attack. McCulloch reported only that Taylor ordered him "to engage the enemy before day and carry his works at the point of the bayonet." Clearly, however, the Texans killed many wounded and otherwise defenseless blacks. Casualties were high on both sides. Confederate losses totaled 44 killed and about 130 wounded, 12 percent of the brigade, testifying to the ferocity of the hand-to-hand fighting. The Federals initially reported 101 killed and 285 wounded, many of whom later died. One black regiment eventually reported 128 killed, almost half its strength.[62]

Federal officials made no formal protest to the Confederates regarding the remorseless killing of black soldiers at Milliken's Bend, but those captured soon became an issue of dire controversy. When General Smith heard rumors on June 13 that black prisoners had been taken, he wrote Taylor, "I hope this may not be so, and that your subordinates . . . may have recognized the propriety of giving no quarter to armed negroes and their officers. In this way we may be relieved from a disagreeable dilemma." Taylor did not respond directly to Smith's statement, but in his official report he remarked that "unfortunately" the blacks and their white officers were indeed in his possession. "I respectfully ask instructions as to the disposition of these prisoners," he inquired of Smith. Ignorance of official Confederate policy prompted Smith to write the War Department for guidance. In 1862 the War Department had approved the army's vow to execute captured black soldiers, but President Davis had modified the

61. *O.R.*, 24(2):462–65 (first quotation 465, second quotation 462); Bearss, "Trans-Mississippi Attempt to Relieve Vicksburg," pt. 2, p. 55; Richard Taylor, *Destruction and Reconstruction*, p. 164; Norman D. Brown, *Journey to Pleasant Hill*, p. 238.

62. *O.R.*, 24(2):459, 469 (quotation); Norman D. Brown, *Journey to Pleasant Hill*, p. 236; Quarles, *Negro in the Civil War*, p. 224.

policy by requiring individual states to prosecute them as slaves inciting insurrection. Until now, however, neither the army nor any state
(South Carolina being the only state where blacks were held prisoners) had gone so far as to execute any black soldiers. Just a few weeks
after the soldiers at Milliken's Bend were captured, the Louisiana legislature passed a law requiring a mandatory death penalty for any
slave caught bearing arms against the Confederacy.[63]

Despite this official policy, in mid-July Secretary of War James A.
Seddon instructed General Smith to avoid giving no quarter to black
troops and to consider black prisoners "as deluded victims" deserving
to be "treated with mercy and returned to their owners." Seddon's
apparent magnanimity actually reflected a growing concern among
Confederate authorities that any executions would not only bring retaliation in kind from the Federals but also that France and England
would continue to withhold full diplomatic recognition and support
for the Confederacy.[64]

In mid-June, General Grant learned that a Confederate deserter,
Thomas Cormal, claimed to have seen a mass hanging of all the
blacks as well as a white captain captured at Milliken's Bend. "General
Taylor and command were drawn up to witness the execution," Cormal testified. Grant immediately wrote Taylor protesting the alleged
incident. Taylor strongly denied the accusation, assuring Grant that
"had any officer or negro been hung the fact must have come to my
knowledge." Grant accepted Taylor's explanation and admitted, "I
could not credit the story, though told so straight, and I am now truly
glad to hear your denial." A similar rumor later circulated that Confederates had executed the two white officers captured at Milliken's
Bend, but no evidence emerged to warrant a Federal investigation.
The state of Louisiana never prosecuted the black prisoners, and although their final disposition remains unclear, most likely they were
reenslaved or used by the army as laborers, typifying the fate of other
such captives in the South. The Confederacy's refusal to treat blacks

63. *O.R.*, series 2, 6:21–22 (first quotation); *O.R.*, 24(2):459 (second quotation); Berlin, *Freedom*, pp. 567–68, 578; Kerby, *Kirby Smith's Confederacy*,
p. 111.

64. *O.R.*, series 2, 6:115 (quotation); Berlin, *Freedom*, pp. 567–68. See also
Westwood, "Captive Black Union Soldiers in Charleston," pp. 28–44.

as regular prisoners for exchange eventually forced Federal officials to suspend all exchanges. At the same time, the combat effectiveness of the fledgling black troops in Louisiana and South Carolina convinced the North to accept sorely needed manpower in the form of nearly two hundred thousand black volunteers during the remainder of the war.[65]

On September 4, an alarmed General Smith informed Taylor, "The policy of our enemy in organizing negro regiments is being pushed to formidable proportions. Our plantations are made his recruiting stations. . . . Every sound male black left for the enemy becomes a soldier, whom we have afterward to fight." Urging Taylor to move slaves into the interior of the state prior to Federal advances, Smith instructed him to put them to work, if possible, as laborers on army fortifications and facilities. As was the case throughout the South, however, Union troops and gunboats would continue to press deep into Louisiana, giving slaves ever-greater incentive to escape bondage and become soldiers in blue. Neither Taylor nor any other Confederate commander could prevent it.[66]

65. *O.R.*, 24(3):425–26 (first quotation 425), 443–44 (second quotation 444), 469 (third quotation); Leon Mitchell, "Prisoners of War in the Trans-Mississippi," pp. 123–35; Berlin, *Freedom*, pp. 568–70; Knox, *Camp-fire and Cotton-field*, pp. 313–15; Quarles, *Negro in the Civil War*, pp. 224–25. See also Cornish, *Sable Arm*, pp. 163–68.

66. *O.R.*, 22(2):990 (quotation), 994–95; Kerby, *Kirby Smith's Confederacy*, pp. 111–12.

CHAPTER EIGHT

Nemesis of Yankee Invaders

We owe it to him that the State is not now

entirely overrun and occupied by the enemy.

Governor Thomas O. Moore

After the exasperating defeat at Milliken's Bend on June 7, Taylor believed he had finally persuaded General Smith of the futility of attempting to aid Vicksburg. Returning to Alexandria, Taylor instructed Walker to prepare to march his division south to the Teche region in order to move against New Orleans and thereby lure Banks away from Port Hudson. But Smith suddenly countermanded Taylor's orders and retained Walker for continued service near Vicksburg. In the rising temperatures of the Mississippi River's bottomlands, Walker soon saw one-third of his men too sick for duty, giving him good reason to resist Smith's entreaties to resume the fight. Taylor considered Walker's stagnation a ludicrous waste, but as he later put it, "the pressure on General Smith to *do something* for Vicksburg was too strong to be resisted." The best Smith could do was to call part of Colonel William H. Parsons's brigade of Texans (two cavalry regiments and a battery) from Arkansas to make a series of mounted raids opposite Vicksburg during late June. With only limited help from Walker's Division, Parsons performed well, routing enemy positions and disrupting Federal-held plantations along the Mississippi, but ultimately his actions proved inconsequential.[1]

Meanwhile Smith reluctantly allowed Taylor to assemble enough men to make a modest strike southward in an indirect attempt to relieve Port Hudson. His command comprised Mouton's and Green's brigades, along with a 650-man Texas cavalry brigade under Colonel James P. Major, Green's brother-in-law. This gave Taylor no more than three thousand men to move against Brashear City, a fortified enemy position that also happened to block his route to New Orleans. While formulating his plan of attack, Taylor spent an evening at the Merrick plantation in Pointe Coupee Parish. At dinner Mrs. Merrick served champagne, causing Taylor to comment rather impulsively, "I'm astonished, madam, that in these times you can be living in such luxury." Mrs. Merrick explained that he had the good fortune to join them on a special occasion, her daughter's birthday, and that the family's last bottle of champagne had been saved for this reason alone.[2]

Taylor was in no mood to celebrate anything just yet. He quickly decided to direct a complicated assault on Brashear City, where the surrounding waters of Berwick Bay and the dense swamps in the vicinity appeared virtually impenetrable. On June 19 he sent Major's cavalry on a daring sweep of more than 150 miles through enemy territory east toward Donaldsonville, then south toward Thibodaux, and finally west to cut off the railroad line that offered the Federal garrison at Brashear City its only avenue of retreat. At the same time, a coordinated attack against the fort was scheduled for dawn on the twenty-third. An advance party of only three hundred men, led by Major Sherod Hunter of Green's brigade, would attempt a surprise amphibious movement across Grand Lake and through the swamps to the rear of the fort. Making preparations in the vicinity of New Iberia, Taylor's soldiers assembled more than fifty watercraft—boats, skiffs, flats, and even sugar coolers. "By night and by day the work of

    1. Kerby, *Kirby Smith's Confederacy*, pp. 114–15; Richard Taylor, *Destruction and Reconstruction*, p. 166 (quotation); Bailey, "A Texas Cavalry Raid," pp. 138–52; Bailey, *Between the Enemy and Texas*, pp. 133–47.

    2. Kerby, *Kirby Smith's Confederacy*, pp. 115–16; Richard Taylor, *Destruction and Reconstruction*, pp. 166–67; Roland, *Louisiana Sugar Plantations*, pp. 132–33 (quotation 132).

collecting together and making small boats went bravely on," a Texan recalled. Ordered to prepare three days' rations, the men of Hunter's Mosquito Fleet, as they called themselves, had no idea of their destination, so secretive was Taylor about their mission. Near sunset on June 22 they departed to the cheers of their comrades, who would march down Bayou Teche and provide little more than artillery support once the Mosquito Fleet arrived for the attack.[3]

Arriving in position at dawn on the twenty-third, Taylor ordered Green to unleash a long-range artillery barrage across Berwick Bay's eight-hundred-yard expanse, the signal for Hunter to begin his charge. "Instantly the whole bay was in a blaze," recalled a Louisianan. The Federals in the fort defending Brashear City scrambled to their heavy guns and returned the fire. Hunter was nowhere in sight. After paddling twelve treacherous miles across Grand Lake, his valiant Mosquito Fleet had become lost in the swamps and was still several miles from Brashear City. "At the sound of [Green's] guns Major Hunter . . . halted and asked us whether we would follow him now in broad daylight and make a desperate effort to capture the place," remembered one of his weary men. "Of course all voted to try the thing, and on we went." Often knee-deep in mud and water, they slogged through the swamps for more than an hour before emerging upon an open field to see a large enemy camp near the fort. At first they recoiled at the sight of so many troops; but Hunter rallied them with some choice profanity, and they began moving in line of battle toward the camp. The shocked Yankee soldiers "formed with astonishing rapidity but we rushed with that 'demonic Texan yell' upon them and they had only time to fire one round at us before we were right at and among them with our bayonets," recalled a Confederate. "Resistance ceased at once," Taylor later noted.[4]

3. Finch, "Surprise at Brashear City," pp. 403–16; Richard Taylor, *Destruction and Reconstruction*, pp. 167–68; Kerby, *Kirby Smith's Confederacy*, pp. 115–17; Noel, *Old Sibley Brigade*, pp. 51–53 (quotation 51).

4. "Capture of Brashear City: A Rebel Account," p. 174 (first quotation); Noel, *Old Sibley Brigade*, pp. 53–55; C. H. Walde to J. B. Barry, September 1, 1864 (second and third quotations), Barry Papers; Finch, "Surprise at Brashear City," pp. 416–20; Richard Taylor, *Destruction and Reconstruction*, pp. 168–69 (fourth quotation 169).

Although Hunter's men had the upper hand, the shooting did not end as quickly as Taylor remembered. Because the Federals had considered the position virtually immune to intrusion, most of the nearly two thousand soldiers stationed there were convalescents who offered easy targets in the first few minutes of smoky chaos and panic. The regular garrison, raw recruits commanded by inexperienced officers, splintered into groups that either waved white handkerchiefs of surrender or kept firing, prompting the attackers to shoot indiscriminately at the armed and unarmed alike. The southerners seemed especially keen on subduing the garrison's small contingent of black troops, most of whom fled into the swamps rather than risk capture. By the time Taylor crossed Berwick Bay with Green's and Mouton's men, Hunter's band of raiders had taken almost seventeen hundred prisoners. "Our captors were the most ragged, dirty-looking set of rascals I had ever seen," recalled a Federal soldier. "The only thing uniform among them was dirt—shirts, pants, skin being all of a fine mud color . . . on the whole a good-natured, jolly set of country boys." Another prisoner noted that the Confederates "at once commenced to loot the town and camps, and get drunk." "It was a scene of wildest excitement and confusion," wrote Taylor. "The sight of such quantities of 'loot' quite upset my hungry followers."[5]

One question remained unanswered: where was Colonel Major's cavalry? Assigned several days earlier the task of sweeping around to secure the railroad line running east from Brashear City, Major and his Texans had been ripping into enemy outposts from Thibodaux to Lafourche Crossing, "with double-barrelled shot-guns and border rifles cracking like champagne corks . . . [and] yelling like Comanches," according to one Yankee. Well fortified with captured Federal commissary whiskey, they had spent a Saturday night singing a drunken version of "Dixie," carrying a refrain about recapturing New Orleans. As Mouton's Louisianans now attempted to restore order in Brashear City, Taylor sent Green's troopers down the railroad line, where they soon heard an engine gaining steam and pulling away, its

5. Finch, "Surprise at Brashear City," pp. 421–26; "Capture of Brashear City," p. 78 (first quotation); Bosson, *Forty-Second Massachusetts Volunteers*, pp. 276 (second quotation), 282–83; Richard Taylor, *Destruction and Reconstruction*, p. 169 (third quotation).

cars loaded with more than four hundred escaping enemy soldiers. Early the next morning Green's men found the train halted near the Bayou Boeuf bridge with Major's errant cavalry blocking its path and rounding up prisoners.[6]

Taylor's strategy had worked to perfection. Considering that so much could have gone wrong in such a combined operation, he astounded even himself. "I felt that sacrifices were due to Fortune," he later confessed. Not only had he seized Brashear City and its railroad line—the key to reconquering the Lafourche region—but he had also bagged twelve large guns, more than five thousand new rifles, and an estimated $2 million worth of supplies. "The quantity of quartermaster's and commissary and ordnance supplies captured at this place exceeds belief," he reported to General Smith. A bemused Federal soldier, alluding to the reputation General Banks had already achieved in Virginia, observed, "Banks was once more Commissary for the Confederacy." Bogged down in the trenches before Port Hudson, Banks wrote General Emory at New Orleans that the news of Brashear City's surrender seemed "incredible." Now left with only about a thousand troops to defend New Orleans against Taylor, Emory retorted sharply, "You need no longer be incredulous."[7]

A Yankee prisoner later described to Emory what he saw at Brashear City: "Taylor, black beard and mustache . . . in citizen's dress . . . seemed to have charge of the operations. . . . The rebels seemed much elated at the amount of spoil they took. . . . They all talked of going to New Orleans." Taylor reflected this pervasive confidence in a dispatch to General Smith. Returning briefly to Alexandria on the twenty-seventh, Taylor abruptly informed Smith that, because "results of great interest can be accomplished . . . I have ordered Major General Walker's division to proceed immediately to Berwick Bay;

6. Kerby, *Kirby Smith's Confederacy*, pp. 117–18; Duganne, *Camps and Prisons*, pp. 122–29 (quotation 123); Richard Taylor, *Destruction and Reconstruction*, pp. 169–70; *O.R.*, 26(1):217–20, 225–26.

7. Winters, *Civil War in Louisiana*, pp. 284–89; Richard Taylor, *Destruction and Reconstruction*, pp. 170–71 (first quotation 171); Kerby, *Kirby Smith's Confederacy*, p. 118; *O.R.*, 26(1):210–12 (second quotation 210–11); Flinn, *Campaigning with Banks*, p. 89 (third quotation); Finch, "Surprise at Brashear City," p. 430 (fourth and fifth quotations).

Richard Taylor's dressing kit, carried throughout the war
(Zachary Taylor Collection, Louisiana State Museum,
photograph by Jan White Brantley).

thence I shall send it into the Lafourche country." He also reminded
Smith, "I had decided upon the same plan" prior to Smith's retention
of Walker near Vicksburg. Despite Walker's obvious inability to do
anything to aid Vicksburg, Smith again thwarted Taylor's intentions,
notifying him succinctly, "I shall order Walker's division to you whenever operations about Vicksburg will permit."[8]

Even without Walker's help, Taylor was determined to push into
the Lafourche region and on toward New Orleans. Remaining at

8. Frank W. Loring to William H. Emory, July 5, 1863 (first quotation),
Emory Papers; *O.R.*, 26(1):211 (second and third quotations) and (2):206–7
(fourth quotation 107).

Brashear City to strengthen the fort's defenses and send the captured supplies into the interior, he ordered Mouton, Green, and Hunter to move east toward the Mississippi. Mouton marched swiftly to Thibodaux, where he forced a Federal outpost to surrender without a fight, and by July 1 his men held Boutte Station, only twenty miles from New Orleans. "They moved quickly from place to place," wrote a Federal soldier, "leaving stragglers and scouting squads occupying all of the roads in the region . . . looting where they could." Southern loyalists rejoiced at Mouton's arrival. "Another glorious victory yesterday," exclaimed a planter. "It is supposed [the Confederates] will now march on New Orleans." As the Confederate resurgence spread, freedmen working on the region's hundreds of confiscated plantations fell into a state of alarm and fled to the swamps. Many, however, refused to submit to the terror, and as one Yankee recalled, they "demanded arms, declaring that they will fight to the death, rather than return to bondage."[9]

Farther upriver at Donaldsonville, on June 28, shortly after midnight, Tom Green's Texans dismounted and attacked a substantial enemy earthwork, Fort Butler, defended by fewer than two hundred Federals. "The affair was unfortunate," wrote Taylor, "but, like the Irishman at Donnybrook, Green's rule was to strike an enemy whenever he saw him." Green failed to carry the fort, suffering heavy casualties during an initial assault. According to one of the defenders, just as Green prepared to make another attempt, a Federal gunboat in the vicinity "discovered the whereabouts of the Confederates and under cover of the fog got into position and gave them a broadside that caused a general stampede." Despite Green's setback, Taylor effectively took control of the river during the first week in July, sending twelve large guns from Brashear City to positions below Donaldsonville to menace transports carrying vital supplies from New Orleans to Banks's siege army at Port Hudson. "Taylor's guns, placed at convenient points along the river, pounded away at the gunboats

9. Richard Taylor, *Destruction and Reconstruction*, pp. 171, 173; Kerby, *Kirby Smith's Confederacy*, p. 118; *O.R.*, 26(1):211–13; Bosson, *Forty-Second Massachusetts Volunteers*, p. 308 (first quotation); Roland, *Louisiana Sugar Plantations*, pp. 117 (second quotation), 98; Duganne, *Camps and Prisons*, p. 130 (third quotation).

and succeeded more than once with the use of red-hot shot in setting fire to transports or in driving them ashore," a Federal soldier affirmed.[10]

On July 4 Taylor informed General Smith that a spy recently sent to New Orleans had returned with sensational news. "The city is greatly excited," Taylor reported. Its citizens were already proclaiming impending liberation from Yankee occupation. "I may succeed in establishing important relations there, so as to justify a *coup*," Taylor asserted further. "If any opportunity, however slight, offers, I will throw myself into New Orleans, and make every effort to hold it. . . . At all events, I have used every exertion to relieve Port Hudson, and shall continue to the last." Pleasantly astonished at this, Smith replied, "The results are beyond my expectation. Should the siege of Port Hudson be raised, your campaign will be crowned with entire success." At New Orleans, General Emory despaired so deeply for the city's safety that he dispatched an impassioned message to Banks imploring him to send troops back to New Orleans immediately. As a Federal officer put it, "General Emory plainly told General Banks he must choose between Port Hudson and New Orleans." But Banks refused to abandon the struggle for Port Hudson. Realizing that neither Vicksburg nor Port Hudson could hold out after the fall of either one, Banks was still determined to upstage Grant as the conquering hero of the Mississippi Valley. Although he had lost many men to casualties and disease, he now believed that with one final assault Port Hudson would be his.[11]

On July 7, just as Banks prepared to send his men into action, news arrived that Pemberton had surrendered to Grant at Vicksburg on July 4. Confederate commander Franklin Gardner's Port Hudson garrison, rapidly running out of food and ammunition, capitulated to Banks the next day, July 8. Two days later Taylor received word that

10. *O.R.*, 26(1):226–30; Winters, *Civil War in Louisiana*, pp. 290–92; Richard Taylor, *Destruction and Reconstruction*, pp. 172–73 (first quotation 172); Townsend, *Sixteenth New Hampshire Volunteers*, pp. 254–62 (second quotation 259); Putnam, *Memories of My Youth*, p. 271 (third quotation).

11. *O.R.*, 26(1):212–14 (first quotation 212, second quotation 212–13) and (2):109 (third quotation); Edmonds, *Guns of Port Hudson*, 2:120, 176, 269; Irwin, "Capture of Port Hudson," pp. 596–97 (fourth quotation).

both Port Hudson and Vicksburg had fallen. With his scouts pushing to within sixteen miles of New Orleans, Taylor had appeared on the verge of a supreme triumph. "A few hours more, and the city would have been wild with excitement," he asserted. Now he blamed everything on Smith's detention of Walker's Division near Vicksburg. "The unwise movement toward Vicksburg retarded operations at Berwick [Bay] and on the river, and Port Hudson fell," he later declared. "The time wasted on these absurd movements cost us the garrison of Port Hudson, nearly eight thousand men." Although he refrained from insulting Smith directly with such accusations, Taylor repeated them to his adjutant, Eustace Surget, arguing strongly, "The plan I had arranged for an attack on New Orleans fell through as soon as I was advised that Walker's division would not join me. . . . Whether the city would have been held is another question." Banks's soldiers tended to support Taylor's claims. Not only did they agree that the loss of New Orleans would have forced Banks to desert Port Hudson, but some also admitted that Banks's weakened and demoralized army would have soon suffered complete defeat at Taylor's hands. "Even we youngsters were able to realize the serious consequences that were likely to come upon our army and upon our control of the State through Taylor's successes," admitted one Yankee.[12]

Prior to July the Confederacy had experienced a rising tide of hope. While Grant and Banks floundered at Vicksburg and Port Hudson, Union forces at Charleston and in Tennessee likewise appeared stymied. Meanwhile Robert E. Lee's Army of Northern Virginia, fresh on the heels of a startling victory at Chancellorsville, was marching into Pennsylvania. Northerners had scant reason to anticipate anything but a long summer of sustained frustration. But the sudden succession of Confederate reverses at Gettysburg, Vicksburg, and Port Hudson transformed the face of the war. Southern armies were now bleeding themselves and becoming prisoners in unparalleled numbers. After the loss of the Mississippi Valley, the Trans-

12. Irwin, "Capture of Port Hudson," p. 597; Richard Taylor, *Destruction and Reconstruction*, pp. 173, 166 (first quotation 173, second quotation 173, 166); *O.R.*, 26(2):110–11 (third quotation 111); Flinn, *Campaigning with Banks*, p. 90; Townsend, *Sixteenth New Hampshire Volunteers*, pp. 238–39; Putnam, *Memories of My Youth*, p. 271 (fourth quotation).

Mississippi Department could no longer funnel supplies across the
river, and General Smith could no longer look to the Confederate
government for guidance in formulating a coordinated military policy. Smith found himself burdened with virtual autonomy and full
responsibility in defending a vast region comprising almost half of all
Confederate-held territory.[13]

With Banks's forces now free from the siege of Port Hudson, Taylor had no choice but to abandon the Lafourche region. "My army is
bagged, and the string is tied, yet I shall make every effort to save it,
but without any hopes," he allegedly told a citizen at Brashear City. To
his adjutant Surget, however, he wrote in a less desperate tone, simply
reporting that recent events had rendered his "present position in the
Lafourche extremely hazardous, and not to be justified on any military grounds. The defenses of [Berwick Bay] are far from satisfactory, and the entrance of a hostile fleet [of gunboats] would ruin my
little army." On July 13, however, Taylor witnessed Green's fourteen
hundred Texans in a spirited fight against six thousand men sent by
Banks from New Orleans. Several miles south of Donaldsonville, on
Bayou Lafourche, Green attacked with vengeance in mind for the
defeat he had suffered two weeks earlier. "The gallant noble Green,
dismounting from his horse, placed himself at the head of his old
regiment, captured the enemy's guns, and drove his forces into the
fort [at Donaldsonville]," Taylor reported. A Confederate soldier recalled, "I passed over the battlefield, saw Yankees lying in every direction . . . [and] saw all manner of wounds, but the most of the Yankees
were shot through the head." [14]

With Banks now convinced he was facing some nine to twelve thousand southern troops, Green had afforded Taylor's men extra time to
evacuate the Lafourche region. Although clearly elated at Green's
victory, Taylor complained to Surget of feeling "fatigued and jaded

13. Edmonds, *Gun of Port Hudson*, 2:369–70; Parks, *Edmund Kirby Smith*,
pp. 280–82.

14. Richard Taylor, *Destruction and Reconstruction*, pp. 173–74; Beecher,
114th N.Y.S.V., p. 241 (first quotation); *O.R.*, 26(2):110–11 (second quotation
111) and (1):230–32, 214–15 (third quotation 215); Bosson, *Forty-Second
Massachusetts Volunteers*, pp. 371–74; Oltorf, *Marlin Compound*, pp. 128–30
(fourth quotation 129).

beyond description." Yet he still managed to oversee the removal of
the remaining captured supplies from the fort at Berwick Bay plus a
herd of cattle confiscated earlier and left in the area by the enemy.
On July 21 Taylor moved his forces up Bayou Teche toward Vermilionville. The Federals reoccupied Brashear City and Berwick Bay the
next day, in the process resuming their pillaging of plantations and
farms in the Lafourche and southern Teche regions.[15]

The twin disasters of Vicksburg and Port Hudson, together with
the lost hope of recapturing New Orleans, plunged morale among
Confederate soldiers in the Deep South to an all time nadir. Much to
Taylor's distress, his troops began deserting at unprecedented rates.
Previously tolerant of what he viewed as periodic and temporary desertions, he soon lost so many men that he sent a message to Major
General John Bankhead Magruder, commander in Texas, urging
him to set up pickets along the Sabine River to arrest deserters crossing the border. "Many of these men are bringing disgrace upon the
service and their State, by taking off stolen horses and other property," wrote Taylor. "If the enemy means to overrun and occupy Louisiana, it is within his power to do so." Magruder suggested that Taylor
order his own cavalry to handle the problem, failing to understand
that Green's Texas horsemen were the very ones deserting. In mid-
August, Mouton's Louisiana infantry brigade, itself reduced by desertions to barely three hundred men, marched at Taylor's behest from
Vermilionville to New Iberia to help subdue a mutiny among Green's
remaining troopers.[16]

Amid the epidemic of desertions, Taylor tried to relieve public
alarm over the prospect of Federal soldiers terrorizing the state as
they had done in the spring. In early August he issued a proclamation
that contradicted his knowledge of true conditions. "It is determined
to defend to the last degree South and West Louisiana," he declared.
"Our forces are certainly sufficient to repel a new invasion. . . . We
may feel secure against any new attempt of the enemy." Only Walker's

15. Richard Taylor, *Destruction and Reconstruction*, pp. 174–76; *O.R.*,
26(2):110–11 (quotation 111); Kerby, *Kirby Smith's Confederacy*, pp. 119–20.

16. Ethel Taylor, "Discontent in Confederate Louisiana," pp. 421–22;
O.R., 26(2):116–18 (quotation 117), 241; Kerby, *Kirby Smith's Confederacy*, pp.
120–21.

Texas Division remained intact to uphold Taylor's public assurances. Yet by September even that stalwart unit showed signs of disintegrating. "There is great dissatisfaction in the army here," wrote Captain Elijah P. Petty, one of Walker's best officers. "Men are insubordinate and . . . I would not be surprised if this army was comparatively broken up. Men say that they will go home and let the Confederacy and war go to hell." After Walker ordered Petty's company to help put down a stir of mutiny in the ranks, Petty noted, "The desertion furor has about ceased, the prospect of getting shot having deterred some and the bad material having most been expended. . . . Things look much better here now."[17]

With the depletion of manpower among Green's and Mouton's forces, however, authorities in Shreveport prodded enrolling officers to find more conscripts. One enrolling officer in northern Louisiana, long since frustrated with his task, scoffed at the new demands, claiming that the only men left in his district were "armed deserters, desperadoes, Yankee scouts, spies, and traitors." By mid-October an estimated eight thousand deserters and delinquent conscripts were listed as absent from the rolls of Taylor's army. With all of Arkansas but the southern tier now in enemy hands, and with Magruder demanding the return of Texas troops from Louisiana, General Smith became so desperate for more soldiers that he privately accepted the radical idea of arming slaves who would be willing to defend the Confederacy in exchange for their freedom. Meanwhile Taylor shifted his available forces from one position to another in southeastern and eastern Louisiana, resisting parties of enemy raiders sent by Banks to probe Confederate strength. "Last month we marched over 290 miles," a Louisiana officer wrote in early October, "and we have been on the go every day, so far, this month. I suppose, however, it is considered successful strategy by *some*. The military genius of this Department is as far superior to any other as Louisiana rum is to old French brandy."[18]

17. Opelousas *Courier*, August 8, 1863 (first quotation); Norman D. Brown, *Journey to Pleasant Hill*, pp. 251–52 (second quotation), 256 (third quotation).

18. Kerby, *Kirby Smith's Confederacy*, pp. 121 (first quotation), 190–91, 237–40; Bragg, *Louisiana in the Confederacy*, pp. 256–57; Hyatt diary, pp. 67–68 (second quotation).

Jean Jacques Alfred Alexander Mouton, commander of Louisianans under Taylor
(Jenkins Rare Book Company).

Whatever Confederate strategy might have lacked in genius at the time, Federal strategy seemed hardly more inspired. Banks had decided, and Grant had agreed, that the most important military results could be gained by attacking and capturing the southern stronghold at Mobile, but the Union high command disagreed. The French monarchy's recent establishment of a military protectorate over Mexico presented the danger of a Confederate-Mexican alliance, prompting President Lincoln to encourage Banks to launch an invasion of Texas. The South's lifeline of open trade across the Rio Grande through Mexico had been a source of irritation also, and with exiled Unionist Texans asserting that a strong base of popular support would welcome an invasion, Lincoln pushed Banks to act. In early September Banks reluctantly sent ten thousand men on troop transports, protected by several gunboats, from New Orleans to Sabine Pass on the Texas coast with orders to take possession of the nearby railroad line that would allow quick access to Houston and Galveston. When General Smith learned of the expedition, he ordered Taylor to prepare to march to Texas, arguing that his Texans would surely desert anyway and would rush to defend their home state. But the tiny Texas garrison posted at Sabine Pass needed no help in rebuffing the carelessly exposed Federal vessels and forcing them to return to New Orleans.

Although ecstatic over the victory, Magruder insisted that the attack portended much worse, and he continued to press Smith to send troops from Louisiana to protect Texas.[19]

Neither Smith nor Taylor believed circumstances warranted abandoning Louisiana just yet, and Taylor even revived the idea of making a strike toward New Orleans in order to distract Banks if he attempted another amphibious assault on the Texas coast. Taylor's officers seemed equally eager to push east again. "It was Green's firm belief," observed one of his men, "that he could 'drive the Yankees into the Mississippi, or make them take to their boats.'" Worrying that Taylor might not wait for the enemy to make the first move, Smith warned, "You as well as myself know our means are too limited to risk any general engagement without some reasonable chance of success." As if to complicate matters even more, by September 25 Smith once again viewed Arkansas as the key strategic goal in the Trans-Mississippi, not only because the Federal presence there seemed to threaten Shreveport but also because he believed the people of Arkansas and the allied Indian tribes were despairing. "Should the enemy advance from Little Rock," Smith wrote Taylor, "Arkansas is decidedly the place for concentration. A success there clears the Indian Territory, whilst it redeems the Arkansas Valley." He therefore told Taylor to be ready to move north at any time.[20]

Anxious to know Banks's strength and purpose, Taylor sent Mouton and Green toward Morganza, east of Opelousas, against an enemy outpost of fewer than a thousand men at Morgan's Ferry on Bayou Fordoche. On September 29, in a driving rainstorm, the southerners attacked, surprising the Federals and taking more than 450 prisoners. At Opelousas Taylor interrogated some of the prisoners, and he gradually began to piece together the information he desired. A massive enemy army had assembled at Brashear City under Major General William B. Franklin, a talented but contentious officer who had been expelled from the Army of the Potomac as a scapegoat

19. Winters, *Civil War in Louisiana*, pp. 294–96; Kerby, *Kirby Smith's Confederacy*, pp. 186–90; *O.R.*, 26(2):220–21.

20. Kerby, *Kirby Smith's Confederacy*, pp. 240–42; Noel, *Old Sibley Brigade*, p. 63 (first quotation); *O.R.*, 26(2):250–53 (second quotation 250), 255–56 (third quotation 256).

for the Union debacle at Fredericksburg the previous December. Now Banks gave Franklin the means to redeem himself as well as to erase the embarrassing memory of Sabine Pass. Along with Banks's Nineteenth Army Corps, Franklin garnered a large detachment from the Thirteenth Army Corps, seasoned midwesterners who had served with Grant during the Vicksburg campaign. The entire force totaled no less than thirty thousand men.[21]

Franklin clearly intended to march overland to Texas, but Taylor remained uncertain whether the invaders would move directly west or northwesterly up the Red River toward Shreveport. Both Smith and Taylor expected the latter, since the Red River Valley offered the Yankee army much better foraging than did the barren prairies and swamps of southwestern Louisiana. Banks had given Franklin complete authority to decide the army's route. But after an uncontested seizure of New Iberia on October 3, Franklin slowed his pace as he continued north toward Vermilionville. "The enemy moves with the greatest caution," reported Taylor on the eleventh. "Nothing can induce his cavalry to separate 500 yards from his infantry supports." Franklin seemed unable to decide in which direction to go, and Taylor's use of mounted attacks against vulnerable points in Franklin's column made his progress even more faltering and uncertain. A Yankee soldier noted, "Our generals, who made war according to rule, were disgusted with the irregular tactics of the Confederates, who played swordfish to the whale." So effective was this harassment that Federal officers estimated Confederate strength at upward of twenty-five thousand men. Taylor, however, began to worry that the Yankees might indeed be preparing to strike west toward the Sabine, a movement that would ruin his ability to operate along interior lines of supply and communication. If they moved up the Red River, at least he would be able to fall back to existing supply bases while maintaining direct lines of communication with Shreveport.[22]

21. Kerby, *Kirby Smith's Confederacy*, pp. 242–43; Richard Taylor, *Destruction and Reconstruction*, pp. 179–80; *O.R.*, 26(1):328–32; Winters, *Civil War in Louisiana*, pp. 296–97; Edmonds, *Yankee Autumn*, pp. 12–13, 16, 153.
22. Kerby, *Kirby Smith's Confederacy*, pp. 243–44; *O.R.*, 26(1):386–87 (first quotation 386), 384; Harding, *Miscellaneous Writings*, p. 331 (second quotation).

Seeking to gain a definite answer to this nagging question, Taylor dispatched a party of cavalrymen on a raid against an enemy tele-graph station near Vermilionville. On the thirteenth the raiders roared into the station, brushed aside the stupefied guards, and car-ried away copies of secret messages that confirmed Franklin's inten-tion to continue pushing his army northward. When Federal units occupied Opelousas on the twenty-first, Taylor informed Smith that the enemy had made "no appearance of a movement west" and that "all conclusions point to a farther advance in this direction." For sev-eral days Taylor had pressed Smith to authorize an all-out assault in order to repel the Federals before they completed the handiwork Banks had begun several months earlier in laying waste to the Red River Valley. Although Tom Green's Texas cavalry had received a sharp rebuff from several midwestern regiments at Buzzard's Prairie north of Vermilionville on October 15, Taylor still believed he could inflict enough damage on Franklin's masses to force a halt to the in-vasion. Smith lacked Taylor's confidence. "Difficult as you may find it," wrote Smith, "you must exercise great caution in your operations. You must restrain your own impulses as well as the desires of your men. The Fabian policy is now our true policy. In the present state of the public mind, a defeat to your little army would be ruinous in its effects. When you strike, you must do so only with strong hopes of success." [23]

Smith's warning placed the onus of a possible defeat squarely on Taylor's shoulders, but by now Taylor was completely willing to accept such a risk. "Notwithstanding the smallness of our forces, compared with the enemy, General Taylor was determined to give battle if the enemy advanced," observed a private in Walker's Division. The Tex-ans seemed especially agitated over the prospect of Yankees setting foot in the Lone Star State. "I had rather dy [sic] forty times than for them to run over our country like they have this, but I think they will have a warm time of it before they do it," asserted another of Walker's men. "I intend to try and kil [sic] all of them I can before they get

23. Edmonds, *Yankee Autumn*, pp. 153–56, 163–68, 195–98, 211–12; Kerby, *Kirby Smith's Confederacy*, pp. 244–45; *O.R.*, 26(1):389–90 (first quota-tion 389) and (2):341–42 (second quotation 341).

there." By October 24 Franklin's advance units had marched through
the town of Washington, several miles north of Opelousas, and were
pressing toward the main Confederate position. Three miles outside
of Washington, Taylor had laid a trap. Walker's Division, along with
Major's cavalry regiment and six artillery batteries, waited in nearby
woods and ditches, ready to ambush Franklin's unsuspecting soldiers.
As Colonel Oran M. Roberts's Eleventh Texas Infantry began skirmishing with the foremost elements of the column in an effort to lure
it forward, a peculiar civilian suddenly appeared on horseback galloping toward the enemy. It was a "well-dressed matronly looking
lady" waving and shouting furiously, "Come on and let us whip the
darned Yankees!" recalled one of the astounded Confederates. Inspired by this bizarre display of gallantry, Roberts's men "charged
with a tremendous yell, she being in the lead." The Federals quickly
retreated back down the road to Washington.[24]

At this point Franklin dreaded the idea of facing any more southerners, male or female. Not only had foraging become difficult in this
destitute region, forcing him to spread his brigades out along the
route, but he also chafed at what he perceived as inadequate cavalry
to resist the continual torment from Green's mounted troops. Franklin reported that Confederate horsemen "hover on all sides of an infantry force, producing an annoyance the severity of which cannot be
appreciated unless it be felt. The only way of meeting this method of
warfare is to keep a large force mounted. This force should be the
main force of the army." He had already begged Banks for more cavalry, or just more horses in order to convert infantry to mounted regiments, but Banks's official requests to the Union high command had
met with stern refusals. Unwilling to push on, Franklin withdrew below Opelousas to reconsider the situation. There he received a surprising message from headquarters in New Orleans saying that
Banks had taken a force aboard steamers down the coast in order to
make a landing somewhere in Texas. The message instructed Franklin to continue making "as much show as possible" so that "the enemy

24. Blessington, *Walker's Texas Division*, pp. 135–36 (first quotation 136);
O.R., 26(1):390; Edmonds, *Yankee Autumn*, pp. 114 (second quotation), 239–
41 (third and fourth quotations 241).

should regard the movement in your direction as the real one." Franklin had unwittingly become a diversion in Banks's erratic strategy for conquering Texas.[25]

Taylor seemed satisfied to keep up a menacing presence, but Tom Green had other ideas. Ordered by Taylor simply to "pursue and harass the enemy," Green took his cavalry division and three regiments from Walker's Division (the Eleventh, Fifteenth, and Eighteenth Texas), led by Colonel Roberts, and three artillery batteries. On November 3, seven miles south of Opelousas on Bayou Bourbeau, Green encountered the rear guard of Franklin's army, a division of midwesterners commanded by Brigadier General Stephen G. Burbridge. Late in the morning Green decided to attack. Caught off guard, Burbridge struggled to align his regiments but could not prevent them from breaking ranks. "We drove them Back one mile and a half to their main encampment before which was a deep ravine," recalled Lieutenant Colonel James E. Harrison of the Fifteenth Texas, "and here th[e]y made a desperate stand. . . . A shout and a rush [and] then our Rifles told on their routed confused masses." Assaulted from the rear by a regiment of Federal cavalry, Harrison turned his soldiers around and ordered them to open fire and charge, a tactic that produced "a scene of wild confution [sic], Men tumbling from Horses, screaming, Others throwing up their hands for mercy, Horses running wildly over the field without riders."[26]

The fighting lasted for about three hours, finally ending in an artillery duel after Federal reinforcements arrived. "This little battle has never figured much in history," wrote a Texas private, "but it was quite an event with us that took part in it." Green reported 125 casualties, inflicting 154 on the enemy and taking about 500 prisoners, including 30 officers. "Too much praise cannot be given to General Green and the troops engaged," Taylor reported proudly. "The exact moment when a heavy blow could be given was seized in a masterly

25. Starr, *Union Cavalry in the Civil War*, 3:484–86 (first quotation 485); Edmonds, *Yankee Autumn*, pp. 263–64 (second quotation 263).

26. *O.R.*, 26(1):393–95 (first quotation 393); Barr, "Battle of Bayou Bourbeau," pp. 83–91; Edmonds, *Yankee Autumn*, pp. 277–91; Blessington, *Walker's Texas Division*, pp. 142–43; Barr, *Polignac's Texas Brigade*, pp. 30–31 (second and third quotations 31).

manner." The Federals officially described Bayou Bourbeau as a victory, but the men in the ranks knew otherwise. "A few more such victories would not leave us many men," remarked a Yankee soldier. Most of the midwesterners blamed Franklin, one of them declaring, "If we had a general with as much spunk as a mouse, we would have turned about and whipped them soundly. This was the first time the 13th Army Corps ever turned its back."[27]

Franklin had endured all the heat he could stand. By mid-November his force had withdrawn to New Iberia, where it set up camp for the coming winter. Meanwhile Banks, with five thousand men, gained a foothold in southern Texas, occupying Brownsville, disrupting Confederate trade along the lower Rio Grande, and thwarting southern hopes of gaining aid from the French regime in Mexico. Banks had not even come close to achieving Lincoln's goal of rallying latent Unionism in Texas, but at least he had carried out part of his mission. Had Franklin been willing to march and fight rather than worry and hesitate, the threat of a real invasion of Texas would have stretched Taylor's meager manpower to its limits. With most of Arkansas and Indian Territory under Federal control, the specter of another offensive toward Texas from southern Louisiana remained patently ominous. For the time being, however, General Smith seemed inclined to ignore Taylor's precarious good fortune, deciding instead to praise his talents. Reporting to the War Department on November 8, Smith described Taylor as "cautious, yet bold; always prepared for and anticipating the enemy; concentrating skillfully upon his main force, holding it in check, and crippling its movements; promptly striking his detached columns, routing and destroying them." Based on these accolades, it seemed that Taylor had become the Stonewall Jackson of the Trans-Mississippi.[28]

On the very day Smith bestowed these plaudits, however, he also sent a stern letter to Taylor expressing deep personal anger over an

27. Blessington, *Walker's Texas Division*, pp. 143–44; Edmonds, *Yankee Autumn*, pp. 281 (first quotation), 309 (third and fourth quotations); *O.R.*, 26(1):395, 359, 391–92 (second quotation 392).

28. Edmonds, *Yankee Autumn*, pp. 350–62; Winters, *Civil War in Louisiana*, pp. 297–300; Geise, "Isolation," p. 40; Kerby, *Kirby Smith's Confederacy*, pp. 246–47; *O.R.*, 26(1):384–85 (quotation).

anonymous editorial that had appeared four days earlier in the *Louisiana Democrat*. Published in Alexandria, the town where Taylor maintained his headquarters, the editorial lambasted Smith for willfully exposing Louisiana to Federal invasion, branded him incompetent to command the department, and demanded his resignation. Although he wisely refrained from holding Taylor responsible for this diatribe, Smith asked him to suppress such attacks, since "they go abroad with the impression of your sanction or as being the re-echo of your views." Furthermore, Smith claimed to have sacrificed much for the defense of Louisiana even while its citizens were the only ones in the Trans-Mississippi Department abusing his character and actions. "I have, feeling the importance of your command, stripped the other districts of troops," he reminded Taylor, "and you have now under your orders more than one-half of the effective force of the department." Regardless, Smith assured Taylor that the incident would not alter "the cordial relations existing between us."[29]

With this letter Smith shrewdly enclosed a copy of his report to the War Department extolling Taylor's achievements during the recent campaign. At any rate, Taylor was in no mood to dwell on past acrimony with Smith. He seemed willing to forget Smith's stubborn refusal to send Walker's Division to help attempt to recapture New Orleans in June. Likewise, Smith's ill-timed suggestion to withdraw in the face of Franklin's invading hordes only a few weeks earlier hardly mattered now. For the time being at least, the lion's share of Louisiana remained in Confederate hands, and Taylor felt compelled to defend his commander's honor. Rather than simply badgering the *Louisiana Democrat* into silence, he wrote a lengthy rejoinder to the infamous editorial, prefacing his statements by emphasizing that this marked the first time he had ever responded formally to a newspaper. Taylor affirmed that "repeatedly has General Smith urged the importance of a vigorous preparation for defence at all points [in Louisiana]." Even during the enemy's seizure of most of Arkansas, Smith had retained in Louisiana the troops originally drawn from Arkansas, "though the homes of the people of that State are doubtless as dear to them as

---

29. *O.R.*, 26(2):394–95 (first quotation 394, second and third quotations 395); *Louisiana Democrat* (Alexandria), November 4, 1863; Kerby, *Kirby Smith's Confederacy*, pp. 247–48.

ours to us." Taylor argued the same point in regard to Texas troops serving in Louisiana. In conclusion, he asserted forcefully that if Louisianans truly believed Smith to be incompetent, "they differ *in toto* not only from all the commanders under whom he has served, but from all the officers who have served under him."[30]

Taylor knew, however, that he could not even begin to quell the misgivings and resentment Louisianans maintained toward Smith. Governor Thomas Moore, for one, had emerged as one of Smith's most antagonistic critics during the past year, confronting him personally with the accusation that, by providing inadequate numbers of troops, he had readily accepted and even abetted Louisiana's vulnerability. Smith responded to Moore with a sardonic rebuke, claiming that so much of Arkansas never would have fallen had he not sent troops to Louisiana and that if Moore wanted more soldiers, he should raise them himself. By the end of 1863, even with most of Louisiana relatively secure, Moore still refused to give Smith any credit. Instead he accorded all acclaim to Taylor. "We owe it to him that the State is not now entirely overrun and occupied by the enemy," Moore wrote President Davis in late December. "General Taylor found literally nothing here. He had to develop resources, and to awaken the public from their apathy. . . . Designing and factious men invented unscrupulous stories of misconduct. . . . His adherence to the plain path of duty soon excited admiration." Davis replied with satisfaction, "Your emphatic commendation of . . . Maj. Gen. R[ichard] Taylor . . . convinces me that I was not mistaken in my estimate of his fitness to perform the duties to which he was assigned."[31]

Taylor clearly deserved such gratitude. Yet like his mentor Stonewall Jackson during the Shenandoah Valley Campaign, he had profited as much from his enemies' fears and blunders as from his own daring and prowess. Banks's gargantuan force had dispensed only an inkling of the devastation that would surely come with another inva-

30. Clipping from *Louisiana Democrat* (Alexandria), November 20, 1863 (quotations), in Smith Papers.

31. *O.R.*, 26(2):221–22; Thomas O. Moore to Jefferson Davis, December 26, 1863 (first quotation), Richard Taylor Papers, Confederate Service Record Files; Jefferson Davis to Thomas O. Moore, April 12, 1864 (second quotation), Moore Papers.

sion. To have any chance of resisting such power, Taylor would have to continue to rely upon General Smith's willingness to let him retain his Texas units, Walker's infantry and Green's cavalry. Even on the defensive, however, Taylor never let go of the dream of wresting New Orleans from Federal hand's. Yet at the same time, with just as much fervor, Smith continued to look toward Arkansas and Missouri, reiterating to Taylor in late November his "great . . . anxiety and desire to drive the Federals from Little Rock and occupy the Arkansas Valley." Responding to Taylor's suggestion that another probe into the Lafourche region might prove effective, Smith repeated bluntly, "The occupation of that country by us . . . is of but little military importance." Just beneath the surface of their mutual respect and sense of duty festered their sharp divergence in strategic goals. Whether driven by personal prejudice or honest conviction, their differences were stark, immutable, and explosive.[32]

32. *O.R.*, 26(2):439 (quotations). See also 22(2):1110–11.

CHAPTER NINE

Hero of the Red River Valley

Though some of his movements savored of rashness,

when calmly weighed, they showed the good judgment

and military genius that conceived them.

Private Joseph P. Blessington

"This is Genl. Taylor's Country. He has set his heart to defend it," declared Captain Elijah Petty of Walker's Division in January of 1864. Expecting Banks to prosecute total war more vicious and destructive than Louisiana might be able to bear, Taylor spent the winter making preparations. "We shall be put on our mettle during the spring," he warned General Smith. Concurring in this opinion, Smith reported to President Davis, "The only true line of operations by which the enemy can penetrate the department is the valley of the Red River, rich in supplies; with steam-boat navigation for six months of the year, it offers facilities for the co-operation of the army and navy, and enables them to shift their base as they advance into the interior." This logic was soon confirmed by Taylor's spies in New Orleans, whose reports convinced him that a Federal campaign up the Red

River "could be relied on with as much confidence as if the plans had been laid here instead of in New Orleans."[1]

As a highly important defensive measure, Taylor established several supply depots along the Red River Valley northwest of his headquarters at Alexandria. As a painful necessity, however, he urged citizens in the southern half of the state to abandon their homes. Most refused to heed his warning. Determined to leave nothing there of any value for the Yankees to seize, Taylor ordered his officers to confiscate horses, mules, and wagons, and to burn privately owned cotton. Carrying personal doubts about the true need for burning cotton, however, he expressed displeasure to General Smith. "It is at the very moment that we are withdrawing all protection from the citizen, leaving him to the enemy's mercy, that we destroy the only means of supporting his family," Taylor argued in mid-January. But within a few weeks he had become completely disgusted with planters' widespread sales of cotton for Federal currency paid by speculators in New Orleans. "The possession of any large amount of cotton will in the end destroy the patriotism of the best citizen," he reported on February 21. "Stringent orders have been given to burn all cotton, baled or in seed, within the enemy's reach."[2]

The destruction of Confederate patriotism was exactly what Abraham Lincoln sought by encouraging Banks to allow speculators to tempt planters throughout the lower Mississippi Valley to sell their cotton for shipment to northern markets. From the beginning of the war, southern planters' hopes for continued profits had fostered an overproduction of cotton, much to the detriment of the Confederate cause. By resisting voluntary relinquishment of their slaves for military projects, planters forced Confederate authorities to conscript too many soldiers for menial labor rather than combat. By growing cotton they also denied the armies food and other supplies for fighting the war, thus requiring military commanders to inflict impressments

1. Norman D. Brown, *Journey to Pleasant Hill*, p. 304 (first quotation); *O.R.*, 34(2):879 (second quotation), 895–96 (third quotation 895), and (1):572–73 (fourth quotation 573).

2. Winters, *Civil War in Louisiana*, pp. 319–24; Richard Taylor, *Destruction and Reconstruction*, p. 182; *O.R.*, 34(2):852–53 (first quotation 853), 971–72, 977–78 (second quotation 978).

upon the southern population at large, often to abusive extremes. Because of such impressments, Taylor's soldiers were almost as unwelcome among the citizenry as were the Federals. "Provisions are getting very scarce . . . [and] in fact the citizens have not enough for their own use in many places," wrote one of Walker's men in early 1864. "It is truly distressing to see the vast havoc war has made on this country, which once abounded in wealth and prosperity, but it is all gone now."[3]

The public outcry against impressments and the burning of cotton only added to Taylor's burden of responsibility, and he began to suffer from the strain. By late February his chronic rheumatoid arthritis had flared up so intensely that he requested a sixty-day leave of absence. "Since my connection with the service . . . I have not asked an indulgence, but my health compels me to do so now," he wrote despondently to Smith. But Smith would not accept Taylor's request. "You know there is no one to take your place, even temporarily, without great injury to the cause. The Dept. can not do without you," he insisted. Showing utmost concern, he asked Taylor to "write frankly and let me know what the matter really is." Promising to "explain or remedy" any action that might have proved disagreeable, Smith closed with a personal note, "Remember me to Mrs. Taylor and the children," and then signed his name "with feelings of friendship."[4]

Despite their disagreements during the past year, Smith's admiration for Taylor had grown steadily. "Taylor is the only district commander on whom I can rely," he declared to an Arkansas senator in January. "He is a good soldier and a man of ability, and could he only forget his habits and training as a politician, would be all that could be asked." Smith also understood quite well that Taylor's anguish ran deeper than the pain of his physical illness. His troop strength had

3. Powell and Wayne, "Self-Interest and the Decline of Confederate Nationalism," pp. 29–45; Lebergott, "Why the South Lost," pp. 58–74; Geise, "Kirby Smith's War Department," pp. 55–56; Bragg, *Louisiana in the Confederacy,* pp. 174, 201–3; Ethel Taylor, "Discontent in Confederate Louisiana," pp. 416–20; Connor, *Dear America,* pp. 91–92 (quotation).

4. Richard Taylor to Edmund Kirby Smith, February 28, 1864 (first quotation), and Smith to Taylor, March 4, 1864 (second, third, and fourth quotations), Taylor Papers, Jackson Barracks.

fallen to about sixty-five hundred after an unusually harsh winter marked by poor food, sickness, and scores of desertions. To make matters worse, in December Smith had sent Tom Green's cavalry division back to Texas in response to Magruder's pleas for aid against a Federal raid up the Texas coast. Left with only Colonel William G. Vincent's Second Louisiana Cavalry for scouting and skirmishing, Taylor petitioned Smith repeatedly for more horsemen simply to track down deserters and conscript evaders and to fight jayhawkers. So badly did he desire Green and any other Texans to help defend Louisiana against the impending enemy invasion, he even offered to relinquish his command to Magruder. "But it was 'a far cry' to Shreveport," Taylor reflected, "and the emergency seemed less pressing in the rear than at the front." [5]

Taylor also objected to General Smith's expanding bureaucratic system, later describing it as "on a scale proportioned rather to the extent of his territory than to the smallness of his force." Smith's agents had continually depleted Taylor's infantry by requiring work details, especially for the construction of river defenses at Shreveport, "to the great discontent of the officers in the field." Besides, Taylor had always considered it a waste of men and artillery to rely on fixed fortifications designed only to thwart naval advances up the Red River. Protesting loudly when Smith ordered him to rehabilitate Fort DeRussy near the mouth of the Red, he again argued that such a position could not resist an infantry assault, "and should the enemy advance in heavy force now we would inevitably lose the guns and material at DeRussy." But he dutifully instructed Walker's Texas Division to put aside their rifles and take up shovels to work on the fort. "If I can complete DeRussy, so as to get it off my hands, it will be a great relief," Taylor reported. [6]

5. *O.R.*, 34(2):868–70 (first quotation 869), 992–93, 999–1000; Kerby, *Kirby Smith's Confederacy*, p. 287; Bergeron, *Uncle Silas*, pp. 143–47; *O.R.*, 34(1):488–89; Richard Taylor, *Destruction and Reconstruction*, pp. 182–85 (second quotation 185).

6. Richard Taylor, *Destruction and Reconstruction*, p. 183 (first and second quotations); Geise, "Kirby Smithdom," pp. 22–24; James L. Nichols, *Confederate Engineers*, pp. 58–60; *O.R.*, 34(2):1024 (third quotation) and (1):489–91 (fourth quotation 491).

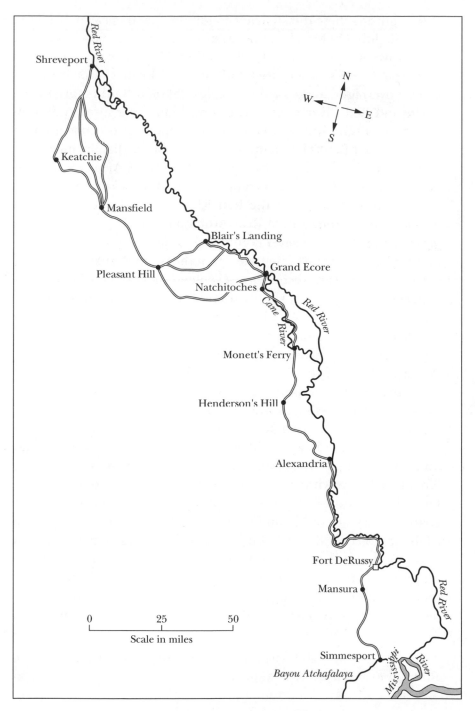

Map 6. Red River Valley

Recognizing these dissatisfying conditions, Smith gave in to Taylor, if only slightly. On March 5, the day after he received Taylor's request for a leave of absence, Smith telegraphed Magruder with orders to send Tom Green's cavalry back to Louisiana. Taylor's disposition improved overnight, and so did his health. "Should Banks move by the Teche and Red River we ought to beat him," he assured Smith on March 11. "Even without Green I should hope to give a good account of Banks." But Banks had more in store for Taylor than he imagined. Ten thousand veterans, borrowed from Sherman's Army of the Tennessee, had already boarded troop transports at Vicksburg and were penetrating the mouth of the Red River. An even more fearsome menace came in the form of Rear Admiral David D. Porter's thirteen gigantic ironclads and several gunboats, a fleet boasting at least two hundred guns. At the same time, from the south, Banks was marching up along Bayou Teche with seventeen thousand soldiers of the Nineteenth Corps and a supply train of more than a thousand wagons, many of them laden with luxury items. Hordes of noncombatants and camp followers joined in, and on occasion the swollen column stretched to a length of more than twenty miles. Including Porter's sailors and the men loaned by Sherman, Banks commanded more than thirty thousand effectives, the most enormous military force the Trans-Mississippi West had ever seen.[7]

Authority for the Red River Campaign came from the highest quarters. Lincoln's longstanding desire to put Louisiana and Texas under Unionist political control and to crush any prospect of a Confederate alliance with the French regime in Mexico coincided perfectly with General-in-Chief Henry W. Halleck's more purely military goals. Halleck not only wanted to secure the Mississippi River from all threats to Federal vessels, but he also believed that a strike through Shreveport into East Texas would ruin the region's vital military industries, agricultural production, and supply lines to the Rio Grande, thereby rendering most of the Trans-Mississippi useless to the Confederate war effort. For several months Banks had been anxious to

7. *O.R.*, 34(2):1027 and (1):490 (first quotation); Ludwell H. Johnson, *Red River Campaign*, pp. 40–48, 79–91, 100; Kerby, *Kirby Smith's Confederacy*, pp. 287–91.

David D. Porter, skeptical Union admiral
(Jenkins Rare Book Company).

mount a campaign against Mobile, a target the Union high command had agreed would become his major responsibility as part of a coordinated invasion of the Deep South in the late spring. But Banks's insatiable political ambition soon compelled him to view the Red River Valley as a plum too inviting to resist. By solidifying Unionist hegemony in Louisiana and then marching into Texas, while also capturing an estimated 150,000 to 300,000 bales of cotton for shipment to New England's largely idle cotton mills, Banks expected to seal his chances for attaining his ultimate goal: the presidency of the United States. Contrary to later charges, he never considered seizing cotton for personal financial gain. One of his staff officers remarked at the time, "His thirst is not for money, but for power."[8]

8. Waldo W. Moore, "Defense of Shreveport," pp. 394–96; Kerby, *Kirby Smith's Confederacy*, pp. 283–92; Ludwell H. Johnson, *Red River Campaign*, pp. 3–48; Harrington, *Fighting Politician*, pp. 151–53, 160–61; Pellet, *114th New York Volunteers*, p. 239 (quotation).

While Banks's forces moved north, Major General Frederick Steele, Federal commander in Arkansas, pushed his fifteen thousand troops southwestward toward Shreveport, where he hoped to combine them with Banks's. With hundreds of miles of hostile territory preventing regular communications, however, Banks and Steele lacked a unified command system to coordinate their long-range pincer movement against Shreveport. Considering the fact that Banks had never actually won a single battle as a field commander, neither Lincoln nor Halleck had much confidence in him. Yet Banks and his officers were already acting like indomitable conquerors, and Steele predicted that the outnumbered Confederates would flee all the way to the Gulf without a fight.[9]

By March 12 Taylor remained completely unaware that enemy transports carrying the ten thousand men from Sherman, together with Porter's mighty fleet of ironclads, had started steaming up the Red River. Expecting for the time being to contend with only Banks's force down on Bayou Teche, Taylor prodded Smith's headquarters to "hurry up Green as rapidly as possible and send me as many of the detailed men at Shreveport as can be spared." Impatient with Walker to finish the construction work at Fort DeRussy, Taylor instructed him to prepare to move south for a rapid concentration against Banks. "When Green gets up, we should make short work of Banks," he assured Walker. The next day Walker reported the presence of twenty-seven Federal troop transports and Porter's fleet on the lower Red River. Fort DeRussy, Walker predicted, "must fall as soon as [it is] invested . . . which would enable the enemy to throw his whole force up Red River as high as Alexandria." Bristling at Walker's warning, Taylor urged him to attack the Yankees before they reached the fort. "Close, sharp, quick fighting is our game where there is any reasonable chance of success," he insisted. "Any severe check to the head of their column would probably break up this expedition." Exhorting Walker to "take more than ordinary hazards" to prevent the enemy's advance, Taylor reminded him of the stakes hanging in the balance:

9. Hattaway and Jones, *How the North Won*, pp. 518–20; Waldo W. Moore, "Defense of Shreveport," pp. 396–97; Kerby, *Kirby Smith's Confederacy*, pp. 292–94; Winters, *Civil War in Louisiana*, pp. 325–28.

"I repeat, the loss of our [guns] at DeRussy and the occupation of Alexandria by the Federals would be a great disaster."[10]

Taylor's provocations, however, seemed irrelevant to Walker. Certain that an attack would endanger his entire division, he ordered a withdrawal, leaving DeRussy's garrison of three hundred men to the enemy's mercy. The ten thousand Federals, hardened midwesterners commanded by grouchy old Brigadier General A. J. Smith, disembarked at Simmesport on March 13, and the next day they marched thirty miles upriver. Late in the afternoon Smith ordered two brigades to assault DeRussy. Aided by erratic shelling from Porter's vessels, the Yankees charged over the earthworks so swiftly that the whole affair resembled a grand practice maneuver. Porter compared the southerners' resistance to "the antics of Chinamen, who build canvas forts, paint hideous dragons on their shields, turn somersets . . . and then run away at the first sign of an engagement." Although Taylor later admitted the necessity of Walker's withdrawal, he also asserted that, had he known of the fort's total vulnerability, he would have ordered an evacuation of its garrison and guns. Embittered less at Walker than at General Smith's unfounded faith in DeRussy, he later summed up the incident with a bald bit of mockery: "Thus much for our Red River Gibralter."[11]

On the afternoon of March 15 Porter reached Alexandria with a vanguard of several vessels. There he learned that Taylor and his staff had waited until the last minute to insure the removal of supplies and public property before fleeing northward to reorganize his command. With no choice but to wait for Banks and his lumbering column to come up from the south and rendezvous at Alexandria, Porter and A. J. Smith allowed their own men to occupy the town. Although Porter later claimed that "the inhabitants were respectfully treated, and everything was as quiet as a New England village," his

10. *O.R.*, 34(1):490–91 (first quotation 491), 492 (third quotation), 493 (fourth and fifth quotations); Richard Taylor to John G. Walker, March 12, 1864 (second quotation), Walker Papers.

11. Ludwell H. Johnson, *Red River Campaign*, pp. 89–93; James L. Nichols, *Confederate Engineers*, pp. 61–62 (first quotation 61); John Scott, *Thirty-Second Iowa*, p. 280; *O.R.*, 34(1):495–96; Richard Taylor, *Destruction and Reconstruction*, pp. 186–87 (second quotation 186).

Admiral Porter's fleet at Alexandria on the Red River
(Jenkins Rare Book Company).

sailors quickly began seizing all the cotton bales they could find. According to a local citizen, Smith's men "made an indiscriminate onslaught upon every private residence, appropriating to themselves everything valuable." When Banks arrived on the nineteenth, he attempted to restore order, but the cotton speculators he had brought howled at the sight of sailors claiming bales as naval prizes of war redeemable by the government in cash. Banks ordered all cotton turned over to the army for confiscation by the Treasury Department. Porter refused to obey, and the speculators decided to scramble for at least a part of the several thousand bales of remaining booty. Many of the bales were in fact being brought into town by jubilant runaway slaves. Taylor had already tried to burn as much cotton as his troops could locate, and now he redoubled his efforts as he withdrew northward, thus intensifying competition among the voracious cotton mongers. Among the speculators was Taylor's brother-in-law and former New Orleans sugar factor, Martin Gordon, Jr.[12]

12. Kerby, *Kirby Smith's Confederacy*, pp. 295–96; Ludwell H. Johnson, *Red River Campaign*, pp. 94–96, 101–5; Bergeron, *Uncle Silas*, pp. 151–52; Porter,

Although his quest for cotton had soured, Banks did not shirk his role as political leader. Announcing permanent Federal occupation of the region, he persuaded several hundred citizens to take oaths of allegiance to the Union. He then staged an election for choosing delegates to the upcoming convention in New Orleans to form a new state constitution as part of Lincoln's reconstruction plan. Most of Alexandria's citizens remained intractable, hardly enthusiastic in their loyalty to the South yet thoroughly appalled at Yankee venality, especially when Banks opened a recruiting office and awarded hefty bounties for joining the army. One citizen characterized these recruits as notorious anti-Confederate jayhawkers. Three mounted companies, dubbed the Louisiana Scouts, were formed for "the patrolling of the country adjacent; they scoured it, visiting upon individuals their vengeance and vindictiveness. . . . In remote parts of the parish they burnt the dwellings of those who were supposed to have been active in pointing out or in aiding in arresting [Confederate] conscripts."[13]

About thirty miles north of Alexandria at a supply depot near the residence of Carroll Jones, a prominent free black, Taylor gathered his forces, two divisions that actually resembled brigades in strength—a total of barely seven thousand men. Along with Walker's Texas Division, he had Mouton's Louisianans, now also designated as a division after the recent addition of a small brigade of Texans under the command of Brigadier General Camille A. J. M. de Polignac, a French aristocrat with professional experience in the Crimean War and as a mercenary in Central America. Offering himself to the Confederacy at the beginning of the war, he served as a staff officer under both Beauregard and Bragg before gaining command of the new brigade of Texans in late 1863. Taylor hoped Polignac would feel comfortable serving under the French-speaking Mouton, but Mouton

---

Naval History, p. 497 (first quotation); *Official Report Relative to Federal Troops*, pp. 145–46 (second quotation 146); Flinn, *Campaigning with Banks*, p. 96; Orton S. Clark, *One Hundred and Sixteenth New York Volunteers*, pp. 147–48; Tregle, "Thomas J. Durant," p. 497.

13. Ludwell H. Johnson, *Red River Campaign*, pp. 108–10; Kerby, *Kirby Smith's Confederacy*, p. 296; Flinn, *Campaigning with Banks*, p. 96; *Official Report Relative to Federal Troops*, pp. 147–48 (quotation).

Camille Armand Jules Marie de Polignac, French professional soldier
(*Johnson and Buell,* Battles and Leaders of the Civil War).

found this self-styled "Lafayette of Confederacy" rather untamed in his penchant for drinking and gambling. Taylor had to quiet a potential mutiny among Polignac's Texans by promising to transfer him if they found him incompetent in combat. Within a few weeks, however, the Texans relaxed under the jaunty foreigner's tutelage, fondly referring to him as General Polecat. "They got on famously, and he made capital soldiers out of them," Taylor recalled proudly.[14]

"Bad times are coming," one of Mouton's officers had predicted prior to the fall of Alexandria. During the rapid withdrawal northward Taylor's men marched without rest and received only one meal a day. "The men are weary and foot sore, broke down and jaded," wrote Captain Petty of Walker's Division. "Even the horses have fagged under it." Another of Walker's soldiers noted, "Our men have

14. Ludwell H. Johnson, *Red River Campaign*, pp. 87, 96; Lonn, *Foreigners in the Confederacy*, pp. 167–70, 447–48; Barr, *Polignac's Texas Brigade*, pp. 21–23, 28–29, 38; Arceneaux, *Acadian General*, pp. 118–19; Richard Taylor, *Destruction and Reconstruction*, pp. 183–84 (quotation 184), 187–88.

suffered very much, but marched like heroes. . . . It remains to be seen what can be done by fighting." Despite the presence of a supply depot at Carroll Jones's, food quickly became scarce again. Adopting Stonewall Jackson's method of movement, Taylor sent his supply wagons farther north to allow for quick marching, thus leaving his troops without tents and blankets. According to yet another Texan, however, "All endured with comparatively little murmuring or complaining, and it shows a spirit which nothing could break or conquer." Expecting a fight within a few days, soldiers gathered nightly for religious services of preaching, singing, and praying.[15]

Taylor also hoped that the arrival of Colonel William G. Vincent's Louisiana cavalry from its reconnaissance of Banks's army would finally give him some means of scouting enemy movements from Alexandria. But when Vincent's horsemen rode into camp, Taylor found them "jaded by constant service and long marches." With Tom Green's troopers still en route from Texas, Taylor would remain in dire need of cavalry support. On March 19, however, he received a measure of good news from General Smith. Concerned about Banks's rapid and forceful encroachment, Smith had already ordered two more Texas cavalry regiments and four infantry regiments to join Green's command as quickly as possible. He had also instructed Major General Sterling Price, district commander in Arkansas, to rely on his cavalry in resisting Steele and to send most of his infantry, about four thousand men, to Shreveport. With these reinforcements, Smith asserted, "we must dispose of Banks." Encouraged by this, Taylor responded, "I shall cheerfully undertake to dispose of Banks and any other force which may be thrown against me." Suggesting, however, that first Taylor might have to withdraw forty-five miles upriver to Natchitoches, Smith asked whether he could hold out there. "I shall hold all I can," Taylor answered, realizing that unless the promised reinforcements arrived soon he might be overwhelmed.[16]

15. Hyatt diary, p. 179 (first quotation); Norman D. Brown, *Journey to Pleasant Hill*, p. 379 (second quotation); Theophilus Perry to Harriet Perry, March 17, 1864 (third quotation), Person Family Papers; *O.R.*, 34(1):497–98; Blessington, *Walker's Texas Division*, pp. 175–76 (fourth quotation 176).

16. *O.R.*, 34(1):496–500 (first quotation 498, second quotation 497, third quotation 499); Castel, *General Sterling Price*, p. 173.

On March 21 the enemy inflicted the very blow Taylor could least afford to sustain. Colonel Vincent's cavalry, having spent the past several days scouting and skirmishing with enemy parties north of Alexandria, was camped near Henderson's Hill, about twelve miles south of Taylor's headquarters. That night, with a cold, windy rain and hail storm making for a miserable encampment, Vincent's weary men fell victim to trickery from jayhawkers who stole the Confederate countersign and then guided a mounted regiment of Yankees past the pickets. The enemy quickly surrounded the camp and charged through it, taking about 250 prisoners, the majority of Vincent's force, and capturing a four-gun artillery battery. Although Taylor refused to assign any blame at the time, he later complained, "Vincent's pickets found their [camp] fires more agreeable than outposts." Some of those who escaped admitted that too few pickets had been on duty. Regardless, the incident dramatized Taylor's vulnerability and coerced him into an unpleasant decision. "This disaster leaves me with little or no means of obtaining information in front of a very large force of the enemy's cavalry," he reported. "I am therefore compelled to fall back . . . and wait until I can effect a junction with General Green." [17]

"It is Taylor's idea to fight with desperation as soon as he can get cavalry, and contest every inch of ground," noted one of Walker's men. "I shall fight like I was standing on the threshold of my door." Yet few of his comrades shared his enthusiasm after marching through the mud to Beasly's, a supply depot about twenty-five miles southwest of Natchitoches. "General Taylor . . . I think has managed very badly," complained one sullen Texan. "This is the hardest soldiering I have ever seen. I have been very tired, very sleepy and very hungry." With food again becoming scarce and foraging difficult in the sparsely settled piney woods surrounding the camp, Taylor implored Smith's staff almost every day for a week to send provisions.

17. Ludwell H. Johnson, *Red River Campaign*, pp. 96–97; Ewer, *Third Massachusetts Cavalry*, pp. 137–39; Richard Taylor, *Destruction and Reconstruction*, p. 188 (first quotation); Blessington, *Walker's Texas Division*, pp. 177–78; *O.R.*, 34(1):501 (second quotation).

"There was much discontent," wrote Captain Petty, "many men's patriotism rising no higher than their stomach's."[18]

At the same time Taylor tried to monitor enemy movements. But intelligence remained sketchy, mainly because his few available scouts offered easy prey to bushwhacking jayhawkers. "The whole country between [here] and Alexandria swarms with these outlaws, who are allied with the enemy," Taylor reported on March 26. "The arrival of . . . Green's regiments will change the whole aspect of affairs." Having reminded Smith repeatedly that Green's cavalry would justify an immediate offensive toward Alexandria, Taylor discovered on the twenty-eighth that the Federals were advancing in force. Expecting Green to take several more days to join him, Taylor prepared to withdraw another forty miles to a supply depot at Pleasant Hill, a small town northwest of Natchitoches. Not only would he be giving up what he considered a good strategic position, but he would be losing Natchitoches to the enemy without a fight. The worst in a series of unexpected setbacks, this withdrawal, he reported, represented "a great calamity."[19]

Fortunately for Taylor, circumstances had hampered Banks from vigorously prosecuting his grand campaign. Already a week behind schedule when his soldiers joined Porter and A. J. Smith at Alexandria on March 25, Banks had to spend several days dealing with the squabbles over cotton seizures and soliciting the town's citizens to participate in the election of delegates to the constitutional convention. Then he had to coax a resistive and insolent Admiral Porter into pushing his fleet up and over the falls of the Red River at Alexandria, where evidence of an unseasonally low water level confirmed Porter's fears about the safety of continued navigation. Then, on the twenty-sixth, Banks received a startling letter from Grant, who had only re-

18. Theophilus Perry to Harriet Perry, March 23, 1864 (first quotation), Person Family Papers; Richard Taylor, *Destruction and Reconstruction*, p. 188; Connor, *Dear America*, p. 95 (second quotation); Hyatt diary, p. 184; *O.R.*, 34(1):505–7, 510–11; Norman D. Brown, *Journey to Pleasant Hill*, p. 383 (third quotation).

19. *O.R.*, 34(1):510 (first quotation), 505–7, 511 (second quotation); Richard Taylor, *Destruction and Reconstruction*, p. 188.

cently replaced Halleck as general-in-chief of Union armies. Anxious to bolster Sherman's impending invasion of Georgia, Grant informed Banks that he must send A. J. Smith's ten thousand men back to Sherman by the middle of April if he did not expect to capture Shreveport by May 1. All hopes of heroics for Banks now depended upon utmost speed. He could tolerate no more distractions.[20]

For Taylor, the withdrawal to Pleasant Hill seemed all the more distasteful because he had to destroy even more cotton. Soldiers burned thousands of bales between Alexandria and Natchitoches, the flames often spreading from storage barns to plantation houses and slave cabins. "In fact the road all the way to Natchitoches, a distance of 18 miles one could say was a solid flame," wrote a witness, "and the air was completely permeated with the smell of burning cotton. My heart was filled with sadness at the sight of those lovely plantations in flames." A Federal soldier marveled, "This was one of the curious phases of the war—to see the rebels bent on the destruction of their own property."[21]

Meanwhile Taylor's men continued to suffer. "During all this march we have not [had] a single tent, and when it rains which is frequently the case we have to lay and take it," noted one of Mouton's officers. "We have nothing but bull beef, corn bread, dirty clothes and sore feet." One of Walker's Texans wrote to his wife, "The men are literally starving here. A great many are talking of leaving the field." Concerned even more about his family's increasing burden of hardship at home, he expressed bitter resentment over Texas's confiscation and rationing laws. "When times get so that your women and children are to be put on half rations . . . it will be time for us to wind it up," he declared. Reflecting on the two hellish years since he had first been wounded at Shiloh, Mouton's officer echoed the thoughts of many a demoralized Confederate with a single, searching question: "Will the war *ever* end?"[22]

20. Ludwell H. Johnson, *Red River Campaign*, pp. 101–10; Kerby, *Kirby Smith's Confederacy*, pp. 296–97.

21. Bearss, *A Louisiana Confederate*, p. 102 (first quotation); Bering and Montgomery, *Forty-Eighth Ohio*, p. 129.

22. Hyatt diary, pp. 188–89 (first quotation 188, fourth quotation 189); S. W. Farrow to Josephine Farrow, March 29, 1864 (second and third quotations), Farrow Papers.

A more immediate question, however, plagued Dick Taylor: where were his reinforcements? During the withdrawal to Pleasant Hill he received at least a partial answer. From his brother-in-law Confederate congressman Duncan Kenner he learned that the reinforcements from Arkansas had already arrived at Shreveport and that General Smith had detained them there. According to Kenner, Smith had interpreted Taylor's repeated vows to fight Banks once Green arrived as meaning that Taylor did not want these extra troops. Taylor promptly dispatched a letter to Smith on the twenty-eighth, reminding him that Green was now more than ten days late. Although he had admitted that the Federal offensive in Arkansas might require sending these troops back to fight, Taylor could "scarcely conceive how this could be interpreted into a declaration that I did not want re-enforcements." Protesting Smith's apparent lack of "anxiety" in the matter, Taylor concluded, "When Green joins me, I repeat, I shall fight a battle for Louisiana, be the forces of the enemy what they may."[23]

To this Smith issued a circumspect response explaining that the reinforcements at Shreveport needed ammunition and that, because the enemy movement from Arkansas now appeared serious, he would have to wait another three or four days before deciding whether to send the promised troops to Taylor. Having originally hoped to strengthen Taylor for a strike against Banks, Smith now hesitated. Attempting to restrain his mounting anger, on the thirtieth Taylor retorted, "I respectfully suggest that the only possible way to defeat Steele's movement [from Arkansas] is to whip the enemy now in the heart of the Red River Valley." Had the reinforcements come forward, he concluded, "I could have fought a battle for the department today. To decline concentration when we have the means, and when the enemy is already in the vitals of the department, is a policy I am too obtuse to understand." When he learned on the thirty-first that Green would probably take another ten days to arrive, Taylor heaped all his frustration on Smith, claiming that had he known of Green's delay he would have already attacked Banks and risked de-

23. *O.R.*, 34(1):512–13 (quotations 513); Parks, *Edmund Kirby Smith*, pp. 380–81; Warner and Yearns, *Biographical Register of the Confederate Congress*, pp. 144–45.

feat rather than abandon most of Louisiana without fighting. "The fairest and richest portion of the Confederacy is now a waste," Taylor moaned. "Louisiana may well know her destiny. Her children are exiles; her labor system is destroyed. . . . I shall never cease to regret the error."[24]

Despite his vacillation, Smith was clearly exercising the grand strategy he had planned from the beginning of the campaign. Short of losing Shreveport, he had never worried about how much territory he might have to give up; instead, he wanted only to exploit the advantage of operating along interior lines, drawing the Federals deeper into an unfamiliar region and then concentrating to defeat one enemy column before it could combine with the other. "Our role must be a defensive policy," he reminded Taylor, emphasizing that "the destruction of either of the little armies at our disposal would be fatal to the whole cause." Besides, Smith argued, with fifty thousand Federals operating in the Trans-Mississippi, "we do good service" by keeping them from participating in the vital Virginia and Georgia campaigns. Finally, Smith also denied Duncan Kenner's accusation that he had believed Taylor did not want reinforcements. "While . . . [you] have always given me a hearty and cordial support, I object to the tone of your letter, which is an unjust complaint," Smith stated flatly.[25]

Taylor responded sharply on April 3, defending Kenner's honor and refusing to accept Smith's denial. "I certainly would have been the first commander possessing ordinary sense who voluntarily declined re-enforcements while retreating before a superior force," he protested. Seeing no reason to apologize for his complaints against Smith, Taylor remarked indignantly, "I am fully impressed with what is due from a subordinate to his military superior." As for Smith's strategic arguments, Taylor remained unconvinced. Although he had agreed before the campaign that Confederate forces must withdraw before concentrating to defeat one enemy column and then the other, Taylor had become increasingly anxious to gain reinforce-

24. *O.R.*, 34(1):513–15 (first quotation 514, second quotation 514–15, third quotation 515).
25. Kerby, *Kirby Smith's Confederacy*, p. 299; *O.R.*, 34(1):516–17 (first and second quotations 516, third quotation 517).

ments to keep Banks from advancing so far. Stonewall Jackson had demonstrated in the Shenandoah Valley the necessity of surrendering territory in order to concentrate against a divided enemy. But unlike Jackson, Taylor now saw the heartland of his home state gutted by total war. "Like the man who has admitted the robber into his bedchamber instead of resisting him at the door, our defense will be embarrassed by the cries of wives and children," he asserted.[26]

In a deliberate attempt to goad Smith into a decision, on the fourth Taylor stated that if necessary he would even join a strike against Steele in Arkansas. "Action, prompt, vigorous action is required," he declared. "While we are deliberating the enemy is marching. King James lost three kingdoms for a mass. We may lose three states without a battle." By now several of Green's cavalry units had finally arrived, and the rest were expected within two days. Taylor would wait no longer than this for Smith to take the initiative. "Unless I receive instructions to the contrary," he warned, "I shall move on Natchitoches . . . and thus check the further advance of Banks's column." Echoing Taylor's resolve, one of Walker's men wrote, "We have run until our patience has oozed out. A fight I think will help us now."[27]

By April 6 Taylor had lost his chance to fight Banks at Natchitoches because the Yankees were already well on their way to Pleasant Hill. By heading away from the Red River at Grand Ecore, however, Banks did not purposely pursue Taylor; he simply believed this route offered the only possible approach to Shreveport. Although Banks could have taken a more direct route along the river, Federal maps did not show the road. Refusing to waste too much time scouting the area, Banks had in mind Grant's order to send A. J. Smith's men back to Sherman by the middle of the month. Banks thus willingly abandoned the protection afforded by Porter's fleet of daunting ironclads. He saw nothing risky in the decision. Certain that Taylor would continue to withdraw, Banks informed the Union high command he would capture Shreveport within a few days and then "pursue the enemy into the interior of Texas, for the sole purpose of dispersing or destroying his forces." Soldiers in the ranks reflected their com-

26. *O.R.*, 34(1):519 (first and second quotations), 522 (third quotation).

27. Ibid., pp. 522–23 (first quotation 522, second quotation 523), 518, 520–21; Norman D. Brown, *Journey to Pleasant Hill*, p. 387 (third quotation).

mander's unbridled confidence as they marched toward Pleasant Hill. Along the route they encountered civilian refugees who claimed that Taylor was amassing his forces to make a stand at Mansfield, just north of Pleasant Hill. "I recollect this distinctly," a Union officer recounted. "They said the rebels were boasting that here was the place they were going 'to begin to bury the Yankees.'" But Banks's men scoffed at these predictions and joked with each other about the fine vacation they would have in Shreveport.[28]

Moving from Pleasant Hill to Mansfield, Taylor now had about eighty-eight hundred troops after the arrival of the rest of Green's cavalrymen. A small number of Louisiana militiamen also appeared, having responded to a call from their energetic new governor, Henry Watkins Allen. On April 2 Allen had issued a public proclamation appealing for volunteers. "I love every swamp and every pine-clad hill in your now beleaguered state," he exclaimed. "Rally in defense of your wives and children. . . . The enemy must be met. We will conquer him and you shall be free." Appeals to patriotism aside, Allen also issued orders requiring every able-bodied man to enroll in the militia, bluntly instructing his conscript officers, "If any man resists you with deadly weapons, you will cause him to be shot dead on the spot." Allen's methods of persuasion, along with the public anger and terror induced by Banks's advance, brought results. "Consternation and alarm everywhere prevailed among the citizens," observed one of Walker's soldiers. "Old men shouldered their muskets and came to our assistance, to help drive back the invader."[29]

After a winter of wretched encampments in freezing cold and rain in Texas, Green's troopers seemed more eager than ever. "We were, if anything, overjoyed at the prospects of returning to Louisiana with

28. Ludwell H. Johnson, *Red River Campaign*, pp. 110–16 (first quotation 111); U.S. Congress, *Report of the Joint Committee on the Conduct of the War*, p. 188 (second quotation); Ewer, *Third Massachusetts Cavalry*, p. 152.

29. Richard Taylor, *Destruction and Reconstruction*, pp. 189–90; Winters, *Civil War in Louisiana*, pp. 317–19; Kerby, *Kirby Smith's Confederacy*, pp. 301–2; *O.R.*, 34(1):534; Galveston *Tri-Weekly News*, April 10, 1864 (first quotation); Cassidy, "Louisiana," pp. 103–5; Cassidy and Simpson, *Henry Watkins Allen*, p. 123 (second quotation); Blessington, *Walker's Texas Division*, p. 179 (third quotation).

our favorite chieftain [Green] to our favorite General—Taylor," one of them recalled. Another, seeing Taylor for the first time, was impressed by his demeanor. "He is a small man—dark complexion—dark hair and eyes—plain in dress and in his manner in all respects. If he is not a good general, I am sure he has the good of his country at heart." Colonel Xavier B. Debray, commander of one of the Texas cavalry units, found Taylor somewhat less genial. Upon reporting for duty Debray received a cool welcome, Taylor stiffly informing him that had not his troopers performed so well in skirmishing with the enemy while en route he would have been arrested and court-martialed. At this Debray expressed complete surprise, whereupon Taylor upbraided him and stated that he and his regiment had arrived from Texas ten days late. Insulted by the reproach, Debray explained that his unit had traveled more than 250 miles, encumbered by a wagon train carrying badly needed supplies. A native Frenchman, Debray spoke with an accent that seemed to assuage Taylor's anger. Extending his hand, he responded in French to the feisty officer, "I see that you are not a politician." A day or two later, when Colonel Walter P. Lane's cavalry regiment arrived at Mansfield, it happened to pass Taylor, sitting on his horse at a street corner. One of the Texans heard Taylor remark, "Boys, I am glad to see you."[30]

Despite his bitter resentment over losing so much of Louisiana to the Federals, Taylor found himself in a remarkably fortunate position at Mansfield. Not only was Banks's army more than fifteen miles from the safety of Porter's fleet, but the Union commander had also strung out his column along a narrow, muddy road enveloped by a dense forest offering little forage and water. "Such a thing as subsisting an army in a country like this could only be achieved when men and horses could be induced to live on pine trees and rosin," a soldier observed. Taylor also realized that, once beyond Mansfield, Banks had a choice of three much better roads veering back toward the Red River to rejoin Porter for the final forty miles to Shreveport. But General Smith perceived no special advantage in Taylor's position. In a

30. Noel, *Old Sibley Brigade*, p. 74 (first quotation); Smith and Mullins, "Diary of H. C. Medford," p. 212 (second quotation); Debray, *Debray's Texas Cavalry*, pp. 15–16 (third quotation 16); Yeary, *Reminiscences of the Boys in Gray*, p. 781 (fourth quotation).

letter to Taylor on April 5 he argued that, because Banks's and
Steele's columns were still two hundred miles apart, a concentration
just now against either one would prove extremely premature.
"When we fight it must be for victory," Smith asserted. "Defeat not
only loses the department, but releases the armies employed against
us here for operations beyond the Mississippi." Seeking to impress his
views upon Taylor, Smith decided to ride to Mansfield for a personal
meeting on the sixth.[31]

After surveying the troops in camp near Mansfield, Smith and Taylor discussed the ramifications of fighting Banks. Smith later claimed
that Taylor surmised Banks was having great trouble advancing his
column. But according to Taylor's version, Smith considered weathering a siege in Shreveport or even withdrawing all the way into
Texas. Taylor objected vociferously, arguing that if Shreveport fell,
the Louisiana and Arkansas regiments would probably desert. Besides, "from the interior of Texas we could give no more aid to our
brethren east of the Mississippi than from the Sandwich Islands," he
argued. By now, however, Smith had agreed at least to send the four
thousand reinforcements under Brigadier General Thomas J.
Churchill from Shreveport to Keatchie, a little more than halfway to
Mansfield, to await Taylor's orders. Yet Smith still refused to authorize
Taylor to resist an advance by Banks. Having specified nothing else in
his meeting with Taylor, Smith returned to Shreveport.[32]

On April 7 a strong wind from the south brought the clear sounds
of heavy gunfire to Taylor's headquarters, compelling him to make a
hard ride toward the action. A few miles down the road he saw about
fifty frazzled Texas cavalrymen galloping toward him, obviously running from the fight. But before he could berate them, one shouted,
"General! If you won't curse us, we will go back with you." Amused at
this reminder of his talent for colorful language, Taylor merely nod-

31. Kerby, *Kirby Smith's Confederacy*, pp. 302–3; Ludwell H. Johnson, *Red
River Campaign*, pp. 117–22; Flinn, *Campaigning with Banks*, p. 99 (first quotation); Richard Taylor, *Destruction and Reconstruction*, p. 191; *O.R.*,
34(1):525–26 (second quotation 526).

32. Edmund Kirby Smith, "Defense of the Red River," pp. 369–71; Richard Taylor, *Destruction and Reconstruction*, pp. 190–91 (quotation 191); Kerby,
Kirby Smith's Confederacy, p. 303.

ded and led them back toward the gunfire. About three miles north of Pleasant Hill, at Wilson's Farm, he found several regiments of Tom Green's troopers clashing with a portion of Brigadier General Albert L. Lee's cavalry division. "Putting in my little re-enforcements, I joined [Green], and enjoyed his method of handling his wild horsemen," Taylor recalled. Although outnumbered, Green gave this Federal advance guard a sharp jolt. According to one Yankee cavalryman, "Green fought so stubbornly that reinforcements were sent for, in order to repel the fiery attack of the Confederates." Confronted by this additional enemy strength, Green ordered his men to withdraw. To one of his officers, Colonel Augustus C. Buchel, he remarked, "We haven't had much show yet, but we will give them hell tomorrow."[33]

Recognizing the collision at Wilson's Farm as proof of Banks's intention to push forward, about 9:00 P.M. Taylor sent a message to Smith asking for permission to "hazard a general engagement." An answer, he emphasized, must come before sunrise the next day, April 8. Yet according to J. E. Sliger, a lieutenant privy to events at Taylor's headquarters, Taylor had already decided to stand and fight. He made certain, therefore, that the courier bearing his message would not reach Smith until the morning of the eighth, thus preventing Smith's reply from reaching him until late in the day. As expected, Smith reacted negatively to Taylor's request. His reply, somewhat vaguely worded, again discouraged Taylor from giving battle, advising him instead to hold his ground but also to "compel the enemy to develop his intentions." On one point, however, Smith made himself clear: "Let me know as soon as you are convinced that a general advance is being made [by the enemy] and I will come to the front." Brigadier General William R. Boggs, Smith's chief of staff, later blamed this scheme on Smith's personal physician and confidant, Dr. Solomon A. Smith (no relation to the General). "Taylor was to harass Banks up to the last moment," Boggs recalled, "and then General Kirby Smith was to move down with additional troops, take command, and carry off the glory of the pitched battle. In the meantime

33. Richard Taylor, *Destruction and Reconstruction*, p. 192 (first and second quotations); Ludwell H. Johnson, *Red River Campaign*, pp. 124–25; Noel, *Old Sibley Brigade*, p. 77; Ewer, *Third Massachusetts Cavalry*, p. 143 (third quotation); Bitton, *Reminiscences of Levi Lamoni Wight*, p. 31 (fourth quotation).

we, at departmental headquarters, were having reviews, balls and a gay time generally." Regardless, because of Taylor's delayed message, Smith's reply would not reach Taylor until late afternoon on the eighth.[34]

Meanwhile Taylor sent orders to Churchill to march at dawn from Keatchie, twenty miles distant. He also instructed Walker and Mouton, whose troops were camped north of Mansfield, to prepare to move into position a few miles south of town. On the evening of the seventh the ladies of Mansfield held a party, with Taylor and his generals in attendance as honored guests. Several of the ladies appealed to him personally, begging him not to let the Yankees capture the town. In a sublime demonstration of chivalry he promised that Banks would first have to pass over his body. His soldiers seemed more ardent than ever in their hopes of battle. " 'Fight, fight,' was the expression of the boys" in camp, a Texan recalled. "I never saw men so eager for a chance to try their pluck, and that against overwhelming odds." Early on the morning of the eighth, a warm spring day, Mouton's and Walker's divisions marched through the streets of Mansfield, their bands playing "Dixie" as the town's women and children threw garlands at their feet and cried out for them to save their homeland.[35]

As the soldiers marched out of town, they passed Taylor, Mouton, Walker, and Green, deep in discussion on the roadside. Private Joseph P. Blessington remembered Taylor's imposing presence at that moment. "He has a glorious pair of dark eyes that scintillate beneath his heavy brows and dark hair," wrote Blessington. "A heavy, curved mustache covers his well-formed mouth. Such is his appearance, and his fighting qualities are in accordance." At 9:40 A.M. Taylor sent another message to General Smith, reporting that the enemy was plainly moving forward. "I consider this as favorable a point to en-

34. Richard Taylor, *Destruction and Reconstruction*, pp. 193–94; *O.R.*, 34(1):526 (first quotation), 528 (second and third quotations); Sliger, "How General Taylor Fought the Battle of Mansfield," pp. 456–57; Boggs, *Military Reminiscences*, pp. 75–76 (fourth quotation 76).

35. Richard Taylor, *Destruction and Reconstruction*, p. 193; Goodloe, "Service in the Trans-Mississippi," p. 31; Gravis, *Twenty-Five Years on the Outside Row*, pp. 29–30 (quotation); Blessington, *Walker's Texas Division*, p. 183; Bonner, "Sketches of the Campaign of 1864," pt. 1, p. 462.

gage him as any other," he stated with feigned indifference. Mounted on a black horse and with a single staff officer at his side, he spent the remainder of the morning supervising the placement of his troops. He had selected the position the day before while returning from the action at Wilson's Farm. Situated about three miles south of Mansfield, the Confederate battle line ran along Sabine Crossroads, named for the road heading west toward the Sabine River. From the edge of a pine forest the southerners looked south across cleared farmland offering a firing range of about a thousand yards. A gently rising slope known as Honeycutt Hill, covered with timber, occupied the horizon. Near the center of Taylor's line, in a forward position, Colonel Debray's cavalry regiment straddled the Mansfield road. To the far right Taylor placed Brigadier General Hamilton P. Bee's two regiments of Texas cavalry, flanked on the inside by Walker's Division, whose lines extended across the Mansfield road. From here Mouton's regiments formed a long leftward arch, with Brigadier General James P. Major's cavalry, part of Green's command, occupying the far left flank. Green himself and the rest of his troopers were already probing and skirmishing with the enemy's advance units, now only a few miles up the road. Twelve artillery batteries, a total of sixty guns, stood at intervals along the line. Without Churchill's reinforcements, still on their way from Keatchie, Taylor had only about eighty-eight hundred men to face Banks's army.[36]

Throughout the morning distant clashes between mounted skirmishers filled the air with sharply resonating cracks of gunfire, agitating the waiting Confederate infantrymen. "We are ready and eager to meet the damned rascals," one of them jotted in his diary. About noon Taylor rode down the line to the left and spoke to Mouton's Louisianans, saying that he wanted them "to draw first blood" since they were "fighting in defense of their own soil." Suddenly a group of cavalry skirmishers came galloping in from the front, pursued by about a hundred Federal horsemen "shouting sooe! sooe! as though they were driving hogs." Nearing the trees where Mouton's men stood

36. Blessington, *Walker's Texas Division*, pp. 183–86 (first quotation 184); *O.R.*, 34(1):526 (second quotation), 525; Richard Taylor, *Destruction and Reconstruction*, p. 193; Kerby, *Kirby Smith's Confederacy*, pp. 304–5; Ludwell H. Johnson, *Red River Campaign*, pp. 132–33.

hidden, the Yankees opened fire, a bullet striking Taylor's saddle. "The charge . . . was a gallant one, for they came within 20 feet of our line," a southerner recalled. A single volley of rifle fire from the Louisianans cut through men and horses, throwing the surprised Federals into "the wildest confusion . . . [all] hurrying from the field and we right on their heels, taking many prisoners," according to a Confederate. Sustained cheering erupted along Mouton's line. With order soon restored and the men back in their original positions, Taylor passed in front of them, offering congratulations for their initial success.[37]

Far across the field, in the woods atop Honeycutt Hill, Union officers began receiving sobering reports from their skirmishers and scouts. Taylor's army had finally stopped retreating and apparently intended to make a stand. About 1:00 P.M. Banks arrived at the front and spoke with a nervous Albert Lee, his cavalry commander. Lee told Banks that he needed reinforcements at once in order to face an estimated fifteen to twenty thousand Confederates. Although Banks had left behind large contingents of troops in Alexandria and Natchitoches, he still had about eighteen thousand men in his invading column. Agreeing to provide Lee with extra infantry, he ordered up Major General William Franklin's Thirteenth Corps, but unfortunately Franklin would require at least three or four hours to arrive because Lee's train of supply wagons stood directly in his path, stretching for several miles along the narrow road through the pine forest. For several days Lee had wanted to send his wagons to the rear in order to have Franklin's infantry close at hand. Yet Franklin, with Banks's approval, had refused, saying that Lee should take care of his own wagons. By 3:30 P.M., with Franklin's corps still on its way, Banks impatiently ordered Lee to advance. Banks believed that Taylor's show of force was a bluff. Lee objected, insisting that if he advanced he would surely be "most gloriously flogged." Banks yielded reluctantly. Lee had at his disposal only his own cavalry division and two

37. Hyatt diary, p. 190 (first and fourth quotations); Richard Taylor, *Destruction and Reconstruction*, p. 195 (second quotation); Duaine, *Dead Men Wore Boots*, p. 55 (third quotation); Haas, "Diary of Julius Giesecke," p. 47 (fifth quotation); Bearss, *A Louisiana Confederate*, p. 106.

Nathaniel P. Banks in all his martial splendor
(Jenkins Rare Book Company).

infantry brigades under Brigadier General Thomas E. G. Ransom, a total of about forty-eight hundred men. Worried that Taylor might attack at any moment, Lee ordered his officers to take advantage of their elevated defensive position and form battle lines.[38]

By mid-afternoon Taylor's impatience began to match that of Banks. Federal batteries had begun a long-range artillery duel, and Taylor's scouts reported the presence of infantry at the front; but the enemy still showed no signs of aggression. Taylor knew that the Union column had stretched itself out to more than twenty miles in length, and he suspected that his own forces outnumbered the Federals then present at the front. Instead of simply waiting for Banks to attack, Taylor considered taking the battle to Banks. "The value of

38. Ludwell H. Johnson, *Red River Campaign*, pp. 124–29, 133–34 (quotation 134).

the 'initiative' in war cannot be overstated," he later observed. "The 'defensive' is weak, lowering the morale of the army reduced to it . . . and keeping commander and troops in a state of anxious tension." Having seen this principle demonstrated to the point of audacity by Stonewall Jackson, Taylor exhibited an equally important Jacksonian trait: boundless disdain for an enemy's abilities. "My confidence of success in the impending engagement," he explained, "was inspired by accurate knowledge of Federal movements, as well as the character of their commander, General Banks, whose measure had been taken in the Virginia campaigns of 1862 and since."[39]

About 3:30 P.M. Taylor rode to Walker's position and conversed with him for nearly twenty minutes, when intense skirmishing by Mouton's troops on the left prompted him to ride in that direction. By now Taylor had reached a critical decision. Seeing Polignac, he shouted, "Little Frenchman, I am going to fight Banks here, if he has a million men!" He quickly found Mouton and ordered him to attack at once. Mouton met briefly with Polignac, exhorting him passionately, "Let us charge them right in the face and throw them into the valley." With this, he drew his saber and led his division forward. It was a few minutes past 4:00 P.M. on a day the Confederate Congress had designated for national fasting, humiliation, and prayer.[40]

Returning to the center, near the Mansfield road, Taylor scanned the scene with his field glasses and puffed calmly on a cigar. Sitting with one leg draped across his saddle in a manner identical to the posture his father had assumed at Buena Vista, he seemed the very image of Old Rough and Ready himself. It remained to be seen whether he would achieve the same grand result. He had resolved to circumvent General Smith's strategy and specific instructions, first by giving Smith no chance of deciding whether to make a stand against an enemy advance, and now, even worse, by initiating an attack himself. Always the gambler, he was placing everything at risk—his reputation, his army, and his state. While watching Mouton's men ad-

39. Richard Taylor, *Destruction and Reconstruction*, pp. 17 (first quotation), 194–97 (second quotation 194).

40. Blessington, *Walker's Texas Division*, p. 186; Dorsey, *Henry Watkins Allen*, pp. 261 (first quotation), 263 (second quotation); Richard Taylor, *Destruction and Reconstruction*, p. 196; Kerby, *Kirby Smith's Confederacy*, p. 304.

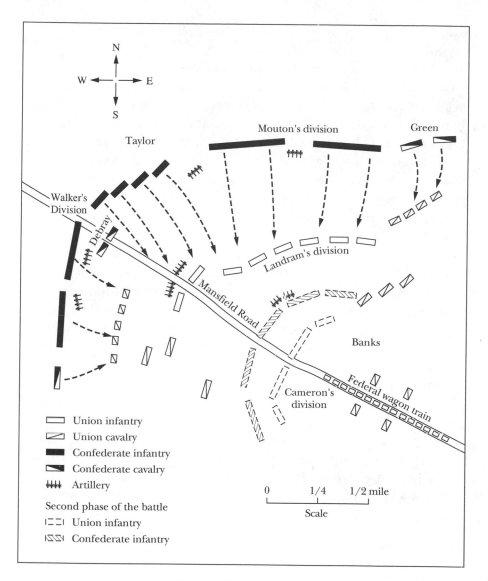

N

W ← → E

S

Mouton's division

Green

Taylor

Walker's
Division

Debray

Mansfield Road

Landram's division

Banks

Federal wagon train

Cameron's
division

Union infantry
Union cavalry
Confederate infantry
Confederate cavalry
Artillery

Second phase of the battle
Union infantry
Confederate infantry

0   1/4   1/2 mile

Scale

Map 7. Battle of Mansfield, April 8, 1864

vance, he remarked quite placidly to Debray that today he was
fighting "with a rope around his neck."[41]

"The charge made by Mouton across the open was magnificent,"
Taylor stated in his official report. One astounded Federal soldier recalled that as the Louisianans moved forward "their lines extended so
far that I could not see the ends on either flank." Another wrote,
"Masses of rebels, no less than four lines in depth, emerged from the
woods and charged with impetuous force, yelling like crazed demons." The Yankees let forth what Taylor described as "a murderous
fire of artillery and musketry." Yet Mouton's men pressed onward.
"Shots plow gaps through them, shells burst in their midst and form
caverns in the mass of living men," wrote a Federal. "But . . . others,
taking the places of their dead comrades, march rapidly on." Rushing
down into a ravine and up the wooded hill, they approached a rail
fence where the enemy held a strong position. About two hundred
yards from the fence they wavered under a storm of rifle fire and
grapeshot, falling to the ground to exchange several rapid volleys.
Here Mouton rallied them with renewed confidence. "He was all the
time in a glee of laughter," recalled a Louisianan, "cheering his men
and officers, telling them that our arms would be victorious today."
When Polignac noticed his Texans suddenly faltering under a barrage of enemy bombshells, he yelled in broken English, "Come on
boys, come on, these things do make a hell of a noise but don't hurt
much." The mounted officers, presenting easy targets, drew particularly heavy fire from the cheering Yankees. Confederate casualties
mounted quickly. Among the many dead lay Mouton himself, his
body covered with wounds.[42]

41. Bartlett, *Military Record of Louisiana*, pt. 3, p. 13; Debray, *Debray's Texas
Cavalry*, p. 17 (quotation).

42. *O.R.*, 34(1):564 (first and fourth quotations); Stanyan, *Eighth New
Hampshire Volunteers*, pp. 412 (second quotation), 402–3 (third quotation
403); Woods, *Ninety-Sixth Ohio Volunteers*, p. 59 (fifth quotation); Bering and
Montgomery, *Forty-Eighth Ohio*, pp. 131–32; Smith and Mullins, "Diary of H.
C. Medford," p. 227 (sixth quotation); L. J. Storey to A. M. Hill, February 21,
1908 (seventh quotation), Hill Papers; Richard Taylor, *Destruction and Reconstruction*, p. 196; Ludwell H. Johnson, *Red River Campaign*, pp. 134–35. Some
sources indicate that Mouton was killed by a group of skirmishers who had

Just as the fighting along Mouton's line became most ferocious, General Smith's courier reached Taylor. Snatching the message from the courier's hand, Taylor read Smith's orders and responded triumphantly, "Too late sir, the battle is won. It is not the first time I have fought with a halter around my neck." At this point, however, the battle was neither won nor lost. Taylor might have believed Mouton was delivering a decisive blow. But more likely, he refused to consider stopping the attack and giving up the advantage he believed he held over the enemy. Although Taylor admitted in his official report that he "ordered Mouton to open the attack," General Smith later chose to overlook Taylor's overt disobedience. "The battle of Mansfield was not an intentional violation of my instructions on General Taylor's part," Smith contended. Rather, Mouton had attacked "without waiting for orders from Taylor." This was not the first instance of Smith's toleration of Taylor's impetuosity, and it would not be the last.[43]

Having sent Mouton forward on the left, Taylor expected the Federals on the right to have weakened their own position by shifting troops to resist Mouton's charge. Therefore he ordered Walker to "feel the enemy in the woods on the right, make him show himself, and attack." Across the field the Texans advanced. "Every man moved off quickly, with a confident and determined step," one of them recalled. "Rising the crest of the hill, we were met by a terrible fire from the enemy's battery," wrote another. "We pressed forward under a terrific storm of shot and shell into a point of timber[,] . . . moved rapidly to the right to get out of range, and again pressed forward." Then came the command to charge. Walker's men dashed to within fifty paces of a rail fence that secured the enemy's line. A sustained

been outflanked and forced to surrender. Seeing the soldiers lay down their arms, Mouton rode forward, but the Yankees, noticing his high rank, quickly picked up their guns and fired at him. Louisiana infantrymen then rushed forward and retaliated by shooting and killing all of the Yankees. See Arceneaux, *Acadian General*, p. 132; Bergeron, *Uncle Silas*, p. 158; "Battle of Mansfield," p. 413.

43. Dorsey, *Henry Watkins Allen*, p. 263 (first quotation); *O.R.*, 34(1):564 (second quotation), 480, 485; Edmund Kirby Smith, "Defense of the Red River," p. 371 (third and fourth quotations).

blast of musket and artillery fire burst forth upon them. "In this fearful charge, there was no flinching or murmuring," asserted a Texan. "At last the fence is gained; over it our troops go [and] a loud and prolonged Texas yell deafens the ear; their cheers rise in one great range of sound over the noise of battle, and are heard far down the lines to the left, where the Louisiana boys are at it."[44]

After Mouton's death, Polignac took command of the troops on the left, and Green's cavalry began to outflank resistance there. With Walker pressing on the right, the Federals found themselves in a huge nutcracker. The Confederates forced their way up Honeycutt Hill, surrounding and capturing entire regiments, many of which had run out of ammunition. Still the Union artillery continued to fire rapidly. "Again and again . . . [we] poured double charges of grape and canister into the ranks of the enemy, mowing great swaths through its serried columns," wrote a Federal. But in a few minutes the southerners swarmed among the batteries, capturing several artillery pieces, turning them around, and firing at the backs of retreating Federal infantry. About 5:00 P.M. Franklin finally arrived with some thirteen hundred fresh troops and held a line about a half-mile behind the first one. General Banks was there as well, his hat removed for better recognition, bravely riding about and urging his troops to withstand the onslaught. "He looked cool and calm, though rather perplexed," a soldier recalled.[45]

Thanks to Franklin's reinforcements, the Federals defied Taylor's relentless pressure for almost an hour before buckling. Then panic swept over them as they retreated headlong into the train of supply wagons obstructing the road in the rear. Banks's convoluted organization of his column along the road, the result of his own limitless confidence and impatience, was proving doubly fatal. Not only had the wagons hampered troops in reaching the front, but now they also

44. Houston *Daily Telegraph*, April 18, 1864 (first and third quotations); Blessington, *Walker's Texas Division*, pp. 187–89 (second quotation 187, fourth quotation 188–89); Bonner, "Sketches of the Campaign of 1864," pt. 1, p. 464.

45. Ludwell H. Johnson, *Red River Campaign*, pp. 135–36; Ewer, *Third Massachusetts Cavalry*, p. 148 (first quotation); Hatch, *Dearest Susie*, pp. 84–87 (second quotation 86).

blocked the only path of retreat through the dense pine forest. Banks implored his men to form new lines, but none listened. "It was every man for himself, and 'Dick' Taylor take the hindmost," one of them admitted. Another recalled seeing "men without hats or coats, men without guns or accoutrements, cavalrymen without horses, and artillerymen without cannon, wounded men bleeding and crying at every step . . . all in a state of fear and frenzy." The Confederates closed in with a merciless fury. One of Walker's Texans wrote, "Cheer after cheer bursts forth from our lines, as the enemy is seen fleeing. . . . Through the woods and along the road, our cavalry and artillery completely slaughter them. Horses and men, by hundreds, roll down together; the road is red with their blood."[46]

Many Yankees managed to escape only because parties of ravenous Confederates merely pushed them aside to leap on the wagons and revel in the supplies. One recalled specifically that "Banks' wagons . . . were labeled 'Austin,' 'San Antonio,' 'Houston,' 'Galveston,' etc.," in honor of anticipated conquests. The booty included exotic canned foods and fancy clothing, even white paper collars. A rumor later circulated that Taylor sent a message to Banks regarding the collars, saying "that his men had baked them, boiled them, fried them and stewed them, and found them of no use, and he would like to exchange them for hard bread." But Taylor's men found the massive quantities of liquor in the wagons singularly agreeable, making their victory all the sweeter.[47]

At 6:00 P.M. Taylor dashed off a dispatch to Smith: "We have driven the enemy this hour 3 miles. . . . We are still driving him. We have lost some valuable officers, among others the gallant and chivalric Mouton. . . . I shall push the enemy to the utmost." When Smith received this message at Shreveport late that night, he refused to believe that Taylor had done more than clash with Banks's advance guard. The

46. Ludwell H. Johnson, *Red River Campaign*, pp. 136–37; Byam, "Swapping Stories in Texas," p. 314 (first quotation); Beecher, *114th N.Y.S.V.*, p. 311 (second quotation); Blessington, *Walker's Texas Division*, p. 189 (third quotation).

47. Stanyan, *Eighth New Hampshire Volunteers*, p. 404; Yeary, *Reminiscences of the Boys in Gray*, p. 627 (first quotation); Orton S. Clark, *One Hundred and Sixteenth N.Y.S.V.*, p. 166 (second quotation).

Monument to Taylor's victory at Mansfield,
erected by his daughters Elizabeth and Myrthe
(Edward M. Boagni).

real battle, Smith assured his staff, would take place north of Mansfield. Perceiving his chance for field command, he hurried south to
join Taylor.[48]

Just when it seemed that Banks's entire army might stampede back
to the Red River, bluecoated reinforcements from the Nineteenth
Corps, a division of more than five thousand men commanded by
William Emory, pushed their way forward through the retreating
rabble. "Turn back! Turn back! All is lost at the front!" many in the
beaten mob screamed, but Emory's men persisted, ignoring the mass

48. *O.R.*, 34(1):527 (quotation), 480; Boggs, *Military Reminiscences*, pp.
76–77.

panic. Shortly before sunset, near a place called Pleasant Grove, several miles south of Sabine Crossroads, Emory deployed his brigades atop a ridge overlooking a creek. "They had scarcely formed," he wrote, "before . . . the enemy [came] rushing and yelling as if they had everything their own way." Although Taylor lacked sufficient cavalry support, he ordered his disorganized infantry to charge through a large plum and peach orchard, up the ridge, and into the teeth of the Federal battle line. Seeing the troops approach, Emory shouted, "Men, you must hold this position at all hazards; before the enemy gets past here they must ride over me and my little gray mare."[49]

One of the Yankees described Taylor's attack: "On they came, flushed with victory and spoils, to which the liquors had not a little bit contributed." Darkness was beginning to fall in long shadows. With the Nineteenth Corps' brass band trumpeting a feverish chorus of "Hail Columbia," Emory's men opened fire on the unsuspecting southerners. "Then came the terrible shock," wrote one of Taylor's officers. "Volley after volley resounded from the hill. . . . The very air seemed dark and hot with balls, and on every side was heard their dull, crushing sound, as they struck that swaying mass, tearing through flesh, bone, and sinew." Taylor reformed his lines and sent them forward again, with the same horrible result. A Federal veteran recalled, "Our men loaded and fired with such rapidity, that it seemed . . . like one continuous explosion. Such discharges from such rifles would check a stronger rebel force than this. The musketry of Champion Hill and Shiloh did not exceed that of Sabine Cross Roads." Operating now in darkness, in a final desperate effort Taylor ordered a concentrated assault on the enemy right flank, but again the Federals held their ground. Taylor now realized that any further attacks would prove futile. The engagement at Pleasant Grove had lasted only fifteen or twenty minutes, and Emory had prevented the annihilation of Banks's army. "As it was," a Texan confessed, "much of the prestige of success gained in the day, was lost in the blood of

49. Ludwell H. Johnson, *Red River Campaign*, pp. 137–39; Woods, *Ninety-Sixth Ohio Volunteers*, pp. 65–66 (first quotation 66); William H. Emory, "Summary of the Red River Campaign," manuscript in Emory Papers, pp. 9–13 (second quotation 13); Beecher, *114th N.Y.S.V.*, pp. 312–13 (third quotation 312).

the fearless, undistinguished heroes who fell in this deadly night charge."[50]

As an unusually cold night set in, the combatants camped only a few hundred yards apart, the Confederates retaining possession of the creek, the only source of water in the vicinity. Forbidden from lighting fires that would reveal their small numbers, and shivering without blankets in the cold, the Yankees huddled on the ground eating hardtack and listening, as one recalled, "to the sounds of jollity and mirth . . . from our victorious neighbors, the 'Johnnies.' The wagon train they had captured was freighted rather heavily with liquor, and judging from the noise and their known love for the article, it suffered heavily." With the rest of his army retreating toward Pleasant Hill and the shortage of water proving unbearable, Banks decided to withdraw Emory's division about midnight. Of this movement one of his soldiers recounted, "It had been a good day's work for the rebels, and its sobering effect on us can be imagined. . . . Darkness and gloom hung around us like a pall."[51]

Despite the costly twilight struggle at Pleasant Grove, Taylor would allow nothing to mar his grandest victory. At 10:30 P.M. he sent word to General Smith that "late in the evening we met the Nineteenth Army Corps; repulsed and drove them back." In his official report he also claimed that "there was no straggling, no plundering," and that "the vast captured property was quietly taken to Mansfield and turned over untouched to the proper officers." Summing up the day's climactic action, he later observed, "The defeat of the Federal army was largely due to the arrogance and ignorance of General Banks, who attributed my long retreat to his own wonderful strategy." Yet

50. McDaniel memoir, p. 79 (first quotation); Woods, *Ninety-Sixth Ohio Volunteers*, pp. 66–67; Pellet, *114th New York Volunteers*, pp. 197–98; Bonner, "Sketches of the Campaign of 1864," pt. 1, pp. 464–65 (second and fourth quotations 465); Blessington, *Walker's Texas Division*, pp. 189–91; Beecher, *114th N.Y.S.V.*, p. 313 (third quotation); Orton S. Clark, *One Hundred and Sixteenth New York Volunteers*, pp. 156–57; Winters, *Civil War in Louisiana*, pp. 340–46.

51. *O.R.*, 34(1):565; Hoffman, *Camp, Court and Siege*, p. 91; Orton S. Clark, *One Hundred and Sixteenth New York Volunteers*, pp. 157–58 (first quotation); Ludwell H. Johnson, *Red River Campaign*, pp. 146–47; McDaniel memoir, pp. 80–81 (second quotation).

Taylor's success actually arose from a remarkable series of fortuitous twists in the campaign. Although Banks expected to march unmolested all the way to Shreveport, Taylor never planned to lure him into a trap at Mansfield. Had Green arrived with his reinforcements in time to fight Banks and Porter on the Red River as Taylor hoped, Taylor's little army would have been grossly outnumbered and outgunned. Similarly, had he fought without waiting for Green's reinforcements—as he claimed he should have—he would have courted complete disaster. Green's delay, coupled with Banks's decision to do without Porter's naval support and to turn toward Pleasant Hill and Mansfield, worked unexpectedly to Taylor's benefit. All he needed was for Banks to form a long, clumsy column that prohibited troops from moving rapidly to the front at Mansfield. In this Banks complied perfectly. Although the invasion's disruption of Louisiana's civilian population outraged Taylor, he could not have hoped for a better advantage than at Mansfield. By deciding to attack, however, he did show audacious tactical skill. Already resolved to ignore General Smith's expressed wishes, and surmising the enemy's weakness at the front, Taylor dealt Banks a crippling blow. "As a soldier he has been wonderfully successful," wrote an admiring Private Joseph P. Blessington. "Though some of his movements savored of rashness, when calmly weighed, they showed the good judgment and military genius that conceived them."[52]

Although Emory's heroics at Pleasant Grove had given Banks hope of salvaging the campaign, the battle of Mansfield would stand as one of the most humiliating Union defeats of the entire war. Of the 12,000 Federals who saw action, almost 700 were killed or wounded, and more than 1,500 soldiers and another 1,000 noncombatants fell prisoner. Banks also lost 20 artillery pieces, more than 200 supply wagons, and almost 1,000 horses and mules. Yet the fighting also ex-

---

52. *O.R.*, 34(1):527 (first quotation), 565 (second quotation); Richard Taylor, *Destruction and Reconstruction*, pp. 197–98 (third quotation); Ludwell H. Johnson, *Red River Campaign*, pp. 141–45; Blessington, *Walker's Texas Division*, p. 184 (fourth quotation). At least one source indicates that, after the fight at Pleasant Grove, Taylor put his men to work until the middle of the night sending captured supply wagons back to Mansfield. See Oltorf, *Marlin Compound*, p. 138.

acted a high toll on Taylor's troops: about 1,000 killed or wounded of
the 8,800 engaged. Returning to Mansfield, Taylor spent time making sure the wounded received proper care. Then he waited appre-
hensively for Churchill's late-arriving reinforcements. Far into the
night he contemplated the day's rapturous yet imposing results. "I
was saddened by the recollection of the many dead," he later confessed, "and the pleasure of victory was turned to grief." Many of the
fallen Louisianans had been neighbors and friends. "Above all, the
death of the gallant Mouton affected me," he wrote. "I thought of his
wife and children, and of his father, Governor Mouton." More than
two-thirds of the casualties had come during Mouton's courageous
charge.[53]

That same night a Texas soldier writing in his diary touched on his
comrades' deepest emotions, giving an angry appraisal of the war's
pervasive meaning: "It grieves me, when I reflect upon the fall of so
many of our brave men. . . . We are fighting for our property and our
homes; they, [the Yankees] for the flimsy and abstract idea that a negro is equal to an Anglo American." Among the meager shreds of
pride Union soldiers took with them from the field at Mansfield, one
came in the form of a battle flag somehow captured from a Texas
color-bearer. Prominently visible on the flag were a few emphatic
words: "Texans never can be slaves."[54]

53. Kerby, *Kirby Smith's Confederacy*, p. 306; Ludwell H. Johnson, *Red River
Campaign*, pp. 139–41; Richard Taylor, *Destruction and Reconstruction*, p. 198
(quotations).

54. Smith and Mullins, "Diary of H. C. Medford," p. 220 (first quotation);
Kirkland, *Pictorial Book of the War of the Rebellion*, p. 312 (second quotation).

CHAPTER TEN

Outraged Subordinate

General Taylor has gained an imperishable fame and the unlimited

confidence of his army.

Galveston Tri-Weekly News

"Time is everything to us," Taylor emphasized in a hurried dispatch to Walker at 1:30 A.M. on April 9. Convinced that he had demoralized Banks's troops so badly that they would retreat all the way to the Red River and reunite with Porter's powerful fleet, Taylor refused to let them escape his grasp. By now Churchill's Arkansas and Missouri regiments, slightly more than four thousand soldiers, had completed their twenty-mile march from Keatchie to Mansfield. Rather than allow them any rest, Taylor ordered Churchill to have his men prepare two days' rations and push on toward the front. "Arkansas and Missouri have the fight in the morning," Taylor informed Walker. "They must do what Texas and Louisiana did today." Reminding him that Banks's army consisted of "Yankees whom we have always whipped . . . [and] many recruits who will make no fight," Taylor stressed the urgency of pressing them at dawn. "The safety of our whole country depends upon it," he insisted.[1]

1. Richard Taylor to [John G. Walker, April 9, 1864] (quotations), Walker Papers; Richard Taylor, *Destruction and Reconstruction*, p. 198; Ludwell H. Johnson, *Red River Campaign*, pp. 152–53.

Taylor then galloped ahead and joined Green's cavalry shortly before sunrise to coordinate the advance pursuit along the road to Pleasant Hill. "Daybreak of the morning of the 9th found our Brigade in their saddles and on the go," a Texas trooper recalled. Along the road they passed burning wagons, dead and wounded Federals, and the charred remains of farmhouses. Green's men captured scores of Union stragglers and rear guard skirmishers and sent them back to Mansfield. At 7:20 A.M. Taylor reported that General Banks himself "came very near being captured." Some of the prisoners were decked out in bright Zouave uniforms, their bloomer-style pants and other exotic trappings eliciting a barrage of jokes and taunts from their captors. "They wore dainty red caps with tassels and made a sight for the Texans to look at," a Confederate recounted. "Some of [the Texans] threw down their guns and declared that if they were to fight any more women they would go home."[2]

At 10:40 A.M. Taylor came within two miles of Pleasant Hill and sent a message to General Smith reporting that enemy skirmishers were "making something of a stand for the purpose of gaining time." Believing that Banks would continue retreating, Taylor sought to block the road running east from Pleasant Hill to Blair's Landing on the Red River to keep him from reuniting with Porter. A detachment of Green's troopers covered the road to Blair's Landing while Taylor instructed the rest to probe farther toward Pleasant Hill. On the town's northern periphery Green's scouts spotted the Federal army formed in a protracted semicircle along a wooded plateau that overlooked a meandering ravine and open field of abandoned farmland. Although shaken by the disaster at Mansfield, Banks seemed determined to redeem himself by resuming the campaign. He knew the Confederates had sustained heavy casualties, and he did not believe Taylor would be so bold as to attack again. At the same time, however, he sent most of his remaining supply wagons back to Grand Ecore, accompanied by battered elements of the Thirteenth Corps and all

2. Richard Taylor, *Destruction and Reconstruction*, pp. 198–99; Noel, *Old Sibley Brigade*, p. 79 (first quotation); Ludwell H. Johnson, *Red River Campaign*, p. 153; Smith and Mullins, "Diary of H. C. Medford," pp. 220–21; *O.R.*, 34(1):528 (second quotation); Blessington, *Walker's Texas Division*, p. 193; Yeary, *Reminiscences of the Boys in Gray*, p. 627 (third quotation).

but a thousand of Albert Lee's cavalry. Free of the long train of wagons that had slowed him down, Banks hoped to make a lightning-swift strike toward Shreveport. He informed Porter of his intention to push forward that very evening in a nonstop forced march. With A. J. Smith's midwestern "gorillas" now at his immediate disposal, Banks had about twelve thousand men to accomplish the task.[3]

Waiting restlessly for Churchill's regiments to arrive, Taylor sat alone on a pine log, deep in thought, whittling on a stick. When Churchill finally appeared shortly after noon, Taylor spoke with him at length and also received several scouting reports. One came from a worried Brigadier General Hamilton Bee, who claimed that at least twenty-five thousand Federals lay ready and waiting to receive an assault. Taylor dismissed this as nonsense. Bee later asserted, "General Taylor himself told me . . . that the superb line of battle I had watched all day, with its serried lines compact and entrenched, and which he had not seen, 'was a mere feint to cover the retreat of their wagon trains.'" Unshakable in this assumption, Taylor decided to attack. He would have to rely heavily on Churchill's troops, but they had just marched forty-five miles in thirty-six hours. "A glance showed that his men were much too exhausted," Taylor noted, so he allowed these footsore and thirsty soldiers two hours' rest, but nothing more. "I did not wish to lose the advantage of the *morale* gained by success on the previous day," he later explained.[4]

About 3:00 P.M. Churchill began moving his troops toward a position on the far right. Taylor had given him the crucial responsibility of opening the battle with a charge meant to outflank the Federal line. To Churchill's left Taylor placed Walker's Division, ordered to work in tandem with Churchill once the enemy's flank began to collapse. Near the center, along the Mansfield road, Green stood ready with his cavalry. Taylor instructed him to sweep through Pleasant Hill and chase the collapsing enemy line once Churchill and Walker had gained the advantage. Until then two brigades of dismounted cavalry

3. *O.R.*, 34(1):528–29 (quotation 528); Richard Taylor, *Destruction and Reconstruction*, pp. 199–200; Johnson, *Red River Campaign*, pp. 147–54.

4. John Scott, *Thirty-Second Iowa*, p. 196; Bee, "Battle of Pleasant Hill," pp. 184–85 (first quotation 184); Richard Taylor, *Destruction and Reconstruction*, pp. 199–200 (second quotation 200, third quotation 199).

Thomas J. Churchill, commander of Arkansans and Missourians at Pleasant Hill
(*Johnson and Buell*, Battles and Leaders of the Civil War).

would apply pressure to the Federals on the left, in the woods east of the Mansfield road. "As no offensive movement by the enemy was anticipated," Taylor reasoned, "he would be turned on both flanks, subjected to a concentric fire, and overwhelmed." Polignac's division, having suffered the brunt of combat at Mansfield, stood in reserve. "Rely on the bayonet," Taylor advised his officers as he rode among the ranks. "We [have] neither time nor ammunition to waste."[5]

"The day was a beautiful one," a Yankee soldier recalled. Before the war Pleasant Hill had been a favorite vacation retreat for northern Louisiana's prominent families. Now, as another Federal observed, "Appearances indicated that for long years to come there would not be heard at Pleasant Hill the sound of mirth or the soft music of its former days." With Churchill in position on the right, about 4:30 P.M. Taylor ordered Major Joseph Brent to create a diversion by moving his artillery to within seven hundred yards of the enemy center and opening fire. For about thirty minutes Brent's guns

5. Richard Taylor, *Destruction and Reconstruction*, pp. 200–201 (first quotation 201); *O.R.*, 34(1):566–67 (second quotation).

pulverized the small enemy battery there, forcing it to withdraw. Then Churchill made his move. His Arkansans and Missourians advanced from the right in a long wave, running out of the woods and down the slope toward the shallow ravine. There a brigade of Federals crouched for cover, one of them recalling that Churchill's men "advanced at a charging pace, delivering a very heavy fire as they advanced." Within a few minutes Walker turned loose his own troops, one of whom later wrote, "Every man became his own leader," rushing forward "with a wild, reckless impetuosity." Then the whole length of the Confederate line unleashed what a Federal officer described as "a most hideous yell, such as Texans and Border ruffians alone can give." Churchill's crazed soldiers descended into the ravine, wielding their muskets like clubs and chasing the shattered enemy brigade up the hill toward the town.[6]

Stirred by this grand sweep of infantry on his right, Tom Green sensed that the rout had begun. He ordered Bee to lead two mounted regiments under Buchel and Debray down the Mansfield road against the center of the Federal line. Colonel Buchel protested rigorously, claiming that his men would surely be slaughtered. But Green was adamant. Buchel said he would obey the order himself but that he would not lead his men unless they volunteered to follow him. This they heartily agreed to do, moving forward at a full gallop, all yelling and with their sabers drawn. "Their cavalry . . . came upon us like a hurricane," a Federal wrote. "Their excited horses with open mouths and distended nostrils, came like a herd of wild buffaloes stampeded by a prairie fire." But the charge proved premature because Walker's infantry had not advanced nearly as far as Green believed. Less than two hundred yards from the enemy, Bee's horsemen caught a blistering volley from a regiment hidden in a clump of woods to their left, sending scores of startled horses and riders reel-

6. Pellet, *114th New York Volunteers*, pp. 193–94 (first quotation 194); Orton S. Clark, *One Hundred and Sixteenth New York Volunteers*, p. 160 (second quotation); *O.R.*, 34(1):567; Richard Taylor, *Destruction and Reconstruction*, p. 201; Ludwell H. Johnson, *Red River Campaign*, pp. 155–56; Henry Marvin Benedict, *A Memorial of Lewis Benedict*, pp. 79–82 (third quotation 79, fifth quotation 80); Bonner, "Sketches of the Campaign of 1864," pt. 2, p. 10 (fourth quotation).

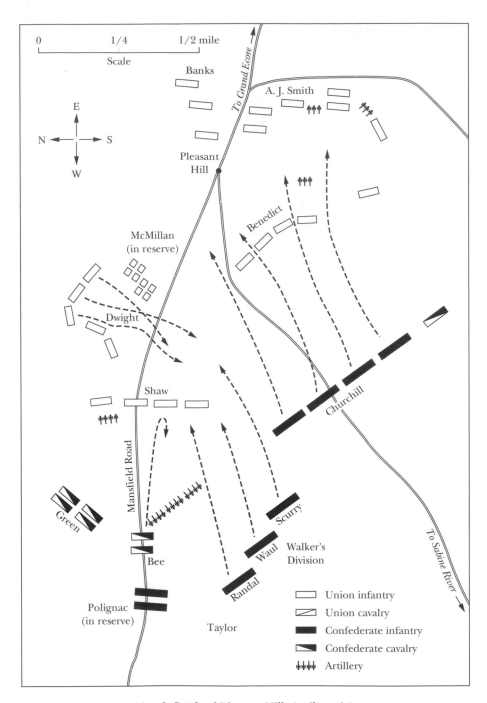

Banks

A. J. Smith

To Grand Ecore

Pleasant
Hill

McMillan
(in reserve)

Benedict

Dwight

Shaw

Churchill

Mansfield Road

Green

Scurry

Bee

Waul   Walker's
Division

Polignac
(in reserve)

Randal

Taylor

To Sabine River

Map 8. Battle of Pleasant Hill, April 9, 1864

ing to the ground. Then the enemy line in front opened up on them. "The range was close and deadly," a Yankee recalled. "If anything in the destruction of human life could be grand and fearfully sublime, that charge surely was."[7]

In a matter of minutes Colonel Debray lost a third of his men, and his own horse fell over on him, pinning him to the ground. Suffering a badly sprained ankle, Debray worked himself free by leaving his boot behind and managed to limp back to the rear. There Taylor noticed him and called out, "Why! Colonel, are you wounded?" "No, General, I am slightly hurt," Debray replied with dry disappointment, "but as you can see, I was sent on a bootless errand." Reassured, Taylor quipped, "Never mind your boot, you have won your spurs." Debray's comrades could hardly afford to indulge in such levity. Buchel fell mortally wounded just as he reached the enemy line. According to a Union officer there, the southern cavalrymen "who were not either killed or wounded jumped from their horses, and concealing themselves in the ravines and among the small pines, escaped to the rear." Hamilton Bee, who had two horses shot out from under him, called the charge "disastrous." But Taylor, as usual, defended Green's decision. "The charge was premature and cost valuable lives," he conceded, "but was of use in moral effect." Few of the lucky survivors would have agreed.[8]

Soon Walker's Division began veering leftward toward the same center position of the Federal line. Charging wildly, and without even returning the enemy's fire, the Texans met such a brutal series of vol-

7. Richard Taylor, *Destruction and Reconstruction*, p. 204; Ludwell H. Johnson, *Red River Campaign*, p. 156; Yeary, *Reminiscences of the Boys in Gray*, p. 362; Bitton, *Reminiscences of Levi Lamoni Wight*, pp. 32–33; Barkley, "Battle of Pleasant Hill," pp. 25–26 (first quotation 25); John Scott, *Thirty-Second Iowa*, pp. 139–40 (second quotation 139). On Buchel, see Lonn, *Foreigners in the Confederacy*, pp. 193–94, 449. See also Hauschild, *Runge Chronicle*, pp. 70–73.

8. Debray, *Debray's Texas Cavalry*, p. 18 (first and second quotations); Spencer, *Terrell's Texas Cavalry*, pp. 38–39; Shaw, "Battle of Pleasant Hill," p. 406 (third quotation); Yeary, *Reminiscences of the Boys in Gray*, p. 362; *O.R.*, 34(1):608 (fourth quotation); Richard Taylor, *Destruction and Reconstruction*, p. 204 (fifth quotation).

leys that they took cover in the ravine within 125 yards of the Yankees. Some inched even closer, to the protection of a rail fence. A
terrific exchange of gunfire ensued. "Their ranks were so fearfully
thinned that their dead and wounded covered the ground like un-
shocked sheaves of grain in harvest time," a Federal recorded. Walker
himself fell wounded with a painful contusion of the groin, and Taylor galloped over to determine its seriousness. Undaunted, Walker
said he would continue leading his men even if he had to be carried
on a stretcher, but Taylor ordered him taken to the rear. Walker's absence proved especially disruptive. All three of his brigade commanders had become so entangled in the fighting that they could not even
send reports to Taylor regarding their movements. Charge after dis-
jointed charge pushed back the enemy line only gradually, and at an
awful cost, leaving the ground littered with Confederate casualties.
Pine trees and thickets screened Taylor's view of the action, as did the
thick clouds of smoke covering the field. A Federal soldier recalled
that "the smoke of battle hung over us so densely that the sun was
entirely obscured." After more than an hour of this murderous fighting, Taylor summoned Polignac's division to add its firepower. Several
of the Federal regiments, assaulted at various times on two or three
sides and running low on ammunition, prayed for relief. The Thirty-
second Iowa was cut off and surrounded, but its officers refused to
surrender.[9]

Far to the right Churchill's troops had pressed steadily toward the
town, driving the enemy before them. The Confederate line thus
gradually took on an S-shaped appearance from end to end. "It was
a sight worth seeing," a Yankee wrote of Churchill's advance, "that
long line of butternut uniforms, advancing . . . faster and faster . . .
enveloping the Third Brigade and sweeping it along as if it were

9. Bonner, "Sketches of the Campaign of 1864," pt. 2, pp. 9–10; Gould,
"Autobiography and Diary of Robert Simonton Gould," typescript, p. 67;
Barkley, "Battle of Pleasant Hill," p. 26 (first quotation); Richard Taylor, *De-
struction and Reconstruction*, p. 203; Houston *Daily Telegraph*, April 18, 1864;
O.R., 34(1):567–68; Pellet, *114th New York Volunteers*, p. 210 (second quota-
tion); Benson, "Battle of Pleasant Hill," pp. 24–25; John Scott, *Thirty-Second
Iowa*, p. 159.

chaff." But suddenly they came upon a completely unexpected sight: a massive line of Federal reserves under A. J. Smith. "There are the western boys," shouted one of Churchill's men. "We will catch hell now." A torrent of rifle and artillery fire cut through their ranks. "The graybacks lay in heaps in our front," a Yankee recalled. Churchill attempted to make a stand, but an additional brigade of A. J. Smith's soldiers emerged suddenly from the woods on the Confederate right flank. In a classic turning movement they drove toward the side and rear, and Churchill's line began to crumble. Instead of having outflanked the enemy, Churchill was now shocked to find himself being outflanked in the worst way. Seizing the opportunity to deal a crushing blow, Smith ordered his entire command to attack. "To the southern men it was an appalling sight," wrote a Federal. "They gazed upon it for just one moment, and flesh and blood could stand no longer, and turning tail, they ran." [10]

Churchill tried to rally his men, but because the brush and trees hindered his officers from forming effective lines, the enemy onslaught continued unabated. "The ground was covered with dead and dying," noted a Federal soldier, "but I felt just [as] cool as I should [be] driving the same amount of cattle." Soon Churchill's fleeing lines began pressing backward upon Walker's right flank, manned by Brigadier General William R. Scurry's brigade. "Come on boys," Scurry yelled to his Texans, "you have got your chance at last." Shedding their knapsacks and blankets, they swept forward to reinforce Churchill. "It was a fine sight," a Confederate recalled, "that charge of Scurry's brigade to the death-struggle. . . . The enemy poured into them a cruel, crushing fire." Scurry waved his hat and cried out, "Scurry's brigade may be annihilated, but must never retreat." Alarmed by this dramatic Federal counterthrust, Taylor ordered Walker's other two brigade commanders, Colonel Horace Randal and

10. Orton S. Clark, *One Hundred and Sixteenth New York Volunteers*, p. 162 (first quotation); Frank Moore, *Rebellion Record*, 8:543 (second quotation); Van [?] to his wife, April 12, 1864 (third quotation), Miscellaneous Manuscripts Collection, Historic New Orleans Collection; Ludwell H. Johnson, *Red River Campaign*, p. 160; Richard Taylor, *Destruction and Reconstruction*, p. 202; Benson, "Battle of Pleasant Hill," p. 27 (fourth quotation).

Brigadier General Thomas N. Waul, to help their compatriots. "Thank God," Scurry declared as Randal's and Waul's men surged forward, "my brigade is saved."[11]

With daylight waning, the battle had reached a most critical and desperate stage. Taylor sent Polignac and Green forward to fortify Walker and Churchill. "My boys, follow your Polignac," the Frenchman bellowed. They responded with an emotional rage, chilling those around them with a one-word battle cry: "Mouton!" Thus began the bloodiest combat of the day, both sides hurling themselves back and forth, firing at close range and hacking away at each other in hand-to-hand fighting. "The army was swaying all along the lines," wrote a southerner, "brave men melting before the blazing cannon and charging infantry." A Confederate captain recalled that he "ran up near the enemy and found Gens. Green, Taylor, and Major right up in the thickest of the fight, encouraging the men." Although approaching twilight began to darken the battlefield, Taylor perceived a gradual weakening in the Federal line, and he prodded his troops into attempting a final series of assaults. Their strength all but spent, however, they faltered in the effort. Many became so confused in the murky shadows that they fired on their own comrades.[12]

As darkness rapidly enshrouded the scene, both armies lost the will to continue the killing. Taylor left a cavalry picket at the northern edge of the battlefield and ordered a general withdrawal to a point about six miles to the rear, where his bedraggled force camped near a stream that provided the only available water in the area. The Federals made no effort to pursue. A disappointed Texan recalled, "It appeared too much like a retreat; we believed then, and still think we had gained a victory." Another expressed a more realistic view: "The

11. *O.R.*, 34(1):605; Van [?] to his wife, April 12, 1864 (first quotation), Miscellaneous Manuscripts Collection, Historic New Orleans Collection; Ludwell H. Johnson, *Red River Campaign*, pp. 160–61; Blessington, *Walker's Texas Division*, pp. 195–96 (second, third, fourth, and fifth quotations 196); Richard Taylor, *Destruction and Reconstruction*, p. 203.

12. *O.R.*, 34(1):568; Blessington, *Walker's Texas Division*, pp. 197–99 (first and second quotations 198); Bonner, "Sketches of the Campaign of 1864," pt. 2, pp. 10–11; Bitton, *Reminiscences of Levi Lamoni Wight*, p. 32 (third quotation); Oltorf, *Marlin Compound*, p. 138 (fourth quotation); Richard Taylor, *Destruction and Reconstruction*, pp. 204–5.

enemy was badly cut up and was willing to let our men go without following them. Darkness closed the fight and found both parties whipped and thousands killed and wounded." Much like the previous day's fighting at Pleasant Grove, the Federals had prevailed against Taylor's aggressive determination to rout them entirely. Yet they realized that Banks had once again only narrowly avoided total disaster. Upon finding A. J. Smith after the battle, an exhilarated General Banks extended his hand in gratitude and declared, "You have saved my army." "By God! I know it, sir," snarled Smith, fully aware that Banks personally deserved neither credit nor salvation.[13]

On the battlefield that night parties from both armies tried to attend to the wounded, many of whom would die before daylight. A Federal surgeon found a ghastly field of slaughter. He saw "headless trunks, scattered limbs, and bodies torn into fragments. . . . Yonder, where swept the canister and grape, thick lie the blackened and bloody dead; and scattered rows show plainly where dense lines faced musketry." Dehydrated and cold from loss of blood, the wounded cried out incessantly for water and fire to relieve them from their suffering. "The wails and cries of agony . . . are still ringing in my ears," wrote a Yankee. "There is scarcely a soldier that would not prefer the hottest engagement rather than spend such a night amid such scenes as we witnessed on the 9th of April." The next day the dead were heaped into shallow common graves as buzzards swarmed and flocked to gorge themselves on the hundreds of dead horses littering the field. A few months afterward, during the sweltering temperatures of summer, the burial grounds swelled up and cracked open with a sickening stench, bringing hordes of green flies to the hillsides.[14]

During the evening after the battle Taylor spoke briefly with a

13. Richard Taylor, *Destruction and Reconstruction*, p. 205; Bonner, "Sketches of the Campaign of 1864," pt. 2, pp. 11–12 (first quotation); Oltorf, *Marlin Compound*, p. 138 (second quotation); Frank Moore, *Rebellion Record*, 8:541 (third and fourth quotations); Winters, *Civil War in Louisiana*, pp. 348–55.

14. Woods, *Ninety-Sixth Ohio Volunteers*, p. 70 (first quotation); Pellet, *114th New York Volunteers*, pp. 212–13 (second quotation); Norman D. Brown, *Journey to Pleasant Hill*, p. 412; Barkley, "Battle of Pleasant Hill," p. 30.

crestfallen Thomas Churchill. He "seemed much depressed," Taylor recalled. "I gave such consolation as I could." Churchill admitted that, had he moved only a half-mile more to the right, he would have out-flanked the enemy and "a brilliant success would have been achieved." Churchill placed much of the blame on a local citizen Taylor had sent along to serve as a guide. According to one of Churchill's soldiers, the guide "mistook his orders . . . so we were too far to the left and hence were flanked." Taylor later criticized Churchill for failing to use his cavalry to detect the true location of the enemy's flank. Banks's generals later acknowledged the position's vulnerability. Regardless, Taylor regretted allowing Churchill to lead this pivotal attack. "I should have conducted it myself" with Polignac's division, he professed. "All this flashed upon me the instant I learned of the disorder on my right. Herein lies the vast difference between genius and common-place: one anticipates errors, the other discovers them too late."[15]

Although Taylor dwelled on Churchill's broken fortunes, he should have judged the assault on the Federal center as equally detrimental. Because Banks had not expected Taylor to take the offensive, he had simply allowed his generals to position their own units in piecemeal fashion. Several gaps therefore existed in their lines, the largest one directly between the Federal left and center, the very spot facing Walker's Division when the battle began. But because Walker failed to connect with Churchill's left during the initial charge, this huge gap remained unexploited. Instead, Walker's men veered left-ward into the heart of the Federal center, which stood concentrated in the vicinity of the Mansfield road. Soon afterward Walker fell wounded. Had he been on the field to coordinate his errant brigades, he might have guided them toward the gap, forcing a breakthrough that would have disrupted the Federals and made Churchill's retreat much less calamitous. As it turned out, Walker's right, anchored by Scurry's brigade, became bogged down in the trees, thickets, and smoke and ran up against enemy troops that had deftly shifted from the far left. Scurry apparently never noticed the gap in the enemy

15. Richard Taylor, *Destruction and Reconstruction*, pp. 205 (first quotation), 200–202 (second quotation 202), 206 (fourth quotation); Wallace diary, April 9, 1864 (third quotation); *O.R.*, 34(1):568, 602; Ludwell H. Johnson, *Red River Campaign*, pp. 155, 167–68.

line to his right. When Churchill's retreating mob collapsed on him, Scurry had to face the brunt of A. J. Smith's pursuing force, and Taylor's entire army was quickly thrown on the defensive. As the sun began to set, the battle of Pleasant Hill ended in a bloody stalemate with the Federals clearly holding the upper hand.[16]

Like Stonewall Jackson in the Shenandoah Valley, Taylor had pushed the offensive advantage gained at Mansfield to its logical extreme at Pleasant Hill. Treacherous terrain and poor generalship seemed to have rendered the enemy prone to annihilation. Also like Jackson at Port Republic, Taylor failed to direct his troops effectively primarily because he underestimated the Federals' ability to repulse him. Believing that Banks's defenses at Pleasant Hill were merely designed to cover a withdrawal to the Red River, Taylor rushed into the battle. Yet he did not possess the overwhelming numbers Jackson had held at Port Republic to sustain him through this tactical error and carry him to victory. His advance scouting should have been more thorough, especially on the far right, where Churchill was outflanked. Deprived of the benefits of superior strength on the right, coordinated pressure at the center, and tactical finesse against the enemy's weakest points, Taylor saw his already weary soldiers falter against relatively fresh, determined Union troops who inflicted heavy damage at the most critical moments. Three short hours of fighting punished both armies severely. Of 12,500 men engaged, Taylor lost about 1,200 in killed and wounded and more than 400 captured. Banks's 12,200 men suffered almost 1,400 casualties. Most of the Federal losses came in the first hour, during Churchill's initially successful attack. At Mansfield, Taylor's boldness and good fortune had produced victory. Now boldness had betrayed him and good fortune had eluded him. During the fading minutes of the battle he readily confessed to his men that "it was his fault." As he later noted in his memoirs, a complete triumph might have been realized, "but for my blunder at Pleasant Hill."[17]

16. Ludwell H. Johnson, *Red River Campaign*, pp. 166–68; Pellet, *114th New York Volunteers*, p. 209.

17. Ludwell H. Johnson, *Red River Campaign*, pp. 168–69; Gould, "Autobiography and Diary of Robert Simonton Gould," p. 69 (first quotation); Richard Taylor, *Destruction and Reconstruction*, p. 206 (second quotation).

That night Taylor camped with some of Bee's cavalry only a few hundred yards from the battlefield. Totally exhausted after several days without rest, he fell into a deep sleep. About 10:00 P.M., however, he awoke to face General Edmund Kirby Smith. Having just covered the sixty-five miles from Shreveport, Smith appeared decidedly disgruntled. "Bad business, bad business, General," said Smith. "I don't know, General. What is the trouble?" Taylor asked. Smith answered instantly, "Banks will be upon you at daylight tomorrow with his whole army." Unruffled, Taylor retorted, "Well, General, if you will listen, you will hear Banks's artillery moving out now on their retreat." Unmoved, Smith repeated his assertion. He expressed particular concern about the wretched condition of Taylor's army, which he had just passed en route. "Our repulse at Pleasant Hill was so complete," Smith later observed, "that had Banks followed up his success vigorously he would have met but feeble opposition to his advance on Shreveport." But as Taylor and Smith sat by the camp fire drinking coffee and discussing the situation, stragglers from the battlefield brought reports that the Federals indeed were deserting Pleasant Hill and turning back toward Grand Ecore.[18]

Banks had been forced into a bitter decision. Although the commander had repeated his desire to continue the campaign, the consensus among his generals was that they had endured enough bloodshed under his dreadful leadership. Food and ammunition were running low, and the town's wells were dry. "Of forage there was none," noted an officer. "Taylor had raked the region as with a fine tooth comb." Moreover, Banks's generals mistakenly surmised that Taylor still had at least twenty thousand troops to resist any further progress. To make matters worse, because Banks had already sent most of his supply wagons back to Grand Ecore, Federal surgeons found themselves without enough medical necessities to tend to the wounded. With the battlefield in Confederate hands, Banks had to

18. Richard Taylor, *Destruction and Reconstruction*, pp. 205–6, 213; Bee, "Battle of Pleasant Hill," p. 185; Sliger, "How General Taylor Fought the Battle of Mansfield," p. 458 (first, second, third, and fourth quotations); Edmund Kirby Smith, "Defense of the Red River," p. 372 (fifth quotation).

leave his surgeons to beg help from their southern counterparts. When A. J. Smith learned that many of his wounded would be left behind, he became so infuriated that he considered staging a mutiny and giving William B. Franklin command of the army. Finally, however, this crusty old officer could only weep for his fallen soldiers. About midnight the army began moving toward Grand Ecore. "We did not *run* from Pleasant Hill," a Yankee later remarked to a comrade, "but you will have to agree that we struck a gait that didn't have a bit of lost motion in it." Along the way Smith's men loudly cursed the name of "Mr. Banks," and even his own northeastern troops howled derisive songs in honor of "Napoleon P. Banks." The thick pine forest of northern Louisiana had stung and smothered him like a Russian winter.[19]

"General Taylor has gained an imperishable fame and the unlimited confidence of his army," proclaimed a Texan newspaper correspondent immediately following Banks's withdrawal. Instead of having to brace his beaten-down army for another fight, Taylor stood transformed into the most heroic figure west of the Mississippi. By unwittingly intimidating Banks into withdrawing, he had converted Pleasant Hill from a tactical defeat into a strategic victory. Caught up in the euphoria, Taylor issued a proclamation to the army on April 11, acclaiming the "glories of Pleasant Hill" won by his men. "This was emphatically the soldier's victory," he declared. "In spite of the strength of the enemy's position ... your valor and devotion triumphed over all." Fortune seemed to have swung back in his favor, and he could scarcely wait to finish the job. He immediately ordered Bee's cavalry to harass the Union column's rear guard all the way to Grand Ecore, where the exasperated Federals dug in and waited for what they believed to be a huge Confederate force to assault them at any moment. "Banks, with the remains of his beaten army, was before us, and the fleet of Porter, with barely enough water to float upon,"

19. Ludwell H. Johnson, *Red River Campaign*, pp. 162–65, 215 (third quotation), 206 (fourth quotation); Harrington, *Fighting Politician*, pp. 157–58; Ewer, *Third Massachusetts Cavalry*, pp. 161–62 (first quotation); John Scott, *Thirty-Second Iowa*, p. 142; Byam, "Swapping Stories in Texas," p. 314 (second quotation).

Taylor recalled. "We had but to strike vigorously to capture or destroy both."[20]

General Smith, however, sternly dispelled any plans of making serious targets of Banks and Porter. "Our troops were completely paralyzed and disorganized by the repulse at Pleasant Hill," he later argued. "Before we could reorganize at Mansfield and get into condition to advance . . . the enemy had been reinforced and entrenched at Grand Ecore." But in a letter to Missouri governor Thomas C. Reynolds on April 14 Smith exuded a different tone. "The victory [at Pleasant Hill] though not complete is glorious. We have lost severely but have gained more in moral strength than have been lost numerically," Smith boasted. "The enemy have fallen back . . . demoralized and in great confusion. . . . Banks had 28,000 men engaged on the 9th and acknowledged half an hour more of daylight would have lost him his whole army." Whatever might have been Smith's motive in writing such an overtly positive letter, its distinct agreement with Taylor's own view of the situation signaled the genesis of a duplicity in Smith that would vex Taylor from this point forward.[21]

Smith had already decided that he would take Taylor and most of his army north to Arkansas, combine it with Price's force, and destroy Steele. "Steele's column from Arkansas [still] caused him much uneasiness," Taylor recalled. But Taylor resisted, pointing out that Steele would have to march at least a hundred miles to reach Shreveport and that Price was badgering him every step of the way. Furthermore, once Steele learned of Banks's "misfortune," he would surely give up the campaign and turn back to Little Rock. But that was exactly what Smith wanted to prevent. Steele's army would remain vulnerable only

20. Galveston *Tri-Weekly News*, April 24, 1864 (first quotation); *O.R.*, 34(1):596 (second and third quotations); Ludwell H. Johnson, *Red River Campaign*, pp. 165–66, 206–7, 215–16; Richard Taylor, *Destruction and Reconstruction*, pp. 205, 213–14 (fourth quotation).

21. Edmund Kirby Smith, "Defense of the Red River," p. 372 (first quotation); Edmund Kirby Smith to Thomas C. Reynolds, April 14, 1864 (second quotation), item 159 in Rosenbach Company, *History of America in Documents*, p. 48.

as long as it continued to advance deeper into Confederate territory. The "prize" to be gained from Steele's defeat consisted of "the Arkansas Valley and the powerful fortifications at Little Rock," Smith insisted.[22]

Smith waited in Shreveport while Taylor grudgingly prepared his troops for the Arkansas expedition. But he simply could not forget about Banks. On April 11 he wrote Smith, "If [Steele] is retreating . . . let me push my whole force south as rapidly as possible, to follow and prevent the escape of the enemy. I will strike for New Orleans, or, at least, Algiers." Should Banks escape, Taylor added, "I shall deserve to wear a fool's cap for a helmet." To this Smith made a stubborn response, arguing that Steele posed a far greater danger to Shreveport and East Texas, whereas Banks would probably retreat all the way to Alexandria. Only by eradicating Steele could "great results" be attained. "Arkansas will be saved politically and the reoccupation of the Arkansas Valley accomplished . . . and the road opened to Missouri," Smith asserted. Besides, a campaign against New Orleans seemed impossible since the Union navy had control of the Mississippi River. Smith also chided Taylor, reminding him that the people of Arkansas had displayed a "patient, uncomplaining spirit" and that "the prompt and unselfish behavior of Price in pushing on his whole infantry force to your support" surely deserved reciprocation.[23]

Unfazed by Smith's logic, Taylor continued to stew. In an attempt to appease him, Smith rode back to Mansfield on April 13. After several hours of arguing he promised that if Steele began to retreat during Taylor's march to Arkansas, Taylor could then halt his troops, turn them back, and try to overtake Banks on the Red River. "The loss of valuable time incurred by a wild-goose chase after Steele was most annoying," Taylor observed, "but I was hopeful that it might be recovered." The next day he set out for Shreveport with Churchill's and Walker's divisions. Meanwhile, Polignac took his small command

22. Richard Taylor, *Destruction and Reconstruction*, p. 213 (first and second quotations); Parks, *Edmund Kirby Smith*, pp. 393–94; Edmund Kirby Smith, "Defense of the Red River," p. 372 (third quotation).

23. *O.R.*, 34(1):530–31 (first and second quotations 530, third, fourth, and fifth quotations 531). See also Castel, *General Sterling Price*, pp. 184–85.

down to Grand Ecore to join Green and Bee in a token effort to menace Banks.[24]

When Taylor arrived at Shreveport on the evening of the fifteenth, he received the most shattering jolt of his military career. In a terse exchange with Smith he learned that Steele had turned eastward, back toward Little Rock, but that Smith still intended to pursue him with Churchill's and Walker's troops. To Taylor, this was nothing short of a humiliating betrayal. He stood speechless as Smith insisted that Steele would have to retreat all the way across the Ouachita River before Shreveport's safety could be assured. "I was further informed that my presence with the troops was not desired," Taylor recalled, "and that I would remain in nominal command at Shreveport, but might join the force near Grand Ecore if I thought proper." Smith stated "all this with the curt manner of a superior to a subordinate, as if fearing remonstrance." Taylor realized that any argument would prove futile. Smith seemed obsessed with Steele.[25]

Strangely, the next day Smith issued an unofficial order promoting Taylor to the rank of lieutenant general. This well-deserved advancement would meet with swift confirmation in the Confederate Congress, where respect for Taylor's abilities had grown since his arrival in Louisiana. Smith also added an unexpected proviso: if he fell during the Arkansas campaign, command of the Trans-Mississippi Department would go to Taylor. Smith explained the decision in a letter to President Davis: "Of the three district commanders, Major Generals Magruder, Price, and Taylor, the latter is the junior, and [yet] the only one of the three I consider suited to take charge of the affairs of the department." If Smith expected Taylor to accept this honor as consolation, it seemed empty and cruelly ironic. Neither a promotion nor command of the department would mean anything if Banks and Porter slipped through his fingers. Learning that Smith had also condescended to send him a pontoon train to help, Taylor later growled, "Doubtless General Kirby Smith thought that a pontoon

24. *O.R.*, 34(1):571–82; Richard Taylor, *Destruction and Reconstruction*, p. 217 (quotation); Ludwell H. Johnson, *Red River Campaign*, p. 182.

25. Richard Taylor, *Destruction and Reconstruction*, p. 218 (quotations); *O.R.*, 34(1):480–81; Ludwell H. Johnson, *Red River Campaign*, pp. 182–83.

train would supply the place of seven thousand infantry and six bat-teries."[26]

As if to underscore Taylor's unfulfilled opportunity, Admiral Por-ter's fleet had been subjected to a harrowing experience just navigat-ing the increasingly shallow waters of the Red River. By April 10 Por-ter had progressed about a hundred miles upriver from Grand Ecore to Loggy Bayou, the point at which he had agreed to meet Banks before descending upon Shreveport. But here Porter received a cryp-tic message from Banks saying that the army was falling back to Grand Ecore and that the fleet should do the same. Porter knew he was in grave trouble. Dreading an attack from pursuing Confederate troops, he managed to reach Blair's Landing, forty-five miles above Grand Ecore, before encountering serious opposition. There, late in the afternoon of the twelfth, Tom Green stood waiting with several regiments of Texas cavalry and a battery of artillery.[27]

Taylor had sent Green from Pleasant Hill the previous day to block the fleet's escape. One of his officers recalled that Green "talked freely about the danger of this attack; but felt the necessity of constant ac-tion, and knew that Gen. Dick Taylor was expecting great things of him." Ordering his men to dismount, Green led them to the river where they began riddling the Union ironclads and troop transports with a sensational display of firepower. Porter quickly responded, fir-ing his heavy guns against the Texans. Still on horseback, Green halted near the riverbank to give orders when a shell exploded over-head. A single piece of grapeshot tore off the top of his skull, killing him instantly. By sundown the disheartened Texans had mostly given up the fight. A Federal officer observed, "The rebels fought with un-usual pertinacity for over an hour, delivering the heaviest and most concentrated fire of musketry that I have ever witnessed." Porter's fleet then steamed to Grand Ecore to meet Banks.[28]

26. O.R., 34(1):476 (first quotation); Richard Taylor, *Destruction and Recon-struction*, p. 218 (second quotation).

27. Ludwell H. Johnson, *Red River Campaign*, pp. 207–11; Kerby, *Kirby Smith's Confederacy*, pp. 308–9.

28. Richard Taylor, *Destruction and Reconstruction*, pp. 215–16; Walter G. Smith, *Life and Letters of Thomas Kilby Smith*, pp. 117–18 (first quotation 118);

Tom Green's attack on Porter's fleet at Blair's Landing
(Jenkins Rare Book Company).

Already in an angry mood, Taylor considered Porter's escape, coupled with Green's death, profoundly disturbing. He heaped immediate blame on General Smith's departmental supply system, which had been expected to deliver a pontoon bridge to Bayou Pierre to enable Colonel Arthur P. Bagby's cavalry brigade to join Green at

Barr, "Battle of Blair's Landing," pp. 204–12; Gallaway, *Ragged Rebel*, pp. 90–101; Spencer, *Terrell's Texas Cavalry*, pp. 42–43; Bailey, *Between the Enemy and Texas*, pp. 170–79 (second quotation 178).

Blair's Landing. Because the pontoon bridge was delayed, Bagby's men waited and then crossed the bayou on a ferry, preventing them from reaching Blair's Landing until the fighting had ended. Likewise, Green himself had been able to cross the bayou with only part of his force. "The fleet . . . would have been under the fire of two thousand riflemen and eighteen guns and suffered heavily, especially the transports, crowded with troops," Taylor later argued. "As it was, we accomplished but little and lost General Green." In the span of a few days Taylor had been deprived of both Mouton and Green, his most valued and revered officers. "For many weary months these two have served with me. . . . [and] my heart has learned to love them," Taylor stated in a proclamation to his army. "To have been their beloved friend and trusted commander is the highest earthly honor I can ever attain."[29]

For three days, April 16–19, Taylor remained at Shreveport writing reports and sending supplies to his small force of cavalry and Polignac's division, now barely twelve hundred infantrymen, near Grand Ecore. Riding down to join them, he was accompanied by Major General John A. Wharton, a Texan who had achieved an excellent record as a cavalry officer in the Army of Tennessee. Wharton would take Green's place as cavalry commander. Taylor and Wharton reached Polignac's camp near Grand Ecore on the evening of the twenty-first. The next morning Banks evacuated the town and began a rapid retreat south through Natchitoches along the road to Alexandria. For several days Banks had considered resuming the drive toward Shreveport. But with Porter grousing about the river's falling water level and Sherman demanding the return of A. J. Smith's troops, Banks gave up all hope of realizing his gigantic ambitions. As for Taylor's own fleeting ambitions, the only advantage he could exercise over Banks was a psychological one. Although Banks believed that Confederate numbers still equaled his own command of more than 25,000 men, Taylor actually had barely 5,000. Having already sent 2,000 cavalrymen under Bee around the enemy column, Taylor intended to cut off Banks's retreat at Monett's Ferry, a point forty-five

29. Richard Taylor, *Destruction and Reconstruction*, pp. 214–16 (first quotation 215); *O.R.*, 34(1):571; Richard Taylor, *General Orders, No. 58* (second quotation).

miles to the south. Here Banks would face the difficult task of crossing the Cane River, giving Bee a magnificent chance to trap the Yankees and let Taylor crush them.[30]

While Taylor nipped at Banks's heels, A. J. Smith's gorillas churned
forward in the forefront of the Union column, bent on looting or
destroying all the property that had escaped their grasp during the
march to Mansfield. After torching the few structures standing at
Grand Ecore, they continued their vandalism along the road to Monett's Ferry. Outraged at the spectacle, Taylor reported: "The destruction of this country by the enemy exceeds anything in history.
For many miles every dwelling-house, every negro cabin, every
cotton-gin, every corn-crib, and even chicken-houses, have been
burned to the ground." He encountered hundreds of civilian victims,
mostly "weeping women and children," some of whom told him that
Banks's own northeastern soldiers had tried in vain to restrain Smith's
men. Capturing some of the perpetrators, Taylor threatened them
with severe punishment, but as he later noted, "they asserted, and
doubtless with truth, that they were acting under orders."[31]

With these scenes of devastation only magnifying his lost chance to
stifle the Federals at Grand Ecore, Taylor redoubled his determination for Bee to make amends for everything. "If Bee stood firm at
Monett's [Ferry]," he recounted, "we were in a position to make Banks
unhappy . . . separated as he was from the fleet, on which he relied to
aid his demoralized forces." But the shallow water levels, having
cursed Porter on the Red River, delivered Banks an unexpected blessing when his army reached the Cane River at Monett's Ferry on the
twenty-third. With Bee in a commanding position on the southern
side of the river at the low-water crossing, the Yankees relied on guidance from a local slave in locating a seldom-used ford about two miles

30. Richard Taylor, *Destruction and Reconstruction*, pp. 218–20; Ludwell H.
Johnson, *Red River Campaign*, pp. 214–23; Lubbock, *Six Decades in Texas*, pp.
537–39; Porter, *Naval History*, pp. 517–19. For a good biographical study of
Wharton, see Paul A. Scott, "John A. Wharton."

31. Ludwell H. Johnson, *Red River Campaign*, pp. 223–25; *O.R.*, 34(1):581
(first quotation); Pellet, *114th New York Volunteers*, p. 225; Bergeron, *Uncle
Silas*, p. 163; Richard Taylor, *Destruction and Reconstruction*, p. 235 (second
and third quotations).

Hamilton P. Bee, isolated challenger to Banks's army at Monett's Ferry
(Tulane University).

upriver to their right. Here several regiments crossed the river. Caught off guard by this sudden movement against his left flank, Bee had to divide his force to meet the assault. Then a simple Federal cavalry feint downriver on Bee's right seemed to confirm in his mind sketchy rumors of enemy troops landing below the mouth of the Cane from the transports with Porter's fleet. Certain that both of his flanks would soon fold, and intimidated by artillery fire on his center, Bee decided to withdraw in the afternoon, having sustained only fifty casualties.[32]

With Bee out of the way, Banks had an open road to Alexandria, where protection from Porter's fleet on the Red River awaited him. Taylor was thoroughly galled. Bee had occupied "the strongest [position] in the State," Taylor claimed in his official report, and had he

32. Richard Taylor, *Destruction and Reconstruction*, pp. 220–21 (quotation 220); Meiners, "Hamilton P. Bee," pp. 36–39; Ludwell H. Johnson, *Red River Campaign*, pp. 225–33.

held out just "a few hours longer, even the small force under my command [in the enemy rear] must have compelled the surrender of
Banks' Army." Testimony from Yankee prisoners, along with some
captured correspondence, confirmed Taylor's contention. One soldier admitted that "at no time did we feel as gloomy, or have such
doubts over the safety of the army . . . as at the battle of Cane River."
Another recalled that "the capture of almost everything pertaining to
our army was expected by most of us." In a searing letter to Bee on
the twenty-ninth Taylor spared no criticism. "Had you done your
duty I would have sung your praises," he wrote. "That you are not a
commander is surely not your fault, but were I to leave you in a position to ruin my plans again, I would be responsible." Taylor then dismissed Bee from duty and ordered him to report to Shreveport to
await further instructions.[33]

Taylor later pointed to Bee's lack of experience as an independent
commander as the most glaring reason for his failure. Taylor and
Wharton both had sent several messages to him emphasizing the crucial importance of making a stand. Yet, according to Taylor, Bee "had
neglected to study the ground or strengthen his position." Then, instead of harassing the Federal column once it crossed the river, he
took his men some thirty miles west to Beasly's, the nearest supply
depot, too far away to do Banks any further damage. In his own defense, Bee reported that he had received none of Taylor's insistent
messages, that he actually had only a few hours to fortify his position,
and that only shortly before the fight began did he realize he would
have to confront the great majority of Banks's army rather than
merely an advance guard. "Those who, distant from the scene, imagined that the enemy, demolished and disorganized, were fleeing before our triumphant forces, might have expected other results," he
wrote, "but those who saw that splendid [Federal] army spread over
the valley of the Cane River as far as the eye could reach were not

33. Richard Taylor to W. R. Boggs, June 1, 1864 (first quotation), Brent
Papers, Tulane University; Beecher, *114th N.Y.S.V.*, p. 333 (second quotation); Orton S. Clark, *One Hundred and Sixteenth New York Volunteers*, p. 170
(third quotation); Pellet, *114th New York Volunteers*, pp. 225–26; Richard Taylor to Hamilton P. Bee, April 29, 1864 (fourth quotation), Confederate District of West Louisiana, Record Book.

surprised that the road had to be yielded to them." He also explained that he withdrew to Beasly's because his men had gone without food for two days. Because Bee had underestimated the distance to Beasly's, his force arrived there too weary to turn back in time for further action against Banks's column.[34]

Embarrassed by recurring rumors of his incompetence, Bee asked General Smith to call a military court of inquiry to clear his name. But Smith evaded the issue by only sympathizing with Bee and dismissing the need for an inquiry. Other prominent officers, including Wharton himself, came to his support, but Bee's reputation remained so badly tarnished that he issued a public circular defending his position. Not until early 1865 did he regain a position in the army. Considering the paucity of troops under Bee at Monett's Ferry, Taylor's plan to cut off and surround Banks appeared suspect to most observers. Holding an overall advantage of five to one, rugged generals like A. J. Smith and William Emory would not have allowed Banks to surrender without first leading their men in a desperate battle to escape. But Taylor knew the situation demanded daring, and Bee had proved no match for the challenge. Because Bee had also made the mistake of speaking out in support of General Smith's decision to take Walker's Division to Arkansas, Taylor was all the more prone to censure Bee as harshly as possible. "I have always thought," Bee wrote Smith after the war, "that [Taylor's] treatment of me at Monett's [Ferry] was to destroy or weaken my testimony in the controversy between yourself and him." Bee's shortcomings aside, Taylor left no doubt as to the ultimate blame for Monett's Ferry. In a disgusted tone he announced to Smith on April 24, "My unfortunate trip to Shreveport and the loss of Walker's division have assuredly saved Banks' army from utter destruction." Writing privately to Walker, Taylor's personal adjutant Eustace Surget moaned, "I wish to God your Division had been with us, and Banks' army would never have reached Alexandria—*certain*."[35]

34. Richard Taylor, *Destruction and Reconstruction*, p. 221 (first quotation); Ludwell H. Johnson, *Red River Campaign*, p. 226; Meiners, "Hamilton P. Bee," pp. 40–43; *O.R.*, 34(1):610–14 (second quotation 613).

35. Meiners, "Hamilton P. Bee," pp. 42–44; Bee, *Dear Sir*; Ludwell H. Johnson, *Red River Campaign*, pp. 233–34; Hamilton P. Bee to Edmund

As the Federals marched the final twenty miles to Alexandria, A. J. Smith's midwesterners took enough time to continue their marauding escapades. "Smith's men made a clean sweep," wrote a Federal cavalryman. "From Cane River to Alexandria the country was in ruins." One of Taylor's men reported, "[In] many instances . . . they have set houses on fire while the women and children were in them." A Yankee perversely compared the march to the Israelites' deliverance, noting that the army was "guided by a pillar of fire by night and a pillar of cloud by day." Taylor prodded his soldiers to keep up a continual series of attacks on the enemy column's rear and flanks. "Without food for man or horse, our men seem animated by a determination to quench the incendiary fires lighted by the vandals in their [own] blood," he reported.[36]

Until now General Smith had actually considered sending Walker's Division back to Taylor. Realizing that Banks might decide to advance from Grand Ecore to Shreveport, Smith had halted Walker's Division near Minden, Arkansas, keeping it in readiness to return to Louisiana to help Taylor. But on the twenty-fifth Taylor learned that Smith had ordered Walker to resume his march into Arkansas. More astonished than angered, Taylor informed Smith, "My plans for following and driving the enemy were to a great extent based upon the assurance that Walker's division would be at my disposal." He also complained that Smith had ordered Brigadier General St. John R. Liddell, whose small cavalry force was harassing Porter from the Red River's eastern bank, to send two siege guns and a portion of his command to Arkansas as well. These disruptions, Taylor asserted, "render my plans for the future so uncertain that I am almost disheartened." Then, two days later, Taylor received a copy of Smith's congratulatory proclamation praising Taylor's army for its triumphs at Mansfield and Pleas-

Kirby Smith, May 18, 1879 (first quotation), Smith Papers; *O.R.*, 34(1):580–81 (second quotation 581); Eustace Surget to John G. Walker, ca. April 30, 1864 (third quotation), Walker Papers.

36. Ewer, *Third Massachusetts Cavalry*, p. 166 (first quotation); Oltorf, *Marlin Compound*, pp. 140–41 (second quotation 141); Beecher, *114th N.Y.S.V.*, pp. 336–37 (third quotation); Stanyan, *Eighth New Hampshire Volunteers*, p. 437; *O.R.*, 34(1):583 (fourth quotation).

ant Hill. The text mentioned nothing about Taylor himself. Personally insulted and embarrassed, he fumed to Smith that this was the
first time he had known such a proclamation to ignore a commanding
officer but that it was certainly consistent with Smith's recent treatment of him. "Whatever place my name is destined to occupy in the
golden book of the Republic I expect to engrave it there with the
point of my sword," Taylor snapped. Even with a low fever now reducing his strength, he vowed to "persevere to the end" despite any
injustice and unkindness Smith might inflict on him. "The cause for
which I have sacrificed fortune is paramount, and shall have my life
if need be," he concluded.[37]

The next day, April 28, Taylor received a letter from Smith explaining the necessity of sending Walker's troops to Arkansas. Walker had
already marched too far to return in time to help prevent Banks from
reaching Alexandria, Smith argued; furthermore, Steele still posed a
threat to Shreveport, thus "endangering the fruit of your victories."
Smith also reminded Taylor, "In both a political and military point of
view, everything is to be gained for the department." As far as Smith
was concerned, Taylor's Louisiana campaign was all but finished. He
even suggested that Taylor come to Arkansas with his increased rank,
where "ultimate and substantial results" would be achieved.[38]

His patience and physical strength already worn to a thread, Taylor
became completely unhinged when he read Smith's letter. In a passionate reply he offered an embittered summary of the whole controversy. Smith had duped and betrayed him, he claimed. Holding
Walker for fifteen days at a point only seventy miles away, Smith had
used this distance as an excuse to keep Walker for himself. One indis-
putable fact stood above all others, Taylor argued: Steele had clearly
given up any intention of marching on Shreveport. He had already
retreated more than one hundred miles, "completely foiled in his
plans by General Price with his raw cavalry." Turning the tables on
Smith, Taylor asked pointedly, "Why not suppose that Banks would
advance from Alexandria?" Had Smith only allowed Taylor to keep

37. *O.R*, 34(1):581–84 (first quotation 582, second quotation 583, third,
fourth, and fifth quotations 584). Smith's order regarding Mansfield and
Pleasant Hill is printed in ibid., p. 549.

38. Ibid., pp. 534–35 (quotations 534).

his command intact after Pleasant Hill, "Banks' army would have been destroyed; the fleet would have been in our hands or blown up by the enemy." Expanding this argument to its logical conclusion, Taylor struck at the very heart of Smith's most cherished ambitions. "By this time . . . I would have been on my way with the bulk of my army to join Price at Camden, enriched with captured spoils of a great army and fleet; Steele would have been brushed from our path as a cobweb before the broom of a housemaid; we would have reached St. Louis, our objective point, by midsummer and relieved the pressure from our suffering brethren in Virginia and Georgia," he declared. "All this is as true as the living God. . . . You might have had all the glory."[39]

As for his increased rank, Taylor denied having sought it and now declined to accept it from Smith. "I have learned from my ancestors that it is the duty of a soldier to conduct himself as to dignify titles and not derive importance from them," he insisted. After more than a year of supporting Smith's policies, even when "fatally wrong," Taylor could no longer submit himself to do his "whole duty." With this, he issued an abrupt request: "I ask that you take steps to relieve me as soon as it can be done without injury to the service." When Smith received this bombshell on May 8, he displayed his usual tolerance. Calling the letter "not only improper but unjust," he returned it to Taylor, stating that it must have been written "in a moment of irritation or sickness."[40]

Meanwhile Taylor's small force at Alexandria presented a ridiculous match for Banks's masses. With the recent arrival of reinforcements, Federal strength had ballooned once again to more than thirty thousand. Yet Banks viewed his situation as anything but enviable. First he would have to wait for Porter's fleet to return, and then Banks and Porter together would have to devise a way for the heavy ironclads to navigate the treacherous falls at Alexandria, where the water's depth had dropped in places to only a few inches. Taylor began to believe he might hold the Federals at bay until Walker's Divi-

39. Ibid., pp. 541–42 (first and second quotations 541, third and fourth quotations 542).

40. Ibid., pp. 542–43 (first and second quotations 542, third quotation 542–43, fourth quotation 543).

sion finished its fighting in Arkansas and returned to Alexandria. "Such was the condition to which this large [enemy] force had been reduced by repeated defeat," Taylor recalled, "that we not only confined it to its works, driving back many attacks on our advanced positions, but I felt justified in dividing my little command in order to blockade the river below, and cut off communication with the Mississippi." Taylor's renewed zeal manifested itself in a private letter from his adjutant Eustace Surget to Walker. "We have run the Yankees to earth in Alexandria, which our cavalry now surrounds on all sides and keeps the devils in a constant panic by shooting into their pickets every night at various points," Surget exclaimed. "Banks 'wishes every gunboat was in hell and he with them.'"[41]

By the time his fleet reached Alexandria on April 28, Admiral Porter was confessing amazement that even one vessel remained afloat. He had been forced to destroy the *Eastport*, colossus of the ironclads, after it ran aground under pressure from Confederate sharpshooters and artillery. Polignac's men had continually raked the fleet with the most violent firing Porter had ever seen, leaving three other gunboats incapacitated and two troop transports destroyed. By now Taylor's cavalry had also effectively blockaded Alexandria from below, sinking or capturing several incoming supply vessels. Fearing that Banks might actually take the army and desert him, Porter sent word to Secretary of the Navy Gideon Welles saying that he might have no choice but to scuttle the entire fleet, leaving Taylor with enough salvageable material to construct half a dozen ironclads. When Banks asked Porter to do this very thing, Porter refused, claiming that A. J. Smith had vowed to stay and defend the fleet with his troops if Banks and his northeasterners tried to evacuate Alexandria.[42]

During the next several days and nights Taylor orchestrated a masterful exercise in deception and torment, shifting his men around Alexandria to harass enemy pickets, sending drummers and buglers

41. Ludwell H. Johnson, *Red River Campaign*, pp. 254–55; Richard Taylor, *Destruction and Reconstruction*, p. 225 (first quotation); Eustace Surget to John G. Walker, ca. April 30, 1864 (second quotation), Walker Papers.

42. Ludwell H. Johnson, *Red River Campaign*, pp. 236–41, 255–57; Richard Taylor, *Destruction and Reconstruction*, pp. 221–29; Porter, *Naval History*, p. 529.

forward to sound battle calls, lighting a multitude of decoy camp fires, and rolling empty wagons over fence rails to imitate the sound of a force several times the numbers he actually possessed. When the Yankees got up enough courage to leave their entrenchments, the Confederates used enticing yet evasive hit-and-run tactics. "Remember my story about the whale," he instructed cavalry commander John Wharton. "When he has been harpooned and entangled he will make surges; then the boat's crew in pursuit of him has only to drop back and wait a little—then forward and grab him again!" Taylor's men also removed or destroyed virtually all forage within the enemy's reach. "We will play the game the Russians played in the [French] retreat from Moscow," he reported. By May 10 he considered Alexandria "as closely besieged as ever was Vicksburg." Portraying Banks's men as "disheartened, sullen, and disinclined to fight," Taylor also pointed out their lack of food and their susceptibility to disease. "All captured horses are like scarecrows and show want of forage," he stated. "From present appearances the end is drawing near."[43]

The scarcity of supplies in the area soon heaped suffering upon Taylor's men as well. "For thirty days we had practically nothing to eat," wrote a cavalryman. On May 3 Taylor issued a circular announcing the execution of two privates in the Nineteenth Texas Cavalry for the offense of "marauding and stealing." This was clearly a case of two hungry Confederates caught in the act of taking food from civilians. Their deaths, however, would serve as examples to all soldiers tempted into "pillaging or taking stock without orders." Future violators would face immediate execution in the field, without appeal to higher authority. Taylor also stipulated that officers who failed to report such crimes would be court-martialed as "aiders and abettors of robbers and thieves."[44]

43. Ludwell H. Johnson, *Red River Campaign*, pp. 258–59; Bergeron, *Uncle Silas*, p. 164; Dorsey, *Henry Watkins Allen*, p. 265; Richard Taylor to John A. Wharton, ca. May 5, 1864 (first quotation), Confederate District of West Louisiana, Record Book; *O.R.*, 34(1):588–91 (second quotation 589, third quotation 590, fourth and fifth quotations 591).

44. Gallaway, *Ragged Rebel*, p. 110 (first quotation); Richard Taylor, General Order No.——, Headquarters, Dist. West La., In the Field, May 3, 1864 (second, third, and fourth quotations), manuscript in Holmsley Papers.

For the Federals, the problem of getting Porter's fleet over the falls had become an all-consuming dilemma. Only one proposal, credited to the obscure but brilliant Lieutenant Colonel Joseph Bailey, appeared even marginally practical: a massive wing dam that would stretch from opposite sides of the Red River's 750-foot expanse. If successful, the dam would provide enough depth for the fleet to shoot through the narrow main channel. Soldiers worked around the clock, demolishing entire buildings in Alexandria, cutting nearby timber, and dumping quarried stone and dirt into the water. Consistent with United States Army custom, black troops performed the most demanding and dangerous work. After several days of mishaps and delays, the increasingly anxious Admiral Porter went so far as to secure Banks's assurance that his soldiers would stay and finish the project even if they had to eat mule meat to survive. By now, however, Banks knew that he needed the fleet's protection every bit as much as Porter needed the army's.[45]

Every day during these few weeks Taylor engaged a score or more of special couriers and staff officers, sending them in a steady stream to the telegraph station at Shreveport with messages to Smith in Arkansas describing the enemy's vulnerability at Alexandria. "It was impossible to believe that General Kirby Smith would continue to persist in his inexplicable policy, and fail to come, ere long, to my assistance," he recalled. In particular, Taylor's repeated contention that the Federal fleet could not pass the falls seemed consciously designed to add potency to his appeals for Smith to send reinforcements from Arkansas. "Day after day we strained our eyes to see the dust of our approaching comrades," wrote Taylor. "Not a camp follower among us but knew that the arrival of our men from the North would give us the great prize in sight." But reinforcements never appeared. "From first to last," Taylor railed in his memoirs, "General Kirby Smith seemed determined to throw a protecting shield around the Federal army and fleet."[46]

By now Taylor should have realized Smith was too busy chasing Steele to worry about anything else. After learning of Banks's set-

45. Ludwell H. Johnson, *Red River Campaign*, pp. 249–50, 260–66.
46. Richard Taylor, *Destruction and Reconstruction*, pp. 221 (first quotation), 231 (second quotation), 229 (third quotation).

Porter's massive ironclads passing through Bailey's dam and over the falls at Alexandria (Jenkins Rare Book Company).

backs at Mansfield and Pleasant Hill, by late April Steele had taken his hungry and disorganized force in a retreat back across the Ouachita River. Smith pursued him all the way, finally overtaking him at Jenkins' Ferry on the Saline River on April 30. Smith finally had his grand chance to lead an army in combat and to realize his dream of liberating Arkansas. But from the first shot he botched the battle, throwing his six thousand men across a muddy field in a succession of frontal assaults that allowed the firmly entrenched Federals, with only four thousand effectives, to shred the Confederate lines. Two of Walker's three brigadiers, Scurry and Randal, fell mortally wounded along with almost a thousand other casualties. Beaten into submission after several hours of fighting, Smith pulled back and watched helplessly as Steele's troops resumed their retreat.[47]

Despite the horrendous result, Smith still had the temerity to claim

47. Ludwell H. Johnson, *Red River Campaign,* pp. 183–205; Kerby, *Kirby Smith's Confederacy,* pp. 211–14. See also Bearss, *Steele's Retreat from Camden.*

Jenkins' Ferry as a victory. Writing to his mother on May 5, he boasted, "I have just passed through the most brilliant and successful campaign of the war." It was a preposterous assertion, and it could not have carried more irony. Smith had suffered a repulse far worse than the one Taylor had experienced at Pleasant Hill, where Smith described Taylor's troops as "broken and scattered." On the contrary, Smith reported to the War Department that Steele had been "signally defeated," and to President Davis he later swaggered, "The battle closed at 1 o'clock, a complete victory. . . . The rise of the river, which flooded the bottom for some miles, and the exhausted condition of our men prevented pursuit." Much like Taylor at Pleasant Hill, he saw a tactical defeat transformed into a strategic victory only because of Steele's retreat after the battle. But from the beginning of the campaign Smith had yearned to eliminate Steele, recapture Arkansas, and set the stage for a forceful sweep into Missouri. Now Steele was escaping to the safety of Little Rock's fortifications, leaving Smith with little more than a badly mauled army.[48]

48. Edmund Kirby Smith to his mother, May 5, 1864 (first quotation), Smith Papers; Kerby, *Kirby Smith's Confederacy*, pp. 314–15; Ludwell H. John-

With the fighting in Arkansas at an end, Smith could no longer ignore Taylor's pleas for help. He immediately ordered Walker and Churchill to march their weary troops back to Louisiana as quickly as possible. But Smith still refused to believe that Taylor could do any harm to Banks and Porter at Alexandria. Leaving the matter entirely in Taylor's hands, he advised, "While I do not wish to restrain you in your operations . . . you cannot exercise too much caution in risking a general engagement or in too far committing your whole force to a position on the river below Alexandria beyond the power of retreat in the event of a disaster."[49]

Walker and Churchill would reach Taylor far too late to do any good. By May 13 all of Admiral Porter's precious ironclads, their outer armor and stores of stolen cotton removed to allow extra buoyancy, had barreled through the small opening in Colonel Bailey's dam as throngs of soldiers cheered their approval. A deliriously happy Porter blessed the dam and called it the most marvelous engineering stunt in history. After watching Banks and Porter frustrate themselves for so long, Taylor could hardly stomach such a miracle. During the dam's construction General Liddell's contingent of Confederate cavalry had made only a few flimsy attempts to disrupt operations from the opposite riverbank near the falls. "The rebels made a great mistake in not interfering with our work," wrote a Federal soldier. "Had they done so, they might have embarrassed us seriously. . . . But they never fired a shot." Taylor castigated Liddell severely for this failure, but Liddell disputed him, claiming that the small force of six hundred men under his command could have done nothing to prevent the dam's completion. "I think that Taylor was at last convinced that he had foolishly thrown away, for lack of good common sense, all his chances," Liddell later contended. "He now had to exercise all his cunning to find someone to bear the blame."[50]

---

son, *Red River Campaign*, pp. 203–5; *O.R.*, 34(1):485 (second quotation), 477 (third quotation), 481–82 (fourth quotation).

49. *O.R.*, 34(1):537 (quotation).

50. Ludwell H. Johnson, *Red River Campaign*, pp. 260–66; Winters, *Civil War in Louisiana*, p. 368; Hoffman, *Camp, Court and Siege*, p. 101 (first quotation); Nathaniel C. Hughes, *Liddell's Record*, p. 183 (second quotation).

Proud and antagonistic, Liddell had detested Taylor from their first meeting a few months earlier. "I found Taylor very self-important and self-opinionated in his general expression of men and things," he recalled. Given a stunted cavalry command with orders to collect recruits and impress horses and supplies in the northern part of the state, Liddell looked upon his men as little better than masquerading deserters and draft evaders seeking soft duty. He also considered Taylor's impressment policy extremely distasteful, especially after witnessing its demoralizing impact upon the civilian population. After performing the thankless task of annoying Porter's fleet as it ascended and then descended the Red River, Liddell reached a point on the eastern bank near Alexandria and urged Taylor to occupy the town before Banks's army arrived, in order to keep Porter from passing the falls. This suggestion Taylor ignored, much to Liddell's touchy displeasure. Afterward, when Taylor criticized him for failing to thwart the construction of Bailey's dam, Liddell lost his last ounce of patience. He immediately requested to be relieved from command, and Taylor complied. "I was pleased at the prospect of getting rid of this wretchedly mismanaged business under the guidance of a foolish man," Liddell later observed. Like Hamilton Bee at Monett's Ferry, Liddell had been the victim of too few men and too little respect for Taylor to avoid serving as a scapegoat.[51]

While Porter's fleet made its escape, A. J. Smith's "gorillas" added the crowning infamy to their record of ravagement by calmly setting fires throughout Alexandria. For several days Smith's men had made their intentions common knowledge to soldiers and civilians alike. Unwilling to challenge Smith directly, Banks cleverly avoided making any serious attempts to prevent the conflagration. Apathy alone would suffice as his final gesture of gratitude to the town in which Unionist elections and army enlistments had seemed so important to him just two months earlier. Smith's men spent the early morning of May 13 spreading flammable materials at strategic points and joking that they were "preparing the place for Hell." Then they applied their torches. Fanned by high winds, the mounting inferno spread unchecked. Smith himself rode through the streets bellowing, "Hur-

51. Nathaniel C. Hughes, *Liddell's Record*, pp. 172–74 (first quotation 173), 178–83 (second quotation 183).

A. J. Smith, scourge of the Red River Valley
(*Johnson and Buell,* Battles and Leaders of the Civil War).

rah, boys, this looks like war!" Some of Banks's northeastern troops
tried to help citizens fight the flames. Families ran screaming toward
the river and begged soldiers for deliverance on the departing Federal transports, but even relatives of army recruits were denied permission to board. Four hours later Alexandria was a smoldering
wasteland.[52]

Alexandria's destruction served as the final humiliation for Taylor
in his agonizing effort to prevent the escape of Banks's army and Porter's fleet. "The enemy left Alexandria after midday to-day, burning
the place," he stated in a snappish message to General Smith. "Two
houses only [are] reported left between the ice-house and railroad."

52. *Official Report Relative to Federal Troops*, pp. 149–85 (first quotation 151,
second quotation 152); Van Alstyne, *Diary of an Enlisted Man,* pp. 320–21;
Ludwell H. Johnson, *Red River Campaign,* pp. 267–72.

*William T. Sherman, advocate of total war
(Jenkins Rare Book Company).*

Attributing the barbarous acts of A. J. Smith's men to experience gained under General Sherman, a good friend to Taylor before the war, Taylor cited in his memoirs several lengthy quotations from wartime correspondence in which Sherman justified his pitiless treatment of civilians during the Atlanta campaign. "It could hardly be expected," Taylor concluded, "that troops trained by this commander would respect *the humanities*." Upon reading Taylor's memoirs, Sherman directed a response to David F. Boyd, one of Taylor's officers and a close mutual friend during Sherman's prewar career in Louisiana. Referring to A. J. Smith as "one of the kindest souls living," Sherman blamed such "vandalism" on the usual run of skirmishers, servants, camp followers, and refugees. "Nobody ought to know better than Dick Taylor that no general can prevent such acts, especially in a case of civil war, the worst of wars," Sherman claimed.[53]

53. *O.R.*, 34(1):591 (first quotation); Richard Taylor, *Destruction and Reconstruction*, pp. 235–37 (second quotation 237); William T. Sherman to David F. Boyd, April 29, 1879 (third and fourth quotations), Boyd Papers. For an in-

The next day, May 14, Taylor dutifully pursued Banks southward along the Red River. "I have not the pretension to fight a general battle with my little force against four times their number," he reported, "but I hope to force the enemy to destroy large amounts of property, and harass and worry him until he reaches the Mississippi." At Mansura, on the sixteenth, the Confederates circled around Banks's column and blocked the road on a broad plain. Artillery on both sides sustained an uproarious duel that finally ended with Taylor's withdrawal in the face of the Federals' determined advance. "By being overwhelmed—not whipped—we were compelled to leave the road," a Texan recalled. Two days later at Yellow Bayou, near the remains of Simmesport, Taylor allowed Wharton to lead a fruitless attack against the enemy's rear guard, anchored by A. J. Smith's veterans. "What Taylor would not risk at Mansura, he did risk [at Yellow Bayou] on the 18th," wrote a Yankee cavalryman. Several southern officers protested the attempt, but Wharton insisted on a total assault. After losing more than six hundred casualties, Taylor watched Banks's bluecoats stream across the Atchafalaya River to safety.[54]

With the long campaign drawing to a close, Taylor could not help but repeat his irate resentment toward Edmund Kirby Smith. "Nothing but the withdrawal of Walker's division from me has prevented the capture of Banks' army and the destruction of Porter's fleet," he expounded. "I feel bitterly about this, because my army has been robbed of the just measure of its glory and the country of the most brilliant and complete success of the war."[55]

As if to vent his discontent even further, Taylor revived the ongo-

---

teresting defense of Sherman's methods, see Brinsfield, "Military Ethics of General William T. Sherman," pp. 87–103.

54. Ludwell H. Johnson, *Red River Campaign*, pp. 272–76; *O.R.*, 34(1):592–95 (first quotation 592); Orton S. Clark, *One Hundred and Sixteenth New York Volunteers*, pp. 179–80; Noel, *Old Sibley Brigade*, pp. 88–89 (second quotation 89); Ewer, *Third Massachusetts Cavalry*, pp. 182–85 (third quotation 183); Goodloe, "Service in the Trans-Mississippi," p. 32; Bergeron, *Uncle Silas*, pp. 168–69; Barr, *Polignac's Texas Brigade*, pp. 45–47; Gallaway, *Ragged Rebel*, pp. 114–21; Bailey, *Between the Enemy and Texas*, pp. 185–87.

55. *O.R.*, 34(1):594 (quotation).

ing struggle against deserters and jayhawkers by issuing a stern proclamation to the citizens of six parishes in southwestern Louisiana. Demanding that all men still owing military service come forward before June 1, he warned that those failing to comply "will be considered as Jayhawkers and shot down on sight." As for actual jayhawkers, he ordered his commander of scouts to "shoot down the parties without further delay. This whole element of disloyalty must be eradicated and . . . their women and children must be banished from the country and their residences burned." But the war had already disrupted life in Louisiana far too much for Taylor's reprisals to make much difference. The plague of deserters and jayhawkers would soon become even more irrepressible.[56]

Taylor's abhorrence for disloyalty took a particularly unsavory turn in his treatment of William B. Hyman, an Alexandria lawyer. Suspecting Hyman of traitorous motives for defending alleged deserters and jayhawkers, Taylor had ordered him banished to Mexico in January. An enraged Hyman claimed to be the victim of "a lie fabricated by Richard Taylor and instigated by personal malice," and he appealed to General Smith and Governor Allen for help. Although both Smith and Allen considered him troublesome and obnoxious, they intervened on his behalf. Hyman returned from exile to Alexandria in early June, but Taylor had him arrested again, allegedly remarking that now "he would send the damn hound where Gov. Allen and Genl. Smith could not interfere [and] that Gov. Allen should learn that the Bayonet was to rule in this Department." Taylor then ordered Hyman taken beyond the Federal lines to New Orleans. Disturbed by this high-handed punishment, Governor Allen issued a public proclamation in July vowing to protect the legal and constitutional rights of anyone persecuted unjustly by military power. "While I am Governor of the State of Louisiana, the bayonet shall not rule her citizens," he affirmed. Ironically, the next year Hyman received appointment as chief justice of the Unionist state government's supreme court, a

56. Richard Taylor, *To the People of St. Landry* (first quotation); Richard Taylor to R. W. Martin, May 23, 1864 (second quotation), Confederate District of West Louisiana, Record Book, April 11–May 19, 1864; Bragg, *Louisiana in the Confederacy*, pp. 198–201, 256–59; Ethel Taylor, "Discontent in Confederate Louisiana," pp. 426–28.

position he held until 1868. Perhaps Taylor's draconian actions had pushed Hyman into becoming an outright Unionist, or perhaps he had been a latent one all along.[57]

Even after the May 18 defeat at Yellow Bayou, Taylor seemed eager to try to carry the war once again into the lower part of the state. "If the water permits I will cross the Atchafalaya, bring up Walker's division and push for the La Fourche, and blockade the Mississippi," he informed Smith. A few days later he issued a laudatory proclamation to his troops, calling them "a band of conquering heroes." Referring to New Orleans's plight, he avowed, "The fairest city of the South languishes in the invader's grasp. Her exiled sons mourn her fate. . . . Soldiers! this army marches toward New Orleans, and although it do[es] not reach the goal, the hearts of her patriot women shall sound high with joy, responsive to the echoes of your guns."[58]

By May 23 Taylor's vision of battling the enemy on the Mississippi and pushing to New Orleans had become a faint mirage. Describing his troops' chronic shortages of basic supplies—food, clothing, and horses—he reported to Smith, "It will be impossible to act upon the defensive, much less upon the offensive." But as usual, the fate of lower Louisiana seemed the least of Smith's concerns. With Banks and Porter now out of the way, his steadfast goal of mounting a campaign into Arkansas and Missouri animated him even more strongly. "The disposable force of the department will be concentrated in that direction," Smith informed Taylor. "You should accompany the column from your district. Your presence will add to its efficiency and increase the prospects of success."[59]

When Taylor received these instructions on the twenty-fourth, he responded with a lengthy epistle ridiculing Smith's hopes. Although he agreed that a Missouri campaign would "have an important bearing on the war in both its political and military aspects," Taylor refused to contemplate any new campaign for the present. "The several

57. Lathrop, "Disaffection in Confederate Louisiana," pp. 308–18 (first quotation 313, second quotation 314, third quotation 315).
58. *O.R.*, 34(1):594–95 (first quotation 595); Richard Taylor, *General Orders No.——* (second and third quotations).
59. *O.R.*, 34(1):595 (first quotation), 538 (second quotation).

commands are utterly worn down with marching and fighting," he argued. In the meantime, he added, Smith should work a radical transformation of the Trans-Mississippi Department's inefficient supply system. Blaming the recurring lack of supplies on Smith's Byzantine bureaucracy, Taylor compared "the rage for what is termed organization" to an absurdly "disproportioned garment—all ruffles and no shirt." The "Shreveport maelstrom" had siphoned off valuable men for labor details, while troops in the field went without pay, food, and clothing, their requisitions "lost in a maze of red tape and circumlocution." Believing a Missouri campaign should wait until the cooler months of autumn, Taylor urged Smith to spend the summer making necessary preparations. With his health now suffering a rapid decline, Taylor repeated his request to be relieved from duty.[60]

Straining to maintain his composure, Smith took several days to formulate a reply. In a thorough and deliberate rebuttal, he rejected each of Taylor's aspersions on the supply system, ascribing most problems to the severe handicaps and shortages strangling the whole department. The various bureaus, he asserted, "are but few in number and have few employees." In a separate letter Smith also responded to Taylor's earlier accusations of bad faith in the detachment of Walker's Division for the campaign against Steele. "This unjust complaint, though repeated, remained unnoticed," Smith reminded him. "It was attributed to your ill health, and that irritability of disposition which at Mansfield, on April 10, you regretted and begged me to bear with." But now Smith meant to set the record straight. Walker's Division, he insisted, had been detached only because Taylor himself had agreed to it. "The fruits of your victory at Mansfield were secured by the march of that column [to Arkansas]," Smith contended. "The complete success of the [Red River] campaign was determined by the overthrow of Steele at Jenkins' Ferry."[61]

Smith's arrogant response regarding Walker's Division, coupled with his claim to martial fame at Jenkins' Ferry, stretched the truth

60. Ibid., pp. 543–45 (first and second quotations 543, third and fourth quotations 545).

61. Ibid., pp. 538–40 (first quotation 539), 545–46 (second quotation 545, third quotation 546).

beyond the breaking point. Realizing Taylor's sensitivity and obstinate conviction on this matter, Smith should have shown greater wisdom by simply dropping it. No one, however, could have predicted Taylor's utterly vituperative reaction. On June 5 he erupted with an astounding diatribe that laid bare his contempt for Smith's behavior. Repeating his indignation over the illogical pursuit of Steele's "comparatively insignificant" retreating force in Arkansas, Taylor then condemned Smith for describing Jenkins' Ferry as the Red River Campaign's climactic success. "I am at a loss to conceive what connection the fruits of Mansfield have with the fight at Jenkins' Ferry," he declared. "We do not today hold one foot more of Arkansas than if Jenkins' Ferry had never been, and we have a jaded army and 1,000 less soldiers." Calling the whole campaign a "hideous failure," he lamented that "the fruits of Mansfield have been turned to dust and ashes" only because Smith had willfully allowed Banks and Porter to escape. Worst of all, "Louisiana, from Natchitoches to the Gulf, is a howling wilderness and her people are starving," he exclaimed. "Arkansas is probably as great a sufferer." Claiming that he had too often accepted public blame for Smith's "grave errors," he concluded defiantly, "After the desire to serve my country, I have none more ardent than to be relieved from longer serving under your command."[62]

This time Taylor got his wish. On June 10, the very day the Confederate Congress issued a joint resolution praising Taylor for his "brilliant successes" at Mansfield and Pleasant Hill, Smith dismissed him and named Walker the new commander of the District of West Louisiana. But the controversy did not end there. In a highly defensive move, Smith dumped the matter into the lap of Jefferson Davis himself, sending the president copies of his recent heated correspondence with Taylor. "I would have arrested General Taylor on the receipt of his first letter," Smith informed Davis, "but acknowledging his merits as a soldier and feeling kindly disposed toward him, I passed it by." Calling Taylor's letters "improper and disrespectful," Smith also claimed that Taylor had criticized him openly. "The public interest required that one of us be relieved," he argued. Smith now offered to

62. Ibid., pp. 546–48 (first and fifth quotations 548, second, third, and fourth quotations 547).

resign as commander of the department "with no feeling of envy," should Davis desire it.[63]

By accusing Taylor of fostering a conspiracy against him, Smith presented a decidedly distorted picture. Public derision toward Smith had been gaining strength for several months throughout war-torn Louisiana, so much that he confided several times to his wife and close friends that he wished he could give up his burdensome position. He also knew that politicians in Richmond had been pressuring Davis to remove him. "Facts will be misrepresented and distorted by certain parties in Louisiana who are waging a bitter war against me," Smith told Davis. This remark reflected Smith's particular antagonism toward E. Warren Moise, a highly influential Natchitoches judge leading the campaign to have Smith ousted. T. R. Heard, a supporter of Smith at Shreveport, told David Boyd, "General Taylor . . . has allowed himself to be ruled by that old Democratic politician Moise and [his] clique."[64]

As one of a legion of anti-Smith partisans, Taylor had merely added fuel to a fire burning hotter all the time. Judge Thomas C. Manning of Alexandria wrote Braxton Bragg on July 9 asking him to use his considerable influence with President Davis to deliver Louisiana from Smith's rotten regime. "His usefulness here is at an end, or, rather, it never had a beginning," proclaimed Manning. "The people of this State cling to Taylor as the very sheet anchor of their salvation . . . and if he be removed I believe they will give up in despair." Two months later Judge Moise articulated to former governor Thomas Moore his agitation over rumors that Rapides Parish might support the pro-Smith candidate in the upcoming congressional election. "By God! If you do—you deserve all you have suffered," Moise ranted, "and I have no sympathy for those who are willing and knowing victims of [Smith's] immeasurable stupidity. What we want now of all other things is to send to Congress a bitter opponent of Smith."

63. Kerby, *Kirby Smith's Confederacy*, pp. 320–21; *O.R.*, 34(1):597, 540–48 (first quotation 540, second, third, and fourth quotations 541).

64. Parks, *Edmund Kirby Smith*, pp. 414–19; *O.R.*, 34(1):478–82 (first quotation 482); T. R. Heard to David F. Boyd, July 7, 1864 (second quotation), Boyd Papers.

Henry Gray, the anti-Smith candidate, won the election with 65 percent of the vote.[65]

Despite the mounting clamor against Smith, President Davis tried to ignore the Taylor-Smith feud. Neither did he comment on Smith's dismissal of Taylor, nor did he express concern over Smith's offer to resign. But Davis did make himself clear regarding Smith's refusal to concentrate against Banks's huge force. On this crucial issue the president plainly supported Taylor's ardent desire to keep Banks from escaping down the Red River. "This was so obvious," Davis wrote Smith on August 8, "that I expected you to act without waiting for orders so as to counteract the movement [Banks] was reported to be making [across the Mississippi] with the troops you had lately defeated." Davis also showed little patience for Smith's longstanding strategic fixation on liberating Arkansas and Missouri to the benefit of the Confederate cause east of the Mississippi. "If our forces on the west side of the river should allow the enemy to leave that section and . . . defeat those on the east side, your projected campaign [into Arkansas and Missouri] could not fail to end in disaster," Davis asserted.[66]

Smith responded to these scathing criticisms in a peevish tone, explaining that his small number of troops could not have kept Banks from escaping. "You say that I should have followed the movements of the enemy," Smith wrote Davis. "This was simply impossible." But Davis refused to accept Smith's rationalization. As late as December the president was still harping on "the withdrawal of so large a portion of the army of the enemy heretofore employed in the Trans-Mississippi Department and their concentration against our forces on this side of the Mississippi River." He would never forget that Smith had failed to take "vigorous measures" to "follow your victories in April as would have prevented the enemy from sending troops" to the East. Davis's opinion of Smith thus deteriorated from displeasure

65. *O.R.*, 41(2):992–93 (first quotation 993); E. Warren Moise to Thomas O. Moore, September 24, 1864 (second quotation), Moore Papers; Bragg, *Louisiana in the Confederacy*, pp. 268–70; Dorsey, *Henry Watkins Allen*, pp. 269–77; William K. Scarborough, *Diary of Edmund Ruffin*, p. 714; Thomas C. Manning to Thomas O. Moore, March 30, 1865, Moore Papers.

66. *O.R.*, 41(1):102 (quotations).

to disfavor, and by the end of the war, according to one account, he spoke of Smith "with marked acerbity."[67]

In his memoirs Taylor carried Davis's logic even further by claiming that Smith's "sheer stupidity and pig-headed obstinacy" had cost the Confederacy a sterling chance to turn the tide of the war. "In all the ages since the establishment of the Assyrian monarchy," wrote Taylor, "no commander has possessed equal power to destroy a cause. Far away from the great centers of conflict in Virginia and Georgia, on a remote theatre, the opportunity of striking a blow decisive of the war was afforded." After Banks's escape, troops from his Nineteenth Corps went to Virginia, arriving "in time to save Washington from General [Jubal A.] Early's attack," while others, including A. J. Smith's men, reinforced Sherman in his campaign through Georgia and the Carolinas. Likewise, had Porter's fleet fallen into southern hands, "we would have at once recovered possession of the Mississippi, from the Ohio to the sea, and undone all the work of the Federals since the winter of 1861." To any rational observer Taylor's assertions must seem farfetched if not fanciful. Even without reinforcements from the Trans-Mississippi, Federal armies east of the river had already become formidable. Moreover, Porter would have destroyed his ironclads before losing them to the Confederates. By accusing General Smith of blindly and forcibly committing a monstrous blunder, Taylor displayed a festering animosity that always haunted him.[68]

Except for his verbose and useless official pleadings to President Davis, Smith held no ill will toward Taylor. During the latter part of the Red River Campaign he spoke with Brigadier General Liddell regarding Taylor's removal of Liddell after Banks's and Porter's escape from Alexandria. Smith listened patiently to Liddell's complaints about Taylor's "contradictory orders" and "childishness and

67. Ibid., 34(1):482–88 (first quotation 487) and 41(1):123–24 (second and third quotations 123); Eckert, *"Fiction Distorting Fact,"* p. 49 (fourth quotation).

68. Richard Taylor, *Destruction and Reconstruction*, pp. 229–31 (first quotation 231, second quotation 229–30, third and fourth quotations 230). For an indication of Taylor's acceptance of the Trans-Mississippi's minimal impact on the outcome of the war, see Richard Taylor to Dabney H. Maury, May 8, 1876, Brock Papers.

absurdities unbecoming an officer." After briefly examining some of
these orders, Smith remarked, "General Taylor's mind is affected by
the paralysis he had some years since, and is hardly responsible." Liddell insisted that if Taylor was truly ill he was therefore unfit for duty.
But Smith denied this. According to Liddell, "General Smith still continued to apologize for and mitigate Taylor's follies, evidently influenced by the kindest feelings. He never gave me the slightest intima-
tion of difference[s] between them." After the war, when Taylor's
memoirs were published, Smith's friends and several former officers
urged him to respond with his own version of events in the Trans-
Mississippi. Dabney Maury, for one, admitted Taylor to be "a good
friend . . . but with a bitter tongue and pen on occasion." Yet Smith
declined to write anything except a short article for *Century Magazine*,
(subsequently published in *Battles and Leaders of the Civil War*) in which
he avoided controversy and spoke of Taylor only in respectful and
complimentary terms.[69]

Had he chosen to dredge up his ugly battle with Taylor, however,
Smith would have faced an extremely difficult task in defending his
own position. Most observers at the time, and since, denounced his
decision to pursue Steele at the cost of giving Banks and Porter time
to break free of Taylor's grasp after the battles at Mansfield and Pleasant Hill. "The move against Steele was a mistake," wrote Colonel H.
T. Douglas, one of Smith's own staff officers. "If the entire available
Confederate force had been massed . . . on both sides of the Red
River . . . General Banks' army might have been destroyed and with it
Admiral Porter's fleet." John G. Walker concurred, arguing strongly
that "Smith was not the leader to comprehend the true line of action,
and . . . against the opinion and advice of all his principal subordinates, he unwisely determined . . . [to move] against the Federal army
still at Camden under Steele. To this fatal blunder Banks was in-
debted for his safety." Even Taylor's old nemesis Liddell admitted,
"General Smith, it is clear, should have kept his forces together and
pushed [forward against Banks], and he will always be censured for
this neglect." Smith's modern biographer, Joseph H. Parks, although

69. Nathaniel C. Hughes, *Liddell's Record*, p. 184 (first, second, and third
quotations); Parks, *Edmund Kirby Smith*, pp. 506–7 (fourth quotation 506);
Edmund Kirby Smith, "Defense of the Red River," pp. 369–74.

largely sympathetic toward his subject, concluded that "it was poor strategy to order Walker from Minden to Camden. Walker's division should have been sent back to [the] Red River Valley, probably to join with Liddell's force operating on the north bank of the river."[70]

By emphasizing Smith's error in failing to concentrate against Banks and Porter, however, the chorus of criticism against him overlooks his most damaging weakness: his personal ambition for military glory. Although Smith had hidden the trait well, the huge responsibilities and frustrations of serving as departmental commander had grated on him for more than a year prior to the Red River Campaign. When Banks reached Mansfield, Taylor's calculated deceit robbed Smith of his prerogative of coming down from Shreveport and taking command of the army. Smith chose to ignore this indiscretion—a gesture made easier because of Taylor's victory—but he used Taylor's setback at Pleasant Hill as an excuse to turn against Steele. Smith then proved far more deceitful than Taylor. Having promised to allow Taylor to pursue Banks and Porter if Steele began a withdrawal, Smith broke his word, taking Walker's troops to chase Steele and leaving Taylor with a skeleton force. Smith did not attempt to justify this decision in Taylor's presence, nor could his vague and contradictory correspondence and reports afterward fully explain his reasoning. His true intentions soon became evident on the field of battle. Smith saw Steele as easy prey, a chance for certain glory, and his ludicrous claim of total victory at Jenkins' Ferry unmasked the ambition that had motivated him from the beginning of the campaign. Taylor's ridicule of Jenkins' Ferry as a fiasco made a gross mockery of Smith's pride. All of Taylor's previous outbursts of indignation paled when compared to this single provocation. Smith could not tolerate being branded a failure as a field commander.[71]

70. H. T. Douglas, "Trans-Mississippi Department," p. 153 (first quotation); Walker, "War of Secession," typescript, p. 56 (second quotation); Nathaniel C. Hughes, *Liddell's Record*, p. 181 (third quotation); Ludwell H. Johnson, *Red River Campaign*, pp. 279–81; Parks, *Edmund Kirby Smith*, p. 413 (fourth quotation). For a vociferous defense of Smith's actions by one of his staff officers, however, see *O.R.*, 34(1):550–60. See also Dorsey, *Henry Watkins Allen*, pp. 264–68.

71. Smith's muddled reasoning regarding his decision to pursue Steele is evident in *O.R.*, 34(1):480–81, 484–85, 531–35, 538, 545–46.

On a more fundamental level Smith's ambition also nourished his grand strategy in the Trans-Mississippi Department. In looking toward Arkansas and Missouri he saw his best opportunity for dealing the enemy a sensational blow that would earn him lasting prestige. Yet like Sterling Price, his district commander, he fell victim to the delusion that citizens in those two states would rise up to help throw off the Federal yoke, while in fact consistent support for the Confederacy remained weak or nonexistent, especially in Missouri. With St. Louis as his monumental goal, Smith spurned the idea of challenging Federal control of the Mississippi River and recapturing New Orleans, which he considered hopelessly lost. This prejudice had produced a series of disagreements with Taylor during 1863, but after each clash, Smith and Taylor managed to resume their cordial, even friendly relationship. The Red River Campaign, however, not only exposed Smith's desire for military accolades but also proved that his ambition had blinded him to the catastrophic effects of total war upon a civilian population. His indifference toward the devastation of Louisiana's heartland infuriated Taylor far more than anything else.[72]

Although Taylor's love for Louisiana prejudiced him toward protecting her citizens and pushing to free New Orleans from Federal dominance, he never sought the kind of public glory Smith craved. Having to watch his home state suffer only intensified his sense of duty to serve it, even when his recurring illness made the task physically excruciating. He asserted emphatically that, had the Red River Campaign proved a complete success, Smith could have claimed all the glory for himself. Taylor had encountered such towering ambition once before in a commanding officer—Stonewall Jackson—but in Taylor's eyes Smith could not begin to measure up to Jackson. Despite the personal affability between them, Taylor never respected Smith as a soldier and never viewed him as having a selfless sense of duty to the Confederacy. Herein lay the most immediate source of Taylor's repugnance toward Smith's decisions and statements.

Had Smith exuded military authority and competence as a com-

72. On the tenuous viability of Arkansas and Missouri as strategic goals, see Castel, *General Sterling Price*, p. 284.

mander, Taylor would have tolerated his ambition just as he had tolerated Jackson's, but only up to a point. Total war—the destruction of property and the complete disruption of lives, along with the attendant evils of heavy-handed conscription, mass desertions, ruthless jayhawkers, violations of civil rights, and arbitrary impressments—had torn Louisiana apart. Taylor's own plantation and the lives of his two young sons were part of the awful toll. Smith's apparent apathy confirmed to Taylor that unmitigated ambition had overwhelmed Smith's capacity as a commander.

Stonewall Jackson did not live long enough to see his own Shenandoah Valley wracked by total war. Yet no Confederate commander, not even Jackson, could have prevented the calamities inflicted by Federal armies ravaging the South. With fewer soldiers every month to put forth resistance, generals like Smith had little choice but to employ the kind of defensive strategy displayed during the Red River Campaign—withdrawing or maneuvering to a position of perceived advantage before fighting. As a result, nothing restrained the Yankees from plundering or destroying whatever lay in their paths. Taylor's unwillingness to accept such a fate for his home state, coupled with Smith's refusal to give him the opportunity for gaining revenge against Banks, pushed Taylor past the boiling point. Yet even after Smith's illogical decision to take Taylor's troops to Arkansas to chase Steele, and even after Smith's outrageous attempt to call Jenkins' Ferry the climactic victory of the campaign, Taylor had absolutely no right to insult Smith so unconscionably. Utterly unprofessional and insubordinate in his remarks, he deliberately forced Smith to relieve him. Smith did overreact by appealing to President Davis for approval, but his postwar inclination to lay aside all personal bitterness toward Taylor showed a magnanimity Taylor himself seemed incapable of exercising.

A symptom of the South's incapacity to withstand the maelstrom of total war, the collision between Taylor and Smith would rank as one of the most notorious of the Civil War. Indeed, it was one of a continual series of such feuds, just the kind of behavior the embattled Confederacy could least afford from its top general officers. In this context, Sarah Dorsey, Governor Allen's confidant and one of Smith's most vocal defenders, described Taylor as fairly as possible: "He was one of our best fighting-men,—a trifle too impatient and passionate, with perhaps not sufficient sense of subordination. In truth, he was both a very able and a very imperious man." Edmund Kirby Smith doubtless would have agreed.[73]

73. Dorsey, *Henry Watkins Allen*, p. 260 (quotation).

CHAPTER ELEVEN

Dutiful Departmental
Commander

He's the biggest man in the lot. If we'd had more

like him, we would have licked the Yankees long ago.

Nathan Bedford Forrest

When Taylor reached Natchitoches in mid-June 1864, the town council provided a large and well-furnished house for him and his family.
"I think this is but a fair indication of the feelings of our people generally to Taylor," Duncan Kenner informed Judah P. Benjamin. Taylor welcomed the reprieve, coming after what he considered "two
years of devotion to work—work so severe, stern, and exacting as to
have prevented me from giving the slightest attention to my family,
even when heavily afflicted." Here he remained for more than a
month.[1]

Having ignored General Smith's remonstrances, President Davis
officially promoted Taylor to lieutenant general on July 18. Among
the seventeen Confederate officers who achieved this distinguished

1. Duncan F. Kenner to Judah P. Benjamin, July 31, 1864 (first quotation),
Miscellaneous Manuscripts Collection, Historic New Orleans Collection;
Richard Taylor, *Destruction and Reconstruction*, p. 239 (second quotation).

rank during the war, Taylor was the first without West Point training. Only Nathan Bedford Forrest and Wade Hampton, both promoted later, were also non–West Pointers. As part of this unprecedented decision, Davis put Taylor in command of the Department of Alabama, Mississippi, and East Louisiana. He succeeded two prominent predecessors, Leonidas Polk and Stephen D. Lee, both of whom Davis had pulled away to serve as corps commanders in the Army of Tennessee.[2]

About the same time, Braxton Bragg, acting on his own initiative as Davis's administrator of military operations, ordered Smith to allow Taylor to take Walker's and Polignac's infantry divisions across the Mississippi. With both Mobile and Atlanta threatened by Federal forces, the Trans-Mississippi Department offered the only source of reinforcements. Seeking to rid himself of Smith forever, Taylor intended to cross the river on his own, but an angry General Smith forced Taylor to take total responsibility for moving the troops. Taylor then formulated a scheme for ferrying them across, but by August 18, the date planned for the movement, he feared that at least half of his men, including several officers, would mutiny and desert to avoid leaving western Louisiana. The Texans of Walker's Division proved particularly rebellious. "At one time, some two or three companies deliberately walked off and started toward Texas but were arrested and brought back," noted a Louisianan. Taylor ordered a captain and ten other ringleaders court-martialed and shot.[3]

On August 26, according to one soldier, Taylor "spoke freely and amicably, telling us that it is his intention to have us cross the river, and promising us a brilliant operation if only he can have us on the other bank." But two days later he realized the futility of the movement. Enemy gunboats, placed at intervals along the Mississippi, had become too numerous. Gaining Smith's permission to go by himself, Taylor and his body servant Tom Strother, accompanied by a single guide, took a canoe in the dark of night from a point near the mouth

2. Dufour, *Nine Men in Gray*, p. 35; Hattaway, *General Stephen D. Lee*, pp. 99–125.

3. Kerby, *Kirby Smith's Confederacy*, pp. 324–29; Parks, *Edmund Kirby Smith*, pp. 420–30; Blessington, *Walker's Texas Division*, pp. 273–74; Bearss, *A Louisiana Confederate*, p. 155; Bergeron, *Uncle Silas*, p. 155 (quotation).

of the Red River, their horses swimming across with them. "A gunboat was lying in the river a short distance below," he recalled, "and even the horses seemed to understand the importance of silence, swimming quietly alongside our frail craft."[4]

Arriving at Woodville in southwestern Mississippi in early September, Taylor located a telegraph office and informed the War Department in Richmond of his safe passage. Here he learned that the forts at the entrance to Mobile Bay had fallen into enemy hands and, far worse, that Sherman had captured Atlanta. Until now the Confederacy's hopes of wearing down the North had seemed surprisingly bright. Taylor's triumph on the Red River had stalled Union designs on Texas from the east and Alabama from the south, and Robert E. Lee was exacting horrifying casualties on Grant's army in Virginia. Yet President Davis's sudden decision to replace Joseph Johnston with the young and impulsive General John Bell Hood as commander of the Army of Tennessee in Georgia had proved worse than barren. After Hood's forced evacuation of Atlanta, the North redoubled its resolve to prosecute the war, insuring Lincoln's reelection in November and dooming the Democratic party's demand for a negotiated peace with the South. Even before his arrival east of the Mississippi, however, Taylor considered northern victory inevitable. "Upon what foundations the civil authorities of the Confederacy rested their hopes of success, after the campaign of 1864 fully opened, I am unable to say," he later observed, "but their commanders in the field, whose rank and position enabled them to estimate the situation, fought simply to afford statesmanship an opportunity to mitigate the sorrows of inevitable defeat."[5]

Despite flagging confidence, Taylor took hold of his new assignment with accustomed determination. He arrived at departmental

4. Bearss, *A Louisiana Confederate*, p. 159 (first quotation); Dufour, *Nine Men in Gray*, p. 35; Richard Taylor, "Last Confederate Surrender," in *Annals of the War*, p. 67; Richard Taylor, *Destruction and Reconstruction*, pp. 240–41 (second quotation).

5. Richard Taylor, *Destruction and Reconstruction*, pp. 240–41 (quotation 240); McPherson, *Ordeal by Fire*, pp. 409–22; Woodworth, *Jefferson Davis and His Generals*, pp. 289–90.

headquarters in Meridian, Mississippi, on September 5 and assumed command the next day. Almost immediately he received a telegram from Davis advising him to send Major General Nathan Bedford Forrest's cavalrymen, about four thousand strong, into Tennessee to disrupt Sherman's supply lines. Forrest happened to be passing through Meridian that evening, intending to take his men south to help defend Mobile. This afforded Taylor the opportunity to meet the vaunted cavalry officer face to face for the first time.[6]

Taylor's initial impression of Forrest was scarcely encouraging: "He was a tall, stalwart man, with grayish hair, mild countenance, and slow and homely of speech." Informing Forrest that Mobile appeared secure for the present, Taylor instructed him to prepare his cavalry to strike northward into Tennessee. But Forrest voiced nervous concerns about logistics, supplies, and other contingencies. "I began to think he had no stomach for the work," Taylor recalled. Continuing to hash over the difficulties with Taylor, Forrest sent for Major L. J. Fleming, a railroad superintendent officer, and asked him about the prospect of sending supplies via the Mobile and Ohio Railroad. Fleming made a swift, positive response. "Forrest's whole manner now changed," noted Taylor. "In a dozen sharp sentences he told of his wants, said he would leave a staff officer to bring up his supplies, asked for an engine to take him back north twenty miles to meet his troops, informed me he would march with the dawn, and hoped to give an account of himself in Tennessee."[7]

Taylor's admiration for Forrest grew steadily from this first somewhat uncertain encounter. Normally a tower of self-assurance and assertiveness, Forrest, quite simply, had been caught off guard. Taylor's commanding presence had made an instantaneous, disarming impact on him. "Forrest admitted that he was more awed by Dick Taylor's power of will than any man he ever met," wrote one of his officers, "or, as he expressed it, 'I lost my charm when I met Dick Taylor.'" Upon leaving Meridian, Forrest was heard to say of Taylor, "He's the

6. *O.R.*, 39(2):816, 818–19; Richard Taylor, *Destruction and Reconstruction*, p. 242.

7. Richard Taylor, *Destruction and Reconstruction*, pp. 242–43 (first quotation 242, second and third quotations 243).

Nathan Bedford Forrest, peerless Confederate cavalry commander
(*Johnson and Buell,* Battles and Leaders of the Civil War).

biggest one in the lot. If we'd had more like him, we would have licked the Yankees long ago."[8]

Although Forrest had already attained fearsome stature as a cavalry raider, his role during the last several months had restricted him to resisting Federal thrusts from Tennessee. This he had accomplished with his usual brilliance. But now, instead of fighting on the defensive or merely supporting the garrison at Mobile, he had a ripe chance once more to exercise his genius for inflicting havoc behind Federal lines. After making the necessary preparations, Forrest took his troopers into northern Alabama and then veered upward into Middle Tennessee. During a short, two-week span in late September and early October he destroyed railroad tracks, burned trestles and bridges, and captured several dozen wagonloads of supplies, hun-

8. Ibid., pp. 243–45; Chalmers, p. 479 (first quotation); Osborne, "Kentucky's Gifts to the Confederacy," p. 200 (second quotation).

dreds of horses, and thousands of arms, leaving about a thousand enemy casualties in his wake. Sherman reacted by dispatching two divisions from Atlanta. Other enemy reinforcements from across Tennessee converged at the same time, keeping nearly thirty thousand Federals distracted in an attempt to stop Forrest. Yet for all this disruption, Forrest's raid annoyed Sherman only slightly. His army was already accumulating great quantities of supplies, allowing him to set his sights on cutting southward all the way through Georgia.[9]

Meanwhile Taylor went to Mobile to confer with his close friend Major General Dabney H. Maury, the garrison's commander. "Intelligent, upright, and devoted to duty, [Maury] gained the respect and confidence of the townspeople," Taylor affirmed, "and was thereby enabled to supplement his regular force of eight thousand of all arms with a body of local militia." Mobile protected key railroad lines to Alabama's interior, but Taylor expected no serious enemy threat until the following spring. With this in mind, he instructed Maury to build up defensive works on the eastern side of Mobile Bay and at Spanish Fort and Fort Blakely. "It was a great comfort to find an able officer in this responsible position, who not only adopted my plans, but improved and executed them," he remembered.[10]

Taylor then went north to Selma, in central Alabama, a railroad hub that seemed to offer means of sending supplies gathered from his department to Hood's Army of Tennessee. Grasping this prospect, Taylor established his headquarters at Selma on September 20. During the previous two weeks he had traveled throughout the department by himself or with a single staff officer, and by engaging all kinds of persons in informal exchanges he had begun to perceive the true temper of public morale. "Citizens were universally depressed and disheartened," he recalled. Most of all, people blamed the loss of Atlanta and the army's degenerate condition on Davis's rejection of Johnston in favor of Hood. "From conversations in railway carriages and on river steamers I had gathered this, and nothing but this, since my arrival," he noted. Although inclined to agree with these malcontents, he did not show it at the time. Years later he admitted that John-

---

9. *O.R.*, 39(1):542–49; Henry, *Forrest*, pp. 345–65.

10. Richard Taylor, *Destruction and Reconstruction*, pp. 245–47 (quotations 247).

Dabney H. Maury, effective officer and favored friend of Taylor
(*Johnson and Buell,* Battles and Leaders of the Civil War).

ston probably had erred in deciding to make a gradual withdrawal all the way to Atlanta without initiating a strong counteroffensive against Sherman. Yet Taylor also contended that Davis should have at least allowed Johnston to defend the city before shelving him. "Had [Johnston] abandoned Atlanta without a struggle, his removal would have met with the approval of the army and the public," he argued. The president's fear that Johnston would indeed abandon Atlanta had prompted him to give the much more aggressive Hood command of the army. Atlanta soon fell anyway, only making Hood all the more unpopular, and Taylor blamed Davis for the resulting mess. "Certainly, no more egregious blunder was possible than that of relieving [Johnston] from command in front of Atlanta," he concluded.[11]

The public rancor over Johnston's fate could not distract Taylor from a more fundamental problem: the sheer lack of enough sol-

11. *O.R.*, 39(2):859; Richard Taylor, *Destruction and Reconstruction*, pp. 248–49 (first and second quotations 249), 44 (third and fourth quotations). See also McNeill, "Survey of Confederate Soldier Morale," pp. 1–25.

diers. On September 25 he sent Bragg a confidential letter with a re-markable proposal. "Unless Sherman can be forced from his present position there is but little to be accomplished in this Department," Taylor asserted. "It appears to me we have put forth our entire strength on this side of the Mississippi, and if we have to face another campaign it is difficult to see whence we are to draw reserves to fill up our ranks." The only hope of salvaging the situation lay in the Trans-Mississippi Department, not as a source of troops for the war east of the river, but as a theater of vigorous military operations and with Bragg as its new commander. More than fifty thousand troops could be raised there, Taylor insisted. "That Department is the proper scene for the employment of your administrative abilities," he told Bragg. Once Bragg replaced Edmund Kirby Smith, Taylor would then also seek to gain transfer back to the Trans-Mississippi. "If I can be of any service to the cause it is by remaining in the field with troops I thoroughly know, and on a theater of operations familiar to me," he concluded.[12]

Dubious about the potential value of his new command, Taylor also plainly continued to harbor bitter umbrage toward Smith. Lost op-portunities in Louisiana, especially the dream of liberating New Or-leans, would presumably merit rejuvenation and redemption with Bragg and Taylor in control. Even now Smith persisted in his un-abashed hope of reclaiming Missouri, sending Sterling Price on a far-flung raid that would end in failure. But Bragg had no intention of supporting Taylor's pet scheme. Instead, he envisioned Taylor as a corps commander with the Army of Tennessee. This could be realized by having Taylor trade places with the petulant Lieuten-ant General William J. Hardee, who had been railing for several weeks about Hood having replaced Johnston. "With Taylor in Har-dee's place this army would be invincible," Bragg declared to Presi-dent Davis.[13]

Hood also considered Taylor a highly desirable candidate for Har-

12. Richard Taylor to Braxton Bragg, September 25, 1864 (quotations), Richard Taylor Letter Book.

13. Nathaniel Cheairs Hughes, *General William J. Hardee*, pp. 243–44 (quo-tation 244).

John Bell Hood, reckless commander of the Army of Tennessee
(Jenkins Rare Book Company).

dee's position, but Davis viewed Taylor's role as a departmental com-
mander as more important within the context of grand strategy.
Stirred by the oppressive might of Sherman's invasion, the president
came south in late September to make speeches in South Carolina,
Georgia, and Alabama in hopes of reviving the plummeting morale
of soldiers and citizens. He was also struggling to decide the Army of
Tennessee's next move, and he seemed particularly anxious to gain
Taylor's advice. On September 27 Taylor met Davis in Montgomery.
After a day consumed by meetings with Alabama state officials and
prominent citizens, Davis took Taylor to his private quarters about
10:00 P.M. They discussed at length the concept of Hood moving the
army north into Tennessee to lure Sherman away from Atlanta. Davis
considered Hood's force strong enough to warrant the strike, but
Taylor disagreed, arguing that the Federal garrisons at Chattanooga
and Nashville would free Sherman, once he had gathered enough
supplies, to continue his invasion of Georgia at will. Davis still hoped
reinforcements could be gained from the Trans-Mississippi, but Tay-

lor ruled out the idea, explaining the logistical problems of crossing the Mississippi and the adamant public resistance west of the river.[14]

"The President listened attentively to this, and asked, 'What then?'" Taylor recounted. The only practical strategy, he answered, would be to send the army north of Atlanta to break up the railroad line supplying Sherman, force him to fight, and then fall back northwestward to safety in the vicinity of Blue Mountain in northeastern Alabama. Taylor also suggested, as had Hardee and others, that Davis transfer General P. G. T. Beauregard from his duties at Charleston to take command of the army. "At the same time, I did not disguise my conviction that the best we could hope for was to protract the struggle until spring," Taylor noted. Davis said he was "distressed to hear such gloomy sentiments," but Taylor asserted that he felt obligated to speak bluntly and that, on the contrary, he had not succumbed personally to despair. "It was for statesmen, not soldiers, to deal with the future," he professed.[15]

After conversing with Taylor all night, Davis left Montgomery the next morning. Taylor believed he had persuaded the president to adopt his recommendations. But Davis decided upon only a superficial course of action. Instead of replacing Hood with Beauregard, he set up a new administrative structure called the Military Division of the West, with Beauregard in command. It encompassed Taylor's department as well as the Army of Tennessee and therefore overlapped amorphously into Georgia and Tennessee. Hardee took over Beauregard's former command, the Department of South Carolina, Georgia, and Florida. Taylor discovered the true ramifications of the new arrangement when he met with Beauregard two weeks later at Blue Mountain. Beauregard had not replaced Hood. Instead, he exercised only an uncertain, almost advisory authority. Davis still had ultimate control over Hood's movements. By elevating Beauregard, the president obviously meant to deflect the public outcry against Hood while also leaving him in command of the army. "Unless Beauregard took

14. McMurry, *John Bell Hood*, pp. 152–53; Woodworth, *Jefferson Davis and His Generals*, pp. 290–91; Richard Taylor, *Destruction and Reconstruction*, pp. 250–51.

15. Richard Taylor, *Destruction and Reconstruction*, pp. 251–52 (quotations); Woodworth, *Jefferson Davis and His Generals*, pp. 291–92.

charge of Hood's army, there was nothing for him to do except to command me," Taylor later observed. "Here was a repetition of 1863 [when] Johnston was sent with a roving commission to command Bragg in Tennessee, Pemberton in Mississippi, and others in sundry places. The result was that he commanded nobody." [16]

Emphasizing to Beauregard the temporary wisdom of having Hood operate north of Atlanta against Sherman's supply lines, Taylor expressed his "readiness to take any command, division, brigade, or regiment to which [Beauregard] might assign me, and, above all, the necessity of prompt action." As if he had been left on the sidelines of the war, Taylor ached to have more impact than merely directing Forrest's cavalry, Maury's Mobile garrison, and "a few scattered men watching the enemy in various directions—all together hardly constituting a command for a lieutenant general, my rank." But Beauregard needed Taylor in his current post, attending to his duties as departmental commander and coordinating the concentration of supplies for the army. In fact Hood had already embarked on the very plan Taylor had suggested to Davis, moving his troops above Atlanta, destroying railroad tracks, and effectively enticing Sherman away from the city. But when Beauregard conferred with Hood on October 21, he discovered the dauntless Texan had decided that in order to lure Sherman out of Georgia he would have to seize a new initiative: a diversionary campaign into Tennessee.[17]

Although Beauregard doubted Hood's ability to succeed, he approved the plan and sent a report to Richmond. When Davis made no reply, Beauregard assumed the president's compliance in the campaign. At any rate, Beauregard urged Hood to move rapidly against the Federal forces defending Tennessee. Returning to explain matters to Taylor, Beauregard confessed that, after making a heated protest, he had finally "declined to interfere" in Hood's audacious campaign, especially when no objection came from Davis. "I could not

16. Cooper, "Jefferson Davis," pp. 198–201; Williams, *Beauregard*, pp. 241–43; McMurry, *John Bell Hood*, p. 158; Richard Taylor, *Destruction and Reconstruction*, pp. 252–53 (quotation 253).

17. Richard Taylor, *Destruction and Reconstruction*, pp. 253–54 (first quotation 253–54, second quotation 253); McMurry, *John Bell Hood*, pp. 159–61; Williams, *Beauregard*, pp. 242–43.

Pierre Gustave Toutant Beauregard, perplexed advisor to Taylor and Hood
(Jenkins Rare Book Company).

blame Beauregard," Taylor recorded. "There was nothing to be said and nothing to be done, saving to discharge one's duty to the bitter end." Taylor quickly prepared to send supplies to the army via the Mobile and Ohio Railroad, and he ordered Forrest to cooperate with Hood. Undaunted by Hood's movements, however, Sherman was preparing to abandon his supply lines at Atlanta and storm through the heart of Georgia.[18]

Having already experienced the chaos and demoralization of total war in Louisiana, Taylor expected the worst. More clearly than any other prominent Confederate officer, he realized that the existing methods of military and local civilian administration would probably not be able to save the Lower South from the combination of Sherman's concentrated invasion and assiduous enemy pressure against

18. Connelly, *Autumn of Glory*, pp. 483–90; Cooper, "Jefferson Davis," pp. 202–4; McMurry, *John Bell Hood*, pp. 161–63; Hood, *Advance and Retreat*, pp. 271–77; Richard Taylor, *Destruction and Reconstruction*, p. 254 (quotations).

numerous other peripheral points. The horror of total war required unified resistance, concentrated and potent. But President Davis's complex system of military departments, each having various districts and subdistricts with their own commanders and troops, presented a firmly entrenched maze of decentralized authority that made coordination and cooperation extremely difficult and often impossible. Designed to protect territory more than to produce the battlefield victories the Confederacy now so desperately needed, the departmental system also catered to state governors and legislatures, reducing valuable combat leaders like Taylor to the level of political intermediaries and glorified commissary and quartermaster officers. Similarly, Forrest's troopers and other potentially powerful cavalry commands often spent too much time resisting enemy raids or launching raids of their own rather than remaining available to lend support to the armies. With limited resources, dwindling manpower, and erratic civilian morale facing him, small wonder Taylor had wanted to return to the Trans-Mississippi or find a position somewhere in the army.[19]

By giving Beauregard superdepartmental command over most of the western theater, Davis had merely made a gesture toward infusing the necessary degree of centralized control. Caught in the midst of Davis's labyrinth, Beauregard struggled to understand the president's rather vague instructions and sporadic responses, while Hood continued to operate as a virtually independent army commander intent on careening recklessly into Tennessee. Conditions in the western theater required a defensive concentration that would result in major victories against Sherman. Seeing Sherman going deeper into Georgia, and with winter approaching, Hood would have improved his chances for stalling and defeating the isolated Federal army by operating on the defensive, along interior lines in Georgia, much like Taylor did during the Red River Campaign in Louisiana. Likewise, Beauregard would have proved more effective, if only as an advisor, and Taylor would have been able to employ more reliable means for sending supplies and whatever reinforcements he could muster from his department.[20]

19. Connelly and Jones, *Politics of Command*, pp. 166–95; J. P. Dyer, "Cavalry Operations in the Army of Tennessee," pp. 210–25.

20. Vandiver, "Jefferson Davis," pp. 11–13.

Hood's Tennessee campaign, a long-range offensive riddled with risks rather than with clear benefits, not only removed the advantage of a defensive concentration against Sherman but also placed a severe strain on the departmental system's ability to meet the army's needs. First, instead of striking rapidly into Tennessee, Hood was forced to turn steadily westward through northern Alabama, seeking to cross the Tennessee River at a point where Federal troops had not yet established control. This unexpected detour, accomplished without even consulting Beauregard, took Hood all the way to Tuscumbia, in the northwestern part of the state, by the end of October. He remained there for more than two weeks, waiting for necessary supplies that Taylor had difficulty forwarding because of deteriorating railroads and a lack of enough mechanics to produce new track quickly. "We had no means of repairing the long lines of railway," Taylor recalled. "Even when unbroken by [enemy] raids, wear and tear rendered them inefficient from an early period of the struggle." Hood also decided to wait for Forrest to return from a raid in western Tennessee, and then bad weather hampered the army's movements as well. Fully cognizant of Hood's intentions by now, Sherman had already detached about thirty thousand men from his own force, sending them north under Major General George H. Thomas to reinforce troops near Nashville. "I well knew the delay at Tuscumbia would accrue to the advantage of Sherman," Hood later acknowledged. "I believed, however, I could still get between Thomas's forces and Nashville, and rout them. . . . These convictions counterbalanced my regret that Sherman was permitted to traverse Georgia 'unopposed,' as he himself admits."[21]

The hellish problem of supplying Hood only compounded the administrative nightmare confronting Taylor as departmental commander. On the eve of the Tennessee campaign, an admiring Forrest sent words of encouragement, painting a decidedly cheerful picture of Taylor's regime. "Twelve months ago I entered your department

21. Connelly, *Autumn of Glory*, pp. 485–90; Williams, *Beauregard*, pp. 244–45; *O.R.*, 39(3):845–47, 880, 903–4, 913; Richard Taylor, *Destruction and Reconstruction*, pp. 247–48 (first quotation); Woodworth, *Jefferson Davis and His Generals*, pp. 294–98; Hood, *Advance and Retreat*, p. 278 (second quotation).

and found the people groaning under the most cruel and merciless oppression," wrote Forrest. "They were despondent and traitors exultant. I leave the department in security and the people hopeful." Although grateful for such sentiments, Taylor perceived a far different state of affairs. Reporting to Secretary of War James A. Seddon in late October, he confessed, "Since reaching the department I have visited nearly every section of it [and] have found its condition to be certainly very deplorable." Most of the command structure was in disarray, prompting him to compile a "long list of officers for whom there is no appropriate or necessary duty" and who should be reassigned or decommissioned. Writing to his various district commanders about the same time, Taylor asserted, "The number of posts within this department is very large, certainly exceeding fifty, at points where the necessity . . . by no means exists. . . . Besides the pernicious influence which is exerted by these innumerable hiding places from active service, the expense of keeping them up" seemed reason enough to abolish most of them.[22]

Corrupt officers at many of these posts engaged in secret traffic with the enemy by exchanging Confederate-owned cotton for gold or sterling, thus depriving the army of the supplies that should have been acquired according to the government's new policy of allowing such trade. These officers also acted as middlemen negotiating illegal subcontracts with civilians to trade privately owned cotton to the enemy for food and merchandise. Describing to Secretary Seddon these "immense frauds upon the government," Taylor bemoaned the "evil effects of the system both upon the citizens and soldiery." In an effort to stem the abuses, he issued harsh orders to restrict cotton trading to the procurement of supplies for military use. But with the civilian population suffering from glaring shortages of basic provisions, the temptation to engage in illegal trading proved overwhelming. "You cannot form a conception of the demoralization existing everywhere in regard to trading in cotton," reported Brigadier General George B. Hodge, commander of the District of Southwest Mississippi and East Louisiana. "I am looked upon as the common enemy

22. *O.R.*, 39(3):915 (first quotation), 860–63 (second quotation 860), 848–49 (third quotation).

of every age, sex, and condition. You could not credit it were I to attempt to describe to you the universal desire to engage in the trade." Hodge had recently seized from citizens almost a thousand bales in small lots of two and three bales each. "So you see I am not popular. . . . My life is a very lonely one," he grumbled.[23]

In Louisiana Taylor had burned cotton to prevent its confiscation by invading enemy forces. Now he was forced to regulate a revised Confederate trading policy designed to help the army while clamping down on private traffic. Planters' insistence on producing cotton largely to the exclusion of other commodities, all in the hopes of continuing profits, had left the army unable to benefit fully from the South's greatest economic asset. "We set up a monarch . . . King Cotton, and hedged him with a divinity surpassing that of earthly potentates," Taylor asserted in his memoirs. "There was a complete mental derangement on this subject. . . . Our people were much debauched by it." Attempts to enforce the army's trading policy proved the absurd extent of the South's cotton mania. Officers who replaced those guilty of profiteering on government-owned cotton usually took up the same vice. But the more stringently enforced restrictions against civilian trading brought Taylor a more palpable kind of grief. Women with "suffering children" and "whose husbands were in the war or already fallen, would beseech me for permits to take cotton through the lines," he recalled. Although he appealed to the War Department for authority to allow these families to trade with the enemy, his requests were denied. "This did not give food and clothing to their children, and they departed, believing me to be an unfeeling brute." They were left but one recourse: to trade the cotton illegally.[24]

Even worse public demoralization resulted from a proliferation of unauthorized military impressments of private property. Post commanders routinely cooperated with Confederate provost guard of-

23. Ibid., pp. 860–61 (first quotation 861), 898–99 (second and third quotations 899), and (2):863–64.
24. Lebergott, "Why the South Lost," pp. 72–73; Richard Taylor, *Destruction and Reconstruction*, pp. 287–88 (first quotation 287, second and third quotations 288); *O.R.*, 45(2):777, 802.

ficers and soldiers, operating in the guise of military police, to intimidate citizens into surrendering their property. "The land swarmed with these vermin, appointed without due authority, or self-constituted, who robbed the people of horses, mules, cattle, corn, and meat," Taylor recounted. "The wretched peasants of the middle ages could not have suffered more from the 'free companies' turned loose upon them." Taylor had never seen public abuse on this scale in Louisiana. Deeply incensed, he banished the provost guard from his department and instructed army officers and local officials to treat all violators of impressment regulations as marauders and thieves. Although illegal seizures soon declined, the hardship of enduring even authorized impressments still caused widespread discontent, especially after the severe winter of 1864–65.[25]

As in Louisiana, destitution aggravated the frequency of soldiers deserting to return home to care for their afflicted families. Many deserters, however, became fugitive jayhawkers bent on plundering the countryside. Mississippi seemed especially plagued by this malignancy. Legal authority in the state nearly evaporated, with sheriffs abdicating their offices, judges failing to ride their circuits, and grand juries refusing to return indictments for fear of violent retaliation from bands of as many as eight hundred mounted jayhawkers. "The state is now under the tacit rule of deserters, thieves, and disloyal men and women," a citizen declared in the spring of 1864. Writing in mid-October to Major General Franklin Gardner, commander of the District of North Mississippi, Taylor asserted, "There are immense numbers of absentees from the army within your district." He prodded Gardner to "leave no efforts untried to ferret them out and enforce their prompt return to their colors." Realizing as he had in Louisiana that circumstances demanded discretion, however, Taylor suggested that deserters who surrendered voluntarily "be permitted to do so with the assurance they will neither be shot nor otherwise severely punished." By the end of 1864 Governor Charles Clark was offering

25. Richard Taylor, *Destruction and Reconstruction*, pp. 254–55 (quotation); Radley, *Rebel Watchdog*, pp. 238–40; *O.R.*, 39(3):861–62 and 45(2):688–89, 701–2; Bettersworth, *Confederate Mississippi*, pp. 81–84; McMillan, *Disintegration of a Confederate State*, pp. 88–89.

amnesty to any army deserter who would agree to join the state militia in order to track down other deserters.[26]

Although Taylor repeatedly looked to the state reserve and militia system to keep public order and lend military and logistical support to the army, the epidemic of desertions and lawlessness undermined his authority at every turn. In a confidential letter to President Davis in late November, Judge Robert S. Hudson of Leake County, Mississippi, alleged, "The State reserves is composed mostly of persons liable to and deserters from the general Confederate service; and the State militia is composed mostly of deserters and persons belonging or liable to the other two branches of service. This is not only true of privates generally, but of officers also." Deserters and conscripts often enlisted under false names in the reserves or the militia to evade army service. "A large number of persons calling themselves 'scouts' and 'independent companies' . . . are nothing less than murderers, plunderers, blockade-runners, and Yankee communicants," wrote Judge Hudson. "They are principally young men and deserters. . . . The citizen is their victim in his purse and property."[27]

Obstructive state statutes and defiant politicians also worked to foil Taylor's appeals for help from the militias. "The laws of Alabama on the subject of the State militia are of such a character as to enable us to derive no benefit from them," he reported to Beauregard in late October. "No authority exists to order the greater portion of the militia out of their own counties. . . . In Mississippi the militia can only be called out for thirty days at a time, fresh calls or proclamations having to be made at the expiration of each thirty days." Governor Thomas H. Watts of Alabama applied earnest pressure to have the militia laws amended, but the legislature delayed making a decision and finally refused to take action. Mississippi's Governor Clark assured Taylor of his desire to cooperate but then resisted relinquishing militia units to army supervision and control. Completely frustrated over the lack of militia even to reinforce the tiny Confederate garrison at Mobile, a strategic point vital to the ultimate security of both

26. Dubay, "Mississippi," pp. 128–29; Harris, *Presidential Reconstruction in Mississippi*, p. 11 (first quotation); *O.R.*, 39(3):838–39 (second and third quotations 839), 806 (fourth quotation), and 49(1):930–31, 950–51.

27. *O.R.*, 45(1):1246–48 (quotations 1247) and 49(1):941.

Alabama and Mississippi, Taylor informed the Confederate high command in mid-November, "Should the enemy operate seriously against Mobile the place must fall."[28]

During an inspection at Mobile, Taylor encountered several hundred slaves laboring on the city's fortifications. Like many of the bondsmen captured during Taylor's command in Louisiana, they had fallen into Forrest's hands during a recent raid behind enemy lines in Tennessee, allowing Taylor no opportunity to return them to their masters. Concerned about their welfare, he visited their camps and spoke to one of their "leaders," inquiring about the food they were receiving. "Thank you, Massa General," the slave replied, "they give us plenty of good victuals; but how do you like our work?" Taylor affirmed that they had "worked very well." The slave then commented, "If you will give us guns we will fight for these works, too. We would rather fight for our own white folks than for strangers." Taylor had no doubt that "this was true." Although he never advocated such a policy, several other high-ranking officers, including Robert E. Lee, would soon press for the emancipation of slaves whose masters were willing to let them take up arms, but this radical notion did not reach fruition until shortly before the end of the war, too late for any black Confederate units to see combat. Despite Taylor's confidence in their desire to fight, only a minuscule number throughout the South actually volunteered. In the fall of 1864 Jefferson Davis was having a hard enough struggle with the Confederate Congress over his proposal to buy freedom for slaves to work on military projects. Davis also eventually supported the idea of emancipation for black soldiers, but both proposals proved so antithetical to most southerners' determination to protect slavery that Congress balked angrily at the president's arguments. The fact that these overtures had gained serious consideration in late 1864, however, underscored the South's desperate circumstances.[29]

Taylor was at Meridian on November 16 when he received an as-

28. Ibid., 39(3):855–57 (first quotation 856), 910 (second quotation), and 45(2):683, 688, 722–24; McMillan, *Disintegration of a Confederate State*, pp. 98–109; Bettersworth, *Confederate Mississippi*, pp. 56, 69–75.

29. Richard Taylor, *Destruction and Reconstruction*, pp. 256–57 (quotations 257); Durden, *Gray and Black*, pp. 101–42, 187–290.

tonishing telegram from Beauregard. Scouting reports indicated that
Sherman was on the march from Atlanta toward Augusta or Macon
with more than sixty thousand men. Beauregard ordered Taylor to
come immediately "with the available forces you can spare from your
department and assume command of all troops in Georgia operating
against Sherman." But with Forrest assisting Hood and only skeleton
forces defending Mobile and other points, and with the militia units
of Mississippi and Alabama tightly in the clutches of jealous politicians, Taylor had nothing to offer but himself. The only troops standing in Sherman's path consisted of Major General Joseph Wheeler's
cavalry, ten thousand at the very most, and a few thousand green
Georgia militia soldiers, mainly draft evaders, teenage boys, and men
too old for conscription. "You will cut and block up all dirt roads in
advance of [Sherman]; remove or destroy supplies of all kinds in his
front," Beauregard instructed Taylor. "Wheeler's cavalry will harass
his flanks and rear."[30]

Beauregard was now scurrying around northern Alabama and
Mississippi trying to equip Hood with enough supplies to coax him
into finally moving his army into Tennessee. But he took enough time
on the seventeenth to dash off another nervous telegram to Taylor:
"Adopt Fabian system. Don't run risk of losing your active forces and
guns . . . to hold any one place or position, but harass at all points.
Hannibal held heart of Italy sixteen years, and then was defeated. Be
cool and confident, and all will yet be right." Aware that Hannibal at
least had enjoyed the advantage of not facing Sherman, Taylor sent a
brief telegram to Wheeler, simply advising him, "Hang on enemy's
rear and flanks doing all you can to impede his march and destroy
everything on his line of march that cannot be saved."[31]

Taylor went immediately to Montgomery, where he took advantage
of railroad connections that carried him to Macon in central Georgia.
He arrived at dawn on November 22. "It was the bitterest weather I
remember in this latitude," he wrote. "The ground was frozen and

30. *O.R.*, 45(1):1213 (quotations). See also Samuel Cooper to Richard Taylor, November 30, 1864, Taylor Papers, Jackson Barracks.

31. *O.R.*, 45(1):1214–18 (first quotation 1218); Richard Taylor to Joseph
Wheeler, November 19, 1864 (second quotation), Richard Taylor Private Telegram Book.

some snow was falling." At Macon he conferred with Major General Howell Cobb, commander of the District of Georgia. A former Speaker of the United States House and member of Buchanan's cabinet, Cobb had served in the Confederate Congress before joining the army. Offering to take Taylor on an inspection of the town's fortifications, Cobb admitted having only some inexperienced conscripts to defend against Sherman's troops, who had been sighted only twelve miles to the north the previous day. Calmly warming himself next to a fireplace in Cobb's home, Taylor declined to inspect the fortifications and instead asked Cobb to "order work upon them to be stopped, so that his men could get by a fire, as I then was and intended to remain." Macon was "the safest place in Georgia," Taylor insisted. An incredulous Cobb nervously complied. In a few minutes Brigadier General William W. Mackall, in charge of building the town's fortifications, arrived and questioned Cobb's order to halt work. Taylor explained that if the Yankees had wanted to take Macon they would have done so already. "This greatly comforted Cobb, who up to that moment held me to be a lunatic," he recalled.[32]

Unlike Cobb, Taylor perceived that Sherman intended to march as rapidly as possible toward his prime objective, the Atlantic coast, rather than waste time seizing every town along the route. While Cobb and Taylor were eating breakfast, a scouting report informed them that the enemy had turned east of Macon, confirming Taylor's supposition. Soon Governor Joseph E. Brown, one of the president's most despised political enemies, arrived to see Taylor, much to Cobb's displeasure since he and the governor were not even on speaking terms. Smoothing over their animosity, Taylor welcomed Brown, who had just fled for his safety from Milledgeville, the state capital. Accompanying him were Robert A. Toombs, state adjutant general, and Gustavus W. Smith, commander of the Georgia militia, both of whom had resigned in dissatisfaction from the army as general officers. At that very moment Smith's militia, also known as Joe Brown's army in honor of the governor's stubborn disobedience to Confederate conscription, was headed east into Sherman's path. Learning this, Taylor advised Smith to retrieve his men instantly. But Smith acted too late

32. Richard Taylor, *Destruction and Reconstruction*, pp. 257–58 (first quotation 257, second, third, and fourth quotations 258).

to avert bloodshed. Although he had ordered his officers to avoid a fight, the militia ran up against the Yankees near Griswoldville, about ten miles from Macon, sustaining heavy losses although performing boldly throughout the day.[33]

Taylor then ordered Smith to prepare to move his force south to Savannah via rail connections through Albany and Thomasville. Lapsing into an irritated frame of mind, Taylor wired Beauregard, "I can accomplish nothing by remaining here. Telegraph me today at this place what you wish me to do." "Await my arrival at Macon," Beauregard replied. Two days later, on the twenty-fourth, Beauregard reached Macon, approved the evacuation of Smith's militia, and ordered Taylor to proceed as well to Savannah to confer with General Hardee, commander of the city's garrison. Remaining in Macon, Beauregard sent Hood a strained telegram: "Sherman's movement is progressing rapidly toward Atlantic Coast. . . . It is essential you should take offensive and crush enemy's force in Middle Tennessee."[34]

Taylor arrived at Savannah late at night on November 29 and spent the next two days there. "Hardee's force was inadequate to the defense of Savannah," Taylor recalled. He advised Hardee to "prepare to abandon the place before he was shut up" inside by Sherman. Although Wheeler's cavalry had been clashing with Yankee troopers and nipping at Sherman's flanks almost every step of the way, the massive invading army had cut a swath of havoc at least fifty miles wide through the state, pillaging and destroying property, tearing up railroad tracks, and terrorizing civilians. Sherman reached Savannah on December 10, established communications with the Union navy off the coast, and called up siege guns from the Union garrison at Port Royal, South Carolina. Meanwhile Hardee, acting under Beauregard's direct supervision, made plans to evacuate the city according

33. Ibid., pp. 259–60; William Y. Thompson, *Robert Toombs*, pp. 214–15; Gustavus W. Smith, "Georgia Militia During Sherman's March," p. 667; McInvale, "'All That Devils Could Wish For,'" pp. 117–30.

34. Richard Taylor, *Destruction and Reconstruction*, p. 260; Richard Taylor to P. G. T. Beauregard, November 22, 1864 (first quotation), Richard Taylor Private Telegram Book; *O.R.*, 45(1):1237 (second quotation), 1242–43 (third quotation 1243).

to Taylor's suggestions. Holding out as long as possible in the face of Sherman's demand to surrender, on the twentieth he led his small force across a pontoon bridge spanning the Savannah River and then regrouped to resist Sherman's further advance through South Carolina.[35]

While passing through Georgia on the return trip to his department, Taylor chanced to meet Major Henry Wirz, commandant of the prisoner of war stockade at Andersonville. Wirz seemed acutely concerned about the prisoners' sufferings, complaining that he had no blankets or wagons for transporting fuel to keep the men from freezing. He showed Taylor copies of requisitions he had submitted to army authorities for assistance, and Taylor endorsed them in hopes of gaining action on Wirz's behalf. "He appeared to be earnest in his desire to mitigate the condition of his prisoners," Taylor recalled. Referring to the North's postwar vengeance toward Wirz, which resulted in the only legally sanctioned death of a Confederate officer, Taylor noted, "There can be little doubt that his execution was a 'sop' to the passions of the 'many-headed.'"[36]

Taylor had left Savannah so suddenly because President Davis had telegraphed him on December 1 saying that he would be "needed in the West." Returning to Meridian, he soon learned of Hood's suicidal assault at Franklin on November 30 and then of his complete repulse at Nashville on December 15 and 16. "It is painful to criticize Hood's conduct of this campaign," Taylor later observed. "He was a splendid leader in battle, and as a brigade or division commander unsurpassed; but, arrived at higher rank, he seems to have been impatient of control." Hood had openly condemned Johnston's defensive maneuvers north of Atlanta in July, and throughout the Tennessee campaign he consistently ignored Beauregard's direction and authority. But Davis had wanted an aggressive general to lead the Army of Tennessee, and Hood filled the bill. "Unwillingness to obey is often interpreted by governments into capacity for command," Taylor concluded sardonically. Although Hood took sole responsibility for his

35. Richard Taylor to Lafayette McLaws, November 27, 1864, Taylor Papers, Jackson Barracks; Richard Taylor, *Destruction and Reconstruction*, pp. 261–64 (quotations 262); Williams, *Beauregard*, pp. 247–48.

36. Richard Taylor, *Destruction and Reconstruction*, p. 264 (quotations).

Tennessee catastrophe, Davis, to his discredit, afterward blamed
Beauregard for devising the campaign and then mismanaging it. Re-
gardless, Hood's defeat and the fall of Savannah had brought the
Confederacy to its knees.[37]

Taylor received a strong indication of the condition of Hood's army
in a blunt letter from Forrest in early January. "The Army of Tennessee was badly defeated and is greatly demoralized," Forrest reported,
"and to save it during the retreat from Nashville I was compelled almost to sacrifice my command." Thanks to Forrest's cavalry, Hood's
surviving troops had narrowly escaped across the Tennessee River. A
few days later Taylor saw for himself these broken remnants in camp
at Tupelo, Mississippi. "This was my first view of a beaten army," he
recalled, "and a painful sight it was. Many guns and small arms had
been lost, and the ranks were depleted by thousands of prisoners and
missing. Blankets, shoes, clothing, and accouterments were wanting."
Exposed to the icy weather, many fell victim to frostbite and some
died. Taylor immediately utilized the Mobile and Ohio railroad line
to begin transporting the men to Meridian, where shelter and supplies were available.[38]

Even now, however, the president was pressuring Beauregard to
send as many soldiers as possible to help Hardee against Sherman in
South Carolina. This prompted Taylor to send a telegram to Davis on
January 9, 1865. "The army needs rest, consolidation, and reorganization," he contended. "If moved in its present condition, it will prove
utterly worthless." Refusing to accept excuses for the men, Davis insisted, "The presence of those veterans will no doubt greatly increase
the auxiliary force now with Hardee." On the fifteenth Taylor again
informed the president that "an attempt to move Hood's army at this
time would complete its destruction." Although Beauregard firmly
supported Taylor's views, arguing that the Mobile garrison needed

37. Richard Taylor to P. G. T. Beauregard, December 1, 1864 (first quotation), Richard Taylor Private Telegram Book; Richard Taylor, *Destruction and
Reconstruction*, pp. 264–65 (second and third quotations 265); Connelly, *Autumn of Glory*, pp. 489–90.

38. *O.R.*, 45(2):756–57 (first quotation 756); Chalmers, "Forrest and His
Campaigns," pp. 482–83; Richard Taylor, *Destruction and Reconstruction*, pp.
266–67 (second quotation 267).

reinforcements more than Hardee did, Davis conceded only that Taylor should retain one corps from the army along with Forrest's cavalry. "To this I hoped you would be able to add many reserves and militia," he told Taylor.[39]

In the midst of this controversy Beauregard was taking steps to remove Hood from command of the army and replace him with Taylor. Having already gained the president's permission, Beauregard found his task made easier when Hood asked to be relieved on January 13. But in a letter to Davis on January 18 Taylor protested the appointment, asserting, "The army and the public unanimously desire General Johnston. This alone will restore confidence. . . . Johnston should be sent at once. The safety of the country demands it." Taylor again suggested that he could "do more in the Trans-Mississippi, either in crossing troops or creating a diversion." Catching wind of Taylor's impending appointment, officers and men in the army petitioned the president to give them Johnston instead of Taylor. Soon afterward the Confederate Congress passed a resolution imploring Davis to restore Johnston. Senator Louis T. Wigfall, one of Davis's most strident critics, declared, "No one but the President's worst enemy would advise him to . . . place in command his own brother-in-law."[40]

Disregarding this clamor, Davis considered the matter closed. On January 23, 1865, Taylor reluctantly assumed command of the Army of Tennessee, retaining as well his authority over the Department of Alabama, Mississippi, and East Louisiana. Davis, however, still expected that most of the army would move east to reinforce Hardee. By January 30 Taylor agreed. "Sherman's movements render a victory necessary to us at once, and it will require all our means to insure it," he telegraphed Beauregard. Strangely enough, neither Davis nor

39. *O.R.*, 45(2):772 (first quotation), 778–80 (second quotation 779), 785 (third quotation), 789, 791 (fourth quotation). See also Richard Taylor to P. G. T. Beauregard, January 15, 1864, Richard Taylor Letter Book.

40. Williams, *Beauregard*, p. 249; *O.R.*, 45(2):781, 784–85, 789, 805; Richard Taylor to Jefferson Davis, January 18, 1865 (first and second quotations), Richard Taylor Letter Book; McMurry, *John Bell Hood*, p. 183; Connelly, *Autumn of Glory*, p. 517; Vandiver, "Proceedings of the Second Confederate Congress," pp. 303–6 (third quotation 306).

Beauregard ever expected Taylor to accompany the army he was supposed to command. He would have his hands full in his own department. In any case, the once grand Army of Tennessee hardly constituted an army at all any more. Hood had marched into Tennessee with almost forty thousand men, but casualties and desertions had reduced that number by about half. Even after absorbing Hardee's troops and other units in the Carolinas, the army offered a pathetic challenge to Sherman. With Beauregard now on the scene in South Carolina, command fell to him by default, but the thunderous public demand for Johnston's appointment only intensified. Finally, Robert E. Lee added his own name to the list of petitioners, and President Davis, although more contemptuous than ever toward Johnston, capitulated in disgust. On February 23 Johnston resumed command of the Army of Tennessee, such as it was.[41]

Johnston faced a monstrous challenge, but Taylor was just as badly fixed. Expecting simultaneous advances by George H. Thomas's Army of the Cumberland from the north and Brigadier General E. R. S. Canby's large force threatening Mobile from the south, Taylor had far too few soldiers to protect his department. Beauregard, for one, fully appreciated Taylor's poverty of manpower. On January 24 he informed the president that, even after diverting part of the Army of Tennessee to the Mobile garrison, Taylor's entire department would still have only about twenty thousand men, a liberal estimate at best. "Unless Kirby Smith is compelled to reinforce Taylor, or to attack St. Louis or New Orleans, it will be impossible to defend successfully the states of Mississippi and Alabama," Beauregard warned. A month later, as Sherman pushed relentlessly through South Carolina, Beauregard envisioned an even more fantastic scenario, a desperate plan he believed would win the war. He telegraphed Davis, urging him to send twenty thousand men from Virginia to form a concentration with the Army of Tennessee in the Carolinas against Sherman, "to give him battle there and crush him; then to concentrate all forces against Grant [in Virginia], and then to march on Washington and dictate a peace." Receiving no reply to this bizarre proposal, Beauregard scribbled a note on the back of his retained copy of the telegram:

41. *O.R.*, 49(1):929, 949 (quotation); Horn, *Army of Tennessee*, pp. 422–23; Connelly, *Autumn of Glory*, pp. 517–22.

"Not answered by the President—as he usually did when the responsibility was too great or any recommendation came from me."[42]

During February and early March the enemy's designs against Taylor seemed stymied. But he had enough problems just keeping his department from lurching into bankruptcy. Typifying a crisis that plagued all parts of the Confederacy, he notified Secretary of War John C. Breckinridge on February 14: "Unless something is done promptly to meet the current expenses of this department it will be useless to attempt to hold the country comprising it. . . . Without cash payments, railroads, steam-boats, citizens, and soldiers will no longer work, sell, or fight." The government's system of taxation and sales of bonds had completely failed to produce enough revenue to sustain the war effort. Instead of paying their taxes and buying bonds, most planters had simply invested their money in growing more cotton, thus crippling the government financially. Aware that the Treasury had no funds to give him, Taylor asked for authority to sell Confederate-owned cotton to the Federals for hard specie to pay his debts. Within a few weeks his request met approval. At the same time, however, he ordered his officers to be prepared to burn all cotton, government and private alike, "whenever the enemy's movements may make it necessary . . . to prevent its falling into the hands of the enemy."[43]

"I had long dismissed all thought of the future," Taylor later admitted. "The duty of a soldier in the field is simple—to fight until stopped by the civil arm of his government, or his government has ceased to exist[,] . . . and the month of March came round to raise the curtain for the last act of the bloody drama." Scouting reports indicated that Thomas would move from Tennessee into central Alabama, where the South's richest deposits of iron and coal fostered the production of heavy ordnance, navy ironclads, munitions, and other weaponry vital to the Confederate struggle. "At Selma was a foundry, where the best ordnance I have seen was made of Briarsfield iron,"

42. O.R., 49(1):929 (first quotation); Roman, Military Operations of General Beauregard, 2:355 (second quotation); P. G. T. Beauregard to Jefferson Davis, February 21, 1865 (third quotation), item 221 in Rosenbach Company, History of America in Documents, p. 64.

43. O.R., 49(1):978–79 (quotation), 1044, 1059–60 and (2):1122–23; Lebergott, "Why the South Lost," pp. 66–74.

Taylor recalled, "and, as this would naturally attract the enemy's attention . . . I endeavored to prepare for him." The defense of Alabama would depend totally on Forrest's cavalry, which had spent the past two months recovering from Hood's Tennessee campaign while also performing the odious task of tracking down jayhawkers and deserters. "Desertion in the army is now an epidemic," Beauregard commiserated from North Carolina on March 7. "They deserted by hundreds from the [railroad] cars on the way here. The same complaint reaches us from Lee's army. Only an active campaign and some brilliant successes can put a stop to that disorder."[44]

General Lee, now burdened with the role of general-in-chief of southern armies, could provide Taylor with only the vaguest sort of advice and encouragement. "I recommend that you concentrate your troops as much as possible so as to collect an army strong enough to defeat the columns of the enemy in detail," Lee wrote on March 15. "Place valuable stores and government property as far as practicable in places of safety." Taylor especially wanted to evacuate as much equipment and munitions from Selma as possible, but Commander Catesby ap R. Jones, in charge of the huge Naval Gun Foundry and Ordnance Works at Selma, reported: "Our machinery is very heavy and there is a great deal of it. Under favorable circumstances it would require weeks to remove it, and it would be months before we could get it in operation elsewhere." On March 16 Taylor met with Forrest at his headquarters at West Point, Mississippi, to plan a strategy for defending the region north of Selma. Ten days later scouts reported three Federal cavalry columns moving southward from Tennessee. Taylor dispatched a reassuring message to Robert E. Lee: "My intention is to meet and whip these detached columns before they can advance far into the country or unite with each other."[45]

44. Richard Taylor, *Destruction and Reconstruction*, pp. 266–67 (first quotation 266–67, second quotation 267); McMillan, *Alabama Confederate Reader*, pp. 288–91; James Pickett Jones, *Yankee Blitzkrieg*, pp. 39–40, 46–50, 75–79; *O.R.*, 49(1):1041–42 (third quotation 1042).

45. Robert E. Lee to Richard Taylor, March 15, 1865 (first quotation), Taylor Papers, Jackson Barracks; *O.R.*, 49(1):1060 (second quotation), and (2):1160–61 (third quotation 1161); Chalmers, "Forrest and His Campaigns," pp. 484–85; James Pickett Jones, *Yankee Blitzkrieg*, pp. 50–52, 58.

The Yankees confronting Forrest were not mere detached elements from Thomas's army but in fact represented the largest mounted force ever assembled on American soil, three divisions totaling 12,500 cavalrymen commanded by the dynamic twenty-seven-year-old Brigadier General James H. Wilson. Wilson's troopers also enjoyed the support of 250 supply wagons, guarded by an additional 1,500 soldiers he intended to mount with captured horses along the way. Most impressive of all, every man was armed with a Spencer repeating carbine, a new rifle capable of delivering seven shots, and with rapid breech reloading. To fight this swarming horde of invaders, Forrest had mustered all the cavalrymen he could find, as many as 10,000 according to some estimates, but probably no more than 7- or 8,000. "His whole force [was] inferior to Wilson's," Taylor observed, "but he was a host in himself, and a dangerous adversary to meet at any reasonable odds." Wilson quickly sought to render the odds as unreasonable as possible. "The Federal commander moved with unusual rapidity, and threw out false signals," Taylor admitted. By the twenty-ninth Wilson's main strike force of horsemen had reached Elyton, present-day Birmingham, where they initiated their mission of destroying blast furnaces, rolling mills, and ironworks along a route stretching southward to Montevallo. The sudden obliteration of this industrial corridor, the source of some of the world's finest iron, meant a sure death for Selma's military production. By the morning of the thirty-first Wilson was poised to hammer Selma itself, only about fifty miles farther south.[46]

Meanwhile Taylor had hurried to Selma, arriving there on the twenty-ninth to supervise Forrest's operations. Having learned that Canby had begun besieging Mobile a few days earlier, Taylor telegraphed Forrest at midnight on the thirtieth: "Our object is to defeat the enemy as far north of [Selma] as we can. . . . This force we can easily whip, and then raise the siege of Mobile." The next day he repeated to Forrest, "If you can beat the force in your front we can relieve Mobile." But Wilson's cavalrymen had moved so swiftly and

46. James Pickett Jones, *Yankee Blitzkrieg*, pp. 58–64; Henry, *Forrest*, pp. 422–29; Chalmers, "Forrest and His Campaigns," pp. 484–85; Starr, *Union Cavalry in the Civil War*, 1:29–34; Richard Taylor, *Destruction and Reconstruction*, pp. 267–68 (quotations 268).

deceptively that Forrest had trouble concentrating his scattered brigades. He had only a few thousand men gathered south of Montevallo when Wilson caught them out of position late on the thirty-first, sparking two days of running combat that forced the outnumbered Confederates into a continual withdrawal. "I can make no fight until I can concentrate," a disturbed Forrest wired Taylor. At Ebenezer Church on April 1 he decided to make a stand behind quickly constructed defensive works. "Forrest fought as if the world depended on his arm," wrote Taylor. After a series of sharp assaults, Wilson's men broke through, compelling the southerners to retreat all the way to Selma. During the fight Forrest himself sustained a slashing saber wound on his arm.[47]

On the morning of April 2 the valiant band of Confederates found refuge behind Selma's breastworks. "Forrest appeared, horse and man covered with blood, and announced the enemy at his heels," Taylor recounted. "I felt anxious for him, but he said he was unhurt and would cut his way through." News of Wilson's approach had the town reeling in pandemonium. Exacerbating the chaos, Taylor ordered all transportable government property out of the enemy's reach. "Long trains of cars loaded with stores and prisoners were being dispatched [westward] toward Demopolis," wrote one of Forrest's men. "Steamers at the landing were being loaded with other stores of all description to be sent up the [Alabama] river to Montgomery. The streets were thronged with wagons and drays, laden with boxes, barrels, and parts of machinery, and being driven in confusion in all directions." Leaving Forrest to defend the town, late that afternoon Taylor jumped aboard the last available means of railroad transportation, a small yard engine, just as a body of Wilson's troopers appeared. "Before headway was attained the enemy was upon us, and capture seemed inevitable," Taylor recalled. But the Yankees fired wildly, with

47. Richard Taylor to Nathan Bedford Forrest, March 30 (first quotation), 31 (second quotation), 1865, Richard Taylor Private Telegram Book; James Pickett Jones, *Yankee Blitzkrieg*, pp. 64–73; Starr, *Union Cavalry in the Civil War*, 1:34–36; Henry, *Forrest*, pp. 429–31; Nathan Bedford Forrest to Richard Taylor, April 1, 1865 (third quotation), Brent Papers, Louisiana State Museum; Richard Taylor, *Destruction and Reconstruction*, p. 268 (fourth quotation).

little effect. "The driver and stoker, both negroes, were as game as possible," wrote Taylor, "and as we thundered across Cahaba bridge, all safe, raised a loud 'Yah! yah!' of triumph, and smiled like two sable angels."[48]

Incredibly, most of Forrest's cavalrymen were still scattered and had not yet joined him. Distracted by roving contingents of Wilson's men, their officers had misunderstood Forrest's orders to concentrate against the enemy's main force, and now they were bogged down trying to cross a series of swollen steams somewhere northwest of Selma. The night before departing Selma, Taylor had telegraphed Robert E. Lee to convey this piece of bad news, explaining that Wilson's success had resulted directly from "the failure of Forrest's command to join him in time." Left with no reinforcements to help defend Selma, Forrest recruited several hundred civilian volunteers along with some equally inexperienced local militiamen. Adding this ragtag bunch to his already depleted ranks, he had no more than four thousand men to face about nine thousand Federals. With sunset approaching, Wilson's troopers dismounted and charged the town's breastworks, firing their Spencer carbines as they advanced. "The massive lines poured out an unceasing stream of leaden hail, to which the return fire was that of a skirmish detachment," a Confederate recalled. Forrest's men held their positions courageously, but most of the civilians and militiamen froze in panic and fled. The Yankees bolted through the gaps. "The scene was one of wild confusion," a southerner recounted. "The Confederates, beaten from their breastworks, rushed to their horses, while the streets were choked with soldiers and citizens hurrying wildly to and fro." Forrest escaped with less than half his force, and Wilson's men soon put the torch to Selma's ordnance and munitions factories, burning many other buildings in the process. That same night Lee evacuated Richmond. Grant's troops entered the Confederate capital the next day.[49]

48. Richard Taylor, *Destruction and Reconstruction*, pp. 268–69 (first quotation 268, third and fourth quotations 269); Dinkins, "Last Campaign of Forrest's Cavalry," p. 177 (second quotation).

49. James Pickett Jones, *Yankee Blitzkrieg*, pp. 80–95; Richard Taylor to Robert E. Lee, April 1, 1865 (first quotation), Richard Taylor Private Telegram Book; Starr, *Union Cavalry in the Civil War*, 1:37–43; Dinkins, "Last

After spending a few days in Selma, Wilson turned toward Montgomery and continued east into Georgia, destroying railroad lines and everything else of military value in his path while attempting to avoid damaging private property. "[Wilson's] soldierly qualities are entitled to respect," Taylor later noted, "for of all the Federal expeditions of which I have any knowledge, his was the best conducted." Having tasted defeat for the first time, Forrest received a brief telegram from Taylor stating the obvious: "It is useless to fight [the] enemy until we are strong enough to whip him." Proceeding immediately to Mobile, Taylor spent two days conferring with Maury and departed believing the garrison would continue to resist Canby's siege. Returning to his headquarters at Meridian on April 5, Taylor wired Forrest, "At Mobile everything goes on well. Yankees have gained nothing thus far." But during the next several days Canby's vastly superior force gradually prevailed, capturing Fort Blakely and its 2,800 defenders on April 9. By the twelfth Maury had evacuated Spanish Fort, escaping the city with the 4,500 soldiers still under his command and moving them by rail northward to Meridian. "Forrest and Maury [together] had about eight thousand men, but tried and true," Taylor recalled. "Cattle were shod, wagons overhauled, and every preparation for rapid movement made." [50]

On the fourteenth Taylor dispatched a telegram to President Davis, who had established the Confederacy's temporary headquarters at Danville, Virginia. Taylor asked whether he should move his command to Georgia or remain at Meridian and preserve his communication and supply lines, thereby enabling a concentration of Confederate forces in his department and even allowing Davis to carry on the war west of the Mississippi River. "[A] decision should be had at once as to which of the two courses to adopt," Taylor stated. "Ignorant of the policy of the Government, I cannot decide." But Davis had al-

---

Campaign of Forrest's Cavalry," p. 177 (second and third quotations); McMillan, *Alabama Confederate Reader*, pp. 413–16.

50. James Pickett Jones, *Yankee Blitzkrieg*, pp. 110–11, 154–56, 185–87; Richard Taylor, *Destruction and Reconstruction*, pp. 269–71 (first quotation 269, fourth quotation 271); *O.R.*, 49(2):1206–7 (second quotation 1207, third quotation 1206), 1234–35.

ready fled Danville and was now in North Carolina, where Johnston and Beauregard were trying to convince him that the Army of Tennessee stood in danger of complete annihilation at Sherman's hands. Receiving no reply, Taylor sent a duplicate telegram on the twentieth, channeling it through Howell Cobb in Georgia. Davis never received either telegram. His communication with the entire Confederacy west of the Carolinas had been disrupted by Sherman's troops.[51]

About this time news reached Taylor that Lee had surrendered the Army of Northern Virginia to Grant on April 9. "The surrender of Lee left us little hope of success," Taylor reflected, "but while Johnston remained in arms we must be prepared to fight our way to him." Forrest and Maury agreed with his determination. "Granting the cause for which we fought to be lost," he affirmed, "we owed it to our own manhood, to the memory of the dead, and to the honor of our arms, to remain steadfast to the last." The troops reacted to the decision "not with noisy cheers, but solemn murmurs of approval." Not long afterward Taylor received word that Lincoln had been assassinated. When he announced this to a group of soldiers, "they were silent with amazement, then asked if it was possible that any Southern man had committed the act." They seemed relieved when Taylor said that "the wretched assassin had no connection with the South, but was an actor, whose brains were addled by tragedies and Plutarch's fables." True enough, John Wilkes Booth had no official connection to the Confederate cause, but he was indeed a southerner. Like the northern fanatic John Brown in 1859, Booth had consummated a private vendetta of violence against his enemy, and with a gargantuan impact. In a fitting twist of fate, as a member of a Virginia militia unit a few years earlier, he had helped carry out Brown's hanging.[52]

On April 19 Canby sent a letter to Taylor proposing a suspension of hostilities, an idea Taylor found increasingly attractive. Three days later he made a cordial but guarded reply, suggesting that "a personal interview between us, although informal in its inception and charac-

51. Richard Taylor to Jefferson Davis, April 14, 1865 (quotation), Richard Taylor Private Official Telegrams; *O.R.*, 49(2):1255; Ballard, *Long Shadow*, pp. 74–90.

52. Richard Taylor, *Destruction and Reconstruction*, pp. 271–72, 279 (first, second, third, and fifth quotations), 278 (fourth quotation).

Edward R. S. Canby, Union conqueror of Mobile
(Lawrence T. Jones III).

ter, may be attended with results consonant with the views which we,
I think, both entertain." Because Canby had left Mobile temporarily,
several days passed before he responded. Meanwhile Taylor received
news on the twenty-fourth that Johnston and Sherman had negotiated their own truce, which, Taylor explained to Forrest and Maury,
was "for [the] purpose of final settlement." Staff officers from both
Johnston and Sherman had come with instructions for Taylor and
Canby to adopt the same course. Forrest, however, resisted all notions
of a final surrender. The next day he issued a proclamation to his
cavalrymen denouncing rumors that had "magnified a simple flag of
truce" from Taylor to Canby "into a mission for negotiating the terms
of surrender" of the department. "It is the duty of every man to stand
firm at his post and true to his colors," Forrest declared.[53]

53. *O.R.*, 49(2):440 (first quotation), 1263–64 (third and fourth quotations
1263); Richard Taylor to Nathan Bedford Forrest and Dabney H. Maury,
April 24, 1865 (second quotation), Richard Taylor Private Official Telegrams; Delaney, "Surrender of General Richard Taylor," p. 46; Richard Taylor, *Destruction and Reconstruction*, p. 274.

Canby responded to Taylor on the twenty-sixth and suggested a meeting at Magee's farm, twelve miles north of Mobile, to be held on the twenty-ninth. Taylor had no other means to make the trip than a railroad handcar, "the motive power of which was two negroes." He arrived at Magee's farm with one staff officer to find Canby attended by a brigade of soldiers and a bevy of officers, all in formal military attire, a glaring contrast to "our rusty suits of Confederate gray," he noted. "General Canby met me with much urbanity," Taylor recalled. After a short session of private negotiations they emerged having agreed to a truce that could be revoked only after forty-eight hours' notice by either side. "A bountiful luncheon was soon spread, and I was invited to partake of pates, champagne-frappe, and other 'delights,' which, to me, had been as lost arts," Taylor recorded. "The joyous poppings of champagne corks," he confessed, were "the first agreeable explosive sounds I had heard for years." As the celebrants sat down to begin their feasting, a military brass band outside the house struck up a hearty rendition of "Hail Columbia," prompting Canby to excuse himself and stride to the door. "The music ceased for a moment," Taylor recalled, "and then the strain of 'Dixie' was heard." Thanking Canby for his gracious and respectful gesture, Taylor requested "Hail Columbia" once more and "expressed a hope that Columbia would be again a happy land, a sentiment honored by many libations." The fact that a Union brass band knew how to play "Dixie" must have made it all the easier for Taylor to believe as much.[54]

Within two days Taylor learned from Canby that the truce between Johnston and Sherman had been rejected by President Andrew Johnson. Sherman had brashly attempted to exert military authority for accomplishing the South's quick restoration to the Union by including in his terms to Johnston a recognition of existing southern state governments as well as a general amnesty for Confederate officials. As a result, Canby informed Taylor that their own truce must be terminated. Within hours Taylor learned that Wilson's troopers had cap-

---

54. *O.R.*, 49(2):481, 1267; Richard Taylor, *Destruction and Reconstruction*, pp. 274–75 (first, second, third, and fifth quotations 274, seventh quotation 275); Richard Taylor, "Last Confederate Surrender," in *Annals of the War*, p. 69 (fourth and sixth quotations).

tured President Davis and that Johnston had decided to surrender to Sherman on the same terms Grant had given Lee, leaving political matters in the hands of Federal officials. This left Taylor no choice but to opt for the same kind of surrender to Canby. John Bell Hood, who happened to be passing through Meridian at the time, tried to convince Taylor to move his command across the Mississippi and combine forces with Edmund Kirby Smith. Taylor dismissed the idea, arguing that recent floods had made the river too treacherous to attempt a crossing. Yet many of the soldiers under Taylor's command, even in their diminished condition, wanted to keep fighting. "At Meridian several hundred officers of all grades . . . were willing and anxious to fight to the last in any manner they could," one of them recalled. Taylor spurned all such pleas. "It seemed absurd for the few there present to continue the struggle against a million men," he asserted.[55]

Having no reason to doubt his decision at the time, after the war Taylor claimed to entertain second thoughts when former soldiers began proclaiming "from the hustings and in print . . . that they were anxious to die in the last ditch." Public approval of such declarations helped elevate "the heroes uttering them" to politically powerful positions, "and popular opinion in our land," he noted derisively, "is a court from whose decisions there is no appeal on this side of the grave." This bit of sarcasm was foreshadowed in more graphic terms in Taylor's warnings to his men against carrying on further resistance to the enemy, especially guerrilla-style warfare. Notifying Forrest, Maury, and the rest of his general officers on May 2 that he intended to "make every effort to secure an honorable and speedy cessation of hostilities," he emphasized the necessity of restraining and holding their commands together. "Unless the troops remain intact," Taylor admonished, "they will be hunted down like beasts of prey, their families will be persecuted, and ruin thus entailed not only upon the sol-

---

55. Richard Taylor, "Last Confederate Surrender," in *Annals of the War*, pp. 69–70; Delaney, "Surrender of General Richard Taylor," p. 47; McMurry, *John Bell Hood*, p. 189; Todhunter, "Col. Todhunter's Account of the Closing Events," p. 398 (first quotation); Richard Taylor, *Destruction and Reconstruction*, pp. 275–76 (second quotation 276).

diers themselves, but also upon thousands of defenseless Southern women and children."[56]

The next day Taylor sent a more personal letter to his trusted friend Maury, fully justifying his decision. "You will explain to your troops that a surrender . . . will not be the consequence of any defeat . . . but is simply, so far as we are concerned, yielding upon the best terms and with a preservation of our military honor to the logic of events," he insisted. "The cause for which we have struggled for four years was a just one at the beginning of the war, and it is as just now. . . . Say to them that their fate will be mine." Maury would hold strong memories of his relationship with Taylor during the war, particularly during this period. He later professed, "In the last year and in the very last days of the nation we had fought to establish we were closely allied in upholding her existence, and in decently ending her life. . . . In that gloomy month of May, Taylor and Forrest alone were unappalled, and maintained a serene front."[57]

On May 4 Taylor met with Canby at Citronelle, forty miles north of Mobile. "Conditions of surrender were speedily determined, and of a character to sooth the pride of the vanquished," he recalled. Soldiers were allowed to keep their personal property, including horses, and officers retained their sidearms. Canby agreed to provide the men transportation to their homes as well as food for their journeys. Taylor maintained control of all railroads and steamboats for this purpose. Over the next several days Federal officers at Meridian issued paroles to more than forty thousand men, a figure attesting to the gigantic number of deserters, draft evaders, chronic absentees, reserve forces, and militiamen in Taylor's department, all of whom had

56. Richard Taylor, *Destruction and Reconstruction*, p. 276 (first and second quotations); *O.R.*, 49(2):1275 (third and fourth quotations). Although Taylor's letter of May 2 in the *O.R.* is addressed only to Maury, his retained manuscript copy shows that it was addressed to Forrest, Maury, and the rest of the general officers in his department. See Richard Taylor to Nathan Bedford Forrest, Dabney H. Maury, et al., May 2, 1865, Richard Taylor Letter Book.

57. *O.R.*, 49(2):1278–80 (first quotation); Maury, "Reminiscences of General Taylor," p. 568 (second quotation).

Richard Taylor's Colt pistol, carried during the war
(Zachary Taylor Collection, Louisiana State Museum,
photograph by Jan White Brantley).

made little or no contribution to the war effort. Staying at Meridian until the last one had been paroled, Taylor and his steadfast body servant, Tom Strother, now a free man, went to Mobile. There Canby offered to take them to New Orleans, where he planned to receive the surrender of the Trans-Mississippi Department. "General Canby most considerately took me, Tom, and my two horses on his boat to New Orleans," Taylor remembered, "else I must have begged my way." This was an exaggeration of course, but he realized the Confederate money in his pocket was now worthless, "and my battered old sword could hardly be relied on for breakfasts, dinners, and horse feed."[58]

Upon arriving in New Orleans, Taylor promptly sold his horses in order to pay for transporting his wife and children from Natchitoches, where they had stayed during his eight-month absence from Louisiana. Tom found his family in New Orleans. "His wife and children [were] all right," Taylor later wrote with satisfaction, also mentioning that afterward Tom became "prosperous." While waiting for his family to arrive, Taylor met with Confederate officers, including Lieutenant General Simon B. Buckner, chief of staff to Edmund

58. Richard Taylor, "Last Confederate Surrender," in *Annals of the War*, p. 70 (first quotation); *O.R.*, 49(2):1283–84 and series 2, 7:717–18; Richard Taylor, *Destruction and Reconstruction*, pp. 276–79 (second and third quotations 279).

Kirby Smith, and Sterling Price, regarding their imminent surrender to Canby. On May 25, at the St. Charles Hotel, Taylor was present at the invitation of both parties to witness the formal surrender of the Trans-Mississippi Department by Buckner, who acted on Smith's behalf. For Taylor the war was finally over. "I shared the fortunes of the Confederacy," he recalled, "and can say, as Grattan did of Irish freedom, that I 'sat by its cradle and followed its hearse.'" [59]

Taylor had achieved a lustrous record as a southern officer, rising from the status of voluntary civilian advisor to the rank of lieutenant general and departmental commander. No other senior general in the Confederate Army came from such an obscure beginning to gain such high rank and authority. Among non–West Pointers Taylor's reputation as a battlefield commander was surpassed only by Forrest, Hampton, and Patrick R. Cleburne. He surely would have rivaled them and perhaps even eclipsed them had not his fragile health cut short a promising career as a combat officer in the Army of Northern Virginia. Secretary of War Randolph had hoped that Taylor's transfer to Louisiana would provide the catalyst for recapturing New Orleans. Taylor made this great but elusive goal the continual focal point of his actions in Louisiana, convincing himself that only by liberating the city could the South hope to reclaim the Mississippi Valley and win the war, a belief his superior, Edmund Kirby Smith, repeatedly ridiculed and rejected. [60]

The conflict with Smith reached a climax soon after Taylor's stunning triumph at Mansfield and his strategic victory at Pleasant Hill, glorious accomplishments that together crushed the Federal invasion of northern Louisiana and assured the security of Texas. Smith's selfish refusal to allow Taylor to capitalize on this advantage and open a path to New Orleans certainly justified his resignation. But his insubordinate and insulting behavior toward Smith must stand as a case of deliberate misconduct, the lone, and major, blot on his record and reputation. The pain of Taylor's physical condition doubtless contributed to his rage against Smith, but more than anything else, the upheaval and decimation inflicted by total war upon Louisiana's popu-

59. Richard Taylor, *Destruction and Reconstruction*, pp. 70 (first quotation), 279–80 (second quotation 280); Heyman, *Prudent Soldier*, pp. 234–35.
60. Bergeron, "General Richard Taylor," pp. 35–47.

lation inflamed him to react so disrespectfully. The baneful effects of total war also dominated Taylor's administration of the Department of Alabama, Mississippi, and East Louisiana, strangling him with desertions, jayhawking, illegal cotton trading, and steadily declining public morale. Left with little more than Forrest's cavalry and a precarious transportation and supply system to aid the Army of Tennessee's erratic response to Sherman's invasion, Taylor likewise had deficient means to defend Mobile and thwart Wilson's thrust through Alabama.

Pointing to the North's wealth of manpower and industrial strength before the war, Taylor expressed grave disapproval of the Confederacy's adherence to democratic excesses and localized prerogatives when the situation demanded a centralization of political authority and military purpose. The deep undercurrent of poor army discipline, especially among cavalrymen, Taylor learned to accept as a necessary evil, particularly after he went to the Trans-Mississippi. But as the incessant strain of total war engulfed soldiers and citizens, he battled not only jayhawkers and cotton traders but also state politicians who refused to support him with their militias. The Confederacy's decentralized departmental military system, rife with superfluous and corrupt personnel and hampered by poor coordination between departments, frustrated him continually. Finally Taylor came face to face with the government's capricious army command system, a loosely knit structure bereft of the effective planning and communication that would have been available from a real military staff system. With Jefferson Davis trying to run everything at once, by the last year of the war the president had lost all means of gaining any help from the Trans-Mississippi Department while he grappled to maintain control of the western theater of war. Finding it impossible to placate the Confederate Congress and the public at large after dismissing Johnston, he appointed the fretful Beauregard as a military administrator with vague responsibilities while demanding that the spasmodic Hood perform decisively as a virtually independent commander of the Army of Tennessee.

The Confederate nation's dearth of political and military unity, born of southerners' devotion to democratic liberty, decentralized authority, and economic individualism, stalked Taylor even after he surrendered. While he was still at Meridian supervising the final paroles in his department, a prominent Alabama railroad executive at Mobile became rankled over the low rates Canby had authorized to pay for transporting the thousands of southern soldiers to their homes. Considering himself finally free from Taylor's power, the executive ordered his agent at Meridian to stop giving passes to the parolees. Taylor instantly wired Canby at Mobile and asked him to escort this sterling entrepreneur back to Meridian under armed guard. Maury recalled of the incident, "What was the horror of the man when a [Federal] corporal and file of soldiers took him from his home and bore him up to Taylor, into whose presence he came with well-grounded fear, for report said the general had shot men for less crimes than that." Taylor glowered at his victim and "administered in his fluent style such a tongue-lashing as only he could utter." Then he exclaimed, "General Canby and I will teach you a lesson that will last you the rest of your miserable life!" First threatening to turn the rascal over "to those soldiers whom you have attempted to wrong . . . [to] hang you as high as Haman upon one of these tall pines," he paused for a second and instead issued a piercing command: "Go, and at once countermand your orders!"[61]

This very sort of ambitious greed and narrow self-interest among so many southerners had discouraged Taylor at first from joining the Confederate cause. Predicting that the South would lose the war, he had fully expected that too much of the population would display only limited nationalistic unity. Yet afterward he chose to contradict his own painfully accurate prediction. "The conduct of the southern people" during the war had been "admirable," he asserted in his memoirs. "Submitting to the inevitable," they displayed "fortitude and dignity." Likewise refusing to acknowledge the hundreds of thousands of slaves who took advantage of the war to seek freedom, many of them volunteering to fight the very soldiers Taylor had commanded, he wrote that they "worked quietly in the fields until removed by the Federals." White southerners "struggled in all honorable ways, and for what?" he asked. "For their slaves? Regret for their loss has neither been felt nor expressed." Here Taylor penetrated to the source of the conflict, both within the South and between the South and the North. Having convinced himself that political neces-

61. Maury, *Recollections*, p. 226 (quotations).

RICHARD TAYLOR

sity rather than his own vital stake in slavery had compelled him, like other southerners, to fight for the Confederacy, he repeated his abhorrence toward the northern Republican majority and its claim that slaveholders like himself had brought on secession and war. So deeply did he loathe the uncontrolled democracy of antislavery northerners that he was willing to forget the self-destructive form of democracy practiced by greedy, short-sighted southerners throughout the war.[62]

"[The] extinction of slavery was expected by all and regretted by none," Taylor insisted, speaking more for himself than for other whites in the South, especially former slaveholders. With slavery obliterated, he briefly anticipated lenient treatment from the Confederacy's conquerors. "Yet, great as were [southerners'] sufferings during the war, they were as nothing compared to those inflicted upon them after its close," he professed. "These had committed the unpardonable sin, had wickedly rebelled against the Lord's anointed, the majority." Taylor quickly persuaded himself that the Civil War had entered a far more sinister and disgraceful phase: Reconstruction.[63]

62. Richard Taylor, *Destruction and Reconstruction*, pp. 288–91 (first quotation 291, third quotation 288), 257 (second quotation). On the abusive extremes of economic individualism among Confederate civilians, see Faust, *Confederate Nationalism*, pp. 48–57. See also Escott, "Failure of Confederate Nationalism," pp. 26–27.

63. Richard Taylor, *Destruction and Reconstruction*, pp. 288–89 (first and second quotations 288, third quotation 289).

Democratic Party Insider

[Taylor is] the brightest, most far-seeing man

I have ever met from the South.

Samuel Latham Mitchell Barlow

Richard Taylor no longer harbored any ambivalence about the righteousness of the southern cause. A Whiggish, nationalistic, conservative southerner who had hesitated to follow the Confederacy into war, he now began to perceive the North's victorious Republican majority as a greater danger than ever, both to the South's integrity and to true national unity. Almost as soon as he laid down his sword, he engaged his equally potent talent for personal persuasion in the realm of political warfare, this time within the highest circles of power.

His most immediate motive was clear-cut. After learning that Federal authorities had imprisoned Jefferson Davis at Fort Monroe, Virginia, on a charge of treason against the United States, Taylor resolved at once to go to Washington to speak with President Andrew Johnson in an attempt to gain Davis's release. "It was a bold thing to do," noted Dabney Maury. "Few of us would risk ourselves in Washington then." Reasoning that he might influence some Republicans who had been Whigs during his father's presidency, Taylor felt an overwhelming sense of duty to save Davis from humiliation. "If Mr.

Davis had sinned, we were all guilty," he affirmed, "and I could not rest without making an attempt for his relief." [1]

Leaving his wife and daughters in the care of his Bringier family in-laws in New Orleans, Taylor gained General Canby's permission to make the trip. He quickly raised enough money from friends to secure passage on an ocean steamer in mid-July. Arriving in New York City a week later, he called upon Samuel Latham Mitchell Barlow, a wealthy attorney with immensely powerful connections in the Democratic party. Thirty-nine years old, the same age as Taylor, Barlow had worked behind the political scenes with southern Democrats since 1856, when he helped achieve Buchanan's presidential nomination at the national convention in Cincinnati. Taylor first met Barlow during the 1860 Democratic convention in Charleston, where they joined Senator Slidell in the failed attempt to prevent fire-eater William Yancey from splitting the party. Taylor and Barlow enjoyed an instant affinity during their brief encounter in Charleston, and in New York they rekindled it, forging a friendship that would become one of the most forceful relationships in postwar national politics. [2]

At first Taylor merely considered Barlow as a powerful man to approach for both advice and money to help him in his quest to gain Jefferson Davis's freedom. Barlow proved extremely cooperative, and in the process he convinced Taylor to act as his personal envoy for gathering political information in Washington. Displaying huge confidence in Taylor, Barlow described him as "the brightest, most far-seeing man I have ever met from the South." Upon arriving at the capital in late July, Taylor took a room at Willard's Hotel, a favorite crossroads for politicians and lobbyists. There an unidentified acquaintance told him that rumors of a new southern plot to assassinate government leaders had provoked Secretary of War Edwin M. Stanton to issue an order prohibiting former Confederates from entering

1. Maury, "Reminiscences of General Taylor," p. 568 (first quotation); Richard Taylor, *Destruction and Reconstruction*, p. 293 (second quotation).

2. Strangely, Taylor made no specific mention of Barlow in his memoirs. Richard Taylor, *Destruction and Reconstruction*, p. 293; House, "Barlow Papers," pp. 341–49; Rosenblum, "Two Americanists," pp. 14–15; Roy F. Nichols, *Disruption of American Democracy*, pp. 14–15, 294; Meade, *Judah P. Benjamin*, p. 105.

Samuel Latham Mitchell Barlow, Democratic party kingpin
(Maury A. Bromsen).

Washington without his personal permission. "My informant appre-
hended my arrest, and kindly undertook to protect me," Taylor recounted. Resourceful as well as discreet, this informant contacted
President Johnson, who immediately sent Taylor a written pass rendering him immune from Stanton's clutches. Johnson also invited
Taylor to visit him at the White House.[3]

3. Milton, *Age of Hate*, pp. 227–28 (first quotation 228); Richard Taylor,
Destruction and Reconstruction, pp. 293–94 (second quotation 294).

President Andrew Johnson
(Library of Congress).

"I was ushered in to the President—a saturnine man, who made no return to my bow, but, after looking at me, asked me to take a seat," Taylor recalled. A Tennessean of common yeoman stock, a white supremacist yet also an enemy of large slaveholders' political power before the war, Johnson was a zealous Unionist whose experience in the Senate and service as military governor of his war-torn state had impressed Lincoln to select him for the vice-presidency in 1864. Painfully serious and dangerously stubborn, the new president had recently vowed retribution upon Confederate leaders. But without warning he had begun to alter his thinking. "He had now somewhat abated his wolfish desire for vengeance," Taylor observed with pleasant surprise, "and asked many questions about the condition of the South, temper of the people, etc." As an erstwhile conservative Democrat with no desire to see Radical Republicans use Reconstruction as a tool to hold the South political hostage, Johnson wanted to shape a swift and complete restoration of the former Confederate states to the Union. Flattered besides that so many former slaveholders such as Taylor were suddenly fawning over him in hopes of luring him back into the Democratic fold as their national party leader, Johnson shared their fear that the Radicals would solidify power even further by giving freedmen full citizenship, including the right to vote.[4]

Dealing with a man as unpredictable as Johnson, however, required all the dexterity Taylor could summon. At one point in their conversation the president mentioned that a Louisiana citizen had just visited him claiming that during the war Taylor had tried to hang him for being a Unionist. "Mr President, he has lied to you," Taylor retorted placidly. "General, did you not hang Union men in Louisiana?" Johnson queried. "Oh yes," Taylor answered. "I hanged many Union men in Louisiana who were spies and traitors to our cause and in our army; but I never tried to hang one that I did not do it, and so your complainant must have lied to you." Hardly amused, Johnson pressed the issue no further.[5]

In responding to Johnson's questions about the southern situation, Taylor mentioned the fact that Governors Charles Clark of Mississippi and Thomas H. Watts of Alabama had been imprisoned by Federal military authorities. "[Johnson] made memoranda of their cases, as well as those of many other prisoners, confined at different forts from Boston to Savannah, all of whom were released within a short time," Taylor recalled. Although he was one of many prominent southerners petitioning Johnson to pardon former Confederate leaders, Taylor believed he had gained a dramatic accomplishment. Satis-

4. Richard Taylor, *Destruction and Reconstruction*, p. 294 (quotations); Gambill, *Conservative Ordeal*, pp. 26–31; Cox and Cox, *Politics, Principle, and Prejudice*, pp. 50–59; Brock, *American Crisis*, pp. 31–32. On Johnson's racial attitudes, see Bowen, *Andrew Johnson and the Negro*, pp. 45–79, 122–35.

5. Maury, "Reminiscences of General Taylor," p. 568 (quotations).

fied with the president's receptive demeanor for the present, he decided to delay for a few days speaking with him about Davis. In the meantime he sought out Secretary of State William H. Seward, an old Whig who still had fond memories of his days in the Senate as a powerful northern advisor to Taylor's father during his presidency. "He greeted me cordially and asked me to dine," Taylor remembered. At Seward's residence Taylor enjoyed a splendid loin of veal, prompting the secretary to comment that he "had killed the fatted calf to welcome the returned prodigal." But he seemed less inclined to help this wayward southern son gain the inheritance he was seeking. Davis's plight elicited Seward's concern but no promise of assistance.[6]

Returning to the White House to see the president, Taylor simply asked for permission to visit Davis at Fort Monroe, but Johnson "pondered for some time, then replied that I must wait and call again." In the interim Taylor encountered General Ulysses S. Grant, whom he had known since the Mexican War. Grant showed unusual interest in Taylor's mission. "He came frequently to see me, was full of kindness, and anxious to promote my wishes," Taylor remembered. But Grant admitted his "ignorance of and distaste for politics and politicians" and only professed "a desire for the speedy restoration of good feeling between the sections, and an intention to advance it in all proper ways." Seeing President Johnson again, Taylor found him willing to discuss the South's political future but still hesitant to let him visit Jefferson Davis. Johnson's personality began to annoy Taylor. "I found that he always postponed action, and was of an obstinate, suspicious temper," Taylor recounted. Although intelligent, Johnson "could not rise above the level of the class in which he was born and to which he always appealed." Distrustful of better-educated men, he seemed "narrow and dogmatic." Considering Taylor's request too delicate politically to act upon, Johnson suggested that he approach Radical Republican congressional leaders and persuade them to make formal recommendations. "I immediately addressed myself to this unpleasant task," Taylor recalled.[7]

6. Richard Taylor, *Destruction and Reconstruction*, p. 295 (quotations); Dorris, *Pardon and Amnesty under Lincoln and Johnson*, pp. 244–77.

7. Richard Taylor, *Destruction and Reconstruction*, pp. 297–99 (first, second, third, fourth, and fifth quotations 297, sixth quotation 298, seventh quota-

Girding up his courage, Taylor first called upon Thaddeus Stevens of Pennsylvania, the Radicals' chief firebrand in the House. Stevens proved glibly honest in his opinions. Referring to the Constitution as a "worthless bit of old parchment," he asserted that a rehabilitation of the old Union would be senseless now. White southerners should remain stripped of all power, their land confiscated and given to the freedmen, who now deserved full suffrage rights, he argued. The Confederacy's "leading traitors" should have been "promptly strung up," he insisted further, causing Taylor to reflect, "Here, I thought, he looked lovingly at my neck." But now too much time had passed to warrant such executions, Stevens said, and Johnson was "silly" to keep Taylor from visiting Jefferson Davis. But Stevens slyly refused to admit this openly because he wanted Johnson to take responsibility for such a decision. From here Taylor visited several other Republican members of the House, "the cuttle-fish of the party," he termed them, "whose appointed duty it was to obscure popular vision by clouds of loyal declamation." They "sharpened every question of administration, finance, law, [and] taxation on the grindstone of sectional hate." He made no headway with them.[8]

Taylor then decided to try his hand with the most powerful Radical in the Senate, Charles Sumner of Massachusetts. Sumner seemed affable yet distinctly distant and condescending toward his southern visitor. "A rebel, a slave-driver, and, without the culture of Boston, ignorant, I was an admirable vessel into which he could pour the inexhaustible stream of his acquired eloquence," Taylor observed. Like Stevens, Sumner left no doubt as to the Radicals' most precious goal: black suffrage. To this contention Taylor responded in a conciliatory yet typically paternalistic tone, suggesting that education for blacks should precede suffrage, since even the great mass of white Americans arguably lacked complete competence for self-government. But Sumner asserted passionately that "the ignorance of the negro was due to the tyranny of the whites," which only proved to Taylor that

tion 299). Taylor's opinion of Johnson's temperament receives support in Bowen, *Andrew Johnson and the Negro*, pp. 139–56.

8. Richard Taylor, *Destruction and Reconstruction*, pp. 299–300 (first, second, and third quotations 299, fourth and fifth quotations 300).

Thaddeus Stevens
(Jenkins Rare Book Company).

the Radicals were willing to ignore the "incapacity" of blacks. Listening to Sumner ramble on, Taylor began to perceive him as "over-educated," that he had "retained, not digested his learning." Yet Taylor also considered him "the purest and most sincere man of his party. . . . Without vindictiveness, he forgave his enemies as soon as they were overthrown." Unable to penetrate Sumner's oratorical fog, he did not even mention his desire to see Jefferson Davis.[9]

Thoroughly foiled, Taylor then pestered Johnson so unmercifully that the president finally issued him a pass to go to Fort Monroe to meet with Davis. He arrived there in early August. "It was with some emotion that I reached the casemate in which Mr. Davis was confined," Taylor recalled. After a silent grasp of hands, Davis stated, "This is kind, but no more than I expected of you." Telling Davis that "his calamities had served to endear him to all," Taylor comforted him

9. Ibid., pp. 300–301 (first quotation 300, second, third, and fourth quotations 301). On the Radical Republicans' goals during 1865, see Trefousse, *Radical Republicans*, pp. 309–28. See also Donald, *Charles Sumner and the Rights of Man*, pp. 218–36.

Charles Sumner
(Jenkins Rare Book Company).

further by promising to gain permission for Davis's family to visit him. For more than a year afterward Taylor often involved himself in seeking Davis's exoneration, pressuring government officials and reassuring his wife, Varina Howell Davis, of eventual success. Writing to her husband in April 1866, Varina Davis noted, "Dick Taylor has . . . been affectionate as a brother and son." He also consulted with Charles G. Halpine, a New York journalist who had orchestrated a scheme to serve as ghostwriter of a sensational book, *The Prison Life of Jefferson Davis*, supposedly authored by Davis's attending physician, Dr. John J. Craven. Already seeing the political advantage of catering to prosouthern interests, President Johnson eagerly endorsed Halpine's secret efforts. A brilliant piece of Democratic propaganda, the book stirred up public sympathy by deliberately distorting Davis's sufferings. In May 1867 the prosecution began to waver, and Davis gained release on bail. Finally, more than a year and a half later, Johnson granted amnesty to all remaining former Confederates who had been denied certain rights as citizens, thus absolving Davis. Taylor later described his own role in the affair as "a simple discharge of duty." [10]

During his interviews with Johnson in the summer of 1865 Taylor reported exciting prospects for the Democratic party to his political backer Samuel Barlow. "I urged [upon the president] the importance of his securing the affection of the Southern people," he wrote Barlow confidently on July 28. "No time should be lost in establishing personal relations with Johnson . . . [to] secure great results for the country." Barlow quickly informed other northern Democratic leaders of Taylor's opinions. "[Taylor] says Mr. Johnson must be supported, at the North, no matter what he may do that we think wrong or injudicious; as otherwise he will never get right," Barlow affirmed. Only through Johnson's leadership would Reconstruction prove mild enough to restore southern Democrats to power in their home states and enable them to send representatives to Congress. This alone would allow the Democratic party to achieve majority ascendancy over the Republicans on a national scale as before the war. Success hinged primarily on one hurdle: preventing Republicans from giving black southerners the right to vote. [11]

Taylor's duty to the South's political fortunes did not divert him very long from attending to his personal welfare. Returning to New Orleans from Washington in late November 1865, he endeavored to improve his blighted finances. "The man of Uz admitted that naked he came into the world, and naked must leave it," he later reflected, "but to find himself naked in the midst of it tried even his patience." Hearing of his circumstances, some of his former slaves offered to give him money, but he gratefully declined this affectionate gesture

10. Richard Taylor, *Destruction and Reconstruction*, pp. 301–3 (first and second quotations 302, third and fifth quotations 303); Strode, *Jefferson Davis*, pp. 245 (fourth quotation), 265, 267; Eckert, "*Fiction Distorting Fact*," pp. xl–xlviii; Hanchett, "Reconstruction and Jefferson Davis," pp. 280–89. For a full description of the legal and political controversy regarding the case against Davis, see Dorris, *Pardon and Amnesty under Lincoln and Johnson*, pp. 278–312.

11. Richard Taylor to Samuel Barlow, July 28, 1865 (first quotation), Barlow Papers; Cox and Cox, *Politics, Principle, and Prejudice*, pp. 59–66 (second quotation 60–61); Gambill, *Conservative Ordeal*, pp. 35–37.

of generosity. His political services to Barlow having afforded him some temporary funds, he shared them with his impecunious friends, including Dabney Maury. Writing to Barlow in December, Taylor grumbled, "The last few months in your society has rather unfitted me for a hard campaign against poverty." Although Federal authorities were now allowing many prominent former Confederates to recover their confiscated properties, Taylor never tried to reclaim his plantation, Fashion, preferring instead to hold a life right in the property and to allow the government to lease it to another planter. Deriving no income from Fashion, he did not even attempt to pay the local taxes accrued against it. Having repaid none of the huge personal prewar debt owed to his mother-in-law, Aglae Bringier, and brother-in-law Martin Gordon, Jr., in early 1866 Taylor decided to file for bankruptcy in federal district court in order to clear his financial standing. Neither Bringier nor Gordon made any claim to Fashion, thus allowing Taylor to retain his life right in the property.[12]

Meanwhile he did his best to retrieve the personal fortune he had enjoyed before the war. Learning that the Louisiana legislature was about to award a private lease to operate the New Basin Canal, a waterway linking the heart of New Orleans with Lake Pontchartrain, Taylor lobbied to gain the lease for himself. Sixty feet wide, six feet deep, and more than six miles long, the canal was clearly the most important in the state because of the large and frequent commercial shipments on barges connecting the city with steamers on the lake, thus allowing direct passage to and from the Gulf Coast. The canal's additional function as part of New Orleans's overburdened water-drainage system made it a public service like many others that politicians saw fit to lease to private contractors rather than risk incurring unforeseen maintenance expenses. On March 6, 1866, Taylor secured a fifteen-year lease, agreeing to pay $36,000 after the first year, $37,000 after the second, and steadily higher rates thereafter to the

12. Richard Taylor, *Destruction and Reconstruction*, p. 279 (first quotation); Jackson Beauregard Davis, "Life of Richard Taylor," p. 116; Maury, *Recollections*, p. 234; Richard Taylor to Samuel Barlow, December 1, 1865 (second quotation), Barlow Papers; White, *Freedmen's Bureau in Louisiana*, pp. 48–49; Deliberation of Creditors of Richard Taylor, March 12, 1866, Succession Papers of the Estate of Richard Taylor.

sum of $85,000 the final year. "The tolls from the canal will yield fifty thousand a year at once, and double that sum within ten years," he announced excitedly to Barlow. When Varina Howell Davis passed through New Orleans in mid-March, she wrote her husband, "Dick Taylor looks well, has leased the canal here at a large sum, and expects to make a large amount by it." [13]

The New Basin Canal lease seemed like a financial coup for Taylor, but when the due date for the first year's payment approached in early 1867, he faced a quandary. Unexpected expenses from repairing and deepening the canal had left him without enough funds. In January 1867 he sought help from his wealthy brother-in-law Duncan Kenner, an inveterate and calculating businessman whose expanding investments in sugar plantations, sulphur mines, levee constructions, utility and manufacturing companies, banks, railroads, and New Orleans real estate had already put him well on the way to recovering and expanding the fortune he had held before the war. Taylor sold half-interest in the canal to Kenner for an unspecified amount, and a year later, in March 1868, he borrowed $100,000 at 8 percent interest from Kenner on a personal loan, "pledging all revenues and profits that might be derived from the operation of the canal." Yet this did not release him from his obligations to the state under the lease. Much like his indebtedness to Aglae Bringier and Martin Gordon, Jr., during the 1850s, Taylor's exploitation of Kenner's good graces as an in-law reached extreme proportions, and still he floundered financially. Throughout the lease he remained unable to pay the state a single dollar of rental on the canal. [14]

13. Jackson Beauregard Davis, "Life of Richard Taylor," p. 116; U.S. Department of the Interior, Census Office, *Report on the Agencies of Transportation*, p. 751; *Transit Riders' Digest*, April 2, 1962, February 18, 1963, March 6, 1967, in Clippings File, Historic New Orleans Collection; John Smith Kendall, *History of New Orleans*, 2:633–34; Jackson, *New Orleans in the Gilded Age*, pp. 145–49; Richard Taylor to Samuel Barlow, February 9, 1866 (first quotation), Barlow Papers; Strode, *Jefferson Davis*, pp. 240–41 (second quotation 241).

14. Memorandum of an agreement between Richard Taylor and Duncan F. Kenner, January 21, 1867, Duncan F. Kenner Papers, Louisiana State University; copy of document stating Richard Taylor's indebtedness to Duncan F. Kenner for $100,000 at eight percent interest, March 17, 1868 (quotation),

Richard Taylor immediately after the war
(author's collection).

Taylor's recurring financial problems hardly discouraged him from resuming his role as an aristocratic socialite and gambler, an expensive lifestyle that projected an image of success. By early 1866 the Metairie Jockey Club had reorganized with Taylor in the thick of its management, planning races and appraising the local horseflesh for betting potential. In January 1867, the very month he sold half-interest in the New Basin Canal to Kenner, he served with Kenner on the reception and invitation committee for the jockcy club's festive ball initiating the special winter racing event. The Metairie track rapidly regained its antebellum standing as one of the finest in the nation, operating under the jockey club's supervision until 1872, when internal squabbles induced the track's owners to sell out to a group of businessmen who converted the site into the Metairie Cemetery.

Succession Papers of the Estate of Richard Taylor; William K. Scarborough, "Slavery—The White Man's Burden," p. 107; Craig A. Bauer, "A Leader among Peers," pp. 402–9; Jackson Beauregard Davis, "Life of Richard Taylor," p. 116.

Meanwhile Taylor also reaffirmed his genteel standing as a member of the Boston Club, New Orleans's exclusive domain for Louisiana's most prominent male citizens. In August 1865 he served on the committee that reorganized the club, whose membership soon counted former Confederate generals Simon B. Buckner, Randall Lee Gibson, Harry Hays, and John Bell Hood as well as the ubiquitous Kenner. In December 1868 Taylor was elected the club's president, a position he retained for five annual terms.[15]

In January 1869 the Boston Club held a grand ball at its sumptuous new quarters on Carondelet Street. "There were over three hundred ladies and gentlemen present, and no limits to the grandeur, grace, beauty, elegance, luxury and enjoyment of the occasion," the New Orleans *Times* reported. "Fountains of champagne flowed perpetually, tempting inevitably the thirsty and the curious to frequent draughts." Taylor used such society to keep his famous wit finely honed. During a dinner party a loquacious man seated at his table was droning on about recent advances in science, proclaiming, "Yes, gentlemen, science has made such strides that we now take Mercury in our arms, measure his weight, and span his form!" Suddenly Taylor erupted, "We do, indeed sir. And we take Venus in our arms, and do the same thing!" Yet Boston Club members, Taylor included, did not confine their attentions strictly to leisure and merrymaking. As before the war, the club fomented political action. According to its historian, "During the Reconstruction days the Boston Club was the gathering place of the leaders of the white element . . . [and] grew into public utterance as an expression standing for the supremacy of the white man and the perpetuation of the white man's institutions." Jefferson Davis, as well as Taylor's old Army of Northern Virginia comrade Dick Ewell, and other southern luminaries frequented the club during their visits to New Orleans. Whether at the club's gaming tables or

15. Richard Taylor to Samuel Barlow, June 1, 1866, Barlow Papers; Jackson Beauregard Davis, "Life of Richard Taylor," p. 117; *Metairie Jockey Club Ball, Winter Meeting, New Orleans, January 1st, 1867*, printed invitation in Louis A. Bringier Family Papers; Talbot, *Turf, Cards and Temperance*, pp. 62–65; Landry, *History of the Boston Club*, pp. 86–103, 270; Craig A. Bauer, "A Leader among Peers," pp. 441–47.

in its drawing rooms discussing politics, Taylor found the atmosphere highly congenial.[16]

In January 1867 Taylor participated in a solemn event that glorified the cause for which white southerners had recently fought and died. The body of General Albert Sidney Johnston, then buried at St. Louis Cemetery in New Orleans, was disinterred for reburial in Texas, his home state. "I was honored by a request to accompany the coffin from the cemetery to the steamer," Taylor recalled. The other pallbearers were P. G. T. Beauregard, Braxton Bragg, Simon B. Buckner, John Bell Hood, James Longstreet, Randall Lee Gibson, and Harry Hays. As the hearse rolled through the streets of New Orleans, thousands of people crowded the sidewalks, all silent in reverent tribute to the soldier who had carried great promise for the Confederacy until his death at Shiloh in the spring of 1862. "As I gazed upon [the coffin] there arose [in me] a feeling of the Theban who, after the downfall of the glory and independence of his country, stood by the tomb of Epaminondas," Taylor lamented.[17]

Two years later Taylor received an opportunity to serve the memory of the Confederacy in a practical and permanent way. Dissatisfied with the spate of histories and memoirs of the war published so far, most of them written by northerners who either slighted or ridiculed the Confederacy, Dabney Maury decided to form an organization to collect original sources and solicit recollections of southern officers and soldiers. "General Dick Taylor cordially encouraged me," Maury remembered, "and in May of [1869] I called a meeting by quiet personal requests of nine or ten gentlemen" in New Orleans. Taylor attended this meeting and another in April that formally established the Southern Historical Society. Besides Taylor and Maury, charter members included Bragg, Beauregard, Buckner, Hays, and Gibson,

16. Landry, *History of the Boston Club*, pp. 158 (first quotation), 115 (fourth quotation); James Cooper Nisbet, *Four Years on the Firing Line*, pp. 58–59 (second and third quotations 59); *Historical Sketch Book and Guide to New Orleans*, p. 95; Hamlin, *"Old Bald Head,"* p. 197; Richard Taylor, *Destruction and Reconstruction*, p. 89.

17. Johnston, *Albert Sidney Johnston*, pp. 699–701; Richard Taylor, *Destruction and Reconstruction*, p. 285 (quotations).

with Dr. Benjamin M. Palmer, the fiery Presbyterian preacher, elected
president. Giving membership to anyone who subscribed to its rather
modest magazine, the society had trouble attracting support. But
when its leaders decided to move their headquarters to Richmond in
1873, a group of Virginians, headed by the cantankerous Jubal A.
Early, took over the organization and set it on solid footing, soon producing the *Southern Historical Society Papers*, a fine journal that appeared regularly for almost forty years. Early's acerbic hatred for
Yankees, especially Republicans, along with his worship of the late
Robert E. Lee, provided an extra push to insure the society's success.
Apart from helping establish the society, Taylor declined involvement
in its prodigious activities, but he continued giving Maury encouragement. "You rightly assume me to be interested in the success of your
Society," Taylor affirmed in May 1876. "'Tis the only institution that
can preserve a record of the civilization of the South—now passed
away." [18]

Taylor's standing as an elite member of conservative southern society only served to intensify his involvement in the bitter and de-
ranged politics of Reconstruction. By early 1866 northern and southern Democrats alike had begun to doubt President Johnson's
intention to abandon the Republican party and embrace Democratic
principles outright. Johnson's decision to keep Stanton and Seward in
his cabinet and his apparently conciliatory behavior toward moderate
Republicans disturbed Democrats most of all. He seemed ambivalent,
unwilling to alienate Republicans and hesitant to confront Congress
directly. Although he now considered the Union restored, often repeating his conviction that the southern states had the right to control
suffrage, Johnson also conceded that the South should protect the
lives and property of freedmen and that Congress had the power to
accept or reject elections of southern congressional candidates.
Meanwhile Republicans in Congress ignored Johnson's view of an instantly reconstructed Union. Alarmed by the continual rise of former
Confederates to power in the South and by the proliferation of south-

18. Maury, *Recollections*, pp. 251–52 (first quotation 251); Mahan, "Final
Battle," pp. 27–37; Foster, *Ghosts of the Confederacy*, pp. 50–62; Connelly and
Bellows, *God and General Longstreet*, pp. 42–43; Richard Taylor to Dabney H.
Maury, May 8, 1876 (second quotation), Brock Papers.

ern laws discriminating against freedmen and controlling their labor—the infamous Black Codes—Congress passed the Civil Rights
Act of 1866 granting freedmen full citizenship and legal rights, including suffrage. Johnson promptly lost his air of conciliation toward
the Republicans and vetoed the measure. Enacted over Johnson's
veto, the Civil Rights Act found more complete expression in June in
the Fourteenth Amendment, with Congress requiring the southern
states to ratify it for readmission to the Union and representation in
Congress. The North speedily opted for ratification, but all the former Confederate states, except Tennessee, refused, leaving the
amendment in temporary abeyance. In spite of his home state's compliance, Johnson openly discouraged the South from submitting to
ratification.[19]

In Louisiana the political climate rapidly degenerated into a circus
of volatility. Unionist politicians, led by Governor James Madison
Wells, despising the legislature with its many former Confederates,
decided to reconvene the constitutional convention of 1864 in New
Orleans in order to write black suffrage into the constitution and
thereby push to gain readmission to the Union under the Fourteenth
Amendment. Taylor, like most conservatives, loathing black suffrage
as "the objective point of radical effort," believed the Unionists had
"no more authority [to meet] than they had to call the British Parlia-
ment." On Saturday, July 28, he agreed to confer with Mayor John T.
Monroe, police officials, and a group of concerned merchants to attempt to reduce the swelling public tension over the convention's
scheduled meeting on Monday. On Sunday Mayor Monroe issued a
proclamation asking citizens to ignore the convention and assuring
them that President Johnson would certainly nullify its actions. Convinced that this gesture would prove sufficient to stifle public outrage,
Taylor personally took the mayor's words to heart and actually forgot
about the convention.[20]

19. Gambill, *Conservative Ordeal*, pp. 38–51; Cox and Cox, *Politics, Principle, and Prejudice*, pp. 68–77, 85–86, 105–10, 125–34; Bowen, *Andrew Johnson and the Negro*, pp. 135–38; Carter, *When the War Was Over*, pp. 241–45.
20. Rable, *But There Was No Peace*, pp. 43–49; Richard Taylor, *Destruction
and Reconstruction*, pp. 304–5 (quotation 304); Vandal, *New Orleans Riot*, pp.
166–70.

Shortly after noon on Monday, July 30, just as the convention assembled at the Mechanics' Institute in the heart of the city, Taylor
happened to step off a tramway car in the vicinity. "I heard pistol
shots and saw a crowd of roughs, Arabs, and negroes running across
Canal Street," he recalled. Several hundred local whites, mostly
young men, enraged at seeing a large group of prominent blacks jamming the streets outside the meeting hall, had started firing pistols,
swinging clubs, and chasing the blacks. According to Taylor, "The
crowd seemed largely composed of boys of from twelve to fifteen, and
negroes." He moved cautiously toward the action. Suddenly a terror-
stricken black man ran past him, pursued by a white teenager bran-
dishing a pistol. Taylor stopped the pursuer and demanded to know
what he was doing. "He said the niggers were having a meeting at
Mechanics' Institute to take away his vote," Taylor recounted. Taylor
asked him "how long he had enjoyed that inestimable right" of suffrage. The youth stood silent, put his weapon in his pocket, and
walked away. By now the riot raged out of control. The young whites,
joined by many ex–Confederate soldiers, lower class laborers, and
even some fairly well dressed citizens, plowed into the blacks, few of
whom were armed. Police and firemen, called to quell the chaos, actually participated in the savagery. Brigadier General Absalom Baird,
left in command of Federal occupation troops during Major General
Philip H. Sheridan's absence, failed to arrive with his men until mid-
afternoon to restore order. By the end of the day thirty-four blacks
and three white Unionists lay dead, and more than a hundred were
wounded. Only one of the white rioters had been killed. The Unionist
cause in Louisiana fell into disarray, shocked and paralyzed.[21]

Igniting a pattern of violence against freedmen that would contam-
inate the South throughout Reconstruction, the New Orleans riot laid
bare the mounting fear among most white southerners over the prospect of blacks exercising even the least bit of political power. Republicans reacted with effusive horror. More than any other event, the riot
inflamed legions of moderate Republicans into adopting the Radical
argument that pictured Democrats as unrepentant Copperheads and

21. Richard Taylor, *Destruction and Reconstruction*, p. 305 (quotations); Vandal, *New Orleans Riot*, pp. 171, 194–202; Rable, *But There Was No Peace*, pp.
49–54; Joseph G. Dawson, *Army Generals and Reconstruction*, pp. 39–42.

treasonous rebels who refused to accept the results of a horrendous war that supposedly had saved the Union and ended tyranny over blacks. Like other genteel Democrats, Taylor regretted such violence, but like virtually all Democrats, he regretted its political effect far more. He later contended that the "perpetrators of the bloody deeds" would have received harsh punishment had civil law taken effect. "But this did not suit the purposes of the Radicals. . . . One would conclude that the Radical leaders prompted the assassination of Lincoln and the murder of negroes; for they alone derived profit from these acts," he observed cynically. "Favorite generals kept lists in their pockets, proving time, place, and numbers, even to the smallest piccaninny." Likewise, he viewed the organized terror of the Ku Klux Klan as a fiction conjured up by the Radicals. "I failed, after many inquiries, to find a single man in the South who had ever heard of [the Klan], saving the newspapers," Taylor asserted. Although he admitted "there were many acts of violence," he blamed the "pestilent" Radicals' political exploitation of "ignorant blacks" for the upheaval. "The whites killed them; and this was to be expected," Taylor concluded, because these were merely common whites, the same racist "breed" he had predicted before the war would brutalize the slaves if emancipated. "Certainty of death could not restrain the colored lambs, impelled by an uncontrollable ardor to vote the Radical ticket."[22]

The Fourteenth Amendment had become a political battlefield. President Johnson had already rejected the amendment out of hand, urging the southern states to reject it. With the growing danger of Democrats and Republicans, North and South, viewing each other as utterly illegitimate forms of political opposition, Johnson called Taylor to Washington in early August. "I explained all the circumstances, as far as I knew them, of the recent murders" in New Orleans, Taylor recalled. Already prone to adopt Taylor's opinion, Johnson angrily

22. Rable, *But There Was No Peace*, pp. 55–58; Vandal, *New Orleans Riot*, pp. 211–17; Carter, *When the War Was Over*, pp. 248–52; Richard Taylor, *Destruction and Reconstruction*, pp. 305–7 (first quotation 305, second quotation 306, third, fourth, fifth, and sixth quotations 307). Activities of the Ku Klux Klan in Louisiana are fully evident in Trelease, *White Terror*, pp. 127–36. See also Vandal, "Policy of Violence in Caddo Parish," pp. 159–82.

blamed Radical agitation for the tragedy and refused to take action against the rioters. "The President had gone back to wise, lawful methods, and desired to restore the Union under the Constitution," Taylor reflected, "and in this he was but following the policy declared in his last utterance by President Lincoln." Holding "many interviews" with Johnson and with "influential men from various parts of the country," Taylor hammered against the Radicals, particularly Secretary of War Stanton, whom he viewed as "constantly betraying" Johnson to Republican "enemies" in Congress. Taylor repeatedly urged the president to dismiss Stanton from the cabinet, arguing that by failing to do so he was "injuring" the South. General Grant expressed to Taylor his own indignation toward Stanton. "My position as Lieut. Gen. is a mere shadow," Grant told Taylor. "I cannot do the first thing toward disciplining the army without being hampered by endless orders from the Sec. of War." Taylor quickly relayed Grant's complaints to Johnson, but the president still balked at the idea of removing Stanton. "In truth," Taylor observed, "President Johnson, slave to his own temper and appetites, was unfit to control others."[23]

Anxious to render the Radicals impotent, however, Johnson had adopted a scheme to form a new political coalition composed of Democrats and moderate and conservative Republicans prior to the 1866 congressional elections in the fall. A National Union convention, scheduled to meet in Philadelphia in mid-August, would seek to steer northern opinion back toward giving the southern states the right to control suffrage and allowing them to send representatives to Congress, thus circumventing the Fourteenth Amendment. As if to prove his restraint, Johnson encouraged southerners to select as convention delegates former Whigs and conservative Democrats who had opposed or reluctantly accepted secession in 1861. Although organizers in Louisiana had already selected Taylor as a delegate, he hesitated to participate. "Averse to appearing before the public, I was reluctant to go to this Convention," he maintained, "but the President, who felt a

23. Brock, *American Crisis*, pp. 158–61; Richard Taylor, *Destruction and Reconstruction*, pp. 308–10 (first quotation 308, second, third, fourth, and sixth quotations 309); undated and unpublished interview with Richard Taylor (fifth quotation).

deep interest in its success, insisted, and I went." Soon after reaching Philadelphia, Taylor became the target of a local newspaper editorial that condemned him as "a rebel who, with hands dripping with loyal blood, had the audacity to show himself in a loyal community." To his defense came Joshua J. Guppey, former colonel of the Twenty-third Wisconsin whom Taylor had treated with kindness as a prisoner three years earlier at the battle of Bayou Bourbeau. Having received an immediate parole from Taylor to return home to care for his sick wife, Guppey was now a convention delegate himself, and he visited Taylor with several Wisconsin colleagues, offering "to make the newspaper office a hot place." Declining Guppey's demonstration of friendship and respect, Taylor noted, "This was the difference between brave soldiers and non-fighting politicians, who grew fat by inflaming the passions of sectional hate."[24]

On August 14 the delegates jammed into a specially constructed "wigwam" building with thousands of spectators. The opening ceremony witnessed northern and southern delegates walking together down the center aisle to a deafening, wall-shaking round of cheering. "Negro-worshipers from Massachusetts and slave-drivers from South Carolina entered the vast hall arm in arm," Taylor recalled. When the tumult finally began to ebb, Taylor stood up in his chair, and in an uncharacteristic burst of emotion shouted, "Three cheers for the thirty-six states of the Union!" The crowd responded in ecstasy, carrying on the frenzy of unity for several more minutes. Former major general John A. Dix of New York, serving as chairman, delivered an opening speech stating the convention's purposes, which Taylor recorded as "to renew fraternal feeling between the sections, heal the wounds of the war, obliterate bitter memories, and restore the Union of the fathers." There was no debate to spoil the event. The platform, decided in advance by committee, praised President Johnson extravagantly and repeated the South's right to control suffrage and elect

24. Carter, *When the War Was Over*, pp. 237–38, 246–47; Perman, *Reunion without Compromise*, pp. 198–211, 217–21; Gambill, *Conservative Ordeal*, pp. 64–68; Richard Taylor, *Destruction and Reconstruction*, pp. 310 (first quotation), 180–82 (second, third, and fourth quotations 182); Edmonds, *Yankee Autumn*, p. 398.

representatives to Congress. After three days the National Union convention adjourned, its heady delegates believing their patriotic example would serve to guide the country toward defeating the Republicans in November.[25]

Despite his enthusiasm in Philadelphia, Taylor relapsed into skepticism when he returned to Washington. "The President was charmed by the Convention," he noted. "Believing the people—his god—to be with him, his crest rose, and he felt every inch a President." Taylor repeated the necessity of getting rid of Stanton and also suggested to Johnson that he replace Secretary of State Seward with General Dix. "The President took kindly to the proposition concerning Dix," Taylor recalled, "and I flattered myself that it would come off." Volunteering to interview Dix on the matter, Taylor took the night train to New York. "Gen. Dix was delighted," he remembered. "He became enthusiastic over [Johnson's] peace policy." As they spoke, a messenger entered the room and handed Dix a telegram. He rose to read it and then gave it to Taylor. It was a message from Seward appointing Dix as minister plenipotentiary to France. "I was astonished, in fact dumfounded for the instant," Taylor recalled. Dix asked what it could mean, and Taylor replied, "Johnson, in a fit of indignation or drunkenness, has either told Seward that he did not intend to keep him in the State Dept. or else the information has gone to him through another source." Taylor returned immediately to Washington, where he found a note from Grant requesting his presence. Grant said that he had misjudged Stanton. "In fact," Grant explained, "I believe that [Stanton] intends to do everything for the promotion of a solid peace in the South." Taylor now understood what had happened regarding Dix. "The truth flashed before me in an instant," he recalled. Not only had Stanton's spies in the White House informed Seward of Johnson's intentions to replace him with Dix, but Stanton himself had also badgered Grant into running interference against Taylor.[26]

25. Richard Taylor, *Destruction and Reconstruction*, pp. 310–11 (first and third quotations 310); Wagstaff, "Arm-In-Arm Convention," pp. 101–19 (second quotation 101).

26. Richard Taylor, *Destruction and Reconstruction*, pp. 311–12 (first and second quotations 311); undated and unpublished interview with Richard Taylor (third, fourth, fifth, sixth, and seventh quotations).

Stanton and Seward had checkmated Taylor completely, but the Radicals had no need for such intrigues in the larger political arena. Johnson's vision of a grand National Union party soon proved "of as little avail as the waving of a lady's fan against a typhoon," Taylor reflected. Radicals successfully painted the new movement as a vehicle for southern demands, with Democrats dominant over Republicans. Then in late August and early September the president embarked on his infamous "Swing Around the Circle," a speech-making tour through the Midwest designed to solidify support for his new coalition in the upcoming congressional elections. At every stop audiences stunned and angered him with verbal abuse for his prosouthern stand. Johnson only succeeded in strengthening his enemies. In November 1866 the Radicals and their moderate Republican cooperatives won a series of jolting victories, solidifying control of Congress with a two-thirds majority in both houses. According to Taylor, the Radicals' furious reaction to Johnson's combative tactics "taught the lesson that is ever forgotten, namely, that it is an easy task to inflame the passions of the multitude, an impossible one to arrest them. From selfish ambition, from thoughtless zeal, from reckless partisanship, from the low motives governing demagogues in a country of universal suffrage, men are ever sowing the wind, thinking they can control the whirlwind."[27]

With the Republicans now poised to launch a Radical-inspired agenda for even stronger Reconstruction measures in Congress, General Grant advised Taylor to seek compliance with their requirements under the Fourteenth Amendment for the South's restoration to the Union. "I would like exceedingly to see one Southern State . . . ratify the amendment, to enable us to see the exact course that would be pursued," Grant informed Taylor in late November. "I believe it would much modify the demands that might be made." To a group of leading southerners asking his opinion, Grant stated the issue in more specific terms: "When you get home, urge your people to accept negro suffrage." Fully aware of the Radicals' added potency, Taylor frantically lobbied every southern congressman who would listen, ar-

27. Richard Taylor, *Destruction and Reconstruction*, pp. 310–11 (first quotation 310, second quotation 311); Perman, *Reunion without Compromise*, pp. 222–31; Gambill, *Conservative Ordeal*, pp. 69–71.

guing for compromise and moderation. "General Dick Taylor has been for some time in Washington riding his jaded political hobby horse—Expediency," noted a political observer. "He has proposed to accept universal suffrage for the South for all who can read and write." But the Radicals had no intention of allowing the South to use literacy tests to discriminate against black voters. In March 1867 the new Republican-dominated Congress passed a series of Reconstruction Acts dividing the South into five military districts and requiring states to call constitutional conventions, elected by universal suffrage, for ratification of the Fourteenth Amendment. Ramrodded through over Johnson's veto, the acts empowered district army commanders to enroll black voters and to protect them at the polls. Radical Reconstruction had begun, insuring enough Republican power in the South to secure final ratification of the Fourteenth Amendment. Taylor later asserted, "Congress . . . [made] a whipping-post of the South . . . inflicting upon it every humiliation that malignity could devise." [28]

Left with no options, southern Democratic leaders seemed ready to submit to Congress, yet hoping at the same time to retain power by currying favor with the many thousands of enfranchised freedmen. Taylor, along with former Confederate generals Beauregard and Longstreet in Louisiana and Robert E. Lee and Jubal Early in Virginia, were among the first to speak out in favor of complying with the Reconstruction Acts. Taking advantage of his influence with Johnson, Taylor induced him to appoint Major General Winfield Scott Hancock, the Union hero of Gettysburg, as district commander over Louisiana and Texas. An avowed Democrat with conservative principles, Hancock offered a welcome contrast to the hated Sheridan, whom Taylor branded "the Lieutenant-General of the Radicals." Indeed, according to Taylor, Hancock was "a gentleman . . . [who] recognizes both the great duties of a soldier of the Republic—to defend its flag and obey its laws." As Taylor probably anticipated, however, Hancock took a loose view of the Reconstruction Acts. With the prospect of so-called cooperation between Democrats and black vot-

28. Richardson, *Personal History of Ulysses S. Grant*, pp. 534–35 (first and second quotations 535); Marks and Schatz, *Between North and South*, p. 278 (third quotation); Perman, *Reunion without Compromise*, pp. 270–78; Richard Taylor, *Destruction and Reconstruction*, p. 313 (fourth quotation).

ers already evaporating after the election of a Republican-controlled constitutional convention in Louisiana, Hancock attempted to weaken every vestige of rising Republican power. Emboldened by the resulting turmoil, Democrats drew their battle lines even more tightly. In December Louisiana's white citizens sent scores of petitions to the president and Congress complaining that "the white population are powerless, subject to the domination of the negro race" because of "vast frauds and irregularities." Damning Louisiana's white Republican leaders as "designing men" who advocated confiscation of plantations and encouraged black sharecroppers to quit working, the petitioners predicted "a conflict of races which must result in the desolation of the country."[29]

Applauding Hancock for his dedication to "law and justice," Johnson had also finally seized upon Taylor's earlier insistence that Stanton must depart the cabinet. No decision could have been more ill-timed. In defiance of Congress's recent Tenure-of-Office Act requiring the president to gain permission from the Senate to remove any official the Senate had originally approved, Johnson dismissed Stanton in August. Congress soon initiated impeachment measures against the president, forcing him to stand trial in the Senate in the spring of 1868. Taylor recalled disgustedly, "President Johnson . . . fought his fight in his own way, had his hands completely tied, and barely escaped impeachment [conviction]." Believing himself vindicated, the president in fact had already obliterated his credibility as a candidate for election in the fall. Democratic power brokers looked upon Johnson as a pariah, while the nation's military idol, General Grant, stood out as the obvious choice for the Republican nomination. Having returned to New Orleans early in the year, Taylor recognized the monstrous challenge of finding a Democrat who might

29. Perman, *Reunion without Compromise*, pp. 278–97; Richard Taylor, *Destruction and Reconstruction*, pp. 322 (first quotation), 308 (second quotation); Joseph G. Dawson, *Army Generals and Reconstruction*, pp. 68–75; *Memorial. To His Excellency the President, and to the Hon. Senators and Representatives in Congress of the United States*, printed petition form dated December 23, 1867 (third and fourth quotations), in Johnson Papers. On Sheridan, see Richter, "General Phil Sheridan," pp. 131–54. On Hancock, see Jordan, *Winfield Scott Hancock*, pp. 200–212.

compete with Grant's popularity. "It was a conviction of this danger," he wrote Sam Barlow in March, "which made me so desirous of keeping Grant away from the Radicals last year."[30]

During the first half of 1868 Taylor tended to business in New Orleans and paid minimal attention to the Democratic party's national follies. In the summer, to no one's surprise, Grant accepted the Republican nomination, Taylor later judging, "The Radical Satan took him up to the high places and promised him dominion over all in view." Meanwhile Democratic leaders flailed about in choosing a candidate. Barlow and his New York clique finally forced the nomination upon an exceedingly reluctant Horatio Seymour, the former wartime governor of New York whose opposition to the Union cause had already rendered him almost as obnoxious as Johnson in Republican eyes. In early June, Taylor took his family on a vacation to Niagara Falls. By August they were in New York City enjoying the hospitality of Barlow's family in their palatial residence at Number 1 Madison Avenue. Taylor added his energy to the campaign, but Seymour's prospects remained murky at best. In August former Confederate brigadier general William Montague Browne, a friend of Barlow's, arrived from Georgia hoping to gain Barlow's and Taylor's help in raising $15,000 to campaign for Seymour in his home state. Receiving a lukewarm response, Browne left with only $500. Taylor remained with his family in New York City through the election in November, helping Barlow while also enjoying gambling at his favorite card game, whist, and betting on the local horse races. Meanwhile many of his fellow Democrats in Louisiana erupted in a violent effort to intimidate Republican voters, assaulting and killing blacks and whites alike in New Orleans and across the state. As a result, on election day Louisiana tallied a titanic majority for Seymour, while the rest of the former Confederate states went Republican (except for Georgia, where massive violence also broke out, and three other states not yet qualified). Thanks to the votes of about half a million

30. Gambill, *Conservative Ordeal*, pp. 108–10 (first quotation 109); Richard Taylor, *Destruction and Reconstruction*, pp. 312–13 (second quotation); Richard Taylor to Samuel Barlow, March 29, 1868 (third quotation), Barlow Papers.

southern freedmen, Grant won almost 53 percent of the total popular vote and a huge electoral majority.[31]

Taylor returned to New Orleans in December to grapple with meeting expenses on the New Basin Canal while also attempting to satisfy Barlow on a personal loan of several thousand dollars. "I am trying to pay my debt by installments," he informed Barlow. He also mentioned that the people of the state were waiting to learn the policies of the new gubernatorial administration. Although Louisiana had voted for Seymour, several months earlier the Republicans had managed to secure the election of one of their own, Henry Clay Warmoth, as governor. A young, handsome bachelor, Warmoth was born in Illinois, moved to Missouri in 1860, and was a Federal lieutenant colonel stationed in Louisiana near the end of the war. He opened a law practice in New Orleans in 1865 and became involved in politics, giving him the image of a dreaded carpetbagger. Once he took office, however, Governor Warmoth proved more moderate than any Republican had imagined. Seeking to ingratiate himself with local Democrats, he appointed several to state offices and aligned himself with a coalition of moderate Republicans and Democrats in the legislature. Early in Warmoth's administration, a prominent New Orleans citizen, Dr. W. Newton Mercer, honored him with a grand dinner attended by many influential Democrats, including Taylor and Duncan Kenner. "This dinner seemed to be most offensive to the colored Lieutenant-Governor [Oscar J. Dunn] and the radical white men who affiliated with him," Warmoth recalled, "many of whom I had been obliged to offend or disappoint in various ways, especially in vetoing bills passed by the Legislature in which they had large financial interests." Warmoth especially wanted "the advice, help, and friendly cooperation of the ablest men of the State . . . [and] found them in Dr. W. Newton Mercer, Joseph H. Oglesby, General Richard Taylor, Dun-

31. Richard Taylor, *Destruction and Reconstruction*, pp. 314 (quotation) 260; Gambill, *Conservative Ordeal*, pp. 131–54; Coulter, *William Montague Browne*, pp. 173–74; Richard Taylor to Samuel Barlow, June 2, August [?], 1868, Barlow Papers; Robert C. Wood to his wife, October [?], 1868, Wood Papers; Rable, *But There Was No Peace*, pp. 76–79; Dauphine, "Knights of the White Camelia," pp. 173–90.

Henry Clay Warmoth, resourceful Republican governor of Louisiana
(Library of Congress).

can F. Kenner, and John G. Gaines." Anxious to promote railroads and other internal improvements, Warmoth feathered his own nest by purchasing and selling state bonds, profiting from inside trading deals made at crucial times.[32]

P. B. S. Pinchback, a black state senator, summed up the politics of Warmoth's administration by proclaiming, "As a race [we] are between the hawk of Republican demagogism and the buzzards of Democratic prejudice." With the dominant white Republican leaders interested mainly in getting blacks to vote for them, civil rights faded further into the background. Warmoth's graft and influence peddling set the tone for a government of politicians in both parties reaping and dispensing the spoils of office. "By this time the charming

32. Richard Taylor to Samuel Barlow, December 14, 26 (first quotation), Barlow Papers; Current, *Those Terrible Carpetbaggers* pp. 242–45; Binning, "Henry Clay Warmoth," pp. 216–17, 287–90; Warmoth, *War, Politics and Reconstruction,* pp. 88–89 (second quotation 89), 81 (third quotation).

credulity of the negroes had abated," Taylor noted, "and they answered the statement that slave-drivers were murdering their race . . . by saying that slave-drivers, at least, did not tell them lies nor steal their money." In early 1872, however, Warmoth began to lose control of the Republican party machinery to the so-called Custom House faction, a rival group of Republicans whose power stemmed from manipulating Federal patronage through the United States Custom House in New Orleans. Having already joined the Liberal Republican party, a national anti-Grant movement with Democratic support, Warmoth agreed to combine his faction with Louisiana Democrats for the upcoming governor's race. In searching for a viable candidate, Democratic leaders approached Taylor. "Many of my friends here are most eager to make me the next governor," Taylor informed Barlow, "but I am too poor to take office." The Democratic nomination went instead to John McEnery. The Custom House Republicans tabbed William P. Kellogg, whom Taylor labeled "a commonplace rogue." With Warmoth's government henchmen still in control of counting votes, fraud became so blatant that Republicans demanded a bipartisan election board to review the voting. When Warmoth attempted to manhandle the board, the Republicans set up their own board, declared Kellogg the winner, and convened their own legislature with enforcement by local Federal troops. Both sides appealed to President Grant and Congress for official recognition. In December, Taylor added his name to a congressional petition by a group representing "a large preponderance of the moral worth, intelligence, and wealth of the city of New Orleans." Complaining that "soon the conservative element of the State will have no representation whatever," the petition denounced Governor Kellogg for perpetrating a "scheme of outrageous misgovernment."[33]

For more than six months Louisiana reeled in political chaos. The presence of the Federal troops barely kept the conflict from lurching

---

33. Joe Gray Taylor, "Louisiana: An Impossible Task," p. 223 (first quotation); Joe Gray Taylor, *Louisiana Reconstructed*, pp. 227–46; Richard Taylor, *Destruction and Reconstruction*, pp. 318–19 (second quotation 319), 322 (fourth quotation); Richard Taylor to Samuel Barlow, February 2, 1872 (third quotation), Barlow Papers; *Address of the Citizens of Louisiana*, pp. 1 (fifth quotation), 12–14 (sixth quotation 12–13).

President Ulysses S. Grant
(*Johnson and Buell,* Battles and Leaders of the Civil War).

into violence. "I have never seen this people in such a state of excitement," Taylor wrote Barlow in early January 1873. Again, on February 1, he moaned, "No description can give you an adequate idea of the depression of the country and people. There is no trade, no business, and no confidence. . . . We have two governments . . . and no one can foresee the result." Desperate for a solution, a large group of Democrats appealed to Taylor, "they believing that my acquaintance and influence with Grant would certainly secure them the deliverance they were looking for," he recounted. Although Grant had won a second term by decisively whipping Liberal Republican Horace Greeley, he was well on his way to establishing the most incompetent and corrupt administration in American history. "The influence of this on the public was most disastrous," Taylor reflected. "Already shortened by the war, the standard of morality, honesty, and right was buried out of sight." Obviously Governor Warmoth's chicanery did not qualify as part of this trend when Taylor presented his arguments to Grant in late February. Dining at the White House with the president and his family, Taylor described the "infamous [Kellogg] government which had been fastened upon" Louisiana. Grant soon became "convinced that a grievous wrong had been committed and was anxious to undo it," Taylor later contended.[34]

After several weeks of negotiations with the president and various members of the cabinet and Congress, Taylor began to feel confident of impending success. "Parties were in hostile array in New Orleans," he noted, "but my friends [there] were restrained by daily reports of the situation in Washington. Only my opinion that there was some ground for hope could be forwarded." By now Grant knew that Reconstruction in the South had reached a crisis point. Although Louisiana embodied the most flagrant example of the Republican party's failure to build broad support among southern whites, almost all Republican regimes had grown too dependent on Federal patronage and military force in maintaining power, often to the detriment of

34. Richard Taylor to Samuel Barlow, January 8 (first quotation), February 1 (second quotation), 24, 25, 1873, Barlow Papers; undated and unpublished interview with Richard Taylor (third, fifth, and sixth quotations); Richard Taylor, *Destruction and Reconstruction*, pp. 314–17 (fourth quotation 314–15), 319–20.

civil rights and opportunities for blacks. With the northern public already growing weary of such problems, conservative and moderate Republican leaders in the North began to lose faith in sustaining the Reconstruction governments. Unable to come to a consensus on the Louisiana fiasco, Congress hesitated to take the initiative. Suddenly, just as Congress was about to adjourn, Grant issued a message to the Senate declaring that without immediate congressional action he would have no choice but to uphold Kellogg's Republican government. According to Taylor, the Radicals had called in their political markers in order to dictate the president's strategy, knowing that by publicly placing the burden on Congress at the last minute, Grant would then be free to act in favor of Kellogg. As everyone expected, Congress did nothing. The Radicals "had swerved Grant from an honest intention to do right," Taylor surmised. After learning of this shocking development, Taylor went at once to the White House, and without even asking Grant for an explanation, told him, "This world is big enough for us both, and hereafter we can live in it apart." Saying nothing more, he departed and never saw Grant again.[35]

"Among my own friends, I was charged with selling them out," Taylor recalled. Louisiana Democrats treated him as "an object of distrust." Soon afterward, violence tore through the state, forcing Grant to authorize the army to protect Kellogg's administration. Democrats repeatedly used organized intimidation and terrorism over the next three years, especially during elections, taking advantage of the army's inconsistent reaction and Grant's deepening reluctance to prop up Louisiana's unstable Republican regime in its irresponsible exploitation of black votes. Louisiana thus became the president's most aggravating problem, a domestic crisis contributing to a decline in Republican power in the North and subverting the purpose of Reconstruction itself. Believing himself betrayed, Taylor looked upon Grant with more pity than enmity. "Of a nature kindly and modest, President Grant was assured by all about him that he was the delight of the Radicals, greatest captain of the age, and saviour of the nation's

35. Richard Taylor, *Destruction and Reconstruction*, pp. 320–21 (first quotation 321); Gillette, *Retreat from Reconstruction*, pp. 104–21; Joe Gray Taylor, "Louisiana: An Impossible Task," pp. 221–30; undated and unpublished interview with Richard Taylor (second and third quotations).

life," Taylor later asserted. "It was inevitable that he should begin by believing some of this, and end by believing it all. . . . [He] finished by hating Southerners and Democrats." [36]

Having lost his political prestige and influence among Louisiana Democrats, Taylor also faced the ire of Governor Kellogg's Republican machine. Lashing out against Taylor for his chronic inability to meet payments to the state on the New Basin Canal lease, the legislature annulled his contract and lodged a legal judgment against him for several hundred thousand dollars, which Taylor refused to pay. Wasting no time in removing himself from the scene of conflict, he eagerly responded to a request from Samuel Barlow to go to England and act as Barlow's agent in a series of business deals involving British banks and investors in stock companies with international connections. Leaving his family in New Orleans, Taylor journeyed to London in May 1873 and remained for more than a year. The English businessmen and government officials he encountered proved difficult and often uncooperative, but the aristocracy seemed charmed by his lineage as the son of a United States president, treating him like an American prince. After meeting the Prince of Wales, the future Edward VII, Taylor wrote Barlow, "The Prince of Wales has fallen alarmingly in love with me. . . . He has had me elected an honorary member of the Marlborough Club, which is reserved for reigning princes and their sons." The prince also awarded him membership in the British Turf Club, hosting him at various horse racing events and entertaining him at his magnificent country palace, Sandringham. [37]

Taylor enjoyed his English sojourn to the fullest. He gambled at whist, bet on horse races, and caroused at all hours of the day and night with the prince and his entourage. On one notable occasion, at the derby, Taylor sat with the prince and his younger brother, the

36. Undated and unpublished interview with Richard Taylor (first quotation); Richard Taylor, *Destruction and Reconstruction*, pp. 321–22 (second quotation 321), 325–26 (third quotation); Joe Gray Taylor, *Louisiana Reconstructed*, pp. 267–313; Gillette, *Retreat from Reconstruction*, pp. 116–35.

37. Richard Taylor, *Destruction and Reconstruction*, p. 329; Jackson Beauregard Davis, "Life of Richard Taylor," pp. 117–18; Richard Taylor to Samuel Barlow, June 7, December 6, 17, 1873, January 26, March 2, 23 (quotation), April 7, May 11, July 13, 1874, Barlow Papers.

Duke of Edinburgh. Learning that Taylor and the prince had bet fifty
guineas each on a certain horse, the duke casually turned to Taylor
and asked him to walk to the betting stand and place a similar wager
for him. "Pardon me, Your Highness," replied Taylor, "the stand is
quite as near to you as to me." The duke stalked off in a huff, but the
prince remarked, "I am so glad you told Edinburgh that. What a deal
of cheek he has to be asking my guest to lay his bets for him!" Recalling his visit to the lavish confines of Sandringham, Taylor compared
the hospitality to treatment received in the mansion of a Virginia,
South Carolina, or Louisiana planter. Taken to the palace in one of
the prince's private carriages, Taylor was escorted to his room by the
prince himself. After a light luncheon in the early evening, he enjoyed the company of the Princess of Wales on a tour of the palace,
noting its superb artwork and decoration. Later in the evening a formal dinner was served, with several aristocratic guests also in attendance. The princess was enthralled with Taylor, so much that she mentioned that she would be glad to have him call on her during her visit
to London during the winter. He readily complied, taking her to the
Marlborough Club for a game of whist. During a break in the game
the lord chamberlain to the princess informed him in private that "it
is not customary for gentlemen to call on Her Royal Highness as you
have done." Taylor was so embarrassed that he later offered a personal apology to the prince. "Oh," the prince replied with a knowing
look, "you American gentlemen are so fascinating that we have to
guard against you."[38]

Upon returning to the United States in August 1874, Taylor met
his wife, Mimi, at Niagara Falls for a vacation of several weeks. When
they returned to New Orleans in the fall, Mimi fell gravely ill with a
fever. "The health of Mrs. Taylor continues uncertain, otherwise I
would leave this wretched land [and] make you a visit," Taylor wrote
Barlow in January 1875. In March, Mimi's strength declined rapidly,
and on the sixteenth she died. She was barely forty-one years old.
"My devoted wife was relieved from her suffering, long and patiently
endured, originating in grief for the loss of her [two young sons] and

38. Maury, "Reminiscences of General Taylor," p. 568 (first and second
quotations); Morrison, *Memoirs of Henry Heth*, pp. 210–14 (third quotation
213, fourth quotation 214).

exposure during the war," Taylor recalled. "Smitten by this calamity, to which all that had gone before seemed as blessings, I stood by her coffin, ere it was closed, to look for the last time upon features that death had respected and restored to their girlish beauty." At Taylor's side was Jefferson Davis, hoping to offer some measure of comfort. Reaching to touch Mimi's brow, Davis lost his composure and wept profusely. "His example completely unnerved me for the time," Taylor remembered, "but was of service in the end. For many succeeding days he came to me, and was as gentle as a young mother with her suffering infant." Mimi was buried in Metairie Cemetery in New Orleans.[39]

With support from his three daughters, Louise Margaret, twenty-three, Elizabeth, twenty, and Myrthe Bianca, ten, Taylor tried to endure the loss of his wife. Two weeks after Mimi's death he wrote Barlow, "My children are well and join me in love to you." In May 1875 Taylor took his daughters to Winchester, Virginia, where his sister Betty and her husband Philip Dandridge offered to care for them during Taylor's absences. Taylor soon decided to take up permanent residence in the town, the scene of his first triumph as a brigade commander during the war. Shortly after arriving he suffered a relapse of rheumatoid arthritis, leaving him unable to move from his bed for several weeks. "This may be a healthy climate," he informed Barlow, "but I am the unfortunate exception to prove the rule."[40]

Taylor found living in Virginia extremely appealing for several reasons beyond the convenience of having his sister's family nearby. Virginia was his ancestral home, and he was proud to claim citizenship in the Old Dominion. From a practical standpoint, he enjoyed a closer proximity to his dear friend Barlow, whose financial and political interests now demanded more time and energy. While working on Bar-

39. Richard Taylor to Samuel Barlow, July 13, November 27, December 20, 1874, January 15 (first quotation), March 9, 1875, Barlow Papers; Morrison, *Memoirs of Henry Heth*, p. 210; Richard Taylor, *Destruction and Reconstruction*, pp. 303–4 (second quotation 303, third quotation 304).

40. Tucker, *Descendants of the Presidents*, p. 104; Richard Taylor to Samuel Barlow, March 30 (first quotation), May 18, June 15, August 6 (second quotation), 1875, Barlow Papers; Jackson Beauregard Davis, "Life of Richard Taylor," p. 118.

Jefferson Davis, ca. 1875
(Jenkins Rare Book Company).

Richard Taylor. Retouched photograph, ca. 1875
(Edward M. Boagni).

low's behalf in England, he had encountered problems from potential investors in Barlow's business schemes who happened to own Virginia state bonds. Virginia had issued the bonds in 1871 in an effort to fund its prewar debt, but stagnant economic conditions had left the state unable to pay the interest, angering British bondholders over the $10 million they had invested. Intent on enhancing Barlow's wealth as well as on reclaiming Virginia's financial standing abroad, Taylor approached politicians in Richmond with a plan to raise taxes for funding and to issue new bonds to settle the state's debt. "I have no doubt a satisfactory arrangement can be affected with foreign bondholders," he assured Barlow in August. In November, Taylor returned to London to urge patience on the part of the investors. "The British bondholder, conveniently ignoring his greed for large interest, believes the outside world in a combination to swindle him," Taylor complained. Yet he soon felt confident of achieving success. "I am spending your money freely, as I am ashamed to say, I have done before," he joked to Barlow. At the end of the month he boasted, "I seem to have won the hearts and confidence of the city." Upon Taylor's return, several members of the Virginia legislature reacted favorably to his plan, but continual weakness in the state's economy put strains on the budget that left the matter suspended indefinitely.[41]

Meanwhile Taylor had also fulfilled his public duty by accepting an appointment to the board of trustees of the Peabody Fund, a multimillion-dollar endowment to American education established by the late George Peabody. Elected to the board in 1871, Taylor attended annual meetings beginning in 1872. Giving priority to normal schools in the South, the Peabody trustees reflected a paternalistic, conservative attitude by discouraging racial integration in education and by favoring white schools over black in awarding gifts.[42]

Spending most of his time working as Barlow's paid political lobbyist, Taylor also helped formulate strategy for the Democratic party's 1876 presidential campaign. With Republicans steadily losing credibility over the scandals of Grant's administration and the embarrassing events of Reconstruction, Democrats worked feverishly to find a strong candidate. Barlow favored his longtime friend and fellow attorney Samuel J. Tilden, now the governor of New York, a modest but stern reformer who had crushed the Tweed ring in New York City. As early as November 1874 Taylor had begun assessing and influencing Tilden's chances in the South. In January 1875 he informed Barlow, "As matters now stand Tilden will have the delegates from the Gulf States and can be nominated without difficulty." After corresponding with a host of Democratic leaders, Taylor asserted in April,

41. Maury, "Reminiscences of General Taylor," p. 568; Richard Taylor to Samuel Barlow, August 27 (first quotation), November 3, 12 (second quotation), 19 (third quotation), 26 (fourth quotation), December 23, 1875, January 9, 26, 31, March 7, 11, 1876, Barlow Papers.

42. Jackson Beauregard Davis, "Life of Richard Taylor," p. 117; Richard Taylor to Samuel Barlow, June 12, 1872, Barlow Papers; Vaughn, *Schools for All*, pp. 141–59; James D. Anderson, *Education of Blacks in the South*, pp. 79–87; Dillingham, *Foundation of the Peabody Tradition*, pp. 1–8.

Samuel J. Tilden, 1876 Democratic presidential candidate
(Jenkins Rare Book Company).

"Very many influential people in every quarter share my views, many of whom are members of the next Congress and will be [delegates] at the Democratic Convention." By the spring of 1876 he was spending time in Washington rubbing shoulders with congressional Democrats and reporting enthusiastically to Barlow, "I succeeded in gaining important strength for Tilden in Tennessee, Kentucky, and Missouri, where he was weak." In June, at the Democratic convention in St. Louis, Taylor helped whip the southern delegates into line for Tilden. With the nomination secured, an ecstatic Barlow sent Tilden congratulations spiced with a special bit of flattery: "Gen. Taylor is I think more gratified than he could have been at his father's nomination."[43]

43. Richard Taylor to Samuel Barlow, November 27, 1874, January 15 (first quotation), March 9, April 16 (second quotation), 1875, April 8 (third quotation), May 18, 1876, Barlow Papers; Jackson Beauregard Davis, "Life of Richard Taylor," p. 115; Samuel Barlow to Samuel J. Tilden, June 29, 1876 (fourth quotation), Tilden Papers. On Tilden's presidential campaign and the subsequent electoral controversy, see Flick, *Samuel Jones Tilden*, pp. 288–324, 360–402.

Taking much of the credit for Tilden's success, Taylor offered the nominee sober advice a few days later. "As I confidently anticipated the result, I have not been unduly elated," he wrote. "Avoid crowds and interviews. Say all you deem necessary in your letter of acceptance. Then keep silent and let your friends conduct the campaign under your general instructions." In November, Tilden won the popular vote by about 250,000 over the Republican candidate Rutherford B. Hayes, but accusations of Democratic fraud in Louisiana, South Carolina, and Florida, and controversy over one elector in Oregon, left the electoral vote in dispute. Tilden needed only a single electoral vote for victory. Already recognized as the most influential southern lobbyist in Congress, Taylor went to work to compel the politicians to settle the matter. Southerners were outraged, and rumors of potentially violent mass upheaval against a Hayes victory alarmed Taylor. "Decided progress is made every day in consolidating the purposes of our friends [in Congress] and impressing the other side with a sense of the gravity of the situation . . . [and] impressing on the South the necessity of prudence and abstinence," he wrote Barlow on December 18. A few days later he noted, "I think the army people about Washington will push for a settlement. They recognize the fact they will be ruined if a row comes off."[44]

With the Senate in Republican hands and the House now controlled by Democrats, committees in both houses failed to formulate a consensus for ending the crisis in early 1877. "Do not expect any near solution to the political problem," Taylor warned Barlow on January 7. "There is hardly a chance of agreement." But two days later he reported, "It is certain that in the next fortnight we will move on the enemy in a way to make things horrible for them. Our people in the House are firm and united." He also observed, "I have been afraid of the Senate . . . mooning about a tribunal [to decide the election], which is another name for surrender; but I am now satisfied that the House will not listen to such nonsense." Almost immediately, however, northern Democrats, already worried about the economic panic that might result from southern demands, began to falter amid accu-

44. Richard Taylor to Samuel J. Tilden, July 5, 1876 (first and second quotations), Tilden Papers; Richard Taylor to Samuel Barlow, December 18 (third quotation), 20, 22 (fourth quotation), Barlow Papers.

sations from Republicans that the Democratic party would surely support a new rebellion in the South if Congress declared Hayes the winner. A compromise proposal involving a special, fifteen-man electoral commission to recount the votes—the tribunal Taylor feared—quickly gained congressional approval. "It is sad indeed—even should we win the toss [in selection of commission members], but losing it buries the National Democratic Party forever," Taylor lamented. On January 18 he confessed, "I see no alternative but to hold together and support this scheme, hoping for success. No one will take the trouble to preach our funeral if we fail." Taylor threw the blame for the debacle squarely on the Senate Democrats: "Our people in that body have been for so long in a hopeless minority that victory never enters their heads."[45]

By January 23 Taylor had completely reversed his pessimistic predictions about the electoral commission's viability. The commission included ten members of Congress evenly divided along partisan lines, but Taylor believed that the remaining five members from the Supreme Court would recognize the strength of the Democratic votes in Florida and Louisiana and thus give the election to Tilden. "There can be no longer a doubt about Tilden's success . . . and that the era of the 'Carpetbaggers' has passed away," he assured Barlow. "These are great achievements, and, in my small way, I have contributed to the result. . . . The battle is won, now comes the division of the spoils." Then, to his utter horror, on February 28 the final ruling, following an unforeseen change in the commission's Supreme Court membership, awarded Hayes all the disputed electoral votes, making him the victor. As Taylor later observed, "Justice was done—that justice ever accorded by unscrupulous power to weakness." Miserable beyond measure, he wrote Barlow, "I am in this wretched den, surrounded by the wreck of our hopes." The so-called Compromise of 1877—a secret agreement between Hayes and southern leaders who agreed to support the commission's decision in exchange for the removal of

45. Richard Taylor to Samuel Barlow, January 7 (first quotation), 9 (second and third quotations), 16 (fourth quotation), 18 (fifth quotation), 14 (sixth quotation), 1877, Barlow Papers; Michael Les Benedict, "Southern Democrats in the Crisis of 1876–1877," pp. 489–503. See also Rable, "Southern Interests and the Election of 1876," pp. 347–61.

Federal troops from the South, a southerner in the cabinet, and future congressional appropriations for a southern railway route to the
Pacific—proved anticlimactic. Hayes was inclined to remove the
troops in any case, the cabinet appointment was for postmaster general, and the Pacific railway project would depend on the mercurial
behavior of Congress. The South had entered the election crisis holding a weak hand, and all of Taylor's maneuverings could not alter the
balance of political power.[46]

Immediately after the election disaster, Taylor vowed to "put politics as far in the past as I have, long since, the war." But Barlow refused to let him rest. Over the next two years Taylor continued to
lobby Congress for a bill to provide funds for railroad promoter
Thomas A. Scott's Texas and Pacific southern line, a project in which
Barlow held a heavy financial stake. Unfortunately for Taylor and
Barlow, lawmakers seemed to lack cohesion on issues, and in particular they resisted spending money on railroads, so Taylor gradually
saw his efforts thwarted by an "utter want of organization and proper
agents on the floor of Congress." At the same time, however, Barlow
invited Taylor more frequently to visit him in New York City and at
his vacation retreat at Newport, on Long Island, and he began prodding Taylor to write his memoirs of the war and politics. Taylor often
absented himself from his home in Winchester for several weeks at a
time, leaving his daughters with his sister's family. A nephew, Robert
C. Wood, Jr., described their feelings in a letter to his wife during a
visit to Winchester in late 1877: "The girls are fearfully dissatisfied
and feel their father's frequent and protracted absences very bitterly. . . . In a word, their life here is a perfect blank." Later he added,
"They are terribly homesick [for Louisiana] and are trying to induce
their father to arrange for them to return to New Orleans. He is
rarely with them. He complains of poverty but continues to live in
grand style in Newport, New York, and elsewhere."[47]

46. Richard Taylor to Samuel Barlow, January 23, 26, February 1 (first
quotation), 28 (third quotation), 1877, Barlow Papers; Richard Taylor, *Destruction and Reconstruction*, p. 327 (second quotation); Michael Les Benedict,
"Southern Democrats and the Crisis of 1876–1877," pp. 509–20.
47. Richard Taylor to Samuel Barlow, February 28 (first quotation), January 7, 23, 1877, January 6, 7, 13, February 10, 20, 22 (second quotation), 26,

Along with the enjoyment of Barlow's hospitality, Taylor found a pleasant antidote to Washington's political machinations in the friendship of Henry Brooks Adams and his wife Clover. Grandson of John Quincy Adams and son of Charles Francis Adams, Henry Adams had recently moved to Washington after teaching history for several years at Harvard. Wealthy, genteel, and intellectually gifted, Adams not only intended to write a biography of Albert Gallatin, but he also had become fascinated with politics and power, noting in his classic autobiography that he had decided his "function in life . . . was as stable-companion to statesmen, whether they liked it or not." Cultivating a jaundiced view of democracy, Adams exuded an aristocratic attitude that struck a harmonious chord with Taylor, whose self-image as a charming southern cavalier of colonial ancestry proved a perfect complement to Adams's own sense of Massachusetts Brahmin superiority. Echoing Taylor's disdain for partisan politics, Adams commented on the times: "The system of 1789 had broken down, and with it the eighteenth-century fabric of *a priori*, or moral, principles. Politicians had tacitly given it up. Grant's administration marked the avowal." Having first met Taylor during a visit at the White House in 1850 when still a boy, Adams observed, "The families were intimate; so intimate that their friendliness outlived generations, civil war, and all sorts of rupture."[48]

Henry and Clover Adams rarely ventured out into Washington society, preferring instead to let the varied luminaries come to them. Every day during the week their townhouse was the scene of a flurry of scrupulously selected politicians, government insiders, and other congenial bon vivants who assembled for afternoon tea. Honored with a standing invitation, Taylor made a habit of appearing almost daily at 5:00 P.M., bearing a bouquet of flowers. "Such a quaint little society you never saw or imagined," Clover wrote to a favorite confi-

28, March 9, 10, 1879, Barlow Papers; Rothman, *Politics and Power*, pp. 192–203; House, "Barlow Papers," p. 351; Robert C. Wood, Jr., to his wife, October 28 (third quotation), November 4 (fourth quotation), 1877, Wood Papers.

48. Samuels, *Henry Adams*, pp. 1–27; Friedrich, *Clover*, pp. 199–202; Henry Adams, *Education*, pp. 317–18 (first quotation), 280–81 (second quotation), 46 (third quotation).

dant. "It is like a dream of the golden age." Temperamental and often caustic in her judgments, however, Clover at first described Taylor as rather "a light weight for a man who has commanded armies and led national councils." But soon she touted him as "one of the best of the rebel Major Generals, a great friend of the Prince of Wales, [and] a first-rate whist-player." Taylor sometimes joined the Adamses for dinner as well, staying long into the night conversing and bantering over literature, history, and politics. In only a few weeks' time he became one of their closest and most valued friends.[49]

In late 1877 Taylor decided to confront the task of writing his memoirs. Only a year earlier he had declined Dabney Maury's request for an article suitable for publication in the *Southern Historical Society Papers*. "One who has made history, even in a small way, is rarely happy in writing it," Taylor argued. He did manage to turn out a brief article on his surrender to Canby as part of a series of Civil War reminiscences published in the Philadelphia *Weekly Times*, and Maury reprinted it verbatim in the March 1877 issue of the *Southern Historical Society Papers*. Beyond this Taylor refused to apply his literary talents. But Barlow's persistence finally forced him to make an attempt at producing a fuller story. "Your nagging has driven me to scribbling," Taylor groused in December 1877. During 1878 two preliminary articles appeared in the *North American Review*, a prominent conservative journal of politics and history. The articles covered Taylor's experiences during Stonewall Jackson's Shenandoah Valley Campaign. Encouraged by Barlow's positive reaction, and always mindful that he depended on Barlow's generosity for his livelihood, he continued writing about the war as well as Reconstruction. By January 1878 Taylor had composed 165 pages of foolscap manuscript. "I have made an audience of the household and read each day's work," he wrote Barlow from Winchester. "I think for five weeks my average working has been ten hours a day, so your commands have been obeyed." In order to write competently about the war in Louisiana, however, he saw the need to go to New Orleans to consult records kept by his former artillery officer Joseph Brent. Taylor's daughters were delighted when he

49. Contosta, *Henry Adams*, pp. 62–63; Levenson et al., *Letters of Henry Adams*, 2:349 (first and third quotations); Friedrich, *Clover*, pp. 204–8 (second quotation 207).

Henry Brooks Adams, aristocratic intellectual. Sketch by Samuel Laurence
(Massachusetts Historical Society).

agreed to take them on the trip. Brent's wife recalled that, once Taylor reached New Orleans, he went to work immediately. During his writing sessions "he would walk back and forth, as if deep in thought, and then, seating himself, would write with great rapidity and precision— as if every sentence had already been formulated in his mind."[50]

50. Richard Taylor to Dabney H. Maury, May 8, 1876 (first quotation), Brock Papers. Taylor's article in the Philadelphia *Weekly Times* subsequently appeared with other articles from the series in *Annals of the War*, pp. 67–71. In the meantime the article also appeared as "Last Confederate Surrender," in *Southern Historical Society Papers*, 3:155–58. Richard Taylor, "Reminis-

In June 1878 Taylor set himself to correcting and revising his manuscript, "a dreary, slow business, but necessary," he complained to his
nephew Robert Wood. As for finding a publisher, he depended on
Barlow, whose contacts in New York City put the author in touch with
William H. Appleton of D. Appleton and Company, a venerable pub-
lishing house that had already produced several excellent Civil War
memoirs and histories. Taylor hoped the book would be published in
the fall of 1878, but it did not appear for distribution until early
spring the following year. Taylor's chosen title, *Destruction and Reconstruction: Personal Experiences of the Late War*, referred to the South's
defeat and subsequent difficulties in peace. Advance reviews appearing in New York newspapers proved extremely favorable. The New
York *Herald* declared, "His volume must be pronounced by far the
most creditable attempt made by a Southern writer to portray and
interpret the most critical epoch in the history of this country." Jacob
D. Cox, a former Union general writing in the northern journal *The
Nation*, however, described the book as "both useful and mischievous:
useful . . . [as a] contribution to the history of the time . . . and mischievous because the writer . . . teaches contempt for popular government, worship for aristocracy . . . and a general belief that the
triumph of the Government in the late war was the ruin of civilization." Taylor's former friend and nemesis William T. Sherman commented in a letter to David F. Boyd that he considered Taylor "brilliant in conversation, but not profound," and that his text "stigmatizes
good men." Although Sherman emerged in the narrative as one of
Taylor's most salient targets of criticism, he had to admit that "on the

---

cences of the Civil War," pp. 77–96; Richard Taylor, "Stonewall Jackson and
the Valley Campaign," pp. 238–61; Richard Taylor to Samuel Barlow, December 30, 1877 (second quotation), January 4 (third quotation), 8, 1878,
Barlow Papers; undated statement by Mrs. Rosella K. Brent (fourth quotation), Wood Papers. In 1926 Taylor's daughter Betty donated the original
manuscript of *Destruction and Reconstruction* to the Louisiana Historical Society, but Tulane University, now the repository of the society's archives, has no
record of it. The manuscript's location remains a mystery. See Lafargue,
"Manuscript of General Richard Taylor's 'Destruction and Reconstruction,'"
pp. 46–58.

whole when [Taylor] narrates events under his own eyes . . . he is honest, fair, and just."[51]

Southern reviewers generally praised Taylor's memoirs, quibbling only with some minor facts and points of interpretation. "We find ourselves riveted to its pages in the 'wee small hours' of the morning," claimed one. Dabney Maury's appraisal in the *Southern Historical Society Papers* was of course highly laudatory, citing Taylor's "abounding metaphor," his "vivid pen-pictures," and "the brilliant and unexpected flashes of thought clothed in wonderful modes of expression." In private, however, some of Taylor's former Confederate comrades blasted the book. Jedediah Hotchkiss, Stonewall Jackson's topographer during the Valley Campaign, asserted that Taylor presented "more fiction than fact," especially regarding the battle of Port Republic, and that his "subordinate officers have denounced its statements in no measured terms." P. G. T. Beauregard declared flatly, "I think it could be called more properly 'The Romance of Destruction and Reconstruction,' for it is everything but accurate. . . . [A]s General Grant said during our Louisiana troubles, 'General Taylor talks well, but like all great talkers, he often draws on his imagination for his facts.'"[52]

Considering Taylor's penchant for dispensing criticism in wide swaths and with deep cuts, the various objections to *Destruction and*

51. Richard Taylor to Robert C. Wood, Jr., June 16, 1878 (first quotation), Wood Papers; Richard Taylor to Samuel Barlow, January 9, 1879, Barlow Papers; Richard Taylor, *Destruction and Reconstruction* (1879), reviews following p. 274 (second quotation); Cox, "General Richard Taylor's Reminiscences," pp. 287–89 (third quotation 287); William T. Sherman to David F. Boyd, April 29, 1879 (fourth and fifth quotations), Boyd Papers. See also "Review of *Destruction and Reconstruction*," *Magazine of American History*.

52. "Review of *Destruction and Reconstruction*," in *Southern Historical Society Papers*, 7:256 (first quotation); Maury, "Reminiscences of General Taylor," p. 567 (second quotation); Jedediah Hotchkiss to Robert L. Dabney, August 4, 1897 (third quotation), Hotchkiss Papers; P. G. T. Beauregard to J. F. H. Claiborne, May 15, 1879 (fourth quotation), Claiborne Papers. For another lengthy and extremely critical review (apparently unpublished) of *Destruction and Reconstruction*, see Confederate general Jubal A. Early's thirty-nine-page manuscript in the Early Papers.

Reconstruction among northerners and southerners alike seem under-
standable. He exercised a stridently opinionated and judgmental
style, and as Sherman perceived so well, Taylor's narrative is most accurate and enlightening in describing events that fell directly under
his observation. Moreover, because he had direct access to records
kept by Brent from the Louisiana campaigns, those chapters of the
book stand out as the best. Douglas Southall Freeman, modern historian of the Army of Northern Virginia, admitted that "Taylor's
treatment of Jackson's Valley Campaign helped to fix the pattern of
all subsequent narrative as late as [1898]." Yet he also noted astutely
that Taylor "wrote charmingly but sketchily of the operations." More
recently William G. Piston has correctly saddled Taylor's book with
much of the blame for James Longstreet's subsequent defamation at
the hands of Lost Cause apologists, especially regarding the Lee-
Longstreet controversy at Gettysburg. The fact that Taylor was not at
Gettysburg, Shiloh, and several other pivotal battles, however, did not
prevent him from commenting on them and passing judgment on
their participants. Finally, taken on its own terms, *Destruction and Reconstruction*'s merits far outweigh its weaknesses. If used carefully, as
should be done with any personal testimony written years afterward,
the book's content easily justifies its reputation as an outstanding primary source on the Civil War era. Freeman rated Taylor as "the one
Confederate general who possessed literary art that approached first
rank . . . [with] so much literary charm and so observant an analysis
of character." *Destruction and Reconstruction*, Freeman affirmed, was
"written with the unmistakable touch of cultured scholarship."[53]

53. Freeman, *Lee's Lieutenants*, 3:819 (first quotation), 1:737 (second quo-
tation); Piston, *Lee's Tarnished Lieutenant*, pp. 142–43, 148; Freeman, *South to
Posterity*, pp. 84–87 (third quotation 85, fourth quotation 86). See also Aaron,
Unwritten War, pp. 246–48.

Epilogue

His last thoughts were of you and his family.

Betty Dandridge to Jefferson Davis

Taylor was in Washington lobbying for the Texas and Pacific Railroad
project on March 3, 1879, when he wrote Barlow saying that he was
"recovering from a wretched cold." Two days later he suffered an attack of rheumatoid arthritis. "I was stricken down severely and can
hardly hold up my head," he complained. "Will come to you as soon
as I can move." Although still weak after several days, he went to Barlow's home in New York City and began reading and correcting page
proofs of his book, scheduled for final publication in early April. By
March 20 he had developed symptoms of dropsy, extensive accumu-
lations of fluid in body organs and cavities, commonly the result of
heart disease and cardiac failure. Barlow secured the services of Dr.
Austin Flint, Jr., who began treatments to relieve the affliction. Learning of Taylor's illness, Henry Adams wrote Barlow: "Our regard for
the General is very strong and our relations with him for a year past
have been so close that his absence is a serious loss. On the other hand
we were fully prepared for the worst. . . . I honestly think he has been
reckless . . . and has gone on with indifferences to consequences."
Under Dr. Flint's care Taylor's condition improved, and he finished
his work on the book. About April 1, however, he suffered an acute

relapse. "We watch with great anxiety the news from General Taylor," wrote Adams. "There is a great deal of chatter about him." [1]

Slipping in and out of consciousness, Taylor continued to weaken, and there seemed no hope of recovery. His sister Betty Dandridge came from Winchester to comfort him. On April 11 he remained unconscious most of the day but rallied in the late afternoon and took Holy Communion from an Episcopal clergyman. About 8:00 A.M. the next day he died. The funeral took place on April 13 at the Church of the Transfiguration on Twenty-ninth Street. A silver plate on the coffin bore an inscription: "Richard Taylor, died April 12, 1879, aged 53 years and 2 months and 16 days." The pallbearers were Barlow, William M. Evarts (President Hayes's secretary of state, yet a longtime friend of Taylor), Hiester Clymer (Democratic congressman from Pennsylvania), and Thomas F. Bayard (Democratic senator from Delaware). "I should have come on to the funeral under any ordinary circumstances, but I couldn't run with that political crowd," Henry Adams informed Barlow. "The poor old General would have lifted his coffin lid and smiled his most sardonic smile, if I had seen him escorted to the grave by politicians." [2]

Taylor's body was taken to New Orleans for burial in Metairie Cemetery alongside his wife in a family crypt. Shortly afterward Betty Dandridge sent Jefferson Davis a copy of *Destruction and Reconstruction*, published the week before Taylor's death, bearing a heartfelt inscription: "I take this opportunity to send you the final product of my dear brother's hand. His last thoughts were of you and his family." Writing to a friend in late April, Davis reflected, "You do not overestimate Genl. D[ick] Taylor. He was as true as he was bright, and his friendship was warmest when most needed. His loss is to me a very great and profoundly sad one." In a tribute published in the *Southern Historical Society Papers*, Dabney Maury admitted that "[Taylor's] abso-

1. Richard Taylor to Samuel Barlow, March 3 (first quotation), March 7, 1879 (second quotation), Barlow Papers; *Record of the Class of 1845 of Yale College*, p. 200; Riley, "General Richard Taylor," p. 81; Levenson et al., *Letters of Henry Adams*, 2:354–55 (third quotation 354, fourth quotation 354–55).

2. New Orleans *Picayune*, April 13, 1879; New York *Times*, April 13, 1879; *Record of the Class of 1845 of Yale College*, pp. 200–201 (first quotation 201); Levenson et al., *Letters of Henry Adams*, 2:357 (second quotation).

Taylor family crypt, Metairie Cemetery, New Orleans
(James A. Mundie, Jr.).

lute self-reliance amounted to a total irreverence for any man's opinion," but he also offered "testimony to many kindly acts of this gifted
man." Nearly two years later Henry Adams's wife remarked, "We all
miss General Taylor . . . and no one takes his place."[3]

Two months before he died Taylor published an article in the *North
American Review*. Titled "A Statesman of the Colonial Era," the article
offered a biographical sketch of George Mason, the Virginia Revolutionary era political leader. Seeking to revive public appreciation for
his subject's accomplishments, Taylor depicted Mason as a sparkling
manifestation of Virginia's past role in providing educated, refined,
and courageous gentlemen to lead the nation. "Equally opposed to
the tyranny of monarchs and majorities, they asserted the rights of
individuals . . . controlled by dignity and self-respect," he wrote. As if
to project himself admiringly in Mason's place, Taylor described a
pastoral childhood in the "daily life of the Virginia gentry," Mason's
"taste for books and habits of study," and the fact that, although
"averse to a public career," Mason responded from "a sense of duty
alone" to the call to serve in politics, even at the risk of his precarious
finances and delicate health. "It is remarkable that a man without
professional training should have been placed at the head of committees, consisting of the ablest lawyers of the day, to deal with purely
legal subjects," Taylor affirmed.[4]

Fully recognizing Mason's "liberal tendencies," however, Taylor described in detail the Virginian's monumental accomplishments: the

3. Elizabeth Taylor Dandridge to Jefferson Davis, undated inscription
(first quotation), in a copy of *Destruction and Reconstruction* in the possession
of Edward M. Boagni, Baton Rouge; Rowland, *Jefferson Davis*, 8:384 (second
quotation); Maury, "Sketch of General Richard Taylor" (third quotation
345); Thoron, *Letters of Mrs. Henry Adams*, p. 259 (fourth quotation). Taylor's
daughter Louise Margaret (1852–1901) never married; Elizabeth (1854–
1936) married Colonel Walter R. Stauffer of New Orleans and had seven
children; Myrthe Bianca (1864–1942) married Isaac H. Stauffer, brother of
Walter Stauffer, and had two children. Tucker, *Descendants of the Presidents*,
p. 104.

4. Richard Taylor, "A Statesman of the Colonial Era," pp. 149–51 (first
quotation 149, second and third quotations 150, fourth quotation 151), 156–
57 (fifth quotation 157, sixth quotation 156).

Fairfax Resolves against the Crown; the Declaration of Rights, which served as the basis for the Declaration of Independence; his arguments in the Constitutional Convention for popular election to the House of Representatives; and his unconditional insistence on adoption of a Bill of Rights to the Constitution. Mason also opposed "with great fire and energy" the constitutional compromise that allowed the slave trade to continue until 1808, "declaring slavery to be a source of national weakness and demoralization[,] . . . this by a Virginia planter, himself a large owner of slaves." Mason thus foresaw "the difficulties and dangers of the slave question." Partly because of the slave-trade clause, but more generally because of the broad implied powers given the federal government over the states, Mason finally opposed ratification of the Constitution. In this regard, Taylor used Mason's position to condemn the upheaval of Reconstruction. "[Mason] urged independent States to create a common servant, the Federal Government, as a useful agent," Taylor argued. "He has seen the creature they called into being rend, like Frankenstein, its creators, disperse their assemblies at the point of the bayonet, and deprive their citizens of every legal right. . . . [A]ny calamity may be predicted of a land wherein millions of people have forgotten George Mason, to worship 'Old John Brown.'"[5]

Despite the recent collapse of Reconstruction, Taylor remained bitter about the Radical Republicans' legacies in American politics. The South's "enemies have sewn the seeds of a pestilence . . . [a] poison, the influence of three fourths of a million of negro voters," Taylor asserted in the final pages of *Destruction and Reconstruction.* "Greed of office, curse of democracies, will impel demagogues to grovel deeper and deeper in the mire in pursuit of ignorant votes." Bemoaning the disappearance of the South's "old breed of statesmen," he urged "respect for the memories and deeds of our ancestors." He then recited a list of Founding Fathers—Washington, Adams, Hamilton, Jay, Marshall, and Madison (but not Jefferson)—and praised their paramount legacy: strong, immutable political traditions, "the mighty influences in restraining peoples." Comparing those traditions to divine starlight

5. Ibid., pp. 151–60 (first quotation 157, second quotation 157–58, third quotation 151, fourth quotation 159–60).

shining from above, he concluded, "Once break the continuity of the stream, and men will deny its heavenly origin, and seek its source in the feeble glimmer of earthly corruption."[6]

In glorifying George Mason's Revolutionary radicalism while also calling forth the traditions of Federalist nationalists such as Washington, Hamilton, and Marshall, Taylor displayed a fundamental intellectual dilemma among nineteenth century American conservatives. Although obviously proud of the popular rebellion against England manifested in Mason's Declaration of Rights and its offspring, the Declaration of Independence, Taylor decried the continual evolution and extension of rights and liberties for the common man manifested in America's nineteenth-century democratic politics. Along with other Whiggish, genteel conservatives, including New England aristocrats like Henry Adams, Taylor refused to view the Declaration of Independence as the legitimate taproot of democratic power, its most recent expressions being the violent destruction of slavery and the racial conflict of Reconstruction. In particular, conservative southerners like Taylor could not reconcile their nationalistic pride in a vigorous, Federalist-inspired Union with their defense of states rights and local self-government by whites. In Taylor's view, America's greatest tragedy was that unrestrained democratic power, embodied in the Republican party's northern majority, had brazenly exploited the issues of slavery and black political power to wrest control of the federal government from prosouthern Democrats, thereby inflicting the Civil War and Reconstruction upon the South.

In criticizing the violence that erupted from democracy's doctrine of progress for the common man, Taylor refused to recognize his own role in conservatism's conspicuous entanglement in the democratic struggle for power. Projecting an outward posture of intellectual detachment and disdainful sarcasm, he discounted his own pursuit of personal wealth, his genteel racism, and his stake in politics, blasting abolitionists and fire-eaters alike for their dangerous fanaticism and then denouncing the Republican achievement of suffrage for freedmen, more because blacks seemed ignorant than because they were black. Alarmed by the growing masses, North and South,

6. Richard Taylor, *Destruction and Reconstruction*, pp. 330–31 (first quotation 330–31, second, third, and fourth quotations 331).

who sought material, racial, and political advantage, Taylor adhered to a self-image grounded in the southern plantation system's ideal of benevolent paternalism and aristocratic duty to the welfare of all, a value system he considered the only hope of tempering the epidemic of democracy. Comparing the North to Cromwell's Puritans and the South to Royal Cavaliers, he called for sectional harmony mirroring the "earnest council" between the peaceful, conservative leaders who "cement[ed] the fabric of England's greatness" during the postrevolutionary Restoration.[7]

As a practical and necessary compromise of his ideals, Taylor joined the South's pervasive participation in a national democratic system centered upon economic capitalism, social friction, and race conflict. Taylor the planter-businessman, slaveholder, politician, and postwar entrepreneur and Democratic power broker hardly reflected true aristocratic security and ideological purity. Unlike his disillusioned friend Henry Adams, who finally rejected politics as dirty and destructive, Taylor immersed himself in America's tumultuous contest of competing interests. Adams's wife Clover observed perceptively, "General Taylor disbelieves in democracy and universal suffrage, but [he] is too much a man of the world to wail over the inevitable."[8]

Only in his devotion to the Confederacy did Taylor act effectively upon the plantation system's paradigm of selfless public duty. His splendid service in Virginia under Stonewall Jackson, taken at the risk of his uncertain health, followed by his resourceful defense of Louisiana, accomplished at the cost of his own plantation's destruction and the deaths of his two young sons, attest to his sacrificial loyalty to the southern cause. Seeking neither undeserved authority nor public glory, Taylor faltered but once—in his strident personal reaction to General Edmund Kirby Smith's foolish ambition during the Red River Campaign. Steadfast to the end of the war, even after he considered the Confederacy's independence utterly hopeless, Taylor finally gave enhanced dignity to defeat and surrender. Thus his reputation as a gentleman warrior—a southern soldier prince—endures.

7. Taylor, "A Statesman of the Colonial Era," p. 160 (quotation).
8. Samuels, *Henry Adams*, p. 28 (quotation).

BIBLIOGRAPHY

PRIMARY SOURCES

Manuscripts

Barlow, Samuel Latham Mitchell. Papers. Huntington Library. San Marino, Calif.

Barry, James Buckner. Papers. Barker Texas History Center. University of Texas.

Boyd, David French. Papers. Louisiana State University.

Bragg, Braxton. Papers. William R. Perkins Library. Duke University.

Brent, Joseph L. Papers. Louisiana Adjutant General's Office. Jackson Barracks, New Orleans.

Brent, Joseph L. Papers. Louisiana State Museum. Louisiana Historical Center.

Brent, Joseph L. Papers. Tulane University.

Bringier, Louis A., Family. Papers. Louisiana State University.

Bringier Family. Genealogy Collection. Historic New Orleans Collection.

Brock, Robert Alonzo. Papers. Huntington Library.

Butler, Thomas W. Papers. Louisiana State University.

Claiborne, J. F. H. Papers. Southern Historical Collection. University of North Carolina.

Confederate District of West Louisiana. Record Book, April 11–May 23, 1864. Tulane University.

Confederate States of America Archives. Army Units. Louisiana Volunteer Papers, 1861–63. William R. Perkins Library. Duke University.

Conner, Mary Savage. "Mary Savage Conner of the Historic and Exclusive Second Creek Settlement: Her Journal, 1846–1850." Typescript compiled by and in the possession of Mary B. Gorman, Redwood, Mississippi.

Davis, Jefferson. Papers. Louisiana Historical Association Collection. Tulane University.

Davis, Jefferson. Papers. Miami University.

Early, Jubal A. Papers. Manuscript Division. Library of Congress.

Emory, William H. Papers. Beinecke Library. Yale University.

Farrow, Sam W. Papers. Barker Texas History Center. University of Texas.

Gould, John, ed. "Autobiography and Diary of Robert Simonton Gould." Typescript in John Simonton Gould Papers. Barker Texas History Center. University of Texas.

Hill, A. M. Papers. United Daughters o the Confederacy Library, Waco, Tex.

Holmsley, James Monroe. Papers. Barker Texas History Center. University of Texas.

Hotchkiss, Jedediah. Papers. Manuscript Division. Library of Congress.

Hyatt, Arthur W. Diary. Typescript at Louisiana State University.

Johnson, Andrew. Papers. Manuscript Division. Library of Congress.

Kingsley Memorial Collection. Yale University Archives.

Lyman, W. R. "Cross Keys and Port Republic." Typescript at Tulane University.

McDaniel, Benjamin F. Memoir. Barker Texas History Center. University of Texas.

Miscellaneous Manuscript Collections. Louisiana State University.

Miscellaneous Manuscripts Collection. Filson Club.

Miscellaneous Manuscripts Collection. Historic New Orleans Collection.

Moore, Thomas O. Papers. Louisiana State University.

Person Family. Papers. William R. Perkins Library. Duke University.

Pierson Family. Papers. Tulane University.

Pugh, R. L. Papers. Louisiana State University.

Sibley, Henry Hopkins. Letters. New York Historical Society.

Smith, Edmund Kirby. Papers. Southern Historical Collection. University of North Carolina.

Stauffer, Walter J. Papers. Louisiana State University.

Stokes, Anson Phelps. Autograph Collection. Yale University Archives.

Succession Papers of the Estate of Richard Taylor. New Orleans Public Library.

Taylor, Richard. Letter Book. Department of Alabama, Mississippi, and East Louisiana, September 25, 1864–May 9, 1865. Tulane University.

Taylor, Richard. Papers. Confederate Service Record Files. National Archives.

Taylor, Richard. Papers. In the possession of Edward M. Boagni, Baton Rouge, La.

Taylor, Richard. Papers. Louisiana Adjutant General's Office. Jackson Barracks, New Orleans.

Taylor, Richard. Papers. Louisiana State Museum. Louisiana Historical Center.

Taylor, Richard. Private Official Telegrams, March 18–May 8, 1865. Tulane University.

Taylor, Richard. Private Telegram Book. Department of Alabama, Mississippi, and East Louisiana, September 7, 1864–April 3, 1865. Tulane University.

Taylor, Zachary. Collection. Louisiana State Museum.

Taylor, Zachary. Family Bible. Virginia Historical Society.

Taylor, Zachary. Papers. Manuscript Division. Library of Congress.

Tilden, Samuel Jones. Papers. New York Public Library.

Trist, Nicholas P. Papers. Manuscript Division. Library of Congress.

Trist Family. Papers. Historic New Orleans Collection.

Undated and unpublished interview with Richard Taylor by an anonymous
  reporter from the New York *Herald*. New York Public Library.
United States Army. Records of Continental Commands, 1821–1920.
  Department of the Gulf. Civil Affairs Office. Record Group 393. National
  Archives.
United States Treasury Department. Records of the Third Special Agency. Civil
  War Special Agencies of the Treasury Department. Record Group 366.
  National Archives.
Walker, John G. Papers. Southern Historical Collection. University of North
  Carolina.
Walker, John G. "The War of Secession West of the Mississippi River During the
  Years 1863–4-& 5." Typescript at United States Army History Institute,
  Carlisle Barracks, Pennsylvania.
Wallace, James T. Diary. Southern Historical Collection. University of North
  Carolina.
Wood, Trist. Papers. Southern Historical Collection. University of North
  Carolina.
Yale College Autograph Album Collection. Yale University Archives.
Yale College Student Record Books. Yale University Archives.

Books, Pamphlets, and Broadsides

Adams, Henry. *The Education of Henry Adams: An Autobiography*. Boston, 1918.
Address of the Citizens of Louisiana, to the People of the United States. Washington,
  D.C., 1872.
Allen, John Fisk. *Memorial of Pickering Dodge Allen by His Father*. Boston, 1867.
American Book Prices Current, 1965–1970 Index. New York, 1974.
Anderson, John Q., ed. *Brokenburn: The Journal of Kate Stone, 1861–1868*. Baton
  Rouge, 1972.
———. *Campaigning with Parson's Texas Cavalry Brigade, C.S.A.: The War Journals
  and Letters of the Four Orr Brothers, 12th Texas Cavalry Regiment*. Hillsboro, Tex.,
  1967.
Anderson Galleries. *Library of the Late Major William H. Lambert. Part III. Civil
  War*. New York, 1914.
Barron, Samuel B. *The Lone Star Defenders: A Chronicle of the Third Texas. Texas
  Cavalry, Ross' Brigade*. New York, 1908.
Bartlett, Napier. *Military Record of Louisiana: Including Biographical and Historical
  Papers Relating to the Military Organizations of the State*. 1875. Reprint. Baton
  Rouge, 1964.

Bearss, Edwin C., ed. *A Louisiana Confederate: Diary of Felix Pierre Poche.* Natchitoches, La., 1972.

Beck, Brandon, and Charles S. Grunder. *Three Battles of Winchester.* Berryville, Va., 1988.

Bee, Hamilton P. *Dear Sir—I send herewith copies of a correspondence. . . .* San Antonio, 1864. Broadside dated December 8, 1864, in Garnett A. Dibrell Collection, Texas State Archives.

Beecher, Harris H. *Record of the 114th Regiment, N.Y.S.V.* Norwich, N.Y., 1866.

Benedict, Henry Marvin. *A Memorial of Brevet Brigadier General Lewis Benedict, Colonel of 162d Regiment N.Y.V.I.* Albany, 1866.

Bergeron, Arthur W., ed. *Reminiscences of Uncle Silas: A History of the Eighteenth Louisiana Infantry Regiment.* Baton Rouge, 1981.

Bering, John A., and Thomas Montgomery. *History of the Forty-Eighth Ohio Vet. Vol. Inf.* Hillsboro, Ohio, 1880.

Berlin, Ira, ed. *Freedom: A Documentary History of Emancipation, 1861–1867, Selected from the Holdings of the National Archives.* Series 2, *The Black Military Experience.* London, 1982.

Beveridge, Charles E., and McLaughlin, Charles C., eds. *The Papers of Frederick Law Olmsted.* Vol. 2, *Slavery and the South, 1852–1857.* Baltimore, 1981.

Bitton, Davis, ed. *The Reminiscences and Civil War Letters of Levi Lamoni Wight.* Salt Lake City, 1970.

Blessington, Joseph P. *The Campaigns of Walker's Texas Division.* New York, 1875.

Boggs, William R. *Military Reminiscences of Gen. Wm. R. Boggs, C.S.A.* Durham, N.C., 1913.

Booth, Andrew B., comp. *Records of Louisiana Confederate Soldiers and Louisiana Confederate Commands.* 3 vols. New Orleans, 1920.

Bosson, Charles P. *History of the Forty-Second Regiment Infantry, Massachusetts Volunteers, 1862, 1863, 1864.* Boston, 1886.

Boyd, David French. *Reminiscences of the War in Virginia.* Edited by T. Michael Parrish. Austin, 1989.

Breeden, James O., ed. *Advice among Masters: The Ideal of Slave Management in the Old South.* Westport, Conn., 1980.

Brent, Joseph L. *The Lugo Case: A Personal Experience [and] Capture of the Ironclad, "Indianola."* New Orleans, 1926.

———. *Memoirs of the War between the States.* New Orleans, 1940.

———. *Mobilizable Fortifications, and Their Controlling Influence in War.* Boston, 1885.

Brown, E. R. *The Twenty-Seventh Indiana Volunteer Infantry in the War of the Rebellion.* Washington, D.C., 1899.

Brown, Norman D., ed. *Journey to Pleasant Hill: The Civil War Letters of Captain Elijah P. Petty, Walker's Texas Division, C.S.A.* San Antonio, 1982.

Bryner, Cloyd. *Bugle Echoes: The Story of the Illinois 47th*. Springfield, Ill., 1905.

Buck, Samuel D. *With the Old Confeds: Actual Experiences of a Captain in the Line*. Baltimore, 1925.

Burdette, Robert J. *The Drums of the 47th*. Indianapolis, 1914.

Butler, Benjamin F. *Private and Official Correspondence of Gen Benjamin F. Butler during the Period of the Civil War*. 5 vols. Norwood, Mass., 1917.

Calendar of the Jefferson Davis Postwar Manuscripts. New York, 1970.

Cannon, Newton. *The Reminiscences of Sergeant Newton Cannon*. Edited by Campbell H. Brown. Franklin, Tenn., 1963.

Carpenter, George N. *History of the Eighth Regiment, Vermont Volunteers, 1861–1865*. Boston, 1886.

Catalogue of Officers and Students in Yale College, 1844–5. New Haven, 1844.

Champomier, P. A. *Statement of the Sugar Crop Made in Louisiana in 1850–51 [–1862]*. New Orleans, 1851–62 [issued annually].

Chesnut, Mary Boykin. *Mary Chesnut's Civil War*. Edited by C. Vann Woodward. New Haven, 1981.

Clark, James S. *Life in the Middle West: Reminiscences of J. S. Clark*. Chicago, 1916.

Clark, Orton S. *The One Hundred and Sixteenth Regiment of New York State Volunteers*. Buffalo, 1868.

Cogley, Thomas S. *History of the Seventh Indiana Cavalry Volunteers*. Laporte, Ind., 1876.

Connor, Seymour V., ed. *Dear America: Some Letters of Orange Cicero and Mary America (Aikin) Connor*. Austin, 1971.

Cooke, John Esten. *Stonewall Jackson; a Military Biography*. New York, 1866.

Correspondence between the War Department and General Lovell, Relating to the Defenses of New Orleans. Richmond, 1863.

Cummer, Clyde L., ed. *Yankee in Gray: The Civil War Memoirs of Henry E. Handerson, with a Selection of His Wartime Letters*. Cleveland, 1962.

Dabney, Robert Lewis. *Life and Campaigns of Lieut. Gen. Thomas J. Jackson*. New York, 1866.

Dana, Charles A. *Recollections of the Civil War*. New York, 1898.

Debray, Xavier B. *A Sketch of the History of Debray's 26th Regiment of Texas Cavalry*. 1884. Reprint. Waco, Tex. 1961.

De Forest, John William. *A Volunteer's Adventures: A Union Captain's Record of the Civil War*. New Haven, 1946.

Dorsey, Sarah H. *Recollections of Henry Watkins Allen*. New York, 1866.

Douglas, Henry Kyd. *I Rode with Stonewall*. Chapel Hill, 1940.

Dowdey, Clifford, and Louis H. Manarin, eds. *The Wartime Papers of Robert E. Lee*. Boston, 1961.

Duganne, Augustine J. H. *Camps and Prisons: Twenty Months in the Department of the Gulf*. New York, 1865.

Dumond, Dwight L., ed. *Southern Editorials on Secession.* New York, 1931.

Eby, Cecil D., ed. *A Virginia Yankee in the Civil War: The Diaries of David Henry Strother.* Chapel Hill, 1961.

Edgar, Thomas H. *History of Debray's (26th) Regiment of Texas Cavalry, Embracing Roster and Casualties.* Galveston, 1898.

Ewer, James K. *The Third Massachusetts Cavalry in the War for the Union.* Maplewood, Mass., 1903.

Fearn, Frances, ed. *Diary of a Refugee.* New York, 1910.

Field, Henry M. *Bright Skies and Dark Shadows.* New York, 1890.

Fleming, Walter L., ed. *General W. T. Sherman As College President.* Cleveland, 1912.

Flinn, Frank M. *Campaigning with Banks in Louisiana.* Lynn, Mass., 1887.

Freeman, Douglas Southall. *A Calendar of Confederate Papers.* Richmond, 1908.

Freeman, Douglas Southall, ed. *Lee's Dispatches: Unpublished Letters of General Robert E. Lee, C.S.A., to Jefferson Davis and the War Department of the Confederate States of America, 1861–1865.* New York, 1957.

Gallagher, Gary W., ed. *Fighting for the Confederacy: The Personal Recollections of General Edward Porter Alexander.* Chapel Hill, 1989.

Gordon, John B. *Reminiscences of the Civil War.* New York, 1903.

Goree, Langston James, V, ed. *The Thomas Jewett Goree Letters.* Vol. 1, *The Civil War Correspondence.* Bryan, Tex., 1981.

Gould, John M. *History of the First-Tenth-Twenty-ninth Maine Regiment . . . May 3, 1861, to June 21, 1866.* Portland, Maine, 1871.

Grant, Ulysses S. *Personal Memoirs of U. S. Grant.* 2 vols. New York, 1885–86.

Gravis, Peter W. *Twenty-Five Years on the Outside Row of the Northwest Conference.* 1892. Reprint. Brownwood, Tex., 1966.

Harding, George C. *The Miscellaneous Writings of George C. Harding.* Indianapolis, 1882.

Hatch, Carl E., ed. *Dearest Susie: A Civil War Infantryman's Letters to His Sweetheart.* New York, 1971.

Henkels, Stan V., Auction Commission Merchant. *Catalogue No. 1148. The Beauregard Papers (General P. G. T. Beauregard of the Confederate States Army) Being the Letters of Various Confederate Generals to Him, and . . . His Own Letters in Answer.* Philadelphia, 1915.

Hesseltine, William B., ed. *Three against Lincoln: Murat Halstead Reports the Caucuses of 1860.* Baton Rouge, 1960.

Historical Sketch Book and Guide to New Orleans and Environs. New York, 1885.

Hoffman, Wickham. *Camp, Court and Siege: A Narrative of Personal Adventure and Observation During Two Wars 1861–1865, and 1870–1871.* New York, 1877.

Hood, John B. *Advance and Retreat: Personal Experiences in the United States and Confederate States Armies.* New Orleans, 1880.

Howard, McHenry. *Recollections of a Maryland Confederate Soldier and Staff Officer under Johnston, Jackson and Lee*. 1914. Reprint. Dayton, Ohio, 1975.

Hughes, Nathaniel C., ed. *Liddell's Record*. Dayton, Ohio, 1985.

Irwin, Richard B. *History of the Nineteenth Army Corps*. New York, 1892.

Johns, Henry T. *Life with the Forty-ninth Massachusetts Volunteers*. Pittsfield, Mass., 1864.

Johns, Jane Martin. *Personal Recollections*. Decatur, Ill., 1912.

Johnson, Charles B. *Muskets and Medicine, or Army Life in the Sixties*. Philadelphia, 1917.

Johnson, Robert Underwood, and Clarence Clough Buell, eds. *Battles and Leaders of the Civil War*. 4 vols. New York, 1887.

Jones, J. William, et al., eds. *Southern Historical Society Papers*. 52 vols. and index. 1876–1959. Reprint. New York, 1977–80.

Jones, Samuel C. *Reminiscences of the Twenty-second Iowa Volunteer Infantry*. Iowa City, 1907.

Kelly, Henry B. *Port Republic*. Philadelphia, 1886.

Kirkland, Frazier. *The Pictorial Book of Anecdotes and Incidents of the War of the Rebellion*. Hartford, Conn., 1867.

Knox, Thomas W. *Camp-fire and Cotton-field: Southern Adventure in Time of War*. New York, 1865.

Levenson, J. C., et al., eds. *The Letters of Henry Adams*. 3 vols. Cambridge, Mass., 1982.

Lewis, Richard. *Camp Life of a Confederate Boy, of Bratton's Brigade, Longstreet's Corps, C.S.A.* Charleston, S.C., 1883.

Long, Andrew D. *Stonewall's "Foot Cavalryman."* Austin, 1965.

Lubbock, Francis R. *Six Decades in Texas*. Austin, 1900.

McClendon, William Augustus. *Recollections of War Times by an Old Veteran*. Montgomery, Ala., 1909.

McDonald, Archie P., ed. *Make Me a Map of the Valley: The Civil War Journal of Stonewall Jackson's Topographer, Jedediah Hotchkiss*. Dallas, 1973.

McGregor, Charles. *History of the Fifteenth Regiment, New Hampshire Volunteers, 1862–1863*. Concord, N.H., 1900.

McHatton-Ripley, Eliza. *From Flag to Flag*. New York, 1889.

McIntosh, James T., ed. *The Papers of Jefferson Davis*. Vol. 3, *July 1846–December 1848*. Baton Rouge, 1981.

Marks, Bayly Ellen, and Mark Norton Schatz, eds. *Between North and South, A Maryland Journalist Views the Civil War: The Narrative of William Watkins Glenn, 1861–1869*. Rutherford, N.J., 1976.

Marshall, Albert O. *Army Life; from a Soldier's Journal*. Joliet, Ill., 1884.

Maury, Dabney Herndon. *Recollections of a Virginian in the Mexican, Indian, and Civil Wars*. New York, 1894.

Moore, Edward A. *The Story of a Cannoneer under Stonewall Jackson*. Lynchburg, Va., 1910.

Moore, Frank, ed. *The Rebellion Record: A Diary of American Events*. 12 vols. New York, 1862–71.

Moors, J. F. *History of the Fifty-Second Regiment Massachusetts Volunteers*. Boston, 1893.

Morrison, James L., Jr., ed. *The Memoirs of Henry Heth*. Westport, Conn., 1974.

Murray, Henry A. *Lands of the Slave and the Free: or, Cuba, the United States, and Canada*. London, 1857.

Myers, F. M. *The Comanches: A History of White's Battalion, Virginia Cavalry, Laurel Brig., Hampton Div., A.N.V., C.S.A.* Baltimore, 1871.

Neese, George M. *Three Years in the Confederate Horse Artillery*. New York, 1911.

Nisbet, James Cooper. *Four Years on the Firing Line*. Edited by Bell Irvin Wiley. 1914. Reprint. Jackson, Tenn., 1963.

Noel, Theophilus. *A Campaign from Santa Fe to the Mississippi, Being a History of the Old Sibley Brigade*. Shreveport, 1865.

Northrup, Solomon. *Twelve Years a Slave*. Auburn, N.Y., 1853.

Oates, William Calvin. *The War between the Union and the Confederacy and Its Lost Opportunities, with a History of the 15th Alabama Regiment*. New York, 1905.

Official Journal of the Proceedings of the Convention of the State of Louisiana. New Orleans, 1861.

Official Report Relative to the Conduct of Federal Troops in Western Louisiana, During the Invasions of 1863 and 1864, Compiled from Sworn Testimony, under Direction of Governor Henry W. Allen. Edited by David C. Edmonds. 1865. Reprint. Lafayette, La., 1988.

Olmsted, Frederick Law. *A Journey in the Seaboard Slave States, with Remarks on Their Economy*. New York, 1856.

Oltorf, Frank Calvert. *The Marlin Compound: Letters of a Singular Family*. Austin, 1968.

Order of Exercises at Commencement, Yale College, August 21, 1845. New Haven, 1845.

Parke-Bernet Galleries. *American Historical Autographs, Portraits, and Views Collected by the Late Grenville Kane . . . Public Auction Sale, Tuesday, December 4*. New York, 1945.

Pellet, Elias P. *History of the 114th Regiment, New York State Volunteers*. Norwich, N.Y., 1866.

Porter, David D. *Incidents and Anecdotes of the Civil War*. New York, 1885.
———. *The Naval History of the Civil War*. New York, 1886.

Powers, George W. *The Story of the Thirty Eighth Regiment of Massachusetts Volunteers*. Cambridge, Mass., 1866.

Proceedings of the National Democratic Convention, Convened at Charleston, S.C., April 23, 1860. Washington, D.C., 1860.

Putnam, George Haven. *Memories of My Youth, 1844–1865.* New York, 1914.

Rainwater, P. L., ed. *A Civilian's Recollections of the War between the States, by H. S. Fulkerson.* Baton Rouge, 1939.

Record of the Class of 1845 of Yale College. New York, 1881.

Reed, Joseph W., Jr., ed. *Barbara Leigh Smith Bodichen: An American Diary, 1857–8.* London, 1972.

Richardson, Albert D. *A Personal History of Ulysses S. Grant.* Hartford, Conn., 1868.

———. *The Secret Service, the Field, the Dungeon, and the Escape.* Hartford, Conn., 1865.

Ripley, Eliza. *Social Life in Old New Orleans.* New York, 1912.

Rosenbach Company. *The History of America in Documents.* Part 3. Philadelphia, 1951.

Rowland, Dunbar, ed. *Jefferson Davis, Constitutionalist: His Letters, Papers, and Speeches.* 10 vols. Jackson, Miss., 1923.

Russell, William H. *The Civil War in America.* Boston, 1861.

———. *My Diary North and South.* Boston, 1863.

Samson, William H., ed. *Letters of Zachary Taylor from the Battlefields of the Mexican War.* Rochester, N.Y., 1908.

Scarborough, William K., ed. *The Diary of Edmund Ruffin.* Vol 3., *A Dream Shattered, June, 1863–June, 1865.* Baton Rouge, 1989.

Scott, John. *Story of the Thirty-Second Iowa Infantry Volunteers.* Nevada, Iowa, 1896.

Sherman, William T. *The Memoirs of Gen. W. T. Sherman.* 2 vols. New York, 1892.

Simon, John Y., ed. *The Papers of Ulysses S. Grant.* Vol. 16. Carbondale, Ill., 1990.

Slaughter, Philip. *A Sketch of the Life of Randolph Fairfax.* Richmond, 1864.

Smedes, Susan Dabney. *Memorials of a Southern Planter.* Edited by Fletcher M. Green. 1887. Reprint. New York, 1965.

Sprague, Homer B. *History of the 13th Infantry Regiment of Connecticut Volunteers.* Hartford, Conn., 1867.

Spurlin, Charles, ed. *West of the Mississippi with Waller's 13th Texas Cavalry Battalion, C.S.A.* Hillsboro, Tex., 1971.

Stanyan, John M. *A History of the Eighth Regiment of New Hampshire Volunteers.* Concord, N.H., 1892.

Statement of So Much of the Proceedings of the National Democratic Convention at Charleston, April, 1860, As Led to the Withdrawal of the Delegates from Certain States. N.p., n.d.

Stephens, Alexander H. *A Comprehensive and Popular History of the United States.* Chattanooga, Tenn., 1882.

Stevenson, Benjamin F. *Letters from the Army, 1862–1864.* Cincinnati, 1886.
Stevenson, James. *History of the Sixteenth Indiana Mounted Infantry.* New Orleans, 1864.
Stirling, James. *Letters from the Slave States.* London, 1857.
Strode, Hudson, ed. *Jefferson Davis: Private Letters, 1823–1889.* New York, 1966.
Stuart-Wortley, Lady Emmeline. *Travels in the United States, etc., During 1849 and 1850.* New York, 1851.
Talbot, J. R. *Turf, Cards and Temperance, or Reminiscences of a Checkered Life.* Bristol, R.I., 1882.
Taylor, Richard. *Destruction and Reconstruction: Reminiscences of the Late War.* New York, 1879.
―――. *Destruction and Reconstruction: Reminiscences of the Late War.* Edited by Richard B. Harwell. New York, 1955.
―――. *General Orders, No. 58, Head Quarters Dist. Western La., April 13th, 1864.* Mansfield, La., 1864. Broadside at Mansfield Battle Park Museum.
―――. *General Orders No.――. Soldiers of the Army of Western Louisiana: Headquarters District [of] Western Louisiana, In the Field, May 23d, 1864.* N.p., 1864. Circular at University of Georgia.
―――. *To the People of St. Landry, Calcasieu, Vermillon, Lafayette, St. Martin and St. Mary [Parishes]. Head Quarters, District of Western Louisiana, In the Field, May 18th 1864.* N.p., 1864. Broadside at Tulane University.
―――. *To the People of the Parishes of St. Mary, St. Martin, and Lafayette . . . Nov. 8, 1862.* New Iberia, La., 1862. Broadside at Museum of the Confederacy, Richmond.
Thorndike, Rachel Sherman, ed. *The Sherman Letters: Correspondence between General Sherman and Senator Sherman from 1837 to 1891.* New York, 1894.
Thoron, Ward, ed. *The Letters of Mrs. Henry Adams, 1865–1883.* Boston, 1936.
Tiemann, William F. *The 159th Regiment Infantry, New York State Volunteers.* Brooklyn, 1891.
Townsend, Luther T. *History of the Sixteenth Regiment, New Hampshire Volunteers.* Washington, D.C., 1897.
U.S. Bureau of the Census. *Agriculture in the United States in 1860.* Washington, D.C., 1864.
U.S. Congress. *Report of the Joint Committee on the Conduct of the War, at the Second Session, Thirty-Eighth Congress. Red River Expedition. Fort Fisher Expedition. Heavy Ordnance.* Washington, D.C., 1865.
U.S. Department of the Interior, Census Office. *Report on the Agencies of Transportation in the United States.* Washington, D.C., 1883.
U.S. House of Representatives. *Report of the Committee of Claims on the Petition of Richard Taylor, Made the Thirteenth of February, 1805. January 11, 1810.* Washington, D.C., 1810.

U.S. War Department. *The War of the Rebellion: A Compilation of the Official Records of the Union and Confederate Armies.* 127 vols. and index. Washington, D.C., 1880–1901.

Van Alstyne, Lawrence. *Diary of an Enlisted Man.* New Haven, 1910.

Warmoth, Henry Clay. *War, Politics and Reconstruction: Stormy Days in Louisiana.* New York, 1930.

Welby-Gregory, Victoria A. M. Z. (Stuart-Wortley). *A Young Traveler's Journal of a Tour in North and South America During the Year 1850.* London, 1855.

Wilson, James H. *Under the Old Flag.* 2 vols. New York, 1912.

Woods, J. T. *Service in the Ninety-Sixth Ohio Volunteers.* Toledo, 1874.

Worsham, John H. *One of Jackson's Foot Cavalry.* New York, 1912.

Yeary, Mamie. *Reminiscences of the Boys in Gray, 1861–1865.* Dallas, 1912.

Articles and Parts of Books

Barkley, A. J. "The Battle of Pleasant Hill, Louisiana: Recollections of a Private Soldier." *Annals of Iowa* 3 (April 1897): 23–31.

Barr, Alwyn, ed. "William T. Mechling's Journal of the Red River Campaign, April 7–May 10, 1864." *Texana* 1 (Fall 1963): 363–79.

"The Battle of Mansfield." *Southern Bivouac* 3 (April 1885): 412–15.

Bee, Hamilton P. "Battle of Pleasant Hill—An Error Corrected." *Southern Historical Society Papers* 8 (April 1880): 184–86.

Beers, Henry A. "Yale College." *Scribner's Monthly,* April 1876, pp. 762–84.

Benson, S. F. "The Battle of Pleasant Hill, Louisiana." *Annals of Iowa* 7 (October 1906): 5–35.

Bonner, T. R. "Sketches of the Campaign of 1864." *The Land We Love* 5 (October 1868): 459–66; 6 (November 1868): 7–12.

Boyd, David French. "Gen. W. T. Sherman. His Early Life in the South and His Relations with Southern Men." *Confederate Veteran* 18 (September 1910): 409–14.

———. "Major Bob Wheat, Commander of the Famous Louisiana Tigers." New Orleans *Daily Item,* August 25, 1896.

Bradwell, I. G. "Soldier Life in the Confederate Army." *Confederate Veteran* 26 (January 1916): 20–25.

Byam, W. W. "Swapping Stories in Texas." *Blue and Gray* 4 (November 1894): 313–15.

Campbell, A. H. "The Lost War Maps of the Confederates." *Century Magazine,* January 1888, pp. 479–81.

"Capture of Brashear City." In Frank Moore, *Rebellion Record,* 7:75–84.

"Capture of Brashear City: A Rebel Account." In Frank Moore, *Rebellion Record*, 7:173–75.

Chalmers, James R. "Forrest and His Campaigns." *Southern Historical Society Papers* 7 (October 1879): 451–86.

Cox, Jacob D. "General Richard Taylor's Reminiscences." *The Nation*, April 24, 1879, pp. 287–89.

Currie, Stephen, ed. "Zachary Taylor, Plantation Owner." *Civil War History* 30 (June 1984): 144–56.

Dabney, Robert L. "Stonewall Jackson." *Southern Historical Society Papers* 11 (April–May 1883): 145–58.

Davis, Stephen, ed. "A Federal Writes of Port Republic: 'Some One Has Blundered.'" *Civil War Times Illustrated* 19 (November 1980): 30–33.

Davis, Varina Howell. "Gen. Zachary Taylor. Mrs. Jefferson Davis' Recollections of Him." Undated clipping in biographical files, United Daughters of the Confederacy Library, Waco, Tex.

DeLoney, Edward. "The Union Broken." *De Bow's Review*, May 1860, pp. 604–7.

Dinkins, James. "The Last Campaign of Forrest's Cavalry." *Confederate Veteran* 25 (May 1927): 177–79.

Douglas, H. T. "The Trans-Mississippi Department." *Confederate Veteran* 25 (April 1917): 153–54.

Douglas, Henry Kyd. "Stonewall Jackson and His Men." In *The Annals of the War Written by Leading Participants North and South*, pp. 642–53. Philadelphia, 1879.

Fenner, Charles E. "Richard Taylor." In *The Library of Southern Literature*, edited by Edwin A. Alderman and Joel Chandler Harris, 12:5199–5203. 17 vols. Atlanta, 1910.

Goodloe, P. H. "Service in the Trans-Mississippi." *Confederate Veteran* 23 (January 1915): 31–32.

Grant, Ulysses S. "The Vicksburg Campaign." In Johnson and Buell, *Battles and Leaders*, 3:493–539.

Haas, Oscar, ed. "The Diary of Julius Giesecke, 1863–1865." *Texas Military History* 4 (Spring 1964): 27–54.

Hall, Charles B. "Notes on the Red River Campaign of 1864." In *War Papers Read Before the Commandry of the State of Maine, Military Order of the Loyal Legion of the United States*, 4:264–81. Portland, Maine, 1915.

Harrison, Jon, ed. "The Confederate Letters of John Simmons." *Chronicles of Smith County, Texas* 14 (Summer 1975): 25–57.

Heath, William H. "Battle of Pleasant Hill, Louisiana." *Annals of Iowa* 7 (October 1906): 48–54.

Henderson, Frank D. "Boys of '63." *Confederate Veteran* 32 (March 1924): 86.

Hewitt, J. E. "The Battle of Mansfield, Louisiana." *Confederate Veteran* 33 (May 1925): 172–73, 198.

Huntington, James F. "Operations in the Shenandoah Valley, from Winchester to Port Republic, 1862." In *The Shenandoah Campaigns of 1862 and 1864 and the Appomattox Campaign, 1865: Papers of the Military Historical Society of Massachusetts*, 6:3–29. Boston, 1907.

Imboden, John D. "Stonewall Jackson in the Shenandoah Valley." In Johnson and Buell, *Battles and Leaders*, 2:282–98.

Irwin, Richard B. "The Capture of Port Hudson." In Johnson and Buell, *Battles and Leaders*, 3:586–99.

———. "The Red River Campaign." In Johnson and Buell, *Battles and Leaders*, 4:345–68.

"Jackson and Ewell: The Latter's Opinion of His Chief." *Southern Historical Society Papers* 22 (January–December 1892): 26–33.

Lamb, John. "Malvern Hill, July 1, 1862." *Southern Historical Society Papers* 25 (January–December 1897): 208–21.

Lanier, T. L. "The Surrender of Vicksburg." *Confederate Veteran* 2 (August 1894): 248–49.

Maury, Dabney H. "Reminiscences of General Taylor." *Appleton's Journal*, n.s. 6 (June 1879): 567–69.

———. "Sketch of General Richard Taylor." *Southern Historical Society Papers* 7 (July 1879): 343–45.

Morris, George R. "The Battle of Bayou des Allemands." *Confederate Veteran* 34 (January 1926): 14–16.

Osborne, Thomas D. "Kentucky's Gifts to the Confederacy." *Confederate Veteran* 13 (May 1905): 200–204.

Palfrey, John C. "Port Hudson." In *The Mississippi Valley, Tennessee, Georgia, Alabama, 1861–1865. Papers of the Military Historical Society of Massachusetts*, 8:21–63. Boston, 1910.

"The Plunderers in Louisiana." *De Bow's Review*, November 1866, p. 538.

"Proceedings of the First Confederate Congress, Third Session in Part, January 29–March 19, 1863." *Southern Historical Society Papers* 48 (September 1941).

Ragan, Cooper K., ed. "The Diary of Captain George W. O'Brien, 1863." *Southwestern Historical Quarterly* 67 (July 1963): 28–54; (October 1963): 235–46; (January 1964): 413–33.

"Review of *Destruction and Reconstruction*." *Southern Historical Society Papers* 7 (May 1879): 256.

"Review of *Destruction and Reconstruction*." *Magazine of American History* 3 (August 1879): 522–23.

Roby, T. K. "Reminiscences of a Private." *Confederate Veteran* 23 (December 1915): 548–50.

Shaw, William T. "The Battle of Pleasant Hill." *Annals of Iowa* 3 (April–July 1898): 401–23.

———. "The Red River Campaign." *Confederate Veteran* 25 (March 1917): 116–18.

Sliger, J. E. "How General Taylor Fought the Battle of Mansfield, La." *Confederate Veteran* 31 (December 1923): 456–58.

Smith, Edmund Kirby. "The Defense of the Red River." In Johnson and Buell, *Battles and Leaders*, 4:369–74.

Smith, Gustavus W. "The Georgia Militia During Sherman's March to the Sea." In Johnson and Buell, *Battles and Leaders*, 4:667–69.

Smith, Rebecca, and Marion Mullins, eds. "The Diary of H. C. Medford, Confederate Soldier, 1864." *Southwestern Historical Quarterly* 34 (January 1931): 203–30.

"The Southern Historical Society: Its Origin and History." *Southern Historical Society Papers* 18 (January–December 1890): 349–65.

Strother, David Henry. "Personal Recollections of the War by a Virginian." *Harper's New Monthly Magazine*, March 1867, pp. 423–49.

Taylor, Charles E. "The Signal and Secret Service of the Confederate States." *Confederate Veteran* 40 (September–October 1932): 338–40.

Taylor, Richard. "The Last Confederate Surrender." In *The Annals of the War Written by the Leading Participants North and South*, pp. 67–71. Philadelphia, 1879.

———. "The Last Confederate Surrender." *Southern Historical Society Papers* 3 (March 1877): 155–58.

———. "Reminiscences of the Civil War." *North American Review* 125 (1878): 77–96.

———. "A Statesman of the Colonial Era." *North American Review* 128 (February 1879): 148–60.

———. "Stonewall Jackson and the Valley Campaign." *North American Review* 126 (1878): 238–61.

Thorpe, Thomas Bangs. "Sugar and the Sugar Region of Louisiana." "Louisiana." *Harper's New Monthly Magazine*, October 1854, pp. 746–67.

Todhunter, Ryland. "Col. Todhunter's Account of the Closing Events." *Confederate Veteran* 15 (September 1907): 398.

"Up the Mississippi." *Emerson's Magazine and Putnam's Monthly*, October 1857, pp. 433–56.

Vandiver, Frank E., ed. "Proceedings of the Second Confederate Congress, Second Session in Part, December 15, 1864–March 18, 1865." *Southern Historical Society Papers* 52 (1959).

Walshe, B. T. "Recollections of Gaines's Mill." *Confederate Veteran* 7 (January 1899): 54–55.

Newspapers

Clippings File, Historic New Orleans Collection.
The Confederate States (New Iberia, La.), November 15, 1862.
Galveston *Tri-Weekly News*, April 10, 1864.
Houston *Daily Telegraph*, April 18, 1864.
New Orleans *Daily Crescent*, January 10, 1862.
New Orleans *Daily Delta*, November 6, 1861.
New Orleans *Picayune*, April 13, 1879.
New Orleans Price Current, Commercial Intelligencer, and Merchants' Transcript, Annual Statement, September 1, 1865.
New York *Times*, April 13, 1879.
Opelousas *Courier*, September 6, 1862.

SECONDARY SOURCES

Books

Aaron, Daniel. *The Unwritten War: American Writers and the Civil War*. Madison, Wis., 1987.
Adams, Randolph G. *Three Americanists*. Philadelphia, 1939.
Adams, William H. *The Whig Party of Louisiana*. Lafayette, La., 1973.
Anderson, James D. *The Education of Blacks in the South, 1860–1935*. Chapel Hill, 1988.
Anderson, John Q. *A Texas Surgeon in the Civil War*. Tuscaloosa, Ala., 1957.
Andrews, J. Cutler. *The North Reports the Civil War*. Pittsburgh, 1955.
———. *The South Reports the Civil War*. Princeton, N.J., 1970.
Arceneaux, William. *Acadian General: Alfred Mouton and the Civil War*. Lafayette, La., 1981.
Ashby, Thomas A. *The Valley Campaigns*. New York, 1914.
Ashworth, John. *"Agrarians" and "Aristocrats": Party Ideology in the United States, 1837–1846*. Atlantic Highland, N.J., 1983.
Bailey, Anne J. *Between the Enemy and Texas: Parson's Texas Cavalry Brigade in the Civil War*. Fort Worth, 1989.
Ballard, Michael B. *A Long Shadow: Jefferson Davis and the Final Days of the Confederacy*. Jackson, Miss., 1986.

Baker, Jean H. *Affairs of Party: The Political Culture of Northern Democrats in the Mid-Nineteenth Century*. Ithaca, N.Y., 1983.

Barr, Alwyn. *Polignac's Texas Brigade*. Houston, 1964.

Bateman, Fred, and Thomas Weiss. *A Deplorable Scarcity: The Failure of Industrialization in the Slave Economy*. Chapel Hill, 1981.

Bauer, K. Jack. *Zachary Taylor: Soldier, Planter, Statesman of the Old Southwest*. Baton Rouge, 1985.

Bearss, Edwin C. *The Campaign for Vicksburg*. 3 vols. Dayton, Ohio, 1985–86.

———. *Steele's Retreat from Camden and the Battle of Jenkins' Ferry*. Little Rock, 1967.

Bergeron, Arthur W. *Guide to Louisiana Confederate Military Units, 1861–1865*. Baton Rouge, 1989.

Beringer, Richard E., et al. *Why the South Lost the Civil War*. Athens, Ga., 1986.

Berlin, Ira. *Slaves without Masters: The Free Negro in the Antebellum South*. New York, 1974.

Bettersworth, John K. *Confederate Mississippi: The People and the Policies of a Cotton State in Wartime*. Baton Rouge, 1944.

Blassingame, John W. *Black New Orleans, 1860–1880*. Chicago, 1973.

———. *The Slave Community: Plantation Life in the Ante-Bellum South*. New York, 1979.

Bledstein, Burton J. *The Culture of Professionalism: The Middle Class and the Development of Higher Education in America*. New York, 1976.

Boles, John B. *Black Southerners, 1619–1869*. Lexington, Ky., 1983.

Boller, Paul F., Jr. *Presidential Wives*. New York, 1988.

Bowen, David Warren. *Andrew Johnson and the Negro*. Knoxville, 1989.

Bragg, Jefferson Davis. *Louisiana in the Confederacy*. Baton Rouge, 1941.

Brock, W. R. *An American Crisis: Congress and Reconstruction, 1865–1867*. New York, 1963.

Brogan, D. W. *American Aspects*. London, 1964.

Brown, Richard D. *Modernization: The Transformation of American Life, 1600–1865*. New York, 1976.

Brown, Thomas. *Politics and Statesmanship: Essays on the American Whig Party*. New York, 1985.

Brown, Thomas McPherson. *Rheumatoid Arthritis: Its Causes and Its Cure*. New York, 1988.

Burch, Philip H., Jr. *Elites in American History: The Civil War to the New Deal*. New York, 1981.

Burns, Rex. *Success in America: The Yeoman Dream and the Industrial Revolution*. Amherst, Mass., 1976.

Bushong, Millard K. *General Turner Ashby and Stonewall's Valley Campaign*. Verona, Va., 1980.

Butler, Pierce. *Judah P. Benjamin*. Boston, 1907.

Caldwell, Stephen A. *A Banking History of New Orleans*. Baton Rouge, 1935.

Carpenter, Jesse T. *The South As a Conscious Minority, 1789–1861: A Study in Political Thought*. New York, 1930.

Carter, Dan T. *When the War Was Over: The Failure of Self-Reconstruction in the South, 1865–1867*. Baton Rouge, 1985.

Casey, Powell A. *The Story of Camp Moore [and] Life at Camp Moore among the Volunteers As Told in Letters, Diaries, and Newspaper Accounts*. N.p., 1985.

Cassidy, Vincent H., and Amos E. Simpson. *Henry Watkins Allen of Louisiana*. Baton Rouge, 1964.

Casso, Evans J. *Francis T. Nicholls: A Biographical Tribute*. Thibodaux, La., 1988.

Castel, Albert. *General Sterling Price and the Civil War in the West*. Baton Rouge, 1968.

Chambers, Lenoir. *Stonewall Jackson*. 2 vols. New York, 1959.

Channing, Steven A. *Crisis of Fear: Secession in South Carolina*. New York, 1970.

Clement, William E. *Plantation Life on the Mississippi*. New Orleans, 1952.

Cohn, Douglas A. *Jackson's Valley Campaign*. Washington, D.C., 1986.

Connelly, Thomas Lawrence. *Autumn of Glory: The Army of Tennessee, 1862–1865*. Baton Rouge, 1971.

Connelly, Thomas Lawrence, and Barbara L. Bellows. *God and General Longstreet: The Lost Cause and the Southern Mind*. Baton Rouge, 1982.

Connelly, Thomas Lawrence, and Archer Jones. *The Politics of Command: Factions and Ideas in Confederate Strategy*. Baton Rouge, 1973.

Contosta, David R. *Henry Adams and the American Experiment*. Boston, 1980.

Cooper, William J., Jr. *Liberty and Slavery: Southern Politics to 1860*. New York, 1983.

———. *The South and the Politics of Slavery, 1828–1856*. Baton Rouge, 1978.

Copeland, Fayette. *Kendall of the Picayune*. Norman, 1943.

Cornish, Dudley Taylor. *The Sable Arm: Black Troops in the Union Army, 1861–1865*. 1956. Reprint. New York, 1987.

Coulter, E. Merton. *William Montague Brown: Versatile Ango-Irish American, 1823–1883*. Athens, Ga., 1968.

Cox, Lawanda, and John H. Cox. *Politics, Principle, and Prejudice, 1865–1866: Dilemma of Reconstruction America*. London, 1963.

Cremin, Lawrence A. *American Education: The National Experience, 1783–1876*. New York, 1980.

Cunningham, Edward. *The Port Hudson Campaign, 1862–1863*. Baton Rouge, 1963.

Current, Richard N. *Those Terrible Carpetbaggers*. New York, 1988.

David, Paul A., et al. *Reckoning with Slavery: A Critical Study in the Quantitative History of American Negro Slavery*. New York, 1976.

Davis, Burke. *They Called Him Stonewall: A Life of Lt. General T. J. Jackson, C.S.A.*
    New York, 1954.
Davis, Edwin H., ed. *Heritage of Valor: The Picture History of Louisiana in the*
    Confederacy. Baton Rouge, 1964.
Dawson, Joseph G., III. *Army Generals and Reconstruction: Louisiana, 1862–1877.*
    Baton Rouge, 1982.
Diggins, John Patrick. *The Lost Soul of American Politics: Virtue, Self-Interest, and the*
    Foundations of Liberalism. New York, 1984.
Diket, A. L. *Senator John Slidell and the Community He Represented in Washington,*
    1853–1861. Washington, D.C., 1982.
Dillingham, George A. *The Foundation of the Peabody Tradition.* Lanham, Md.,
    1989.
Donald, David Herbert. *Charles Sumner and the Rights of Man.* New York, 1970.
———. *Liberty and Union.* Lexington, Mass., 1978.
Dorris, Jonathan Truman. *Pardon and Amnesty under Lincoln and Johnson: The*
    Restoration of the Confederates to Their Rights and Privileges, 1861–1898. Chapel
    Hill, 1953.
Dowdey, Clifford. *The Seven Days: The Emergence of Lee.* Boston, 1964.
Duaine, Carl L. *The Dead Men Wore Boots: An Account of the 32nd Texas Cavalry,*
    C.S.A., 1862–1865. Austin, 1966.
DuBose, John W. *The Life and Times of William Lowndes Yancey.* 2 vols.
    Birmingham, Ala., 1892.
Dufour, Charles L. *Gentle Tiger: The Gallant Life of Roberdeau Wheat.* Baton
    Rouge, 1957.
———. *Nine Men in Gray.* New York, 1963.
Durden, Robert F. *The Gray and the Black: The Confederate Debate on Emancipation.*
    Baton Rouge, 1972.
———. *The Self-Inflicted Wound: Southern Politics in the Nineteenth Century.*
    Lexington, Ky., 1985.
Dyer, Brainerd. *Zachary Taylor.* Baton Rouge, 1946.
Eaton, Clement. *The Growth of Southern Civilization, 1790–1860.* New York, 1961.
———. *Jefferson Davis.* New York, 1977.
———. *The Mind of the Old South.* Baton Rouge, 1967.
Eckert, Edward K. *"Fiction Distorting Fact": The Prison Life, Annotated by Jefferson*
    Davis. Macon, Ga., 1987.
Edmonds, David C. *The Guns of Port Hudson: The River Campaign (February–May,*
    1863) [and] The Guns of Port Hudson: The Investment, Siege and Reduction. 2 vols.
    Lafayette, La., 1983–84.
———. *Yankee Autumn in Acadiana: A Narrative of the Great Texas Overland*
    Expedition through Southwestern Louisiana, October–December, 1863. Lafayette,
    La., 1979.

Eliot, Ellsworth, Jr. *Yale in the Civil War.* New Haven, 1932.

Fabos, Julius Gy., Gordon T. Milde, and V. Michael Weinmayr, *Frederick Law Olmsted, Sr.: Founder of Landscape Architecture in America.* Amherst, Mass., 1970.

Faulk, Odie B. *General Tom Green: Fightin' Texan.* Waco, Tex., 1963.

Faust, Drew Gilpin. *The Creation of Confederate Nationalism: Ideology and Identity in the Civil War South.* Baton Rouge, 1988.

———. *James Henry Hammond and the Old South: A Design for Mastery.* Baton Rouge, 1982.

Fehrenbacher, Don E. *Constitutions and Constitutionalism in the Slaveholding South.* Athens, Ga., 1989.

———. *The South and Three Sectional Crises.* Baton Rouge, 1980.

Fessenden, Francis. *Life and Public Services of William Pitt Fessenden.* 2 vols. Boston, 1907.

Flick, Alexander C. *Samuel Jones Tilden: A Study in Political Sagacity.* New York, 1939.

Fogel, Robert William. *Without Consent or Contract: The Rise and Fall of American Slavery.* New York, 1989.

Foner, Eric. *Reconstruction: America's Unfinished Revolution, 1863–1877.* New York, 1988.

Foster, Gaines M. *Ghosts of the Confederacy: Defeat, the Lost Cause, and the Emergence of the New South, 1865–1913.* New York, 1987.

Freeman, Douglas Southall. *Lee's Lieutenants: A Study in Command.* 3 vols. New York, 1942–44.

———. *The South to Posterity: An Introduction to the Writing of Confederate History.* New York, 1939.

Friedrich, Otto. *Clover.* New York, 1979.

Gallaway, B. P. *The Ragged Rebel: A Common Soldier in W. H. Parson's Texas Cavalry, 1861–1865.* Austin, 1988.

Gambill, Edward L. *Conservative Ordeal: Northern Democrats and Reconstruction, 1865–1868.* Ames, Iowa, 1981.

Gates, Paul W. *Agriculture and the Civil War.* New York, 1965.

Genovese, Eugene D. *The Political Economy of Slavery: Studies in the Economy and Society of the Slave South.* New York, 1965.

———. *Roll, Jordon, Roll: The World the Slaves Made.* New York, 1974.

———. *The World the Slaveholders Made: Two Essays in Interpretation.* New York, 1969.

Gillette, William. *Retreat from Reconstruction, 1869–1879.* Baton Rouge, 1979.

Glatthaar, Joseph T. *Forged in Battle: The Civil War Alliance of Black Soldiers and White Officers.* New York, 1990.

Govan, Gilbert E., and James W. Livingood. *A Different Valor: The Story of General Joseph E. Johnston, C.S.A.* Indianapolis, 1956.

Green, George D. *Finance and Economic Development in the Old South: Louisiana Banking, 1804–1861*. Stanford, Calif., 1972.

Greenberg, Kenneth S. *Masters and Statesmen: The Political Culture of American Slavery*. Baltimore, 1985.

Greer, James G. *Louisiana Politics, 1845–1861*. Baton Rouge, 1930.

Grossman, Lawrence. *The Democratic Party and the Negro*. Urbana, Ill., 1976.

Gunby, A. A. *Life and Services of David French Boyd*. Baton Rouge, 1904.

Gutman, Herbert G. *The Black Family in Slavery and Freedom, 1790–1925*. New York, 1976.

Hair, William Ivy. *Bourbonism and Agrarian Protest: Louisiana Politics, 1877–1900*. Baton Rouge, 1969.

Hale, Laura Virginia. *Four Valiant Years in the Lower Shenandoah Valley, 1861–1865*. Front Royal, Va., 1986.

Hamilton, Holman. *Zachary Taylor: Soldier in the White House*. Indianapolis, 1951.
———. *Zachary Taylor: Soldier of the Republic*. Indianapolis, 1941.

Hamlin, Percy Gatling. *"Old Bald Head" (General R. S. Ewell): The Portrait of a Soldier*. Strasburg, Va., 1940.

Hargrove, Hondon B. *Black Union Soldiers in the Civil War*. Jefferson, N.C., 1988.

Harrington, Fred Harvey. *Fighting Politician: Major General N. P. Banks*. Philadelphia, 1948.

Harris, William C. *Presidential Reconstruction in Mississippi*. Baton Rouge, 1967.

Hatcher, Edmund N. *The Last Four Weeks of the War*. Columbus, Ohio, 1892.

Hattaway, Herman. *General Stephen D. Lee*. Jackson, Miss., 1976.

Hattaway, Herman, and Archer Jones. *How the North Won the Civil War*. Urbana, Ill., 1983.

Hauschild, Henry J. *The Runge Chronicle: A German Saga of Success*. Austin, 1990.

Heitmann, John Alfred. *The Modernization of the Louisiana Sugar Industry, 1830–1910*. Baton Rouge, 1987.

Henry, Robert Selph. *"First With the Most" Forrest*. Indianapolis, 1944.

Hesseltine, William B. *Confederate Leaders in the New South*. Baton Rouge, 1950.

Hewitt, Lawrence Lee. *Port Hudson, Confederate Bastion on the Mississippi*. Baton Rouge, 1988.

Heyman, Max L. *Prudent Soldier: A Biography of Major General E. R. S. Canby*. Glendale, Calif., 1959.

Hochfield, George. *Henry Adams: An Introduction and Interpretation*. New York, 1962.

Hofstadter, Richard. *Academic Freedom in the Age of the College*. New York, 1955.

Holt, Michael F. *The Political Crisis of the 1850s*. New York, 1978.

Horn, Stanley F. *The Army of Tennessee: A Military History*. Indianapolis, 1941.

Howard, Perry H. *Political Tendencies in Louisiana*. Baton Rouge, 1971.

Howe, Daniel W. *The Political Culture of the American Whigs*. Chicago, 1979.

Hughes, Nathaniel Cheairs, Jr. *General William J. Hardee: Old Reliable*. Baton Rouge, 1965.

Hughes, Robert M. *General Johnston*. New York, 1893.

Hyman, Harold M. *A More Perfect Union: The Impact of the Civil War and Reconstruction on the Constitution*. Boston, 1975.

Jackson, Joy J. *New Orleans in the Gilded Age: Politics and Urban Progress, 1880– 1896*. Baton Rouge, 1969.

Johannsen, Robert W. *The Frontier, the Union, and Stephen A. Douglas*. Urbana, Ill., 1989.

Johnson, Allen, and Dumas Malone, eds. *Dictionary of American Biography*. 20 vols. and index. New York, 1928–37.

Johnson, Ludwell H. *Red River Campaign: Politics and Cotton in the Civil War*. Baltimore, 1958.

Johnson, Thomas Cary. *The Life and Letters of Robert Lewis Dabney*. Richmond, 1903.

Johnston, William Preston. *The Life of Albert Sidney Johnston*. New York, 1878.

Jones, Archer. *Confederate Strategy from Shiloh to Vicksburg*. Baton Rouge, 1961.

Jones, Charles C. *A Roster of General Officers, Heads of Departments, Senators, Representatives, Military Organizations, &C., &C., in Confederate Service During the War Between the States*. Richmond, 1876.

Jones, James Pickett. *Yankee Blitzkrieg: Wilson's Raid through Alabama and Georgia*. Athens, Ga., 1976.

Jones, Terry L. *Lee's Tigers: The Louisiana Infantry in the Army of Northern Virginia*. Baton Rouge, 1987.

Jordan, David M. *Winfield Scott Hancock: A Soldier's Life*. Bloomington, Ind., 1988.

Keller, Morton. *Affairs of State: Public Life in Late Nineteenth Century America*. Cambridge, Mass., 1977.

Kendall, John Smith. *History of New Orleans*. 2 vols. Chicago, 1922.

Kerby, Robert L. *Kirby Smith's Confederacy: The Trans-Mississippi South, 1863– 1865*. New York, 1972.

King, Albert L. *Louis T. Wigfall: Southern Fire-Eater*. Baton Rouge, 1970.

Kolchin, Peter. *Unfree Labor: American Slavery and Russian Serfdom*. Cambridge, 1987.

Landry, Stuart O. *History of the Boston Club*. New Orleans, 1938.

Lewis, Lloyd. *Sherman: Fighting Prophet*. New York, 1932.

Linderman, Gerald F. *Embattled Courge: The Experience of Combat in the American Civil War*. New York, 1987.

Longacre, Edward G. *From Union Stars to Top Hat: A Biography of the Extraordinary General James Harrison Wilson*. Harrisburg, Pa., 1972.

Lonn, Ella. *Foreigners in the Confederacy*. Chapel Hill, 1940.

———. *Salt As a Factor in the Confederacy*. University, Ala., 1965.

Lytle, Andrew. *Bedford Forrest and His Critter Company*. New York, 1960.

McCoy, Drew R. *The Last of the Fathers: James Madison and the Republican Legacy*. Cambridge, 1989.

McCrary, Peyton. *Abraham Lincoln and Reconstruction: The Louisiana Experiment*. Princeton, N.J., 1978.

McKitrick, Eric L. *Andrew Johnson and Reconstruction*. Chicago, 1960.

McMillan, Malcolm C. *The Alabama Confederate Reader*. University, Ala., 1963.

———. *The Disintegration of a Confederate State: Three Governors and Alabama's Wartime Home Front, 1861–1865*. Macon, Ga., 1986.

McMurry, Richard M. *John Bell Hood and the War for Southern Independence*. Lexington, Ky., 1982.

McPherson, James M. *The Negro's Civil War: How American Negroes Felt and Acted during the War for the Union*. New York, 1965.

———. *Ordeal by Fire: The Civil War and Reconstruction*. New York, 1982.

McWhiney, Grady. *Braxton Bragg and Confederate Defeat*. New York, 1969.

———. *Southerners and Other Americans*. New York, 1973.

Maddex, Jack P., Jr. *The Virginia Conservatives, 1867–1897: A Study in Reconstruction Politics*. Chapel Hill, 1970.

Mantell, Martin E. *Johnson, Grant, and the Politics of Reconstruction*. New York, 1973.

Meade, Robert Douthat. *Judah P. Benjamin: Confederate Statesman*. New York, 1943.

Menn, Joseph K. *The Large Slaveholders of Louisiana in 1860*. New Orleans, 1964.

Messner, William F. *Freedmen and the Ideology of Free Labor: Louisiana 1862–1865*. Lafayette, La., 1978.

Miller, Helen Hill. *George Mason: Gentleman Revolutionary*. Chapel Hill, 1975.

Milton, George Ford. *The Age of Hate: Andrew Johnson and the Radicals*. New York, 1930.

———. *The Eve of Conflict: Stephen A. Douglas and the Needless War*. Boston, 1934.

Mitchell, Betty L. *Edmund Ruffin: A Biography*. Bloomington, Ind., 1981.

Moore, Alison. *He Died Furious*. Baton Rouge, 1983.

———. *The Louisiana Tigers, or the Two Louisiana Brigades of the Army of Northern Virginia, 1861–1865*. Baton Rouge, 1961.

Moore, James Tice. *Two Paths to the New South: The Virginia Debt Controversy, 1870–1883*. Lexington, Ky., 1974.

Moorman, J. J. *The Virginia Springs, and Springs of the South and West*. Philadelphia, 1859.

Morgan, Edmund S. *American Slavery, American Freedom: The Ordeal of Colonial Virginia*. New York, 1975.

Mushkat, Jerome. *The Reconstruction of the New York Democracy, 1861–1874*. Rutherford, N.J., 1981.

Nevins, Allan. *The Emergence of Lincoln*. Vol. 2, *Prologue to the Civil War, 1859–1861*. New York, 1950.

Nichols, James L. *Confederate Engineers*. Tuscaloosa, Ala., 1957.

Nichols, Roy F. *The Disruption of American Democracy*. New York, 1948.

Nisbet, Robert. *History of the Idea of Progress*. New York, 1980.

Noll, Arthur H. *General Kirby-Smith*. Sewanee, Tenn., 1907.

Oakes, James. *The Ruling Race: A History of American Slaveholders*. New York, 1982.

———. *Slavery and Freedom: An Interpretation of the Old South*. New York, 1990.

Oates, Stephen B. *Confederate Cavalry West of the River*. Austin, 1961.

Olsen, Otto H., ed. *Reconstruction and Redemption in the South*. Baton Rouge, 1980.

Overdyke, W. Darrell. *The Know-Nothing Party in the South*. Baton Rouge, 1959.

Parks, Joseph H. *General Edmund Kirby Smith, C.S.A.* Baton Rouge, 1954.

Perman, Michael. *Reunion without Compromise: The South and Reconstruction, 1865–1868*. Cambridge, 1973.

———. *The Road to Redemption: Southern Politics, 1869–1879*. Chapel Hill, 1984.

Persons, Stow. *The Decline of American Gentility*. New York, 1973.

Piston, William G. *Lee's Tarnished Lieutenant: James Longstreet and His Place in Southern History*. Athens, Ga., 1987.

Plummer, Alonzo H. *Confederate Victory at Mansfield*. Mansfield, La., 1969.

Polakoff, Keith Ian. *The Politics of Inertia: The Election of 1876 and the End of Reconstruction*. Baton Rouge, 1973.

Potter, David M. *The Impending Crisis, 1848–1861*. New York, 1976.

Pratt, Fletcher. *Stanton: Lincoln's Secretary of War*. New York, 1953.

Pressly, Thomas J. *Americans Interpret Their Civil War*. Princeton, N.J., 1954.

Quarles, Benjamin. *The Negro in the Civil War*. Boston, 1953.

Rable, George C. *But There Was No Peace: The Role of Violence in the Politics of Reconstruction*. Athens, Ga., 1984.

Radley, Kenneth. *Rebel Watchdog: The Confederate States Army Provost Guard*. Baton Rouge, 1989.

Raphael, Morris. *The Battle in the Bayou Country*. Detroit, 1976.

Reed, Germaine M. *David French Boyd: Founder of Louisiana State University*. Baton Rouge, 1977.

Reinders, Robert C. *End of an Era: New Orleans, 1850–1860*. New Orleans, 1964.

Reniers, Perceval. *The Springs of Virginia: Life, Love and Death at the Waters, 1775–1900*. Chapel Hill, 1941.

Reynolds, Donald E. *Editors Make War: Southern Newspapers in the Secession Crisis.* Nashville, 1970.

Rice, C. Duncan. *The Rise and Fall of Black Slavery.* New York, 1975.

Ripley, C. Peter. *Slaves and Freedmen in Civil War Louisiana.* Baton Rouge, 1976.

Roark, James L. *Masters without Slaves: Southern Planters in the Civil War and Reconstruction.* New York, 1977.

Robertson, James I., Jr. *The Stonewall Brigade.* Baton Rouge, 1963.

Roland, Charles P. *Louisiana Sugar Plantations during the American Civil War.* Leiden, Netherlands, 1957.

Roman, Alfred. *The Military Operations of General Beauregard in the War Between the States, 1861 to 1865.* 2 vols. New York, 1884.

Roper, Laura W. *FLO: A Biography of Frederick Law Olmsted.* Baltimore, 1973.

Rothman, David J. *Politics and Power: The United States Senate, 1869–1901.* Cambridge, Mass., 1966.

Royster, Charles. *Light-Horse Harry Lee and the Legacy of the American Revolution.* Cambridge, 1982.

St. Aubyn, Giles. *Edward VII: Prince and King.* New York, 1979.

Samuels, Ernest. *Henry Adams: The Middle Years.* Cambridge, Mass., 1958.

Scarborough, Ruth. *Belle Boyd: Siren of the South.* Macon, Ga., 1983.

Scarborough, William K. *The Overseer: Plantation Management in the Old South.* Baton Rouge, 1966.

Schmitz, Mark. *Economic Analysis of Antebellum Sugar Plantations in Louisiana.* New York, 1977.

Sefton, James E. *Andrew Johnson and the Uses of Constitutional Power.* Boston, 1980.

Seip, Terry L. *The South Returns to Congress: Men, Economic Measures, and Intersectional Relationships, 1868–1879.* Baton Rouge, 1983.

Shackelford, George Green. *George Wythe Randolph and the Confederate Elite.* Athens, Ga., 1988.

Shore, Laurence. *Southern Capitalists: The Ideological Leadership of an Elite, 1832–1885.* Chapel Hill, 1986.

Shugg, Robert W. *Origins of the Class Struggle in Louisiana: A Social History of the White Farmers during Slavery and After, 1840–1875.* University, La., 1939.

Silbey, Joel H. *A Respectable Minority: The Democratic Party in the Civil War Era, 1860–1868.* New York, 1977.

Singal, Daniel Joseph. *The War Within: From Victorian to Modernist Thought in the South, 1919–1945.* Chapel Hill, 1982.

Sitterson, J. Carlyle. *Sugar Country: The Cane Sugar Industry in the South, 1753–1950.* Lexington, Ky., 1953.

Smith, Walter G. *Life and Letters of Thomas Kilby Smith.* New York, 1898.

Soltow, Lee. *Men and Wealth in the United States, 1850–1870.* New Haven, 1975.

Somers, Dale A. *The Rise and Fall of Sports in New Orleans, 1850–1900*. Baton Rouge, 1972.

Somkin, Fred. *Unquiet Eagle: Memory and Desire in the Idea of American Freedom, 1815–1860*. Ithaca, N.Y., 1967.

Spencer, John W. *Terrell's Texas Cavalry*. Burnet, Tex., 1982.

Sproat, John G. *"The Best Men": Liberal Reformers in the Gilded Age*. New York, 1968.

Stafford, G. M. G. *General Leroy Augustus Stafford, His Forebears and Descendants*. Baton Rouge, 1969.

Stampp, Kenneth B. *The Peculiar Institution: Slavery in the Ante-Bellum South*. New York, 1956.

———. *The Southern Road to Appomattox*. El Paso, 1969.

Starr, Stephen Z. *The Union Cavalry in the Civil War*. 3 vols. Baton Rouge, 1979–85.

Stephenson, Richard W. *Civil War Maps: An Annotated List of Maps and Atlases in the Library of Congress*. Washington, D.C., 1989.

Sterkx, H. E. *The Free Negro in Ante-Bellum Louisiana*. Rutherford, N.J., 1972.

Stokes, Anson Phelps. *Memorials of Eminent Yale Men*. 2 vols. New Haven, 1914.

Summers, Mark W. *Railroads, Reconstruction, and the Gospel of Prosperity: Aid under the Radical Republicans, 1865–1877*. Princeton, N.J., 1984.

Sutherland, Daniel E. *The Confederate Carpetbaggers*. Baton Rouge, 1988.

Takaki, Ronald T. *A Pro-Slavery Crusade: The Agitation to Reopen the African Slave Trade*. New York, 1971.

Tanner, Robert G. *Stonewall in the Valley: Thomas J. Jackson's Shenandoah Valley Campaign, Spring 1862*. Garden City, N.Y., 1976.

Taylor, Joe Gray. *Louisiana Reconstructed, 1863–1877*. Baton Rouge, 1974.

———. *Negro Slavery in Louisiana*. Baton Rouge, 1963.

Taylor, William R. *Cavalier and Yankee: The Old South and American National Character*. Garden City, N.Y., 1963.

Thomas, Emory M. *The Confederate Nation, 1861–1865*. New York, 1979.

Thompson, Edgar T. *Plantation Societies, Race Relations, and the South: The Regimentation of Populations*. Durham, N.C., 1975.

Thompson, Jerry. *Henry Hopkins Sibley: Confederate General of the West*. Natchitoches, La., 1987.

Thompson, Margaret Susan. *The "Spider Web": Congress and Lobbying in the Age of Grant*. Ithaca, N.Y., 1985.

Thompson, William Y. *Robert Toombs of Georgia*. Baton Rouge, 1966.

Thornton, J. Mills, III. *Politics and Power in a Slave Society: Alabama, 1800–1860*. Baton Rouge, 1978.

Trefousse, Hans L. *Andrew Johnson: A Biography*. New York, 1989.

————. *The Radical Republicans: Lincoln's Vanguard for Racial Justice.* New York, 1969.

Trelease, Allen W. *White Terror: The Ku Klux Klan Conspiracy and Southern Reconstruction.* New York, 1971.

Tucker, R. Whitney. *The Descendants of the Presidents.* Charlotte, N.C., 1975.

Tunnell, Ted. *Crucible of Reconstruction: War, Radicalism and Race in Louisiana, 1862–1877.* Baton Rouge, 1984.

Vandal, Gilles. *The New Orleans Riot of 1866: Anatomy of a Tragedy.* Lafayette, La., 1983.

Van Deburg, William L. *The Slave Drivers: Black Agricultural Labor Supervisors in the Antebellum South.* Westport, Conn., 1979.

Van Deusen, John G. *The Ante-Bellum Southern Commercial Conventions.* Durham, N.C., 1926.

Vandiver, Frank E. *Rebel Brass: The Confederate Command System.* Baton Rouge, 1956.

Vaughn, William P. *Schools for All: The Blacks and Public Education in the South, 1865–1877.* Lexington, Ky., 1974.

Wall, Bennett H., ed. *Louisiana: A History.* Arlington Heights, Ill., 1984.

Warner, Ezra J. *Generals in Blue: Lives of the Union Commanders.* Baton Rouge, 1964.

————. *Generals in Gray: Lives of the Confederate Commanders.* Baton Rouge, 1959.

Warner, Ezra J., and W. Buck Yearns. *Biographical Register of the Confederate Congress.* Baton Rouge, 1975.

Weaver, Richard M. *The Southern Tradition at Bay: A History of Postbellum Thought.* New Rochelle, N.Y., 1968.

Wender, Herbert. *Southern Commercial Conventions, 1837–1859.* Baltimore, 1930.

White, Dana F., and Victor A. Kramer, eds. *Olmsted South: Old South Critic, New South Planner.* Westport, Conn., 1979.

White, Howard A. *The Freedmen's Bureau in Louisiana.* Baton Rouge, 1970.

Whitten, David O. *Andrew Durnford: A Black Sugar Planter in Antebellum Louisiana.* Natchitoches, La., 1972.

Wiebe, Robert H. *The Opening of American Society: From the Adoption of the Constitution to the Eve of Disunion.* New York, 1984.

Wilkinson, Andrews. *Plantation Stories of Old Louisiana.* Boston, 1914.

Williams, T. Harry. *P. G. T. Beauregard: Napoleon in Gray.* Baton Rouge, 1955.

Wilson, Edmund. *Patriotic Gore: Studies in the Literature of the American Civil War.* New York, 1962.

Winters, John D. *The Civil War in Louisiana.* Baton Rouge, 1963.

Woodward, C. Vann. *The Burden of Southern History.* Baton Rouge, 1960.

————. *Reunion and Reaction: The Compromise of 1877 and the End of Reconstruction.* Boston, 1951.

Woodworth, Steven E. *Jefferson Davis and His Generals: The Failure of Confederate Command in the West*. Lawrence, Kans., 1990.

Wooster, Robert A. *The People in Power: Courthouse and Statehouse in the Lower South, 1850–1860*. Knoxville, 1969.

———. *The Secession Conventions of the South*. Princeton, N.J., 1962.

Wright, Gavin. *Old South, New South: Revolutions in the Southern Economy since the Civil War*. New York, 1986.

———. *The Political Economy of the Cotton South: Households, Markets, and Wealth in the Nineteenth Century*. New York, 1978.

Wright, George C. *Life behind a Veil: Blacks in Louisville, Kentucky, 1865–1930*. Baton Rouge, 1985.

Wright, Marcus J. *Texas in the War, 1861–1865*. Edited by Harold B. Simpson. Hillsboro, Tex., 1965.

Wyatt-Brown, Bertram. *Southern Honor: Ethics and Behavior in the Old South*. New York, 1982.

———. *Yankee Saints and Southern Sinners*. Baton Rouge, 1985.

Wyeth, John Allen. *Life of General Nathan Bedford Forrest*. New York, 1901.

Yoes, Henry E. *A History of St. Charles Parish*. Norco, La., 1973.

Articles and Parts of Books

Alexander, Thomas B. "The Dimensions of Continuity across the Civil War." In *The Old South in the Crucible of War*, edited by Harry P. Owens and James J. Cooke. Jackson, Miss., 1983.

Bailey, Anne J. "A Texas Cavalry Raid: Reaction to Black Soldiers and Contrabands." *Civil War History* 35 (June 1989): 138–52.

Barr, Alwyn. "The Battle of Bayou Bourbeau, November 3, 1863: Colonel Oran M. Roberts' Report." *Louisiana History* 6 (Winter 1965): 83–91.

———. "The Battle of Blair's Landing." *Louisiana Studies* 2 (Winter 1963): 204–12.

———. "Confederate Artillery in Western Louisiana, 1862–1863." *Civil War History* 5 (Winter 1963): 74–85.

———. "Texan Losses in the Red River Campaign, 1864." *Texas Military History* 3 (Summer 1963): 103–10.

———. "Tom Green: The Forrest of the Trans-Mississippi." *Lincoln Herald* 88 (Summer 1986): 39–41.

Bearss, Edwin C. "The Civil War Comes to the Lafourche." *Louisiana Studies* 5 (Summer 1966): 97–155.

———. "The Seizure of the Forts and Public Property in Louisiana." *Louisiana History* 2 (Fall 1961): 401–9.

———. "The Trans-Mississippi Confederate Attempt to Relieve Vicksburg."
    McNeese Review 15, pt. 1 (1964): 46–70; 16, pt. 2 (1965): 46–67.
Benedict, Michael Les. "Southern Democrats in the Crisis of 1876–1877: A
    Reconsideration of *Reunion and Reaction*." *Journal of Southern History* 46
    (November 1980): 489–524.
Bergeron, Arthur W. "Free Men of Color in Gray." *Civil War History* 32
    (September 1986): 247–55.
———. "General Richard Taylor As a Military Commander." *Louisiana History*
    23 (Winter 1982): 35–47.
Boney, F. N. "The Southern Aristocrat." *Midwest Quarterly* 21 (Autumn 1979):
    140–56.
Bowman, Shearer Davis. "Antebellum Planters and *Vormarz* Junkers in
    Comparative Perspective." *American Historical Review* 85 (October 1980):
    779–808.
Brinsfield, John W. "The Military Ethics of General William T. Sherman: A
    Reassessment." In *The Parameters of War: Military History from the Journal of the
    U.S. Army War College*, edited by Lloyd J. Matthews and Dale E. Brown, pp.
    87–103. Washington, D.C., 1987.
Canney, Donald J. "The Battle of Port Republic." *Blue and Gray Magazine* 2
    (December 1984–January 1985): 24–33.
Carriere, Marius. "Political Leadership of the Louisiana Know-Nothing Party."
    Louisiana History 21 (Spring 1980): 183–95.
Cassidy, Vincent H. "Louisiana." In *The Confederate Governors*, edited by W. Buck
    Yearns, pp. 91–107. Athens, Ga., 1985.
Coles, Harry L., Jr. "Some Notes on Slaveownership and Landownership in
    Louisiana, 1850–1860." *Journal of Southern History* 9 (August 1943): 381–94.
Cooper, William J., Jr. "The Politics of Slavery Affirmed: The South and the
    Secession Crisis." In *The Southern Enigma: Essays on Race, Class, and Folk Culture*,
    edited by Walter J. Fraser, Jr., and Winfred B. Moore, Jr., pp. 199–215.
    Westport, Conn., 1983.
———. "A Reassessment of Jefferson Davis As War Leader: The Case from
    Atlanta to Nashville." *Journal of Southern History* 36 (May 1970): 189–204.
Dauphine, James G. "The Knights of the White Camelia and the Election of
    1868." *Louisiana History* 30 (Spring 1989): 173–90.
Davis, Jackson Beauregard. "The Life of Richard Taylor." *Louisiana Historical
    Quarterly* 24 (January 1941): 49–126.
Davis, Stephen. "A Georgia Firebrand: Major General W. H. T. Walker." *Georgia
    Historical Quarterly* 64 (Winter 1979): 447–60.
Dawson, Jan C. "The Puritan and the Cavalier: The South's Perception of
    Contrasting Traditions." *Journal of Southern History* 44 (November 1978): 597–
    614.

DeBats, Donald A. "An Uncertain Arena: The Georgia House of Representatives, 1808–1861." *Journal of Southern History* 56 (August 1990): 423–56.

Delaney, Caldwell. "The Surrender of General Richard Taylor to General E. R. S. Canby at Citronelle, Alabama, May 4, 1865." In *A New Nation, A War, A Young Hero, and a Surrender*, edited by Albert B. Moore, pp. 45–49. Montgomery, Ala., 1965.

Dew, Charles B. "The Long-Lost Returns: The Candidates and Their Totals in the Louisiana Secession Election." *Louisiana History* 10 (Fall 1969): 353–69.

———. "Who Won the Secession Election in Louisiana?" *Journal of Southern History* 36 (February 1970): 18–32.

Diggins, John Patrick. "Comrades and Citizens: New Mythologies in American Historiography." *American Historical Review* 90 (June 1985): 614–38.

Diket, A. L. "Slidell's Right Hand: Emile La Sere." *Louisiana History* 4 (Summer 1963): 177–205.

Donald, David Herbert. "The Confederate As a Fighting Man." *Journal of Southern History* 25 (May 1959): 178–93.

Dubay, Robert W. "Mississippi." In *The Confederate Governors*, edited by W. Buck Yearns, pp. 108–29. Athens, Ga., 1985.

Dyer, J. P. "Some Aspects of Cavalry Operations in the Army of Tennessee." *Journal of Southern History* 8 (May 1942): 210–25.

Escott, Paul D. "The Failure of Confederate Nationalism: The Old South's Class System in the Crucible of War." In *The Old South in the Crucible of War*, edited by Harry P. Owens and James J. Cooke, pp. 15–28. Jackson, Miss., 1983.

Finch, L. Boyd. "Surprise at Brashear City: Sherod Hunter's Sugar Cooler Cavalry." *Louisiana History* 25 (Fall 1984): 403–34.

Fitzhugh, Lester N. "Texas Forces in the Red River Campaign, March–May, 1864." *Texas Military History* 3 (Spring 1963): 15–22.

Foner, Eric. "Politics, Ideology, and the Origins of the American Civil War." In *A Nation Divided: Problems and Issues of the Civil War and Reconstruction*, edited by George M. Frederickson, pp. 15–34. Minneapolis, 1975.

Foster, Gaines M. "Guilt over Slavery: A Historiographical Analysis." *Journal of Southern History* 56 (November 1990): 665–94.

Frederickson, George M. "Aristocracy and Democracy in the Southern Tradition." In *The Southern Enigma: Essays on Race, Class, and Folk Culture*, edited by Walter J. Fraser, Jr., and Winfred B. Moore, Jr., pp. 97–104. Westport, Conn., 1983.

Geise, William Royston. "The Department Faces Total Isolation, February–July, 1863." *Military History of Texas and the Southwest* 15, no. 1 (1979): 35–47.

———. "General Holmes Fails to Create a Department, August, 1862–February, 1863." *Military History of Texas and the Southwest* 14, no. 3 (1978): 169–78.

———. "Hindman and Hebert Divide Command, June–July, 1862." *Military History of Texas and the Southwest* 14, no. 2 (1978): 107–19.

———. "Isolation, July–December, 1863." *Military History of Texas and the Southwest* 15, no. 2 (1979): 31–41.

———. "Kirby Smithdom, 1864." *Military History of Texas and the Southwest* 15, no. 4 (1979): 17–35.

———. "Kirby Smith's War Department, 1864." *Military History of Texas and the Southwest* 15, no. 3 (1979): 45–62.

Gerster, Patrick, and Nicholas Cords. "The Northern Origins of Southern Mythology." *Journal of Southern History* 43 (November 1977): 567–82.

Hamilton, Holman. " 'A Youth of Good Morals': Zachary Taylor Sends His Only Son to School." *Filson Club Quarterly* 26 (October 1953): 304–7.

Hanchett, William. "Reconstruction and the Rehabilitation of Jefferson Davis: Charles G. Halpern's *Prison Life*." *Journal of American History* 56 (September 1969): 280–89.

Harwood, Thomas F. "The Abolitionist Image of Louisiana and Mississippi." *Louisiana History* 7 (Fall 1966): 281–308.

Hattaway, Herman, and Archer Jones. "Lincoln As Military Strategist." *Civil War History* 26 (December 1980): 293–303.

Hendrix, James P. "The Efforts to Reopen the African Slave Trade in Louisiana." *Louisiana History* 10 (Spring 1969): 97–124.

Hennessey, Melinda M. "Race Violence in Reconstruction New Orleans: The 1868 Riot." *Louisiana History* (Winter 1979): 77–91.

Hesseltine, William B. "Four American Traditions." *Journal of Southern History* 27 (February 1961): 3–32.

House, Albert V. "The Samuel Latham Mitchell Barlow Papers in the Huntington Library." *Huntington Library Quarterly* 28 (August 1965): 341–52.

Jeanfreau, Vance Lynn S. "Louisiana Know-Nothings and the Elections of 1855–1856." *Louisiana Studies* 4 (Fall 1965): 222–64.

Jones, Archer. "Some Aspects of George W. Randolph's Service As Confederate Secretary of War." *Journal of Southern History* 26 (August 1960): 299–314.

Kendall, Lane C. "The Interregnum in Louisiana in 1861." *Louisiana Historical Quarterly* 16 (April 1933): 175–208; (July 1933): 374–408; (October 1933): 639–69.

Kolchin, Peter. "American Historians and Antebellum Southern Slavery." In *A Master's Due: Essays in Honor of David Herbert Donald*, edited by William J. Cooper, Jr., Michael F. Holt, and John McCardell, pp. 87–111. Baton Rouge, 1985.

———. "Reevaluating the Antebellum Slave Community: A Comparative Perspective." *Journal of American History* 70 (December 1983): 579–601.

Lafargue, Andre. "The Manuscript of General Richard Taylor's 'Destruction and Reconstruction.'" *Louisiana Historical Quarterly* 13 (January 1930): 46–58.

Lang, Walter P., Jr., J. Frank Hennessee, and William E. Bush. Jr. "Jackson's Valley Campaign and the Operational Level of War." In *The Parameters of War: Military History from the Journal of the U.S. Army War College*, edited by Lloyd J. Matthews and Dale E. Brown, pp. 28–51. Washington, D.C., 1987.

Lathrop, Barnes F. "Disaffection in Confederate Louisiana: The Case of William Hyman." *Journal of Southern History* 24 (August 1958): 308–18.

———. "Federals 'Sweep the Coast': An Expedition into St. Charles Parish, August, 1862." *Louisiana History* 9 (Winter 1968): 62–68.

———. "The Lafourche District in 1861–1862: A Problem in Local Defense." *Louisiana History* 1 (Spring 1960): 99–129.

———. "The Lafourche District in 1862: Confederate Revival." *Louisiana History* 1 (Fall 1960): 300–319.

———. "The Lafourche District in 1862: Invasion." *Louisiana History* 2 (Spring 1961): 175–201.

———. "The Lafourche District in 1862: Militia and Partisan Rangers." *Louisiana History* 1 (Summer 1960): 230–44.

Lebergott, Stanley. "Why the South Lost: Commercial Purpose in the Confederacy, 1861–1865." *Journal of American History* 70 (June 1983): 58–74.

McCrary, Peyton, Clark Miller, and Dale Baum. "Class and Party in the Secession Crisis: Voting Behavior in the Deep South, 1856–1861." *Journal of Interdisciplinary History* 8 (Winter 1978): 429–57.

McInvale, Morton R. "'All That Devils Could Wish For': The Griswoldville Campaign, 1864." *Georgia Historical Quarterly* 60 (Summer 1976): 117–30.

McNeill, William J. "A Survey of Confederate Soldier Morale during Sherman's Campaign through Georgia and the Carolinas." *Georgia Historical Quarterly* 55 (Spring 1971): 1–25.

McPherson, James M. "Antebellum Southern Exceptionalism: A New Look at an Old Question." *Civil War History* 29 (September 1983): 230–44.

Mahan, Harold Eugene. "The Final Battle: The Southern Historical Society and Confederate Hopes for History." *Southern Historian* 5 (Spring 1984): 27–37.

Main, Gloria. "Inequality in Early America." *Journal of Interdisciplinary History* 7 (1976–77): 559–82.

Meiners, Fredericka. "Hamilton P. Bee in the Red River Campaign of 1864." *Southwestern Historical Quarterly* 78 (July 1974): 21–44.

Mitchell, Reid. "The Creation of Confederate Loyalties." In *New Perspectives on Race and Slavery in America: Essays in Honor of Kenneth M. Stampp*, edited by Robert H. Abzug and Stephen E. Maizlish, pp. 93–108. Lexington, Ky., 1986.

Moody, Vernie Alton. "Slavery on Louisiana Sugar Plantations." *Louisiana Historical Quarterly* 7 (April 1924): 191–301.

Moore, Waldo W. "The Defense of Shreveport—The Confederacy's Last Redoubt." In *Military Analysis of the Civil War: An Anthology*, edited by the editors of *Military Affairs*, pp. 394–404. Millwood, N.Y., 1977.

Olsen, Otto H. "Historians and the Extent of Slave Ownership in the Southern United States." *Civil War History* 18 (June 1972): 101–16.

Onwood, Maurice. "Impulse and Honor: The Place of Slave and Master in the Ideology of Planterdom." *Plantation Society in the Americas* 1 (1979): 31–56.

Owen, Thomas M. "William Strother, of Virginia, and His Descendants." *Publications of the Southern History Association* 2 (April 1898): 147–73.

Padgett, James A. "The Letters of Colonel Richard Taylor and of Commodore Richard Taylor to James Madison, together with a Brief Sketch of Their Lives." *Register of the Kentucky State Historical Society* 36 (October 1938): 330–44.

Pease, Jane H. "A Note on Patterns of Conspicuous Consumption among Seaboard Planters, 1820–1860." *Journal of Southern History* 35 (August 1969): 381–93.

Pessen, Edward. "How Different from Each Other Were the Antebellum North and South?" *American Historical Review* 85 (December 1980): 1119–49.

Powell, Lawrence N., and Michael S. Wayne. "Self-Interest and the Decline of Confederate Nationalism." In *The Old South in the Crucible of War*, edited by Harry P. Owens and James J. Cooke, pp. 29–45. Jackson, Miss., 1983.

Prichard, Walter. "The Effects of the Civil War on the Louisiana Sugar Industry." *Journal of Southern History* 5 (August 1939): 315–32.

———. "Routine on a Louisiana Sugar Plantation under the Slavery Regime." *Mississippi Valley Historical Review* 14 (September 1927): 168–78.

———, ed. "A Tourist's Description of Louisiana in 1860." *Louisiana Historical Quarterly* 21 (October 1938): 1110–1214.

Rable, George C. "Southern Interests and the Election of 1876: A Reappraisal." *Civil War History* 26 (December 1980): 347–61.

Richter, William L. "General Phil Sheridan, the Historians, and Reconstruction." *Civil War History* 33 (June 1987): 131–54.

Riley, Harris D., Jr. "General Richard Taylor, C.S.A.: Louisianan, Distinguished Military Commander, and Author, with Speculations on His Health." *Southern Studies* 1 (Spring 1990): 67–86.

Ripley, C. Peter. "The Black Family in Transition: Louisiana, 1860–1865." *Journal of Southern History* 41 (August 1975): 369–90.

Roland, Charles P. "Louisiana and Secession." *Louisiana History* 19 (Fall 1978): 389–99.

Rosenblum, Joseph. "Two Americanists: Samuel L. M. Barlow and Henry
    Harrisse." *American Book Collector* 6 (March–April 1985): 14–25.
Scarborough, William K. "Slavery—The White Man's Burden." In *Perspectives
    and Irony in American Slavery*, edited by Harry P. Owens, pp. 103–35. Jackson,
    Miss., 1976.
Schmitz, Mark. "The Transformation of the Southern Sugar Cane Sector,
    1860–1930." *Agricultural History* (January 1979): 270–85.
Sellers, Charles Grier, Jr. "Who Were the Southern Whigs?" *American Historical
    Review* 59 (January 1954): 335–46.
Shalhope, Robert E. "Race, Class, Slavery, and the Antebellum Southern Mind."
    Journal of Southern History 37 (November 1971): 557–74.
Siegel, Fred. "The Paternalist Thesis: Virginia As a Test Case." *Civil War History*
    25 (September 1979): 246–61.
Sitterson, J. Carlyle. "Financing and Marketing the Sugar Crop of the Old
    South." *Journal of Southern History* 10 (May 1944): 188–99.
Taylor, Ethel. "Discontent in Confederate Louisiana." *Louisiana History* 2 (Fall
    1961): 410–28.
Taylor, Joe Gray. "The Foreign Slave Trade in Louisiana after 1808." *Louisiana
    History* 1 (Winter 1960): 36–43.
———. "Louisiana: An Impossible Task." In *Reconstruction and Redemption in the
    South*, edited by Otto H. Olsen, pp. 202–35. Baton Rouge, 1980.
———. "A New Look at Slavery in Louisiana." In *Louisiana's Black Heritage*,
    edited by Robert R. Macdonald, John R. Kemp, and Edward F. Haas, pp.
    190–208. New Orleans, 1979.
———. "Slavery in Louisiana during the Civil War." *Louisiana History* 8 (Winter
    1967): 27–33.
Tregle, Joseph G., Jr. "Thomas J. Durant, Utopian Socialism, and the Failure of
    Presidential Reconstruction in Louisiana." *Journal of Southern History* 45
    (November 1979): 485–512.
Vandal, Gilles. "The Policy of Violence in Caddo Parish, 1865–1884." *Louisiana
    History* 32 (Spring 1991): 159–82.
Vandiver, Frank E. "Jefferson Davis and Unified Army Command." *Louisiana
    Historical Quarterly* 38 (January 1955): 1–13.
Venable, Austin L. "The Conflict between the Douglas and Yancey Forces in the
    Charleston Convention." *Journal of Southern History* 8 (May 1942): 226–41.
Wagstaff, Thomas. "The Arm-In-Arm Convention." *Civil War History* 14 (June
    1968): 101–19.
Westwood, Howard C. "Captive Black Union Soldiers in Charleston—What to
    Do?" *Civil War History* 28 (March 1982): 28–44.
White, Melvin J. "Duncan Farrar Kenner." In Johnson and Malone, *Dictionary of
    American Biography*, 10:337–38.

Whitten, David O. "Medical Care of Slaves: Louisiana Sugar Region and South Carolina Rice District." *Southern Studies* 16 (Summer 1977): 153–80.

———. "Sugar Slavery: A Profitability Model for Slave Investments in the Antebellum Sugar Industry." *Louisiana Studies* 12 (Summer 1973): 423–42.

———. "Tariff and Profit in the Antebellum Louisiana Sugar Industry." *Business History Review* 44 (Summer 1970): 226–33.

Woodworth, Steven E. "'Dismembering the Confederacy': Jefferson Davis and the Trans-Mississippi West." *Military History of Texas and the Southwest* 20 (Spring 1990): 1–22.

Woody, Thomas. "James Gordon Carter." In Johnson and Malone, *Dictionary of American Biography*, 4:538.

Wooster, Ralph A. "The Secession of the South: An Examination of Changing Interpretations." *Civil War History* 7 (June 1961): 117–27.

———. "The Structure of Government in Late Antebellum Louisiana." *Louisiana Studies* 14 (Winter 1975): 361–78.

———. "Wealthy Southerners on the Eve of the Civil War." In *Essays on Southern History Written in Honor of Barnes F. Lathrop*, edited by Gary W. Gallagher, pp. 133–59. Austin, 1980.

Theses and Dissertations

Barr, Alwyn. "Confederate Artillery in the Trans-Mississippi." M.A. thesis, University of Texas, 1961.

Bauer, Craig A. "A Leader among Peers: The Life and Times of Duncan Farrar Kenner." Ph.D. diss., University of Southern Mississippi, 1989.

Bergeron, Arthur W. "General Richard Taylor: A Study in Command." M.A. thesis, Louisiana State University, 1972.

Binning, Francis Wayne. "Henry Clay Warmoth and Louisiana Reconstruction." Ph.D. diss., University of North Carolina, 1969.

Lathrop, Barnes F. "The Pugh Plantations, 1860–1865: A Study of Life in Lower Louisiana." Ph.D. diss., University of Texas, 1945.

Mitchell, Leon. "Prisoners of War in the Confederate Trans-Mississippi." M.A. thesis, University of Texas, 1961.

Power, J. Tracy. "'There Stands Jackson Like a Stone Wall': The Image of General Thomas J. 'Stonewall' Jackson in the Confederate Mind, July 1861–November 1862." M.A. thesis, University of South Carolina, 1984.

Scott, Paul A. "John A. Wharton: The Forgotten General." Term paper in history at Texas A & M University, fall 1981.

Taylor, Arvilla. "Horse Racing in the Lower Mississippi Valley Prior to 1860."
    M.A. thesis, University of Texas, 1953.
Urquhart, Kenneth T. "General Richard Taylor and the War in Virginia." M.A.
    thesis, Tulane University, 1958.

                                Interview

Interview with Jack S. McIlhenny, Baton Rouge, March 30, 1982.

INDEX